THE VICTORIA HISTORY
OF THE
COUNTIES OF ENGLAND

—

A HISTORY OF
GLOUCESTERSHIRE

VOLUME VII

THE VICTORIA HISTORY
OF THE
COUNTIES OF ENGLAND

EDITED BY C. R. ELRINGTON

THE UNIVERSITY OF LONDON
INSTITUTE OF
HISTORICAL RESEARCH

Oxford University Press, Walton Street, Oxford OX2 6DP

LONDON GLASGOW NEW YORK TORONTO
DELHI BOMBAY CALCUTTA MADRAS KARACHI
KUALA LUMPUR SINGAPORE HONG KONG TOKYO
NAIROBI DAR ES SALAAM CAPE TOWN
MELBOURNE WELLINGTON
and associate companies in
BEIRUT BERLIN IBADAN MEXICO CITY

*Published in the United States by
Oxford University Press, New York*

© *University of London 1981*

ISBN 0 19 722755 4

R 942.41

RA 540847

PRINTED IN GREAT BRITAIN BY
ROBERT MACLEHOSE AND CO. LTD.
PRINTERS TO THE UNIVERSITY OF GLASGOW

INSCRIBED TO THE
MEMORY OF HER LATE MAJESTY
QUEEN VICTORIA
WHO GRACIOUSLY GAVE THE TITLE TO
AND ACCEPTED THE DEDICATION
OF THIS HISTORY

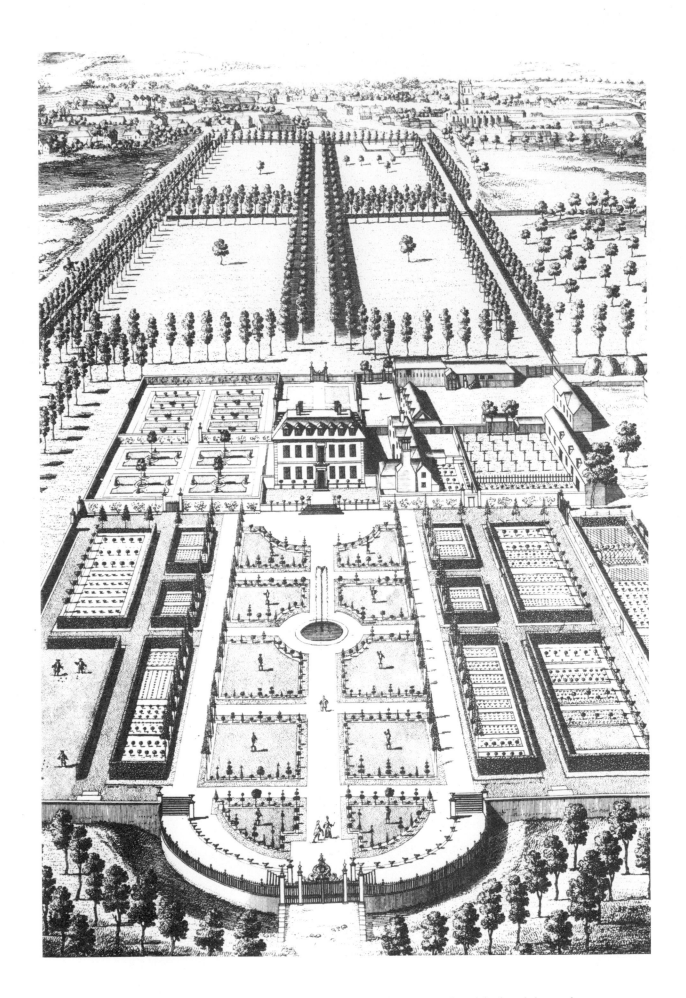

FAIRFORD PARK in the early 18th century, with the town and parish church beyond

A HISTORY OF THE COUNTY OF GLOUCESTER

EDITED BY N. M. HERBERT

VOLUME VII

BRIGHTWELLS BARROW
AND RAPSGATE HUNDREDS

PUBLISHED FOR

THE INSTITUTE OF HISTORICAL RESEARCH

BY

OXFORD UNIVERSITY PRESS

1981

Distributed by Oxford University Press until 1 January 1984
thereafter by Dawsons of Pall Mall

CONTENTS OF VOLUME SEVEN

LIST OF ILLUSTRATIONS

For permission to reproduce material in their possession thanks are offered to the Bodleian Library, Oxford, the Gloucester Divisional Library, the Gloucestershire Record Office, Mr. F. C. Innocent, and the Royal Commission on Historical Monuments (England) for material in the National Monuments Record (N.M.R.). The photograph of Barnsley Park is reproduced by permission of *Country Life*, and that of the Syde door handle by permission of B. T. Batsford Ltd. Photographs dated 1978 and 1979 are by A. P. Baggs.

LIST OF MAPS

The maps were drawn by Mr. A. A. Klaiber, of the Gloucestershire County Planning Department, from drafts prepared by N. M. Herbert and A. R. J. Juřica. Those of Fairford and Lechlade are based on Ordnance Survey Maps 1/2,500 (1903 edn.), that of Bibury on Ordnance Survey Map 6″ (1903 edn.), with later information taken from Ordnance Survey material, Crown Copyright reserved; those of the hundreds in 1845 are based on Ordnance Survey Maps 1″ (1958 edn.), and that of Chedworth on Ordnance Survey Map 6″ (1903 edn.).

EDITORIAL NOTE

VOLUME SEVEN is the sixth to be published of the *Victoria History of Gloucestershire* and the fifth since the revival of the Gloucestershire History in 1958. An outline of the structure and aims of the *Victoria History* as a whole, as also of its origins and progress, is included in the *General Introduction* (1970), and the arrangements by which the Gloucestershire County Council and the University of London collaborate to produce the Gloucestershire History are indicated in the Editorial Note to *Gloucestershire*, Volume Six. Once again it is the General Editor's pleasure to record the University's gratitude for the generosity displayed by the County Council.

The compilation of the *Victoria History of Gloucestershire* has continued to be supervised by the County Council's Recreation and Leisure Committee, and since the publication of Volume Eleven in 1976 the Chairman of that committee (Cllr. P. M. Robins), the county editor of the Gloucestershire History (Dr. N. M. Herbert) and the assistant editor (Dr. A. R. J. Juřica) have remained in office.

The authors and editors of the volume, as of all similar volumes, have drawn widely on the information and advice of many people, too numerous to be mentioned individually here but named in the footnotes to the articles with which they helped. They are all most cordially thanked. For access to records in their possession grateful acknowledgement is made to the Marquess of Bath, Earl St. Aldwyn, of Williamstrip Park, Mr. H. W. G. Elwes, of Colesbourne, Mr. G. J. Phillips, of S. J. Phillips & Sons (Kemble) Ltd., Mr. John Workman, of Sheeps-combe, the Dean and Chapter of Gloucester, the Dean and Chapter of Christ Church, Oxford, the Warden and Scholars of New College, Oxford, the Warden and Fellows of Wadham College, Oxford, and the Keeper of the Oxford University Archives. The Gloucestershire County Record Office and the Gloucester Divisional Library have continued to give their indispensable aid, and the co-operation of the former County Archivist, Mr. B. S. Smith, of the Librarian, Mr. G. R. Hiatt, and of their respective staffs is recorded with particular gratitude. Lastly it is a pleasure to thank Mrs. Margaret Collier for the conscientious and devoted way in which since 1960 she has undertaken the typing of very nearly all the text of the volumes that have appeared since then.

LIST OF CLASSES OF DOCUMENTS
IN THE PUBLIC RECORD OFFICE
USED IN THIS VOLUME
WITH THEIR CLASS NUMBERS

Chancery

		Proceedings
C	1	Early
C	2	Series I
C	3	Series II
C	47	Miscellanea
C	54	Close Rolls
C	60	Fine Rolls
C	66	Patent Rolls
C	78	Decree Rolls
		Masters' Exhibits
C	107	Senior
C	115	Duchess of Norfolk Deeds
		Inquisitions post mortem
C	132	Series I, Hen. III
C	133	Edw. I
C	134	Edw. II
C	135	Edw. III
C	137	Hen. IV
C	139	Hen. VI
C	140	Edw. IV and V
C	142	Series II
C	143	Inquisitions ad quod damnum
C	145	Miscellaneous Inquisitions
C	260	Files (Tower and Rolls Chapel) Recorda

Court of Common Pleas

	Feet of Fines
C.P. 25(1)	Series I
C.P. 25(2)	Series II
C.P. 40	De Banco Rolls
C.P. 43	Recovery Rolls

Duchy of Lancaster

D.L. 10	Royal Charters
D.L. 29	Ministers' Accounts
D.L. 30	Court Rolls
D.L. 42	Miscellaneous Books
D.L. 44	Special Commissions and Returns

Exchequer, King's Remembrancer

E 126	Decrees and Orders, Series IV
E 134	Depositions taken by Commission
E 142	Ancient Extents
E 150	Inquisitions post mortem, Series II
E 164	Miscellaneous Books, Series I
E 178	Special Commissions of Inquiry
E 179	Subsidy Rolls etc.

Exchequer, Augmentations Office

E 301	Certificates of Colleges and Chantries
E 309	Enrolments of Leases
E 310	Particulars of Leases
E 315	Miscellaneous Books
E 318	Particulars for Grants

Ministry of Education

Ed. 7	Public Elementary Schools, Preliminary Statements

Registry of Friendly Societies

	Indexes to Rules and Amendments
F.S. 2	Series I
F.S. 4	Series II

Home Office

H.O. 107	Census Returns 1841 and 1851
H.O. 129	Ecclesiastical Returns

Justices Itinerant

J.I. 1	Eyre Rolls, Assize Rolls, etc.

Ministry of Agriculture, Fisheries, and Food

M.A.F. 68	Agricultural Returns: Parish Summaries

Prerogative Court of Canterbury

Prob. 11	Wills

Court of Requests

Req. 2	Proceedings

Special Collections

S.C. 2	Court Rolls
S.C. 6	Ministers' Accounts Rentals and Surveys
S.C. 11	Rolls
S.C. 12	Portfolios

State Paper Office

S.P. 16	State Papers Domestic, Chas. I

Court of Wards and Liveries

Wards 2	Deeds and Evidences

SELECT LIST OF ACCUMULATIONS
IN THE GLOUCESTERSHIRE RECORD OFFICE

Deposited Collections

D 181   Sewell, Rawlins & Logie of Cirencester (solicitors)

D 182   Mullings, Ellett & Co. of Cirencester (solicitors)

D 184   Craven family

D 269B   Coxwell family of Ablington

D 326   Guise family of Elmore and Rendcomb

D 540   Bazley family of Hatherop

D 678   Sherborne estate

D 936   Dean and Chapter of Gloucester

D 936A   ,,   ,,   ,,

D 1070   Wilmot & Co. of Fairford (solicitors)

D 1388   Mullings, Ellet & Co. of Cirencester (solicitors)

D 1728   Mullings, Ellet & Co.: Barker family of Fairford

D 1740   Dean and Chapter of Gloucester

D 1878   Stowell Park estate

D 2052   Notes on nonconformity in Gloucestershire compiled by Mr. G. Dutton

D 2299   Bruton, Knowles & Co. of Gloucester (estate agents)

D 2525   Bathurst family of Cirencester Park

D 2440   Hicks Beach family of Williamstrip and Witcombe Park

D 2957   Deeds transferred from the Gloucestershire Collection at Gloucester Library

Gloucester Diocesan Records (G.D.R.)

T 1   tithe awards

V 5   glebe terriers
     volumes of the diocesan registry
     wills proved in consistory court

Parish Records

P 44   Bibury

P 44A   ,,

P 130   Eastleach Turville

P 197   Lechlade

P 261   Quenington

Quarter Sessions Records

     Administration

Q/AL   lunatic asylums

Q/AV   victuallers

Q/CI   Clerk of the Peace, indexes

     Registration

Q/REl   elections, land tax

Q/RI   inclosure awards

Q/RNc   papists' estates

Q/RSf   friendly societies

Q/RUm   public works

Q/RZ   miscellaneous

     The Court in Session

Q/SIb   indictment books

Q/SM   minutes

Q/SO   order books

Q/SRh   rolls, highway diversions

Miscellaneous

CH   Charities

DC   County Council deeds

G.B.R.   Gloucester Borough Records

PA   Pamphlets, parish histories

S   Schools

SL   Sale particulars

TS   Thames and Severn Canal records

NOTE ON ABBREVIATIONS

Among the abbreviations and short titles used the following, in addition to those listed in the Victoria History's *Handbook for Editors and Authors*, may require elucidation:

Acreage Returns, 1801   Home Office Acreage Returns of 1801, printed in *Trans. B.G.A.S.* lxviii. 174–83

Acreage Returns, 1901   Board of Agriculture Acreage Returns of 1901, from a MS. copy *penes* the Editor, Victoria History of Gloucestershire

Agric. Returns 1976   Agricultural Returns, Parish Summaries 1976 *penes* Ministry of Agriculture, Fisheries, and Food, Divisional Office, Elmbridge Court, Gloucester

Atkyns, *Glos.*   R. Atkyns, *Ancient and Present State of Glostershire* (1712)

B. & G. Par. Rec.   *Guide to the Parish Records of the City of Bristol and County of Gloucester*, ed. I. Gray and E. Ralph (B.G.A.S. 1963)

B.G.A.S.   Bristol and Gloucestershire Archaeological Society

B.L.   British Library (used in references to documents transferred from the British Museum)

Berkeley MSS.   John Smith, *Berkeley Manuscripts: Lives of the Berkeleys with a Description of the Hundred of Berkeley*, ed. J. Maclean (3 vols. Gloucester, 1883–5)

Bibliotheca Glos.   *Bibliotheca Gloucestrensis: Collection of Scarce and Curious Tracts Illustrative of and Published during the Civil War* (2 vols. Gloucester, priv. print. 1825)

Bigland, *Glos.*   *Historical, Monumental, and Genealogical Collections Relative to the County of Gloucester, Printed from the Original Papers of Ralph Bigland* (3 vols. 1791–1889, issued in parts; vol. iii unpaginated)

Bryant, *Map of Glos.* (1824)   A. Bryant, *Map of the County of Gloucester in the years 1823 & 1824* (1824)

Cat. of Glos. Colln.   *Catalogue of the Gloucestershire Collection in the Gloucester Public Library*, compiled by R. Austin (Gloucester, 1928)

Church School Inquiry, 1846–7   *Result of the Returns to the General Inquiry made by the National Society* (1849)

Ciren. Cart.   *Cartulary of Cirencester Abbey*, ed. C. D. Ross and M. Devine (3 vols. 1964, 1977)

Compton Census   Bishop Compton's Census, 1676, William Salt Library, Stafford

Davis, *Glos. Brasses*   C. T. Davis, *Monumental Brasses of Gloucestershire* (1899)

Eccl. Misc.   *Ecclesiastical Miscellany* (B.G.A.S. Rec. Section, xi, 1976), including a survey of Gloucester diocese, 1603

Educ. Enquiry Abstract   *Education Enquiry Abstract*, H.C. 62 (1835), xli

Educ. of Poor Digest   *Digest of Returns to the Select Committee on Education of the Poor*, H.C. 224 (1819), ix (1)

Finberg, Early Charters of W. Midlands   H. P. R. Finberg, *Early Charters of the West Midlands* (Leicester, 1961)

Finberg, *Glos. Studies*   *Gloucestershire Studies*, ed. H.P.R. Finberg (1957)

Fosbrooke, *Glos.*   T. D. Fosbrooke, *Abstracts of Records and Manuscripts Respecting the County of Gloucester, Formed into a History* (2 vols. Gloucester, 1807)

G.D.R.   Gloucester Diocesan Records (see p. xvi)

Glos. Ch. Bells   H. T. Ellacombe, *Church Bells of Gloucestershire* (Exeter, 1881)

Glos. Ch. Notes   *Gloucestershire Church Notes*, by S. R. Glynne, ed. W. P. W. Phillimore and J. Melland Hall (1902)

Glos. Ch. Plate	*Church Plate of Gloucestershire*, ed. J. T. Evans (B.G.A.S. 1906)
Glos. Colln.	The Gloucestershire Collection, in Gloucester Library, comprising printed works, manuscripts, prints and drawings, etc.
Glos. N. & Q.	*Gloucestershire Notes and Queries* (10 vols. 1881–1914)
Glos. Q.S. Archives	*Gloucestershire Quarter Sessions Archives 1660–89: A Descriptive Catalogue,* compiled by I. E. Gray and A. T. Gaydon (Glos. County Council, 1958)
Glos. R.O.	Gloucestershire Record Office (see p. xvi)
Glos. Subsidy Roll, 1327	*Gloucestershire Subsidy Roll. I Ed. III, 1327* (priv. print. by Sir Thos. Phillipps, n.d. [?1856])
Glouc. Cath. Libr.	Gloucester Cathedral Library
Glouc. Corp. Rec.	*Calendar of the Records of the Corporation of Gloucester,* ed. W. H. Stevenson (Gloucester, 1893)
Glouc. Jnl.	*Gloucester Journal* (established 1722)
Grundy, *Saxon Charters*	G. B. Grundy, *Saxon Charters and Field Names of Gloucestershire* (B.G.A.S. 1935)
Hist. & Cart. Mon. Glouc. (Rolls Ser.)	*Historia et Cartularium Monasterii Sancti Petri Gloucestriae,* ed. W. H. Hart (Rolls Series, no. 33, 3 vols. 1863–87)
Hockaday Abs.	The 'Hockaday Abstracts', being abstracts of ecclesiastical records relating to Gloucestershire, compiled by F. S. Hockaday mainly from diocesan records, in Gloucester Library
Household, *Thames and Severn Canal*	H. Household, *Thames and Severn Canal* (Newton Abbot, 1969)
Inq. p.m. Glos.	*Abstracts of Inquisitiones post mortem for Gloucestershire, 1236–1413, 1625–1642* (6 vols. issued jointly by the British Record Society, Index Library vols. xxx, xl, xlviii, and ix, xxi, xlvii, and the B.G.A.S., 1893–1914)
Kirby, *Cat. of Glouc. Dioc. Rec.*	*Diocese of Gloucester*: vol. i, *Catalogue of the Records of the Bishop and Archdeacons* (Gloucester Corporation, 1968); vol. ii, *Catalogue of the Records of the Dean and Chapter* (Glos. County Council, 1967); compiled by I.M. Kirby
Langston, 'Cath. Missions'	J. N. Langston, 'Catholic Post-Reformation Missions in Gloucestershire', typescript, Glos. Colln. 31840 (6 vols. revised 1957)
Manual of Glos. Lit.	*Bibliographer's Manual of Gloucestershire Literature . . .,* ed. F. A. Hyett and W. Bazeley (3 vols. Gloucester, priv. print. 1895–7)
Margary, *Rom. Roads*	I. D. Margary, *Roman Roads in Britain* (2 vols. 1955)
P.N. Glos. (E.P.N.S.)	*Place-Names of Gloucestershire* (4 vols. English Place-Name Society vols. xxxviii–xli, 1964–5)
Payne, *Glos. Survey*	G. E. Payne, *Gloucestershire: a Survey* (Gloucester, n.d. [1946])
Pleas of the Crown for Glos. ed. Maitland	*Pleas of the Crown for the County of Gloucester, 1221*, ed. F. W. Maitland (1884)
Poor Law Abstract, 1804	*Abstract of Returns Relative to the Expense and Maintenance of the Poor* (printed by order of the House of Commons, 1804)
Poor Law Abstract, 1818	*Abstract of Returns to Orders of the House of Commons Relative to Assessments for Relief of the Poor,* H.C. 294 (1820), xii
Poor Law Com. 2nd Rep.	*Second Report of the Poor Law Commission,* H.C. 595 (1836), xxix (1)
Poor Law Returns (1830–1)	*Account of the Money Expended for the Maintenance and Relief of the Poor for the five years ending 25th March 1825, 1826, 1827, 1828, and 1829,* H.C. 83 (1830–1), xi
Poor Law Returns (1835)	*Account of the Money Expended, 1830, 1831, 1832, 1833, and 1834,* H.C. 444 (1835), xlvii
Proc. C.N.F.C.	*Proceedings of the Cotteswold Naturalists' Field Club*

NOTE ON ABBREVIATIONS

Red Bk. of Worc.	*Red Book of Worcester*, ed. Marjory Rollings (Worcs. Hist. Soc. 1934–9)
R.C.H.M. *Glos.* i	Royal Commission on Historical Monuments (England), *County of Gloucester:* vol. i, *Iron Age and Romano-British Monuments in the Gloucestershire Cotswolds* (1976)
Reg. Bransford	*Calendar of the Register of Wolstan de Bransford, Bishop of Worcester 1339–49*, ed. R. M. Haines (Worcs. Hist. Soc. 1966)
Reg. Cobham	*Register of Bishop Thomas de Cobham, 1317–27*, ed. E. H. Pearce (Worcs. Hist. Soc. 1930)
Reg. Giffard	*Register of Bishop Godfrey Giffard, 1268–1302*, ed. J. W. W. Bund (Worcs. Hist. Soc. 1902)
Reg. Ginsborough	*Register of Bishop William Ginsborough, 1303–7*, ed. J. W. W. Bund (Worcs. Hist. Soc. 1907)
Reg. Mon. Winch.	*Landboc, sive Registrum Monasterii de Winchelcumba*, ed. D. Royce (2 vols. Exeter, 1892–1903)
Reg. Reynolds	*Register of Bishop Walter Reynolds, 1308–13*, ed. R. A. Wilson (Worcs. Hist. Soc. 1927)
Reg. Sede Vacante	*Register of the Diocese of Worcester during the Vacancy of the See*, ed. J. W. W. Bund (Worcs. Hist. Soc. 1893–7)
Reg. Wakefeld	*Calendar of the Register of Henry Wakefield, Bishop of Worcester 1375–95*, ed. W. P. Marett (Worcs. Hist. Soc. 1972)
Rep. Com. Agric. Employment	*First Report of the Commissioners on the Employment of Children, Young Persons, and Women in Agriculture*, App. II [C. 4068-I], H.C. (1867–8), xvii
20th Rep. Com. Char.	*20th Report of the Commissioners Appointed to Enquire Concerning Charities* (Lord Brougham's Commission), H.C. 19 (1829), vii (1)
21st Rep. Com. Char.	*21st Report . . . Concerning Charities*, H.C. 349 (1829), viii (1)
Richardson, *Wells and Springs of Glos.*	L. Richardson, *Wells and Springs of Gloucestershire* (H.M.S.O. 1930)
Roper, *Glos. Effigies*	Ida M. Roper, *Monumental Effigies of Gloucestershire and Bristol* (Gloucester, 1931)
Rudder, *Glos.*	S. Rudder, *New History of Gloucestershire* (Cirencester, 1779)
Rudge, *Agric. of Glos.*	T. Rudge, *General View of the Agriculture of the County of Gloucester* (Gloucester, 1807)
Rudge, *Hist. of Glos.*	T. Rudge, *History of the County of Gloucester* (2 vols. Gloucester, 1803)
Sherborne Mun.	*Calendar of Charters, Rolls, and Other Documents at Sherborne House* (priv. print. 1900)
Smith, *Men and Armour*	*Names and Surnames of All the Able and Sufficient Men in Body Fit for His Majesty's Service in the Wars, within the County of Gloucester, compiled by John Smith, 1608* (1902)
Taylor, *Map of Glos.* (1777)	I. Taylor, *Map of the County of Gloucester* (1777)
Trans. B.G.A.S.	*Transactions of the Bristol and Gloucestershire Archaeological Society*
Verey, *Glos.*	D. C. W. Verey, *Gloucestershire:* vol. i, *The Cotswolds;* vol. ii, *The Vale and the Forest of Dean* (The Buildings of England, ed. N. Pevsner, 1970)
Visit. Glos. 1623	*Visitation of the County of Gloucester, 1623*, ed. J. Maclean and W. C. Heane (Harleian Society xxi, 1885)
Visit. Glos. 1682–3	*Visitation of the County of Gloucester, 1682, 1683*, ed. T. FitzRoy Fenwick and W. C. Metcalfe (Exeter, priv. print. 1884)
Worc. Episc. Reg.	Worcester Episcopal Registers

BRIGHTWELLS BARROW HUNDRED

IN 1086 Brightwells Barrow hundred comprised Coln St. Aldwyns, Williamstrip (then called Hatherop but later a part of Coln St. Aldwyns), Eastleach Martin, Eastleach Turville, Fairford, Hatherop, Kempsford, Lechlade, Quenington, and Southrop (then, like the Eastleaches, called Leach), and was assessed at a total of 102 hides and 4 yardlands.[1] Another Domesday hundred, called Bibury, comprising Aldsworth, Bibury (which then included Barnsley), Arlington (a tithing of Bibury), and Eycot, was assessed at 40 hides.[2] References to Bibury hundred found in the late 13th century[3] presumably relate only to the separate frankpledge jurisdiction enjoyed by the bishop of Worcester, for by 1221 the Bibury hundred manors had for other purposes been included in Brightwells Barrow hundred.[4] Eycot, which became part of Rendcomb parish, remained in Brightwells Barrow hundred in the 14th century.[5] In 1086 Winson, later a chapelry of Bibury, was included under Bradley hundred where it emerged as a separate civil parish.[6]

Brightwells Barrow hundred was one of the group known as the Seven Hundreds of Cirencester[7] which was granted to Cirencester Abbey in 1189. The descent and liberties of the Seven Hundreds have been treated in an earlier volume.[8]

At Bibury the bishops of Worcester retained wide liberties, including return of writs, view of frankpledge, and gallows,[9] and in 1272 the bishop, who had a prison in Barnsley, was disputing with Cirencester Abbey procedure in cases concerning thieves caught but not red-handed.[10] The Bibury liberty covered the area of the former hundred including Ablington (a tithing of Bibury) but the court rolls, surviving from 1382,[11] contain no evidence that Barnsley was represented at the frankpledge court.[12] The suit of Arlington was withdrawn in the mid 13th century[13] and later the lord of the Bibury rectory estate held view of frankpledge.[14] Gloucester Abbey's tenants in Ablington apparently attended a biannual view held in Coln Rogers.[15]

Elsewhere in Brightwells Barrow hundred three manors secured full quittance of hundredal jurisdiction. The lords of Fairford, a member of the honor of Gloucester, claimed view of frankpledge, gallows, pillory, tumbril, and waif in 1287[16] and their court was also the frankpledge court for part of Eastleach Turville and, after the mid 13th century, Arlington.[17] The view was also held on Quenington manor, owned from the mid 12th century by the Knights Hospitallers,[18] and on Southrop manor by

[1] *Dom. Bk.* (Rec. Com.), i. 163v.–164, 165v., 167v., 168v.–169.

[2] Ibid. 164 and v., 165v., 170v.

[3] *Red Bk. of Worc.* 369–70, 376.

[4] *Pleas of the Crown for Glos.* ed. Maitland, p. 41.

[5] *Glos. Subsidy Roll, 1327,* 14; E 179/113/31A rot. 4; *Feud. Aids,* ii. 248, 280.

[6] *Dom. Bk.* (Rec. Com.), i. 169v.; *Census, 1801–1971.*

[7] *Cal. Pat. 1550–3,* 411–12; C 142/107 no. 50.

[8] *Ciren. Cart.* i, pp. 27–9; *V.C.H. Glos.* xi. 152–3.

[9] *Rot. Hund.* (Rec. Com.), i. 177; *Plac. de Quo Warr.* (Rec. Com.), 264; *Rot. Parl.* i. 322.

[10] *Ciren. Cart.* iii, pp. 848–9.

[11] Glos. R.O., D 678, Bibury MSS. pp. 1–24, 126; ct. rolls 63, 64, 77A, 79, 81A, 99A*; ct. roll (formerly D 1375).

[12] Cf. *Red Bk. of Worc.* 369; G.D.R. vol. 381A, f. 88.

[13] *Red Bk. of Worc.* 376.

[14] *Oseney Cart.* (Oxford Hist. Soc.), v, p. 7; Glos. R.O., D 678, ct. roll 64, rot. 3.

[15] Glouc. Cath. Libr., Reg. Abb. Newton, ff. 41v.–42v.; Reg. Abb. Malvern, i, ff. 179v.–180v., 187v.–188v.

[16] *Plac. de Quo Warr.* (Rec. Com.), 253.

[17] *Cal. Inq. p.m.* v, p. 329; cf. *Red Bk. of Worc.* 376.

[18] Cf. *Valor Eccl.* (Rec. Com.), ii. 462.

the early 14th century.[19] In three other manors the rights of the lord of the hundred were limited. Under an agreement made in the 1230s the biannual view of frankpledge for Hatherop manor was held in the manor court by Cirencester Abbey's bailiffs and the lady of the manor received the amercements for an annual composition and enjoyed pecuniary rights in the hue and cry.[20] A similar arrangement was in force at Kempsford, apparently by 1258,[21] but in the later 16th century the view for both places was held by manorial stewards.[22] About 1230 Cirencester Abbey granted the lady of Lechlade the right to a tumbril and pillory and the profits of the biannual

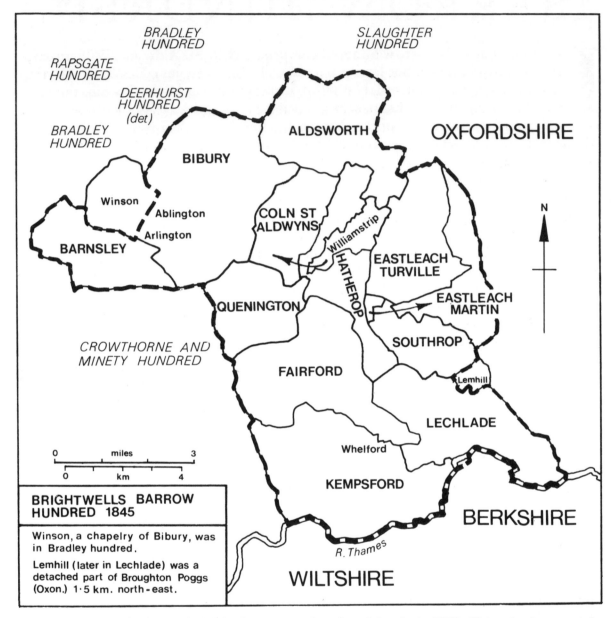

BRADLEY HUNDRED

SLAUGHTER HUNDRED

RAPSGATE HUNDRED

DEERHURST HUNDRED (det)

BRADLEY HUNDRED

ALDSWORTH

OXFORDSHIRE

BIBURY

Winson

Ablington

Arlington

COLN ST ALDWYNS

Williamstrip

EASTLEACH TURVILLE

BARNSLEY

HATHEROP

EASTLEACH MARTIN

QUENINGTON

SOUTHROP

CROWTHORNE AND MINETY HUNDRED

FAIRFORD

Lemhill

LECHLADE

Whelford

KEMPSFORD

0 miles 3

0 km 4

BRIGHTWELLS BARROW HUNDRED 1845

Winson, a chapelry of Bibury, was in Bradley hundred.

Lemhill (later in Lechlade) was a detached part of Broughton Poggs (Oxon.) 1·5 km. north-east.

BERKSHIRE

R. Thames

WILTSHIRE

N

view, which was to be held in her court by the abbey's bailiffs;[23] in the later 13th century the lords of the manor unsuccessfully claimed wider liberties, including gallows, and the free tenants withdrew their suit from the hundred court.[24] In 1367 the abbot of Bruern (Oxon.) laid claim unsuccessfully to gallows on his Eastleach Turville manor.[25]

The remaining places in the hundred were represented at the biannual hundred

[19] *Inq. p.m. Glos.* 1301–58, 248.
[20] Dugdale, *Mon.* vi(1), 507–8; *Ciren. Cart.* ii, p. 623.
[21] *Ciren. Cart.* ii, p. 623; cf. *Inq. p.m. Glos.* 1236–1300, 22.
[22] Glos. R.O., D 1375/496–502; D 2525, ct. roll 7–8 Eliz.;

Glos. Colln. JV1. 5.
[23] *Ciren. Cart.* i, pp. 220–1.
[24] Ibid. ii, p. 548; *Rot. Hund.* (Rec. Com.), i. 177.
[25] *Cal. Pat.* 1367–70, 69.

view of frankpledge at which Coln St. Aldwyns, Eastleach Martin, and part of Eastleach Turville with Williamstrip each formed single tithings.[26] The meeting-place was in the centre of the hundred at the junction of the Droitwich–Lechlade salt-way and a route from Fairford where a barrow was mentioned in 1400;[27] a tree growing on the barrow later gave the name Barrow Elm to the meeting-place.[28] In the early 15th century Gloucester Abbey provided overnight hospitality for the court's officers in near-by Coln St. Aldwyns[29] and in the 1530s the lessee of Hatherop manor entertained Cirencester Abbey's steward holding courts at Barrow Elm.[30] In the later 16th century views were held there in the spring and autumn and the tithings made presentments and paid cert money, that for Coln St. Aldwyns and Eastleach Martin being called hole silver. At those views Williamstrip was sometimes represented separately and representatives of Hatherop, Kempsford, and Lechlade appeared in order to pay cert money and ask permission for the manorial stewards to hold the view or else for the hundredal lords' bailiffs to be sent to hold it.[31] The custom of ward-staff involving watching duty on certain nights, although exacted from Hatherop but not from Kempsford and Southrop in 1394,[32] was limited by the later 16th century to those tithings attending the view and in the autumn they owed a 3d. fine called wake, evidently in place of it.[33]

The twelve parishes of the hundred formed a compact group at the south-eastern corner of the county, extending from high Cotswold downland in the north to flat and relatively low-lying land by the river Thames, which marks the southern boundary. The higher land is mostly on oolitic limestone and the lower on clay. The most notable features of the landscape are the valleys of the rivers Coln and Leach which flow into the Thames near Lechlade. The rich alluvial soil of the southern part has been well suited for meadow land. In contrast the higher land above the valleys was farmed as open fields and common pasture and some landowners compensated a shortage of meadow land with property in Kempsford and other Thamesside parishes near by. Gravel beds in the southern part were not exploited on any scale until the mid 20th century. Architecturally the area is rich in churches of which those at Fairford and Lechlade were rebuilt in the late 15th century. Of several substantial country houses the most notable is the 18th-century Barnsley Park. The most important early routes crossing the hundred were a salt-way from Droitwich to Lechlade, the old Gloucester–London road (the Welsh way) which passed through Barnsley and Fairford, and the Roman Akeman Street running east-north-eastwards from Cirencester, but in the coaching era and later the Cirencester–London road through Fairford and Lechlade and the Cirencester–Oxford road through Bibury were the main roads. The Thames and Severn canal, opened in 1789, crosses the south part of the hundred to meet the Thames just above Lechlade. The only railway line to penetrate the hundred, a branch line from Witney (Oxon.) to Fairford, was in operation from 1873 until 1962.

In the Middle Ages settlements in the hundred were, with the exceptions of Aldsworth and Barnsley, located beside one of the three rivers. Eastleach Martin (known also as Botherop), Southrop, Williamstrip, Hatherop, and its hamlet of Netherton (formerly Netherup) all share a place-name element that recalls their origin as farmsteads dependent on older settlements.[34] The villages and hamlets of the central and northern parts have remained small and Netherton was depopulated in the mid 19th century. In the south the market town of Fairford, established at an important road

[26] *Ciren. Cart.* ii, p. 622.
[27] *Trans. B.G.A.S.* ix. 333.
[28] *P.N. Glos.* (E.P.N.S.), i. 37; Taylor, *Map of Glos.* (1777).
[29] *Ciren. Cart.* ii, p. 622.
[30] S.C. 6/Hen. VIII/3985 rot. 32d.; Glos. R.O., D 540/T 30.
[31] Glos. R.O., D 1375/496–502.
[32] *Ciren. Cart.* ii, pp. 634–5.
[33] Glos. R.O., D 1375/496–502.
[34] *P.N. Glos.* i. 37.

junction and a crossing of the Coln, was a borough from the 12th century. Dominated by John Tame, a wool-merchant, in the late 15th century, it later depended on local trade and road traffic. Lechlade, sited at the head of the navigable Thames close to an important crossing of the river, was a borough and market town from the early 13th century. Later the road traffic and the consignment of goods, particularly cheese, down river to London provided the bulk of its trade. Both towns remained small, their growth possibly inhibited by their proximity to each other.

The land was used extensively for sheep-farming in the Middle Ages, especially by ecclesiastical landowners, including the bishop of Worcester, the Knights Hospitallers, and the abbeys of Cirencester, Gloucester, Lacock (Wilts.), Bruern (Oxon.), and Oseney (Oxon.). A cloth-making industry based on Fairford and mills in the Coln valley was of no great significance, and the hundred remained predominantly agricultural and centred on its estates and large farms. Landowning families, including the Barkers, Coxwells, and Thynnes, had an important influence, and in the northern part of the hundred much land passed into the Hatherop, Williamstrip, and Sherborne estates. The northern part remained sparsely populated in the 1970s when a factory in Quenington was the only significant representative of manufacturing industry. From the mid 20th century there was some expansion in the southern part, for which airfields in Kempsford and Brize Norton (Oxon.) provided employment and which came under the regional influence of Swindon. In the 1970s the hundred with its picturesque scenery was favoured as a residential area, and its rivers, of which the Coln had long been known for trout-fishing, and its flooded gravel pits were developed for recreational purposes.

ALDSWORTH

THE RURAL parish of Aldsworth lies 6.5 km. south-east of Northleach and 5 km. north-east of Cirencester. In 1976 it covered an area of 1,356 ha. (3,350 a.)[1] and was irregular in shape with the boundaries marked by field boundaries save on the west and part of the south where they followed the river Leach and a short section of the Coln St. Aldwyns road. The Leach broke its banks in 1412[2] and 1723,[3] and in 1612 a meeting of the inhabitants of Aldsworth and Bibury was convened to determine its ancient course,[4] but it had ceased to run in that part by 1976.

The land, lying mostly between 122 m. and 152 m., but rising to 168 m. in the north-east and north-west, is on the Great Oolite which is overlaid by Forest Marble on the higher ground in the west and south-east.[5] Formerly there were several quarries.[6] Before inclosure in 1793 most of the parish lay in extensive open fields but from the 13th century the downlands have provided sheep-pastures. There is some meadow land in the Leach valley but by the 16th century estates either had meadows in or took hay from near-by parishes, suggesting a shortage of meadow land in Aldsworth.

The downlands were said c. 1775 to provide excellent hunting[7] and at about that date a race-course was laid out for the Bibury Club, an exclusive private racing club, in the south-eastern corner.[8] A grandstand was designed by Richard Pace of Lechlade in 1800,[9] and the Prince of Wales attended the four-day summer meeting of 1802.[10] The club, which declined after 1814, also met at Burford (Oxon.) from where in 1827 it transferred its meetings to Cheltenham.[11] The Aldsworth race-course apparently remained in use in the mid 19th century[12] and a training groom lived in the parish in the late 1830s,[13] but between 1839 and 1859 the races ceased and the stables were closed.[14] Although the site had been inclosed and the grandstand apparently removed by c. 1881[15] some buildings remained in the early 20th century when the land was still uncultivated.[16] The village contains several buildings built or used in connexion with the racecourse; the jockey stable recorded in the southern

part in 1799[17] was probably that beside the trainer's house which had been converted as cottages by 1912.[18]

Of the land in the north-west part of the parish taken into Lodge park, created mainly in Farmington and Northleach in the mid 17th century,[19] the southern part had been planted by 1799[20] and was later included in Larkethill wood, planted south of the Northleach road in the 19th century.[21] In the north-west, where Conygree was recorded in 1571,[22] was a warren in 1674[23] but in 1799 only a small area adjoining Lodge park remained a warren.[24] In 1839 Lodge park was a deer-park and with other woodland was kept in hand by the lord of the manor.[25] In 1901 the parish had 77 a. of wood and plantation.[26] Allotment gardens south east of the village between the Burford and Eastleach roads were recorded in 1836[27] and, with allotments west of the village in the angle of the Northleach and Cocklebarrow roads, in the early 1920s.[28]

The Cirencester–Oxford road which crosses the parish from south-west to north-east was described as a highway in 1389 when it was flooded and blocked through the neglect of the villagers.[29] The bridge over the Leach, possibly that recorded in the 1260s,[30] was called Burfording bridge in 1412[31] and was out of repair in 1434 through the neglect of the Bibury villagers.[32] The road was turnpiked in 1753.[33] The bridge was partly maintained by the county in 1836,[34] although in the same year a turnpike commissioner contracted with a Bibury mason for its repair.[35] There was a bridge on the Coln St. Aldwyns road by 1413.[36] The roads leading from the village westwards to Cocklebarrow, called Waldron way, north-eastwards to Sherborne, and north-westwards to Northleach were recorded in 1571.[37] All the above-mentioned roads with others were specified in the inclosure award of 1793 when the course of the Northleach road was aligned on the spire of Aldsworth church,[38] a notable landmark which is also the focus for sections of the Cocklebarrow, Sherborne, and Coln St. Aldwyns roads.

There are signs of early settlement including

---

[1] O.S. Area Bk. (1884); Census, 1971. This account was written in 1976.

[2] Glos. R.O., D 936A/M 5, rot. 2.

[3] Ibid. D 678, ct. roll 99A.

[4] Ibid. 81A.

[5] Geol. Surv. Map 1″, solid, sheet 44 (1856 edn.).

[6] Cf. O.S. Map 6″, Glos. XLIV. NE. (1884 edn.).

[7] Rudder, Glos. 221.

[8] Taylor, Map of Glos. (1777); cf. H. A. Evans, Highways and Byways in Oxford and the Cotswolds (1905), 355.

[9] Colvin, Biog. Dict. of Eng. Architects, 427.

[10] Glouc. Jnl. 5 July 1802.

[11] Cf. V.C.H. Oxon. ii. 364–5.

[12] Glos. R.O., Q/RUm 145; Geol. Surv. Map 1″, solid, sheet 44 (1856 edn.).

[13] Glos. R.O., P 8/IN 1/4.

[14] Christ Church, Oxford, MS. Estates 24, f. 179; no evidence is cited for the statement in Glos. R.O., PA 44/1 that races were held until 1847.

[15] O.S. Map 6″, Glos. XLV. NW. (1886 edn.).

[16] Ibid. (1923 edn.); Glos. Colln. KR 1.1.

[17] Glos. R.O., D 1388, Aldsworth inc. map.

[18] Glos. Colln. KR 1.1.

[19] V.C.H. Glos. vi. 122; Glos. R.O., D 678, settlements 49.

[20] Glos. R.O., D 1388, Aldsworth inc. map.

[21] O.S. Map 6″, Glos. XLIV. NE. (1884 edn.).

[22] Glos. Colln. 16209.

[23] Glos. R.O., D 678, settlements 49.

[24] Ibid. D 1388, Aldsworth inc. map.

[25] Ibid. Aldsworth par. val.

[26] Acreage Returns, 1901.

[27] Glos. R.O., Q/RUm 145.

[28] O.S. Map 6″, Glos. XLIV. NE. (1924 edn.).

[29] Glos. R.O., D 678, ct. roll 63, rot. 4.

[30] When Agnes atte brugge was named: Hist. & Cart. Mon. Glouc. (Rolls Ser.), iii. 186.

[31] Glos. R.O., D 936A/M 5, rot. 2.

[32] Ibid. D 678, Bibury MSS. p. 14.

[33] Bibury Road Act, 26 Geo. II, c. 70.

[34] Glos. R.O., CI 2, p. 16.

[35] Ibid. D 1070/I/49.

[36] Ibid. D 936A/M 5, rot. 2d.

[37] Glos. Colln. 16209.

[38] Glos. R.O., D 678, Aldsworth inc. award.

several earth-works and, in the south-east part of the parish, traces of small Iron Age inclosures.[39] The village grew up north of the Cirencester–Oxford road, apparently around two separate focal points, a larger and a smaller green at its western and eastern ends respectively. The larger green, possibly that recorded in the 1260s,[40] lies in a gap between two hills through which a stream runs and was the earlier and more important. The church occupied the hill to the south-west by the 12th century and is set apart from and overlooks the village. The sites of former buildings in the field north-east of the church were suggested by earth-works visible in 1976. In the 1790s a farm-house, Aldsworth Farm, was recorded north-west of the church.[41] East of the church stands the Manor, the rectory farm-house which dates from the 17th century. On the green was a well, probably that recorded in 1412[42] and called Fair well in 1638,[43] and to the east in 1799 stood the village pound,[44] possibly the common park which was out of repair in 1644.[45] The parish house held from the manor in 1541[46] may have been the church house which comprised three cottages in 1743 when the rents were applied to church repairs.[47] The building, which occupied an island on the green,[48] was repaired c. 1794 but was demolished, possibly after 1878.[49] The Barracks, on the north-west side of the green, dates from the early 18th century and Brook Cottage on the south-east side is dated 1728 and bears the name of William Mury, whose ancestors were recorded in the village from the 1260s.[50]

The village grew along two lanes leading up the spur east of the green to join the road from the turnpike to Sherborne at the smaller green. Green Farm on the north side dates from the early 18th century; east of it Harvest Barn was converted as a house c. 1970 and north of it stands a dovecot. A well recorded on the green in 1799[51] was the chief water-supply in the early 20th century until Lord Sherborne supplied most of the village in 1920.[52] A memorial was built on the green after the First World War.[53]

Most of the farm-houses and cottages are of the 19th century. Many earlier buildings recorded around the larger green in 1799 and Aldsworth Farm and some cottages north of the lane to the church

were demolished, apparently before 1824, during the construction of a private carriage-way to Sherborne Park from the turnpike.[54] Lodges were built both on the northern boundary,[55] called Allen's Lodges c. 1882, and south-west of the village.[56] The latter, unoccupied in 1836,[57] is an early-19th-century building. In the northern part of the village are two substantial farm-houses; Blackpits House was rebuilt in 1854[58] and Tayler's Farm House to the east has a main block built or remodelled in 1851[59] and extensive out-buildings. East of the Sherborne road are some later-19th-century estate cottages. A school was built north-east of the western green in 1853. The vicarage and a nonconformist chapel date from the early 20th century and a pair of cottages by the Cirencester road was described as new in 1919.[60] There was some new building in the village in the mid 20th century. In 1976 one cottage remained north of the lane to the church; another there had been recently demolished.

At Wall Farm, 500 m. north of the village, there was a settlement by the mid 12th century when people surnamed of Wall were mentioned.[61] Although it was styled a vill c. 1230[62] it was probably never much more than a farmstead.[63] In 1976 it comprised a farm-house with some cottages and out-buildings. The other outlying farmsteads are post-inclosure. By 1799 there was a farm-house at Cocklebarrow where a rambling house of various dates of the 19th century stood in 1976. There was a barn at Conygree by 1799;[64] the farm-house there dates from the late 19th century[65] and has a secondary back wing dated 1899. The farm-house at Ladbarrow on the south-eastern boundary, where there were farm-buildings by 1799,[66] is a 19th-century building.

In 1086 41 tenants were recorded in Aldsworth[67] and in 1327 27 people were assessed for the subsidy.[68] The parish had 21 households in 1563[69] and 94 communicants in 1603.[70] The population was estimated at 120 c. 1710,[71] and also c. 1775[72] when it was certainly larger, for in 1801 it was 288. From 282 in 1811 it rose to 430 by 1861 and then dropped to 299 by 1901. After a small increase to 312 by 1911 the number of inhabitants continued to fall to 230 by 1951 and to 190 by 1971.[73]

The victualler licensed in 1755[74] presumably

[39] R.C.H.M. *Glos.* i. 2–3.

[40] *Hist. & Cart. Mon. Glouc.* iii. 186.

[41] Glos. R.O., D 678, Aldsworth inc. award; cf. ibid. D 1388, Aldsworth inc. map.

[42] Ibid. D 936A/M 5, rot. 2.

[43] Ibid. D 678, ct. roll 79, rot. 18.

[44] Ibid. D 1388, Aldsworth inc. map.

[45] Ibid. D 678, ct. roll 79, rot. 22.

[46] S.C. 6/Hen. VIII/1248 rot. 9d.

[47] G.D.R. vol. 397, f. 89.

[48] Glos. R.O., D 1388, Aldsworth inc. map.

[49] Ibid. P 8/CW 2/1.

[50] *Hist. & Cart. Mon. Glouc.* iii. 185; Glos. R.O., D 936A/M 2, rot. 6.

[51] Glos. R.O., D 1388, Aldsworth inc. map.

[52] Richardson, *Wells and Springs of Glos.* 46.

[53] O.S. Map 6″, Glos. XLIV. NE. (1924 edn.).

[54] Cf. Glos. R.O., D 1388, Aldsworth inc. map; Bryant, *Map of Glos.* (1824).

[55] Bryant, *Map of Glos.* (1824).

[56] O.S. Map 6″, Glos. XLIV. NE. (1884 edn.).

[57] Glos. R.O., Q/RUm 145.

[58] Ex inf. Mr. G. J. Phillips, of Blackpits Ho.

[59] Date on vane.

[60] Glos. R.O., D 2299/1955; cf. O.S. Map 6″, Glos. XLIV. NE. (1903 edn.).

[61] *Hist. & Cart. Mon. Glouc.* i. 59, 155, 163; ii. 191.

[62] *Oseney Cart.* (Oxford Hist. Soc.), v, p. 32.

[63] Cf. Beresford, *Lost Villages* (1965), 351.

[64] Glos. R.O., D 1388, Aldsworth inc. map.

[65] Cf. O.S. Map 6″, Glos. XLIV. NE. (1884 edn.).

[66] Glos. R.O., D 1388, Aldsworth inc. map.

[67] *Dom. Bk.* (Rec. Com.), i. 165v., 170v.

[68] *Glos. Subsidy Roll, 1327*, 15.

[69] Bodl. MS. Rawl. C.790, f. 24v.

[70] *Eccl. Misc.* 97.

[71] Atkyns, *Glos.* 212.

[72] Rudder, *Glos.* 222.

[73] *Census*, 1801–1971.

[74] Glos. R.O., Q/AV 2, rot. 3.

occupied the inn called the Sherborne Arms in 1793;[75] owned by Lord Sherborne, it stood at the entrance to the village from the turnpike.[76] The early-19th-century building was a private residence in 1976, the inn having moved, probably by 1824, to a site on the turnpike east of the village.[77] A friendly society met at the inn in the 1840s.[78] In the mid 19th century J. W. Taylor, a brewer, lived in the parish,[79] and the Sherborne Arms was owned at the end of the century by the Taylor family's Northleach brewery.[80] It may have been the village inn which in 1912 had the names of horses carved over the doors and windows[81] but in 1891 there was also a beerhouse owned by John Waine.[82]

The Duttons of Sherborne have dominated the life of the parish at least from 1611 when they acquired the principal estate; the physical changes resulting from the creation of a route to Sherborne in the early 19th century have already been mentioned.

MANOR AND OTHER ESTATES. Land in Aldsworth was granted between 1002 and 1004 by Wulfric Spot to Burton Abbey (Staffs.) which exchanged it with King Ethelred for land nearer the abbey in 1008.[83] In 1086 an estate of 11 hides was held by Gloucester Abbey.[84] The abbey, which received other grants of land[85] and was granted free warren in 1354,[86] retained the manor of *ALDSWORTH* until the Dissolution.[87] In 1577 the Crown granted a lease of the manor to Thomas Dutton of Sherborne (d. 1581) and his sons Thomas and William,[88] and William purchased the freehold in 1611.[89] After his death in 1618 the manor passed with Sherborne manor to his son John[90] (d. 1657), and then to John's nephews William (d. 1675) and Ralph, who was created a baronet in 1678. Ralph's son Sir John Dutton, Bt., (d. 1743) was succeeded by his nephew James Lenox Naper who took the name Dutton and was succeeded in 1776 by his son James Dutton. James, created Lord Sherborne in 1784, died in 1820 and the manor then passed with the title in the direct line to John (d. 1862), James (d. 1883), and Edward. Edward (d. 1919) was succeeded by his brother Frederick (d. 1920), whose nephew

James Huntley Dutton[91] sold Ladbarrow farm to Mr. M. C. Willes c. 1939.[92] After James's death in 1949 Cocklebarrow farm was sold to E. R. H. Wills, the second son of Lord Dulverton, but James's son Charles Dutton, Lord Sherborne, remained a considerable landowner in the parish in 1976.[93]

An estate of 2 hides held in 1066 by Balchi had passed by 1086 to the Crown whose tenant was Elward son of Regenbald, a king's thegn.[94] In 1133 Henry I granted the estate, later called *WALL FARM*, with other property formerly held by Elward's father, to Cirencester Abbey[95] which was granted free warren in 1252.[96] The abbey held the estate until the Dissolution.[97] In 1543 it was granted to Richard Andrews and Nicholas Temple,[98] and in 1547 Richard sold it to William Blomer of Cowley.[99] After William's death in 1554 the estate with the tithes of wool and lambs passed to his brother-in-law William Colley of Buscot (Berks.)[1] who died in 1557 leaving as his heir his son Giles, a minor.[2] Giles Colley (d. 1558) was succeeded by his brother Thomas.[3] After Thomas's death in 1603 the estate passed to his son Thomas[4] (d. 1616), whose son Thomas[5] sold it to John Blomer of Hatherop in 1637.[6] John died in 1638 and the estate passed to his son William[7] who released it in 1669 to his elder brother John.[8] It then passed with Hatherop manor and in 1764 was owned by Sir John Webb.[9] Wall farm, which was apparently sold by 1785,[10] was part of Lord Sherborne's estate in 1793 when he was allotted c. 240 a. for the farm and c. 65 a. for the tithes.[11] Thomas Colley's dwelling at Wall mentioned in 1634[12] was presumably on the site of Wall Farm. The 18th-century farm-house was extended later in the century and remodelled internally in the late 19th.

Thomas Lawrence, described as a yeoman in 1608,[13] and Anthony Fettiplace granted an estate of 5½ yardlands to Thomas and Matthew Bennett in 1638. The estate, known later as *GREEN FARM*, was bought from Thomas Bennett's son, Thomas Bennett of Salthrop in Wroughton (Wilts.), in 1676 for John Greenwood of Brize Norton (Oxon.) by his father Thomas. Thomas, by will dated 1678, ordered a division of the estate between John's

[75] Ibid. D 678, Aldsworth inc. award.
[76] Ibid. D 1388, Aldsworth inc. map.
[77] Greenwood, *Map of Glos.* (1824); O.S. Map 6″, Glos. XLIV. NE. (1884 edn.).
[78] F.S. 2/3 no. 435.
[79] *Kelly's Dir. Glos.* (1856 and later edns.).
[80] *Licensed Houses in Glos. 1891*, 160–1; *1903*, 144–5.
[81] Glos. Colln. KR 1.1.
[82] *Licensed Houses in Glos. 1891*, 160–1; also in ibid. *1903*, 144–5.
[83] Finberg, *Early Charters of W. Midlands*, pp. 65–6.
[84] *Dom. Bk.* (Rec. Com.), i. 165v.
[85] *Hist. & Cart. Mon. Glouc.* i. 59, 156, 163.
[86] *Cal. Chart. R. 1341–1417*, 142.
[87] *Red Bk. of Worc.* 370; *Valor Eccl.* (Rec. Com.), ii. 410, 417.
[88] E 310/14/52 f. 7; cf. *Memoirs of the Dutton Family of Sherborne*, 34.
[89] *Sherborne Mun.* 236.   [90] C 142/378 no. 107.
[91] *V.C.H. Glos.* vi. 123; Glos. R.O., D 678, Aldsworth par. 12, 51, 74; *Kelly's Dir. Glos.* (1856 and later edns.); *Memoirs of the Dutton Fam.*; cf. Glos. R.O., photocopy 64B, in which one of the Cresswell fam. was named as lady of the man. in 1764.

[92] Ex inf. Mr. G. J. Phillips.
[93] Ex inf. Rylands & Co., Cirencester, agents to the Sherborne est.; Burke, *Peerage* (1963), 775.
[94] *Dom. Bk.* (Rec. Com.), i. 170v.
[95] *Ciren. Cart.* i, p. 22.
[96] Ibid. pp. 8–9.
[97] *Red Bk. of Worc.* 370; *Valor Eccl.* (Rec. Com.), ii. 464.
[98] *L. & P. Hen. VIII*, xviii (2), p. 53.
[99] Glos. R.O., D 540/T 4.
[1] C 142/102 no. 76; Hockaday Abs. cxc, Eastleach Martin, 1554.
[2] C 142/109 no. 75; cf. *Cal. Pat. 1557–8*, 98.
[3] C 142/185 no. 90.
[4] C 142/280 no. 54.
[5] C 142/357 no. 19.
[6] Glos. R.O., D 540/T 6.
[7] *Inq. p.m. Glos. 1625–42*, ii. 52–4; cf. Bigland, *Glos.* ii. 48, where John's date of death is given as 1640.
[8] Glos. R.O., D 540/T 29.
[9] Bigland, *Glos.* ii. 48; Glos. R.O., D 540/T 50, E 4.
[10] Cf. Glos. R.O., D 540/E 6.
[11] Ibid. D 678, Aldsworth inc. award.
[12] Ibid. D 540/T 31.
[13] Smith, *Men and Armour*, 257.

younger sons, George, Thomas, and Gregory, but in 1691 sole right was acquired by the younger Thomas, who was described in 1694 as of Rotherwas in Dinedor (Herefs.). In 1717 the estate was owned by Charles Greenwood, a papist, and in 1722 by his widow Anne, later Mrs. James, who held *c.* 235 a. in 1746 but had been succeeded by their son Charles Greenwood by 1748.[14] Charles sold the estate in 1766 to John Waine,[15] whose family had held a lease of it since at least 1717.[16] John (d. 1776) was succeeded by his son Thomas[17] (d. 1815), whose son Thomas (d. 1849)[18] held 205 a. in 1839.[19] After Giles Waine's death *c.* 1866 the estate passed to his son John Charles Waine, a minor,[20] who put Green farm, comprising 210 a., up for sale in 1897.[21] It was bought by Robert Garne but after the death of his nephew William Thomas Garne *c.* 1966 the estate, comprising Green and Tayler's farms, was fragmented.[22] Green Farm, which dates from the early 18th century, was described in 1762 as a substantial, well built stone messuage with a malt-house.[23]

The demesne and great tithes of the manor were granted by the bishop of Worcester to Gloucester Abbey in 1100.[24] Oseney Abbey, which in 1151 appropriated Bibury church of which Aldsworth was a chapelry,[25] agreed *c.* 1155 to share with Gloucester Abbey the tithes of the tenants.[26] About 1184 the abbeys agreed to share the tithes from 49 a. held by the manorial ploughmen and from the stipends of the other manorial servants, and Oseney dropped its claim to a rent of 3s. and a load of wheat.[27] Gloucester Abbey, which had a portion for its tithes valued at £2 10s. in 1291,[28] had evidently secured its title to the manorial tithes by 1535 when it received £2 13s. 4d. as a pension or portion from the appropriator for part of the great tithes.[29] That pension or portion was granted to the bishop of Gloucester in 1541[30] and was being paid as a pension in 1713.[31] The manorial tithes, for which the Aldsworth estate was charged by 1724 with an ancient modus,[32] probably the £5 owed to the impropriator in 1771,[33] passed to Lord Sherborne and were commuted at inclosure in 1793.[34]

In 1291 Oseney Abbey held 2 yardlands in Alds-

worth,[35] evidently the endowment of the chapel there which was appropriated to the abbey in 1151 with the mother church of Bibury. With the abbey's tithes the land was considered to form an appropriated rectory in the early 16th century[36] and was regranted in 1546 to the dean and chapter of Christ Church, Oxford.[37] The rectory estate, valued at 100 marks in 1603[38] and at £60 *c.* 1708,[39] included *c.* 250 a. about 1775[40] and the dean and chapter's lessee received 203 a. for their lands and 387 a. for their tithes at inclosure in 1793.[41] A lease of the rectory passed from the owners of the Williamstrip estate to the Waine family in 1767,[42] and in 1793 Lord Sherborne was lessee.[43] Christ Church remained one of the principal landowners in the parish[44] until *c.* 1970 when it sold its property there to the trustees of David Wills.[45] The rectory farm-house, called the Manor, is a substantial 17th-century house described in 1771 as a three-storeyed house of five bays with some twelve rooms.[46] It was dilapidated in 1835 but was restored *c.* 1836[47] when one of the out-buildings to the south-west served as the farm-house.[48] In the mid 19th century the Manor was used as the parsonage, being repaired in 1866,[49] but by 1900 it was a farm-house again.[50] It was sold in the mid 1970s to Capt. P. Percy[51] and extensively restored with the addition of a porch on the main east front and several windows.

ECONOMIC HISTORY. In 1086 Wall farm had 1 plough and 1 *servus* in demesne;[52] the manorial demesne was cultivated by 6 *servi* with 3 ploughs.[53] In the later 12th century the manorial servants included ploughmen[54] and in the mid 13th century labour-services were used on the manorial demesne which was worked by 5 ploughs, of which 4 had 6 oxen each and the fifth 5 draught-beasts. Some of the labour-services were connected with sheep-farming.[55] A lease of the demesne arable was granted in 1514, Gloucester Abbey retaining its flocks in hand.[56] Oseney Abbey's estate, described as a grange in 1271,[57] was administered in 1280 with its property

---

[14] Glos. R.O., D 1388/III/1; Q/RNc 1, p. 188; 2/1, p. 27.
[15] Ibid. D 2440, Aldsworth deed.
[16] Ibid. Q/RNc 1, p. 188; 2/1, p. 27; D 1388/III/1.
[17] Ibid. D 678, Aldsworth par. 108A.
[18] Ibid. D 1388/III/2.
[19] Ibid. D 1388, Aldsworth par. val.
[20] Ibid. D 1388/III/2; cf. *Kelly's Dir. Glos.* (1856 and later edns.).
[21] Glos. R.O., D 1388/SL 8, no. 37.
[22] Ex inf. Mr. Phillips.
[23] Glos. R.O., D 1388/III/1.
[24] *Hist. & Cart. Mon. Glouc.* ii. 41.
[25] *Oseney Cart.* v, pp. 1–2. [26] Ibid. p. 31.
[27] Ibid. pp. 35–6. [28] *Tax. Eccl.* (Rec. Com.), 222.
[29] *Valor Eccl.* (Rec. Com.), ii. 410; the pension was valued at 60s. in ibid. 221; Hockaday Abs. xcix, 1546.
[30] *L. & P. Hen. VIII*, xvi, p. 572; cf. *Cal. Pat.* 1550–3, 375; Hockaday Abs. ccclxxxi, Twyning, 1659.
[31] Glos. R.O., D 1388/III/1; cf. B. L. Lansd. MS. 885, f. 106v.
[32] Glos. R.O., D 678, Aldsworth par. 74.
[33] Christ Church, Oxford, MS. Estates 24, f. 18.
[34] Glos. R.O., D 678, Aldsworth par. 125; Aldsworth inc. award.

[35] *Tax. Eccl.* (Rec. Com.), 237.
[36] *Valor Eccl.* (Rec. Com.), ii. 221, 452.
[37] Hockaday Abs. xcix.
[38] *Eccl. Misc.* 97. [39] Bodl. MS. Top. Glouc. c. 3, f. 211v.
[40] Rudder, *Glos.* 221.
[41] Glos. R.O., D 678, Aldsworth inc. award.
[42] Ibid. Aldsworth par. 104, 111; D 1388/III/1.
[43] Ibid. D 678, Aldsworth inc. award.
[44] *Kelly's Dir. Glos.* (1856 and later edns.).
[45] Ex inf. assistant treasurer, Christ Church, Oxford.
[46] Christ Church, Oxford, MS. Estates 24, f. 18.
[47] Ibid. ff. 63, 93.
[48] Glos. R.O., Q/RUm 145.
[49] Christ Church, Oxford, MS. Estates 24, ff. 151, 187; O.S. Map 6″, Glos. XLIV. NE. (1884 edn.).
[50] O.S. Map 6″, Glos. XLIV. NE. (1903 edn.).
[51] Ex inf. Mr. Phillips.
[52] *Dom. Bk.* (Rec. Com.), i. 170v. [53] Ibid. 165v.
[54] *Hist. & Cart. Mon. Glouc.* i. 159; *Oseney Cart.* v, pp. 35–6.
[55] *Hist. & Cart. Mon. Glouc.* iii. 185–7.
[56] Glouc. Cath. Libr., Reg. Abb. Newton, ff. 69–70v.
[57] *Hist. & Cart. Mon. Glouc.* i. 158; *Oseney Cart.* v, pp. 30–1.

in Bibury but had its own permanent staff;[58] its demesne was let at farm in the early 16th century.[59] All three estates were let at farm in the mid 16th century.[60]

The tenants recorded on Wall farm in 1086 were 4 *villani* and 2 bordars with 2 ploughs.[61] The manor then supported 21 *villani*, 5 bordars, and 2 Frenchmen with 15 ploughs.[62] In the later 12th century the manorial ploughmen held 49 a. apparently by their service on the demesne.[63] In the 1260s 5 free tenants were recorded on the manor; 3, of whom 2 held a ½ hide (96 a.) each, owed cash rents, suit of court, and a heriot of a horse and armour, a fourth owed cash rent, and the fifth, the widow of a smith, owed cash rent and services of a customary nature, including aid, pannage, and a toll on brewing. Of the customary tenants 26 each held a yardland, which comprised 48 a., and two more shared a yardland; the lord had 2½ customary yardlands in hand. One yardlander owed a rent of 12s. a year but from the other yardlands were owed pannage, heriots, and heavy labour-services. Between Michaelmas and Lammas 4 week-works were owed and carrying service might be enforced on the fifth day once every 5 weeks; extra services were required for ploughing, haymaking, sheep-shearing, and burning pitch, used as a sheep-salve. Between Lammas and Michaelmas the yardlander owed 5 harvest-works a week, 4 bedrepes with 4 men, and carrying-service. There were also 5 mondaymen owing cash rents; three of them also owed 1 week-work between the Nativity of John the Baptist (24 June) and Lammas, a day's reaping each week and 3 bedrepes between Lammas and Michaelmas, a day's work at haymaking, and the same customary payments as a yardlander.[64] There was tension between the abbey and its unfree tenants in 1412 when eight of the latter were said to have fled and the abbey to have seized all of its bondsmen's goods and chattels.[65]

In the mid 16th century 2 yardlands of Wall farm were held by copy[66] and several large copyholds were held from the manor including holdings of 3, 3½, and 5½ yardlands.[67] In 1609 fines for customary land were said to be at the will of the lord, and widows were entitled to free bench.[68] In the same year the copyholders petitioned the Crown for the right to hold the manor in fee farm.[69] In 1617 2 free tenants and 15 copyholders held from the manor.[70]

In the 1640s heriots were payable for land held by leases for lives,[71] such as were held by some of the 8 leaseholders recorded on the manor in 1661 with 2 free tenants and 14 copyholders;[72] similar leases were granted in the mid 18th century.[73]

The parish had two large open fields, an east and a west field on opposite sides of the village, first recorded in 1571 when they contained 2,815¾ a.[74] In 1688 a yardland, divided almost equally between them, contained strips of an acre or a half-acre.[75] Some land had been temporarily inclosed by 1584 when pigs were kept on it[76] and in 1718 4 hitchings covered 11 a.[77] By 1739 the fields had been adapted to a three-course rotation by a division of the east field, part of which was then known as the north field.[78]

The parish has little meadow land apart from some by the river Leach.[79] In the 1260s the lord of the manor took 2d. for each horse and 1d. for each ox over a year old pasturing in a several pasture called Haylinge;[80] free men enjoyed common rights there between Michaelmas and Whitsun and from 1271 Oseney Abbey was permitted to pasture 12 oxen during that period and 6 oxen for the rest of the year if the lord had cattle there.[81] Areas of downland, recorded in 1542 as Aldsworth Downs,[82] were used as common pastures. Three areas of downland remained uninclosed in 1799.[83] At Blackpits Downs (170 a.) in the north-east the right to cut furzes in the 18th century was reserved to manorial tenants;[84] Allen's Downs (178 a.), north of Wall Farm, was probably named after the mid-16th-century holders of Sherborne manor;[85] and East Downs (191 a.), a common pasture east of Ladbarrow Farm and recorded from 1571,[86] was the site of the racecourse. Blackpits and Allen's Downs had been inclosed by 1839.[87]

By the mid 13th century sheep-farming was of considerable importance on Gloucester Abbey's estate,[88] a shepherd being recorded in 1281 or 1282.[89] In 1514 the abbey retained in hand two flocks[90] which from 1532 it leased to a farmer; for one of 360 wethers hay was provided from Kempsford and Ampney St. Peter, and the other of 240 ewes was wintered at Maisemore.[91] At the Dissolution Cirencester Abbey, which had pasture rights for 300 sheep with Wall farm, was letting at farm with the demesne a flock, for which hay was provided from

[58] *Oseney Cart.* vi, pp. 193–4.
[59] Ibid. pp. 232, 263.
[60] *Valor Eccl.* (Rec. Com.), ii. 221, 410, 464; see also Hockaday Abs. xcix, 1546, 1557; cxc, Eastleach Martin, 1554; C 3/161/56.
[61] *Dom. Bk.* (Rec. Com.), i. 170v.
[62] Ibid. 165v.
[63] *Oseney Cart.* v, pp. 35–6; *Hist. & Cart. Mon. Glouc.* i. 159.
[64] *Hist. & Cart. Mon. Glouc.* iii. 184–7.
[65] Glos. R.O., D 936A/M 5, rot. 2.
[66] S.C. 6/Hen. VIII/1240 rot. 48; Req. 2/251/47.
[67] Glos. R.O., D 678, Aldsworth par. 126; E 310/14/51 ff. 29, 34.
[68] Glos. R.O., D 678, Aldsworth par. 121.
[69] *Cal. S.P. Dom.* 1603–10, 513.
[70] Glos. R.O., D 678, Sherborne and Aldsworth ct. bk. 1582–1622.
[71] Ibid. Aldsworth par. 18–20.
[72] Ibid. ct. roll 72A.
[73] Cf. ibid. Aldsworth par. 91–7, 100.
[74] Glos. Colln. 16209.

[75] Glos. R.O., D 678, Aldsworth par. 51.
[76] Ibid. 126.
[77] Ibid. D 540/T 50.
[78] Glos. Colln. 16209; cf. Glos. R.O., D 678, Aldsworth inc. award.
[79] Cf. Glos. R.O., D 1388, Aldsworth inc. map.
[80] *Hist. & Cart. Mon. Glouc.* iii. 187.
[81] Ibid. i. 158; *Oseney Cart.* v, pp. 30–1.
[82] *P.N. Glos.* (E.P.N.S.), i. 23.
[83] Glos. R.O., D 1388, Aldsworth inc. map.
[84] Ibid. D 678, Aldsworth par. 85, 124.
[85] *V.C.H. Glos.* vi. 123.
[86] Glos. Colln. 16209; cf. Glos. R.O., D 678, Aldsworth par. 121.
[87] Glos. R.O., D 1388, Aldsworth par. val.
[88] See above.
[89] J.I. 1/278 rot. 51d.
[90] Glouc. Cath. Libr., Reg. Abb. Newton, ff. 69–70v.
[91] Ibid. Reg. Abb. Malvern, ii, ff. 58v.–60; E 310/14/52 f. 7; Glos. R.O., D 678, Aldsworth par. 3A.

Latton (Wilts.), and the sheep-pasture rent was much the most valuable part of the estate; the farm of its tithes of wool and lambs was also valuable.[92] In the later 16th century a large flock was kept on the manor[93] which continued to include meadows in Kempsford and Ampney St. Peter.[94] In the 18th century the manor also had pasture in Sherborne.[95] Two shepherds were listed in Aldsworth in 1608[96] and the manor court was much concerned with the regulation of sheep-pasture in the late 16th century.[97] In 1634 a half-yardland had common rights for 60 sheep, 3 horses, and 3 rother beasts[98] but by 1688 the stint for a whole yardland had been reduced to 60 sheep, 2 horses, and 3 cows.[99] On the eve of inclosure it was estimated that 600 sheep were kept in the parish.[1]

Few early inclosures were recorded. By 1739 92½ a. had been inclosed in the east and north fields and 11 a. at Conygree in the west field.[2] The parish remained largely open until 1793 when it was inclosed under a private Act. The award, which affected 3,158 a., allotted Lord Sherborne 2,228 a. for his open-field land, tithes, and common rights and he shared an allotment of 46 a. with another proprietor, who after various exchanges, took 26 a. As lessee of the dean and chapter of Christ Church Lord Sherborne was awarded 590 a. for their glebe and tithes, the curate 26 a. for his tithes, and Thomas Waine 204 a. The custom whereby the rectory estate provided a bull and boar for the tenant of Aldsworth farm for £5 a year was abolished by the award.[3] After various exchanges, by 1799 Lord Sherborne owned c. 2,417 a. and held a lease of the rectory estate comprising c. 586 a.[4]

As a result of inclosure 470 a. were added to the area under tillage and 1,640 quarters to the annual crop of wheat, barley, oats, and peas and the number of sheep kept trebled.[5] In the early 19th century a considerable proportion of the parish was meadow land and pasture[6] but in 1866 2,893 a. were returned as arable or rotated grass and only 101 a. as permanent grass. Large flocks of sheep, returned at 2,349, were kept then.[7] In 1896 at least 178 a. were lying fallow and in 1926 there were at least 740 a. of permanent grassland but sheep and corn husbandry remained dominant in the later 19th century and early 20th.[8] From the later 19th century, when the parish became noted for its shorthorn cattle through the activity of the Garne family of farmers,[9] more cattle were reared and in 1926 397 cattle, including 72 milk cows, were returned compared with 178, including 62 milk cows, in 1896.[10] The Garnes also kept a flock of pure-bred Cotswold sheep which was the last of its kind when disbanded c. 1970.[11] In 1976 the land was devoted mainly to cereal production and beef-farming. Some dairy cows and pigs were kept and one breeding flock of sheep.[12]

The post-inclosure farms were large and provided the main source of employment. In 1831 4 farmers employed 70 labourers.[13] By 1839 the Sherborne estate had been organized with 6 farms in Aldsworth; they were Cocklebarrow (807 a.), Ladbarrow (591 a.), Blackpits (575 a.), Wall (477 a.), Conygree (146 a.), and one of 226 a. Blackpits and Wall farms were farmed by William Garne. There was also a freehold farm of 205 a.[14] The rectory estate, let at farm in 1808[15] and known later as Manor or College farm,[16] comprised 621 a. in 1919.[17] There were 10 farms in the parish in 1896 and 13 in 1926 when they provided full-time employment for 76 labourers. Three of the farms in 1926 were smallholdings with less than 20 a. each and six had over 300 a. each.[18] In 1976 there were six principal farms; Cocklebarrow, Manor, and Blackpits were farmed by Mr. G. J. Phillips, and the others, Wall, Conygree, and Ladbarrow, separately.[19]

No record has been found of a mill in Aldsworth; in the mid 13th century Gloucester Abbey had its corn milled in Coln St. Aldwyns,[20] and its unfree manorial tenants owed suit of mill there in the mid 14th.[21]

In 1811 53 families were supported by agriculture and 8 by trades; the figures in 1831 were 60 and 15 respectively.[22] Most of the usual village trades were represented in the parish. A smith lived there in the mid 13th century[23] and in the 17th.[24] Henry Collett was smith in 1799[25] and his descendants followed the trade until the early 20th century; the village had a second smith for periods in the late 19th century.[26] In 1839 a new carpenter's shop was recorded,[27] and there were two wheelwrights in the mid 19th century.[28] In the mid 19th century a weaver lived in the parish,[29] where in 1912 linen cloth was made.[30] A butcher was recorded in 1434.[31] The village had a

[92] *Valor Eccl.* (Rec. Com.), ii. 464; S.C. 6/Hen. VIII/1240 rot. 48.
[93] *Memoirs of the Dutton Fam.* 34.
[94] Glos. R.O., D 678, Aldsworth par. 1, 16.
[95] Ibid. 89.   [96] Smith, *Men and Armour*, 257.
[97] Glos. R.O., D 678, Aldsworth par. 126.
[98] Ibid. D 540/T 31.
[99] Ibid. D 678, Aldsworth par. 51.
[1] Rudge, *Agric. of Glos.* 381.
[2] Glos. Colln. 16209.
[3] Glos. R.O., D 678, Aldsworth inc. award.
[4] Ibid. D 1388, Aldsworth inc. map.
[5] Rudge, *Agric. of Glos.* 381.
[6] Rudge, *Hist. of Glos.* i. 246.
[7] M.A.F. 68/26/12; M.A.F. 68/25/23.
[8] M.A.F. 68/1609/2; M.A.F. 68/3295/17.
[9] Glos. Colln. KR 1.1; cf. ibid. J 10.32, 48, 49.
[10] M.A.F. 68/3295/17; M.A.F. 68/1609/2.
[11] C. & A. M. Hadfield, *The Cotswolds* (1966), 20; *The Cotswolds, A New Study* (Newton Abbot, 1973), 288.
[12] Ex inf. Mr. Phillips; Mr. D. C. Wilcox, of Wall Farm.

[13] *Census*, 1831.
[14] Glos. R.O., D 1388, Aldsworth par. val.
[15] Glos. R.O., D 678, Aldsworth par. 113.
[16] *Kelly's Dir. Glos.* (1906 and later edns.); O.S. Map 6″, Glos. XLIV. NE. (1903 and 1924 edns.).
[17] Glos. R.O., D 2299/1955.
[18] M.A.F. 68/1609/2; M.A.F. 68/3295/17.
[19] Ex inf. Mr. Phillips and Mr. Wilcox.
[20] *Hist. & Cart. Mon. Glouc.* iii. 197.
[21] Glouc. Cath. Libr., deeds and seals, x, f. 10.
[22] *Census*, 1811, 1831.
[23] *Hist. & Cart. Mon. Glouc.* iii. 184.
[24] *Cat. Glouc. Wills*, 206; E 179/247/14 rot. 4d.
[25] Glos. R.O., D 1388, Aldsworth inc. map.
[26] *Kelly's Dir. Glos.* (1856 and later edns.); cf. O.S. Map 6″, Glos. XLIV. NE. (1884, 1903, and 1924 edns.).
[27] Glos. R.O., D 1388, Aldsworth par. val.; cf. ibid. III/2.
[28] *Kelly's Dir. Glos.* (1856), 217; (1863), 195.
[29] Glos. R.O., P 8/IN 1/4, entries from 1837 to 1856.
[30] Glos. Colln. KR 1.1.
[31] Glos. R.O., D 678, Bibury MSS. p. 14.

shop and a bakehouse in 1799,[32] and a shop and a post-office in 1976. The trades recorded in the early 20th century included those of a stonemason, shoe repairer, and hurdle-maker.[33] Members of the Howse family were carriers from the mid 19th century and C. J. Howse, a coal-dealer in the early 1930s, had established by 1939 a haulage business[34] which was still operating in 1976.

LOCAL GOVERNMENT. In the late 13th century the manor of Bibury exercised leet jurisdiction over most of Aldsworth but view of frankpledge for the appropriated rectory estate[35] belonged then to Bibury Oseney manor as it did in the 17th and early 18th centuries. In 1191 a joint session of Cirencester Abbey's halimotes of Cirencester and Wall was held at Cirencester dealing with tenurial matters at Wall.[36] The Aldsworth manor court was recorded in the 1260s;[37] court rolls survive for 1351, 1412–13,[38] 1542, 1609, 1617–18, 1622, 1661, and 1670 and there are court papers and estreats for the period 1561–1601.[39] The court, which dealt with tenurial and agrarian matters and, in 1412 and 1413, with the maintenance of buildings, weirs, ditches, and banks, was concerned with the purity of the water-supply in the 17th century. It elected a keeper of the fields in 1617, and in 1661 four tellers, to supervise the use of the commons, and a hayward.

Two churchwardens were recorded in Aldsworth from 1576[40] but in the periods 1787–1842 and 1860–76 there was only one. Their accounts survive for 1764–1878. Between 1795 and 1800 an overseer of the poor paid rents for the church house to the churchwardens, suggesting that the poor were being housed there.[41] The increase in the cost of poor-relief in the late 18th century was considerable; from £52 in 1776 it rose to £268 by 1803 when occasional help was given to 12 people and permanent relief to 23, of whom 13 were maintained in a workhouse, presumably in a neighbouring parish.[42] Although the number receiving regular help dropped slightly, the cost of relief rose to £294 by 1813 before falling to £191 by 1815. The number on occasional aid rose to 29 by 1815.[43] Expenditure, which in 1825 was £212, fell in the late 1820s[44] and in 1834 was £134.[45] In 1836 the

parish became part of the Northleach poor-law union[46] and remained in Northleach rural district[47] until 1974 when it was included in Cotswold district.

CHURCH. There was a chapel at Aldsworth c. 1184,[48] apparently one of the dependent chapels of Bibury church appropriated in 1151 by Oseney Abbey which was taking mortuaries in Aldsworth c. 1235.[49] The chapel's dependent status was recorded in 1276[50] and again in 1563[51] but the right of burial had been acquired by 1683.[52]

From the later 12th century the chapel was served from Bibury. The assignment c. 1195 by Oseney Abbey of a vicarage endowed with some tithes and all the offerings of the chapelry[53] was apparently not secured. Aldsworth had a chaplain in the mid 13th century,[54] and no vicars were recorded in the later Middle Ages. The chapelry was served in 1532 by a curate[55] and in 1535 by a chaplain.[56] In 1546 the advowson of the living, called a vicarage, passed with the impropriate rectory to the dean and chapter of Christ Church, Oxford.[57] By 1540 the obligation of paying the curate had been imposed on the lessee of the rectory estate.[58] The living, described as a curacy in 1576,[59] thus had the characteristics of a perpetual curacy, a status attributed to it in 1736[60] and acquired in 1789 when it was endowed out of Queen Anne's Bounty.[61] From the later 19th century the living was usually styled a vicarage.[62] The dean and chapter of Christ Church, who appointed graduates of the college to hold the living in plurality with Turkdean vicarage between 1736 and 1837,[63] retained the advowson in 1976.[64] The living was united that year with Sherborne with Windrush and Great Barrington with Little Barrington.[65]

The Wall farm tithes, which were part of the vicarage assigned c. 1195 by Oseney Abbey,[66] were possibly taken then by Cirencester Abbey, which certainly held them by 1291 when it had a portion for tithes of 6s. 8d. in Bibury church.[67] After the Dissolution the owner of Wall farm took the tithes of wool and lambs there.[68]

In the mid 16th century the chaplain or curate

[32] Ibid. D 1388, Aldsworth inc. map.
[33] *Kelly's Dir. Glos.* (1902 and later edns.).
[34] Ibid. (1856 and later edns.).
[35] *Red Bk. of Worc.* 370.
[36] *Ciren. Cart.* ii, p. 364.
[37] *Hist. & Cart. Mon. Glouc.* iii. 184.
[38] Glos. R.O., D 936A/M 2, rot. 6; M 5, rot. 2 and d.
[39] Ibid. D 678, ct. rolls 92, 72A; Aldsworth par. 121, 118A, 126; Sherborne and Aldsworth ct. bk., 1582–1622.
[40] G.D.R. vol. 40, f. 166; *Trans. B.G.A.S.* lviii. 183.
[41] Glos. R.O., P 8/CW 2/1.
[42] *Poor Law Abstract,* 1804, 172–3.
[43] Ibid. 1818, 146–7.
[44] *Poor Law Returns* (1830–1), p. 67.
[45] Ibid. (1835), p. 65.
[46] *Poor Law Com. 2nd Rep.* p. 523.
[47] *Census,* 1961.
[48] *Oseney Cart.* v, pp. 35–6.
[49] Ibid. pp. 37–8.   [50] Ibid. pp. 8–9.
[51] Bodl. MS. Rawl. C.790, f. 24v.
[52] Glos. R.O., P 8/IN 1/1.

[53] *Oseney Cart.* v, pp. 36–7.
[54] *Ciren. Cart.* ii, pp. 364–5.
[55] Hockaday Abs. xxv, 1532 subsidy, f. 14.
[56] *Valor Eccl.* (Rec. Com.), ii. 223.
[57] Hockaday Abs. xcix.
[58] Ibid. xxviii, 1540 stipendiaries, f. 15; cf. ibid. xxx, 1544 stipendiaries, f. 16.
[59] Ibid. xlvii, 1576 visit. f. 115.
[60] Ibid. xcix.
[61] See below; cf. G.D.R. vols. 382, f. 47; 384, f. 3.
[62] G.D.R. vol. 385, f. 4; *Kelly's Dir. Glos.* (1870 and later edns.); in 1962 it was called a perpetual curacy; *Glouc. Dioc. Yr. Bk.* (1962–3), 60.
[63] Hockaday Abs. xcix; ccclxxx, Turkdean; cf. G.D.R. vol. 381A, f. 88; Bigland, *Glos.* i. 37–8.
[64] *Glouc. Dioc. Yr. Bk.* (1976), 68–9.
[65] Ex inf. Mr. Wilcox, a churchwarden.
[66] *Oseney Cart.* v, pp. 36–7.
[67] *Tax. Eccl.* (Rec. Com.), 222.
[68] S.C. 6/Hen. VIII/1240 rot. 48; Glos. R.O., D 540/T 4; C 142/357 no. 19.

received a stipend of £4[69] which had been increased to £5 6s. 8d. by 1603 when he also received small tithes worth 53s. 4d.[70] About 1710 the curacy was valued at £6.[71] By 1736 the impropriator had granted a stipend of £20 to the curate, whose income was supplemented by some small tithes, Easter offerings, and rents from the churchyard. He also held two cottages[72] which were probably those on the plot described as the curate's messuage in 1799, north of the lane to the church.[73] The curate's small tithes were from cows and calves in 1750 and c. 1770 when he also took garden pence.[74] In 1789, when the curacy was valued at £23 10s.,[75] the living received an endowment of £200 out of Queen Anne's Bounty to meet a benefaction of £200 by the impropriator.[76] When all the tithes were commuted at inclosure in 1793 the curate was allotted 26 a. and rent-charges of 2s. 2½d. for his tithes.[77] In 1843 Queen Anne's Bounty augmented the living by a grant of £200 to meet another benefaction of £200 by the impropriator.[78] The living was valued at £67 in 1856.[79] The glebe comprised 26 a. until c. 1902[80] when much of it was sold,[81] leaving 7 a. in 1927.[82] There was no glebe in 1976.[83]

There is no early record of a parsonage house. Between 1736 and 1837 the curates probably lived at Turkdean, where a stipendiary curate was licensed to live in 1817[84] and from where the perpetual curate served Aldsworth every other week in 1825.[85] The vicarage house said to be void in 1839[86] was possibly the rectory farm-house, for in 1840 the perpetual curate was assigned a residence in Farmington until a glebe-house was built.[87] At times between 1849 and 1863 the rectory farm-house was occupied by the incumbent or stipendiary curates[88] but in 1866, when it was being repaired, it was declared unfit for the perpetual curate's residence.[89] It was in use as a vicarage in the early 1880s[90] after which the incumbent lived in rented accommodation in the parish.[91] Aided by a grant of £100 in 1895 out of the Warneford Diocesan Charities[92] a new vicarage

was built north-west of the church c. 1905.[93] It was offered for sale in 1976.[94]

The curate serving the living in 1576 evidently did not accept fully the Elizabethan Settlement: at Easter he had worn a cope, and furthermore had worn the surplice on perambulations, had preached only one sermon in two years, and had not taught the catechism.[95] Thomas Roberts, described in 1584 as a conformist,[96] was said in 1593 to be a sufficient scholar but not a preacher.[97] In 1619 the church had neither Bible nor common prayer book but they had been provided by the following year.[98] In 1639 the curacy was disputed by Daniel Cowley and Laurence Griffith; the latter, who claimed to have been nominated first and imprisoned later,[99] recovered the living. Griffith, described in 1650 as a preaching minister,[1] had been suspended by 1671,[2] and in 1674 it was said that he was making £80 a year from performing clandestine marriages,[3] an enterprise which in 1677 attracted persons from Lydiard Tregoze (Wilts.).[4] He had been succeeded by 1682.[5] In the 18th and 19th centuries many of the curates were non-resident[6] but in 1743 Aldsworth was served once a week.[7] John Bellingham, perpetual curate 1839–65, served the living by stipendiary curates from 1851, but in 1866 his successor, Edward Hallet Todd who lived at Windrush, served in person.[8] In 1970 a priest-in-charge was appointed pending the union of benefices.[9]

The parish church of ST. BARTHOLOMEW, named before 1784[10] but sometimes called St. Peter's from 1745,[11] comprises chancel with south vestry, nave with north aisle, north and south porches, and west tower with spire.[12] The north arcade is of the late 12th century and the aisle was laid out at that time although the nave may have been subsequently widened. The west tower and north porch were added in the 14th century and about the same time the north aisle was remodelled and enriched with carved decoration as a chapel of St. Catherine; the ornamentation on the outside includes several shields, one of which carries the

[69] Valor Eccl. (Rec. Com.), ii. 223; Hockaday Abs. xcix, 1546.
[70] Eccl. Misc. 97.
[71] Atkyns, Glos. 211.   [72] G.D.R., V 5/9T 1.
[73] Glos. R.O., D 1388, Aldsworth inc. map.
[74] G.D.R. vol. 381A, f. 88; Rudder, Glos. 221–2.
[75] G.D.R. vol. 382, f. 47.
[76] C. Hodgson, Queen Anne's Bounty (1845), pp. clxxvi, cclxxxiii.
[77] Glos. R.O., D 678, Aldsworth inc. award; cf. Ibid. Aldsworth par. 125.
[78] Hodgson, Queen Anne's Bounty, pp. ccxxxii, cclxxxiii.
[79] G.D.R. vol. 384, f. 3.
[80] Kelly's Dir. Glos. (1902), 19.
[81] Christ Church, Oxford, MS. Estates 24, f. 328.
[82] Kelly's Dir. Glos. (1927), 25.
[83] Ex inf. Mr. Wilcox.
[84] See above; Hockaday Abs. xcix.
[85] G.D.R. vol. 383, no. cccxxi.
[86] Glos. R.O., D 1388, Aldsworth par. val.
[87] Hockaday Abs. xcix.
[88] Ibid; Christ Church, Oxford, MS. Estates 24, ff. 151, 179, 187.
[89] Hockaday Abs. xcix.
[90] O.S. Map 6″, Glos. XLIV. NE. (1884 edn.).
[91] Christ Church, Oxford, MS. Estates 24, ff. 234, 270, 282.
[92] Glos. N. & Q. vi. 107–8.

[93] Evans, Highways and Byways in Oxford and the Cotswolds, 354; Glos. R.O., D 1381/2; O.S. Map 6″, Glos. XLIV. NE. (1924 edn.).
[94] Ex inf. Mr. Wilcox.
[95] G.D.R. vol. 40, f. 166.
[96] Hockaday Abs. xlix, state of clergy 1584, f. 30.
[97] Ibid. lii, state of clergy 1593, f. 9.
[98] Trans. B.G.A.S. lviii. 183.
[99] Ibid. 194.
[1] Ibid. lxxxiii. 94.
[2] Glos. R.O., P 44/MI 1, f. 14.
[3] Sherborne Mun. 90.
[4] Hist. MSS. Com. 55, Var. Coll. I, Wilts., i, p. 155; cf. Glos. R.O., D 2052.
[5] Hockaday Abs. xcix.
[6] See above.
[7] G.D.R. vol. 397, f. 89.   [8] Hockaday Abs. xcix.
[9] Glouc. Dioc. Yr. Bk. (1975), 50; ex inf. Mr. Wilcox.
[10] Bigland, Glos. i, 37; cf. Rudge, Hist. of Glos. i. 247; Kelly's Dir. Glos. (1870 and later edns.); O.S. Map 6″, Glos. XLIV. NE. (1903 edn.).
[11] G.D.R. vol. 397, f. 89; cf. H.O. 129/341/1/10/13; O.S. Map 6″, Glos. XLIV. NE. (1884 edn.); Glos. R.O., D 2299/1955; incorrectly called St. Mary's in Kelly's Dir. Glos. (1856), 217; (1863), 195.
[12] For an illustrated description of the ch. c. 1916, see Trans. B.G.A.S. xli. 189–93.

arms of Oseney Abbey,[13] and on the inside are shields bearing a clawed foot and a crowned heart. The south porch was added and the south wall of the nave rebuilt in the 15th century. The spire may also belong to that period.

The church was restored between 1842 and 1843 largely at the cost of Lord Sherborne, who provided new open pews. The roof was rebuilt and a clerestory added, the south porch was converted as a vestry, and the chancel floor was relaid. A western gallery was rebuilt then;[14] it had an external entrance and was removed after 1921.[15] In 1877 the chancel and chancel arch were rebuilt to designs by J. R. Clarke and the vestry was added.[16]

The north door survives from the 14th century and that to the porch is dated 1636. In the south porch the east window contains fragments of 15th-century glass. Only two of the monuments recorded before 1784 survived in 1976.[17] There are three early-15th-century bells, probably cast by Robert Hendley of Gloucester or his assistant,[18] and repaired by subscription c. 1868,[19] and a modern sanctus bell. The plate includes a chalice of 1724 and a paten of 1727.[20] The registers survive from 1683.[21]

NONCONFORMITY. A house was registered as a meeting-place in 1742,[22] and another house, for use by Independents, in 1754.[23] In 1907 the Wesleyan Methodists built a chapel in the village.[24] It had a congregation of c. 8 in 1976 when it was served once a week from Fulbrook (Oxon.).[25]

EDUCATION. In 1818 the parish had no school[26] but by 1833 three day-schools had been established in which children were educated at their parents' expense; one had 12 children, another begun in 1821 had 5, and the third begun in 1832 had six.[27] A Sunday School, attended by 61 children in 1825[28] and by 48 in 1833, was supported by Lady Sherborne.[29] Attendance had risen to 51 by 1847 when an associated day-school with 32 children was supported by subscriptions, payments, and Lady Sherborne, but had no schoolroom. Another day-school supported by payments and with a schoolroom was attended by 20 children in 1847.[30] Aldsworth C. of E. school was built in 1853 by Lord Sherborne,[31] who supported it in 1856.[32] In 1871 when it had an average attendance of 53 it was supported by school pence and voluntary contributions;[33] it was receiving a government grant in 1879.[34] Attendance rose to 60 by 1885[35] and 74 by 1904;[36] in 1936 the average attendance was 57.[37] There were 19 children on the roll in 1976 drawn from Aldsworth and neighbouring parishes.[38]

CHARITIES FOR THE POOR. None known.

BARNSLEY

THE SMALL rural parish of Barnsley lies 6·5 km. north-east of Cirencester and is irregular in shape, extending from Ready Token at the junction of the Welsh way and Akeman Street on the south-east to the valley of the Winterwell brook below the Foss way on the west. The parish contains 876 ha. (2,163 a.)[39] and has been subject to no boundary changes. It lies mainly at 120–40 m., the ground formed by Forest Marble except on the north boundary where the underlying Great Oolite emerges.[40] Apart from an ancient park and a common pasture called Barnsley Wold in the north-west of the parish, the land was occupied by open fields until inclosure in 1762.

The name of the parish was recorded c. 800 as 'Bearmodeslea'[41] and in later centuries often took the form Bardesley. The original clearing to which the name was applied was perhaps at the park, the oldest part of which is probably the area in the north including the site of a Roman villa and a related field-system.[42] The park was certainly in existence by 1197[43] and was the site of one of the ancient manor-houses.[44] In the Middle Ages it covered 100 a. inclosed by stone walls;[45] it was grazed by deer[46] and administered by a parker.[47] A keeper of the park was still employed in the late

[13] U. Daubeny, *Ancient Cotswold Churches*, 118–19; and for the aisle, see below, plate facing p. 141.
[14] Christ Church, Oxford, MS. Estates 24, ff. 127, 130, 135; Glos. R.O., P 8/CW 2/1.
[15] Daubeny, *Ancient Cotswold Churches*, 119; cf. *Trans. B.G.A.S.* xli. fig. 54.
[16] Verey, *Glos.* i. 84; *Kelly's Dir. Glos.* (1879), 554; (1885), 349; *Trans. B.G.A.S.* xli. 189 gives the date as 1890.
[17] Cf. Bigland, *Glos.* i. 38.
[18] *Glos. Ch. Bells*, 29; cf. ibid. 3–5; *Trans. B.G.A.S.* xlii. 149.
[19] Glos. R.O., P 8/CW 2/1.
[20] *Trans. B.G.A.S.* lxiii. 232; cf. *Glos. Ch. Plate*, 4.
[21] *B. & G. Par. Rec.* 45.
[22] Hockaday Abs. xcix.   [23] Glos. R.O., D 2052.
[24] Date on bldg.; the date is given as 1908 in *Kelly's Dir. Glos.* (1910), 23.
[25] Ex inf. Mr. Wilcox; notice outside chap.
[26] *Educ. of Poor Digest*, 289.
[27] *Educ. Enquiry Abstract*, 300.
[28] G.D.R. vol. 383, no. cccxxi.
[29] *Educ. Enquiry Abstract*, 300.
[30] *Church School Inquiry, 1846–7*, 2–3.
[31] Ed. 7/34/3.
[32] *Kelly's Dir. Glos.* (1856), 217.
[33] Ed. 7/34/3.
[34] *Kelly's Dir. Glos.* (1879), 554.
[35] Ibid. (1885), 350.
[36] *Public Elem. Schs. 1906*, 181.
[37] *Bd. of Educ., List 21, 1936*, (H.M.S.O.), 118.
[38] Ex inf. Mr. Wilcox.
[39] *Census*, 1971. This account was written in 1975.
[40] Geol. Surv. Map 1″, drift, sheet 235 (1905 edn.).
[41] Finberg, *Early Charters of W. Midlands*, p. 44.
[42] R.C.H.M. *Glos.* i. 9–11.
[43] *Camd. Misc.* xxii (Camd. 4th ser. i), p. 71.
[44] C 145/103 no. 17.
[45] *Inq. p.m. Glos. 1301–58*, 229.
[46] Ibid. 1236–1300, 135; *Cal. Pat. 1272–81*, 177.
[47] J.I. 1/274 rot. 2d.

15th century[48] but by 1542 it had been disparked.[49] The original inclosure evidently survived, however, and was apparently considerably enlarged when Brereton Bourchier built a new manor-house, Barnsley Park, there in the early 18th century; Bourchier was said to have a pleasant grove and a large park c. 1710,[50] and in 1730 the outlying parts of the park were described as inclosures. In the later 18th century the park covered over 300 a.[51] A further extension to the south-east took place in 1794 when the Barnsley–Ablington road was diverted.[52] The 83 a. of woodland recorded in the parish in 1841[53] were mainly in the park, which remained well planted in 1975.

Barnsley village grew up south of the park at the cross-roads of two of the most important routes of the county, the Cirencester–Oxford road, turnpiked in 1753,[54] and the old London–Gloucester road,[55] often called the Welsh way. The latter was named from the use made of it by Welsh drovers, who were often recorded at Barnsley in the 1770s, pasturing their cattle overnight in the Ten Acres behind Barnsley House.[56] The Welsh way was probably the Tame's path recorded in the west of the parish in the 17th century,[57] the name presumably recalling journeyings by that family between Fairford and Rendcomb.[58] Usually, however, the Welsh way was called Gloucester way (or road) in the west part of the parish and London way (or road) in the east.[59] The Cirencester–Oxford road took a different route through the village before it was turnpiked. In 1675 it ran on the east rather than the west side of the church,[60] and Clapton's Lane running east of Barnsley House[61] may represent its old course into the south end of the village; alternatively, a road that ran over Wayboll hill west of the turnpike until the late 18th century[62] may have been the original course in that end of the village.

The village street that Barnsley forms on the Cirencester–Oxford road seems thus to be mainly the product of re-routing of the road in 1753, and the regularity of the street is contributed partly by the addition of estate cottages in the 19th century. A few of the houses date from an earlier period, including a cottage on the west side of the street, which has an early plan with a passage entry. The end of the 17th century and the beginning of the 18th, when Brereton Bourchier was lord of the manor, evidently saw considerable expansion and new building in the village. A new farm-house that Bourchier was building in 1703, described as near

the inn,[63] may be the older wing of Church Farm, north of the church, and a cottage west of the church, with a central chimney and gabled elevation, is dated 1698. Licence to build other cottages at the south end of the village was given in 1694 and 1712, the latter being evidently represented by the small cottage beside the road to Ampney Crucis.[64] A greater number of the cottages along the street were added or rebuilt in the 19th century by the Musgrave family; one pair is dated 1811, another pair 1817, and a row of three 1851. A pair of cottages at the north end, adjoining the park, was converted into a dower house c. 1932[65] and in 1975 was the home of Mr. W. H. Wykeham-Musgrave, the former owner of the estate. In the 20th century the village street was carefully preserved against discordant additions.

Near the south end of the village a large new house, originally called the Lower House but later Barnsley House, was built in 1697 by Brereton Bourchier,[66] who perhaps intended it for his own residence, not yet contemplating the building of Barnsley Park. From 1762 until 1932 it was the rectory.[67] The original range with mullioned and transomed windows was given dormers c. 1830 and the west side refronted. In the garden is a late-18th-century Gothic summer-house and a Doric temple, the latter moved from Fairford Park in 1962 by the owner of the house, Mr. D. C. W. Verey, an architectural historian.[68]

Poultmoor Farm by the Bibury road is the only outlying farm-house in the parish. It was built in 1790 by James Musgrave,[69] and the Gothic front may have been intended as an eye-catcher from Barnsley Park.

Tradition ascribes to a member of the Tame family the building of an inn at Barnsley for his own accommodation when travelling between Fairford and Rendcomb.[70] The village certainly had an inn by 1657[71] and it had a good reputation among travellers in the later 17th and early 18th centuries.[72] By 1707 the inn was called the Greyhound.[73] In the 19th century, when the landlord was also a farmer,[74] it was at Greyhound Farm on the main road near the north end of the village;[75] but it had apparently moved there only at the turnpiking of the road in 1753, for a house called the old inn in the same part of the village was mentioned in 1789.[76] In the early years of the 20th century the inn moved from Greyhound Farm to a cottage on the west side of the street, where it remained in 1975.[77] The Greyhound was the only inn in the village in 1788 and again in

[48] *Cal. Pat.* 1485–94, 189.
[49] *L. & P. Hen. VIII*, xvii, p. 161.   [50] Atkyns, *Glos.* 249.
[51] Bodl. MS. d.d. Wykeham-Musgrave, c. 19, settlement 1730; Glos. R.O., D 2383/P 1.
[52] Glos. R.O., Q/SRh 1794 D/2.
[53] G.D.R., T 1/15.
[54] Bibury Road Act, 26 Geo. II, c. 70.
[55] Ogilby, *Britannia* (1675), pp. 29, 110.
[56] Glos. R.O., D 269B/F 13.
[57] G.D.R., V 5/34T 1; Bodl. MS. d.d. Wykeham-Musgrave, c. 18, lease 1690.   [58] Cf. below.
[59] Bodl. MS. d.d. Wykeham-Musgrave, c. 18, 21.
[60] Ogilby, *Britannia* (1675), p. 110, plate 55.
[61] Glos. R.O., D 1390.   [62] Ibid. D 269B/F 106.
[63] Bodl. MS. d.d. Wykeham-Musgrave, c. 18.   [64] Ibid.

[65] Ex inf. Miss M. Wykeham-Musgrave, of Barnsley.
[66] Date and inits. on bldg.
[67] Glos. R.O., D 1390; *Lond. Gaz.* 26 Apr. 1932, pp. 2714–15.
[68] Ex inf. Mr. Verey.
[69] Date and inits. on bldg.; see plate facing p. 45
[70] Atkyns, *Glos.* 249; Bodl. MS. Top. Glouc. c. 3, f. 211v.
[71] Glos. R.O., P 34/CW 2/2.
[72] Ogilby, *Britannia* (1675), p. 29; Hist. MSS. Com. 29, *13th Rep. II, Portland*, ii, p. 299; Bodl. MS. Top. Glouc. c. 3, f. 211v.
[73] Bodl. MS. d.d. Wykeham-Musgrave, c. 18.
[74] *Kelly's Dir. Glos.* (1856 and later edns.).
[75] O.S. Map 6″, Glos. LII. NW. (1884 edn.); cf. Glos. R.O., D 2582/3.
[76] Bodl. MS. d.d. Wykeham-Musgrave, c. 21.
[77] O.S. Map 6″, Glos. LII. NW. (1903 and 1924 edns.).

the late 19th century,[78] but in 1844 the Blackamoor's Head and the Queen's Head were recorded at Barnsley and friendly societies met at both;[79] one may have been the Greyhound under a temporary change of name. A cottage on the east side of the street was being used as a village hall by 1937.[80]

Twenty-four inhabitants of Barnsley were recorded in 1086.[81] Twenty-eight were assessed for the subsidy in 1327,[82] and 59 for the poll tax in 1381.[83] In 1551 c. 93 communicants were recorded[84] and in 1563 28 households.[85] There were said to be 30 families in the parish in 1650,[86] c. 160 inhabitants about 1710,[87] and 217 inhabitants c. 1775.[88] In 1801 the population was 271 and it rose to 318 by 1821, remaining at about that figure until 1861 before falling to 222 by the end of the century. The fall generally continued in the 20th century and there were 150 inhabitants in 1971.[89]

MANORS AND OTHER ESTATES. Barnsley belonged to the bishopric of Worcester from before 822. Bishop Denebeorht leased 6 'manentes' there to a priest, Balthun, and in 855 the bishop's estate at Barnsley was exempted from certain dues by Burgred, king of the Mercians.[90] In 1086 Durand held 3 hides and 1 yardland from the bishop as part of Bibury manor, and another estate of 7 yardlands, not subsequently traced, was held by Eudes.[91]

Durand's estate, later called the manor of BARNSLEY, passed to his nephew Walter of Gloucester who c. 1123 settled it on the marriage of his son Miles.[92] Miles, created earl of Hereford in 1141, died in 1143 and the manor evidently passed with his other estates in turn to his sons Roger (d. 1155), Walter, Henry, and Mahel[93] (d. 1165). Mahel's English estates were subsequently divided between his sisters Margaret, wife of Humphrey de Bohun, and Lucy, wife of Herbert FitzHerbert[94] but the details of the division are obscure and varied from manor to manor.[95] Margaret de Bohun held the whole or part of Barnsley manor c. 1180 when she alienated land at Barnsley with the assent of her son Humphrey,[96] and in 1195 Herbert FitzHerbert's portion of Barnsley was mentioned.[97] In 1209 Margaret's grandson Henry de Bohun, earl of Hereford, held 1 knight's fee at Barnsley under

the bishop of Worcester.[98] Later FitzHerbert's descendants and others held the manor in demesne while the de Bohuns retained an intermediate lordship[99] and the advowson of the church. After the death of Humphrey de Bohun in 1373 his rights passed to his daughter Mary and her husband Henry of Lancaster,[1] later Henry IV. The superior overlordship of the bishop of Worcester is not recorded after 1299.[2]

Herbert FitzHerbert's son Peter (d. 1235)[3] presumably held the manor or a share of it, and it passed to Peter's son Herbert (d. 1248).[4] Herbert's brother Reynold held it in 1258[5] and evidently until his death in 1286,[6] although in 1285 the knight's fee held from the earl of Hereford was said to be shared by Reynold's heir and Robert de Plessis.[7] Reynold's son John held part of the manor in 1292[8] and granted it before 1300 to the elder Hugh le Despenser.[9] The portion of Robert de Plessis, described as a third of the manor but ⅕ knight's fee, was held in right of his wife Ela. On his death c. 1301 it passed to his son John,[10] whose son Edmund de Plessis held it in 1316. In 1323 Edmund granted it to Hugh le Despenser,[11] thus uniting the two parts of the manor.

After Despenser's execution and forfeiture the manor was granted to Edmund, earl of Kent,[12] who was executed in 1330. It was then held briefly by Queen Isabella[13] but in 1331, subject to dower assigned to Maud, widow of Edmund de Plessis,[14] it was placed in the custody of Thomas de Bradeston, who held during the minority of the earl of Kent's sons Edmund (d. 1331) and John.[15] In 1335 Eleanor, widow of Herbert, son of John son of Reynold, also secured dower in the manor.[16] John, earl of Kent, died seised of the manor in 1352[17] and, with the assent of his sister and heir Joan, wife of Thomas Holland, it was settled in dower on his widow Elizabeth.[18] In 1366 an estate, apparently two-thirds of that which Edmund, earl of Kent, had held, was extended as a possession late of William de Grenville,[19] but Elizabeth held the manor in 1374[20] and at her death in 1411. It then passed to Edmund Mortimer, earl of March, as heir of the earls of Kent,[21] who died in 1425[22] and was succeeded by his nephew Richard, duke of York.[23]

[78] Glos. R.O., D 269B/F 39; *Licensed Houses in Glos. 1891*, 42.
[79] Glos. R.O., Q/RZ 1.
[80] Ibid. D 2582/3.
[81] *Dom. Bk.* (Rec. Com.), i. 164v.
[82] *Glos. Subsidy Roll, 1327*, 14.
[83] E 179/113/35A rot. 1; E 179/113/31A rot. 5A.
[84] *E.H.R.* xix. 113.
[85] Bodl. MS. Rawl. C. 790, f. 24.
[86] *Trans. B.G.A.S.* lxxxiii. 94.
[87] Atkyns, *Glos.* 249.   [88] Rudder, *Glos.* 261.
[89] *Census*, 1801–1971.
[90] Finberg, *Early Charters of W. Midlands*, pp. 44, 48.
[91] *Dom. Bk.* (Rec. Com.), i. 164v.
[92] *Ancient Charters* (Pipe R. Soc. x), p. 19.
[93] *Complete Peerage*, vi. 451–7; cf. *Camd. Misc.* xxii, p. 63.
[94] *Trans. B.G.A.S.* lxxix. 175.
[95] Ibid. 196–206.
[96] *Camd. Misc.* xxii, pp. 58–9.
[97] *Pipe R.* 1195 (P.R.S. N.S. vi), 180.
[98] *Bk. of Fees*, i. 39.
[99] *Feud. Aids*, ii. 237.
[1] *Cal. Inq. p.m.* xiii, pp. 141–2; *Cal. Close*, 1381–5, 513.

[2] *Red Bk. of Worc.* 369.
[3] For the FitzHerberts, see *Trans. B.G.A.S.* xix. 295.
[4] J.I. 1/274 rot. 2d.
[5] *Ciren. Cart.* iii, p. 784; *Rot. Hund.* (Rec. Com.), i. 167.
[6] *Cal. Inq. p.m.* ii, p. 364.
[7] *Feud. Aids*, ii. 237.
[8] *Cal. Pat.* 1281–92, 519.
[9] *Cat. Anct. D.* i, A 921; cf. *Cal. Chart. R.* 1257–1300, 489.
[10] *Cal. Inq. p.m.* iv, p. 6; *Feud. Aids*, ii. 247.
[11] *Feud. Aids*, ii. 272; *Cal. Inq. p.m.* vii, p. 344.
[12] *Cal. Chart. R.* 1327–41, 4.
[13] *Cal. Pat.* 1327–30, 519, 521.
[14] *Cal. Close*, 1330–3, 206.
[15] *Cal. Fine R.* 1327–37, 225, 277; *Feud. Aids*, ii. 280.
[16] *Cal. Inq. p.m.* vii, p. 84; *Cal. Close*, 1333–7, 51, 424.
[17] *Cal. Inq. p.m.* x, p. 42.
[18] *Cal. Close*, 1349–54, 530–1.
[19] *Inq. p.m. Glos.* 1359–1413, 40; cf. ibid. 1301–58, 229.
[20] *Cal. Inq. p.m.* xiii, p. 141.
[21] *Inq. p.m. Glos.* 1359–1413, 260–1; C.P. 25(1)/291/63 no. 31.
[22] C 139/19 no. 26.   [23] C 139/24 no. 36.

After the duke's attainder in 1459 the manor was granted for life to his wife Cecily.[24] On Cecily's death in 1495[25] it passed under a reversionary grant of 1492 to Elizabeth, the queen consort,[26] and later it formed part of the jointure of each of Henry VIII's wives.[27]

On Catherine Parr's death in 1548 Barnsley manor passed to Anthony Bourchier under a reversionary grant made originally to John Dudley, earl of Warwick.[28] Anthony died in 1551, leaving his son Thomas, a minor, as his heir.[29] Thomas died in 1579 having settled two-thirds of the manor on his wife Bridget for 16 years. Thomas's son Charles, an infant at his father's death,[30] sold the manor in 1600 to William Bourchier,[31] apparently his brother.[32] From William (d. 1623) the manor passed in direct line of descent to Walter[33] (d. 1648), William (d. 1693), and Brereton (d. 1714).[34] Brereton's heir was his daughter Martha, during whose minority his widow Catherine and trustees held the manor.[35] In 1719 Martha married Henry Perrot of North Leigh (Oxon.),[36] who was succeeded at his death in 1740 by his daughters Martha (d. 1773) and Cassandra (d. 1778).[37]

Cassandra Perrot devised the manor to a relation James Musgrave,[38] who inherited a baronetcy on a cousin's death in 1812. Sir James (d. 1814) was succeeded by his son Sir James (d. 1858) and the second Sir James by his brother, the Revd. Sir William Augustus Musgrave, rector of Chinnor (Oxon.). Sir Augustus (d. 1875)[39] was succeeded by his sister Georgiana, wife of Aubrey Wenman Wykeham. Aubrey and Georgiana, who expanded their surname to Wykeham-Musgrave, both died in 1879 and the manor passed in direct line to Wenman Aubrey (d. 1915), Herbert Wenman (d. 1931), and Wenman Humfry. In 1935 W. H. Wykeham-Musgrave sold the manor-house, Barnsley Park, and the park[40] to Lady Violet Henderson[41] (d. 1956); her son Alexander Gavin Henderson, Lord Faringdon, succeeded but later made the estate over to his nephew, Mr. C. M. Henderson,[42] the owner in 1975. Another large part of the estate was sold in 1935 to the Revd. J. W. H. Toynbee who put it up for sale in 1937.[43] It was bought by various members of the Wykeham-Musgrave family, who formed the Barnsley Estate Co. which retained c. 900 a. in 1975.[44]

In 1327 there were two manor-houses at Barnsley, presumably one for each of the two former portions of the manor. The one standing in the park had evidently belonged to the FitzHerberts, whose portion of the manor included the park, while the one in the village, called Nether Court,[45] had presumably belonged to the de Plessis family. Both houses probably fell into decay in the late Middle Ages, but the Bourchiers later lived at Barnsley in a house in the centre of the village, perhaps on the site of Nether Court. William Bourchier was assessed for tax on 16 hearths in 1672,[46] and the house still stood in a dilapidated state in the late 18th century.[47] By tradition it stood south of the church not far from Barnsley House.[48]

It was probably after his marriage in 1700 to Catherine, a daughter of James Bridges, Lord Chandos,[49] that Brereton Bourchier built a new house, which became known as Barnsley Park, in the old park.[50] It was of five bays by seven and had a symmetrical plan with two large central rooms and smaller rooms in the corners. Whether he had completed the house by the time of his death is not known, for it was enlarged to its present shape by Henry Perrot after 1719.[51] The main west front was extended to nine bays, the central three being brought forward. On the east side a library was added and on the south terminal pavilions, one bay square, which ingeniously recreated the symmetry of the three principal elevations. Inside, the centre of the old house was remodelled to form a hall, extending up through two floors and joined to a communicating passage and gallery by an arcade of two heights, which is pierced through an older wall. That work and that of the three main fronts is in the English baroque style. The redecoration of the interior continued for some time after the exterior was complete; Charles Stanley is said to have been employed on some of the interior plasterwork and may have done that in the hall. It has been suggested that Perrot's building work was much influenced by the contemporary operations of his wife's uncle, the 1st duke of Chandos, at Canons in Great Stanmore (Mdx.) and that some of the craftsmen who worked there were also employed at Barnsley.[52]

The dining-room at Barnsley Park was remodelled from designs by Anthony Keck about 1790. Between 1806 and 1809 John Nash was employed by James Musgrave to carry out internal refitting, including all the woodwork of the library. He also built the orangery on the east lawn and the lodge at the Bibury gate of the park.[53]

[24] *Cal. Pat.* 1452–61, 542; cf. ibid. 1461–7, 131.
[25] *Complete Peerage*, xii (1), 909.
[26] *Cal. Pat.* 1485–94, 370.
[27] *L. & P. Hen. VIII*, i (1), p. 49; vii, p. 176; xii (2), p. 456; xv, p. 52; xvi, p. 240; xix (1), p. 82.
[28] *Cal. Pat.* 1547–8, 220, 254–6.
[29] C 142/93 no. 92.   [30] C 142/185 no. 92.
[31] C.P. 25(2)/147/1920 no. 16.
[32] Cf. *Visit. Glos.* 1682–3, 20, where William's date of death is evidently wrong.
[33] C 142/399 no. 138.
[34] *Visit. Glos.* 1682–3, 21–2; Glos. R.O., P 34/IN 1/2–3.
[35] Bodl. MS. d.d. Wykeham-Musgrave, c. 18, lease 1715.
[36] Glos. R.O., D 189/III/1.
[37] Ibid. D 2383/F 9; mon. in North Leigh ch.
[38] Bodl. MS. d.d. Wykeham-Musgrave, c. 21.
[39] G.E.C. *Baronetage*, ii. 436.
[40] Burke, *Land. Gent.* (1937), 1657–8.

[41] *Glos. Countryside*, Oct.–Dec. 1953, 110.
[42] Burke, *Peerage* (1970), 985.
[43] Glos. R.O., D 2582/3.
[44] Ex inf. Miss Wykeham-Musgrave.
[45] C 145/103 no. 17; cf. *Inq. p.m. Glos.* 1236–1300, 135; *Cal. Pat.* 1281–92, 519.
[46] E 179/247/14 rot. 4.
[47] Bigland, *Glos.* i. 127.
[48] Ex inf. Mr. Verey.
[49] Glos. R.O., P 34/IN 1/2.
[50] Atkyns, *Glos.* 249.
[51] Bigland, *Glos.* i. 127; the dates 1720 and 1721 appear on the rainwater heads.
[52] *Country Life* 2, 9 Sept. 1954, 720–3, 806–9, which has a full description and many photogs.; Verey, *Glos.* i. 98–9; see also below, plate facing p. 28.
[53] Bodl. MS. d.d. Wykeham-Musgrave, c. 22; Glos. R.O., D 2383/E 7.

An estate owned by Robert Moreton in the early 16th century was known as the manor of *BARNSLEY*, but its origin is obscure. Robert died in 1514 and his son and heir William[54] died a minor in 1522, leaving his sisters Dorothy and Elizabeth as his heirs.[55] Elizabeth married Sir George West and later Ralph Rosier[56] and she and Ralph sold the estate in 1568 to Thomas West.[57] West sold it in 1569 to George Fettiplace of Coln St. Aldwyns (d. 1577) who was jointly enfeoffed with his wife Cecily who survived him. It passed to their son John[58] but has not been found recorded after 1605 when it was settled on the marriage of John's son George.[59] It was evidently absorbed into the chief manor which later included all the land of the parish except for the glebe.[60]

About 1180 Margaret de Bohun granted ½ hide at Barnsley to Philip the monk and confirmed his grant of the land to Llanthony Priory. She also granted 1 yardland to William of Stoke and confirmed his grant of it to the priory.[61] Presumably Philip and William were merely her intermediaries in those transactions. Land worth 20s. which she granted to Fulk of St. George to hold for $\frac{1}{10}$ knight's fee apparently also passed to Llanthony.[62] The priory's lands in Barnsley, which were accounted ¼ fee in 1303,[63] were administered with its manor of South Cerney,[64] which was still said to include land in Barnsley in 1605.[65] The bulk of the estate, however, was granted in 1545 to John Pope who sold it the same year to Thomas Webb[66] (d. 1559). Thomas was succeeded by his son John[67] (d. 1582), whose son John died a minor in 1586 when Anne, widow of the elder John, and her husband John Hignell were taking the profits.[68] The estate was evidently absorbed later in the chief manor.

A house and land in Barnsley that had belonged to Holy Trinity chantry in Cirencester church were granted to Anthony Bourchier in 1549.[69]

ECONOMIC HISTORY. In 1086 the estates of Durand and Eudes at Barnsley had a total of 5 demesne teams and 12 *servi*.[70] The part of the manor held by Reynold son of Peter had 140 a. of demesne arable in 1286 and the part held by Robert de Plessis had 60 a. in 1301;[71] in 1327 the united manor had 192 a. At the last date 4 a. of meadow were also recorded and the lord had the first crop of a meadow called Dittenham at Cirencester.[72] The demesne was farmed by 1413.[73]

In 1086 the tenants at Barnsley were 12 *villani* with 6 teams.[74] In 1286 Reynold son of Peter's estate had 2 free tenants, 4 customary yardlanders, 2 half-yardlanders, and 4 cottagers. The yardlander worked 5 days in the week all the year round but the value of his works increased threefold during August and September; he also did 4 bedrepes in the harvest. Two of the cottagers owed only money rents and 4 bedrepes but the other two also owed 1 day's work each week. On the estate of Robert de Plessis in 1301 there were 2 free tenants and 4 customary yardlands shared by 8 tenants. The tenants apparently paid money instead of working[75] and on the combined estate in 1327 the tenants worked or gave money as the lord wished. The estate in 1327 had 10 free tenants, some nevertheless owing heriots, 4 yardlanders and another 2 yardland tenements that were divided among several tenants, 18 half-yardlanders, and 7 cottagers.[76] The Llanthony Priory estate at the Dissolution was made up of 3 customary tenements, one comprising 3 houses and 3 yardlands, another 2 houses and 2 yardlands, and a third merely a garden.[77]

The yardland at Barnsley probably measured 48 a., for in 1670 a ½-yardland estate had 12 a. in each of the two open fields.[78] At that period and until inclosure the usual form of tenure was by leases for three lives with heriots payable.[79]

The two large open fields, recorded in the late 12th century as the west and the east field[80] but later called Upper and Lower field, lay respectively west and east of the village and park. They occupied the greater part of the land of the parish,[81] though in the north-west corner was a common pasture, called Barnsley Wold, covering 169 a.[82] The wold was used for pasturing cows,[83] while the sheep grazed the open fields. A ¼-yardland tenement had common for 1 horse, 2 beasts, and 10 sheep in 1673; the larger holdings had common for up to 112 or even 200 sheep. The larger holdings also had land in a common meadow called Middle Mead, recorded in 1675, and the right to cut furze on ground near Ready Token in the east corner of the parish.[84]

There was apparently little early inclosure of the open fields, although in the 1690s Brereton Bourchier granted leases which reserved his right to make inclosures. He may have planned then and carried out soon afterwards an extension of the park into the fields. It is certain that he permitted some small inclosures in the fields.[85] The parish was inclosed privately in 1762[86] by the Perrots, who were

[54] C 142/29 no. 136.
[55] C 142/40 no. 34.
[56] *V.C.H. Glos.* xi. 117; C 3/287/6.
[57] C.P. 25(2)/259/10 Eliz. Hil. no. 4.
[58] C 142/177 no. 86.
[59] *Sherborne Mun.* 9.
[60] G.D.R., T 1/15.
[61] *Camd. Misc.* xxii, pp. 58–9, 70.
[62] Ibid. 71.
[63] *Feud. Aids*, ii. 247.
[64] *Tax. Eccl.* (Rec. Com.), 232; S.C. 6/Hen. VIII/1224 rot. 8 and d.
[65] C.P. 25(2)/297/3 Jas. I Mich. no. 46.
[66] *L. & P. Hen. VIII*, xx (2), p. 323.
[67] C 142/274 no. 11.
[68] C 142/277 no. 15.
[69] *Cal. Pat.* 1547–8, 329.

[70] *Dom. Bk.* (Rec. Com.), i. 164v.
[71] *Inq. p.m. Glos.* 1236–1300, 135, 227.
[72] C 145/103 no. 17.
[73] S.C. 6/850/24.
[74] *Dom. Bk.* (Rec. Com.), i. 164v.
[75] *Inq. p.m. Glos.* 1236–1300, 135–6, 227.
[76] C 145/103 no. 17.
[77] S.C. 6/Hen. VIII/1224 rot. 8d.
[78] Bodl. MS. d.d. Wykeham-Musgrave, c. 18.
[79] Ibid. c. 18–20.
[80] *Camd. Misc.* xxii, p. 71.
[81] G.D.R., V 5/34T 1–2.
[82] G.D.R., T 1/15.
[83] Cf. Glos. R.O., D 269B/F 34.
[84] Bodl. MS. d.d. Wykeham-Musgrave, c. 18.
[85] Ibid.
[86] Rudder, *Glos.* 260.

the sole landowners.[87] After the inclosure the land was formed into three large farms, leased initially for 14-year terms. The cottages and small holdings continued on 99-year leases determinable on lives with heriots still required.[88]

After inclosure some of the land was evidently converted to pasture for sheep-farming. Sheep-farming had, however, long had a role in the parish: there was a sheep-house on the manorial demesne in the Middle Ages;[89] Thomas Rogers (d. 1515) left 180 sheep to his children;[90] and in 1535 the rector's annual tithes included wool worth £3.[91] The three big post-inclosure farms had a total of 1,100 sheep and 460 lambs in 1778; the largest farm included the wold which had been turned into a sheep-walk and one of the other farms used part of the park for grazing. The farms were, however, predominantly arable in area: in 1778 the largest, with a total of 890 a., had 529 a. of arable, the next, with 440 a., had 350 a. of arable, and the smallest, with 379 a., had 196 a. of arable. The rotation followed included wheat, barley, and oats, with, as fodder crops for the sheep, sainfoin and clover and presumably also turnips. One of the farms produced some butter and cheese and one had 108 a. of meadow land, but dairying was of little importance; the total herd of cows on the farms was 39.[92]

The pattern of farming apparently continued unchanged into the 19th century. There were evidently large flocks in the late 1830s when at least two shepherds were employed in the parish[93] and in 1841 the proportion of arable to grassland, 1,212 a. to 769 a., was much the same as in the late 18th century. There had been, however, some reorganization in the farms. In 1841 c. 1,035 a. were farmed from the Greyhound inn in the village, c. 115 a. from Church Farm, and c. 460 a. from Poultmoor Farm on the Bibury road.[94] Those three farms remained the main ones in the parish in the later 19th century and earlier 20th[95] but there were also a number of smaller ones; 11 agricultural holdings were returned in 1926, all but three of them under 150 a. The later 19th century saw the usual decline in cereal crops; by 1896 permanent grass, returned at 1,042 a., predominated over arable, returned at 869 a., and in 1926 295 a. of the grassland was described as rough grazing.[96] The number of cattle on the farms, kept mainly for beef, was increased during that period, 369 being returned in 1926 compared with 187 in 1866, but sheep were reduced from 1,034 in 1866 to 581 in 1926.[97] By the mid 1970s, however, arable land once more predominated in the parish and cereal cultivation and the raising of beef cattle were the main elements in local farming. The Barnsley estate was then farmed as a single unit from Church Farm, and there was another smaller farm and one small holding worked on a part-time basis.[98]

In relation to its size Barnsley was well supplied with tradesmen; the passing trade brought by the two main roads was probably of some importance. In 1608 the inhabitants included three carpenters, a smith, and a tailor,[99] and the first two trades were regularly represented in the village in succeeding centuries. Shoemakers were also recorded regularly from the 1770s.[1] The village had a blacksmith until the 1890s and a carpenter and a shoemaker until the early years of the 20th century.[2] A glazier was recorded in the parish in 1712,[3] bakers in 1699[4] and 1775, a butcher in 1738,[5] and a wheelwright in 1856.[6] The landlord of the Greyhound had a malt-house adjoining the inn in 1775.[7] There was a shopkeeper in the village in 1879 and two in 1906.[8] In 1831 10 families were supported by trade and 47 by agriculture.[9]

By the early 18th century large freestone quarries were being worked at Quarry hill by the Bibury road on the east side of the parish,[10] and in the 1770s they were said to produce stone almost equal in quality to Bath stone.[11] A mason Richard Norris, not the first of his family to follow that trade at Barnsley, took a lease of one of the quarries in 1725.[12] One was being worked for stone tiles in 1757[13] and slaters have been regularly recorded; two were living in the parish in 1717[14] and the Poole family followed the trade at Barnsley between the 1830s and the First World War.[15] In addition to those at Quarry hill there was Hollington quarry in Upper field, which was recorded from 1635[16] and leased to a Barnsley mason in 1777.[17]

LOCAL GOVERNMENT. No records are known to survive for the Barnsley manor court, which brought in a small sum to the lord of the manor in 1327[18] and was still being held in the mid 18th century.[19] Frankpledge jurisdiction over Barnsley was said to be exercised by the court of the lord of Bibury in 1299 and 1750,[20] but there is no record in the surviving rolls of Barnsley's attendance at the Bibury court.

[87] Cf. G.D.R., T 1/15.
[88] Bodl. MS. d.d. Wykeham-Musgrave, c. 20–1; cf. Glos. R.O., D 269B/F 32.
[89] C 145/103 no. 17; S.C. 6/850/26.
[90] Hockaday Abs. cxii.
[91] Valor Eccl. (Rec. Com.), ii. 452.
[92] Glos. R.O., D 269B/F 32–34.
[93] Ibid. P 34/IN 1/6.
[94] G.D.R., T 1/15.
[95] Kelly's Dir. Glos. (1856 and later edns.).
[96] M.A.F. 68/1609/16; M.A.F. 68/3295/4.
[97] M.A.F. 68/25/3; M.A.F. 68/3295/4.
[98] Ex inf. Mr. J. Russell, of Church Fm.
[99] Smith, Men and Armour, 259.
[1] Glos. R.O., P 34/IN 1/3, 6; Bodl. MS. d.d. Wykeham-Musgrave, c. 20.
[2] Kelly's Dir. Glos. (1856 and later edns.).
[3] Glos. R.O., P 34/IN 1/3.   [4] Ibid. 2.

[5] Bodl. MS. d.d. Wykeham-Musgrave, c. 19–20.
[6] Kelly's Dir. Glos. (1856), 225.
[7] Bodl. MS. d.d. Wykeham-Musgrave, c. 20.
[8] Kelly's Dir. Glos. (1879), 562; (1906), 31.
[9] Census, 1831.
[10] Atkyns, Glos. 249.
[11] Rudder, Glos. 259.
[12] Bodl. MS. d.d. Wykeham-Musgrave, c. 19; Glos. R.O., P 34/IN 1/3, burials 1717.
[13] Bodl. MS. d.d. Wykeham-Musgrave, c. 20.
[14] Glos. R.O., P 34/IN 1/3.
[15] Ibid. 6, baptisms 1830, 1837, 1844; Kelly's Dir. Glos. (1879 and later edns.).
[16] G.D.R., V 5/34T 1.
[17] Bodl. MS. d.d. Wykeham-Musgrave, c. 20.
[18] C 145/103 no. 17.
[19] G.D.R. vol. 381A, f. 88.
[20] Ibid.; Red Bk. of Worc. 369.

There were usually two churchwardens for Barnsley parish but between 1785 and 1844 there was only one. The churchwardens' accounts survive from 1609[21] and the accounts of the two overseers from 1710 until 1781.[22] Two surveyors of the highways were elected in 1673.[23] The usual methods of poor-relief were applied; in 1759 one pauper was provided with a spinning-wheel. In the 1730s there were only c. 3 people receiving permanent relief and the numbers were still only c. 6 in the 1760s.[24] Annual expenditure on the poor was about £100 in the 1780s and it rose to £177 by 1803, when 21 people were on permanent relief.[25] There was no excessive increase in the burden in the following years,[26] perhaps partly because of the concern of the rector Charles Coxwell for matters of poor-relief.[27] During his incumbency Coxwell made two cottages belonging to the rectory available as poorhouses, taking no rent for them until after 1804.[28] In 1836 Barnsley was included in the Cirencester union[29] and later formed part of the Cirencester rural district.[30] In 1974 it was included in Cotswold district.

CHURCH. The church at Barnsley had been built by 1151. It originated as a chapel to Bibury[31] and, although it eventually won full parochial status, it remained within the jurisdiction of Bibury peculiar.[32] It already had its own priest, endowed with some share of the profits of the chapel, by the mid 12th century but the claim by the lady of the manor, Margaret de Bohun, to present the priest was later disputed by Oseney Abbey, appropriators of Bibury church. By an agreement made before 1191 her right to present was upheld and in return she granted to Oseney 2 a. of her demesne land and a moiety of the tithes of 2 yardlands; Oseney's right to take all the tithes of sheaves from the tenants of James Barnsley was also confirmed. The priest serving the church was styled a rector by 1191 but the church, which in some respects remained dependent on Bibury,[33] continued to be referred to as a chapel on occasion until the end of the 14th century.[34] In particular, burial rights were retained by the mother church and Oseney's right to take mortuaries was upheld in 1251.[35] A licence to perform burials at

Barnsley was being sought in 1538[36] and had been secured by 1574.[37] The living, which remained a rectory, was united with Bibury with Winson in 1932.[38]

The advowson was retained by the de Bohuns. After Humphrey de Bohun's death in 1373[39] alternate turns were assigned to his daughters Mary, wife of Henry of Lancaster, later Henry IV, and Eleanor, wife of Thomas of Woodstock, earl of Buckingham,[40] later duke of Gloucester. Eleanor's right passed to her daughter Anne, wife of Edmund Stafford, earl of Stafford,[41] but the Staffords apparently gave up their right to the Crown before 1439.[42] By 1574 the advowson belonged to the lord of the manor Thomas Bourchier and it subsequently descended with the manor, although John Bourchier presented in 1676 and Robert Payne in 1696.[43] In 1975 the patrons of the united benefice with right to alternate presentations were the bishop and Mr. W. H. Wykeham-Musgrave.[44]

Before inclosure the rectory included c. 50 a. of arable in the open fields and beast-, sheep-, and horse-pastures in the fields and the wold.[45] The rector also held a small close of pasture subject to the obligation of providing a bull and boar for the parish. At the inclosure in 1762 the glebe was exchanged with the Perrots for other land, amounting to 36 a.,[46] and by 1841 the glebe had been reduced to 16 a.[47] The portion of the tithes retained by Oseney Abbey in the 12th century was received by the abbey as a rent of 46s. 8d. in 1510,[48] but no later record of it has been found. Later the rector owned all the tithes of the parish and no land was tithe-free. In 1706 most of the tithes were still paid in kind but there was a modus for milk and lambs.[49] By 1767 the occupiers of land were making cash payments, totalling £120, for their tithes and in 1778 the rector secured a new valuation at £190. In 1789 he leased the tithes at the same sum to James Musgrave[50] who owned all the tithable land. In 1841 the tithes were commuted for a corn rent-charge of £320.[51] The living was worth £7 in 1291,[52] £10 in 1397,[53] and £13 15s. 4d. in 1535.[54] The value had risen to £90 by 1650,[55] £120 by 1750,[56] and £200 by 1789.[57] In 1856 it was valued at £288.[58]

The rectory house, mentioned in 1635,[59] is thought to have been at the Tithe House adjoining a

[21] Glos. R.O., P34/CW 2/1–3.
[22] Ibid. OV 2/1.
[23] Ibid. CW 2/2
[24] Ibid. OV 2/1.
[25] Poor Law Abstract, 1804, 172–3.
[26] Ibid. 1818, 146–7; Poor Law Returns (1830–1), p. 67; (1835), p. 65.
[27] Glos. R.O., D 269B/B 14; F 37–8.
[28] Ibid. F 13.
[29] Poor Law Com. 2nd Rep. p. 522.
[30] Census, 1911.
[31] Oseney Cart. (Oxford Hist. Soc.), v, pp. 1, 26–7.
[32] Ibid. pp. 29–30; Rudder, Glos. 260.
[33] Oseney Cart. v, pp. 23–7.
[34] Cal. Pat. 1388–92, 410.
[35] Oseney Cart. v, pp. 27–8.
[36] L. & P. Hen. VIII, xiii (2), p. 279.
[37] Glos. R.O., P 34/IN 1/1.
[38] Lond. Gaz. 26 Apr. 1932, pp. 2714–15.
[39] Reg. Bransford, p. 83; Cal. Inq. p.m., xiii, pp. 141–2.

[40] Cal. Close, 1381–5, 515; 1377–81, 394–5.
[41] Inq. p.m. Glos. 1359–1413, 206, 217–19; Cal. Close, 1402–5, 228.
[42] Cal. Pat. 1436–41, 300, 357, 520.
[43] Hockaday Abs. cxii.
[44] Glouc. Dioc. Yr. Bk. (1975), 48.
[45] Atkyns, Glos. 249; G.D.R., V 5/34T 1.
[46] Glos. R.O., D 1390; D 269B/F 13.
[47] G.D.R., T 1/15.
[48] Oseney Cart. vi, p. 241.
[49] G.D.R., V 5/34T 2.   [50] Glos. R.O., D 269B/F 13.
[51] G.D.R., T 1/15.
[52] Tax. Eccl. (Rec. Com.), 222.
[53] Inq. p.m. Glos. 1359–1413, 206.
[54] Valor Eccl. (Rec. Com.), ii. 452.
[55] Trans. B.G.A.S. lxxxiii. 94.
[56] G.D.R. vol. 381A, f. 89.
[57] Ibid. 382, f. 47.
[58] Ibid. 384, f. 15.
[59] Ibid. V 5/34T 1.

lane called Parsonage Lane on the west side of the village street.[60] It was exchanged with the Perrots in 1762 for the Lower House, later Barnsley House, at the south end of the village.[61] Barnsley House remained the rectory until 1932, from which time the incumbent of the united benefice lived at Bibury.[62]

John Walden, rector of Barnsley, had leave of absence for study in 1305,[63] as did Thomas of Bisley in 1315[64] and Peter Malet in 1343.[65] Malet was a native of France and his revenues from the church were claimed by the Crown.[66] Richard Morris, rector 1574–1600,[67] was described as a good Latinist and divine in 1576[68] but as no preacher in 1593.[69] John Leigh, rector from 1635 until his death in 1654,[70] was described as a constant preacher.[71] His successor Thomas Careless subscribed in 1662 and held the rectory with Cirencester vicarage at his death in 1675.[72] William Walker, rector 1744–61, was also rector of Tackley (Oxon.); Christopher Golding, 1761–4,[73] was warden of Winchester College;[74] and Peter Senhouse, 1764–7, also held the living of Upper Heyford (Oxon.). Charles Coxwell, rector 1767–1829,[75] lived at his house in Ablington during his long incumbency[76] but played an active role in parish affairs.[77] He was also rector of Coberley 1778–82, perpetual curate of Marston Maisey (Wilts.) 1782–1817, vicar of Badgeworth with Shurdington 1789–1806, and vicar of Bibury 1806–9. His curate at Barnsley between 1814 and 1817 was William Augustus Musgrave,[78] later lord of the manor, and another member of the Musgrave family, Richard Adolphus, succeeded Coxwell as rector.[79]

The church of *ST. MARY*[80] comprises chancel with north vestry and south organ chamber, nave with north aisle and porch, and west tower.[81] The Norman church apparently comprised chancel and nave and from that church survive the corbel table, now partly concealed, the chancel arch responds, the north doorway, and the bases of a south doorway.[82] The head of the chancel arch was replaced in the 13th century, and in the 14th the chancel was given two new windows. In the course of the 15th and early 16th centuries the aisle, porch, and tower were

added, the chancel roof was renewed, and the south side of the nave was apparently refenestrated.[83] The aisle was the property of the lords of the manor.[84] The top stage of the tower was added in the early 17th century. During the 18th century box pews and a west gallery were introduced, the nave and chancel were ceiled, and the east window and those of the aisle and nave were replaced by round-headed lights.[85] The interior was described as modernized and neat in 1803.[86]

A thorough restoration was begun in 1843 and supervised successively by J. M. Derrick and J. P. Harrison. The chancel was given a new east window and its other windows were restored, the nave and aisle were refenestrated, the nave was reroofed, the tower arch was rebuilt, a vestry was added on the north of the chancel, and the church was repewed and refitted. Two old windows from Daglingworth church, a Norman light in the chancel (later moved to the organ chamber) and a 13th-century window in the south wall of the nave, were introduced at the restoration.[87] In 1877 a south organ chamber, incorporating some reset Norman detail, was built at the cost of the rector D. G. Compton; the organ is an 18th-century instrument by Samuel Green, rebuilt and enlarged.[88]

The font was replaced c. 1840 by a Norman one, originally from Bradwell (Oxon.), but in 1845 that was returned to Bradwell and a close copy of it made for Barnsley.[89] An Elizabethan or Jacobean oak communion table was introduced at the restoration.[90] There are few monuments, but in the north aisle, moved from the chancel,[91] is a wall tablet to Elizabeth (d. 1691), the first wife of Brereton Bourchier. The plate in 1623 comprised a silver chalice and a pewter flagon;[92] the chalice was replaced in 1795,[93] and a new set of plate, by Keith, was given in 1854.[94] The church has three bells: (i) recast by Edward Neale of Burford in 1677; (ii) recast by Neale in 1660 and again recast in 1828; (iii) recast in 1865.[95] The registers survive from 1574.[96]

NONCONFORMITY. Only two nonconformists were recorded at Barnsley in 1676,[97] apparently

[60] Ex inf. Mr. Verey; cf. Glos. R.O., D 269B/F 106.
[61] Glos. R.O., D 1390; cf. G.D.R., T 1/15.
[62] *Lond. Gaz.* 26 Apr. 1932, pp. 2714–15.
[63] *Reg. Ginsborough*, 104.
[64] Worc. Episc. Reg., Reg. Maidstone, f. 25.
[65] *Reg. Bransford*, p. 97.
[66] Ibid. pp. 310, 314–16; *Cal. Pat.* 1343–5, 21, 39; *Cal. Close*, 1343–6, 219–20.
[67] Hockaday Abs. cxii.
[68] Ibid. xlvii, state of clergy 1576, f. 143.
[69] Ibid. lii, state of clergy 1593, f. 9.
[70] Ibid. cxii; Bigland, *Glos.* i. 128.
[71] *Trans. B.G.A.S.* lxxxiii. 94.
[72] Hockaday Abs. cxii; Bigland, *Glos.* i. 359.
[73] Hockaday Abs. cxii.
[74] Glos. R.O., D 1390.
[75] Hockaday Abs. cxii.
[76] Glos. R.O., D 269B/E 11, E 14, F 25.
[77] Ibid. F 13, F 37–8, B 14.
[78] Ibid. F 13–14.
[79] Hockaday Abs. cxii.
[80] The dedication, recorded only from 1803, was apparently in doubt in 1856; Rudge, *Hist. of Glos.* i. 248; *Kelly's Dir. Glos.* (1856), 225.

[81] For a detailed description of the ch. with many photogs. see *Trans. B.G.A.S.* xli. 173–8.
[82] *Trans. B.G.A.S.* lxxvi. 176; cf. Glos. R.O., P 34/CW 2/2, 1672 acct.
[83] *Trans. B.G.A.S.* lxxvi. 176. A tradition that Sir Giles (*sic*) Tame of Fairford rebuilt the ch., recorded by Atkyns, *Glos.* 249, may have as its basis the fact that Sir Edm. Tame was receiver of Barnsley man. during the early 16th cent. and so may have disbursed money for building work: S.C. 6/Hen. VII/219; S.C. 6/Hen. VIII/1042.
[84] *Trans. B.G.A.S.* lxxvi. 178.
[85] Ibid. 173, 175.
[86] Rudge, *Hist. of Glos.* i. 248.
[87] *Trans. B.G.A.S.* lxxvi. 173–8.
[88] Glos. R.O., P 34/CW 2/3; cf. *Trans. B.G.A.S.* xciii. 168.
[89] *Trans. B.G.A.S.* lxxvi. 177; cf. ibid. xlix. 149–50.
[90] Ibid. lxxvi. 174.
[91] Rudder, *Glos.* 261.
[92] Glos. R.O., P 34/CW 2/1.
[93] Ibid. D 269B/F 45.
[94] *Glos. Ch. Plate*, 14.
[95] *Glos. Ch. Bells*, 32; Glos. R.O., P 34/CW 2/2.
[96] *B. & G. Par. Rec.* 58–9.
[97] Compton Census.

Quakers attached to the Cirencester meeting.[98] A house in Barnsley was registered for use by Quakers in 1740.[99] In 1786 an unidentified dissenting group was using James Shurmur's house.[1] There is no later record of any meeting,[2] although an itinerant preacher visited the village more than once in the 1820s.[3]

EDUCATION. From the beginning of his incumbency in 1767 the rector Charles Coxwell paid women to teach poor children to read.[4] The two schools with a total of 38 children recorded in the parish in 1818[5] may have both been supported by him, for in the early 1820s he was employing two teachers, although they were then teaching a total of only c. 15 children.[6] In 1824 Coxwell also started a Sunday school.[7] The schools were continued by his successors. In 1833 there were two day-schools with a total of 27 children, supported by the rector, a small subscription, and payments from a few of the parents; the Sunday school then had an attendance of 44.[8] Sir James Musgrave is said to have built a schoolroom c. 1842[9] but, if so, it was still not secured to that purpose in 1847, and at the latter date the two day-schools were described as dame schools and were presumably still taught by local, untrained teachers.[10] In 1867 there was a mixed parish school, still supported largely by the rector, G. E. Howman, who also lent his support to a dame school which

served the role of infant school to the main one; c. 40 children attended the schools. A night-school was also held in an attempt to continue the education of the young, many of whom gave up full-time schooling at the age of 7 or 8.[11]

In 1873 a new building for the parish school was provided, apparently at the cost of Sir W. A. Musgrave, and in 1874, known as the Barnsley C. of E. School, it had an average attendance of 35 and was supported by a small government grant, pence, and voluntary contributions.[12] In 1904 the average attendance was 59,[13] and attendance fell steadily in the following years to 14 in 1936.[14] In 1964, when the number on the roll was 12, the school was closed and the children transferred to Ampney Crucis.[15]

CHARITIES FOR THE POOR. Twenty pounds given for the relief of the poor of the parish was out at interest in 1706[16] but is not recorded later. William Wise (d. 1774) left £125 for the poor of Barnsley who did not receive parish relief. The sum was used in 1779 to buy stock which produced an annual income of £6 in the 1820s. Sir James Musgrave (d. 1814) gave as much stock as would produce an annual income of £10 for the poor.[17] In the 1870s part of the income of the two charities was distributed in clothes or coal.[18] In 1975 the two charities each produced £6–7 a year and were distributed in firewood.[19]

BIBURY

THE LARGE RURAL PARISH of Bibury lies 10.5 km. north-east of Cirencester. The ancient parish, which included the hamlets of Arlington and Ablington and the chapelry and village of Winson, was irregular in shape with an area of 2,596 ha. (6,414 a.).[20] Land in the parish belonged to the bishop of Worcester's estate by the river Coln in the early 8th century when land in Ablington was leased to Leppa and his daughter Beage,[21] from whom the first part of the name of the parish derives,[22] but Winson to the north-west comprised three distinct estates in Bradley hundred in 1066.[23] The parish was thus divided between two hundreds and Winson became a separate unit for poor-law purposes, being described as a tithing of Bibury in 1804.[24] From the later 19th century Winson, which comprises 492 ha. (1,216 a.), was accounted a separate civil parish and

in 1975 had its own parish meeting.[25]

The parish is bisected from north-west to south-east by the winding valley of the river Coln, near crossing-points of which the four principal settlements in the parish grew. The valley, which in the north is met at a right-angle by a valley running south-westwards from Downs Barn and on the southern boundary by a stream flowing through Shagborough Bottom, crosses the parish at c. 107 m. Above it the land rises to 168 m. in the west, to 149 m. in the south near Ready Token, and to 158 m. in the north-east before falling to 122 m. at the river Leach, the north-eastern boundary of the parish. The other boundaries, apart from short sections of the northern and southern which are marked by the Coln and the tributary stream mentioned above, follow field boundaries and ancient roads, including

[98] Glos. R.O., D 2052.
[99] Ibid. Q/SO 3.
[1] Hockaday Abs. cxii.
[2] Cf. G.D.R. vol. 383, no. cccxviii.
[3] Glos. R.O., D 269B/B 14.
[4] Glos. R.O., D 269B/F 13.   [5] Educ. of Poor Digest, 291.
[6] Glos. R.O., D 269B/B 14.   [7] Ibid. F 13.
[8] Educ. Enquiry Abstract, 302.
[9] Rep. Com. Agric. Employment, 109.
[10] Church School Inquiry, 1846–7, 2–3.
[11] Rep. Com. Agric. Employment, 109–10.
[12] Ed. 7/34/28.
[13] Public Elem. Schs. 1906, 181.
[14] Bd. of Educ., List 21, 1911 (H.M.S.O.), 158; 1922, 102; 1932, 112; 1936, 119.

[15] Ex inf. county educ. dept.
[16] G.D.R., V 5/34T 2.
[17] 20th Rep. Com. Char. 14–15.
[18] Kelly's Dir. Glos. (1870), 470; (1879), 562.
[19] Ex inf. the vicar of Bibury, the Revd. D. T. Taffinder.
[20] O.S. Area Bk. (1884); Census, 1971. This account was written in 1975.
[21] Finberg, Early Charters of W. Midlands, p. 34; Grundy, Saxon Charters, 40–4.
[22] P.N. Glos. (E.P.N.S.), i. 26.
[23] Dom. Bk. (Rec. Com.), i. 169v.
[24] Poor Law Abstract, 1804, 172–3.
[25] Cf. Census, 1801–1971; ex inf. Mrs. Beryl Bradley, sec. of Bibury par. council.

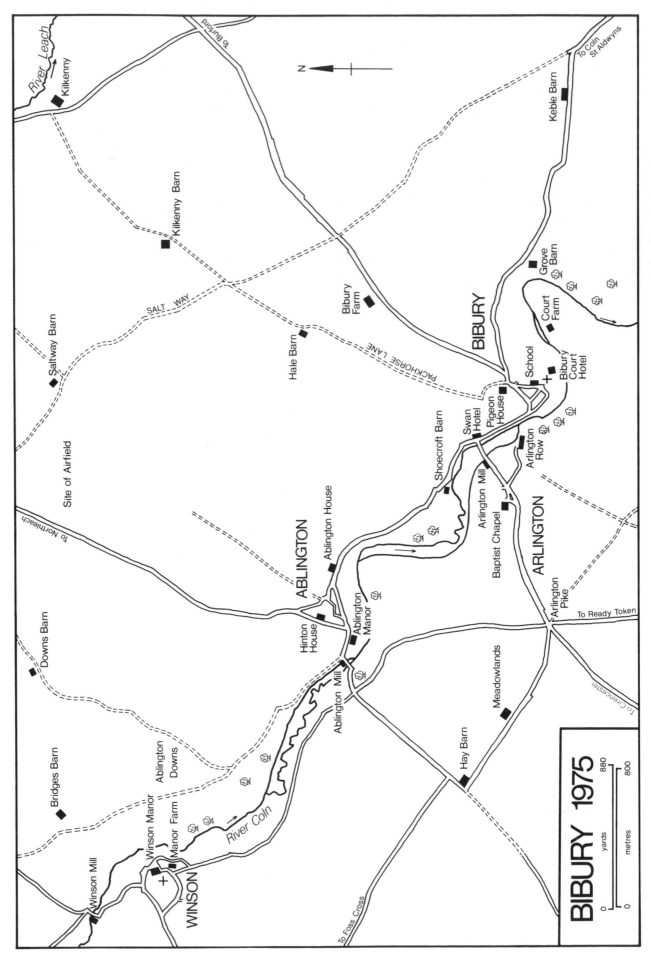

River Leach

Kilkenny

To Burford

N

To Coln St Aldwyns

Keble Barn

Kilkenny Barn

Grove Barn

SALT WAY

Bibury Farm

Saltway Barn

BIBURY

Court Farm

Hale Barn

PACKHORSE LANE

Site of Airfield

School

Bibury Court Hotel

Pigeon House

Swan Hotel

Shoecroft Barn

Arlington Row

To Northleach

Ablington House

Arlington Mill

Baptist Chapel

ABLINGTON

ARLINGTON

Downs Barn

Hinton House

Ablington Manor

Arlington Pike

To Ready Token

Ablington Mill

Meadowlands

To Cirencester

Bridges Barn

Ablington Downs

Hay Barn

Winson Manor

Manor Farm

River Coln

BIBURY 1975

Winson Mill

WINSON

yards   880

800

To Foss Cross

0   metres   0

22

the Roman Akeman Street in the south and a road between Coln Rogers and Barnsley in the west.

The parish lies on the Great Oolite, which on the high ground is overlaid by Forest Marble, but the floor of the Coln valley is formed from fuller's earth from which issue many springs, the most notable rising near the Swan at the north-western end of Bibury village street.[26] There are many disused quarry sites. Apart from heavier land near Ready Token and in the south-west part of Winson, the soil is of good quality, with areas of grassland in the south-west and in Winson.[27] The water-meadows of the Coln valley provide excellent meadow land. The high ground was covered by open fields and extensive commons on which sheep-farming was important. Winson was inclosed in 1726, Bibury and Arlington in 1768, and what was left of the Ablington open fields in 1780, and since then the land has been mainly devoted to arable. A landing strip laid out south of Oldwalls Sheds during the Second World War was retained by the Air Ministry until 1957;[28] traces of the runways survived in 1975 when some of the remaining buildings were used for agricultural purposes.

The woodland in Arlington which measured a league by ½ league in 1066[29] presumably represented Oxhill wood and Shagborough copse in the southern part of the parish. Park-land was recorded in Bibury in 1628.[30] Trees have remained an important feature of the Coln valley landscape, notably around Ablington hamlet where in 1548 or 1549 it was recorded that Henry Daubeney, earl of Bridgwater, and former lord of the manor, had sold 161 elms and ashes to his tenants.[31] In 1575 the manor court ordered each tenant to plant three trees, elms or ashes, a year[32] but in 1581 the number was reduced to two for every yardland.[33] In 1823 a single gale was said to have brought down 100 elms there.[34] In Arlington the activity of wood pickers was under scrutiny in 1814 and a woman was summoned in 1826 for collecting wood.[35] In Winson the main area of woodland is Cadmoor copse. In 1840 86 a. of woodland were recorded in Arlington, Ablington, and Winson tithings[36] and in 1901 the parish had 113 a. of wood and plantation.[37]

The reputation of the Coln as a trout stream has brought renown to Bibury.[38] On Bibury manor a customary payment by the tenants at Midsummer called fish fee was recorded in the 1260s.[39] The bishop's fishery was mentioned c. 1285[40] and in the

later Middle Ages men were frequently presented in his court for fishing.[41] In 1575 a similar presentation was made in Ablington manor court.[42] In the later Middle Ages Oseney Abbey (Oxon.) owned the fishing rights in a stretch of the river at Arlington.[43] The excellence of Bibury trout was noted in the late 17th century,[44] and a trout farm established c. 1906 next to Arlington mill by Arthur Severn[45] served markets at home and abroad in 1975.

Bibury has also become famous as a beauty spot, on account of its setting and its buildings, notably Arlington Row. In 1726 Alexander Pope wrote of 'the pleasing prospect of Bibury' and William Morris in the late 19th century considered Bibury 'surely the most beautiful village in England',[46] but Bibury achieved widespread fame after the publication in 1898 of *A Cotswold Village* by Joseph Arthur Gibbs of Ablington Manor.[47] The tourist trade grew and by 1939 there were two tea rooms and a boarding-house in Bibury and a guest-house in Arlington.[48] Rack Isle, the meadow between the Coln and the leat of Arlington mill, became a wildfowl preserve c. 1956[49] and it was owned with Arlington Row, in front of which it lay, by the National Trust in 1975. The trout farm and the mill, which housed a folk museum and an art gallery, were then tourist attractions.

The growth of Arlington hamlet and Bibury village, the two main settlements, on the west and east sides respectively of crossing-points of the Coln indicates the early importance of the Cirencester–Oxford road, which crosses the parish from south-west to north-east, where it was recorded as Burford way in 1619.[50] From the south-west it originally ran through Arlington Corner, a group of buildings west of Arlington mill, to crossings upstream from the mill. The river and mill leat had been bridged by 1527 when a bequest was made for the repair of bridges in Arlington.[51] The road, which probably took the more direct descent south of the mill when it was turnpiked in 1753,[52] continued behind the site of the Swan and north of Bibury village.[53] Another important route between Cirencester and the Coln, indicated by the reference in 1625 to the lower port way in the southern part of the parish, ran north-eastwards from Ready Token and down Awkward hill (Hawker's hill) past Arlington Row.[54] The route probably disappeared long before 1769 apart from the section down Awkward hill which then provided access from the turnpike to

[26] Geol. Surv. Map 1″, solid, sheets 34, 44 (1856–7 edns.); Richardson, *Wells and Springs of Glos.* 56.

[27] Payne, *Glos. Survey*, 88–9.

[28] Ex inf. Mr. G. J. Phillips, chairman of S. J. Phillips & Sons (Kemble) Ltd., Kemble, which bought the land then.

[29] *Dom. Bk.* (Rec. Com.), i. 164.

[30] Glos. R.O., D 678, Bibury MSS. p. 126.

[31] S.C. 12/2/46 f. 137.

[32] Glos. R.O., D 269B/M 7, rot. 2.

[33] Ibid. rot. 3d.

[34] Ibid. F 117.

[35] Ibid. P 44/CO 1/1.

[36] Ibid. SD 2/1–2.

[37] Acreage Returns, 1901.

[38] Cf. Glos. Colln. RV 43.1.

[39] *Red Bk. of Worc.* 459.

[40] Ibid. 376.

[41] Glos. R.O., D 678, Bibury MSS. pp. 2, 8; ct. roll 63, rot. 4 and d.

[42] Ibid. D 269B/M 7, rot. 2.

[43] *Oseney Cart.* (Oxford Hist. Soc.), vi, p. 262.

[44] B.L. Harl. MS. 4716, f. 6.

[45] Glos. Colln. R 43.7; Glos. R.O., SL 211.

[46] H. A. Evans, *Highways and Byways in Oxford and the Cotswolds* (1905), 302 and n.

[47] Gibbs, *Cotswold Village* (2nd edn. 1899).

[48] *Kelly's Dir. Glos.* (1939), 42–3.

[49] *Glos. Countryside*, Oct.–Dec. 1956, 110.

[50] Glos. R.O., D 678, ct. roll 79, rot. 3.

[51] Hockaday Abs. cxxi, 1528.

[52] Bibury Road Act, 26 Geo. II, c. 70.

[53] Glos. R.O., D 678, map, 1769; Taylor, *Map of Glos.* (1777).

[54] Shropshire R.O. 1578 uncat., Arlington deeds; cf. O.S. Map 1/25,000, SP 10 (1959 edn.).

a bridge. That was a more important crossing than the ford and footbridge on the turnpike[55] where, however, a new bridge was built by subscription in 1770.[56] In 1790 the turnpike was diverted through the village, along the left bank of the Coln as far as the churchyard.[57] The route running behind the Swan fell out of use between 1829 and 1844.[58]

Several other ancient routes crossed the parish. The levying of toll on carts carrying salt across the bishop's estate in the late 13th century[59] points to the importance of the salt-way between Droitwich and Lechlade running across the north-eastern part and recorded in 1388.[60] At Saltway Barn, dated 1732,[61] the route was crossed by an old road from Ablington hamlet to Sherborne and both roads were specified in the inclosure award of 1780 together with a road branching from the salt-way near the northern boundary towards Northleach.[62] Of the route from Ablington the section from Saltway Barn to the road from Coln St. Aldwyns to Northleach in the north-eastern corner had gone out of use by 1840[63] and the remainder was replaced before 1882 by a road to the north-west which joined the salt-way near Oldwalls Sheds.[64] The ridgeway recorded in Winson in 1654[65] was part of the road between Foss Cross and Fairford recorded as Fairford way in 1625;[66] at Arlington Pike it crossed the Cirencester road and a route from Ready Token to Ablington and Winson. Packhorse lane, recorded in 1712 as Packer's lane,[67] ran north-eastwards from Bibury village to join the road to Northleach from Coln St. Aldwyns at Kilkenny and was possibly a continuation of the route from Ready Token to the Coln and important for the wool trade. It fell out of use soon after the turnpiking of the Cirencester–Oxford road[68] and in 1975 was a track. The road from Ablington to Coln St. Dennis, specified in 1780,[69] had become a track by 1840.[70]

The existence of a church at Bibury by 899 suggests that the village, established not far from the site of a Roman villa,[71] was then the most important settlement in the parish. Nevertheless in 1327 it had fewer people assessed for a subsidy than Arlington or Ablington and a considerably lower assessment than Arlington[72] but in 1608 it had more adult males listed than the other settlements.[73] The village had 307 inhabitants c. 1775.[74] An early focal point was the village square, the junction of various routes including Packhorse lane and a road to Coln St.

Aldwyns. On the north side the Pigeon House, so called by 1714,[75] is a small early-16th-century house with cross-passage and central chimney stack surmounted by a carved stone cowl. The principal room was on the first floor to the south of the stack and had an open roof with arch-braced collar-truss and a fireplace hood supported on carved brackets. North of the house is an old stone dovecot restored and reroofed in 1975.[76] Many of the cottages date from the 17th century, including east and south of the square three gabled buildings on a traditional cross-passage plan. The lane leading southwards to the church was built up in that century and east of the church stands Bibury Court, the 17th-century manor-house. During the 17th century the village, which was then called Bywell,[77] expanded north-westwards along the river bank to form a long street which ended at the Swan, recorded from the late 17th century, opposite Arlington mill. The buildings included the church house, mentioned in 1636 and demolished in 1878 to make way for a reading-room,[78] and Westwood Cottage, a 17th-century alms-house restored in the early 20th century. Of the cottages surviving in 1975 many had been much restored in the late 19th century after the closure of the route bypassing the village. Court Farm, a little way east of the manor-house and south of the river, dates from the 17th century and was formerly a mill-house.

On the north-east side of the square an 18th-century cottage, dated 1769,[79] was later enlarged and a cottage on the west side dates from the 19th century. Church House, probably on the site of an early vicarage west of the church, is dated 1802 but is of several periods; in 1975 Sir Tobias Clarke lived there. North-west of the village the Glebe House was built as a vicarage c. 1844. In the later 19th century some estate cottages were built south-east of the Swan, and c. 1953 a small council estate was built outside the village by the Burford road.[80]

Of several outlying post-inclosure farm-houses and barns, Shoecroft Barn was built in 1769 for the vicar's glebe.[81] By the river Leach a farm-house, built for Estcourt Cresswell[82] between 1769 and 1777[83] and called Kilkenny by 1799,[84] is a plain building refronted to the west in the 19th century. It was bought by Lord Sherborne, apparently in 1816.[85] Near by is a large barn dated 1795. Kilkenny Cottages by the Burford road date from the mid 19th

[55] Glos. R.O., D 678, map, 1769; cf. Ogilby, *Britannia* (1675), plate 55.
[56] Date on bridge; Rudder, *Glos.* 284; cf. *Glouc. Jnl.* 27 Nov. 1769.
[57] Glos. R.O., D 1070/VII/1.
[58] Ibid. Q/SRh 1829 Trin. C/3; 1844 Trin.
[59] *Red. Bk. of Worc.* 375.
[60] Glos. R.O., D 678, ct. roll 63, rot. 3.
[61] Date with inits. 'I.M.' on bldg.
[62] Glos. R.O., Q/RI 20.
[63] Ibid. P 44/SD 2/2.
[64] O.S. Map 6″, Glos. XLIV. NW. (1884 edn.).
[65] Christ Church, Oxford, MS. Estates 32, f. 539.
[66] Shropshire R.O. 1578 uncat., Arlington deeds, lease.
[67] Glos. R.O., D 678, ct. roll 77A, rot. 1.
[68] It was not recorded in ibid. map, 1769.
[69] Ibid. Q/RI 20.
[70] Ibid. P 44/SD 2/2.
[71] R.C.H.M. *Glos.* i. 14–15.

[72] *Glos. Subsidy Roll, 1327,* 14–15.
[73] Smith, *Men and Armour,* 258–9, 271.
[74] Rudder, *Glos.* 284.
[75] Glos. R.O., D 247/60.
[76] Ex inf. Sir Colin Crowe who bought the ho. in 1965 and the dovecot in 1972.
[77] Glos. R.O., D 678, ct. roll 79, rot. 8; Ogilby, *Britannia* (1675), p. 110; Bywell hill was recorded from 1382: Glos. R.O., D 678, Bibury MSS. p. 9; ct. roll 79, rot. 6.
[78] Glos. R.O., D 678, Bibury MSS. p. 150; see below.
[79] Date with inits. 'T.I.' on bldg.
[80] Verey, *Glos.* i. 111.
[81] Date and inits. 'W.S.' on bldg.; cf. Glos. R.O., Q/RI 21.
[82] Glos. R.O., D 269B/B 12.
[83] Ibid. D 678, map, 1769; Taylor, *Map of Glos.* (1777); a date stone is indecipherable.
[84] Glos. R.O., D 1388, Aldsworth inc. map.
[85] Ibid. D 2440, Bibury est. papers 1709–1829; cf. Glos. Colln. RQ 43.1.

century. North-east of the village Bibury Farm was also built in the mid 19th century together with some cottages to the south-west.

The settlement at Arlington included two mills in 1066. The hamlet enjoyed an early prosperity based on the manufacture of woollen cloth and by 1327 it had more persons assessed for the subsidy and a higher assessment than Bibury.[86] Many buildings date from the 17th century but the woollen industry declined in the 18th and c. 1775 the estimated population of 255 was smaller than that of Bibury.[87]

In the absence of land by the river suitable for building the hamlet developed up the hillside on the two roads leading to Cirencester. An early focal point was a green south-west of Arlington Corner on which there was a pound in the early 19th century.[88] From the green a lane leads to Awkward hill at the foot of which stands Arlington Row. The row, a long east-west range of uncertain date, but probably late-14th-century, almost spans the valley floor and was originally of one storey and had an open roof. The building, which was well placed to use the abundant water-supply of the leat of Arlington mill, was converted in the 17th century or early 18th into seven small cottages, each of which had an attic. Then or later cottages were added to both ends of the range.[89] The row was bought by the Royal Society of Arts in 1928[90] and conveyed to the Bristol and Gloucestershire Archaeological Trust which repaired it the following year. It was acquired by the National Trust in 1949[91] and was restored in the early 1970s, some of the cottages being amalgamated. West of the row are some 17th-century cottages. At the top of the hill a 17th-century farm-house was converted after 1839 as cottages[92] and a barn among its outbuildings was converted as a house after the Second World War.

The hamlet has several other 17th-century buildings, among them the mill and a cottage north of the green. A house at Arlington Corner has later additions and several cottages around the green date from the 18th century. Arlington Lodge on the south side of the Cirencester road was built in the early 18th century and to the south-west stands Arlington House, an 18th-century building in which a curate lived in the early 20th century.[93] Arlington Manor, on the corner of the lane to Awkward hill, is a 17th-century house with an 18th-century south-west front which dates from a rebuilding of a south wing. In 1839 it was a farm-house on the Barnsley Park estate and the out-buildings to the south included a

barn which is dated 1808[94] and has initials indicating that it was then part of William Hall's estate;[95] the barn had been converted as a house by 1939.[96] In the 19th century the hamlet expanded considerably. A nonconformist chapel, schoolroom, and manse were built near the green and a farm-house to the north-west.[97] Nine houses had been built west of the green by 1836,[98] one of them becoming a police station by 1882.[99] In the 1960s and early 1970s several large detached houses were built in traditional style near the green and south of the Cirencester road where a small private estate was developed on the site of a quarry. To the south and west of Arlington are a few outlying farms and barns built after the inclosures, including Quarryhill (formerly Deanhill) Farm.[1] At Arlington Pike is a small group of late-19th-century cottages and mid-20th-century houses, both council and private. Some way to the north-west is a substantial modern dwelling called Meadowlands.[2]

Evidence of early settlement in and around Ablington is provided by an Iron Age hill fort on the southern rim of the Coln valley and an ancient field-system on the downland to the north.[3] The hamlet, first recorded in 855,[4] grew east of a river crossing on an old route from Barnsley to Sherborne. The bridge which in 1692 needed repairing[5] was possibly that of stone swept away by floodwater in 1795.[6]

In 1327 Ablington, though with a lower assessment, had as many taxpayers as Arlington[7] but in 1608 it had fewer adult males listed than Bibury or Arlington[8] and with 91 inhabitants c. 1775 was the smallest settlement in the parish.[9] The hamlet, which forms a loose collection of dwellings, developed around a small green, on which the former Coln St. Dennis road converged, and along the lane leading eastwards past the 16th-century manor-house. Ablington House, at the eastern end of the hamlet, is a mid-17th-century farm-house, later extended on both sides; its entrance is flanked by 19th-century carved stone lions from the Houses of Parliament.[10] In the 19th and early 20th centuries the house was used for Lower farm[11] but in the 1930s it was owned by Judge A. R. Kennedy[12] (d. 1943)[13] with a small estate of c. 65 a. called Old farm.[14]

In the hamlet are several substantial, 18th-century farm buildings. A barn north of the manor-house was built by John Coxwell in 1727[15] and Manor Farm, a post-inclosure farm-house near by, in 1780 by Charles Coxwell,[16] who also built a barn

[86] *Glos. Subsidy Roll, 1327*, 14–15.
[87] Rudder, *Glos.* 284–5.
[88] Glos. R.O., P 44/SD 2/1.
[89] E. Mercer, *Eng. Vernacular Houses* (H.M.S.O. 1975), 157.
[90] Glos. Colln. RR 43.1; *Trans. B.G.A.S.* l. 375.
[91] Glos. R.O., PA 44/1 (W.I. village hist.); *Trans. B.G.A.S.* li. 19; xcii. 234–5.
[92] Glos. R.O., P 44/SD 2/1; cf. Davie and Dawber, *Old Cotswold Cottages*, plate 23.
[93] Ex inf. Mr. D. C. W. Verey, of Barnsley Ho., Barnsley.
[94] Glos. R.O., P 44/SD 2/1.
[95] See below.
[96] *Kelly's Dir. Glos.* (1939), 42.
[97] Cf. Glos. R.O., P 44/SD 2/1.
[98] Ibid. Q/RUm 147.
[99] O.S. Map 6″, Glos. XLIV. SW. (1884 edn.).

[1] Cf. Glos. R.O., P 44/SD 2/1; IN 3/1; O.S. Map 6″, Glos. XLIV. SW. (1884 edn.).
[2] Cf. O.S. Map 6″, Glos. XLIV. SW. (1884 edn.).
[3] R.C.H.M. *Glos.* i. 13–14.
[4] Finberg, *Early Charters of W. Midlands*, p. 48.
[5] Glos. R.O., D 269B/M 10, rot. 1.
[6] Ibid. F 117.
[7] *Glos. Subsidy Roll, 1327*, 15.
[8] Smith, *Men and Armour*, 258–9.
[9] Rudder, *Glos.* 285.   [10] Verey, *Glos.* i. 112.
[11] Glos. R.O., P 44/SD 2/2; SL 203.
[12] *Kelly's Dir. Glos.* (1931), 42; (1939), 42.
[13] *Who Was Who, 1941–50*, 630.
[14] Ex. inf. Mr. Phillips.
[15] Inscr. on bldg.
[16] Inscr. on bldg.; cf. Glos. R.O., D 269B/E 15, E 18.

north of Ablington House in 1797.[17] Hinton House, a small house dated 1753, was probably built for Samuel Tawney[18] (d. 1756).[19] The house, enlarged on the north in the late 18th and early 19th centuries, belonged to Hinton farm in 1875[20] but in the mid 20th century it was sold separately.[21] Beside the river crossing a house, formerly a mill, dates from the 18th century and a house on the western bank is of the same date. Nineteenth-century buildings include two houses west of the river and a few cottages on the Coln St. Dennis track.[22] There are several modern houses in traditional Cotswold style.

Winson village, 3.5 km. north-west of Bibury, grew west of a ford recorded in 1394[23] and around a small green and along a narrow lane entering it from the south. Two buildings to the north were in Coln St. Dennis parish, namely Winson Mill Farm, which is dealt with under that parish,[24] and Winson mill. The village, which by the 12th century had a chapel, has always been small; its assessment for the subsidy in 1327 was the lowest in the parish[25] and in 1608 it had the smallest number of adult males listed.[26] Manor Farm, west of the lane, has a 17th-century cross-wing to the south but the main front is dated 1729 with initials indicating that it was then enlarged by Thomas Matthews.[27] In 1839 it was owned by Samuel Bridges and in 1975 was a private residence. By the green Winson Manor is a mid-18th-century house and Village Farm is an early-19th-century farm-house which in 1839 belonged to the Barnsley Park estate.[28] In 1882 a pound stood south-west of Village Farm.[29] The village contains extensive stockyards and barns. College Cottage south of the Barnsley road was recorded as a barn in the early 20th century.[30] A school was built in the 19th century and the most substantial 20th-century building is the Clover House at the southern end of the village, dating from the 1930s.[31]

By 1839 there were a few scattered buildings on the downlands south-west of the village, including a keeper's lodge, later called Montreal House, and two barns.[32] The site of Pool House recorded in 1882[33] was occupied by farm buildings in 1975. Oxwold House was built in the early 1960s for David Henriques.[34]

In 1086 88 tenants were listed in the parish.[35] Eighty-three people were assessed for the subsidy in 1327[36] and at least 91 for the poll tax in 1381.[37] In 1551 80 communicants lived in the parish[38] and in 1563 there were 49 households.[39] The population had risen considerably by 1603 when there were 202 communicants,[40] and in 1650 96 families were estimated to live in the parish.[41] The 18th century saw a large increase in the population, from c. 500 about 1710[42] to c. 780 in the 1770s[43] and in 1801 it was 852. It continued to rise to 999 by 1821 and, after falling to 950 by 1831, reached a peak of 1,116 by 1851. It then declined and, despite a small rise between 1901 and 1911, had fallen to 663 by 1921. It then increased to 783 by 1961 but had dropped to 671 by 1971.[44]

In 1635 premises near the river Coln were used for the illicit production and consumption of beer.[45] A house occupied by Francis Crawford and assessed on 3 hearths in 1672[46] was evidently the coaching inn called the Swan, where his widow lived at the end of the century[47] and which stood opposite Arlington mill.[48] The building occupied an important place in the life of the parish in the late 18th and 19th centuries;[49] the tradition that the manor court was held there[50] is perhaps supported by the building of a small lock-up to the north-west in the later 18th century. The inn, which was rebuilt in the 19th century and has 19th-century stabling, was later called the Swan hotel. It remained part of the Bibury estate until 1926[51] and was remodelled and enlarged c. 1930.[52] Of the two victuallers licensed in 1755[53] one possibly occupied the Catherine Wheel recorded south-east of the Swan in 1829.[54] It may have closed soon afterwards, for one of the two beerhouses in Arlington in 1838 was called the Wheel[55] and later the Catherine Wheel;[56] the latter occupied premises south of the Cirencester road in 1975.

A friendly society began meeting at the Swan in 1835.[57] The village reading-room, built in 1878 on the site of the church house by Lord Sherborne,[58] was later enlarged and became the village hall.[59] In the early 1970s it was maintained out of the church lands charity and a trust established by Judge

[17] Inscr. on bldg.
[18] Date and inits. on bldg.
[19] Bigland, *Glos.* i. 184; in the 1770s his descendant John was an under-tenant on the est. of the dean and chapter of Glouc.: Glos. R.O., D 269B/E 13, T 32; Q/RI 20.
[20] Deed *penes* S. J. Phillips & Sons.
[21] Local information.
[22] Cf. Glos. R.O., P 44/SD 2/2; O.S. Map 6", Glos. XLIV. SW. (1884 edn.).
[23] *Ciren. Cart.* ii, p. 634. [24] *V.C.H. Glos.* viii. 28.
[25] *Glos. Subsidy Roll, 1327*, 11, 14–15.
[26] Smith, *Men and Armour*, 258–9, 271.
[27] Cf. Glos. R.O., D 2957/343A.3.
[28] Ibid. P 44/SD 2/1.
[29] O.S. Map 6", Glos. XLIV. SW. (1884 edn.).
[30] Ibid. (1903, 1924 edns.).
[31] Verey, *Glos.* i. 481.
[32] Glos. R.O., P 44/SD 2/1; O.S. Map 6", Glos. XLIV. SW. (1884 edn.).
[33] O.S. Map 6", Glos. XLIV. SW. (1884 edn.).
[34] Ex inf. Mr. Verey.
[35] *Dom. Bk.* (Rec. Com.), i. 164 and v., 169v.
[36] *Glos. Subsidy Roll, 1327*, 11, 14–15.
[37] E 179/113/35A rot. 1d.; E 179/113/31A rott. 3, 5d.
[38] *E.H.R.* xix. 113.
[39] Bodl. MS. Rawl. C. 790, f. 24.
[40] *Eccl. Misc.* 94.
[41] *Trans. B.G.A.S.* lxxxiii. 92, 94.
[42] Atkyns, *Glos.* 277.
[43] Rudder, *Glos.* 288. [44] *Census*, 1801–1971.
[45] Glos. R.O., D 678, Bibury MSS. p. 148.
[46] E 179/247/14 rot. 4d.
[47] B.L. Harl. MS. 4716, ff. 5v.–6.
[48] Glos. R.O., D 247/60.
[49] Ibid. Q/RI 21; P 44A/VE 2/1, entry for 1874; *Glouc. Jnl.* 27 Nov. 1769.
[50] Glos. R.O., PA 44/1.
[51] Ibid. SL 211.
[52] Ibid. D 2299/5126; cf. photog. c. 1900, *penes* Mr. Verey, at Arlington mill.
[53] Glos. R.O., Q/AV 2, rot. 3.
[54] Ibid. Q/SRh 1829 Trin. C/3.
[55] Ibid. D 1554.
[56] Ibid. P 44/IN 3/1.
[57] F.S. 2/3 no. 386; Glos. R.O., Q/RZ 1.
[58] *Kelly's Dir. Glos.* (1889), 673; Glos. R.O., P 44A/VE 2/1; inscr. on bldg.
[59] *Kelly's Dir. Glos.* (1931), 42; (1935), 41.

Kennedy.[60] A social club met in Ablington at the end of the 19th century in a building in the grounds of Ablington Manor.[61]

For over three centuries the Coxwell family dominated events in Ablington and under Charles Coxwell, vicar 1806–9, the whole parish benefited from his philanthropy and interest in education.[62] His grandson Henry Tracey Coxwell (1819–1900) was a pioneer aeronaut.[63] Yeoman families, notably those of Howse, recorded from 1394,[64] Bridges, and Matthews, were prominent in the affairs of Winson for several centuries. Among persons associated with the parish who achieved national prominence were Thomas Tryon (1634–1703), merchant, writer, and vegetarian, who was born at Bibury, and Samuel Bowly (1802–84), slavery abolitionist and temperance advocate, who was the son of an Arlington miller.[65]

Threshing machinery was destroyed in Bibury during the agricultural labourers' riots of 1830;[66] the Arlington tithingman was seeking the offenders on 30 November.[67] The Bibury Club, a private racing club, is dealt with under Aldsworth. In 1951 an old Valentine's day custom of throwing heated coins to children after they had sung was recorded in Bibury.[68]

MANORS AND OTHER ESTATES. The bishopric of Worcester had an estate of 15 'cassati' by the river Coln in the early 8th century and between 718 and 745 Bishop Wilfrith leased 5 'cassati' in Ablington to Leppa and his daughter Beage for their lives.[69] In 1086 the bishop's estate, which included land in Barnsley, comprised 21 hides.[70]

The manor of *BIBURY*, assessed at 1½ knight's fee,[71] was held by the bishops of Worcester, who were granted free warren there in 1254,[72] until 1549. Then, by an exchange of lands, it was acquired by John Dudley, earl of Warwick.[73] Dudley was created duke of Northumberland in 1551[74] and later that year he sold the manor to the Crown.[75] In 1554 it was granted to John Walters and Thomas Carpenter[76] who sold it later that year to Hugh Westwood of Chedworth.[77] The manor, known as Bibury Episcopi in the early 17th century, was more

usually called Bibury Northumberland to distinguish it from Bibury Oseney manor.[78]

Hugh Westwood, who also acquired Bibury Oseney and Arlington manors, died in 1559 leaving as his heir his nephew Robert Westwood.[79] Robert died in the Fleet prison[80] in 1600 and his son and heir William[81] sold the manor c. 1625 to Sir Thomas Sackville.[82] Sir Thomas (d. 1647) was succeeded in turn by his sons John (d. 1647) and Richard (d. 1670),[83] who in turn was succeeded by his sons John (fl. 1685), a lunatic and the ward of Jane Trinder (fl. 1694), and Henry.[84] Henry died in 1712 leaving as his heirs his daughters Elizabeth and Katherine.[85] On the division of his property in 1713 Bibury passed to Elizabeth, the elder,[86] who married Edmund Warneford of Sevenhampton in Highworth (Wilts.) (d. 1724).[87] Elizabeth (d. 1756) left her property to her grandson Estcourt Cresswell, son of her daughter Anne and Thomas Estcourt Cresswell of Pinkney (Wilts.).[88] Estcourt Cresswell, M.P. for Cirencester 1768–74,[89] sold part of the estate in 1816 to James Dutton, Lord Sherborne,[90] and died in 1823 heavily in debt. His will was the subject of a long Chancery lawsuit and in 1829 his son Richard Estcourt Cresswell conveyed most of the Bibury estate to John Dutton, Lord Sherborne,[91] with whose manor of Sherborne it then passed. James Huntley Dutton, Lord Sherborne,[92] owned 3,372 a. in Bibury and Ablington in 1921[93] but sold part of the manor with the manor-house in 1925 to Orme Bigland Clarke[94] who in 1932 succeeded to a baronetcy. Sir Orme (d. 1949) was succeeded by his son Sir Humphrey Orme Clarke,[95] whose son Sir Tobias Clarke[96] owned Court farm in 1975. Lord Sherborne retained Bibury and Kilkenny farms in 1926;[97] Kilkenny had been broken up by 1938 but the two parts were acquired in 1966 and 1967 by S. J. Phillips & Sons (Kemble) Ltd. which had bought Bibury farm from Albert Perry in 1953.[98]

Bibury Court is a large gabled house of the early 17th century commanding a view down the valley. The main range is entered at its centre by a porch on the east bearing the initials of Thomas and Barbara Sackville and the date 1633, and there is a former stair tower on the west. The south end of the range contained the principal rooms and is extended by a contemporary wing projecting eastwards. A similar

[60] Glos. R.O., CH 21.
[61] Gibbs, *Cotswold Village*, 22–3.
[62] Glos. R.O., D 269B/B 13.
[63] D.N.B.
[64] *Ciren. Cart.* ii, p. 634.
[65] D.N.B.
[66] *Glouc. Jnl.* 4 Dec. 1830; 8 Jan. 1831.
[67] Glos. R.O., P 44/CO 1/1.   [68] Ibid. PA 44/1.
[69] Finberg, *Early Charters of W. Midlands*, p. 34.
[70] *Dom. Bk.* (Rec. Com.), i. 164v.
[71] *Feud. Aids*, ii. 247; *Cal. Close, 1346–9*, 231.
[72] *Cal. Pat. 1247–58*, 345.
[73] Ibid. *1548–9*, 255.
[74] *Complete Peerage*, ix. 725.
[75] *Cal. Pat. 1550–3*, 117.
[76] Ibid. *1553–4*, 347–8.
[77] Ibid. 353.
[78] Glos. R.O., D 678, ct. rolls 77A, 78A, 79, 81A, 99A.
[79] C 142/126 no. 80; for grant of livery, see B.L. Add. Ch. 19542.
[80] *Sherborne Mun.* 84; cf. Req. 2/287/31.
[81] C 142/265 no. 59.
[82] Glos. R.O., D 269B/L 2.
[83] Ibid. D 38B/F 1; Gwladys Campbell, *The Web of Fortune* (1965), 186, 192.
[84] Glos. R.O., D 227; D 678, ct. roll 78A; P 44A/CH 3/1, leases 1685; *Sherborne Mun.* 91.
[85] Campbell, *Web of Fortune*, 192.
[86] *Sherborne Mun.* 95.
[87] Ibid. 96–7, 100.
[88] Ibid. 101; Burke, *Land. Gentry* (1898), i. 343.
[89] Campbell, *Web of Fortune*, 197.
[90] Glos. R.O., D 2440, Bibury est. papers 1709–1829, draft release 1826.
[91] Campbell, *Web of Fortune*, 203–7; Glos. R.O., D 2440, est. papers 1814–29; cf. *Sherborne Mun.* 101.
[92] Cf. *V.C.H. Glos.* vi. 123.
[93] *Country Life*, 3 Dec. 1921, suppl. p. iii.
[94] Ex inf. Rylands & Co., Cirencester, agents to the Sherborne est.
[95] Burke, *Peerage* (1963), 514; *Who's Who, 1955*, 557.
[96] Cf. *Who's Who, 1970*, 591.
[97] Glos. R.O., SL 211.
[98] Ex inf. Mr. Phillips.

wing of less ambitious design and containing service rooms was added at the north end of the east front, presumably in the later 17th century. Rain-water heads dated 1759 presumably mark the succession of Estcourt Cresswell and the interior appears to have been remodelled at about that time.[99] Richard Estcourt Cresswell left the house in 1825.[1] In 1838 James Dutton lived there[2] but after inheriting Sherborne he and his successors leased the house.[3] Extensive remodelling in the 1920s removed most of the 17th- and 18th-century features. The house, which remained a private residence until the death of Elfrida, widow of Sir Orme Clarke, in 1963, was sold in 1966 and converted as a hotel in 1968.[4] In 1975 the interior contained a variety of styles from the 17th to the 20th centuries.

An estate of 5 hides in Arlington was held in 1066 by Chenvichelle. It was later granted to Earl Roger who by 1086 had forfeited it to the Crown.[5] Earl Roger's property formed part of the endowment of the honor of Gloucester,[6] from which *ARLINGTON* manor, assessed at 1 knight's fee, was held as a member of Fairford manor.[7] At the division of the honor the overlordship of Arlington manor, assessed at ½ fee by the mid 14th century, passed with Fairford and was granted after the death of Hugh le Despenser in 1349 to his widow Elizabeth in dower.[8]

Land in Arlington was held from Geoffrey de la Mare in the early 13th century.[9] In 1233 during Richard Marshal's rebellion the manor was confiscated from John le Sor and granted during pleasure to William Bluet.[10] In 1253 it was held by Robert le Sor[11] and by 1285 had passed to John le Sor[12] (d. c. 1300).[13] In 1327 John of Pembridge was described as lord of Arlington[14] and his widow Alice was holding about two-thirds of the manor in dower in 1333 when it was settled on Roger Norman of Southampton and his son Roger.[15] The elder Roger had secured the land by 1337 when he was granted free warren[16] but later he held only four-fifths of the demesne.[17] He was succeeded in 1349 by his grandson Giles,[18] during whose minority the wardship was granted in turn to John of Pembridge in 1350[19] and William of Fifehyde in 1359.[20] Giles

died in 1361 leaving as his heir his cousin Margaret, wife of John Chamberlayne,[21] but the manor later passed to William de Shareshull and William of Garsington who sold it in 1363 to Oseney Abbey.[22] Although in 1391 the grant of free warren was confirmed to Roger Norman's kinswoman Alice and her husband Richard Becket,[23] the manor was retained by the abbey[24] and passed with Bibury Oseney manor[25] until 1713 when on the division of Henry Sackville's estate it was granted to his younger daughter Katherine.[26] Katherine (d. 1760)[27] left the manor to her great-nephew Estcourt Cresswell, a minor.[28] Cresswell, owner of the Bibury estate, held Arlington until his death in 1823.[29] In 1829 his son Richard Estcourt Cresswell sold c. 120 a. in Arlington to Michael Hicks Beach of Williamstrip[30] and the manor and certain tithes to Sir James Musgrave of Barnsley Park.[31] The manor passed with Barnsley[32] and was retained by Wenman Humfry Wykeham-Musgrave in 1939.[33] In 1975 most of Arlington belonged to the Barnsley Estate Co.

In 1607 William Westwood sold part of the manor, including a copyhold estate of over 160 a. and other land occupied by Robert Hall, to Charles Cox of London and his brother Christopher. In 1625 that property, comprising over 250 a., was included in a lease for life to Robert who apparently acquired the freehold, for later that year he settled it on the marriage of his son Robert[34] (d. c. 1652).[35] The younger Robert Hall's son William settled the property in 1680 on the marriage of his son William, whose son, also William[36] (d. 1760), was succeeded by his son Richard.[37] Richard, who was allotted 440 a. in 1768,[38] died in 1781 and was succeeded by his son William (d. 1824).[39] By 1839 his estate, including the barn near Arlington Manor, had been acquired by Sir James Musgrave.[40]

The bishop of Worcester's estate included land in Ablington in the early 8th century. In 855 Bishop Alhuun was exempted from all obligations, except the *trinoda necessitas*, in respect of 10 'manentes' in Ablington by Burgred, king of the Mercians,[41] and in 899 Bishop Waerfrith leased 5 'manentes' there to a

[99] For a view of the ho. c. 1780, see Rudder, *Glos.*, and for a modern view, see below, plate facing p. 44.

[1] Glos. R.O., D 269B/F 117.

[2] Ibid. D 1554; *Kelly's Dir. Glos.* (1856), 228; cf. ibid. (1863), 205.

[3] Glos. R.O., D 1388/III/8; *Kelly's Dir. Glos.* (1870–1919 edns.).

[4] Sale partics. *penes* Maj. Cresswell, Charingworth Manor, Ebrington; draft sale partics. *penes* the editor, V.C.H. Glos.; Bibury Court Hotel brochure; inscr. in ch.

[5] *Dom Bk.* (Rec. Com.), i. 164.

[6] Taylor, *Dom. Glos.* 153.

[7] *Feud. Aids*, ii. 237.

[8] See below; *Cal. Close*, 1349–54, 36; cf. C 139/96 no. 3.

[9] Glos. R.O., P 86/CH 1/44.

[10] *Close R.* 1231–4, 333.

[11] *Oseney Cart.* v, pp. 14–16.

[12] *Feud. Aids*, ii. 237.

[13] Cf. *Red Bk. of Worc.* 370; *Feud. Aids*, ii. 248.

[14] *Glos. Subsidy Roll, 1327,* 15.

[15] C.P. 25(1)/286/37 no. 137.

[16] *Cal. Chart. R. 1327–41,* 389.

[17] *Oseney Cart.* v, pp. 13–14.

[18] *Cal. Inq. p.m.* ix, pp. 231–3.

[19] *Cal. Fine R. 1347–56,* 208.

[20] Ibid. 1356–68, 88.

[21] *Cal. Inq. p.m.* xi, p. 207.

[22] *Cal. Pat.* 1361–4, 398; *Inq. p.m. Glos.* 1359–1413, 38.

[23] *Cal. Pat.* 1388–92, 508.

[24] *Cal. Inq. p.m.* xiv, p. 223.

[25] *Oseney Cart.* v, pp. 232, 262–3; *Valor Eccl.* (Rec. Com.), ii. 220–1; *Cal. Pat.* 1547–8, 63; C 142/265 no. 59.

[26] *Sherborne Mun.* 95.

[27] Inscr. in ch.   [28] *Sherborne Mun.* 101.

[29] Cf. Fosbrooke, *Glos.* ii. 466; see above.

[30] Glos. R.O., D 2240, est. papers 1753–1852, est. partics. 1830.

[31] Cf. ibid. D 2957/343A.8.

[32] See above; *Kelly's Dir. Glos.* (1856), 228; (1931), 42.

[33] *Kelly's Dir. Glos.* (1939), 42, where he is called Chris. Wenman; ex inf. Mr. Verey.

[34] Shropshire R.O. 1578 uncat., Arlington deeds.

[35] Cf. Glos. R.O., P 44A/CH 2, churchwardens' accts. at end of vol.

[36] Shropshire R.O. 1578 uncat., Arlington deeds, deeds 1680, 1705.

[37] Glos. R.O., D 1395/III/15; inscr. in ch.

[38] Glos. R.O., Q/RI 21.

[39] Ibid. D 1395/III/15; inscr. in ch.

[40] Cf. Glos. R.O., P 44/SD 2/1; see above, p. 25.

[41] Finberg, *Early Charters of W. Midlands*, p. 48.

BARNSLEY PARK: the south front

FAIRFORD: the east side of the market-place

CHEDWORTH CHURCH from the south

BIBURY CHURCH from the south

priest.[42] From the 12th century the overlordship of *ABLINGTON* manor passed with the bishops' manor of Bibury.[43] Ablington manor, assessed at $\frac{1}{2}$ fee in 1241,[44] was held in 1285 for 1 knight's fee and a rent of 33s. 4d.[45] Later assessed at $\frac{1}{2}$ fee[46] and then in the mid 14th century at $\frac{1}{4}$ fee,[47] it was said in 1574 to be held by the rent alone.[48]

In the early 12th century the manor, comprising 2 hides, was held by Geoffrey de Meysi who gave it with his daughter in marriage to Geoffrey d'Evercy. Geoffrey's son Robert d'Evercy held 1 knight's fee from the bishop in 1166 but was elsewhere said to hold the 2 hides, assessed at $\frac{2}{5}$ fee, and another 6 hides and 4 yardlands.[49] Robert, who gave property in Ablington to Bruern Abbey (Oxon.), was the grandfather of Olympia who with her husband Ralph of Willington was granted a reversionary right in half of the manor in 1207.[50] Ralph, who was holding the 2 hides in 1208 or 1209,[51] acquired $2\frac{1}{2}$ hides there in 1211 from Cecily de Quercy by an exchange of lands.[52] About 1276 a lease of the manor was granted to Roger Clifford by another Ralph of Willington[53] who held the manor in 1285.[54] In 1299 it was held by John of Willington[55] who was granted free warren in 1311.[56] John forfeited the estate in 1322, when custody was awarded to Robert of Aston,[57] but recovered it the following year[58] and was succeeded in 1338 by his son Ralph.[59] Ralph (d. 1348) left as his heir his uncle Reynold but the manor passed to Henry of Willington. Henry (d. 1349) was succeeded by his son John, a minor,[60] and in 1350 custody of the manor was granted to the tenants.[61] John, later Sir John (d. 1378), granted a life-interest to Thomas of Willington, his brother, who survived him. After Thomas's death the manor reverted to Sir John's son Ralph, a minor who was succeeded in 1382 by his brother John, also a minor. In 1384 Ralph's widow Joan, who married Thomas West, received dower in a third of the manor but in 1396 it was said that after Ralph's death Ablington had been held by Thomas West the elder and his wife Alice and after Alice's death by Thomas's son Thomas.[62] John of Willington, an idiot, died in 1396 leaving as coheirs his sister Isabel, wife of William Beaumont, and

nephew John Wrothe, a minor.[63] In 1397 the Crown assigned two-thirds of the manor to Isabel[64] and in 1404 the other third reverted to John and Isabel on the death of Joan West.[65] Until John Wrothe's death in 1412 the Crown evidently retained an interest in the manor,[66] which Isabel held at her death in 1424.[67] It then passed with Westonbirt manor until 1574[68] when Arthur Basset sold it to John Coxwell of Cirencester.[69]

John Coxwell, who had acquired property in Bibury and Coln St. Dennis from Richard ap Owen in 1565,[70] was succeeded in 1618 by his son Nathaniel.[71] Nathaniel, who in 1624 purchased a yardland in Arlington formerly held by Sir Edmund Tame of Rendcomb and then by his sister Isabel,[72] died in 1638 and the manor passed in the direct line to Edward[73] (d. 1645) and John.[74] John conveyed the estate in 1695 to his son Charles[75] (d. 1702), who was succeeded by his son John, a minor. John (d. 1754) was succeeded in turn by his sons John (d. 1762) and Charles,[76] who became rector of Barnsley and vicar of Bibury.[77] From Charles (d. 1829) the estate passed to his son Charles Coxwell, rector of Dowdeswell (d. 1854), who was succeeded by his son Richard Rogers Coxwell Rogers of Dowdeswell.[78] Richard, whose brother Charles Rogers Coxwell (d. 1893)[79] also held lands in Ablington,[80] died in 1895 leaving a son and heir, Godfrey Hugh Wheeler Coxwell Rogers, and two daughters, Ellen, wife of George Edward Beale Browne, and Grace.[81] The daughters' interest in the estate ended with Godfrey's death in 1914[82] when he was succeeded by Richard Hugh Coxwell Rogers who began the break-up of the estate,[83] Lower farm being sold to Lauriston Batten in 1914 and the manor-house to Lt.-Col. C. G. Martyr in 1915. Richard was killed in action in 1915[84] and his successor Miss F. A. Coxwell Rogers sold Manor farm in 1918 to Edward Dutton, Lord Sherborne, who had acquired Lower and Oldwalls farms in 1916.[85] S. J. Phillips bought those farms from the Sherborne estate in 1944 and 1946, and in the latter year he established S. J. Phillips & Sons (Kemble), a limited company.[86]

In the early 16th century non-resident lords leased

[42] Ibid. p. 51.
[43] *Red Bk. of Worc.* 376, 414, 448.
[44] C.P. 25(1)/73/13 no. 231.
[45] *Feud. Aids*, ii. 237.
[46] *Red Bk. of Worc.* 370.
[47] *Cal. Inq. p.m.* ix, pp. 90, 196.
[48] Glos. R.O., D 269B/M 1.
[49] *Red Bk. of Worc.* 438, 414.
[50] *Cal. Pat.* 1364–7, 344; C.P. 25(1)/73/7 no. 77; C.P. 25(1)/282/4 no. 48.
[51] *Bk. of Fees*, i. 39.
[52] C.P. 25(1)/73/3 no. 64.
[53] *Abbrev. Plac.* (Rec. Com.), 190.
[54] *Feud. Aids*, ii. 237.
[55] *Red Bk. of Worc.* 370.
[56] *Cal. Chart. R.* 1300–26, 165.
[57] Cf. *Cal. Close*, 1318–23, 605.
[58] S.C. 6/1147/12 m. 12.
[59] *Cal. Inq. p.m.* viii, pp. 109–10.
[60] Ibid. ix, pp. 90, 196.
[61] *Cal. Fine R.* 1347–56, 254–5.
[62] *Cal. Inq. p.m.* xv, pp. 62, 339–42.
[63] *Inq. p.m. Glos.* 1359–1413, 201–2.
[64] *Cal. Fine R.* 1391–9, 199–200.
[65] *Inq. p.m. Glos.* 1359–1413, 240.
[66] Ibid. 263–4.
[67] C 139/11 no. 28.

[68] C 139/143 no. 30; C.P. 25(2)/66/545 no. 26; *V.C.H. Glos.* xi. 286.
[69] Glos. R.O., D 269B/T 21; cf. *Cal. Pat.* 1555–7, 403–5.
[70] Glos. R.O., D 269B/T 8.
[71] Ibid. T 23.
[72] Ibid. T 9; cf. C.P. 40/1134 Carte rot. 2; Sir Edm.'s father Edm. and grandfather John were among those granted land in Bibury, Arlington, and Ablington by Rob. Throckmorton in 1496: B.L. Eg. Ch. 753.
[73] *Inq. p.m. Glos.* 1625–42, ii. 120.
[74] *Visit. Glos.* 1682–3, 52; Glos. R.O., D 269B/T 1.
[75] Glos. R.O., D 269B/T 21.
[76] Ibid. F 117; *Visit. Glos.* 1682–3, 52–3.
[77] Hockaday Abs. cxxi.
[78] *Visit. Glos.* 1682–3, 53, 146–7; Glos. R.O., D 627/39–40.
[79] Glos. R.O., D 269, pedigree in cat.
[80] Ibid. P 44/IN 3/1; cf. *Kelly's Dir. Glos.* (1870), 474, where he is called Chas. Coxwell Rogers.
[81] *Visit. Glos.* 1682–3, 146–7; Glos. R.O., D 269, pedigree in cat.
[82] Glos. R.O., P 44/IN 3/1, entries 1903–1914; *Kelly's Dir. Glos.* (1902), 39.
[83] Glos. R.O., P 44/IN 3/1; SL 203.
[84] Ibid. P 44/IN 3/1, in which Martyr's initial is given as F.; cf. *Kelly's Dir. Glos.* (1919 and later edns.).
[85] Glos. R.O., P 44/IN 3/2.
[86] Ex inf. Mr. Phillips.

the manor-house to members of the Howse family.[87] The house, apparently set in park-land mentioned in 1575,[88] presumably occupied the same site as Ablington Manor. It is a substantial house of traditional three-roomed plan with a porch on the north side dated 1590 and leading to a former cross-passage. The house was enlarged in the earlier 17th century by the addition of terminal wings on the south side which faces the river Coln. In 1650 John Coxwell set aside certain rooms for his mother Katherine.[89] About 1780 for the Revd. Charles Coxwell the interior was refitted, the south elevation refenestrated, the area between the wings taken in for a staircase, and the roofs partly reconstructed.[90] At that time and during the 19th century considerable additions were made on the east side for service rooms, and a stable court dated 1860 was added. Nevertheless in the later 19th century the Coxwell Rogerses preferred to live at Dowdeswell Court.[91] After Col. Martyr's death in 1936[92] his widow owned the house[93] which his daughter-in-law, Mrs. West, sold to Mr. V. Walker. He sold it in 1975 to Mr. Robert Cooper.[94] Successive owners in the 20th century have refitted the interior. Gardens run down from the house to the river.

In 1227 Ralph of Willington granted 1 hide in Ablington to Gloucester Abbey.[95] After the Dissolution 3½ yardlands passed to the dean and chapter of Gloucester with Coln Rogers manor,[96] from which land, known as College lands, was leased in the later 18th century.[97] The land, which was extended at c. 125 a. in 1789,[98] was leased for 21 years in 1796 to William Hinton[99] (d. c. 1812). His son William, who in 1826 acquired an estate of 72 a. allotted in 1780 to John Howse,[1] evidently bought the land, for in 1840 he owned 208 a. in Ablington.[2] Robert Hinton by will dated 1860 left his property to his cousin John Hinton Bryan of Down Ampney (d. 1867), who was succeeded in turn by his widow Ann (d. 1870) and his son John, under whom the estate, called Hinton farm, was broken up. Richard Rogers Coxwell Rogers bought parts in 1874 and 1875 and Robert Garne of Aldsworth c. 174 a. in 1875. By will dated 1900 Robert left the farm to his nephew William Thomas Garne[3] who sold it c. 1945 to Mr. Jelf from whom an estate of 80 a. was bought by S. J. Phillips & Sons in 1959.[4]

An estate of 5 hides in Winson, held as three manors by Edric, Leuric, and Elric in 1066, had passed by 1086 to Ansfrid de Cormeilles.[5] The manor of *WINSON*, assessed at ½ fee,[6] passed with the honor of Cormeilles. In 1303 the earl of Hereford was recorded as overlord,[7] possibly by virtue of a grant of the overlordship of the honor in 1141 by the Empress Maud to Miles of Gloucester.[8] The manor was held by Richard de Cormeilles in 1192, and by his brother Walter[9] in 1213.[10] Walter died leaving as coheirs four daughters, at least two of whom, Aubrey wife of Richard le Brun and Margaret wife of Walter of Stoke, received a share in the manor.[11] The estate, held from the honor for 1 knight's fee in 1236 by Walter de Baskerville,[12] was held in 1243 by Lucy de Cormeilles from John le Brun,[13] the son of Richard le Brun and Aubrey de Cormeilles.[14]

John le Brun held a quarter of the manor with Elkstone manor at his death c. 1266 and was succeeded by another John le Brun.[15] In 1304 John granted a reversionary right in a third of the manor to John, son of John of Acton,[16] who had succeeded him by 1316.[17] John of Acton forfeited his lands in 1322[18] but recovered them, and his Winson property, sometimes called Winson manor, passed with Elkstone until the early 17th century after which it has not been traced.[19]

A part of Ansfrid de Cormeilles's estate passed through Margaret of Stoke's elder daughter Alice, wife of Robert Archer,[20] to Nicholas Archer. Nicholas granted a life-interest in 60 a. of land and 40s. rent in Winson to William Absalom who may have been the Absalom Clark recorded in 1285.[21] William was still in possession in 1305 when Nicholas's son Nicholas granted a remainder in the property, held by the serjeanty tenure of carrying the king's bow when he was hunting in Gloucestershire forests, to John of Acton.[22] John held it at his death in 1312 when he was succeeded by his son John.[23] Nicholas Archer's widow Alice secured her dower in a third of 70 a. in 1316 or 1317[24] and was still in possession in 1333.[25] The property presumably passed with John of Acton's other property in Winson and Elkstone.

Another part of Winson manor passed through Margaret of Stoke's younger daughter Isabel, wife

[87] Glos. R.O., D 269B/T 2, T 28.
[88] Ibid. M 7, rot. 2.
[89] Ibid. T 1; the rooms of the ho. were listed in an inventory of 1645: ibid. F 3.
[90] Ibid. E 11, E 14.
[91] Gibbs, *Cotswold Village*, 22.
[92] Inscr. in S. window of Winson chap.
[93] *Kelly's Dir. Glos.* (1939), 42.
[94] Ex inf. Mrs. R. Cooper and Mr. Verey.
[95] *Hist. & Cart. Mon. Glouc.* (Rolls Ser.), i. 59–60.
[96] Cf. *L. & P. Hen. VIII*, xvi, p. 573; Hockaday Abs. cxxi, 1550.
[97] Glos. R.O., D 269B/E 13, T 32; Q/RI 20.
[98] Ibid. D 936/E 10.
[99] Deed *penes* S. J. Phillips & Sons.
[1] Ibid.; Glos. R.O., D 936/M 1/2, cts. 5 Nov. 1801, 5 Nov. 1812; Q/RI 20.
[2] Glos. R.O., P 44/SD 2/2.
[3] Deeds *penes* S. J. Phillips & Sons.
[4] Ex inf. Mr. Phillips.
[5] *Dom. Bk.* (Rec. Com.), i. 169v.

[6] Cf. *Feud. Aids*, ii. 238, 278.
[7] Ibid. 246; cf. ibid. 256.
[8] *V.C.H. Herefs.* i. 277 n.
[9] *Pipe R. 1191 & 92* (P.R.S. N.S. ii), 98, 290.
[10] *Bk. of Fees*, i. 50.
[11] *Trans. B.G.A.S.* xl. 115; cf. ibid. xiii. 333.
[12] *Bk. of Fees*, i. 440.
[13] Ibid. ii. 819.
[14] *Trans. B.G.A.S.* xiii. 333.
[15] *Inq. p.m. Glos. 1236–1300*, 37.
[16] C.P. 25(1)/75/39 no. 240.
[17] *Feud. Aids*, ii. 271.
[18] *Cal. Fine R. 1319–27*, 96.
[19] *Inq. p.m. Glos. 1302–58*, 301; *Cal. Inq. p.m.* xv, pp. 19–20; C 142/332 no. 154; C.P. 25(2)/299/21 Jas. I Trin. no. 22.
[20] *Trans. B.G.A.S.* xvi. 70; xl. 115–16.
[21] *Cal. Pat. 1301–7*, 164; *Feud. Aids*, ii. 238.
[22] *Inq. p.m. Glos. 1302–58*, 15–16; C.P. 25(1)/75/40 no. 262.
[23] *Cal. Inq. p.m.* v, pp. 229–30.
[24] *Abbrev. Rot. Orig.* (Rec. Com.), i. 240.
[25] C.P. 25(1)/286/37 no. 137.

of Simon de Sollers,[26] to Thomas de Sollers who in 1278 granted 3 yardlands and 40s. rent to another Simon de Sollers.[27] Simon, who held property in Winson in 1285 and 1316,[28] forfeited rents there in 1322.[29] The estate has not been traced after 1346 when it was held by John de Sollers.[30]

By 1285 part of Winson manor was held by Walter of Burton[31] who in 1304 granted a third of the manor, including 9 messuages, 10 yardlands, and a third of a mill, to Richard of Burton and his heirs.[32] That property was evidently held in 1316 by Thomas of Burton[33] whose son Thomas secured permission to grant 10 messuages, 11½ yardlands, and a third of the mill to Walter of Cirencester in 1344.[34] The property has not been traced after 1346.[35]

The estate of Walter of Cirencester or John de Sollers in 1346 may have formed part of the manor of *WINSON* held by Sir Edmund Tame. Sir Edmund (d. 1534) left it to his wife Elizabeth who died in 1545.[36] Sir Edmund's son and heir Sir Edmund Tame of Rendcomb had died without issue and at a partition made among his three sisters in 1547 Winson manor passed to Margaret, wife of Sir Humphrey Stafford.[37] Sir Humphrey's son John[38] with others conveyed it to John Dryden in 1567.[39] By 1583 the manor of Winson or Dryden's Winson was owned by William Aubrey[40] and after his death in 1595 it passed to his second son Thomas.[41] In 1603 Thomas divided the manor into three parts by grants to John Matthews, William Bridges, and Thomas Howse the younger,[42] members of the principal copyholding families on the estate.[43]

The part acquired by John Matthews, described in 1608 as lord of Winson,[44] was later known as Winson manor and was held by the Matthews family for over a century. A Richard Matthews died in 1620 leaving a son Richard[45] (d. 1669).[46] Richard Matthews, lord of the manor in the early 18th century,[47] settled it on his son Richard in 1711.[48] The younger Richard, who had inherited 423 a. by 1728,[49] sold the manor in 1738 to Alexander Ready of Fairford,[50] from whom it was purchased in 1741 by Charles D'Oyley[51] (d. 1776). The estate passed, evidently with land in Southrop, to his son Charles

(d. 1802),[52] whose heir put up 600 a. in Winson for sale in 1806.[53] By 1836 the estate had been acquired by Sir James Musgrave of Barnsley Park[54] who acquired the other parts of the manor and was described in 1856 as lord of the manor.[55] The estate, which passed with Arlington,[56] was sold in the 1950s to the author Robert Henriques (d. 1967), whose sons Michael and David owned land in Winson in 1975.[57]

Winson Manor is a small double-pile house of c. 1740 with a principal front of 5 bays to the east. The decoration inside and out is in the style associated with the books of James Gibbs. In 1839 it was a farm-house on the Barnsley Park estate[58] and c. 1954 was bought by Mrs. M. Y. Darwin.[59]

The part of the manor acquired by William Bridges, who was mentioned in 1608,[60] was held by his descendants for over two centuries. John Bridges was recorded in 1645.[61] In 1700 Thomas Bridges settled 3 yardlands on his marriage[62] and in 1725 he settled the property, in return for an annuity of £15, on the marriage of his son Thomas[63] who held 181 a. in 1728.[64] The elder Thomas died in 1751 and the younger in 1796.[65] The latter's son, also Thomas, was succeeded in 1808 by Samuel Bridges,[66] who in 1830 exchanged 101 a. with Sir James Musgrave for 48 a. and certain tithes.[67] Samuel died in 1845 and his property passed to his sister Mary. After her death in 1850 it was sold to William Weeks, a relative by marriage, from whom it was bought in 1852 by Sir James Musgrave.[68]

The third part of the manor, which passed to Thomas Howse the younger (fl. 1608),[69] was held by his descendants for over two centuries. Richard Howse (d. c. 1718) left his lands to his son Richard[70] who held 194 a. in 1728.[71] Richard (d. c. 1753) was succeeded by his son Richard[72] (d. c. 1766), whose widow Esther quitclaimed the lands settled on her to his brother and heir John in 1767. John (d. 1807) was succeeded in turn by his sons Richard (d. 1808) and William. William, who held 380 a. in Winson and Coln St. Dennis, sold his property in 1824 to Sir James Musgrave.[73]

In 1086 a priest held 3 hides from Bibury manor.[74] Some land was presumably appropriated with

[26] Cf. *Trans. B.G.A.S.* xvi. 70.
[27] C.P. 25(1)/75/31 no. 31.
[28] *Feud. Aids,* ii. 238, 271.
[29] S.C. 6/1145/15 m. 4.
[30] *Feud. Aids,* ii. 278.
[31] Ibid. 238.
[32] C.P. 25(1)/75/39 no. 238.
[33] *Feud. Aids,* ii. 271.
[34] *Cal. Pat.* 1343–5, 241.
[35] *Feud. Aids,* ii. 278.
[36] C 142/74 no. 86; cf. Hockaday Abs. cxciv, Fairford 1533.
[37] C.P. 40/1134 Carte rot. 2.
[38] *Visit. Glos.* 1623, 260.
[39] C.P. 25(2)/141/1796 no. 22.
[40] C 3/221/48.   [41] C 142/246 no. 99.
[42] *Trans. B.G.A.S.* xvii. 205; cf. Glos. R.O., D 210/4.
[43] C 3/221/48.
[44] Smith, *Men and Armour,* 271.
[45] G.D.R. wills 1621/100.
[46] Bigland, *Glos.* i. 183.
[47] Bodl. MS. Top. Glouc. c. 3, f. 211.
[48] C.P. 25(2)/926/10 Anne Mich. no. 35.
[49] Glos. R.O., D 2957/343A.3.
[50] C.P. 25(2)/1128/12 Geo. II Hil. no. 23.

[51] C.P. 25(2)/1128/15 Geo. II Mich. no. 3.
[52] Glos. R.O., D 2440, Southrop est. papers 1715–1814; cf. ibid. D 2957/343A.19; Rudge, *Hist. of Glos.* i. 250.
[53] Glos. R.O., D 1388/SL 3, no. 19.
[54] Cf. ibid. Q/RUm 147.
[55] *Kelly's Dir. Glos.* (1856), 390.
[56] See above; *Kelly's Dir. Glos.* (1939), 379.
[57] Ex inf. Mr. Verey; *Glos. Life,* Apr. 1973, 50–1.
[58] Glos. R.O., P 44/SD 2/1.   [59] Ex inf. Mrs. Darwin.
[60] Smith, *Men and Armour,* 271.
[61] Glos. R.O., D 269B/F 3.
[62] Ibid. D 2957/343A.1.
[63] Ibid. 2.   [64] Ibid. 3.
[65] Inscrs. in Winson churchyard.
[66] Glos. R.O., D 1388, Winson sale papers, abs. 1851.
[67] Ibid. D 2957/343A.8.
[68] Ibid. D 1388, Winson sale papers, abs. 1851; D 2957/343A.11–18.
[69] Smith, *Men and Armour,* 271.
[70] G.D.R. wills Bibury pec. 124.
[71] Glos. R.O., D 2957/343A.3.
[72] G.D.R. wills Bibury pec. 125.
[73] Glos. R.O., D 1388/III/123; inscrs. in Winson chap.
[74] *Dom. Bk.* (Rec. Com.), i. 164v.

Bibury church and its tithes by Oseney Abbey in 1151,[75] for the abbey, which in 1248 acquired ⅔ yardland in Bibury,[76] held 2 yardlands there in 1291.[77] The appropriated rectory, with which went the peculiar jurisdiction of Bibury church, the tithes of wool and lambs, and all the tithes of the rectory estate, was held by the abbey until the Dissolution[78] and was granted in 1542 to Christ Church, Oxford.[79] The rectory estate, which included land in Arlington, had been resumed by the Crown by 1547 when it was granted to John Harrington.[80] Known later as *BIBURY OSENEY* manor,[81] it was held by various speculators and in 1552 Sir William Sharington sold it to William Herbert, earl of Pembroke, who sold it to Hugh Westwood.[82] Hugh later bought Bibury manor with which it afterwards descended.[83] The rectory was valued at 200 marks in 1603.[84]

In 1620 William Westwood sold the tithes of wool and lambs in Arlington and some land to Elizabeth Clarke and Elizabeth Bedford[85] but in 1632 they were sold back to Sir Thomas Sackville.[86] The Arlington tithes which Sir Thomas had apparently sold to Richard Westwood in 1628[87] were evidently the grain tithes from land once belonging to the rectory estate there which Richard sold to Nathaniel Coxwell in 1629.[88] On the partition of the Sackville estate in 1713 the tithes of wool and lambs in Arlington, Ablington, and Winson passed with Arlington manor.[89] In 1780 Estcourt Cresswell received an allotment of 68 a. for the tithes of wool and lambs in Ablington then inclosed.[90] In 1830 Sir James Musgrave conveyed some of the tithes of wool and lambs in Winson to Samuel Bridges.[91] The tithes of wool and lambs in Arlington and Winson were commuted in 1839 for a rent-charge of £57 3s. 2d., £46 0s. 8d. being awarded to Sir James Musgrave, £5 2s. 6d. to Sir Michael Hicks Hicks Beach, and £6 to Samuel Bridges.[92]

A rent of 8s. from Winson, received by the appropriator in 1280[93] and until the Dissolution, derived from a yardland of glebe belonging to the chapel there.[94] In 1546 the yardland was regranted to the dean and chapter of Christ Church, Oxford,[95] who held 33a. in 1728.[96] The land was sold to the Barnsley Park estate in 1874.[97]

The ½ hide which Cirencester Abbey was said to hold in the parish at 'Walle' in the early 14th century[98] was at Wall Farm in Aldsworth.

ECONOMIC HISTORY: AGRICULTURE.

In 1086 the bishop's estate had a demesne of 4 plough-lands with 11 *servi* and *ancillae*.[99] Bibury manor, which c. 1285 had 2 cart-horses, 4 draught-beasts, and 12 oxen for two ploughs and could support up to 500 sheep and 6 cows,[1] had in 1299 446¼ a. of arable in demesne, on which wheat, barley, and oats were sown as a mixed crop. Only 8 a. of meadow land were in demesne. Labour-services were provided by the tenants who were given a wether and cheese for haymaking and sheaves for harvesting. In 1302 or 1303 surplus labour-services, mostly after the harvest, were sold back to the tenants, some of whom were among the hired farm-servants of 3 ploughmen, a reap-reeve, a smith, and a carter.[2] Although the demesne was apparently leased in 1327 for £20 a year[3] it was kept in hand in the later 14th century and was devoted to corn and sheep husbandry. In the early 1370s dredge and some oats, wheat, barley, and vetches were grown. In 1372 127 harvesters were each paid 5d. for a day's work and the grain was threshed by farm-servants and hired labour. From 1395 the manor was leased out[4] and in the later 15th century the farm of the demesne was £4.[5] The demesne had been taken in hand by the mid 16th century and Hugh Westwood is said to have had 70 kine, as well as 500 sheep and a large barn of corn, at his death in 1559.[6]

Winson manor had 4 ploughs in demesne with 10 *servi* and *ancillae* in 1086.[7] The demesne of Arlington manor, which in 1066 had 4 ploughs with 16 *servi* and *ancillae*,[8] was extended in 1350 at 170 a. of arable, 6 a. of meadow, and some pasture held in severalty[9] and was let at farm in the early 16th century.[10] Ablington manor was leased in the mid 16th century.[11]

In 1280 Oseney Abbey, the appropriator, administered its land in Bibury with its property in Aldsworth, Turkdean, and Winson. The estate, from which much corn, principally barley and some wheat, was sent to the abbey or sold, and on which cattle and pigs were kept, was also organised for sheep-farming. The rectory demesne was let at farm by 1493 when Richard Bagot took a 20-year lease. In 1512 Bagot was granted a lease for 21 years[12] and in 1535 the demesne was farmed by Hugh Westwood.[13]

The appropriator's retention of the tithes of wool

[75] *Oseney Cart.* v, pp. 1–2.
[76] C.P. 25(1)/74/17 no. 349.
[77] *Tax. Eccl.* (Rec. Com.), 237.
[78] *Oseney Cart.* vi, pp. 262–3; *Valor Eccl.* (Rec. Com.), ii. 220, 452.
[79] *L. & P. Hen. VIII*, xvii, pp. 490–2.
[80] *Cal. Pat.* 1547–8, 63.
[81] Glos. R.O., D 678, ct. roll 81A.
[82] *Cal. Pat.* 1550–3, 417–18, 246.
[83] C 142/265 no. 59; *Sherborne Mun.* 95.
[84] *Eccl. Misc.* 94.
[85] C.P. 25(2)/299/18 Jas. I Mich. no. 49; Glos. R.O., D 678, Bibury MSS. p. 75.
[86] C.P. 25(2)/527/8 Chas. I East. no. 6.
[87] Cf. *Sherborne Mun.* 274.
[88] Glos. R.O., D 269B/T 8.
[89] *Sherborne Mun.* 95; cf. Glos. R.O., D 269B/F 79.
[90] Glos. R.O., Q/RI 20.
[91] Ibid. D 2957/343A.8.
[92] Ibid. P 44/SD 2/1.
[93] *Oseney Cart.* vi, pp. 193–4.

[94] Ibid. p. 232; *Valor Eccl.* (Rec. Com.), ii. 221.
[95] Hockaday Abs. cxxi; *L. & P. Hen. VIII*, xxi(2), p. 336.
[96] Glos. R.O., D 2957/343A.3.
[97] Ex inf. assistant treasurer, Christ Church, Oxford.
[98] *Inq. Non.* (Rec. Com.), 409.
[99] *Dom. Bk.* (Rec. Com.), i. 164v.
[1] *Red Bk. of Worc.* 376.
[2] Ibid. 368–74, 504–5.
[3] *Cal. Pat.* 1327–30, 197–8.
[4] Worcs. R.O. 009:1 (BA 2636/160–1).
[5] Glos. R.O., D 678, acct. roll 89.
[6] Req. 2/48/28.
[7] *Dom. Bk.* (Rec. Com.), i. 169v.
[8] Ibid. 164.
[9] *Cal. Inq. p.m.* ix, p. 233.
[10] *Oseney Cart.* vi, pp. 232, 263; cf. *Valor Eccl.* (Rec. Com.), ii. 220.
[11] Glos. R.O., D 269B/T 2, T 28.
[12] *Oseney Cart.* vi, pp. 193–5, 232, 262–3.
[13] *Valor Eccl.* (Rec. Com.), ii. 220.

and lambs rather than those of grain[14] indicates that in the Middle Ages sheep-farming was more important than arable. In 1327 two shepherds were listed in Arlington.[15] In 1280 Oseney Abbey had 766 sheep, including some at Turkdean, and another 80 had been sent to Water Eaton in Kidlington (Oxon.). The abbey's crop included 180 fleeces, besides 65 taken for tithe, and 357 skins.[16] In 1299 there was sufficient pasture for 300 sheep on the bishop's demesne[17] where in 1372 a shepherd looked after 442 wethers, including 171 which had been brought from Withington.[18] In 1389 the sheep from the rectory estate had grazing rights with the bishop's flock from Lammas.[19] In 1507 or 1508 Oseney Abbey wintered 80 wethers in Arlington,[20] where later the lessee of the abbey's rectory estate appears to have been required to erect a sheepfold.[21] The abbey's shepherd, who in 1510 had a stipend of 10s. charged on Arlington manor but earlier had received barley, oats, and salt, used buildings in Bibury and Arlington in 1512;[22] the latter was possibly the sheep-house which had been converted as cottages by 1758.[23]

In 1086 the bishop's estate supported 19 *villani* and 2 bordars with 11 ploughs, a priest with 3 hides and 4 ploughs, and 3 radknights with 4 hides and 4 ploughs.[24] The freeholds of the manor recorded in 1299 were substantial estates, including two in Aldsworth owing suit of court at Bibury. The free tenant of 1 yardland, who owed 2 ploughing-services, 8 autumn bedrepes with 8 men, and carrying-services for two days, was also required to carry writs of the bishop and the steward within the diocese at his own cost and to London, Winchester, and elsewhere for 3½d. a day, and to buy food for the bishop at Cirencester and 'Tornisham'. The same tenant held a mill, ½ hide, and 6 a. of land in Ablington.[25] In 1399 the bishop remitted similar services, including writ-carrying and the duty to serve as beadle, to the tenant of a holding with 8 yardlands in Bibury and Ablington.[26]

Of the 17 customary tenants recorded on Bibury manor in 1299 6 held yardlands and 11 held half-yardlands. The tenant of each yardland owed 4 ploughing-services, 3 bedrepes with 4 men, works at harrowing, threshing, and haymaking, and carrying-services which included fetching wood from Withington. The tenant was expected to perform week-work every day except Saturday for most of the year, to work with 2 men during the harvest, and even to perform carrying-services with pack-horses on Sundays if need arose. The tenant was quit of his

rent of 5s. if all his works were performed. Three more tenants held *enchelondi*, a half-yardland, 16 a., and 16 a. respectively, by service as ploughmen or for cash rent and the services of a third-yardlander, indicating a yardland of 48 a. Of 5 *cotmani* paying rent three also owed services at haymaking and reaping. The customary payments owed by the unfree tenants included pannage, tithing penny, and a toll on brewing and those tenants were obliged to attend a *fustale*. The assized rents of the free and customary tenants were valued at 119s. 6d. and the works at 105s.[27]

In 1280 the tenants on the rectory estate paid 22s. 6d. in assized rents;[28] the rents from the estate in the early 16th century amounted to 56s. 10d.[29] Arlington manor supported 12 *villani* and a bordar with 6 ploughs in 1066.[30] In the early 14th century Roger Norman had 8 tenants at Arlington, of whom 7 owed 10s. each and one 4s.; the holder of the other part of the estate had 5 tenants, 4 of whom owed 10s. for ½ yardland each and the fifth owed 12d.[31] Roger Norman's tenants were listed in 1350 as 3 freeholders and 5 unfree half-yardlanders.[32]

In 1086 9 *villani* and 4 bordars with 5 ploughs were recorded on Winson manor[33] where in 1583 there was some ambiguity over the customary rights of 7 copyholders.[34] In Arlington, where a yardland contained *c.* 80 a., five large tenements, of ½–3 yardlands, were held from the manor by copy for up to 3 lives in 1607.[35] Most of the Arlington copyholds had been enfranchised by the time of inclosure in 1768 when 8 small freeholders received allotments and only one copyholder, who was awarded 58 a.[36] Gloucester Abbey granted leases of several tenements in Ablington in the early 16th century for terms of 70 years or lives with heriots payable.[37] A yardland there comprised 48 a. and from the manor in 1548 or 1549 were held a freehold tenement of 3 yardlands and copyholds of 5½, 4¾, and 4½ yardlands.[38] Although several leaseholders were mentioned in 1731, copyhold tenure persisted there in 1737.[39]

Before the inclosures of the 18th century there were several extensive commons and Bibury, Arlington, Ablington, and Winson each had two fields. Pasture rights in those fields were used primarily for sheep. The Bibury fields, an east and a north (later west) field, were recorded in 1299.[40] In 1626 a stint of 45 sheep to the yardland was ordered in the fields,[41] for which a guardian was appointed in the early 18th century.[42] The east and west fields of Arlington were mentioned in the mid 13th century;[43]

[14] *Oseney Cart.* vi, pp. 194, 262.
[15] *Glos. Subsidy Roll, 1327,* 15.
[16] *Oseney Cart.* vi, p. 195.
[17] *Red Bk. of Worc.* 368.
[18] Worcs. R.O. 009:1 (BA 2636/160).
[19] Glos. R.O., D 678, ct. roll 63, rot. 4.
[20] *Oseney Cart.* vi, pp. 210, 219.
[21] Cf. ibid. p. 262.   [22] Ibid. pp. 232, 262–3.
[23] Glos. R.O., P 44/MI 3.
[24] *Dom. Bk.* (Rec. Com.), i. 164v.
[25] *Red Bk. of Worc.* 369–70.
[26] *Cal. Pat.* 1396–9, 498.   [27] *Red Bk. of Worc.* 370–5.
[28] *Oseney Cart.* vi, pp. 193–4.
[29] Ibid. 232, 262; cf. *Valor Eccl.* (Rec. Com.), ii. 220–1 where the rents are valued at 10s.

[30] *Dom. Bk.* (Rec. Com.), i. 164.
[31] *Oseney Cart.* v, pp. 13–14.
[32] *Cal. Inq. p.m.* ix, p. 233.
[33] *Dom. Bk.* (Rec. Com.), i. 169v.
[34] C 3/221/48.
[35] Shropshire R.O. 1578 uncat., Arlington deeds.
[36] Glos. R.O., Q/RI 21.
[37] Glouc. Cath. Libr., Reg. Abb. Newton, ff. 41v.–42v.; Reg. Abb. Malvern, i, ff. 179v.–180v., 187v.–188v.
[38] E 164/39 ff. 247–248v.
[39] Glos. R.O., D 269B/M 12.
[40] *Red Bk. of Worc.* 368; Glos. R.O., Q/RI 21.
[41] Glos. R.O., D 678, Bibury MSS. p. 22.
[42] Ibid. ct. roll 77A, rott. 4, 5.
[43] *Oseney Cart.* v, p. 17.

the former was also called the south field.[44] Those fields took in furzy ground near Ready Token where some land lay uncultivated in 1734.[45] The east and west fields of Ablington, also recorded in the mid 13th century,[46] were separated by the old Sherborne road[47] and extended beyond the salt-way.[48] From 1639 the practice was recorded of opening the more northerly part of the stubble field to the commoners about Michaelmas and the rest on the feast of SS. Simon and Jude (28 October),[49] and a similar procedure was followed in the early 18th century.[50] In the 17th century two men, sometimes called sheep-tellers, were chosen to enforce the stint in the fields,[51] where the number of sheep commons was abated in the late 17th century and early 18th[52] but on the eve of inclosure in 1780 the stint was 50 sheep, 2 cows, and a horse to the yardland.[53] The cultivation of the Ablington fields, called Bibury and Down fields in 1649,[54] was still regulated by the manor court in the 1730s.[55] The east and west fields of Winson were recorded in 1654.[56]

In 1086 only 10 a. of meadow were recorded in Bibury and 15 a. in Winson.[57] Although meadow land is found by the river Coln, where rich water-meadows have been created by periodic flooding,[58] and in the south-west part of the parish,[59] in the later Middle Ages a lack of good meadows led to the renting of meadow land in Inglesham (Wilts.) for Bibury manor and the rectory estate.[60] In Winson in 1583 there were 3 common lot meadows, Broad mead, Cratlands, and Cadmoor, which were opened by agreement among the copyholders and closed on Lady Day.[61] Broad mead was probably the great meadow which with Cratlands, a water-meadow,[62] was divided between the three principal land-holders, Alexander Ready, Richard Howse, and Thomas Bridges, in 1739.[63] Cadmoor in the south-west remained a common meadow in 1806.[64]

In the mid 13th century the tenants of Bibury manor had common rights in a pasture called Ruyndone for which they owed a ploughing service or paid ½d. if they did not have plough-beasts. By 1299 Ruyndone was the principal pasture on the manorial estate, having been appropriated by the bishop who allowed only the priest and two others to

graze a total of 10 beasts.[65] It probably lay on the site of Bibury Downs, recorded adjoining the river Leach in 1412[66] and pastured with cattle in the mid 18th century.[67]

In Ablington the area between the tributary valley of the Coln and the parish boundary, which was presumably commonable in the early 8th century when it was not part of the property put out to farm by the bishop,[68] included two commons, Ablington Downs[69] and, to the north-east, Ox Down,[70] probably the two commons mentioned in 1384.[71] Under an agreement among the commoners in 1612 the lord of the manor was allowed to hold the northern part of Ablington Downs in severalty and to pasture a flock of 300 during winter in the part remaining common;[72] the area inclosed by the lord was extended at 80 a. in 1680.[73] By 1780 Ox Down had been held in severalty by the lord of the manor for several years.[74] The lord's park was used as a common before 1575 when orders were issued for its conservation.[75] Cow Downs, a common for both cattle and sheep recorded in 1699,[76] lay by the Coln.[77]

In Arlington the main common, Arlington Hay, was in the west adjoining Winson,[78] and was used for cattle in 1595[79] and in the mid 18th century.[80] Winson Wold or Old, in the west part of the parish, was open in 1583 to cattle from Holy Rood Day (3 May) until All Saints when sheep were admitted until Candlemas.[81]

John and Nathaniel Coxwell inclosed open-field land in Ablington by exchange in the early 17th century[82] and several demesne closes were recorded in 1632.[83] From the later 17th century an abatement of the number of sheep commons was ordered because of inclosures and in 1719 three tenants were presented in the manor court for inclosing open-field land.[84] By 1780 760 a. in Ablington were inclosed.[85] Old inclosures in the eastern part of the parish were recorded in 1717.[86]

In Winson most of the open and commonable land was divided and inclosed in 1726[87] by agreement; 1,080 a. were affected[88] and the new holdings were described in a deed of 1728. The principal land-holder, Richard Matthews, held 423 a. and his

[44] Shropshire R.O. 1578 uncat., Arlington deeds, lease 1625; Glos. R.O., Q/RI 21.
[45] Glos. R.O., D 127/8.
[46] *Oseney Cart.* v, pp. 19–20.
[47] Glos. R.O., D 269B/E 10.
[48] Ibid. M 10, rot. 3.
[49] Ibid. M 3; M 9, rot. 3.
[50] Ibid. M 10, rot. 3; M 12.
[51] Ibid. M 3; M 6; M 7, rot. 6 and d.; M 9, rott. 1, 7; M 10, rot. 1.
[52] Ibid. M 5, M 6, M 12.
[53] Ibid. E 13.
[54] Ibid. T 31.
[55] Ibid. M 12.
[56] Christ Church, Oxford, MS. Estates 32, ff. 538–9.
[57] *Dom. Bk.* (Rec. Com.), i. 164v., 169v.
[58] Cf. Glos. R.O., D 269B/E 6.
[59] Payne, *Glos. Survey*, 88–9, 112–13.
[60] *Red Bk. of Worc.* 368, 504; *Oseney Cart.* vi, pp. 194, 262; S.C. 6/1143/18 m. 2.
[61] C 3/221/48.
[62] Cf. Glos. R.O., P 44/SD 2/1.
[63] Ibid. D 2957/343A.4.
[64] Ibid. 5.
[65] *Red Bk. of Worc.* 371.

[66] Glos. R.O., D 936A/M 5, rot. 2.
[67] Ibid. Q/RI 21.
[68] Finberg, *Early Charters of W. Midlands*, p. 34; Grundy, *Saxon Charters*, 40–4.
[69] Bryant, *Map of Glos.* (1824).
[70] Glos. R.O., P 44/SD 2/2.
[71] *Cal. Inq. p.m.* xv, p. 342.
[72] Glos. R.O., D 269B/M 7, rot. 7.
[73] Ibid. T 1.
[74] Ibid. Q/RI 20.
[75] Ibid. D 269B/M 7, rot. 2.
[76] Ibid. M 11.
[77] Ibid. Q/RI 20.
[78] Ibid. D 2957/343A.3.
[79] Shropshire R.O. 1578 uncat., Arlington deeds, grant of part of man. 1607.
[80] Glos. R.O., Q/RI 21.
[81] C 3/221/48.
[82] Glos. R.O., D 269B/T 5/2; cf. ibid. M 3.
[83] Ibid. T 1.
[84] Ibid. M 12.
[85] Ibid. E 6.
[86] Ibid. D 674B/T 90.
[87] E 134/4 Geo. II Mich./8.
[88] Christ Church, Oxford, MS. Estates 32, f. 547.

mother Anne and his brother Thomas had 123 a., Richard Howse 192 a., Thomas Bridges 180 a., and the dean and chapter of Christ Church, Oxford, 33 a.[89] Bibury and Arlington were inclosed by a private Act and the award made in 1768 dealt with 2,551 a. Estcourt Cresswell, the principal beneficiary, was allotted 204 a. in Arlington and, with his father, 1,065 a. in Bibury. Elsewhere in Bibury the vicar took 222 a. for his tithes and a leaseholder 14 a. In Arlington 440 a. and 330 a. were awarded to Richard Hall and Giles Hall respectively, 90 a. to John Taylor, a freeholder and copyholder, and 17 a. to the churchwardens; eight other proprietors received small allotments.[90] The remaining commonable land in Ablington was inclosed under a private Act in 1780. The award, which affected 1,045 a., allotted 780 a. to Charles Coxwell, 72 a. to John Howse, and 68 a. to Estcourt Cresswell, and three sub-tenants of the dean and chapter of Gloucester were awarded a total of 123 a.[91]

There were many farms after the inclosures and most were large. By 1771 the Bibury estate had been organized with four farms comprising 705 a., 401 a., 352 a., and 325 a.,[92] and in 1881 it included Kilkenny farm (786 a.), Bibury farm (733 a.), and a farm (probably that later called Shoecroft) of 149 a.[93] In the early 1780s farms of 815 a. and 605 a. were recorded on the Ablington estate[94] which in 1914 comprised Manor farm (869 a.) and Lower farm (612 a.).[95] In 1921 Lord Sherborne's estate included seven farms in Bibury and Ablington, including Bibury farm[96] which had been reduced to 512 a. by 1926.[97] In 1839 there were farms of 468 a., 322 a., 165 a., two of c. 110 a., and two of c. 30 a. in Arlington and farms of 578 a. and 423 a. in Winson.[98] In 1926 104 labourers found full-time employment in the parish, where there were 22 farms, including 9 with less than 50 a. each.[99] In the mid 1970s Phillips & Sons let out its lands in Ablington but farmed Bibury and Kilkenny.[1] The rest of the land was cultivated in large farms or in a few smallholdings worked part-time.[2]

After inclosure much downland was converted to tillage, a process noted c. 1775,[3] and corn and sheep husbandry remained dominant in the 19th century. In 1866 5,427 a. were returned as arable and temporary grass and only 424 a. as permanent grass, and large flocks, numbering at least 4,194 sheep,

were kept. They were folded on the turnips and grass leys, which with wheat, barley, oats, peas, and beans were the main constituents of the crop rotation.[4] Pastoral farming became more important in the later 19th century and early 20th, and in 1926 3,072 a. of arable and temporary grass and 1,931 a. of permanent grass were returned. There were also 262 a. of rough grazing. Sheep-farming on a large scale continued and the number of cattle kept increased considerably during that period: in 1866 380 cattle, including 69 milk cows, were returned and in 1926 869, including 118 milk cows.[5] At that time Bibury and Kilkenny farms were devoted to cereal production and dairying.[6] In 1975 the principal crops were barley and wheat, the acreage of the latter having increased after the Second World War, and beef- and sheep-farming were important. In the mid 20th century part of Kilkenny had been a pig farm owned by Gillette, a bacon-producing company,[7] and in 1975 there was a pig unit on the site of Pool House in Winson. There were also stud farms in Bibury at Court farm and in Winson at Village farm, on which the poll variety of Hereford cattle was also kept.

MILLS. Five water-mills were recorded in the parish in 1086. Of the two on the bishop's estate[8] one was probably in Ablington. The other, leased from Bibury manor from the late 13th century,[9] was in ruins by 1487.[10] A miller listed in Bibury in 1608[11] probably worked the mill east of Bibury Court belonging to the Bibury estate in 1769.[12] It was in use as a corn-mill in the 1920s[13] but was disused by 1934.[14] The 19th-century mill building was used for storage in 1975 when the 17th-century mill-house was the farm-house for Court farm.

There were two mills on Arlington manor in 1066[15] and the manor had a water-mill in 1350.[16] Arlington mill was worked by Thomas Carter, a fuller, in 1638[17] and from 1670 by Richard Smart, who was described in 1684 as a cloth-maker.[18] The site then also included several corn-mills[19] and, after it had passed to Elizabeth Sackville in 1713,[20] it was used both as a corn- and a fulling-mill.[21] In the early 19th century the mill was worked by Samuel Bowly of Cirencester (d. 1820)[22] and in 1839 by its owner, William Crotch Bowly[23] (d. 1861).[24] The Bowlys used it solely as a corn-mill and in 1859 a steam-

[89] Glos. R.O., D 2957/343A.3.
[90] Ibid. Q/RI 21.
[91] Ibid. 20.
[92] Ibid. D 674B/T 90.
[93] Ibid. D 1388/III/8; cf. *Country Life*, 3 Dec. 1921, suppl. p. iii.
[94] Glos. R.O., D 269B/T 6/7–8.
[95] Ibid. SL 203.
[96] *Country Life*, 3 Dec. 1921, suppl. p. iii.
[97] Glos. R.O., SL 211.
[98] Ibid. P 44/SD 2/1.
[99] M.A.F. 68/3295/8; M.A.F. 68/3295/17.
[1] Ex inf. Mr. Phillips.   [2] Agric. Returns 1976.
[3] Rudder, *Glos.* 284.
[4] M.A.F. 68/26/10; M.A.F. 68/26/12; M.A.F. 68/25/3; M.A.F. 68/25/23.
[5] M.A.F. 68/3295/8; M.A.F. 68/3295/17; M.A.F. 68/25/3; M.A.F. 68/25/23
[6] Glos. R.O., SL 211.
[7] Ex inf. Mr. Phillips; cf. Agric. Returns 1976.

[8] *Dom. Bk.* (Rec. Com.), i. 164 and v., 169v.
[9] *Red Bk. of Worc.* 368, 375, 459, 504; Worcs. R.O. 009:1 (BA 2636/160–1).
[10] Glos. R.O., D 678, acct. roll 89.
[11] Smith, *Men and Armour*, 259.
[12] Glos. R.O., D 678, map, 1769.
[13] O.S. Map 6″ Glos. XLIV. SE. (1924 edn.); Glos. R.O., SL 211.
[14] Glos. R.O., Q/SRh 1934 East.
[15] *Dom. Bk.* (Rec. Com.), i. 164v.
[16] *Cal. Inq. p.m.* ix, p. 233.
[17] *Trans. B.G.A.S.* lviii. 192.
[18] Glos. R.O., D 227; D 678, ct. roll 78A.
[19] Glos. R.O., D 227; TRS 172.
[20] *Sherborne Mun.* 95.
[21] Glos. R.O., D 674B/T 90.
[22] *D.N.B.*; J. Stratford, *Glos. Biographical Notes* (Glouc. 1887), 201–2.
[23] Glos. R.O., P 44/SD 2/1.
[24] Ibid. D 678, sale partics. 1895.

engine was installed and the building strengthened by external butresses.[25] The mill, owned by William Bowly in the early 1890s,[26] was bought by Lord Sherborne in 1895.[27] Milling stopped c. 1913[28] and the building was acquired in 1926 by the tenant Arthur Severn (d. 1949).[29] The engine shed had fallen down by 1965 when the mill was bought by Mr. D. C. W. Verey, who restored the mill and an adjoining cottage for use as a folk museum.[30] The mill with its mill-house, situated on a long mill race, is of various dates from the 17th to the 19th centuries.

A mill in Ablington was among the property granted, probably in the mid 12th century, by Robert d'Evercy to Bruern Abbey (Oxon.)[31] which held it in the mid 1380s.[32] Another mill there was recorded on the bishop's estate from 1299.[33] In the late 14th century and early 15th millers were frequently presented from Ablington for taking toll,[34] indicating possibly that both mills were in use as corn-mills. By 1540 Bruern Abbey's mill had passed to Sir Edmund Tame, who leased it to Ralph Eve, a Cirencester fuller. By 1564 Ralph had built a fulling-mill there.[35] The mill was sold by Richard ap Owen the following year to John Coxwell,[36] who acquired other mills with the manor in 1574.[37] Of the two mills facing each other at the western end of the hamlet in 1777,[38] Ablington mill on the north-eastern bank remained in 1840.[39] It was worked solely as a corn-mill in 1862[40] and 1914[41] but had apparently gone out of use by 1920.[42] The mill, an 18th-century building, was later converted as a house.

The mill recorded in Winson in 1086[43] and mentioned in 1221[44] was called Winson mill by 1527.[45] The mill, north of the village with its buildings mainly in Coln St. Dennis, may be of the 17th century but was remodelled and enlarged to include a miller's house in the 19th century. It was worked as a corn-mill in 1836 by Robert Coles[46] (d. 1862) and then by his son William.[47] It was in use in 1882[48] but was abandoned c. 1912[49] and later converted as a house.

OTHER INDUSTRY AND TRADE. Until the mid 18th century a woollen textile industry was based on the mills in Arlington and Ablington. Benedict of Ghent, who lived in Arlington c. 1300,[50] may have been connected with the wool trade. Arlington had a walker in 1327[51] and possibly a weaver in 1381.[52] In 1608 3 fullers were listed in Ablington and 2 weavers in Arlington.[53] Thomas Tryon as a child was occupied between 1643 and 1646 in spinning and carding in Arlington[54] where fulled cloths were evidently dried on Rack Isle, which was associated with Arlington mill by 1680.[55] Rack Close in Ablington was used for the drying of narrow fulled cloths in 1690.[56] A Bibury weaver was mentioned in 1685 and Benjamin Archer of Arlington, described as a clothier in 1694,[57] had a warehouse which by 1727 had passed to his daughter Sarah, wife of William Field, a Cirencester wool-comber.[58] No later evidence of the woollen cloth industry has been found.

Quarrying was once important. From the earlier 8th century quarries were recorded in Ablington[59] which later had the reputation for the best tiles in the Cotswolds;[60] a field north of Downs Barn was called Slate Quarry Ground in 1840.[61] In 1382 there was a quarry at Bywell hill[62] where a new quarry was mentioned in 1436.[63] A quarry recorded near Ready Token in 1625[64] was being worked in the late 17th century.[65] Two masons were noted in Bibury in 1608,[66] a free mason in 1699,[67] and a mason in the mid 18th century.[68] In the early 18th century masons were recorded in Arlington[69] where in 1777 there was a quarry at Arlington Pike.[70] In the early 19th century the most important quarries were to the south-west, partly in Barnsley.[71] In 1806 2 masons and 5 slaters lived in Bibury[72] and in 1856 there was a stonemason in Bibury and another in Arlington.[73]

Most inhabitants were employed in agriculture

[25] Glos. Colln. R 43.7.
[26] Kelly's Dir. Glos. (1894), 37.
[27] Glos. R.O., D 678, sale partics. 1895.
[28] Ibid. P 44A/PC 3/1, letter 29 Apr. 1913.
[29] Ibid. SL 211; Glos. Colln. R 43.7.
[30] Ex inf. Mr. Verey.
[31] Cal. Pat. 1364–7, 344; C.P. 25(1)/73/7 no. 77; cf. E 315/32 no. 178, which is probably a confirmatory grant to the abbey by the bp. of Worc. in the mid 13th cent.
[32] Glos. R.O., D 678, Bibury MSS. p. 2; ct. roll (formerly D 1375).
[33] Red Bk. of Worc. 370; Cal. Pat. 1396–9, 498; Glos. R.O., D 678, acct. roll 89.
[34] Glos. R.O., D 678, Bibury MSS. pp. 14–20, 24; ct. roll 63, rot. 3.
[35] Ibid. D 269B/T 3.
[36] Ibid. T 8.
[37] Ibid. T 21.
[38] Taylor, Map of Glos. (1777).
[39] Glos. R.O., P 44/SD 2/2.
[40] Ibid. D 627/40.
[41] Ibid. SL 203.
[42] O.S. Map 6", Glos. XLIV. SW. (1924 edn.).
[43] Dom. Bk. (Rec. Com.), i. 169v.
[44] Pleas of the Crown for Glos. ed. Maitland, p. 45.
[45] Hockaday Abs. cxxi, 1528.
[46] Glos. R.O., Q/RUm 147.
[47] Ibid. D 1388, Coles fam. 1847–62; cf. ibid. SL 5, no. 45.

[48] O.S. Map 6", Glos. XLIV. NW. (1884, 1924 edns.).
[49] Cf. Kelly's Dir. Glos. (1910), 367; (1914), 376.
[50] Glos. R.O., P 86/CH 1/45, 47.
[51] Glos. Subsidy Roll, 1327, 15.
[52] E 179/113/31A, rot. 5d.
[53] Smith, Men and Armour, 258.
[54] D.N.B.
[55] Glos. R.O., D 227.
[56] Ibid. D 269B/M 11.
[57] Ibid. P 44A/CH 3/1.
[58] Ibid. D 1388/III/4.
[59] Grundy, Saxon Charters, 42; Glos. R.O., D 269B/E 14.
[60] Rudge, Agric. of Glos. 24.
[61] Glos. R.O., P 44/SD 2/2.
[62] Ibid. D 678, Bibury MSS. p. 9.
[63] Worcs. R.O. 009:1 (BA 2636/160).
[64] Shropshire R.O. 1578 uncat., Arlington deeds.
[65] Ibid. leases 1699, 1701.
[66] Smith, Men and Armour, 259.
[67] Shropshire R.O. 1578 uncat., Arlington deeds.
[68] Glos. R.O., D 181/III/T 3.
[69] Shropshire R.O. 1578 uncat., Arlington deeds, lease 1701; Glos. R.O., D 127/7, 9.
[70] Taylor, Map of Glos. (1777).
[71] Greenwood, Map of Glos. (1824); Bryant, Map of Glos. (1824).
[72] Glos. R.O., D 269B/F 69.
[73] Kelly's Dir. Glos. (1856), 228.

but the usual village trades were regularly represented in Bibury and its hamlets. In 1831 127 families were supported by agriculture and 67, of whom over half came from Arlington, by trade, manufacture, and handicraft.[74]

A smith was recorded on the Bibury estate in 1302 or 1303[75] and in the later 15th century,[76] and trade surnames of villagers assessed for the subsidy in 1327 included those of carter and chapman.[77] In the later 19th century several shopkeepers, a butcher, a baker, a carpenter, a plasterer, a glazier, a tailor, a shoemaker, a saddler, and a surgeon lived there.[78] Among the more unusual trades represented were those of tallow-chandler in 1776[79] and collar-maker in 1787.[80] A farrier worked in the parish in the mid 20th century.[81] In 1975 several shops in the village catered for the tourist trade.

The trades followed in Arlington were more varied, some early ones arising from the cloth industry. In the 1860s calico was manufactured in the hamlet[82] where the tradesmen listed in 1856 were a shopkeeper, a grocer and draper, a butcher, a carpenter, a cooper, a tailor, a shoemaker, a watch-maker, a cattle-dealer, a drillman, and a surgeon.[83] A blacksmith was recorded there from 1698[84] and in 1870 there were two. In the early 20th century trades connected with motoring became significant and Arlington residents in 1939 included 3 motor engineers.[85] In 1975 an agricultural contractor lived at Meadowlands.

Few trades were recorded in Ablington and Winson. Ablington had a shoemaker in 1381[86] and a carpenter in the later 19th century. Residents in the early 20th century included a sack-dealer and in the 1930s a haulier.[87] In 1975 a small firm of agricultural engineers occupied premises at the former airfield near Oldwalls Sheds. In Winson there was a blacksmith in 1672[88] and in the early 20th century,[89] and a joiner in the early 1830s.[90] In 1856 Winson tradesmen included a shopkeeper, a stonemason, a carpenter and postmaster, a butcher, a baker, and a carrier. A dress-maker lived there in 1919 and a tobacco dealer in the 1930s.[91] The village had a post office in 1975.

LOCAL GOVERNMENT. In 1086 Bibury was named as a distinct hundred including Arlington, Aldsworth, and Barnsley[92] but by 1221 the court

attended by the vills of Bibury, Arlington, Aldsworth, Barnsley, and Eycot in Rendcomb implemented orders of the officers of the abbot of Cirencester,[93] lord of Brightwells Barrow hundred. The ascription of hundredal status to Bibury presumably resulted from the liberties held by the lord of the manor, the bishop of Worcester, who in 1276 was excluding the royal bailiffs and claiming return of writs, *vetitum namium*, gallows, and assize of bread and of ale.[94] In 1287 he was summoned to justify his claim to view of frankpledge, waif, free warren, and *vetitum namium*.[95] In 1299 customary tenants were obliged to guard and conduct prisoners to Gloucester.[96] The duty of a free tenant to attend the county court[97] was commuted in 1399.[98] Edward II's confirmation to the bishop of the liberty of return of writs led Cirencester Abbey to complain in 1314 or 1315 that its hundredal rights were prejudiced.[99]

For the Bibury court, mentioned again c. 1270,[1] rolls survive for the periods 1382–90, 1432–77, 1496–8, 1611–44, 1684, 1712–15, and 1723. The court, which was then the court leet for the tithings of Bibury, Ablington, Aldsworth, and Eycot, dealt with the assize of bread and of ale, pleas of debt, bloodshed, hue and cry, sale of meat, fishing, and the maintenance of ditches and roads, besides tenurial and agrarian matters. In the early 17th century presentments were made for playing bowls, not maintaining the butts, and not keeping a crows' net. In some earlier courts tithingmen for Bibury and Aldsworth and a reeve for Bibury were elected and from the 17th century constables for Bibury and Aldsworth and tithingmen for each of the tithings. In 1626 a hayward and two sheep-cleaners were appointed for Bibury.[2]

About 1290 the bishop quitclaimed the suit of Oseney Abbey to the court and view[3] but in 1441 the abbey was presented for holding its own view.[4] Court rolls for Bibury Oseney manor survive for 1427, 1479–80, 1499, 1501–2,[5] and the period 1611–1723 during which it still exercised leet jurisdiction. The court elected its own tithingman[6] but that officer was not recorded in 1627 and 1636 when Bibury, Arlington, Ablington, and Winson each had its own tithingman.[7]

Although the lord of Bibury manor was said in 1697 to have leet jurisdiction over Arlington, Winson, and Barnsley[8] there is no evidence on the

[74] *Census*, 1831.
[75] *Red Bk. of Worc.* 505.
[76] Glos. R.O., D 678, acct. roll 89.
[77] *Glos. Subsidy Roll, 1327*, 14.
[78] *Kelly's Dir. Glos.* (1856), 228; (1870), 474.
[79] Glos. R.O., D 127/15.   [80] Ibid. P 44/OV 3/4/1.
[81] *Cotswold Life*, Aug. 1973, 25.
[82] Glos. R.O., P 44/CW 2/1.
[83] *Kelly's Dir. Glos.* (1856), 228.
[84] Glos. R.O., D 127/5; D 2957/43.4, 6.
[85] *Kelly's Dir. Glos.* (1870 and later edns.).
[86] E 179/113/35A rot. 1d.
[87] *Kelly's Dir. Glos.* (1856 and later edns.).
[88] E 179/247/14 rot. 10.
[89] *Kelly's Dir. Glos.* (1906), 363; O.S. Map 6", Glos. XLIV. SW. (1903 and 1924 edns.).
[90] Glos. R.O., D 182/III/186.
[91] *Kelly's Dir. Glos.* (1856 and later edns.).
[92] Taylor, *Dom. Glos.* 264.

[93] *Pleas of the Crown for Glos.* ed. Maitland, p. 41.
[94] *Rot. Hund.* (Rec. Com.), i. 177.
[95] *Plac. de Quo Warr.* (Rec. Com.), 264.
[96] *Red Bk. of Worc.* 371.
[97] Ibid. 369.
[98] *Cal. Pat.* 1396–9, 498.   [99] *Rot. Parl.* i. 322.
[1] *Oseney Cart.* v, p. 7.
[2] Glos. R.O., D 678, Bibury MSS. pp. 1–24, 126; ct. rolls 63–4, 77A, 78A, 79, 81A, 99A*; ct. roll (formerly D 1375); the location of a sched. of ct. papers 1726–43 and ct. rolls 1753–1836, mentioned in 1900, is unknown: cf. *Sherborne Mun.* 98, 101.
[3] *Oseney Cart.* v, p. 7.
[4] Glos. R.O., D 678, ct. roll 64, rot. 3.
[5] Bodl. MS. Rolls Oxford (Oseney) 1, 92, 98, 21.
[6] Glos. R.O., D 678, ct. rolls 77A, 79, 81A, 99A*; Bibury MSS. pp. 126–8.
[7] Ibid. Bibury MSS. pp. 132, 150.
[8] C.P. 25(2)/833/9 Wm. III East. no. 15.

Bibury court rolls that those tithings attended. Arlington, withdrawn from the bishop's view by Richard de Clare, earl of Gloucester 1243–62,[9] attended the view of the honor of Gloucester held at Fairford,[10] although in 1383 a distraint on the lord of the manor to attend the Bibury court was ordered.[11] The tithingman of Arlington attended the Fairford court during the period 1788–1836.[12] Winson tithing attended the view held in the Bradley hundred court in the early 15th century.[13] Tenants of Gloucester Abbey in Ablington in the early 16th century owed suit twice a year to Coln Rogers manor court.[14]

Court rolls for Arlington manor survive for 1427, 1479–80, 1499, and 1501–2,[15] and for the period 1612–44 when it dealt with agrarian matters.[16] Records of the Ablington manor court include rolls and papers 1574–1737 and draft rolls and original presentments 1652–72. The court was concerned mainly with copyhold and agrarian matters but in 1692 it dealt with the repair of a bridge.[17]

Bibury had two churchwardens in 1498 and 1543.[18] Three churchwardens were recorded from 1576, Bibury, Arlington, and Ablington each having its own,[19] until the mid 19th century after which there were two. Their accounts survive for the periods 1651–7,[20] 1703–26,[21] and 1844–89.[22] In Winson two churchwardens were recorded from 1543[23] and their accounts survive from 1812 to 1915,[24] but by 1939 Bibury and Winson had the same churchwardens.[25]

Bibury had two surveyors of highways whose accounts survive from 1811 to 1836.[26] In 1848 two surveyors each were also chosen for Arlington and Ablington but later they had one each.[27] In 1636, when Bibury parish for poor-law purposes comprised Bibury, Arlington, and Ablington tithings, the overseers of the poor were neglecting to provide accommodation for a poor parishioner although the church house was being used as a poorhouse.[28] The house, which in 1720 was assigned to trustees for the maintenance of the poor and the repair of the highways,[29] was occupied by paupers in 1806[30] but had been leased by 1844.[31] The three tithings each had an overseer in 1720 and later,[32] although in 1781 only two were recorded for the parish. Winson,

which was not rated for poor-relief with the rest of the parish,[33] had clearly become a separate administrative unit by 1636. It had its own constable possibly in 1627[34] and certainly in 1715[35] and a surveyor in 1861.[36] A poorhouse west of Winson village was recorded in 1839.[37]

Between 1776 and 1803 expenditure on poor-relief more than doubled in Bibury from £202 to £570 and in Winson it rose from £63 to £106.[38] After the poor harvest of 1795 the vestry in Bibury agreed to provide cheap flour, and bread and money were later distributed to the poor; in 1799 it was agreed to raise the weekly wage to 9s. and proposals to aid relief in 1800 included selling rice to the poor, distributing bread or money, obtaining spinning work from Witney (Oxon.), and using charity money to buy clothes for the most needy children at Christmas.[39] In 1803 45 people in Bibury were helped regularly and 39 occasionally and in Winson 15 people received aid regularly and 40 occasionally.[40] In the next ten years expenditure almost doubled to £1,057 in Bibury and to £199 in Winson; the numbers receiving regular relief rose to 81 and 32 respectively but those on occasional relief fell in both places. By 1815 there had been a considerable drop in the numbers receiving aid and in the cost of relief which was £651 in Bibury and £107 in Winson.[41] In the late 1820s expenditure averaged £440 in Bibury and £104 in Winson[42] but by 1834 it had risen to £506 in Bibury and had fallen to £78 in Winson.[43] In 1836 Bibury and Winson became part of the Northleach poor-law union[44] and they remained in Northleach rural district until 1974[45] when they were included in Cotswold district.

CHURCHES. A church had been founded at Bibury by 899 when Bishop Waerfrith in leasing land to a priest reserved the church-scot and soul-scot paid to Bibury.[46] A priest was recorded in 1086.[47] In 1151 Oseney Abbey was permitted by the bishop to appropriate the church and its dependent chapels;[48] the latter, at Aldsworth, Barnsley, and Winson, were mentioned in 1276.[49] The abbey was taking mortuaries in Aldsworth and Barnsley in the mid 13th century,[50] and in 1291 the Aldsworth tithes were

[9] *Red Bk. of Worc.* 376.
[10] *Cal. Inq. p.m.* ix, p. 332; *Inq. p.m. Glos.* 1359–1413, 35.
[11] Glos. R.O., D 678, Bibury MSS. p. 2.
[12] Ibid. P 44/CO 1/1.
[13] *Ciren. Cart.* ii, p. 621.
[14] Glouc. Cath. Libr., Reg. Abb. Newton, ff. 41v.–42v.; Reg. Abb. Malvern, i, ff. 179v.–180v., 187v.–188v.
[15] Bodl. MS. Rolls Oxford (Oseney) 1, 92, 98, 21.
[16] Glos. R.O., D 678, ct. roll 79; Bibury MSS. p. 126.
[17] Ibid. D 269B/M 1–12.
[18] Hockaday Abs. xxii, 1498 visit. f. 32; xxix, 1543 subsidy, f. 17.
[19] G.D.R. vol. 40, f. 150; Glos. R.O., P 44A/CH 2, f. 2.
[20] Glos. R.O., P 44A/CH 2: at end of vol.
[21] Ibid. CW 2/1.
[22] Ibid. P 44/CW 2/1.
[23] Hockaday Abs. xxix, 1543 subsidy, f. 17; Glos. Colln. microfilm 23303, presentment July 1619.
[24] *B. & G. Par. Rec.* 295.
[25] Glos. R.O., P 44/VE 2/1.
[26] Ibid. SU 2/1.
[27] Ibid. P 44A/VE 2/1.
[28] Ibid. D 678, Bibury MSS. p. 150.

[29] Ibid. P 44A/CH 3/1; Bigland, *Glos.* i. 181.
[30] Glos. R.O., D 269B/F 69.
[31] Ibid. P 44/CW 2/1, entries for 1844 and 1862.
[32] Ibid. OV 4/1; cf. ibid. D 627/38.
[33] Ibid. P 44/OV 1/1; cf. ibid. D 269B/E 19; for a Winson poor-rate, see ibid. B 11.
[34] Ibid. D 678, Bibury MSS. p. 132.
[35] Ibid. Q/SO 4.
[36] Ibid. Q/RUm 293.
[37] Ibid. P 44/SD 2/1.
[38] *Poor Law Abstract, 1804,* 172–3.
[39] Glos. R.O., D 269B/F 89.
[40] *Poor Law Abstract, 1804,* 172–3.
[41] Ibid. *1818,* 146–7.
[42] *Poor Law Returns* (1830–1), pp. 66–7.
[43] Ibid. (1835), p. 65.
[44] *Poor Law Com. 2nd Rep.* p. 523.
[45] *Census,* 1961.
[46] Finberg, *Early Charters of W. Midlands,* p. 51.
[47] *Dom. Bk.* (Rec. Com.), i. 164v.
[48] *Oseney Cart.* v, pp. 1–2.
[49] Cf. ibid. 8–9.
[50] Ibid. 37–8; Glos. R.O., P 44/MI 1, ff. 4–5.

included in the valuation of the living.[51] Aldsworth and Barnsley later achieved independent status but Winson remained a chapelry.

From the later 12th century Bibury church was served by canons of Oseney Abbey specially nominated to the custody and cure of the church and its chapels.[52] The parish priest ordered in 1339 to induct a canon was probably the official of Bibury peculiar.[53] The process of nominating canons was recorded in 1457.[54] In 1498 the church had two chaplains, one of whom may have served at Winson.[55] No record of the ordination of a vicarage has been found but the priest serving the living was styled vicar in 1532[56] and in 1535 he had a portion of the tithes.[57] After the Dissolution the living was accounted a vicarage. In 1932 Bibury with Winson was united with Barnsley.[58]

Oseney Abbey had presumably claimed a peculiar jurisdiction for the church and its chapels by 1173 when the bishop's rights were safeguarded in an agreement under which the abbey paid £3 a year for the church;[59] that pension was later paid to Worcester Priory.[60] The bishop's right of visitation was upheld in 1276,[61] suggesting that the scope of his jurisdiction was disputed then. For the jurisdiction exercised by the abbey through its official[62] and the peculiar court, recorded in 1280,[63] the bishop received a pension of 10s. in 1347[64] and of 12s. from c. 1380.[65] The peculiar had archidiaconal jurisdiction in the 17th century[66] but exemption from episcopal visitations was persistently claimed from the late 16th[67] and marriage licences were granted in the 17th.[68] In the 17th century and early 18th the official, who might be the vicar, was appointed by the lay rector for terms of 3 or 4 years.[69] The dispute over visitations was not ended by an award of the Court of Arches in 1741 which, besides upholding the bishop's right to hold triennial visitations in Bibury or Barnsley church, protected the peculiar's testamentary jurisdiction and granted its official concurrent authority with the bishop's chancellor in issuing marriage licences within the peculiar.[70] No episcopal visitations were held after 1752.[71] Records of the peculiar's probate jurisdiction survive for the period 1590–1833;[72] other records of the peculiar

include marriage licences for the period 1769–1813,[73] churchwardens' presentments 1619–23, and an act book 1638–9.[74]

After the Dissolution the advowson of the vicarage passed with the rectory estate.[75] The Crown presented to the living in 1548 and the patronage was granted away for one turn in 1561. The Crown presented in 1576 but in 1582 Edward Evans of Mold (Flints.) claimed to be patron. In 1599 John Coxwell of Ablington presented to the living[76] under a grant from Richard Platt, patron for the turn. In 1622 William Westwood sold the next turn to Arthur Crewe of Hawkesbury, from whom it was acquired by Francis Heydon of Shipton Solers. In the late 1620s Heydon was contesting the patronage with Sir Thomas Sackville and Richard Westwood; another claimant to the patronage was Nathaniel Coxwell.[77] Eventually, in 1629, Heydon's presentee was instituted. Richard Westwood unsuccessfully presented in 1641.[78] In 1697 Henry Sackville sold two presentations[79] but at the second in 1756 the bishop collated through lapse. In 1843 William Strahan was patron for the turn.[80] In 1962 Elfrida, Lady Clarke, and W. H. Wykeham-Musgrave had alternate rights of appointment to the united benefice[81] but by 1975 Lady Clarke's interest had been acquired by the bishop.[82]

Oseney Abbey appropriated the tithes with the church in 1151.[83] The Arlington tithes, however, had been acquired by the early 12th century by Lire Abbey (Eure)[84] which c. 1230 agreed to let them at farm to Oseney Abbey.[85] The farm was paid to Sheen Priory (Surr.) from 1414[86] and was recorded in 1607 when the grantee of part of Arlington manor was exempted from payment.[87] Cirencester Abbey had a tithe-portion in the church in 1291 for its property in Aldsworth. No mention was made then of the Winson tithes[88] although in 1224 Oseney Abbey farmed two-thirds of them from a prebendary of Romsey Abbey (Hants).[89]

In 1280 Oseney took the tithes of wool and lambs,[90] the other tithes presumably being set aside for the canon serving the church. By 1535 the vicar had been assigned the grain tithes[91] but the tithes of the rectory estate went to the appropriator.[92] In

---

[51] *Tax. Eccl.* (Rec. Com.), 222; see below.

[52] Cf. *Oseney Cart.* v, pp. 9–10; *Reg. Giffard*, 14; Worc. Episc. Reg., Reg. Brian, i, f. 19v.

[53] *Reg. Bransford*, p. 20; cf. ibid. p. 83.

[54] Worc. Episc. Reg., Reg. Carpenter, i, f. 148v.

[55] Hockaday Abs. xxii, 1498 visit. f. 32.

[56] Ibid. xxv, 1532 subsidy, f. 14.

[57] *Valor Eccl.* (Rec. Com.), ii. 452.

[58] *Lond. Gaz.* 26 Apr. 1932, pp. 2714–15.

[59] *Oseney Cart.* v, pp. 3–4.

[60] Ibid. vi, p. 194; *Tax. Eccl.* (Rec. Com.), 222; *Valor Eccl.* (Rec. Com.), ii. 220.

[61] *Oseney Cart.* v, pp. 8–9; Glos. R.O., P 44/MI 1, ff. 8–9.

[62] Cf. *Reg. Bransford*, p. 83.

[63] *Oseney Cart.* vi, p. 194.   [64] Ibid. v, p. 9.

[65] *Reg. Wakefeld*, p. 167; *Valor Eccl.* (Rec. Com.), ii. 220.

[66] *Trans. B.G.A.S.* lviii. 182–94; Glos. Colln. microfilm 23303.

[67] Glos. R.O., P 44/MI 1, ff. 13–17v.; *Sherborne Mun.* 92–4.

[68] Glos. R.O., P 44/MI 1, f. 14.

[69] *Sherborne Mun.* 83, 87–8, 91, 97–8.

[70] G.D.R. vol. 381A, f. 88; *Sherborne Mun.* 98–9.

[71] *Sherborne Mun.* 103–6; Glos. R.O., D 269B/F 77; Rudder, *Glos.* 286.

[72] *Wills proved in Glos. Peculiar Courts* (Glouc. City Libr. loc. hist. pamphlet no. 2), 3, 11–18.

[73] Glos. R.O., D 269B/F 16.

[74] *Trans. B.G.A.S.* lviii. 182–94; Glos. Colln. microfilm 23303.

[75] *Cal. Pat.* 1547–8, 63; C 142/265 no. 59.

[76] Hockaday Abs. cxxi.

[77] Ibid.; Glos. R.O., D 269B/L 2.

[78] Hockaday Abs. cxxi.

[79] Glos. R.O., D 269B/B 1.

[80] Hockaday Abs. cxxi.

[81] *Glouc. Dioc. Yr. Bk.* (1962–3), 59; Burke, *Peerage* (1963), 514.

[82] *Glouc. Dioc. Yr. Bk.* (1975), 48.

[83] *Oseney Cart.* v, pp. 1–2.

[84] Dugdale, *Mon.* vi (2), 1093–4.

[85] *Oseney Cart.* v, pp. 14–17; cf. ibid. vi, p. 194.

[86] Dugdale, *Mon.* vi (1), 29; *Valor Eccl.* (Rec. Com.), ii. 220.

[87] Shropshire R.O. 1578 uncat., Arlington deeds.

[88] *Tax. Eccl.* (Rec. Com.), 222.

[89] *Oseney Cart.* v, pp. 22–3.

[90] Ibid. vi, p. 194; cf. ibid. p. 262.

[91] *Valor Eccl.* (Rec. Com.), ii. 452.

[92] Cf. Glos. R.O., P 44/MI 1, f. 39.

1576 no tithes were being exacted in Winson[93] but in 1617 the vicar made an assignment of his Winson tithes[94] and in 1730, after inclosure, he was disputing certain tithes there.[95] The open-field tithes taken by him in Bibury and Arlington were commuted at inclosure in 1768.[96] In the 18th century the vicar took a modus in kind or cash for the tithes of milch cows, calves, sows, and gardens, and customary payments of eggs for poultry on Good Friday. His remaining tithes taken in kind[97] were leased to landholders in the early 19th century.[98] Agistment tithes which he claimed in 1824[99] were paid to him the following year.[1] In 1839, when 212 a. formerly belonging to Oseney Abbey were described as tithe-free, the vicar's tithes in Arlington and Winson were commuted for a rent-charge of £650 18s. 6d.[2] His tithes in Ablington were commuted the following year for a rent-charge £364 5s.[3]

The church was worth £26 13s. 4d. in 1291 and included a portion of £2 13s. 4d. paid to the bishop of Worcester[4] from 1285 by Oseney Abbey instead of providing hospitality.[5] In 1535 the clear annual value of the vicarage and Winson chapelry was £13 1s. 4d., the vicar's income being derived principally from the grain tithes, for he had no glebe apart from a small close.[6] In 1650 the living excluding the chapelry provided an income of £103.[7] In the early 18th century the glebe comprised c. 4 a.[8] but in 1768 the vicar was allotted 222 a. in Bibury and Arlington for his tithes there.[9] The glebe was extended at 242 a. in 1838.[10] The value of the vicar's tithes increased considerably with the extension of arable farming in the later 18th century[11] and the living rose in value from £400 in 1750[12] to £1,045 in 1856.[13] Most of the glebe was sold to S. J. Phillips & Sons in 1956.[14]

In 1520 a house on the rectory estate was provided for the canon serving the living.[15] The vicarage recorded in 1617[16] stood by the churchyard[17] and was assessed on 4 hearths in 1672.[18] The house, described in the late 17th century as 'the parson's brave house',[19] was rebuilt in the early 18th.[20] A new vicarage was built in Tudor style north-west of the village c. 1844[21] but between c. 1894 and c. 1906 the vicar lived in a cottage in Arlington.[22] The vicarage was sold with 10 a. of land c. 1965. Saltway Cottage, east of Packhorse lane, then became the vicarage and was enlarged.[23]

Of the canons serving Bibury, Peter Oxenford, appointed in 1453, burdened the church with pensions and wasted its goods before being recalled in 1457. His successor Thomas Walgarcote[24] resigned in 1458 on being elected prior of Chetwode (Bucks.).[25]

The clergy serving the living in 1525 included a curate. William Shelden, vicar from 1548,[26] who could not recite the Commandments or prove the Articles in 1551,[27] was deprived in 1554 for being married. Lawrence Gase, vicar from 1559, was succeeded in 1561 by Richard Bagge[28] who granted him a pension of £4 which they later disputed.[29] Bagge, formerly a baker's apprentice and then a friar, was presented in 1563 for not serving every Sunday, immoral conduct, not being a grammarian, and laxity in enforcing the peculiar jurisdiction, a duty to which he had presumably been appointed by the lay rector. In the same year he was dispensed to hold two benefices[30] but was said to be resident.[31] During the incumbency of the non-resident Lewis Evans, vicar 1566–76, the church was served by curates;[32] in 1576 the curate was said to neglect the church through his work at Winson.[33] David Rice, vicar 1576–99,[34] was excommunicated for violence in Winson chapel but the sentence was lifted in 1577.[35] Rice was described as neither graduate nor preacher in 1584 when he held another benefice.[36]

In 1627 John Randall was presented to the vicarage[37] which was claimed by Robert Knollys, in whose favour Randall resigned in 1629.[38] Knollys (d. 1641), who also held the living of Wick Rissington,[39] involved himself in many lawsuits,[40] including one against Nathaniel Coxwell with whom he had entered into an agreement to secure his title to the living.[41] Against Sir Thomas Sackville he alleged an encroachment on the churchyard during the building of the manor-house.[42] Knollys also claimed all the tithes and the right to hold the peculiar court; in 1631 he suspended his curate for refusing to recognize his court.[43] In 1639 the parishioners com-

[93] G.D.R. vol. 40, f. 159v.
[94] Hockaday Abs. cxxi.
[95] E 134/4 Geo. II Mich./8.
[96] Glos. R.O., Q/RI 21.
[97] Ibid. P 44/MI 1, ff. 38v.–39; D 269B/F 72, F 79.
[98] Ibid. D 269B/F 14, F 80, F 81.   [99] Ibid. B 11.
[1] Ibid. D 2440, Bibury est. papers 1709–1829.
[2] Ibid. P 44/SD 2/1.
[3] Ibid. 2; a vol. of vicar's tithe accts. 1870–84 survives in ibid. D 540/E 13/2.
[4] Tax. Eccl. (Rec. Com.), 222.
[5] Oseney Cart. v, pp. 17–19.
[6] Valor Eccl. (Rec. Com.), ii. 452.
[7] Trans. B.G.A.S. lxxxiii. 94.
[8] Bodl. MS. Top. Glouc. c. 3, f. 211v.; Glos. R.O., P 44/MI 1, f. 41.
[9] Glos. R.O., Q/RI 21.
[10] Ibid. D 1554.
[11] Rudge, Hist. of Glos. i. 251.
[12] G.D.R. vol. 381A, f. 89.
[13] G.D.R. vol. 384, f. 19.
[14] Ex inf. Mr. Phillips.
[15] Oseney Cart. vi, p. 262.
[16] Hockaday Abs. cxxi.
[17] Sherborne Mun. 87.

[18] E 179/247/14 rot. 4d.
[19] B.L. Harl. MS. 4716, f. 6.
[20] Rudder, Glos. 286.
[21] Docs. in ch.
[22] Kelly's Dir. Glos. (1894–1906 edns.).
[23] Ex inf. Mrs. Bradley.
[24] Worc. Episc. Reg., Reg. Carpenter, i, ff. 107, 142v.
[25] Ibid. f. 149.
[26] Hockaday Abs. cxxi.
[27] E.H.R. xix. 113.
[28] Hockaday Abs. cxxi.   [29] C 3/14/89.
[30] Hockaday Abs. cxxi.
[31] Ibid. xlii, 1563 visit. f. 49.
[32] Ibid. xliii, 1566 visit. f. 30; xlvii, 1576 visit. f. 113.
[33] G.D.R. vol. 40, f. 151.
[34] Hockaday Abs. cxxi.
[35] Glos. R.O., P 44/MI 1, f. 13.
[36] Hockaday Abs. xlix, state of clergy 1584, f. 30.
[37] Ibid. cxxi.
[38] Ibid.; Glos. R.O., D 269B/L 2.
[39] V.C.H. Glos. vi. 119.
[40] Cf. Cal. S.P. Dom. 1640, 326.
[41] Glos. R.O., D 269B/L 2.
[42] Cal. S.P. Dom. 1638–9, 93.
[43] Sherborne Mun. 83–7; Cal. S.P. Dom. 1640, 325.

plained that through his litigiousness and consequent absence he neglected services, did not catechize, preached seldom, and did not provide the Sacraments.[44]

Benjamin Winnington, vicar 1641–73,[45] described in 1650 as a constant preacher,[46] was remembered for his long sermons.[47] John Vannam, rector of West Camel (Som.), was vicar 1673–1721,[48] and in 1718 a curate was licensed to serve the church. William Somerville, vicar 1756–1803, appointed curates and in 1774 he was dispensed to hold Aston Somerville rectory.[49] Charles Coxwell, rector of Barnsley and lord of Ablington manor where he lived, was vicar from 1806 until 1809 when he resigned in favour of Sackville Cresswell (d. 1843).[50] F. G. Dutton, vicar 1874–1916, succeeded later, as 5th Baron Sherborne, to the Bibury estate.[51]

In the mid 1540s 18 a. of land, mostly in Ablington, were given for a lamp in the church.[52] The land, valued at 2s. in 1548,[53] was the subject of grants by the Crown until 1609 when it was bought by Nathaniel Coxwell.[54] Property including the church house and land, given for the repair of the church,[55] was administered by trustees in 1656.[56] At the inclosures of the later 18th century the churchwardens were allotted c. 19 a. in Arlington and Ablington for the land.[57] The church house was used as a poorhouse in 1636 and until the early 19th century, but by the mid 19th century the house and several cottages, a shop, and 20 a. of land were leased and the rents applied to church repairs.[58] The house was pulled down in 1878 to be replaced by the reading-room and several cottages.[59] The cottages, which had been brought under a charitable Scheme by 1896,[60] were used as alms-houses in the early 20th century.[61] William Forden of Ampney Crucis by will dated 1683 gave a stock of £5 to the churchwardens for the use of the church. The principal was lent out until 1725 when it was spent on repairs to the church.[62]

The church of ST. MARY, so called by the mid 13th century,[63] is built of rubble and ashlar and has a chancel and an aisled and clerestoried nave with north-west tower and south porch. The underlying plan is that of a large pre-Conquest church, part of whose walls survive almost to roof level in places. It had a simple plan of chancel and nave, there being no evidence for lateral extensions, and the walls were of rubble with long and short quoins and narrow pilaster buttresses of ashlar. The church appears to

have survived without alteration until the later years of the 12th century when a period of major alterations, extending well into the 13th century, began.

The first addition was a north aisle with an arcade of three bays, and later the chancel was extended eastwards to almost double its length and the nave was extended westwards by two bays. Simultaneously the north aisle was extended and the tower was built over its westernmost bay. Finally the south aisle, which has three bays and extends only half the length of the nave, and south porch were added. The only later addition to the plan arose from the rebuilding of the north aisle to a slightly greater width in the earlier 14th century. The original 12th-century doorway was then reset and cusping added to the tympanum. The walls of the nave were heightened in the 15th century when a clerestory was added and a new roof put on. Other windows were also put in, notably those in the south aisle and the west end of the nave. The Wilcox chapel mentioned in 1527 was presumably in one of the aisles.[64]

Repairs to the north aisle and tower were carried out in 1760.[65] About that time a large figure of St. Christopher on the aisle wall was whitewashed over.[66] The church was restored in 1863, apparently by Sir Gilbert Scott,[67] and between 1895 and 1900 by Messrs. Waller.[68] In 1920 the chancel was cleared by moving the choir stalls to the nave and the chancel arch opened to full view by removing the organ to the south aisle.[69] Some of the 19th-century innovations were removed in 1949 when the tiles on the chancel floor were replaced by stone and a red colour wash on the walls was covered with a lime wash.[70]

Several sculptured stones in the Scandinavian and native Saxon tradition were moved from the churchyard to the tower in 1896; one was reset in the external north wall of the chancel c. 1913 when four others were presented to the British Museum.[71] The font, a square bowl on an octagonal stem surrounded by four octagonal shafts, dates from the early 13th century. The church bells mentioned c. 1652[72] numbered five c. 1703[73] and were recast into six by Abraham Rudhall in 1723.[74] The plate includes a chalice and paten of 1681.[75] The church had a clock by 1635.[76] The east window commemorates Lady Elizabeth Dutton (d. 1845) and John William Dutton (d. 1850), mother and brother of Edward Dutton, 4th Baron Sherborne.[77] The

[44] Glos. R.O., D 49/III/2.
[45] Hockaday Abs. cxxi.
[46] Trans. B.G.A.S. lxxxiii. 94.
[47] Rudder, Glos. 287.
[48] Hockaday Abs. cxxi; inscr. in ch.
[49] Hockaday Abs. cxxi.
[50] Ibid.; Glos. R.O., D 269B/B 8.
[51] Kelly's Dir. Glos. (1906), 38; Burke, Peerage (1963), 2215.
[52] E 178/949.
[53] Trans. B.G.A.S. viii. 305.
[54] Cal. Pat. 1548–9, 367; 1566–9, 225; Glos. R.O., D 269B/T 30.
[55] Atkyns, Glos. 276.
[56] Glos. R.O., P 44A/CH 3/1.
[57] Ibid. Q/RI 20–1.
[58] Glos. R.O., D 678, Bibury MSS. p. 150; D 269B/F 69; P 44/CW 2/1, entries for 1844 and 1862.
[59] Glos. R.O., P 44A/VE 2/1.
[60] Ibid. P 44/CH 1.
[61] Ibid. P 44A/CH 4/3.
[62] Ibid. CW 2/1, ff. 22v.–23.
[63] Oseney Cart. v, pp. 20–1; for the ch., see above, plate facing p. 29.
[64] Hockaday Abs. cxxi, 1528.
[65] Glos. R.O., P 44A/CW 2/1.
[66] Rudder, Glos. 286.
[67] Kelly's Dir. Glos. (1870), 474; Verey, Glos. i. 109.
[68] Glos. R.O., P 44/CW 2/2.
[69] Ibid. VE 2/1.
[70] Bibury ch. guide (1964).
[71] H. M. & J. Taylor, A.-S. Archit. (1965), i. 63–6; Glos. R.O., P 44/VE 2/1; Procs. Soc. Antiq. 2nd ser. xxvi. 60–72.
[72] Glos. R.O., P 44A/CH 2, churchwardens' accts.
[73] Bodl. MS. Rawl. B. 323, f. 62.
[74] Glos. R.O., D 269B/F 84; Glos. Ch. Bells, 33.
[75] Glos. Ch. Plate, 21.
[76] Sherborne Mun. 87.
[77] Burke, Peerage (1963), 2214.

registers survive from 1551 but no burials were recorded between 1588 and 1602.[78]

Part of the churchyard called Bisley piece was believed by tradition to have been used for burials of Bisley parishioners while that parish was under interdict.[79]

Architectural evidence shows that at Winson the chapel, dedicated to *ST. MICHAEL* by 1457,[80] existed by the 12th century but the earliest known documentary reference is of 1276.[81] Church-scot, paid by the inhabitants of the chapelry to the bishop,[82] had been appropriated by 1450 or 1451 by Nicholas Poyntz, owner of part of Winson manor,[83] but by 1487 had been recovered by the bishop.[84] The chapelry had its own churchwardens and presumably its own rates for, although in 1639 the churchwardens made payment to the Bibury churchwardens,[85] the chapelry was not rated for the repair of the parish church in 1704.[86] The right of burial, exercised from 1602,[87] was confirmed to the chapel in 1738.[88]

The chapel was served from the parish church in the Middle Ages but may have had its own chaplain in 1498[89] and possibly a stipendiary priest in 1535.[90] In the early 1540s it was served by a curate supported by the lessee of the rectory estate.[91] In 1563 the vicar served in person[92] and in 1576 the curate of Bibury, when he was ordered to stop serving and the vicar to appoint a curate specifically for the chapel.[93] Curates were recorded from the later 16th century until the early 18th;[94] in 1650 the curate had a stipend of £16.[95] In 1738 the chapel had a service every Sunday.[96] Charles Coxwell during his incumbency employed a curate for Winson and Barnsley,[97] but thereafter the chapel was usually served with Bibury church by the vicar or his curate.[98]

The chapel comprises chancel and nave with south porch and west bellcot. The chancel and nave are of the 12th century. There was some enlargement of the windows in the 13th century and in the 14th when the south porch was added and the nave reroofed. The chancel walls were said in 1620 to be on the point of collapse.[99] The chapel was restored in the 19th century, possibly c. 1882 when the east window was presented by Mrs. G. M. Wilson of Ablington Manor.[1] There was some renewal of tracery, the chancel roof was replaced, and the walls were covered with stencil decoration. The font has a 12th-century bowl on a 19th-century base. Most of the other fittings are of the 19th century. The two bells were cast by Thomas Rudhall in 1764.[2] The plate includes a chalice and paten of 1800.[3] In the churchyard are several elaborate tomb-chests. The chapel had its own separate registers from 1577.[4]

NONCONFORMITY. In 1676 ten protestant nonconformists were recorded in the parish.[5] A house in Bibury was registered in 1706 for use by Independents[6] and there was a dissenting preacher in 1715.[7] The meeting may have been that of Congregationalists, founded by a Mr. Jacobs (d. c. 1710), which in 1743 numbered forty,[8] but no record has been found of it after 1750.[9] There were 11 nonconformists in Bibury village in 1806.[10] Premises in Bibury and Ablington were registered for use by nonconformists in 1842.[11]

A house in Arlington was registered by Independents in 1730. The Independents who in 1760 intended holding a meeting in Arlington Row were probably Presbyterians, by whom six children were baptized that year.[12] A newly built house registered in Arlington in 1754[13] may have been used by the Baptists. Their chapel, standing north-west of the green, was rebuilt in 1839[14] when the meeting's connexion with Fairford was severed.[15] In 1806 22 nonconformists were recorded in Arlington[16] but in 1851 the Baptist chapel had an average attendance of c. 220.[17] A legacy of £100 by Molly Taylor (d. 1822) was applied to the minister's salary by 1834.[18] The manse south-east of the chapel, dating from the 1830s, was sold in 1966 and a new one built.[19]

In Winson one nonconformist was recorded in 1676[20] and seven in 1806.[21] A meeting established there before 1800, had an average attendance of 35 in 1851, when it was described as Primitive Methodist,[22] and from the late 19th century occupied a hut east of the Coln Rogers road.[23] The hut was sold in 1965[24] and had been demolished by

[78] *B. & G. Par. Rec.* 64.
[79] Bibury ch. guide (1964); *V.C.H. Glos.* xi. 35; cf. Bodl. MS. Top. Glouc. c. 3, ff. 167v., 211v.
[80] Hockaday Abs. cxxi, 1458.
[81] *Oseney Cart.* v, p. 9.   [82] *Red Bk. of Worc.* 459.
[83] Glos. R.O., D 678, ct. roll 64, rot. 5.
[84] Ibid. ct. roll 89.
[85] *Trans. B.G.A.S.* lviii. 190.
[86] Glos. R.O., P 44A/CW 2/1.
[87] *B. & G. Par. Rec.* 295.   [88] Hockaday Abs. cxxi.
[89] Cf. ibid. xxii, 1498 visit. f. 32.
[90] *Valor Eccl.* (Rec. Com.), ii. 452.
[91] Hockaday Abs. xxviii, 1540 stipendiaries, f. 16; xxx, 1544 stipendiaries, f. 16; cf. *Valor Eccl.* (Rec. Com.), ii. 220.
[92] Hockaday Abs. xlii, 1563 visit. f. 49.
[93] G.D.R. vol. 40, f. 150.
[94] Hockaday Abs. xlix, 1584 visit. f. 30; Glos. R.O., P 44/MI 1, ff. 13–14; *Trans. B.G.A.S.* lviii. 187; Bodl. MS. Top. Glouc. c. 3, f. 211; Hockaday Abs. cxxi, 1735; G.D.R. vol. 397, f. 90.
[95] *Trans. B.G.A.S.* lxxxiii. 92.
[96] Hockaday Abs. cxxi.
[97] Glos. R.O., D 269B/F 14.
[98] Hockaday Abs. cxxi.
[99] Glos. Colln. microfilm 23303.

[1] Cf. *Kelly's Dir. Glos.* (1879), 787; (1885), 624, 365; Burke, *Peerage* (1935), 2512.
[2] *Glos. Ch. Bells*, 71.   [3] *Glos. Ch. Plate*, 21.
[4] *B. & G. Par. Rec.* 295.
[5] Compton Census.
[6] Glos. R.O., D 2052.
[7] Ibid. Q/SO 4.
[8] G.D.R. vol. 397, f. 90.   [9] G.D.R. vol. 381A, f. 89.
[10] Glos. R.O., D 269B/F 69.
[11] Hockaday Abs. cxxi.
[12] Glos. R.O., D 2052; Hockaday Abs. cxxi.
[13] Glos. R.O., D 2052.
[14] *Kelly's Dir. Glos.* (1919), 41.
[15] Glos. R.O., D 2751/3.
[16] Ibid. D 269B/F 69.
[17] H.O. 129/341/1/14/16.
[18] Glos. R.O., D 2751/8.
[19] Ibid. 4.
[20] Compton Census.
[21] Glos. R.O., D 269B/F 69.
[22] H.O. 129/341/2/1/2.
[23] *Kelly's Dir. Glos.* (1897 and later edns.); O.S. Map 6″, Glos. XLIV. NW. (1924 edn.).
[24] Glos. R.O., free ch. surv.

1975. Premises in Winson were registered for use by unidentified nonconformists in 1823 and 1842 and by Baptists in 1843.[25]

EDUCATION. In 1568 a school was being held without licence by John Stone of Bibury.[26] About 1640 Thomas Tryon attended a school in the village.[27] Charles Coxwell, during his incumbency 1806–9, paid four women, two in Bibury, one in Arlington, and one in Ablington, to teach children to read[28] and in 1807 he reported that reading was adequately taught but not writing.[29] In 1818 the poor were educated by private subscription,[30] and in 1833 a boarding school with 26 children and a day-school with 12 boys, begun in 1831, were both run at the parents' expense. There was also a day-school on the Lancastrian system with 60 children, supported by weekly pence, contributions, and £5 a year from Lord Sherborne, who provided the schoolroom.[31] It was replaced by Bibury National school, established in 1845 in a building on the glebe north-west of the church, which was supported by subscriptions and school pence in 1852 when it had an average attendance of 70.[32] The building was enlarged in 1872 to include an infants' department[33] and by 1885 the average attendance was 112.[34] As Bibury C. of E. school it had an average attendance of 118 in 1904,[35] 62 in 1922,[36] and 112 in 1932.[37] In 1975 there were 38 children on the roll of Bibury Primary school.[38]

In the early 19th century an evening-school was formed at Arlington mill by Samuel Bowly[39] but the only school recorded in Arlington in 1833 was the Baptist Sunday school which was supported by subscriptions and had an attendance of 80.[40] In 1845 Arlington British school was opened in a new schoolroom adjoining the Baptist chapel. The school, supported by school pence and voluntary contributions in 1870, was later closed.[41]

There was no school in Winson in 1833.[42] By 1847 there was a C. of E. school, supported partly by subscriptions and payments; some of the 19 children came from Coln Rogers whose rector defrayed half the expenses.[43] Coln Rogers children also attended Sunday school in Winson in 1851.[44] The day-school, a National school by 1856,[45] occupied a small building, altered in 1874, north of the chapel. The school, supported in 1875 by voluntary contributions and school pence, was closed in 1922[46] when its average attendance was 19.[47] The building was unused in 1975.

CHARITIES FOR THE POOR. Hugh Westwood (d. 1559) left the rents from his lands in Ampney St. Peter, Ampney Crucis, and Ampney St. Mary to provide weekly payments and wood and coal for four poor men of Bibury who were to live in an almshouse, for the building of which he gave £40 charged on Arlingham manor. The endowments, however, were appropriated by Robert Westwood (d. 1600) against whom the trustees took legal action. In 1603 a Chancery decree ordered the purchase of a site for the alms-house, to be called Jesus Almshouse, to house four elderly bachelors who were each eventually to receive a coat, 18s. 6d. for firewood a year, and a weekly payment of 1s. 4d. (or 1s. 6d. for the alms-man chosen as master). They were to attend church three times a week.[48] The alms-house had been built by 1607[49] on land belonging to the parish[50] in the northern angle of the village street and the road to the square.[51] It needed repairs in 1829.[52] By the later 19th century women were recipients of the charity.[53] Under a Scheme of 1901 the income was laid out in pensions for two men and the alms-house was repaired for letting; it was sold to Lord Sherborne in 1902.[54]

Katherine Sackville (d. 1760) left £100 for the poor to be administered by her niece Anne Cresswell who at her death in 1791 left a similar sum. Payments from the charities ceased in 1823 and had not been resumed by 1829.[55] In the mid 19th century the charities were used occasionally to buy flannel and calico[56] and from 1914 to pay for dental treatment.[57]

John Smithyer of Arlington[58] left £10 for four or five poor people. The charity, first recorded in 1639,[59] was paid to 4 widows by 1653.[60] About 1691 it was appropriated for the use of the church[61] and from then 10s. a year from the church- or poor-rate was shared among the widows.[62] Payments were made in 1844[63] but ceased before 1866 when it was agreed to resume them.[64] By a bequest, apparently made in 1676, Thomas Tawney left £50 in reversion

[25] Hockaday Abs. cxxi.   [26] Glos. R.O., P 44/MI 1, f. 13.
[27] D.N.B.
[28] Glos. R.O., D 269B/F 14, F 69, F 94.
[29] Ibid. F 20.
[30] Educ. of Poor Digest, 291.
[31] Educ. Enquiry Abstract, 303.
[32] Ed. 7/34/35.
[33] Glos. R.O., D 2186/12; P 44/SC 1.
[34] Kelly's Dir. Glos. (1885), 365.
[35] Public Elem. Schs. 1906, 182.
[36] Bd. of Educ., List 21, 1922 (H.M.S.O.), 102.
[37] Ibid. 1932, 113.
[38] Ex inf. county educ. dept.
[39] Glos. Colln. R 43.7.
[40] Educ. Enquiry Abstract, 303.
[41] Ed. 7/37/Bibury, Arlington Brit. sch.
[42] Educ. Enquiry Abstract, 303.
[43] Church School Inquiry, 1846–7, 5–7.
[44] H.O. 129/341/2/1/1.
[45] Kelly's Dir. Glos. (1856), 390.
[46] Ed. 7/37/377.

[47] Bd. of Educ., List 21, 1922, 109.
[48] 20th Rep. Com. Char. 15–16; Glos. R.O., P 44A/CH 1.
[49] Glos. R.O., P 44A/CH 2; two alms-houses were mentioned in 1672: E 179/116/544.
[50] Glos. R.O., P 44A/CH 3/1.
[51] Ibid. Q/SRh 1829 Trin. C/3.
[52] 20th Rep. Com. Char. 16; cf. Glos. R.O., D 269B/F 69.
[53] Glos. R.O., P 44/CW 2/1.
[54] Ibid. P 44A/CH 4/1, letters 20 July 1900, 28 Aug. 1909; draft conveyance 1902; cf. ibid. SL 211.
[55] 20th Rep. Com. Char. 16–17; inscrs. in ch.
[56] Glos. R.O., P 44/CW 2/1.
[57] Ibid. P 44A/PC 3/1.
[58] John Smithyer the younger was alive in 1607 and 1625: Shropshire R.O. 1578 uncat., Arlington deeds.
[59] Trans. B.G.A.S. lviii. 189.
[60] Glos. R.O., P 44A/CH 2, f. 13v.; cf. Rudder, Glos. 287.
[61] Glos. R.O., P 44A/CW 2/1, f. 22v.
[62] Ibid. passim; 20th Rep. Com. Char. 16.
[63] Glos. R.O., P 44/CW 2/1.
[64] Ibid. P 44A/VE 2/1.

to the poor. The principal was lent out in the early 18th century, a distribution of the interest among the poor being recorded in 1725. The same year the principal was appropriated for paving the church and until 1753 it was held by the vicar, £2 10s. a year derived from church property being distributed at irregular intervals to the poor. In 1753 the principal was transferred to the churchwardens but no record of any distribution has been found between 1754 and 1829 when the £2 10s. was used to buy linen at Easter for poor elderly women.[65]

The above-mentioned charities, together with the church lands charity which included cottages used as alms-houses, were consolidated and brought under a single trust as the United Charities in 1898. Under the Scheme the churchwardens were to pay 10s. and £2 10s. for the Smythyer and Tawney charities but the latter sum had not been paid for many years by the early 1970s when the united charities were benefitting the elderly.[66]

Charles Rogers Coxwell (d. 1893) by will established a Christmas charity for the poor of Ablington. In the early 1970s its income of £7 was shared between seven needy people. The Eric William Bowman Vaughan charity, established in 1926, had an income of £5 in the early 1970s and was distributed in wood at Christmas to c. 32 elderly people.[67]

COLN ST. ALDWYNS

COLN ST. ALDWYNS, known until 1959 as Coln St. Aldwyn,[68] is a rural parish lying 12.5 km. ENE. of Cirencester. The ancient parish, which before 1935 comprised 2,666 a., included Williamstrip, a large detached piece of land to the east almost completely surrounded by Hatherop and Eastleach Turville.[69] The name Williamstrip was recorded from 1287[70] but in 1086 Williamstrip was represented by an estate called Hatherop. That estate was connected tenurially with land in Eastleach Turville[71] with which part of Williamstrip was assessed for the subsidy in 1327,[72] and in the early 15th century Williamstrip and part of Eastleach Turville formed a single tithing.[73] The inclusion of Williamstrip in Coln St. Aldwyns parish by 1505[74] probably originated from the grant of some of its tithes to Gloucester Abbey before 1096.[75] Nevertheless in Williamstrip an estate was said to be in Hatherop parish in the later 16th century[76] and the alternative name of Hatherop was used for another estate in 1554.[77]

The main part of the parish (1,999 a.), roughly rectangular in shape, was bounded on the south by the river Coln and extended northwards to the river Leach, which had ceased to run there by 1976, and beyond. There the Aldsworth road marked the western boundary but elsewhere the boundaries followed lanes and field boundaries,[78] including Hatherop hedge mentioned in 1677.[79] Williamstrip, after changes in its boundaries from the later 18th century including an exchange before 1812 of 61 a. for 92 a. of Hatherop,[80] was an irregularly shaped piece of land of 667 a. extending north-eastwards from Hatherop village to the Leach. It was bounded for short distances by the Hatherop road on the south and the Hatherop–Burford road and Akeman Street on the south-east.[81] In 1935 the two parts of the parish were united geographically and the south-eastern boundary was brought into line with the Hatherop and Hatherop–Burford roads by absorbing 818 a. of Hatherop, to which 57 a. were transferred. The whole of Williamstrip park was thus brought into the enlarged parish, which comprises 1,387 ha. (3,427 a.).[82] The following account relates to the area included in the parish until 1935 and those parts of Hatherop in the park.

The land, which above the valleys of the Coln and Leach rises from 122 m. to over 137 m., is formed by the Great Oolite overlaid on the higher ground by Forest Marble.[83] Until inclosure in 1770 the main part of the parish was largely covered by open fields and there was a common south of the Leach. Meadow land was scarce and Downhall or Downhill meadow, the principal water-meadow by the Coln, lay partly in Hatherop.[84] The Coln was famed as a trout stream by the late 17th century.[85]

Bratch copse, the principal wood in Coln St. Aldwyns, was called Aldwins grove in 1824.[86] In Williamstrip woodland accounted for at least 20 a., mostly ash, c. 1680.[87] Tyning wood was recorded in 1754 together with woodland east of Williamstrip Park house and a small ornamental park north of the house.[88] Williamstrip park, created by Samuel Blackwell between 1769 and 1777, covered a rectangular area bounded on the north by Akeman Street, on the east by the old Hatherop–Burford road, on the south by the Hatherop road and on the west by a lane following the boundary of the main

[65] 20th Rep. Com. Char. 16; Glos. R.O., P 44A/CW 2/1, passim.
[66] Glos. R.O., CH 21; cf. ibid. P 44A/CH 4/3.
[67] Glos. R.O., CH 21.
[68] Census, 1961. This account was written in 1976.
[69] O.S. Area Bk. (1882).
[70] P.N. Glos. (E.P.N.S.), i. 30.
[71] Dom. Bk. (Rec. Com.), i. 167v.; cf. Feud. Aids, ii. 247.
[72] Glos. Subsidy Roll, 1327, 14.
[73] Cf. Ciren. Cart. ii, p. 622.
[74] B.L. Eg. Ch. 770.
[75] Reg. Regum Anglo-Norm. ii, App., no. LXIA.
[76] B.L. Eg. Ch. 809.

[77] Cal. Pat. 1554–5, 88.
[78] O.S. Area Bk. (1882).
[79] G.D.R., V 5/89T 1.
[80] Glos. R.O., D 2440, est. papers 1729–1866, misc. papers; cf. Manual of Glos. Lit. ii. 207.
[81] O.S. Area Bk. (1882).
[82] Census, 1931 (pt. ii), 1971.
[83] Geol. Surv. Map 1", solid, sheets 34, 44 (1856–7 edns.).
[84] Glos. R.O., photocopy 64B.
[85] B.L. Harl. MS. 4716, f. 6.
[86] Bryant, Map of Glos. (1824).
[87] Glos. R.O., D 2134.
[88] Ibid. photocopy 64A.

BIBURY COURT

COLN MANOR

NORTH CERNEY: 19th-century cottages at Calmsden

BARNSLEY: Poultmoor Farm

NORTH CERNEY: Manor House at Woodmancote

EASTLEACH TURVILLE: old cottages

part of the parish. A lake was created north-east of the house.[89] After an exchange of land with Sir John Webb of Hatherop in 1778 the park was enlarged by the inclusion of Downhall meadow and other land and further ornamented.[90] As a deer park it inclosed c. 199 a. about 1785.[91] Home covert to the north-east had been planted by 1824[92] and Cockrup Farm to the west had been taken in by 1881, possibly after road changes in 1871.[93] The park also included a triangular piece of Hatherop in the angle of Akeman Street and the Hatherop–Burford road,[94] until 1870 part of the Hatherop glebe and conveyed the following year to Sir Michael Edward Hicks Beach.[95] In 1901 Coln St. Aldwyns parish contained 119 a. of woods and plantations.[96]

Akeman Street, a route used by the Romans[97] and recorded in 1394,[98] ran north-eastwards from the Coln. It was crossed by the salt-way between Droitwich and Lechlade, and the village grew up south of the junction and above the valley of the Coln, which had been bridged by 1559.[99] Akeman Street, which was connected to the village by the lane along the parish boundary, remained the principal route to Burford until 1777.[1] Then it was replaced by the road through Hatherop, which was straightened, and a road built from Hatherop village north-eastwards to Akeman Street to replace that leading northwards through Williamstrip.[2] The lane from Coln St. Aldwyns village continued beyond Akeman Street to Dean Farm in Hatherop but in 1871 the southern part was closed and the remainder joined to the Aldsworth road by a new road. At the same time a road was built past Williamstrip Farm[3] thereby giving access across Williamstrip where right of way had been claimed in the mid 19th century.[4] The northern part of the salt-way was specified in the inclosure award of 1770 together with other routes, including one from Bratch copse to Dean Farm[5] which had gone out of use by 1862.[6] A private carriage-way from the southern end of the village to Williamstrip Park had been built by 1824.[7]

Until inclosure in 1770 settlement in the main part of the parish was concentrated in the village, where a church had been built at the western end and highest point by the later 12th century. Next to it stand the manor-house and vicarage, and a school and school-house were built near by in the mid 19th century. The main focal point of the village was a

small green lower down where the Aldsworth road meets roads descending southwards along the main street to a 19th-century mill and eastwards towards Hatherop. West of the green Coln Stores, which bears the initials of Sir M. E. Hicks Beach,[8] was built in the late 19th century on the site of a church house[9] and incorporates on the west a fragment of an earlier, possibly 17th-century, building. The plot of land to the west served as a cemetery in 1976. There are several 17th-century cottages in the main street and one north of the Hatherop road is on a traditional cross-passage plan. A house to the south, in the later 18th century the Downhall farm-house, is of various dates from the 17th century.[10] Some 18th-century houses survive around the green but two buildings standing on it in the late 18th century[11] have been demolished. West of the Aldsworth road an early-18th-century house was extended on both sides in the 19th century. In the later part of that century some estate cottages were built to the north. The Mill House south-west of the village, which apparently was built in the later 19th century[12] for letting as a gentleman's residence,[13] was the home of Michael Hugh Hicks Beach in 1914.[14] The most striking 20th-century building is a block of six memorial cottages with a lodge built south-east of the school after the Second World War by Earl St. Aldwyn using masonry from a demolished range of Williamstrip Park.[15] The cottages provided cheap accommodation for retired estate labourers but by 1976 some were let at economic rents.[16]

There was a settlement at Cockrup Farm, north-east of the village, by the mid 13th century, when several people described as of Cockrup lived in the parish.[17] A house was recorded there in 1649[18] and a farm-house from 1745.[19] Cockrup Farm is a late-18th-century house with later cottages to the west and out-buildings, including a range dated 1842, to the east.

The other outlying buildings in Coln St. Aldwyns were built after the inclosure of 1770. Swyre Farm, on a site north of the Leach recorded in 1777,[20] is a simple symmetrically-fronted house of the early 19th century with a back staircase and kitchen wing which had new rooms added to the west in the later 19th century. In 1971 it was bought by the Beshara Trust, a charity established to promote a spiritual orientation to life, and a 19th-century barn was con-

---

[89] Cf. ibid. photocopies 64B, 64H; Williamstrip Mun., penes Earl St. Aldwyn, of Williamstrip Pk., MTD/93/4.

[90] Williamstrip Mun. MTD/93/1; cf. Glos. R.O., D 540/E 3, P 2: a map of the Hatherop est. showing those parts taken into the pk.

[91] Glos. R.O., D 2440, est. papers 1753–1852.

[92] Greenwood, Map of Glos. (1824).

[93] O.S. Map 6″, Glos. LII. NE. (1886 edn.); cf. Glos. R.O., Q/SRh 1871 D/1.

[94] Cf. O.S. Map 6″, Glos. XLIV. SE. (1903, 1924 edns.).

[95] Glos. R.O., D 540/T 63; Williamstrip Mun. MTD/96; MTA/5.

[96] Acreage Returns, 1901.

[97] I. D. Margary, Rom. Roads in Britain (1955), i, p. 147.

[98] Ciren. Cart. ii, p. 634.

[99] Glos. R.O., D 1375/496 rot. 4d.

[1] Cf. ibid. D 540/P 1; Taylor, Map of Glos. (1777).

[2] Glos. R.O., Q/SRh 1777 A/2; cf. ibid. photocopy 64B.

[3] Ibid. Q/SRh 1871 D/1.

[4] Ibid. D 2440, est. papers 1766–1853.

[5] Ibid. P 96B/SD 1/1.

[6] Ibid. D 540/E 10.

[7] Bryant, Map of Glos. (1824). [8] The date is illegible.

[9] Cf. Glos. R.O., D 2240, est. papers 1852–3; see below, p. 52.

[10] Glos. R.O., Q/RNc 2/22; photocopies 64B, 64H; cf. ibid. D 540/T 56.

[11] Ibid. photocopy 64H.

[12] O.S. Map 6″, Glos. LII. NE. (1886 edn.).

[13] Cf. Williamstrip Mun. MTD/111/4; Kelly's Dir. Glos. (1910), 135.

[14] Kelly's Dir. Glos. (1914), 139.

[15] Cf. Trans. B.G.A.S. lxxi. 92.

[16] Ex inf. the vicar, the Revd. G. S. Mowat.

[17] Glouc. Cath. Libr., deeds and seals, i, f. 31; Hist. & Cart. Mon. Glouc. (Rolls Ser.), iii. 196, 201; cf. Glos. R.O., D 936A/M 1, rot. 9.

[18] Glos. R.O., D 1740/E 1, f. 64.

[19] Ibid. D 2440, est. papers 1545–1789, abs. of title; deed 1790.

[20] Taylor, Map of Glos. (1777); cf. Glos. R.O., D 540/P 2.

verted as a meditation centre by the insertion of a central feature surmounted by a many-faceted geodesic dome.[21] At Moor's Farm, partly in Hatherop, where farm buildings were recorded from 1824,[22] a pair of 19th-century cottages stood derelict in 1976.

In Williamstrip, which c. 1775 had a population of 48,[23] Williamstrip Park stands on a site occupied at least since the late 17th century. To the south-west by the Hatherop road Dean Row, a row of cottages recorded in 1764[24] and so called by 1830,[25] was rebuilt as estate cottages in the later 19th century. Williamstrip Farm in the north-east on a site recorded in 1754[26] is an early-19th-century farm-house.[27] Its out-buildings include a barn with an equestrian vane, presumably marking the riding school established there by 1919,[28] and there are some 19th-century estate cottages to the west.

In 1086 22 tenants were recorded in Coln St. Aldwyns and 12 in Williamstrip.[29] The numbers assessed for the subsidy in 1327 were 18 in Coln St. Aldwyns and 10 in part of Williamstrip, the inhabitants of another part being assessed with Eastleach Turville.[30] At least 25 people were assessed in Coln St. Aldwyns for the poll tax in 1381.[31] In 1548 the parish was said to have 106 'houseling people'[32] but only 40 communicants were mentioned in 1551[33] and 23 households in 1563.[34] There were 161 communicants in 1603 and 40 families in 1650,[35] after which the population increased rapidly to an estimated 300 by c. 1710[36] and to 392 by c. 1775.[37] The last figure may be too high, for in 1801 the population was 385. It rose to 441 by 1831 and, after dropping to 428 by 1841, to 523 by 1871. It then fell to 310 by 1931 but in 1951, after the boundary changes of 1935, it stood at 327. By 1971 it had dropped to 263.[38]

An inn in Coln St. Aldwyns belonged to the Hatherop manor estate in 1653 and 1676.[39] Two innholders were licensed in 1755,[40] one of whom possibly occupied the Swan inn mentioned in the late 18th and early 19th centuries.[41] From 1870 the parish had one beer retailer[42] who occupied premises east of the village street called the New inn by

1902.[43] The inn, a two-storey 18th-century building, has been much enlarged and was bought by the trustees of Viscount Quenington in 1917.[44]

In 1803 a friendly society in the parish had 44 members[45] and in 1876 the parish had clothing and coal clubs with 44 and 42 members respectively.[46] A benefit society was begun in 1908.[47] The parish had a lending library in 1833, the books being provided chiefly by the S.P.C.K.[48] A reading-room was opened in 1884[49] but it was inadequate by 1912 when its function was taken over by a new parish room at the top of an old factory.[50] In 1914 the former vicarage barn south-west of the vicarage was converted as a village hall at the expense of Viscount St. Aldwyn.[51] It closed in 1967.[52]

The achievements of holders of Coln St. Aldwyns manor and the Williamstrip estate are noted below. The Hicks Beach family of Williamstrip became the dominant landed interest in the parish before 1845 with the acquisition by Sir Michael Hicks Hicks Beach of the leaseholds of Coln St. Aldwyns manor and the rectory estate. His son Michael Edward provided the village with a piped water-supply in 1878[53] and electric street lighting by 1906.[54]

MANORS AND OTHER ESTATES. Between 779 and 790 Aldred, under-king of the Hwicce, granted an estate of 60 'manentes' in Coln St. Aldwyns, then called *Enneglan*, to Gloucester Abbey.[55] The estate was alienated by Wilstan, abbot from 1058, but Abbot Serlo had recovered it from the archbishop of York[56] by 1086 when it was assessed at 4 hides.[57] The abbey was granted free warren in 1354[58] but by then its manor of *COLN ST. ALDWYNS* was held by a tenant at a rent of 13s. 6d.[59] John de Haudlo, tenant in 1322,[60] died in 1346 when the manor reverted to Isabel, widow of his son Richard.[61] Isabel, who married Robert of Hillesley, died in 1361 and, as her son Edmund de Haudlo had died, her heirs were her daughters Margaret and Elizabeth.[62] Margaret and her husband John of Appleby, who were awarded the manor for the life of Edmund's widow Alice,[63] secured it in 1366[64] and in

[21] Ex inf. the sec., Beshara, Swyre Fm.
[22] Greenwood, *Map of Glos.* (1824); O.S. Map 6″, Glos. XLIV. SE. (1886, 1903, 1924 edns.).
[23] Rudder, *Glos.* 385.
[24] Glos. R.O., photocopy 64B.
[25] Ibid. D 2440, est. papers 1760–1843, presentment of Hatherop man. boundaries; cf. Davie and Dawber, *Old Cotswold Cottages*, plate 75.
[26] Glos. R.O., photocopy 64A.
[27] Cf. Bryant, *Map of Glos.* (1824).
[28] O.S. Map 6″, Glos. XLV. SW. (1923 edn.).
[29] *Dom. Bk.* (Rec. Com.), i. 165v., 167v.
[30] *Glos. Subsidy Roll, 1327,* 13–14.
[31] E 179/113/31A rot. 5d.; E 179/113/35A rot. 1.
[32] *Trans. B.G.A.S.* viii. 278.
[33] *E.H.R.* xix. 113–14.
[34] Bodl. MS. Rawl. C. 790, f. 26v.
[35] *Eccl. Misc.* 98; *Trans. B.G.A.S.* lxxxiii. 94.
[36] Atkyns, *Glos.* 364.
[37] Rudder, *Glos.* 385.
[38] *Census,* 1801–1971.
[39] Glos. R.O., D 540/T 31–2.
[40] Ibid. Q/AV 2, rot. 3.
[41] Ibid. D 936/E 256; Williamstrip Mun. EMS/9; MTA/4.

[42] *Kelly's Dir. Glos.* (1870 and later edns.).
[43] Ibid. (1902), 131.
[44] Cf. Williamstrip Mun. MTC/34/2, 5.
[45] *Poor Law Abstract, 1804,* 172–3.
[46] Glos. R.O., PA 96/1, vol. for 1877.
[47] Ibid. vol. for 1909.
[48] *Educ. Enquiry Abstract,* 311.
[49] Glos. R.O., PA 96/1, vol. for 1885.
[50] Ibid. vols. for 1912–13.
[51] Ibid. vols. for 1914–15.
[52] Ex inf. the vicar.
[53] Glos. R.O., PA 96/1, vol. for 1879.
[54] Ibid. vol. for 1906.
[55] Finberg, *Early Charters of W. Midlands,* p. 40.
[56] *V.C.H. Glos.* ii. 53; *Hist. & Cart. Mon. Glouc.* i. 11.
[57] *Dom. Bk.* (Rec. Com.), i. 165v.
[58] *Cal. Chart. R. 1341–1417,* 142.
[59] *Cal. Inq. p.m.* viii, p. 494; *Inq. p.m. Glos. 1301–58,* 367; cf. ibid. *1359–1413,* 15.
[60] *Cal. Pat. 1321–4,* 320.
[61] *Cal. Inq. p.m.* viii, p. 494; cf. C.P. 25(1)/286/36 no. 96.
[62] *Inq. p.m. Glos. 1301–58,* 367; *1359–1413,* 15.
[63] *Cal. Fine R. 1356–68,* 185–6.
[64] *Cal. Pat. 1364–7,* 276–7.

the early 15th century land there was said to be held from John.[65] The abbey later took the estate in hand but in the early 16th century the demesne was let at farm.[66]

In 1541 the manor was settled on the dean and chapter of Gloucester cathedral[67] who held it until the mid 19th century. Sir Giles Poole farmed the manor in the mid 16th century[68] but it was leased, evidently in 1550 for 90 years, to Sir Anthony Kingston. In 1556, after Sir Anthony's death, Ralph Jennings, to whom the lease had reverted, sold it to George Fettiplace who acquired a lease of the demesne, in which the Jennings family had had an interest, from Jerome Barnard.[69] From the mid 17th century George's descendants farmed the manor under leases for terms of 21 years, generally renewed after 4 to 10 years.[70] The dean and chapter resumed the manorial rights in 1804.[71]

George Fettiplace, a judge, died in 1577 and the estate passed in turn to his wife Cecily and son John[72] (d. 1636). John's heir was his brother Sir Giles Fettiplace of Poulton (Wilts., later Glos.)[73] (d. 1641) who was succeeded by his nephew John Fettiplace.[74] John, who served Parliament as governor of Cirencester,[75] acquired the freehold from the parliamentary commissioners in 1650[76] but took a lease in 1660.[77] By 1677 he had been succeeded by his son Giles, a prominent Quaker,[78] who died in 1702[79] leaving as his heirs his daughters Elizabeth, Frances, and Theophila. They and their descendants held joint leases of the manor.[80] Elizabeth died in 1716[81] and her interest evidently passed to, among others, Rebecca, wife by 1765 of Sir John Bridger of Coombe in Hamsey (Suss.).[82] Their daughter Mary married George Shiffner, created a baronet in 1818.[83] Frances Fettiplace (d. 1717) married John Bellers (1654–1725), a Quaker philanthropist, and their son Fettiplace Bellers (?d. 1750) was a dramatist and philosopher.[84] Theophila Fettiplace married in turn Thomas Church (d. by 1705) and John Partridge (d. by 1720),[85] and her interest passed, apparently with Bourton-on-the-Water manor, to the Ingram family. In 1720 Joseph Ingram and his wife Mary, and later Samuel Ingram (d. c. 1777) and his brother Thomas (d. 1806), were named among the lessees. Thomas's daughter Frances (d. 1834) married John Rice, but a distant cousin, Bowyer Vaux,[86] had apparently acquired her interest by 1833.[87] The lessees who

held c. 1,487 a.[88] sold the lease before 1845 to Sir Michael Hicks Hicks Beach of Williamstrip[89] who already leased c. 217 a. from the dean and chapter.[90] The freehold, which passed in 1855 to the Ecclesiastical Commissioners,[91] was bought in 1860 by Sir Michael Edward Hicks Beach,[92] with whose Williamstrip estate it then passed.

Coln Manor, north of the church, is a large gabled house of various dates and generally of two storeys with attics. The central east-west range incorporates a smaller house, possibly that which had been built by the mid 16th century,[93] of conventional plan, with a cross-passage entered through a north porch, a ground-floor hall to the west, and former service accommodation to the east. Beyond the hall a parlour block is probably of the 17th century and there are additional rooms, perhaps of the same date, in an eastern cross-wing. In 1649 the house was said to have about 6 bays and 19 rooms[94] and in 1672 it was assessed on 12 hearths.[95] A new block with two rooms on each floor was added north of the parlour c. 1700. At that time the house was used for Quaker meetings and John Bellers lived there c. 1710.[96] The hall and some other rooms were refitted in the earlier 18th century when a staircase was put in the parlour end. Later Thomas Ingram lived in the house,[97] which was occupied by tenants in the early 19th century[98] and again in the early 1890s.[99] In 1896, when Sir M. E. Hicks Beach made it his country residence, an access passage was built along the south side of the hall range, the south-eastern room was greatly enlarged, and additions were made on the north-west. Some new panelling was introduced to the principal rooms but some surviving 17th-century panelling may have been refitted in first-floor rooms. The reversal in the house's arrangement, whereby the north wing at the parlour end became kitchens, was probably made then.[1] The house, which after the First World War was the home of Lucy Catherine, widow of the 1st Earl St. Aldwyn,[2] was bought by Hatherop Castle School c. 1968 and used as a sixth-form college until 1974.[3] During that period several rooms were subdivided. In 1976 the house was sold to Mr. Anthony Hunt, a consulting engineer, and all sub-dividing walls were removed and the central range and east wing adapted as offices for his firm.[4] An early-18th-century dovecot and stabling stand north of the house.

[65] Ciren. Cart. ii, p. 631.
[66] Glouc. Cath. Libr., Reg. Abb. Braunche, pp. 122–4; Valor Eccl. (Rec. Com.), ii. 410.
[67] L. & P. Hen. VIII, xvi, p. 572.   [68] Req. 2/133/37.
[69] Cf. C 3/66/7; C 142/107 no. 50; Glos. R.O., D 2019.
[70] Cf. Glos. R.O., D 936/E 67; D 1740/E 30.
[71] Ibid. D 936/E 67; cf. ibid. D 1740/M 1.
[72] C 142/177 no. 86; Req. 2/133/37.
[73] C 142/728 no. 26; cf. Glos. R.O., D 1740/E 1, f. 67.
[74] C 142/701 no. 17; cf. Glos. R.O., D 1740/E 1, f. 63.
[75] Glos. R.O., NC 60, p. 15.
[76] C 54/3451 mm. 14–16.
[77] Glos. R.O., D 936/E 161.
[78] Ibid. NC 60, p. 15.   [79] Ibid. D 2052.
[80] Ibid. D 936/E 67.   [81] 20th Rep. Com. Char. 17.
[82] Glos. R.O., D 936/E 67, E 68; Hockaday Abs. clxvii, 1775.
[83] Glos. R.O., D 936/E 67; V.C.H. Suss. vii. 85; Burke, Peerage (1963), 2216–17.
[84] D.N.B.; Glos. R.O., D 2052.
[85] Glos. R.O., D 936/E 67.

[86] Cf. V.C.H. Glos. vi. 40; Glos. R.O., D 936/E 64, E 67.
[87] Glos. R.O., D 1070/III/3.   [88] Ibid. D 936/E 6, pp. 2–3.
[89] Williamstrip Mun. EMS/12.
[90] Glos. R.O., D 936/E 6, p. 1.
[91] Kirby, Cat. of Glouc. Dioc. Rec. ii, p. xiii.
[92] Glos. R.O., D 2440, est. papers 1860; Williamstrip Mun. MTA/5.
[93] Cf. C 3/66/7; Req. 2/133/37; see above, plate facing p. 44.
[94] Glos. R.O., D 1740/E 1, f. 63.
[95] E 179/247/14 rot. 4.
[96] Atkyns, Glos. 364.
[97] Rudder, Glos. 384; Bigland, Glos. i. 411; Rudge, Hist. of Glos. i. 252.
[98] Churchwardens' acct. bk. 1758–1867, penes the vicar, rates 1813–35; Glos. R.O., D 936/E 160, p. 1.
[99] Kelly's Dir. Glos. (1889), 748; (1894), 128.
[1] Verey, Glos. i. 198; Williamstrip Mun. EM/BP/6.
[2] Kelly's Dir. Glos. (1919 and later edns.).
[3] Ex inf. the vicar.
[4] Ex inf. Mr. A. Hunt.

A farm with land in Coln St. Aldwyns and Hatherop, based on a capital messuage in the former called *DOWNHALL* and later known as Downhall farm, was held from the dean and chapter by John Blomer, lord of Hatherop manor. John (d. 1558) left the farm to his eldest son John[5] but his second son William, lord of Hatherop, later acquired it.[6] In 1769 Sir John Webb sold *c.* 166 a., mostly between the villages of Coln St. Aldwyns and Hatherop, to Samuel Blackwell, lord of Williamstrip,[7] who in 1778 acquired *c.* 81 a. near the two villages from Sir John by exchange for land in Quenington.[8]

In 1066 Dunning held an estate of 2 hides called Hatherop which by 1086 had passed to Roger de Lacy. It was held under him by William Devereux,[9] from whom the estate probably derived the name of *WILLIAMSTRIP*. The estate was held with land in Eastleach Turville with which it was assessed at a knight's fee in the early 14th century[10] and the overlordship passed with that of the Eastleach Turville land to the Verduns and their successors.[11]

In 1303 part of the estate was held by John Devereux, the rest having been granted to Thomas Dun and Bruern Abbey (Oxon.),[12] and by 1402 part, assessed at $\frac{2}{3}$ fee, was held by several people, including Robert Andrews (d. 1437) and possibly Ralph Lingen. In the early 15th century Lingen owned lands there, some of which had once belonged to Robert Moryn.[13] Later John Lingen owned an estate with a capital messuage there which after his death passed to his daughter Joan, a minor in 1554.[14] Joan, who survived her husband, a Mr. Shelley, died in 1610 and her property, known as Williamstrip manor, passed to her cousin Edward Lingen.[15] By 1618 Edward had conveyed it to Henry Powle,[16] a member of a prominent Coln St. Aldwyns family.[17] Henry died in 1643[18] and his son Richard sold the manor in 1657 to his younger brother Henry[19] who inherited Quenington manor. Henry (d. 1692) served as M.P. for Cirencester, East Grinstead (Suss.), and New Windsor (Berks.), and was Speaker of the House of Commons in the Convention Parliament of 1689, becoming Master of the Rolls the following year.[20] He was survived by his daughter Catherine who married Henry Ireton (d. 1711), and after her death in 1714 the estate passed under her will in turn to her cousins John Powle (fl. 1735) and (by 1741) William Forester.[21] In 1751 it was bought from Forester by Humphrey

Mackworth Praed who in 1759 agreed to sell it to Samuel Blackwell. Blackwell, who became M.P. for Cirencester, mortgaged the estate before the sale was completed in 1761 and died in 1785. In 1790 the estate was sold under an Exchequer order of 1788 to Michael Hicks and his wife Henrietta Maria, following an agreement of 1784 between her father William Beach and Blackwell.[22] Michael, who took the name Hicks Beach in 1790 and was M.P. for Cirencester 1794–1818, died in 1830 and Henrietta Maria in 1837. She was succeeded by her grandson Sir Michael Hicks Hicks Beach, Bt., of Beverstone, who in 1854 was M.P. for East Gloucestershire. He died later that year to be succeeded by his son Michael Edward Hicks Beach, the statesman (d. 1916), who became Viscount St. Aldwyn in 1906 and Earl St. Aldwyn in 1915.[23] About 1907 he conveyed his land to his son Michael Hugh, M.P. for Tewkesbury and from 1915 Viscount Quenington, who died in 1916. His son and heir Michael John, who inherited the earldom later that year as a minor,[24] entered his property in 1937[25] and retained 850 ha. (2,100 a.) of the Williamstrip estate in 1976.[26]

Williamstrip Park incorporates part of the house for which Henry Powle was assessed on 15 hearths in 1672.[27] That house, possibly of the early 17th century and perhaps with a courtyard in the centre, was roughly square in plan and the principal elevation, to the south, had a central porch of two storeys with square-sided bays on each side. Internal alterations accompanied the building *c.* 1700 of new fronts to the east and west of 7 bays with sash-windows. Land to the north-east occupied by extensive formal gardens[28] had been landscaped informally by 1754.[29] Mid-18th-century alterations to the house included adding canted bays to the west front and heightening the walls to include the attic storey, central pediments being built on the east and west fronts.[30] In 1791 Sir John Soane appears to have rebuilt the south front on the line of the front of the 17th-century bays and refaced the west front, which to maintain its symmetry was extended to the north, Soane probably being responsible for the segmental bays and central portico. He designed the two-storeyed addition on the north and refitted the library.[31] Some internal alterations were carried out in 1834 and there was much interior redecoration of ground-floor rooms on the south side, including the library, to plans by David Brandon between 1865

[5] C 142/122 no. 64; cf. Glos. R.O., D 540/T 35.
[6] C 142/347 no. 62; cf. C 142/406 no. 50; *Inq. p.m. Glos. 1625–42*, ii. 50–4; Glos. R.O., D 540/E 4.
[7] Williamstrip Mun. MTD/93/4; cf. Glos. R.O., photocopies 64B, 64H.
[8] Williamstrip Mun. MTD/93/1, 7B.
[9] *Dom. Bk.* (Rec. Com.), i. 167v.; cf. *Reg. Regum Anglo-Norm.* ii, App., no. LXIA.
[10] *Feud. Aids*, ii. 247; cf. ibid. 280.
[11] See below; cf. *Cal. Inq. p.m.* vii, pp. 496–7; xv, p. 311.
[12] *Feud. Aids*, ii. 247.
[13] Ibid. 300; *Ciren. Cart.* ii, pp. 631–3.
[14] *Cal. Pat.* 1554–8, 88.
[15] C 142/332 no. 16; cf. Smith, *Men and Armour*, 260.
[16] E 178/3861: the doc. is partly illegible.
[17] Cf. Smith, *Men and Armour*, 260.
[18] Bigland, *Glos.* i. 413.
[19] Glos. R.O., D 2440, est. papers 1545–1789, abs. of title.
[20] *D.N.B.*
[21] Glos. R.O., D 2440, est. papers 1545–1789, abs. of title; G.D.R. vol. 285B, f 35.
[22] Glos. R.O., D 2440, deed 1790; Rudder, *Glos.* proof pages (Glos. Colln.), MS. note on p. 385.
[23] Burke, *Peerage* (1963), 2134–5; for M. E. Hicks Beach, see *D.N.B.* 1912–21.
[24] Victoria Hicks Beach, *Life of Sir Michael Hicks Beach* (1932), ii. 281; Burke, *Peerage* (1963), 2135; inscr. in ch.
[25] Glos. R.O., PA 96/1, vol. for 1938.
[26] Ex inf. Earl St. Aldwyn.
[27] E 179/247/14 rot. 4.
[28] Atkyns, *Glos.* plate at pp. 364–5.
[29] Glos. R.O., photocopy 64A.
[30] Ibid. photocopy 64H; see plate in Rudder, *Glos.*; cf. Bigland, *Glos.* i. 412.
[31] Sir John Soane's Museum, London, XXX, 1, ff. 1–14; cf. *Delineations of Glos.* plate facing p. 90.

and 1866, when the canted bays were presumably added.[32] The house was occupied by tenants in the 1890s.[33] There was some rearrangement in and around the library in 1946 and a range of outbuildings to the north was demolished then.[34] The stables date from the early 18th century. A lodge at the western end of Hatherop village south of the house, designed by Richard Pace in 1822,[35] was demolished in the mid 20th century.[36] The eastern lodge on the Burford road, dating from *c.* 1810,[37] and the lodge east of Coln St. Aldwyns village were rebuilt in the late 19th century.

John Tame, who witnessed a grant of land in Williamstrip, Hatherop, and Eastleach in 1468,[38] with his son Edmund acquired 5 messuages and over 100 a. in Fairford, Williamstrip, and Hatherop from Thomas Mymmes in 1497.[39] John died in 1500[40] and Edmund made further purchases in Williamstrip, including 4 yardlands in 1501 and the property of John Mymmes in 1505.[41] Edmund, who was later knighted, died in 1534[42] and his Williamstrip property descended with his Tetbury lands to the Verney family. Under George Verney (d. 1574)[43] the Williamstrip land, which he settled on his natural brother Richard Verney, was occupied by John Hawkins[44] and in 1606 Francis Verney was party to a fine by which the land, called a manor, was confirmed upon Robert Hawkins.[45] Robert shared the lordship of Williamstrip with Joan Shelley in 1608[46] but later lack of evidence suggests that his property was absorbed by another estate.

In the early 16th century the rectory of Coln St. Aldwyns, which belonged to Gloucester Abbey and included the tithes of Ampney St. Peter chapelry, was let at farm.[47] The farm was £9 16s. 8d. in 1535[48] when the grain tithes evidently belonged to it.[49] In 1541 the rectory passed with the manor to the dean and chapter of Gloucester cathedral,[50] from whom it continued to be farmed.[51] Leases of it were apparently held by Jane Parker in 1563 and by Michael Parker, described in 1572 as parson.[52] It was worth £60 in 1603[53] and included *c.* 217 a. in 1649 when John Fettiplace was lessee.[54] From the later 17th century it was leased to the manorial lessees on similar terms[55] but in 1680 a renewal of Giles Fetti-

place's lease was delayed on the ground that he had no right to take tithes which, as a Quaker, he refused to pay.[56] In the late 17th century the rectorial tithes of the Williamstrip estate were farmed by the landowner for £20 a year.[57] The rectory was worth over £120 *c.* 1710[58] and in 1770 the dean and chapter's lessees were allotted 261 a. in Coln St. Aldwyns for the rectorial tithes of the whole parish.[59] The lease passed with that of the manor[60] to Sir M. E. Hicks Beach who also bought the freehold.[61]

ECONOMIC HISTORY. In 1086 Roger de Lacy's estate had 2 ploughs in demesne with 6 *servi*.[62] On Coln St. Aldwyns manor an extension of cultivation is perhaps indicated by a rise in value from £6 in 1066 to £8 in 1086, when the estate supported 15 ploughs of which 3 were in demesne with 4 *servi*.[63] A permanent staff was retained on the manor in the 1260s when the demesne arable was worked in part by tenant labour-services, some of which were connected with sheep-farming.[64] Gloucester Abbey retained 3 plough-lands on the manor in 1291.[65] In the early 16th century the demesne was let at farm but under a lease granted in 1504 for 70 years or lives the abbey retained its flocks in hand.[66] A survey of 1649 recorded 899 a. as being held in hand by the dean and chapter's lessee, but probably as little as 416 a. in Coln St. Aldwyns, with 41 a. in Kempsford and 19 a. in Hatherop, represented the demesne farm; the remainder was grouped as 15 holdings, ranging in size from 3 a. to 60 a. except for a farm of *c.* 240 a. at Cockrup, and may have been held by tenants on leases or at will. The 416 a. included 180 a. of arable in an open field, 226 a. in pasture closes, and only 8 a. in meadow closes. Additional hay and pasture was provided by the Kempsford land.[67] The rectory estate was let at farm with a customary yardland in the early 16th century, the lease of 1521 being for 51 years or lives.[68] In 1649 it included 207 a. of arable divided between two open fields, *c.* 2 a. of meadow, and *c.* 1 a. of pasture.[69]

The tenants recorded on Roger de Lacy's estate in 1086 were 3 *villani* and 3 bordars with 1 plough. Coln St. Aldwyns manor then supported 11 *villani*

[32] Williamstrip Mun. EMA/22.
[33] Glos. R.O., PA 96/1, vol. for 1891; *Kelly's Dir. Glos.* (1894), 128.
[34] Verey, *Glos.* i. 198–9; ex inf. Earl St. Aldwyn; for a view of the ho., see below, plate facing p. 124.
[35] Colvin, *Biog. Dict. of Eng. Architects*, 427.
[36] Cf. O.S. Map 6″, Glos. LII. NE. (1924 edn.).
[37] Glos. R.O., D 2440, est. papers (1766–1854), depositions 15 May 1850.
[38] B.L. Eg. Ch. 766.
[39] C.P. 25(1)/79/96 no. 32; *Trans. B.G.A.S.* liii. 91.
[40] Mon. in Fairford ch.
[41] B.L. Eg. Ch. 768, 770–1. In 1500 John Mymmes had secured a reversionary right to property in Williamstrip and neighbourhood: C.P. 25(1)/79/97 no. 50.
[42] C 142/74 no. 86; cf. Hockaday Abs. cxciv.
[43] *V.C.H. Glos.* xi. 265, where n. 14 should read C.P. 40/1334 Carte rot. 2.
[44] B.L. Eg. Ch. 809.
[45] *Trans. B.G.A.S.* xvii. 227.
[46] Smith, *Men and Armour*, 260.
[47] Glouc. Cath. Libr., Reg. Abb. Malvern, i, ff. 172v.–173v.; ii, ff. 83v.–84v.
[48] *Valor Eccl.* (Rec. Com.), ii. 410.

[49] Cf. ibid. 447.
[50] *L. & P. Hen. VIII*, xvi, p. 572.
[51] Hockaday Abs. clxvii, 1553.
[52] Ibid. clxvii.
[53] *Eccl. Misc.* 98.
[54] Glos. R.O., D 1740/E 1, ff. 67v.–68v.
[55] Ibid. D 936/E 67, E 68, E 138; D 1740/E 30, E 31.
[56] *Life of Robert Frampton*, ed. T. Simpson Evans (1876), 127; *Glos. N. & Q.* i. 273–4.
[57] Glos. R.O., D 2134.
[58] Atkyns, *Glos.* 364.
[59] Glos. R.O., P 96B/SD 1/1.
[60] Ibid. D 1740/E 30, E 31.
[61] Ibid. D 2440, est. papers 1860; Williamstrip Mun. MTA/5.
[62] *Dom. Bk.* (Rec. Com.), i. 167v.
[63] Ibid. 165v.
[64] *Hist. & Cart. Mon. Glouc.* iii. 196–203.
[65] *Tax. Eccl.* (Rec. Com.), 232.
[66] Glouc. Cath. Libr., Reg. Abb. Braunche, pp. 122–4; *Valor Eccl.* (Rec. Com.), ii. 410.
[67] Glos. R.O., D 1740/E 1, ff. 63–64v.
[68] Glouc. Cath. Libr., Reg. Abb. Malvern, i, ff. 172v.–173v.; ii, ff. 83v.–84v.
[69] Glos. R.O., D 1740/E 1, ff. 67v.–68.

and 7 bordars working 12 ploughs.[70] In the 1260s at least 29 tenements including some in Hatherop and 3 mills were held from the manor. The largest was of three yardlands (a yardland being 80 a.) and there was one of a yardland. Both owed cash rents and heriots in kind and the lord was entitled to wardship, marriage, and relief. Cash rents were owed for a yardland, a half-yardland, and 6 smaller holdings.[71] The customary tenements included 5 yardlands, 5 yardlands each held by two people jointly, and 9 smaller holdings. The holdings of another 7 tenants were not detailed. From October to July each customary yardland owed 4 week-works, services for threshing, ploughing, mowing, making hay, shearing and washing sheep, and carrying hay from Kempsford, and the service once every other week of carrying to Gloucester and of taking corn to sell at Fairford or Lechlade. Extra mowing services were due from one yardlander and the 5 pairs. In August and September 5 week-works and 9 bedrepes with 3 men were required from each yardland. Similar but reduced services were required from the smaller holdings most of whose tenants might have to act as ploughmen. Other customs included aid, toll on ale brewed for sale and on sale of horses, and pannage.[72] Rents of assize totalling 23s. belonged to Gloucester Abbey in 1291.[73]

In 1649 three freeholds, of three yardlands, a yardland, and $\frac{3}{4}$ yardland respectively, were held from Coln St. Aldwyns manor. The dean and chapter's lessee, who could grant copyholds for up to 3 lives, retained one of two yardlands in hand. Of the other 12 copyholds mentioned then 7 were over 40 a. and the remainder included a cottage and a mill.[74] In the mid 17th century some leasehold land was held from that manor,[75] which included 11 copyholds and 11 leaseholds in 1744 when part was worked under William Forester of Williamstrip.[76] By 1770 the dean and chapter's lessees had taken 4 copyholds in hand but another 5 were held by three tenants.[77] Several farms included copyhold land in the early 19th century but by 1812 some copyhold, including 355 a. of Swyre farm, had been replaced by leaseholds, although c. 78 a. at Cockrup[78] were the subject of grants in the manor court as late as 1827.[79] By 1830 c. 195 a. of another farm had become leasehold[80] and the last remaining copyholds were enfranchised at the sale of Coln St. Aldwyns manor in 1860.[81]

In Coln St. Aldwyns, where a west field was mentioned c. 1243,[82] the inclosure and conversion to pasture of 62 a. in 1496 or 1497 led to the abandoning of a house and the departure of 5 people.[83] Neat field, recorded in 1549,[84] was one of two open fields named in 1649, the other, Berry field, including 180 a. of manorial demesne.[85] By 1705 Neat field had been divided into an east and west field[86] but by 1769 all three fields had apparently been amalgamated to form a single open field said to comprise c. 1,950 a.[87] Downhall meadow (c. 13 a.), a water-meadow south-east of the village, was shared with Hatherop manor until 1778 after which it was taken into Williamstrip park.[88] In 1504 the main sheep-pasture in Coln St. Aldwyns manor was called the Bratch,[89] probably that let at farm by 1535,[90] and it comprised 200 a. in 1649.[91] Then the copyholders had small holdings of less than $1\frac{1}{2}$ a. in pasture closes and the yardlander common rights for 4 beasts and 80 sheep in the common fields.[92] The Cow Downs where the stint of cattle was halved in 1657[93] was the main common in 1769 when it included 100 a.[94] It was apparently situated between Bratch copse and the river Leach.[95]

Williamstrip, which contained open-field land in 1381[96] and where several inclosures had been made in Williamstrip Downs by 1713,[97] had been completely inclosed by 1754.[98] In Coln St. Aldwyns most of the land was inclosed in 1770 under a private Act of the previous year, and by the award, which affected c. 1,572 a., the tithes in both parts of the parish were commuted. The dean and chapter's lessees received the largest allotments, 749 a. for the manorial demesne and four copyholds in hand and 261 a. for the rectorial tithes; of their tenants Samuel Blackwell was allotted 196 a. for his leasehold and three persons with leaseholds and copyholds received a total of 186 a. Of the freeholders Sir John Webb was awarded 80 a., which passed with Dean farm in Hatherop, but Samuel Blackwell only 1 a. because his Williamstrip estate was freed from tithes. The vicar received 54 a. for his glebe and tithes. One smallholder was allotted 24 a. and five others a total of 21 a.[99]

After inclosure the parish was given over to cereal production and sheep-farming. In 1801 1,069 a. were sown with crops, wheat and barley occupying the largest areas and then turnips and oats.[1] Sheep were kept for their wool and in the early 19th century cross-breeding increased the quantity but decreased the quality.[2] Flocks numbering c. 1,930

[70] Dom. Bk. (Rec. Com.), i. 167v, 165v.
[71] Hist. & Cart. Mon. Glouc. iii. 196–8.
[72] Ibid. 198–203.
[73] Tax. Eccl. (Rec. Com.), 232.
[74] Glos. R.O., D 1740/E 1, ff. 64v.–66v., 68.
[75] Williamstrip Mun. MTD/95/2.
[76] Glos. R.O., D 936/E 162.
[77] Ibid. P 96B/SD 1/1.
[78] Ibid. D 936/E 3/1, pp. 106–8.
[79] Ibid. D 1740/M 1; D 2440, est. papers 1860.
[80] Ibid. D 2440, est. papers 1802–54, fm. partics. 1802; est. papers 1753–1852, est. partics. 1830.
[81] Williamstrip Mun. MTA/5.
[82] Glouc. Cath. Libr., deeds and seals, i, f. 31.
[83] C 47/7/2 no. 2.
[84] Hockaday Abs. clxvii.
[85] Glos. R.O., D 1740/E 1, ff. 63v.–68.

[86] G.D.R., V 5/89T 3.
[87] Glos. R.O., D 936/E 162.
[88] Ibid. photocopy 64B; Williamstrip Mun. MTD/93/1; Glos. R.O., D 540/P 2.
[89] Glouc. Cath. Libr., Reg. Abb. Braunche, pp. 122–3.
[90] Valor Eccl. (Rec. Com.), ii. 410.
[91] Glos. R.O., D 1740/E 1, f. 63v.
[92] Ibid. ff. 64v.–66.
[93] G.D.R., V 5/89T 3.
[94] Glos. R.O., D 936/E 162; P 96B/SD 1/1.
[95] Ibid. photocopy 64B.
[96] B.L. Eg. Ch. 765.
[97] Glos. R.O., D 1388/III/1.
[98] Ibid. photocopy 64A.
[99] Ibid. P 96B/SD 1/1; cf. ibid. D 540/E 6.
[1] Acreage Returns, 1801.
[2] Rudge, Agric. of Glos. 307.

sheep were kept in 1866, when 1,962 a. were returned as arable and grass leys and 205 a. as permanent grass.[3] In the late 19th century and early 20th there was the usual shift from arable to grass and in 1926 1,210 a. were returned as under arable crops or rotated grass and 996 a. as under permanent grass. Another 77 a. were used for rough grazing. Sheep-farming continued on a considerable scale but more cattle were also reared: 348 cattle, including 54 milk cows, were returned in 1926,[4] compared with c. 133, including c. 18 in milk, in 1866.[5] By 1976, however, much land was under wheat and barley and arable had become more important, but large numbers of sheep and beef cattle were raised then.[6]

After inclosure the land was included in a few, large farms. The three listed on the Coln St. Aldwyns manor estate in 1778 contained 113 a., 209 a., and 688 a. (Swyre farm),[7] and in Williamstrip in 1784 there were farms of 283 a. and 493 a.[8] In 1831 there were 8 farmers in the parish of whom 7 employed 60 labourers.[9] In 1839 215 a. were farmed with land in Hatherop.[10] In 1861 the farms, all belonging to the Williamstrip estate, were Manor (734 a.), Williamstrip (520 a.), Swyre (501 a.), Moor's (264 a.), and Cockrup (181 a.).[11] In 1894 the Coln St. Aldwyn Farming Co-operative Society Ltd. was established to farm Cockrup farm[12] and in 1909 it took a lease of Moor's farm.[13] The society, which was working 575 a. and a corn-mill c. 1911, stopped farming in 1919 and was wound up in 1921.[14] In 1926, when 54 agricultural labourers worked in the parish full-time, there were seven farmers of whom two, with less than 20 a. each, were smallholders and another worked less than 50 a. Of the larger farms one was over 150 a. and three were over 300 a.[15] In 1976 Earl St. Aldwyn directly farmed 607 ha. (1,500 a.) on the Williamstrip estate, and in the enlarged parish there were also two farms with over 200 ha. (494 a.) and 100 ha. (247 a.) respectively.[16]

Two mills were recorded on Coln St. Aldwyns manor in 1086.[17] In the 1260s it had three of which the two that were then held for cash rent, services for mowing and making hay, bedrepes, and other customs, were in Coln St. Aldwyns.[18] In 1340 the tenant of one was granted a lease for 60 years with half of the suit of mill owed by Gloucester Abbey's tenants in Coln St. Aldwyns and Aldsworth.[19] In 1534 a reversionary right in a mill was granted to the lessee of the rectory estate,[20] to which a corn-mill belonged in 1649.[21] That mill, south-west of the village,[22] included two fulling-mills and a gig-mill in 1754[23] but by 1770 was only a corn-mill.[24] It became a saw-mill in the 1920s[25] and continued in use until the 1940s.[26] By 1976 it had been converted as a house.

The mill further downstream at the southern end of the village street, called Kemeys's mill in 1598,[27] was always a corn-mill.[28] It was rebuilt by Sir M. E. Hicks Beach in 1858.[29] It went out of use after 1939[30] and was used for storage in 1976.

There was a smith in Coln St. Aldwyns in 1327[31] but the trade was not recorded in 1608 when non-agricultural occupations were represented by two slaters, two masons, a tailor, a butcher, and a carpenter. There was also a weaver, a wool-driver who had two servants and was presumably engaged in transporting wool by pack-horse, and a loader who may have handled corn for milling. No trades were recorded in Williamstrip then[32] but there was a smithy south-west of Dean Row by 1830[33] and in 1976 the site was occupied by a firm of agricultural engineers. The parish had a carpenter in the 18th century[34] and a wheelwright from 1840 until 1939 at least.[35] There was a cordwainer in 1754 and 1835,[36] and a shoemaker was recorded from 1856 to 1906 and a tailor from 1863 to 1910. In 1856 there were two bakers and two maltsters but those trades disappeared after the 1870s.[37] Mercers were recorded in the 18th century.[38] The number of shopkeepers fell from four in 1856 to one by 1879 but the village then also had the stores[39] run by the Coln Independent Co-operative Society Ltd., founded in 1875 and wound up in 1955.[40] The shop remained open in 1976 as Coln Stores. A laundry set up to the south-west c. 1912[41] closed after the Second World War.[42] In 1976 the village also had a

[3] M.A.F. 68/25/3; M.A.F. 68/26/10.
[4] M.A.F. 68/3295/8.
[5] M.A.F. 68/25/3.
[6] Agric. Returns 1976.
[7] Glos. R.O., D 936/E 256; cf. churchwardens' acct. bk. 1758–1867.
[8] Glos. R.O., D 2440, est. papers 1753–1852.
[9] Census, 1831.
[10] Glos. R.O., D 936/E 160; D 2440, est. papers 1753–1852, est. partics. 1830.
[11] Williamstrip Mun. EMS/17.
[12] Ibid. SCR/2; Glos. R.O., PA 96/1, vol. for 1912.
[13] Williamstrip Mun. MTC/26; MTD/106/8.
[14] Glos. R.O., PA 96/1, vols. for 1912, 1919, 1922.
[15] M.A.F. 68/3295/8.
[16] Ex inf. Earl St. Aldwyn; Agric. Returns 1976.
[17] Dom. Bk. (Rec. Com.), i. 165v.
[18] Hist. & Cart. Mon. Glouc. iii. 196–7; cf. Tax. Eccl. (Rec. Com.), 232.
[19] Glouc. Cath. Libr., deeds and seals, x, f. 10.
[20] Ibid. Reg. Abb. Malvern, ii, ff. 83v.–84v.
[21] Glos. R.O., D 1740/E 1, f. 68.
[22] Cf. Bryant, Map of Glos. (1824).
[23] Glouc. Jnl. 12 Feb. 1754.
[24] Glos. R.O., D 2440, misc. papers.

[25] Cf. O.S. Map 6″, Glos. LII. NE. (1924 edn.); Richardson, Wells and Springs of Glos. 77.
[26] Ex inf. the vicar.
[27] Glos. R.O., D 540/T 29.
[28] Ibid. D 1740/E 1, f. 65v.; D 936/E 162, p. 1.
[29] Date and inits. on bldg.
[30] O.S. Map 6″, Glos. LII. NE. (1924 edn.); Kelly's Dir. Glos. (1939), 136.
[31] Glos. Subsidy Roll, 1327, 14.
[32] Smith, Men and Armour, 260; for the loader cf. O.E.D.
[33] Glos. R.O., D 2440, est. papers 1760–1843, presentment of Hatherop man. boundaries; cf. O.S. Map 6″, Glos. LII. NE. (1924 edn.).
[34] Glos. R.O., D 1070/III/2; D 1740/M 1, ct. 2 Dec. 24 Geo. III.
[35] Kelly's Dir. Glos. (1856 and later edns.).
[36] Glos. R.O., D 2440, est. papers 1754–1854, abs. of title 1848; D 1620.
[37] Kelly's Dir. Glos. (1856 and later edns.).
[38] Glos. R.O., D 213/T 3, covenant to produce deeds 1825.
[39] Kelly's Dir. Glos. (1856 and later edns.).
[40] Glos. R.O., D 1382: the mins. of the soc.
[41] Williamstrip Mun. EMM/16; O.S. Map 6″, Glos. LII. NE. (1924 edn.).
[42] Local information.

post office. A lime-burner was recorded in 1852[43] and a builder and a plasterer in the late 1880s, as well as a saddle and harness maker and a bacon-factor.[44] A cycle repairer lived in the parish in the 1920s and 1930s[45] and there was a garage in the village in 1976.

LOCAL GOVERNMENT. In the early 15th century the biannual view of the hundred court was attended by the tithingman of Coln St. Aldwyns but another tithingman represented the inhabitants of Williamstrip and part of Eastleach Turville.[46] For Coln St. Aldwyns manor[47] court rolls survive for 1293 and 1351 when it dealt with tenurial and agrarian matters.[48] It was apparently held twice a year in 1504[49] but in 1649 it was said to be held at the will of the lord, presumably the dean and chapter's lessee.[50] There are further court rolls for courts held to deal with tenurial matters by the lessees between 1755 and 1794 and by the dean and chapter in 1813 and 1827.[51]

Two proctors of the parish church mentioned in 1519 held property on its behalf.[52] That was one aspect of the duties of the two churchwardens, recorded from 1543,[53] whose accounts survive from 1758.[54] Of the other parish officers a constable was mentioned in 1715[55] and two overseers in 1823.[56] A church house, presumably built on the site of Catland House given to the parish for that purpose by Gloucester Abbey in 1519,[57] included rooms belonging to a holding on Coln St. Aldwyns manor in the mid 17th century.[58] It was used partly as a poorhouse from 1700[59] until 1852 when the house, which by then also included a school-room, was bought by Sir M. H. Hicks Beach.[60] The cost of poor-relief rose considerably from £44 in 1776 to £222 by 1803 when 27 people received permanent and 22 occasional help, and by 1813, when the equivalent numbers were 38 and 13, it was £481. A drop in numbers was reflected in a fall in cost to £361 by 1815.[61] From £389 in 1825 expenditure rose to £480 by 1828 but after 1831 it fell sharply to £297 by 1834.[62] The parish, which became part of the Northleach poor-law union in 1836,[63] remained in Northleach rural district until 1974[64] when it was included in Cotswold district.

CHURCH. A grant of tithes at Coln St. Aldwyns to Gloucester Abbey in 1100[65] suggests the existence of a church there but no record of it has been found before the later 12th century.[66] The church, of which Ampney St. Peter was a chapelry,[67] was appropriated to the abbey in 1217 and a vicarage ordained,[68] to which presentations were recorded from 1274.[69] In 1928 the living was united with Hatherop and Quenington.[70]

The patronage was exercised by Gloucester Abbey which in 1538 granted the next turn to William Mitchell, a Gloucester draper, and two others.[71] In the mid 16th century presentations were made by lessees of the dean and chapter of Gloucester, Jerome Barnard in 1550, Ralph Jennings in 1553, and George Fettiplace in 1557.[72] Robert Westwood was said to be patron in 1584[73] and the Crown presented through lapse of time in 1591. In 1618 John White was patron for a turn. The patronage which from the later 17th century passed with the lease of the manor was resumed by the dean and chapter in the early 19th century. In 1852 the bishop presented by reason of lapse.[74] In 1976 the patronage of the united benefice was shared by the dean and chapter with Sir Thomas Bazley and Earl St. Aldwyn.[75]

In 1217 the vicarage was assigned a portion worth 5 marks[76] and the vicar's portion was presumably comprised in the valuation of the church and its chapel at £7 6s. 8d. in 1291.[77] In 1535 the vicar was taking tithes of wool, milk, calves, pigs, and lambs among others, and had 1 a. of glebe.[78] In the later 17th century £6 13s. 4d. was paid to him by ancient composition for his Williamstrip tithes[79] but in 1705 he was taking all small tithes, except those of the demesne of Coln St. Aldwyns manor and of the rectory estate, mainly in kind.[80] Those from the manor were evidently paid to the impropriated rectory, from the lessee of which the vicar received a stipend of £7 for them. By 1662 it had been raised to £20, and another £10 was added under the inclosure Act of 1769.[81] In 1862 the stipend was charged on Manor farm.[82] An award of £200 from Queen Anne's Bounty in 1765 to meet a grant of £200 by T. Willoughby and Alexander Colston and his wife Sophia[83] was used to buy 17 a. in Quenington.[84] At

[43] Glos. R.O., D 2440, est. papers 1766–1853, mem. 11 Sept. 1852.
[44] Kelly's Dir. Glos. (1885), 435; (1894), 128.
[45] Ibid. (1923 and later edns.).
[46] Ciren. Cart. ii, p. 622. Atkyns, Glos. 364 was wrong in saying that there was a court leet at Coln; cf. Bodl. MS. Rawl. B.323, f. 88.
[47] Cf. Hist. & Cart. Mon. Glouc. iii. 196; Glouc. Cath. Libr., deeds and seals, vi, f. 6.
[48] Glos. R.O., D 936A/M 1, rot. 9; M 2, rot. 1d.
[49] Cf. Glouc. Cath. Libr., Reg. Abb. Braunche, p. 123.
[50] Glos. R.O., D 1740/E 1, f. 66v.   [51] Ibid. M 1.
[52] Glouc. Cath. Libr., Reg. Abb. Malvern, i, f. 142.
[53] Hockaday Abs. xxix, 1543 subsidy, f. 18; G.D.R. vol. 40, f. 158v.; Hockaday Abs. lxiv, 1642 visit. f. 18.
[54] Penes the vicar.   [55] Glos. R.O., Q/SO 4.
[56] Ibid. D 1070/I/65.
[57] Glouc. Cath. Libr., Reg. Abb. Malvern, i, f. 142 and v.
[58] Williamstrip Mun. MTD/95/2.   [59] G.D.R., V 5/89T 3.
[60] Glos. R.O., D 2440, est. papers 1852–3; churchwardens' acct. bk. 1758–1867.
[61] Poor Law Abstract, 1804, 172–3; 1818, 146–7.
[62] Poor Law Returns (1830–1), p. 67; (1835), p. 65.
[63] Poor Law Com. 2nd Rep. p. 523.   [64] Census, 1961.
[65] Hist. & Cart. Mon. Glouc. ii. 41.
[66] Ibid. i. 257; iii. 11.
[67] Cf. Tax. Eccl. (Rec. Com.), 222; Glouc. Cath. Libr., Reg. Abb. Malvern, i, ff. 172v.–173v.; Glos. R.O., D 1740/E 1, f. 68 and v.; D 936/E 160, p. 11.
[68] Hist. & Cart. Mon. Glouc. i. 231.
[69] Reg. Giffard, 64; Worc. Episc. Reg., Reg. Maidstone, f. 52; Reg. Carpenter, i, f. 129.
[70] Lond. Gaz. 2 Nov. 1928, pp. 709–67.
[71] Glouc. Cath. Libr., Reg. Abb. Malvern, ii, f. 172v.
[72] Hockaday Abs. clxvii; cf. Glos. R.O., D 2019; C 3/66/7.
[73] Hockaday Abs. xlix, state of clergy 1584, f. 23.
[74] Ibid. clxvii; Glos. R.O., D 1740/E 1, f. 66v.; D 936/E 67.
[75] Glouc. Dioc. Yr. Bk. (1976), 66–7.
[76] Hist. & Cart. Mon. Glouc. i. 231.
[77] Tax. Eccl. (Rec. Com.), 222.
[78] Valor Eccl. (Rec. Com.), ii. 447; cf. G.D.R., V 5/89T 1.
[79] Glos. R.O., D 2134.   [80] G.D.R., V 5/89T 3.
[81] Glos. R.O., D 936/E 68; cf. ibid. D 1740/E 31.
[82] Par. reg. 1791–1812, penes the vicar, mem.
[83] Hodgson, Queen Anne's Bounty, pp. clxv, cclxxxiv.
[84] G.D.R., V 5/89T 4; cf. par. reg. 1791–1812, mem. 28 Sept. 1826.

inclosure in 1770 the vicar was allotted 53 a. for his commuted tithes as well as 1 a. for glebe.[85] A further grant in 1842 of £200 from Queen Anne's Bounty which met benefactions of £100 by the patron and £270 by the vicar, Horatio James,[86] was used in part for rebuilding the vicarage.[87] The Ecclesiastical Commissioners endowed the living with £163 a year in 1869, with 10 a. of land in 1870, and with 4 a. in 1886.[88] Most of the glebe was sold in 1912 to Michael Hugh Hicks Beach,[89] leaving 2.4 ha. (6 a.) in 1976.[90] The value of the vicarage in 1535 was £8 19s. 5d. clear.[91] It rose to £26 6s. 8d. by 1649,[92] £37 by 1750,[93] £60 by c. 1775,[94] and £104 by 1856.[95]

There was a vicarage house with out-buildings in 1649[96] but the present house south-east of the church began as a small 18th-century house which was largely rebuilt in the 1840s.[97] It was further enlarged in 1857 and 1875[98] and two bay-windows were added and other external alterations made c. 1911.[99]

The appointment of at least six incumbents between 1402 and 1420 possibly reflected the poverty of the living,[1] but when John Russell resigned in 1524 he was awarded a pension of 4 marks from the profits of the church. His successor Thomas Moorcroft (d. c. 1528) was a doctor of medicine.[2] Edward Barnard, vicar 1550–3,[3] lived at Oxford, the living being served in 1551 by an unlearned curate.[4] In 1563 Henry Banner, who was also rector of Quenington, where he lived, served in person[5] but by 1572 he had a curate at Coln St. Aldwyns.[6] Banner, who was presented in 1576 for not teaching the catechism and for preaching only one sermon,[7] resigned to be succeeded that year by William Banner,[8] described as learned in Latin and zealous in religion.[9] John Fifield, vicar 1728–75,[10] served on alternate Sunday mornings and afternoons in 1750.[11] John Keble, also vicar of Blewbury (Berks.) until 1824, held the living from 1782 until he died in 1835.[12] Although he lived at Poulton (Wilts., later Glos.) and then moved to his family house in Fairford, the vicarage being too small, he served in person.[13] His son John, who between 1825 and 1835 was curate,[14] was the Tractarian divine and author of *The Christian Year* published in 1827.[15]

The parochial chaplain recorded in 1340[16] may have been, like the proctor of Blessed Mary mentioned in 1533,[17] connected with a chantry-chapel in the churchyard dedicated to the service of Our Lady. In 1548 the vicar celebrated Mass once a week in the chantry and the endowments, valued at 17s. 4d. clear[18] and comprising 7 a. and 3 cottages in Coln St. Aldwyns, 20 a. in Williamstrip, and a close in Hatherop, were sold the following year.[19]

The parish church was called St. Athelwine's in the later 12th century[20] but the dedication was changed after 1535[21] and before the beginning of the 18th century to *ST. JOHN THE BAPTIST*.[22] It is built of rubble and ashlar and has a chancel with north organ chamber and a nave with north transeptal chapel, south tower, and south porch. The south wall of the nave is substantially of the later 12th century and has a doorway with three enriched orders. The chancel was rebuilt in the 13th century. Its upkeep was later the responsibility of the lessees of the rectory estate.[23] The tower is placed transeptally to the nave but appears to have been entered from the south and to have had a small building against its east wall. The second stage bears the initials of John de Gamages, abbot of Gloucester 1284–1306,[24] and it is possible that it was a chantry for him, the chapel being that to Our Lady mentioned above. In the 14th century the west wall and probably also the north wall of the nave were rebuilt and a new window was put into the south wall. The old south porch, of which only the roof-line survives, may also have been of that date. The roof of the nave was rebuilt to a flatter pitch in the 15th century when the embattled parapet was added. The top stage of the tower, which has crocketed pinnacles and a pierced parapet, was also added in the 15th or early 16th century.

In 1821 a north vestry was built in the church by Michael Hicks Beach.[25] The 19th-century additions and restoration, mostly done between 1853 and 1868, are extensive.[26] The organ chamber was added, a new south porch built, and a canopied entry made into the east face of the tower, the southern doorway having been blocked before 1787.[27] The nave windows were restored, presumably following the

---

[85] Glos. R.O., P 96B/SD 1/1.

[86] Hodgson, *Queen Anne's Bounty*, pp. ccxxx, cclxxxiv; cf. Hockaday Abs. clxvii.

[87] Par. reg. 1791–1812, mem. 1857.

[88] *Lond. Gaz.* 15 Jan. 1869, p. 236; 21 Jan. 1870, p. 413; par. reg. 1791–1812, mem.

[89] Glos. R.O., PA 96/1, vol. for 1912; Williamstrip Mun. MTC/27.

[90] Ex inf. the vicar.

[91] *Valor Eccl.* (Rec. Com.), ii. 447.

[92] Glos. R.O., D 1740/E 1, f. 66v.   [93] G.D.R. vol. 381A, f. 84.

[94] Rudder, *Glos.* 385.   [95] G.D.R. vol. 384, f. 4.

[96] Glos. R.O., D 1740/E 1, f. 67v.

[97] Ibid. PA 96/1, vol. for 1920; D 1381/45, glebe partics. 1888.

[98] Par. reg. 1791–1812, mem.; cf. *Lond. Gaz.* 6 Mar. 1874, p. 1629.

[99] Glos. R.O., PA 96/1, vol. for 1912.

[1] Worc. Episc. Reg., Reg. Clifford, ff. 19, 62, 92; Reg. Peverell, f. 64; Reg. Morgan, i, ff. 3, 16v.

[2] Worc. Episc. Reg., Reg. Ghinucci, ff. 16v., 33.

[3] Hockaday Abs. clxvii.

[4] *E.H.R.* xix. 113–14; *Trans. B.G.A.S.* lx. 104 n.

[5] Hockaday Abs. xlii, 1563 visit. f. 51; clxvii.

[6] Ibid. xliv, 1572 visit. f. 41.   [7] G.D.R. vol. 40, f. 159.

[8] Hockaday Abs. clxvii.

[9] Ibid. xlvii, state of clergy 1576, f. 145.

[10] Ibid. clxvii; Bigland, *Glos.* i. 414.   [11] G.D.R. vol. 381A, f. 84.

[12] Hockaday Abs. clxvii; *Kelly's Dir. Glos.* (1897), 129.

[13] Hockaday Abs. clxvii; G.D.R. vol. 319; vol. 382, f. 16.

[14] Inscr. in ch.; cf. *V.C.H. Glos.* ii. 47; Hockaday Abs. clxvii, 1831.

[15] *D.N.B.*   [16] *Reg. Bransford*, p. 58.

[17] D.L. 30/127/1907, f. 49v.   [18] *Trans. B.G.A.S.* viii. 278.

[19] *Cal. Pat.* 1549–51, 100; Hockaday Abs. clxvii.

[20] *Hist. & Cart. Mon. Glouc.* i. 257; iii. 11; *P.N. Glos.* i. 29–30.

[21] Cf. Glouc. Cath. Libr., Reg. Abb. Malvern, i, f. 142; *Valor Eccl.* (Rec. Com.), ii. 447.

[22] Bodl. MS. Rawl. B.323, f. 88; there was an altar to St. John the Baptist in 1537: Hockaday Abs. clxvii, 1538.

[23] Glouc. Cath. Libr., Reg. Abb. Malvern, i, f. 173; Glos. R.O., D 1740/E 1, f. 68; D 1381/45, glebe partics. 1883.

[24] *V.C.H. Glos.* ii. 61.

[25] Churchwardens' acct. bk. 1758–1867.

[26] Par. reg. 1791–1812, mem.; cf. Glos. R.O., PA 96/1, vol. for 1900.

[27] Bigland, *Glos.* i. 411; for a later print of same view cf. Glos. R.O., PA 96/1, vol. for 1877.

original designs, and the chancel and transept arches renewed. A western gallery, probably that built in the mid 17th century by members of the Powle family,[28] and a gallery in the transept were taken down.

A monument recorded in the later 18th century to George Fettiplace (d. 1577), his wife, and six children was possibly removed from the chancel[29] when it was refitted in 1917 as a memorial to Earl St. Aldwyn and Viscount Quenington and his wife Marjorie, who all died in 1916. The pulpit was then given a 17th-century appearance.[30] The chancel chandelier is dated 1767. There were three bells c. 1703[31] which possibly included the sanctus bell of 1656 by Edward Neale of Burford.[32] In 1725 Abraham Rudhall cast a peal of 6 to which 2 were added by G. Mears of London in 1865.[33] The plate includes a chalice and a paten-cover of 1625, a paten and tankard flagon of 1777, and a cruet of 1813.[34] The registers begin in 1650 but have some gaps, including one between 1727 and 1775, the incumbency of John Fifield.[35]

NONCONFORMITY. Four protestant nonconformists recorded in Coln St. Aldwyns in 1676[36] presumably were Quakers including Giles Fettiplace, who was presented the same year for not coming to church.[37] In 1677 George Fox attended a meeting in Giles's manor-house[38] which was registered as a Quaker meeting-house in 1702.[39] In 1735 there were 6 anabaptists in the parish[40] and in 1860 a group of Congregationalists met in Coln St. Aldwyns under a Fairford minister.[41]

In 1676 there were also two papists in the parish.[42] Eleven were recorded between 1714 and 1724[43] and five in 1735.[44] They presumably attended the mission in Hatherop; after its closure in 1844 a cottage in Coln St. Aldwyns was used as a mass centre for a few years.[45]

EDUCATION. In 1818 two Sunday schools, presumably one for boys and the other for girls, were recorded in Coln St. Aldwyns teaching c. 60 children and supported by voluntary contributions and Lady Bridger's charity[46] from which £2 10s. a year was

paid in the 1820s.[47] In 1833 there were also three day-schools, including a boys' school begun that year where a private benefactor paid for the education of 12 of the 15 boys, and a girls' school with 24 girls of whom 21 were paid for by subscription. In the third school all 12 children were supported by their parents.[48] The girls' day- and Sunday schools had been united by 1846 when they taught 36 children but the boys' day- and Sunday schools, with 16 and 28 respectively, remained separate.[49] The girls' school was held in the church house which was sold in 1852,[50] the sale partly financing the building of a National school, completed in 1856 east of the church.[51] The school, which was mixed and included infants, was supported in 1866 by voluntary contributions, pence, rent from part of the building, £5 from Betton's charity, and an endowment of £2 12s. from the combined Fettiplace and Bridger charity.[52] There were 77 children on the roll in 1876.[53] The classroom was enlarged in 1881[54] but the average attendance fell from 80 in 1885 to 60 in 1897.[55] In 1894 the school was supported partly by Lambert's charity.[56] Attendance dropped from 56 in 1910 to 35 in 1922.[57] In 1929 the juniors were transferred to Hatherop and the school became the infants' school for both parishes[58] but attendance had fallen to 17 by 1936.[59] The school, known later as Coln St. Aldwyns C. of E. Controlled Primary school, closed in 1970 and its 11 children were transferred to Quenington.[60]

CHARITIES FOR THE POOR. Catherine Ireton by will proved 1715 left a rent-charge of £10 for distribution among the Protestant poor of the parish.[61] Between 1777 and 1893 the charity was usually distributed as a coat for a man, a gown for a woman, and as bread. A deficit in 1856 was met by subscription.[62] From 1967 to 1970 the income of £10, derived from investments, was used to provide a cardigan each for a man and a woman, and groceries for two families.[63] Elizabeth Fettiplace (d. 1716) left £20 for the poor but the income was misapplied in the early 19th century.[64] The bequest by Lady Bridger of £50 to the poor,[65] which was used in 1818 to support two Sunday schools,[66] had been amalgamated with the Fettiplace charity by 1838

[28] Atkyns, *Glos.* 364.
[29] Rudder, *Glos.* 385; Bigland, *Glos.* i. 413 n; cf. Roper, *Glos. Effigies*, 625.
[30] Glos. R.O., PA 96/1, vol. for 1918; inscr. in ch.
[31] Bodl. MS. Rawl. B.323, f. 87v.
[32] U. Daubeny, *Ancient Cotswold Churches*, 168.
[33] *Glos. Ch. Bells*, 43: one is dated 1724; par. reg. 1791–1812, mem.
[34] *Glos. Ch. Plate*, 61–2.   [35] *B. & G. Par. Rec.* 109.
[36] Compton Census.
[37] Glos. R.O., D 2052.
[38] Ibid. NC 60, p. 14.   [39] Ibid. Q/SO 3.
[40] G.D.R. vol. 285B, f. 35.
[41] Glos. R.O., D 2052.
[42] Compton Census.
[43] Glos. R.O., Q/SO 4.
[44] G.D.R. vol. 285B, f. 35.
[45] Langston, 'Cath. Missions', i, p. 12.
[46] *Educ. of Poor Digest*, 296; cf. G.D.R. vol. 383, no. xciv.
[47] *20th Rep. Com. Char.* 17.
[48] *Educ. Enquiry Abstract*, 311.

[49] *Church School Inquiry, 1846–7*, 6–7.
[50] Glos. R.O., D 2440, est. papers 1852–3; churchwardens' acct. bk. 1758–1867.
[51] Par. reg. 1791–1812, mem.; Glos. R.O., D 2186/47.
[52] Ed. 7/34/89.
[53] Glos. R.O., PA 96/1, vol. for 1877.
[54] Par. reg. 1791–1812, mem.
[55] *Kelly's Dir. Glos.* (1885), 435; (1897), 129.
[56] Glos. R.O., PA 96/1, vol. for 1895.
[57] *Bd. of Educ., List 21, 1911* (H.M.S.O.), 160; *1922*, 103.
[58] Glos. R.O., PA 96/1, vols. for 1929–30.
[59] *Bd. of Educ., List 21, 1932* (H.M.S.O.), 114; *1936*, 120.
[60] Ex inf. county educ. dept. and the vicar.
[61] Glos. R.O., D 2440, est. papers 1545–1789, abs. of title.
[62] Churchwardens' acct. bks. 1758–1867, 1868–1922.
[63] Glos. R.O., CH 21.
[64] *20th Rep. Com. Char.* 17; churchwardens' acct. bk. 1758–1867: char. accts. for 1807–21 appear after acct. for 1855–6.
[65] *20th Rep. Com. Char.* 17; Lady Bridger was presumably Rebecca, wife of Sir John.
[66] *Educ. of Poor Digest*, 296.

when they were invested in stock.[67] In the later 19th century the National school was assisted by the combined charity,[68] which in 1970 had an income of £3.[69] The charity of James Anthony Lambert who by will dated 1828 left £25 for eight poor people[70] assisted a cloth and coal club in 1876[71] and the National school in 1894.[72] It was applied with the Fettiplace and Bridger charity by 1970 when all the above charities, with a total

income of £13, were amalgamated as the Coln St. Aldwyns United Charities.[73]

Under the will of Edmund James Wilkins, proved 1917, £600 was left for an alms-house. A charity was established which took a lease of two cottages south of the school[74] but in 1973, when the income was £50–100, a new Scheme applied it to individual cases of need[75] and in 1976 it was distributed with the United Charities.[76]

EASTLEACH MARTIN

EASTLEACH MARTIN, often called Botherop, was a small and sparsely populated parish lying on the Oxfordshire boundary 18.5 km. ENE. of Cirencester. The ancient parish contained 1,966 a. (796 ha.) and was elongated in shape, its boundaries formed mainly by field divisions but with the river Leach as the central part of the west boundary. The south part of the parish extended across the Leach and was divided from Southrop on the south by an irregular boundary and from Eastleach Turville on the north-west by a straight track running from Hammersmith Bottom to the south side of Eastleach Turville village; beyond that area lay a detached part of the parish, comprising Homeleaze Farm and 90 a. (36 ha.).[77] The land west of the Leach and the detached part evidently represented two ancient estates called Coate farm and Prior's Coate which, being intermingled with land belonging to Southrop, were inclosed with that parish in 1621.[78] In 1883 the detached part was given to Southrop[79] and in 1935 Eastleach Martin was joined to Eastleach Turville to form the new civil parish of Eastleach with 4,506 a. (1,824 ha.).[80]

Eastleach Martin was called Leach in 1086[81] and was one of four places so named after the river on which they stood; two of them later became known as Eastleach and the others Northleach and Southrop. To distinguish it from its neighbour Eastleach Martin came to be called after one of the patron saints of its church,[82] but the name Botherop, recorded as 'Burythrop' in 1351,[83] has been used almost as frequently for the name of the parish. Botherop had, however, a local significance within the parish, being used to distinguish the area near the Leach, where the church and Botherop Farm stood, from the other areas of the parish called Fyfield and Coate. Presumably there was once some kind of earthwork there, built to guard the crossing of the Leach and matched by another at Greenbury

on the high ground of Eastleach Turville village opposite.

The land of the parish lies mainly at c. 100 m. but in the north it rises from the Leach valley to c. 140 m. The Leach valley is formed by the Great Oolite which in most of the rest of the parish is overlaid by Forest Marble.[84] Until inclosure in 1753 much of the north part of the parish consisted of downland sheep-pastures and much of the south open-field land.[85] The Roman road called Akeman Street crosses the north part of the parish but is no longer in use there, and apart from the Fairford–Burford road, crossing further north, there is no thoroughfare of any significance.

The settlement by the Leach opposite Eastleach Turville village remained undeveloped, comprising only the church and Botherop Farm, the old site of the manor. The rectory stands on its own some way further up the Leach and a school was built above it in the mid 19th century. Near by the lessees of the Botherop farm estate built a substantial Cotswold-style house, called Ravenshill, in the earlier 19th century, before 1841.[86] Further down the Leach there seems once to have been a small hamlet at Coate, judging from the number of inhabitants surnamed of Coate in the 13th and 14th centuries.[87] Later only Coate Mill on the river and Coate Farm to the west remained. Probably from medieval times the bulk of the inhabitants of the parish have lived in the hamlet of Fyfield, anciently called Fifhide, in the south part. The hamlet was settled by the early 13th century[88] and was presumably fairly populous by 1327 when the parish was called Eastleach cum Fifhide.[89] The hamlet had about 17 cottages in 1823 and most of them date from the 18th century, as does the one small farm-house. One of the cottages was a public house in 1823[90] and had perhaps been kept by the innholder recorded in 1755.[91]

In the south-west part of the parish close to

[67] Glos. R.O., D 2440, est. papers 1729–1866, misc. papers.
[68] Ed. 7/34/89.
[69] Glos. R.O., CH 21.
[70] Ibid. D 2440, est. papers 1753–1852.
[71] Ibid. PA 96/1, vol. for 1877.
[72] Ibid. vol. for 1895.
[73] Ibid. CH 21; Char. Com. Reg.
[74] Glos. R.O., PA 96/1, vol. for 1919; inscr. on cottages.
[75] Char. Com. Reg.
[76] Ex inf. the vicar.
[77] O.S. Area Bk. (1882). This account was written in 1976.
[78] See p. 133.
[79] Census, 1891.

[80] Ibid. 1931 (pt. ii).
[81] Dom. Bk. (Rec. Com.), i. 168v.
[82] Cal. Pat. 1301–7, 14.
[83] Glos. R.O., D 936A/M 2.
[84] Geol. Surv. Map 1″, solid, sheet 34 (1857 edn.).
[85] Glos. R.O., D 1740/M 2.
[86] Ibid. D 333/E 2.
[87] Hist. & Cart. Mon. Glouc. (Rolls Ser.), iii. 188–9; Glos. Subsidy Roll, 1327, 14.
[88] Hist. & Cart. Mon. Glouc. i. 269–70.
[89] Glos. Subsidy Roll, 1327, 14.
[90] Glos. R.O., D 1388/SL 3, no. 24.
[91] Ibid. Q/AV 2, rot. 3.

Southrop village a new house, later called Fyfield House, was built by Joseph Small, the lord farmer of the manor, in the early 18th century.[92] After the inclosure two small farm-houses, Sheephouse Farm and Warren Farm (later called Tom Jolly's),[93] were built on the former downland in the north.

Twenty-eight inhabitants of Eastleach Martin were recorded in 1086.[94] Seventeen people were assessed for the subsidy in 1327[95] and 34 for the poll tax in 1381.[96] There were said to be c. 54 communicants in 1551[97] and 14 households in 1563.[98] Thirty-eight families were enumerated in 1650[99] and c. 120 inhabitants in 30 houses about 1710.[1] About 1775 the population was estimated to have risen to 313[2] but it stood only at 210 in 1801. During the first half of the 19th century the population fluctuated but after 1861, when it stood at 216, it declined fairly steadily and there were only 131 people in 1931. The new parish of Eastleach formed in 1935 started with a population of over 400, which fell to 367 by 1951. After some recovery in the following decade it fell again to 320 by 1971.[3]

MANOR AND OTHER ESTATES. The manor of *EASTLEACH MARTIN* or *BOTHEROP* was apparently represented by the estate called Leach held by Drew son of Pons in 1086.[4] It passed to Drew's brother Richard who c. 1127 settled it on his wife Maud. Richard's son Walter,[5] sometimes called Walter de Clifford, granted the manor in 1144 to Gloucester Abbey in exchange for the manor of Glasbury (Brec.).[6] The abbey later received other lands in Eastleach Martin, including an estate at Coate granted by the brothers William and Walter Heyrun before 1179[7] and land in Fyfield granted by Felice, daughter of Osbert of Hailes, in the early 13th century.[8]

The manor was among the former abbey estates settled on the dean and chapter of Gloucester in 1541[9] and until the late 18th century it was held by lords farmers on leases for 3 lives; the dean and chapter's profits from the estate arose from the fines, assessed at $1\frac{1}{2}$ years' valuation in the 18th century, paid for the insertion of new lives into the leases.[10] In 1641 a lease was granted to Charles Trinder of Holwell (Oxon.) and William Blomer, the latter's right passing by 1649 to William Hancock of London and his son William. The whole of the estate was then included in the lease[11] but later one of the demesne farms, called Botherop farm, was leased separately while the lords farmers held the manorial rights and the other demesne farm, called Coate farm. Jane Trinder, widow, had a lease of the manor and Coate farm in 1681[12] and the estate remained in her family until 1717 when John Trinder of Westwell (Oxon.) sold it to Joseph Small. For one moiety of the estate Small was acting on behalf of Richard Cambridge of Pudhill, Woodchester, who sold his interest to Small in 1747.[13] Small (d. 1750) was succeeded by his son Viner Small[14] who in 1765 had to grant the estate to trustees for his creditors, from whom it was bought by Slade Nash of Martley (Worcs.) in 1767. The manor was held for Nash by two trustees,[15] from whom he himself took grants of the two large copyhold estates created after inclosure, Fyfield farm and Downs farm, and the reversion of the other copyholds.[16] Between 1768 and 1789 leases of the manor were made to John Baker and his son John, both of whom were evidently acting for Nash;[17] but those leases were for terms of years only and before 1798 the dean and chapter took the manorial rights into their own hands.[18]

Slade Nash remained in possession of his large copyhold estates and also of the lease of Coate farm.[19] He was succeeded at his death c. 1811 by his son William[20] who died before 1814 holding 1,012 a. in the parish.[21] The Nashes' leasehold and copyhold estates were eventually acquired by Michael Hicks Beach of Williamstrip (d. 1830). In 1858 his great-grandson Sir Michael Edward Hicks Beach sold his rights to the Ecclesiastical Commissioners,[22] who had succeeded the dean and chapter as lords of the manor in 1855.[23] Eastleach was among the estates returned to the dean and chapter at their re-endowment in 1866 but in 1894 it passed once more to the Ecclesiastical Commissioners,[24] whose successors the Church Commissioners sold the bulk of the estate to G. W. White in 1953. That land, comprising 844 a. based on Baxter's Farm (the former Fyfield Farm),[25] was sold by the White family in 1962 to Mr. H. E. Kinch, the owner in 1976.[26]

Coate Farm, standing west of the Leach, was recorded as one of the demesne farm-houses from

[92] Ibid. D 1740/T 41.
[93] Ibid. D 309/P 4.
[94] *Dom. Bk.* (Rec. Com.), i. 168v.
[95] *Glos. Subsidy Roll, 1327*, 14.
[96] E 179/113/35A rot. 2A; E 179/113/31A rot. 5.
[97] *E.H.R.* xix. 114.
[98] Bodl. MS. Rawl. C 790, f. 26.
[99] *Trans. B.G.A.S.* lxxxiii. 94.
[1] Atkyns, *Glos.* 423.
[2] Rudder, *Glos.* 432.
[3] *Census*, 1801–1971.
[4] *Dom. Bk.* (Rec. Com.), i. 168v.
[5] *Trans. B.G.A.S.* iv. 165; *Ancient Charters* (P.R.S. x), 20–1.
[6] *Hist. & Cart. Mon. Glouc.* i. 80, 311–13.
[7] Ibid. 75, 275–9.
[8] Ibid. 269–73.
[9] *L. & P. Hen. VIII*, xvi, p. 572.
[10] Glos. R.O., D 936/E 11, p. 33; cf. ibid. E 165.
[11] Ibid. D 1740/E 1, ff. 72–8v.
[12] Ibid. D 936/E 69.

[13] Ibid. D 309/T 2.
[14] Prob. 11/782 (P.C.C. 307 Greenly). A rather obscure note made in the par. reg. in Mar. 1749 about a stone vault at Cruel hill near Coate Mill probably refers to a burial vault built by Jos. Small for himself and his family (Glos. R.O., P 129/IN 1/1; cf. ibid. D 1740/T 35, lease 1754) and not, as has been stated, to remains of a medieval bldg.: e.g. *Trans. B.G.A.S.* xxii. 118.
[15] Glos. R.O., D 1740/T 34.
[16] Ibid. M 2.
[17] Ibid. D 936/E 69; cf. Rudder, *Glos.* 432; Rudge, *Hist. of Glos.* i. 254.
[18] Glos. R.O., D 1740/M 2.
[19] Ibid.; ibid. E 2, pp. 44–5.
[20] Ibid. M 2, T 38.
[21] Ibid. D 309/E 1.
[22] Ibid. D 1740/T 33.
[23] Kirby, *Cat. of Glouc. Dioc. Rec.* ii, p. xiii.
[24] Ibid. p. xiv; *Lond. Gaz.* 3 July 1866, pp. 3804–7.
[25] Glos. R.O., D 2582/10.
[26] Ex inf. Mr. Kinch.

1518[27] and it may be on the site of the capital messuage belonging to the Heyrun family's estate in the 12th century.[28] In 1649 it was a stone-built house containing hall, parlour, and kitchen, with chambers above and various out-buildings,[29] and it was presumably the house with 7 hearths occupied by William Trinder in 1672.[30] In 1831 the old farmhouse was in decay and used as labourers' cottages[31] and it was described as semi-derelict in 1962;[32] it had been restored by 1976. One wing appears to date from the 17th century. The place of Coate Farm as the chief house on the lord farmer's estate was taken by the New House (later called Fyfield House or Fyfield Manor) built c. 1720 by Joseph Small at the south of the Coate farm land, near to Southrop village. Both Small and his son lived at the New House[33] and it acquired the status of the manor-house.[34] It is a house of modest size, having a south front with a projecting centre of 3 bays with a gabled parapet; alterations made in the mid 20th century gave the front more symmetry.

The ancient site of the manor was by the church at *BOTHEROP FARM*, also called *BLOMERS FARM* from the family that had a lease of it with the demesne lands belonging in 1521.[35] In 1681 the dean and chapter leased the farm for 3 lives to William Dowdeswell of Pull Court, Bushley (Worcs.) and it remained in his family until after the death of his great-grandson William Dowdeswell in 1775,[36] when it included 739 a.[37] Later it was held by members of the Kimber family,[38] and in 1824 a lease was granted to Thomas Bendry who sold it to Thomas Clarke in 1830. In 1882 the estate was put up for sale after the death of H. J. Clarke[39] and by the early 20th century it was part of the Hatherop estate,[40] which retained the land in 1976. In 1649 Botherop Farm was stone-built with a hall, parlour, buttery, milk-house, wool-house, kitchen, and brewhouse on the ground floor, 4 chambers above, and extensive farm buildings.[41] It was evidently the house at Eastleach with 6 hearths in 1672.[42] The north part of the house apparently dates from a rebuilding in the 18th century and a large classical-style block was added in the early 19th.

A hide of land in Eastleach Martin was owned by Great Malvern Priory and evidently represented 4 of the 5 yardlands granted to it with the church by Richard son of Pons c. 1120,[43] and probably the hide that the priory confirmed to the church c. 1144.[44] In 1200, however, the parson of Eastleach, having originally claimed the hide in right of his church in free alms, confirmed it as the lay fee of the priory.[45] The estate, which became known as *PRIOR'S COATE*, was described as 4 yardlands in 1560 when it was granted to John Dodington and John Jackson; it descended with their manor in Eastleach Turville to become part of the Hatherop estate.[46] During the 16th and early 17th centuries, however, Prior's Coate was held by lessees who were also lessees of the Coate farm estate. That arrangement and the fact that the land of the two estates lay intermixed caused confusion, which was not satisfactorily resolved by the inclosure of that part of the parish, completed with Southrop in 1621. In 1633 the owner of Prior's Coate, John Blomer, complained that his land was indistinguishable from Coate farm and that the lessee had deliberately obscured his rights.[47] It seems, however, that a compact block of land north of the Coate farm land had been allotted for Prior's Coate. That land belonged to the Hatherop estate until 1773 when, under the Eastleach Turville inclosure, Sir John Webb exchanged it with the Revd. Benjamin Boyes for land in Eastleach Turville. Benjamin (d. 1814) was succeeded by his son Richard Edmund Boyes, who sold the estate, then comprising 102 a. farmed from a house called the Jostle (later Troutbeck Farm) in Eastleach Turville village, to Sir Michael Hicks Beach of Williamstrip in 1843.[48] Sir Michael Edward Hicks Beach sold it with his other land in the parish to the Ecclesiastical Commissioners in 1858.[49]

ECONOMIC HISTORY. In 1086 there were 4 plough-teams and 9 *servi* on the demesne of the estate of Drew son of Pons.[50] Gloucester Abbey's demesne estate comprised 3 plough-lands in 1291.[51] By the early 16th century the demesne was leased as two farms, Coate farm and Botherop farm.[52] In 1649 Coate farm comprised 261 a. of inclosed land and rights in certain meadows shared with Southrop manor, and Botherop farm comprised 875 a. (including 250 a. in the open fields) with pasture rights and rights in meadow land in Kempsford.[53] Sheep were naturally an important element in demesne farming. Gloucester Abbey's shepherd was mentioned in 1221[54] and the abbey still had its own flock in 1521 when a lease of Botherop farm reserved a sheep-house and part of the pasture land for the use of its shepherd.[55] In 1531, however, pasture for a demesne flock of 400 together with the sheep-house and the

[27] Glouc. Cath. Libr., Reg. Abb. Malvern, i, ff. 104v.–5.
[28] *Hist. & Cart. Mon. Glouc.* i. 75.
[29] Glos. R.O., D 1740/E 1, f. 72.
[30] E 179/247/14 rot. 4.
[31] Glos. R.O., D 936/E 238.
[32] Ibid. D 2582/10.
[33] Ibid. D 1740/T 41.   [34] Ibid. D 309/E 1, P 4.
[35] Glouc. Cath. Libr., Reg. Abb. Malvern, i, ff. 171v.–172.
[36] Glos. R.O., D 936/E 70; for the fam. see *V.C.H. Worcs.* iv. 47–8.
[37] Glos. R.O., D 936/E 165.
[38] Bigland, *Glos.* i. 545; Glos. R.O., D 309/P 4.
[39] Glos. Colln. RF 119.1.
[40] Cf. *Kelly's Dir. Glos.* (1902), 153.
[41] Glos. R.O., D 1740/E 1, f. 72v.
[42] E 179/247/14 rot. 4.

[43] B.L. Campb. Ch. xviii. 11.
[44] Ibid.; the hide was then described as in the field of Southrop, apparently because it lay W. of the Leach where the land of the two parishes was intermixed.
[45] C.P. 25(1)/73/1 no. 3.
[46] *Cal. Pat.* 1558–60, 466; Glos. R.O., D 540/T 6; E 4/1, 3.
[47] Glos. R.O., D 540/T 6; E 4/3; cf. below, p. 133.
[48] Glos. R.O., D 1740/T 37; and for Benjamin's death, ibid. P 180/IN 1/7.
[49] Ibid. D 1740/T 33.   [50] *Dom. Bk.* (Rec. Com.), i. 168v.
[51] *Tax. Eccl.* (Rec. Com.), 232.
[52] Glouc. Cath. Libr., Reg. Abb. Malvern, i, ff. 104v.–105, 171v.–172.
[53] Glos. R.O., D 1740/E 1, ff. 72–73v.
[54] *Pleas of the Crown for Glos.* ed. Maitland, p. 40.
[55] Glouc. Cath. Libr., Reg. Abb. Malvern, i, ff. 171v.–172.

shepherd's house was leased to William Blomer, tenant of Botherop farm.[56] In 1649 a 300-acre sheep-walk for pasturing a flock of that size belonged to the farm in severalty and it had another 150 a. of downland for a flock of 200 ewes; the farm's buildings included a wool-house and a sheep-house.[57] The Prior's Coate estate of Malvern Priory also had its sheep-house in the 16th century.[58]

The tenants on the estate of Drew son of Pons in 1086 were 15 *villani* and 4 bordars working 9 teams.[59] About 1267 the manor included 3 considerable freehold estates, one of a hide belonging to Hugh of Coate, one of 3 yardlands belonging to Sywat of Fifhide, and one of ½ hide belonging to the Heyrun family. There were also 6 yardland estates and 5 12-acre estates which were held for lives and though free of weekly labour-services still owed the other customary burdens. The customary tenants were 13 yardlanders, who owed 5 days' work each week, 20 bedrepes in the harvest, and the usual servile dues, 8 holders of 12-acre estates who owed 3 days' work each week in the harvest and 2 days each week during the rest of the year, and a holder of a messuage and curtilage who owed 1 day a week. The labour-services of the yardlanders included carrying to Gloucester 15 times in the year, and those of the lesser tenants sheep-washing and sheep-shearing. The yardland at Eastleach contained 32 a. in the 13th century[60] but was accounted as 34 a. in the 17th. In 1649 the tenants of the manor were 17 copyholders, the largest holding comprising 4 yardlands; the copies, for which arbitrary fines were levied, could be granted for 3 lives in possession and 3 in reversion.[61]

Two open fields, a north and south field, were recorded at Fyfield in the 13th century[62] and there were presumably then also the Upper and Lower (or North and South) Botherop fields mentioned in 1649. In 1753 Fyfield's two fields covered 470 a. in the south-east part of the parish and were larger than the two Botherop fields which lay in the centre of the parish. The north part of the parish was occupied by downland, a large part of it appropriated in severalty to Botherop farm while c. 150 a. were common,[63] stinted at 30 sheep to the yardland; there were also rights of common in the open fields but those too were limited by the right of the Botherop farm flock to be folded there overnight.[64] Another common of 56 a. lay in the southern tip of the parish and between it and the Leach was the main area of meadow land, a lot meadow containing 17 a.[65]

The land of Eastleach Martin lying west of the Leach and belonging to the Coate farm and Prior's Coate estates was inclosed with Southrop in the

early 17th century.[66] The remainder of the parish was inclosed in 1753 at the instigation of the lord farmer Viner Small, who shared the expense with William Dowdeswell, the lessee of Botherop farm. Small had acquired by purchase, or had allowed to fall in to the manor, 13 of the copyhold estates, for which he was awarded 451 a. including most of the common downland. Dowdeswell was allotted a considerable acreage, including the whole of Botherop Upper field, while the 5 surviving copyholders received a total of 241 a. and the Greenwood family received 122 a. for a freehold estate.[67] Small, whose estate was said to be doubled in value by the inclosure,[68] formed his allotments into two farms, the Downs farm with 110 a. and Fyfield farm with 359 a.[69] Dowdeswell's estate was also much increased in value and he complained when the fine for renewing his lease was increased proportionately by the dean and chapter and no allowance made for his trouble and expense in improving the estate.[70] Additional buildings for his estate were provided at Sheephouse Farm, probably the site of the ancient sheep-house of the estate.

Much of the former downland was evidently ploughed up after the inclosure[71] and three-quarters of the parish were said to be under the plough c. 1780.[72] Following the inclosure the usual sheep - and-corn husbandry of the Cotswolds was the practice in the parish. In 1866, when 1,693 a. were returned as arable and 247 a. as permanent grass, the main constituents in the rotation were wheat, barley, oats, beans, turnips, and grass-seeds.[73] In the early 1820s at least three parishioners worked as shepherds[74] and the flocks returned in 1866 totalled 1,313.[75] Arable farming was not apparently eroded to any significant extent in the later 19th century: in the returns for 1896 only wheat was much reduced in acreage compared with 1866 and oats and roots showed a considerable increase. The number of sheep returned was up to 2,176 in 1896 and more cattle, including dairy cows, were then kept.[76]

In spite of the reorganization at inclosure the tenant land remained copyhold, including the two new farms which Slade Nash, the tenant from 1767, let out on 21-year leases; the houses that had belonged to the estates dismembered to make the new farms were granted on separate copies.[77] In 1814 William Nash's estate included, besides the demesne farm of Coate with 207 a., Fyfield farm with 423 a. based on the farm-house on the north side of Fyfield hamlet, Warren farm (the former Downs farm) with 109 a. farmed from the house later called Tom Jolly's, Homeleaze farm with 80 a. in the detached part of the parish, two other farms of 90 a. and 55 a., and most of the cottages of the

---

[56] Ibid. ii, ff. 50–1.
[57] Glos. R.O., D 1740/E 1, ff. 72v.–73.
[58] Ibid. D 540/E 4/3.
[59] *Dom. Bk.* (Rec. Com.), i. 168v.
[60] *Hist. & Cart. Mon. Glouc.* iii. 187–92.
[61] Glos. R.O., D 1740/E 1, ff. 74–77v.
[62] *Hist. & Cart. Mon. Glouc.* i. 271–2.
[63] Glos. R.O., D 1740/E 1, ff. 73–4; M 2.
[64] Ibid. E 1, f. 77.
[65] Ibid. M 2; cf. ibid. D 309/P 3.
[66] See p. 133.

[67] Glos. R.O., D 936/L 19; D 1740/M 2.
[68] Ibid. D 936/E 11, p. 33.
[69] Ibid. L 19; D 1740/T 39.
[70] Ibid. D 936/E 165.
[71] Ibid. D 2318/III/10.
[72] Bigland, *Glos.* i. 545.
[73] M.A.F. 68/26/10.
[74] Glos. R.O., P 129/IN 1/3.
[75] M.A.F. 68/25/3.
[76] M.A.F. 68/1609/9.
[77] Ibid. D 1740/M 2, ct. 1767; D 2318/III/10.

parish.[78] Copyhold tenure was apparently extinguished by the Ecclesiastical Commissioners when they bought in the estate in 1858.[79] Subsequently most of the estate was let as two farms: Fyfield farm which included the former Warren farm land had 931 a. in 1867, and the Jostle farm, which comprised most of the land west of the river and was based on a farm-house in Eastleach Turville village, had 229 a.[80] The other farms in the late 19th century were Botherop farm, still held on leases for lives and containing 644 a. in 1882,[81] and Homeleaze farm, which had been sold to Lord de Mauley, owner of the Hatherop estate, in 1854 and had 172 a. in 1862, lying partly in Southrop and Eastleach Turville.[82] Fyfield farm (later called Baxter's farm) and Botherop farm, which was farmed with Manor farm in Eastleach Turville from c. 1930, remained the principal farms in the 20th century.[83] In 1976 the former covered 341 ha. (843 a.), used mainly for dairying and growing cereals.[84]

The mill recorded on the estate of Drew son of Pons in 1086[85] was apparently Coate mill on the Leach north-east of Coate Farm. It was evidently worked by Richard the miller whose pond on the river was mentioned in the early 13th century.[86] In 1529, when it was known as Hacker's mill, the mill was leased by Gloucester Abbey to the tenant of Coate farm[87] and it remained part of that estate in the time of the lords farmers. The buildings included a malt-house by 1730 when the mill was leased to a maltster.[88] The limited local trade of Coate mill was emphasized in a valuation of 1831, when it was a small building with 2 pairs of stones,[89] but it continued working for many years afterwards and was apparently rebuilt in the late 19th or early 20th century. From 1920 it was occupied by Robert Hinton who used it to make animal feed and built up a successful business, which was made a limited company in 1934. The water-wheel was replaced by diesel power before 1940, and the firm continued to use the mill until 1965 when it concentrated its operations at Southrop.[90] The buildings at Coate mill were used as cottages in 1976.

The parish has numbered few tradesmen among its inhabitants. In 1608 a weaver was the only tradesman recorded in Eastleach Martin[91] and in 1831 only 2 families in the parish were supported by trade.[92] One of the earliest tradesmen mentioned was Richard the slater c. 1267[93] and of the few recorded later slaters and masons were a high proportion. The parish had a mason, carpenter, and bootmaker in the mid 19th century but from about 1860 it appears to have been almost entirely devoid of tradesmen.[94]

LOCAL GOVERNMENT. A single roll for the court baron of Eastleach Martin manor survives for 1351[95] and there is also a court book for the period 1764–1824. After inclosure the court's business was almost exclusively concerned with the granting of copyholds, although it appointed a hayward in 1798.[96]

The accounts of the churchwardens survive from 1744[97] and there are also vestry minutes from 1843.[98] In the late 18th century and the beginning of the 19th expenditure on the poor was generally lower than for any other parish in the hundred; 16 people received permanent relief in 1803 and 15 in 1813.[99] In the 1820s and 1830s, however, expenditure rose above that of several of the other small parishes in the neighbourhood.[1] Eastleach Martin was one of the places where agricultural machinery was broken in the riots of 1830[2] and there was still unemployment among the labourers in 1844 when one farmer's plan to bring more of his land under the plough was welcomed.[3] Eastleach Martin became part of the Northleach union in 1836[4] and later formed a part of Northleach rural district.[5] In 1974 the combined parish of Eastleach was included in the new Cotswold district.

CHURCH. The church of Eastleach Martin was granted by the lord of the manor, Richard son of Pons, to Great Malvern Priory about 1120, and it was dedicated by the bishop of Worcester soon after Gloucester Abbey acquired the manor in 1144, full tithes and parochial rights being confirmed to it.[6] Licence to Great Malvern to appropriate the church was granted in 1346[7] but never acted upon and the living, for which a parson was recorded in 1200,[8] has remained a rectory. In 1385, however, and until the Dissolution an annual pension of 26s. 8d. was owed to the priory out of the rectory.[9] The advowson was exercised by the priory,[10] though in 1304 the bishop collated, claiming negligence on the part of the priory, and the clerk presented by the priory later that year was forced to withdraw his claim in return for an annual pension.[11] In 1554 Sir John Russell

[78] Ibid. D 309/E 1, P 4.
[79] Ibid. D 1740/T 33; cf. ibid. T 38, lease 1864.
[80] Glouc. Cath. Libr., bk. of maps of re-endowment ests. 1867; cf. Glos. R.O., D 1740/T 37.
[81] Glos. R.O., D 1388/SL 6, no. 109.   [82] Ibid. D 540/E 10.
[83] Kelly's Dir. Glos. (1931), 161.
[84] Ex. inf. Mr. Kinch.
[85] Dom. Bk. (Rec. Com.), i. 168v.
[86] Hist. & Cart. Mon. Glouc. i. 273–5.
[87] Glouc. Cath. Libr., Reg. Abb. Malvern, ii, ff. 14v.–15v.
[88] Glos. R.O., D 1740/T 35.   [89] Ibid. D 936/E 238.
[90] Ex inf. Mr. M. J. Hinton, managing director, R. Hinton & Sons, Yarnold & Gale Ltd.
[91] Smith, Men and Armour, 261.
[92] Census, 1831.
[93] Hist. & Cart. Mon. Glouc. iii. 190.
[94] Glos. R.O., P 129/IN 1/1–3; Kelly's Dir. Glos. (1856 and later edns.).

[95] Glos. R.O., D 936A/M 2.
[96] Ibid. D 1740/M 2.
[97] Ibid. P 129/CW 2/1.
[98] Ibid. VE 2/1.
[99] Poor Law Abstract, 1804, 172–3; 1818, 146–7.
[1] Poor Law Returns (1830–1), p. 67; (1835), p. 65.
[2] Glouc. Jnl. 8 Jan. 1831.
[3] Glos. R.O., D 2440, Eastleach Martin and Langford est. papers 1809–57.
[4] Poor Law Com. 2nd Rep. p. 523.
[5] Census, 1911.
[6] B.L. Campb. Ch. xviii. 11.
[7] Cal. Pat. 1345–8, 478.
[8] C.P. 25(1)/73/1 no. 3.
[9] Reg. Wakefeld, p. 142; Valor Eccl. (Rec. Com.), ii. 446.
[10] e.g. Reg. Bransford, p. 381; Reg. Wakefeld, p. 13; Worc. Episc. Reg., Reg. Carpenter, i, f. 149.
[11] Reg. Ginsborough, 82–3, 131.

presented under a grant from Malvern but later the advowson was exercised by the Crown.[12] The living was united with Eastleach Turville in 1871[13] and Southrop was added to the united benefice in 1930.[14]

The rector of Eastleach Martin apparently retained only one of the five yardlands that Richard son of Pons granted with the church c. 1120 but his glebe probably also included a yardland in Fyfield given to the church by Gloucester Abbey c. 1144.[15] In 1535 he had 48 a. of arable and a small close and he owned all the great and small tithes of the parish.[16] At inclosure in 1753 the rector was awarded 16 a. for his glebe and the tithes were commuted for an annual charge of £133 6s. 8d. apportioned among the occupiers of land in the parish.[17] The rectory house, standing by the Leach some way above the church, was rebuilt by Henry Smith, rector 1688–1702,[18] as a tall building, square on plan, with a hipped roof; various alterations and additions were made later, mainly in the early 19th century. It remained the residence of the incumbent after the formation of the united benefice. The living of Eastleach Martin was valued at £12 in 1291[19] and at a clear value of £9 7s. 2d. in 1535.[20] It was valued at £60 in 1650,[21] at about £80 c. 1710,[22] at about £140 in 1777,[23] and at £191 in 1856.[24]

In 1277 Henry, rector of Eastleach Martin, had leave of absence for 3 years' study[25] and in 1310 John Caleys had leave to be absent in the service of the bishop of Ely.[26] Baldwin Hyde, instituted in 1458,[27] also held a prebend at St. Mary's college in Hastings castle.[28] Richard Hill, who held the living by 1532,[29] was deprived in 1554 for being married. Rowland Searchfield, instituted rector in 1601,[30] was later bishop of Bristol.[31] John Wall, D.D., held the living from 1622[32] until the 1640s but was presumably deprived after the Civil War, part of which he had spent at the king's headquarters at Oxford.[33] In 1650 the cure was being served by John Soane.[34] Edward Beer was instituted in 1651 and, subscribing at the Restoration,[35] remained rector until his death in 1688.[36] William Asplin, author of theological works,[37] was rector 1733–58, holding the living with the vicarage of Horley and Hornton (Oxon.).[38] James Parsons, rector 1758–85, was also rector of Brimpsfield from 1777[39] and lived at Cirencester.[40] His successor the Hon. Francis Knollys was living

on his other benefice at Burford in 1786[41] and the next rector, Hugh Pollard Willoughby, 1827–58, was non-resident for part of his incumbency on the grounds of illness.[42] The parish was thus left in the charge of curates for many years. Benjamin Boyes, owner of an estate in the parish and Eastleach Turville,[43] was the curate in the 1770s and 1780s and also served Eastleach Turville,[44] as did the Tractarian leader John Keble between 1815 and 1825[45] and Rowland Helme Cooper, licensed in 1832. In 1851 Cooper held morning and evening services alternately in each church. He became rector of Eastleach Martin in 1858[46] and remained incumbent of the united benefice after 1871.[47] Joseph Henry Hodges, instituted in 1880, incurred debts which led to the sequestration of the living between 1885 and 1895; in 1894 he was living in London as chaplain to a refuge for the destitute while a curate-in-charge served Eastleach.[48]

The church at Eastleach Martin, recorded from c. 1120, was dedicated to SS. MICHAEL AND MARTIN c. 1144.[49] It is built of limestone rubble, partly rendered, with ashlar dressings, and comprises chancel, nave with north transept and south porch, and west tower. The nave of the 12th-century church survives and retains its original doorways, that on the north (now blocked) being plain in design and that on the south having two orders. The chancel was rebuilt in the early 13th century, when the chancel arch was renewed on the old responds. In the early 14th century the chancel was lengthened and the north transept, porch, and tower were added. The carving of the tracery and reveals of the transept windows is of high quality and the same craftsmen were probably responsible for the east window and for a new south window in the nave. Some minor alterations were made in the 15th century and included a new west window and possibly the tower buttresses and the innermost order to the south doorway.

In 1753 Viner Small was given licence to put up a seat in the north transept and the transept was appropriated to him and successive occupants of the manor estate.[50] A gallery at the west end of the nave was removed in 1864 when some slight restoration was carried out.[51] A more thorough restoration was done in 1886 when the nave was re-roofed.[52]

[12] Hockaday Abs. cxc.
[13] Ex inf. the diocesan registrar.
[14] Glouc. Dioc. Yr. Bk. (1976), 66–7.
[15] B.L. Campb. Ch. xviii. 11.
[16] Valor Eccl. (Rec. Com.), ii. 446. [17] Glos. R.O., D 1740/M 2.
[18] Atkyns, Glos. 423; Hockaday Abs. cxc.
[19] Tax. Eccl. (Rec. Com.), 222.
[20] Valor Eccl. (Rec. Com.), ii. 446.
[21] Trans. B.G.A.S. lxxxiii. 94.
[22] Atkyns, Glos. 422.
[23] Hockaday Abs. cxc.
[24] G.D.R. vol. 384, f. 98.
[25] Reg. Giffard, 92.
[26] Reg. Reynolds, 88.
[27] Worc. Episc. Reg., Reg. Carpenter, i, f. 149.
[28] Cal. Papal Regs. xi. 654.
[29] Hockaday Abs. xxv, 1532 subsidy, f. 11.
[30] Hockaday Abs. cxc.
[31] D.N.B.
[32] Hockaday Abs. cxc.
[33] C 3/449/81.

[34] Trans. B.G.A.S. lxxxiii. 94.
[35] Hockaday Abs. cxc.
[36] Bigland, Glos. i. 545.
[37] D.N.B.
[38] Hockaday Abs. cxc.
[39] Ibid.; cf. Glos. R.O., P 129/IN 1/1.
[40] G.D.R. vol. 319.   [41] Ibid. 382, f. 15.
[42] Hockaday Abs. cxc.
[43] Glos. R.O., D 1740/T 37.
[44] Ibid. P 129/IN 1/2; P 130/IN 1/3.
[45] D.N.B.; Glos. R.O., P 129/IN 1/3; P 130/IN 1/5.
[46] Hockaday Abs. cxc; H.O. 129/341/1/2/2.
[47] Clergy List (1872).
[48] Kelly's Dir. Glos. (1894), 147; G.D.R., D 16/3/13.
[49] B.L. Campb. Ch. xviii. 11. It has sometimes been called SS. Mary and Michael (Atkyns, Glos. 423), a dedication that was used occasionally for Great Malvern Priory, or St. Mary alone: G.D.R. vol. 285B, f. 35.
[50] Glos. R.O., D 1740/T 41; cf. ibid. T 34, lease 1775.
[51] Ibid. P 129/VE 2/1.
[52] Glos. Colln. R 119.1; Kelly's Dir. Glos. (1889), 763.

The nave retains some 16th- and 17th-century pews and the parish chest is dated 1662. The font has an octagonal bowl of the 15th century. In some of the windows are fragments of medieval glass.[53] Two of the three bells are of early date, one possibly of the late 14th century and another by the early-16th-century founder John White of Reading;[54] the other bell was recast by Abel Rudhall in 1739. There is also a sanctus bell of 1616.[55] The plate includes a chalice and paten cover given by the rector Henry Smith in 1689.[56] The base and part of the shaft of a medieval cross stand in the churchyard. The parish registers survive from 1538.[57]

NONCONFORMITY. Baptists registered William Eyles's house at Eastleach Martin in 1775 and their meetings, later held in William's barn, continued until at least 1811.[58] In 1825 it was said that there were no dissenting meetings in the parish[59] and none were recorded later.

EDUCATION. By 1818 day and Sunday schools had been started for teaching the children of Eastleach Martin and Eastleach Turville together.

The schools were in union with the National Society and were probably supported by the curate John Keble.[60] In 1826 a new day-school was started at Eastleach Martin, apparently for that parish alone; in 1833 it was supported by subscriptions and weekly pence and taught 31 children.[61] There was no secured schoolroom,[62] however, until 1863 when a National school to serve both Eastleaches was built in Eastleach Martin east of the church. It had an attendance of c. 75 at the outset,[63] rising to 90 by 1885.[64] In the early 20th century the attendance was c. 70[65] and in 1936 it was 59.[66] In 1974, when the number on the roll had fallen to 9, the school was closed and the children transferred to Southrop.[67]

CHARITIES FOR THE POOR. Henry Smith, rector of Eastleach Martin, left £50 in 1702, the profits to be given to 5 poor people on St. Thomas's day.[68] The principal was lent out to private individuals and the interest was apparently regularly distributed later.[69] In 1970 the charity was amalgamated with the Eastleach Turville charity of Thomas Howes and the joint income of c. £4 a year was allowed to accumulate to await particular cases of need.[70]

EASTLEACH TURVILLE

EASTLEACH TURVILLE was a parish on the river Leach 18.5 km. ENE. of Cirencester. It was roughly oblong in shape and comprised 2,630 a. (1,065 ha.) until 1883 when a triangular area of 154 a. on the northern boundary was transferred to it from Little Barrington.[71] That area was transferred again to the new parish of Barrington in 1935 when Eastleach Turville was amalgamated with Eastleach Martin to form the parish of Eastleach.[72] Eastleach Turville was designated merely as Leach at the time of the Domesday survey[73] and the prefix was not used consistently until after the Middle Ages. The parish was often called Leach (or Eastleach) St. Andrew in the Middle Ages[74] from the dedication of the church, but the form Leach Turville was recorded in 1316[75] and the family name, that of early-13th-century landowners, became the usual way of distinguishing the parish from its eastern neighbour.

The parish lies at between 90 and 150 m., the land

being formed mainly by Forest Marble but with the Great Oolite appearing in the Leach valley.[76] The river Leach, which bisects the parish from west to east before turning southwards to form part of the east boundary, had ceased to run in its upper part by 1976 but was fed from a series of springs below Sheep bridge, and near the village, where it was once exploited for watercress beds,[77] it remained a clear and copious stream. Before inclosure in 1773[78] the Leach provided the boundary between the common downland in the gently rolling north part of the parish and the open fields in the flatter south part. The scenery of the former downland area is varied by clumps of beech, some of them planted in the late 19th century.[79]

The Roman road called Akeman Street, recorded by that name in 1287[80] and mentioned as the foss way in 1691,[81] crosses the parish. In 1773 the stretch of the road in the parish was used as a route from

---

[53] Trans. B.G.A.S. xlvii. 311.
[54] Ibid. xx. 226, 229; xlii. 156.
[55] Glos. Ch. Bells, 46.
[56] Glos. Ch. Plate, 77.
[57] B. & G. Par. Rec. 132.
[58] Hockaday Abs. cxc.
[59] G.D.R. vol. 383, no. xcvi.
[60] Educ. of Poor Digest, 298.
[61] Educ. Enquiry Abstract, 314.
[62] Cf. Church School Inquiry, 1846–7, 8–9.
[63] Ed. 7/34/130.
[64] Kelly's Dir. Glos. (1885), 450.
[65] Public Elem. Schs. 1906, 184; Bd. of Educ., List 21, 1911 (H.M.S.O.), 161.
[66] Bd. of Educ., List 21, 1936, 120.
[67] Ex inf. county educ. dept.
[68] Bigland, Glos. i. 545; cf. Hockaday Abs. cxc.

[69] 20th Rep. Com. Char. 17–18.
[70] Char. Com. Reg.; ex inf. Mrs. M. G. Richardson, of Southrop.
[71] O.S. Area Bk. Eastleach Turville (1882); Little Barrington (1882); Census, 1891. This account was written in 1976.
[72] Census, 1931 (pt. ii).
[73] Dom. Bk. (Rec. Com.), i. 167v.
[74] e.g. Tax. Eccl. (Rec. Com.), 222; Reg. Bransford, pp. 184, 314; Hockaday Abs. cxc, 1554.
[75] Feud. Aids, ii. 272.
[76] Geol. Surv. Map 1", solid, sheet 34 (1857 edn.).
[77] O.S. Map 1/2,500, Glos. LIII. 2 (1899 edn.).
[78] Glos. R.O., D 181/VII/2.
[79] A. P. Ledger, 'Eastleach Martin and Eastleach Turville' (1974, TS. in Glos. R.O. Libr.), 73.
[80] E 315/38 no. 213.
[81] Glos. R.O., D 540/T 35.

Coln St. Aldwyns to Witney[82] but in 1976 the east part was no longer in use, though still clearly evident crossing the fields. The main thoroughfare in the parish has been the Fairford–Burford road, recorded from the late 13th century.[83] It crosses the Leach at Sheep bridge, which also gave access from the village and the south part of the parish to the downland of the north. From Sheep bridge a road formerly crossed the downs to Aldsworth.[84]

Eastleach Turville village grew up on a hill overlooking a crossing-point of the river Leach. Greenbury House at the end of the hill preserves a name that was recorded in 1303[85] and presumably refers to an earthwork built to command the crossing. The church was built below, close to the river, facing Eastleach Martin church; it now appears somewhat set apart from the main village, but there were formerly more cottages near the church.[86] The village developed in a haphazard manner along the hillside and was based loosely on the road leading from the crossing up to the Fairford–Burford road. The cottages were built around a series of pasture closes and small greens, much of the development apparently taking place in the late 17th and early 18th centuries. A recently-built cottage on the close called Playhay in the north-west part of the village was mentioned in 1702, and one built on land taken out of Boleshay, perhaps the later Boltshay at the south end of the village, was mentioned in 1713.[87] Also mentioned in 1713 were two cottages built on land taken out of Perryhay,[88] and land adjoining Crowhay was leased for building in 1725.[89] In 1713 11 tenants had cottages that were built on the manorial waste.[90] Several of the cottages date from the early 18th century, including some which stand on the lane running round the north side of the village, possibly that called Pudding Lane in 1709.[91] A larger number of cottages date from the later 18th century and early 19th, and others, on the main street, were built in the late 19th century by T. S. Bazley, the lord of the manor. One on the south side of the street is dated 1875 and there is a row by the turning to Southrop which incorporates a small clock-tower. A row of five alms-houses was built on the north side of the street by Bazley in 1871[92] but in 1976 was used as cottages. In the mid 20th century a small group of council houses was built on the north side of the village.

The three larger houses of the village are Manor Farm at the west end, which was rebuilt in 1872[93] but may be on the site of one of the old manorhouses, Troutbeck Farm (formerly the Jostle) by the river,[94] a late-17th-century farm-house extended in the early 19th, and Greenberry (or Greenbury) House, occupying a prominent position on the hill above the church. Greenberry House may be 17th-century in origin but it bears the date 1738 and the initials of Richard and Dinah Boyes, who apparently bought the house in that year. Richard (d. 1771)[95] was succeeded by his son Benjamin, curate of Eastleach,[96] and the house later passed, apparently by marriage, to John Fowler (d. 1864), a solicitor,[97] who may have built the tall Gothic-style wing added on the west in the 19th century. Some of the carved stonework of the new wing is said to have come from Tewkesbury Abbey. In 1955[98] the old south wing was modernized and refitted.

Before inclosure in 1773 the only dwelling outside the village appears to have been the house called Eastleach Grove which stood just south of the Leach close to the west boundary of the parish.[99] It was bought before 1740 by John Howe, later Lord Chedworth, whose family used it as a hunting box until 1774.[1] It has not been found recorded after the late 18th century. Following the inclosure three new farm-houses were built in outlying parts of the parish. Macaroni Farm by the road to Hatherop has sash windows while Macaroni Downs Farm and Eastleach Downs Farm on the former downland are in the traditional Cotswold style. Macaroni Downs was presumably a name used for the downland in the late 18th century, probably deriving, as has been suggested, from the 'macaronis', dandies of the period who affected Italian dress; some of them presumably frequented the race-course on the downs in Aldsworth parish.[2]

Fifty-two inhabitants of Eastleach Turville were recorded in 1086,[3] and 28 people, some of them from the part of Williamstrip which was linked tenurially to Eastleach, were assessed for the subsidy in 1327.[4] At least 44 people were assessed for the poll tax in 1381.[5] There were c. 50 communicants in the parish in 1551[6] and 81 in 1603,[7] and in 1650 39 families were enumerated.[8] About 1710 there were said to be 60 houses and c. 200 inhabitants[9] and a considerable expansion of the village was apparently then under way. About 1775 the population was estimated at near 400,[10] and it stood at 370 in 1801. Unusually, the first 30 years of the 19th century saw no rise in population and there was a fall between 1821 and

[82] Ibid. D 181/VII/2.
[83] E 315/32 no. 17.
[84] Glos. R.O., D 181/VII/2.
[85] E 315/35 no. 180.
[86] Ledger, 'Eastleach', 73.
[87] Glos. R.O., D 540/T 16; Q/RNc 1, p. 177; cf. ibid. D 540/E 10.
[88] Ibid. Q/RNc 1, p. 176.
[89] Ibid. D 540/T 15.
[90] Ibid. Q/RNc 1, p. 178.
[91] Ibid. D 540/T 49.
[92] W. Wilkinson, *Eng. Country Houses* (1875), plate 61.
[93] Ibid. plates 11–12.
[94] Glos. R.O., D 1740/T 37.
[95] Bigland, *Glos.* i. 548; Glos. R.O., D 1740/T 37, deed of sale 1738, which refers only to Collins's Ho. adjoining Greenbury Ho.

[96] Glos. R.O., D 1740/T 37; P 130/IN 1/3.
[97] H.O. 107/1969; *Kelly's Dir. Glos.* (1870), 542; inscrs. in ch.
[98] Ex inf. the owner, Mrs. E. M. Honour.
[99] Taylor, *Map of Glos.* (1777); cf. Glos. R.O., D 181/VII/2 (under allotment of roads).
[1] Glos. Colln. RF 120.1.
[2] Ledger, 'Eastleach', 75.
[3] *Dom. Bk.* (Rec. Com.), i. 163v.–4, 167v.
[4] *Glos. Subsidy Roll, 1327*, 14.
[5] E 179/113/35A rot. 2A; E 179/113/31A rot. 5, where the end of the list is lost.
[6] *E.H.R.* xix. 114.
[7] *Eccl. Misc.* 98.
[8] *Trans. B.G.A.S.* lxxxiii. 94.
[9] Atkyns, *Glos.* 624.
[10] Rudder, *Glos.* 434.

1831, but by 1841 an increase had begun and the population then stood at 421. It rose to 506 by 1861 and then a decline set in, quickening with the agricultural depression of the later years of the century. The population was down to 299 by 1901 but made some recovery by 1921 before falling once more to 294 at the time of the union with Eastleach Martin.[11]

The history of the parish has been dominated by the Hatherop estate, which included two of the manors from 1624 and almost the whole village and parish from the 1770s. T. S. Bazley (later Sir Thomas), owner of the estate from 1867, provided a number of improvements for the villagers, including a water-supply pumped up from the Leach to standpipes, street-lamps put up in 1897, and a reading-room[12] which remained in use as the village hall in 1976. A single innholder was recorded in the parish in 1755[13] and the Victoria inn, occupying a cottage on the north side of the main street, was recorded from 1856[14] and remained open in 1976.

MANORS AND OTHER ESTATES. At the time of the Conquest a five-hide estate at Eastleach Turville was held by Aldwin. In 1086 it was held by William Devereux as tenant under Roger de Lacy,[15] whose father Walter had probably acquired it from William FitzOsbern, earl of Hereford.[16] That part of Eastleach, comprising 2 fees in 1236 and 1½ fee in 1285, remained under the overlordship of the Lacy family as a member of their honor of Weobley.[17] After the death of Walter de Lacy in 1241[18] the overlordship passed to his granddaughter and coheir Margery de Lacy who married John de Verdun. John's son Tibbald de Verdun (d. 1309)[19] held it in 1285[20] and was succeeded by his son Tibbald (d. 1316),[21] whose daughter Joan, wife of Thomas de Furnivalle, Lord Furnivalle, was later awarded it in her share of her father's fees.[22] It passed in succession to Thomas's sons Thomas (d. 1365) and William (d. 1383) and then to William's daughter Joan, wife of Thomas de Neville.[23] In 1285 an intermediate lordship under Tibbald de Verdun was held by William Comyn and in a half fee of the 1½ Alina de Blakeford held a further lordship between Comyn and the tenants-in-demesne.[24] The intermediate lordship, which also extended over an associated Williamstrip estate and a group of Herefordshire manors, belonged to Richard Comyn and the heirs of

William Comyn in 1317[25] and to William Comyn of Putley (Herefs.) in 1355;[26] it was recorded until 1486.[27]

Another part of Eastleach Turville belonged originally to Fairford manor and apparently formed the two estates with 4 hides and 3 hides and 3 yardlands respectively which Queen Maud granted away from that manor before 1086 to John the chamberlain and one Baldwin.[28] The earls of Gloucester as overlords of Fairford later had rights over two estates in Eastleach. One was grouped with lands in Rodmarton and Woolford in Thornbury to form a fee called Chamberlains.[29] The other, assessed at one fee, was held by Herbert of St. Quintin c. 1205,[30] by William of St. Quintin in 1263,[31] by another Herbert of St. Quintin in 1285 and 1314,[32] and by Herbert's heirs in 1349,[33] though the St. Quintins only exercised an intermediate lordship over the tenants-in-demesne, a family surnamed Leach. After the death of Earl Gilbert de Clare in 1314 the two fees were apparently subject to some kind of partition between two of his sisters and coheirs, Margaret who married Hugh de Audley, successor to the earldom, and Eleanor who married the younger Hugh le Despenser.[34] Hugh de Audley was said to hold both fees in their entirety at his death in 1347,[35] but Despenser's son Hugh (d. 1349) was said to hold a moiety of the St. Quintins' fee[36] and the moiety passed to his nephew Edward le Despenser (d. 1375)[37] whose wife Elizabeth was granted it during the minority of his heir.[38] In 1386, however, Hugh Stafford, earl of Stafford, the grandson of Hugh de Audley, held the whole of both fees[39] and they subsequently descended with the earldom of Stafford.[40]

The manor of *EASTLEACH* held by William Devereux in 1086 belonged to Sibyl Devereux in 1100.[41] In Henry II's reign it was held by another William Devereux and later passed to his granddaughter, Cecily Devereux, who between 1201 and 1212 contested with Ralph and William of Lechlade ½ hide which had formed part of her mother's marriage settlement.[42] Cecily leased her land at Eastleach for 5 years to Bruern Abbey (Oxon.) in 1216,[43] and she evidently granted part of her manor in fee to Robert de Turville before 1220 when he called her to warrant 12 yardlands to him.[44] Cecily Devereux and Galiana de Turville shared the two fees held from the Lacys in 1243[45] and the latter was presumably Galiana, widow of Robert Gerbert, who

---

[11] *Census*, 1801–1931.   [12] Ledger, 'Eastleach', 71.
[13] Glos. R.O., Q/AV 2, rot. 3.
[14] *Kelly's Dir. Glos.* (1856), 283.
[15] *Dom. Bk.* (Rec. Com.), i. 167v.; cf. W. E. Wightman, *Lacy Fam. in Eng. and Normandy 1066–1194* (1966), 144, 154 n.
[16] Wightman, *Lacy Fam.* 125.
[17] *Bk. of Fees*, i. 439; *Feud. Aids*, ii. 237; cf. *Cal. Inq. p.m.* vi, p. 38.
[18] Wightman, *Lacy Fam.*, pedigree at end.
[19] For the Verduns, see *Complete Peerage*, xii (2), 248–52.
[20] *Feud. Aids*, ii. 237.
[21] *Cal. Inq. p.m.* vi, p. 38.
[22] Ibid. vii, pp. 496–7.
[23] *Complete Peerage*, v. 583–9; *Cal. Inq. p.m.* xv, p. 311.
[24] *Feud. Aids*, ii. 237.
[25] *Cal. Inq. p.m.* vi, p. 38.   [26] Ibid. x, p. 201.
[27] Ibid. *Hen. VII*, i, p. 34.
[28] *Dom. Bk.* (Rec. Com.), i. 163v.–4.

[29] *Earldom of Glouc. Charters*, ed. R. B. Patterson (Oxford, 1973), p. 57; *Cal. Inq. p.m.* iii, p. 250; cf. *Cal. Close*, 1402–5, 218. In most of the references to the fee Didmarton is wrongly substituted for Rodmarton.
[30] *Reg. Mon. Winch.* ii, pp. 522–3.
[31] *Close R.* 1261–4, 287.
[32] *Feud. Aids*, ii. 237; *Cal. Inq. p.m.* v, p. 341.
[33] *Cal. Inq. p.m.* ix, p. 336.
[34] *Complete Peerage*, v. 714.   [35] *Cal. Inq. p.m.* ix, p. 61.
[36] Ibid. p. 336; for the Despensers, see *Complete Peerage*, iv. 269–78.
[37] *Cal. Inq. p.m.* xiv, p. 223.   [38] *Cal. Close*, 1374–7, 307.
[39] *Cal. Inq. p.m.* xvi, p. 167; *Complete Peerage*, xii (1), 174–9.
[40] e.g. *Cal. Close*, 1402–5, 218–19.
[41] *Hist. & Cart. Mon. Glouc.* (Rolls Ser.), ii. 41.
[42] *Cur. Reg. R.* i. 401; vi. 144, 367.
[43] *Cat. Anct. D.* i, B 1228.
[44] *Cur. Reg. R.* ix. 102–3.   [45] *Bk. of Fees*, ii. 819.

granted a lease of 2 plough-lands at Eastleach in 1246.[46] Galiana's estate later passed to Bruern Abbey, probably by her gift,[47] and Bruern also received a yardland c. 1250 from Robert Devereux,[48] who had presumably succeeded to Cecily's estate. In 1285 the abbey answered for three-quarters of a fee held under Tibbald de Verdun and William Comyn while Robert Devereux answered for a quarter. The $\frac{1}{2}$ fee over which Alina de Blakeford then exercised a lordship was shared by Robert and Simon Moryn.[49]

Robert Devereux's manor had passed to John Devereux by 1303[50] and it later passed to Richard de Wydeslade and his wife Eleanor, from whom John's widow, Eve, was claiming dower rights in 1329.[51] Richard de Wydeslade (d. c. 1355) was succeeded by his son Stephen.[52] The estate passed to the Leversage family and later became known as LEVERSAGE'S MANOR.[53] It was held by Edmund Leversage in 1407 when he owed suit to the abbot of Bruern's court for part of it,[54] and Edmund's widow Elizabeth died seised of it in 1422. She was succeeded by her son Robert Leversage[55] (d. 1464), Robert by his son William[56] (d. 1485), and William by his son Edmund[57] (d. 1508). Edmund was succeeded by his posthumous son Robert[58] who died in 1549 when the manor passed to his son William,[59] who sold it in 1559 to James Morris of Little Faringdon (Berks.).[60] Morris also acquired Abbot's manor in Eastleach and the two manors passed to his son John, who sold them in 1595 to William Blomer of Hatherop.[61] They passed, probably before William's death in 1613,[62] to his younger son John,[63] who succeeded to the Hatherop estate in 1624. With that estate the two manors subsequently descended.[64]

During the 13th century Bruern Abbey acquired a considerable estate at Eastleach, later known as ABBOT'S MANOR.[65] Before 1205 William the chamberlain granted the abbey a hide of land in Eastleach,[66] evidently part of the estate granted by Queen Maud to John the chamberlain. The services due from that land and rent from other lands in Eastleach Turville featured in a settlement made between William the chamberlain and his son William in 1227,[67] but apart from Bruern Abbey the subsequent holders of the Eastleach part of the fee called Chamberlains are not known. As mentioned above Bruern also received the estate of Galiana de Turville and part of the estate of Robert Devereux and at the same period, the mid 13th century, it had other land by the gift of Adam of Bidford, also called

Adam the scribe.[68] In 1544 Abbot's manor was granted to Sir Ralph Warren and others[69] and Sir Ralph (d. by 1557) left it to his wife Joan with reversion to his son Richard.[70] By 1560 the manor was once more in the hands of the Crown which granted it to John Dodington and John Jackson[71] who transferred it immediately to John Dodmore. Dodmore sold it in 1561 to James Morris and it passed with Leversage's manor into the Hatherop estate.[72]

The manor at Eastleach held under the St. Quintins and the earls of Gloucester belonged c. 1205 to John of Leach who granted it in marriage with his daughter Ascelina to Richard of Leach (or Eastleach), reserving to himself for life the use of the manor-house and some land.[73] In 1243 the manor was held by Ralph of Leach,[74] who was also called Ralph Ascelin and was apparently the son of Richard and Ascelina. Ralph was succeeded in or soon after 1256 by his son Robert[75] and in 1285 and 1303 the manor was held by another Ralph of Leach.[76] John of Leach held it in 1346[77] and died before 1371[78] to be succeeded by his son William of Leach (fl. 1382).[79] William settled the manor, which became known as PAUNTON'S COURT, on the marriage of his daughter Joan to John Paunton. Joan was presumably the same who held the manor with her husband William Gore in 1405 and 1418 and it later belonged to William Paunton (fl. 1444), son of John and Joan.[80] In 1489 it belonged to another John Paunton who was dead by 1495 when his widow Elizabeth received the manor for life. In the same year Elizabeth leased her life-interest to Thomas Marston who also acquired from her son John Paunton a 41-year lease to run from after her death. In 1496, however, Thomas and John sold their rights to Robert Hawkins and Thomas Wodyngton, who bought out Hawkins. Wodyngton sold the manor in 1498 to Edmund Tame[81] and it descended with the Tame family's lands in Tetbury to the Verney family.[82] In 1604 Sir Richard Verney and Francis Verney sold the manor to William Guise of Elmore, who sold it the following year to Thomas Clutterbuck of King's Stanley.[83] Thomas (d. 1614) was succeeded by his son William (d. 1655),[84] who settled it on his wife Dorcas. On her death before 1668 it passed to their daughter Anne and her husband John Godsalve, a skinner of London. John and Anne were both dead by 1674 when their children sold the manor to John Blomer,[85] with whose Hatherop estate it then descended.

An estate held by a family called Beaufiz during

[46] C.P. 25(1)/74/17 no. 331.
[47] Glouc. Cath. Libr., Reg. Abb. Froucester B, pp. 185–6.
[48] Ciren. Cart. i, p. 221.
[49] Feud. Aids, ii. 237. [50] Ibid. 247.
[51] C.P. 40/279 rot. 325. [52] Cal. Inq. p.m. x, p. 201.
[53] Glos. R.O., Q/RNc i, p. 167.
[54] S.C. 2/175/33; cf. Ciren. Cart. ii, p. 631.
[55] C 139/5 no. 37. [56] C 140/14 no. 31.
[57] Cal. Inq. p.m. Hen. VII, i, p. 34.
[58] C 142/24 no. 53. [59] C 142/90 no. 110.
[60] Glos. R.O., D 540/T 5. [61] Ibid. T 4.
[62] Cf. C 142/347 no. 62. [63] Glos. R.O., D 540/E 4/3.
[64] See below.
[65] Glos. R.O., Q/RNc i, p. 167.
[66] Pipe R. 1205 (P.R.S. N.S. xix), 98; E 315/48 no. 201.
[67] C.P. 25(1)/73/7 no. 92.

[68] E 315/33 nos. 229–30; E 315/36 no. 231; E 315/46 nos. 229, 319; E 315/50 no. 199.
[69] L. & P. Hen. VIII, xxi (1), p. 351.
[70] Cal. Pat. 1555–7, 499–500. [71] Ibid. 1558–60, 466.
[72] Glos. R.O., D 540/T 4–6.
[73] Reg. Mon. Winch. ii, pp. 522–6. [74] Bk. of Fees, ii. 818.
[75] E 315/35 nos. 71, 249; E 315/37 no. 130.
[76] Feud. Aids, ii. 237, 247. [77] Ibid. 280.
[78] E 315/37 no. 231.
[79] E 315/45 no. 31; Cal. Inq. p.m. xvi, p. 167.
[80] B.L. Eg. Rolls 1902–3; Eg. Ch. 795.
[81] B.L. Eg. Ch. 796–805.
[82] V.C.H. Glos. xi. 265, where n.14 should read C.P. 40/1134 Carte rot. 2. [83] Glos. R.O., D 540/T 5.
[84] C 142/343 no. 169; V.C.H. Glos. x. 247.
[85] Glos. R.O., D 540/T 5.

the 13th century may have been a manor[86] and, if so, was possibly that sometimes known as *EASTLEACH TURVILLE FARM*, which Oliver Cromwell and his wife Elizabeth conveyed to Richard Keble and his son Richard in 1598.[87] It was presumably the son who died in 1636 when the manor, subject to dower rights of his wife Elizabeth, passed to his son Richard.[88] Another Richard Keble held the manor in 1706[89] and died before 1718 leaving two daughters and coheirs, Mary and Clara. The two daughters married two brothers, Joseph and Henry Bedwell, and Joseph released his share to Henry in 1722, retaining only a part of the manor-house. Henry died in 1750 and was succeeded by his son Henry who conveyed a moiety of the estate to his aunt Martha Bedwell in satisfaction of debts owed to her as mortgagee. In 1772 Henry and Martha sold the whole estate to Sir John Webb, owner of Hatherop.[90] In 1785 Sir John's estate in Eastleach Turville, comprising the four manors and the rectory estate, held under the dean and chapter of Gloucester, totalled 2,555 a.[91] In 1976 the owner of the Hatherop estate, Sir Thomas Bazley, who then lived in the parish at the house called Eastleach Folly, still owned almost the whole of the ancient parish of Eastleach Turville.[92]

The sites of the various manor-houses are difficult to identify because of the absorption of the manors into the Hatherop estate. A house called the old farm at the site of Abbot's manor was mentioned in 1771[93] and it or the site of Leversage's manor may be represented by Manor Farm on the west side of the village. The manor-house of the Paunton's Court manor was mentioned in 1674[94] but is not identified later. The manor-house of Eastleach Turville farm, which was the home of the Kebles in the 17th century, was described as partly new-built in 1722.[95]

The rectory of Eastleach Turville, formerly belonging to Tewkesbury Abbey, was granted in 1541 to the dean and chapter of Gloucester.[96] In the late 17th and early 18th centuries it was leased for lives to the Saunders family. After a partition between the two sons of Frances Saunders (d. 1704) it descended in two moieties, the owners of which sold them to Sir John Webb in 1771.[97] The rectory was valued at £100 c. 1710 when it included 83 a. of glebe,[98] and in 1769 the tithes alone were valued at £203.[99] The inclosure of 1773 allotted 442 a. for the rectory[1] and that estate continued in the tenure of Sir John Webb and his successors to Hatherop,[2] who bought the freehold from the Ecclesiastical Commissioners in

1857.[3] The house belonging to the rectory estate was described as formerly a considerable mansion in 1801, by which time it was ruinous and used as cottages.[4] It was pulled down c. 1875.[5]

ECONOMIC HISTORY. In 1086 the estates of William Devereux, John the chamberlain, and Baldwin each had 2 teams in demesne and the numbers of *servi* on the estates were 5, 13, and 5 respectively.[6] In 1291 Bruern Abbey's manor had 3 plough-lands in demesne,[7] but the general contraction of arable farming was evident by 1341 when 200 a. of the parish that had been under the plough 50 years earlier were no longer cultivated.[8] Sheep-farming probably became increasingly important; the inhabitants of the parish included 2 shepherds in 1381.[9] Bruern Abbey had had sheep-houses at Eastleach in the mid 13th century when it inclosed a piece of land adjoining them, having bought out the common pasture rights of other landholders,[10] and the abbey had a flock of at least 300 sheep in 1311.[11] Later the right to pasture a flock of 600, known as the ranging flock, was annexed to its manor.[12] The demesne of the manor was let at farm by 1407[13] but the abbey probably retained its flock and pasture rights in hand, for a later lease of the demesne, in 1454, reserved the use of a sheep-house.[14] The demesne of Leversage's manor apparently comprised 174 a. of arable in 1422.[15]

In the 18th century the Webbs' estate included two demesne farms called the old farm and the place farm. In 1717 the former, which evidently represented the demesne of Abbot's manor, comprised 12 yardlands, a few closes, the ranging flock, and pasture for another 660 sheep, while the latter, presumably the former demesne of Leversage's manor, contained 9¾ yardlands with pasture rights.[16] The yardland at Eastleach was estimated variously as 38 a. and 40 a.[17] In 1769 the old farm comprised 426 a. of land, the 1,260 sheep-pastures, and 72 beast-pastures, while the place farm comprised 307 a. of land, 585 sheep-pastures, and 64 beast-pastures.[18]

The tenants on William Devereux's estate in 1086 were 12 *villani* and 1 bordar with 5 plough-teams between them; John the chamberlain's estate had 9 *villani* and 4 bordars with 4 teams; and on Baldwin's estate there was a freeman with one team and 2 bordars.[19] Later evidence about the tenants is not forthcoming until 1415 when the Paunton's Court manor had 17 tenants, mostly yardlanders

[86] e.g. E 315/34 no. 117; E 315/35 no. 71; B.L. Eg. Ch. 786.
[87] *Trans. B.G.A.S.* xvii. 175.
[88] *Inq. p.m. Glos.* 1625–42, ii. 38–40.
[89] C.P. 25(2)/925/5 Anne Mich. no. 22.
[90] Glos. R.O., D 540/T 7–8; in the purchase, as in that of the rectory lease in 1771, Ant. Browne, Vct. Montagu, acted for Sir John.
[91] Ibid. E 6.
[92] Ex inf. Smith-Woolley & Co., Woodstock, agents to the Hatherop est.
[93] Glos. R.O., D 540/T 25; cf. ibid. T 49, lease 1707.
[94] Ibid. T 5.   [95] Ibid. T 8; E 179/247/14 rot. 4.
[96] *L. & P. Hen. VIII*, xvi, p. 572.
[97] Glos. R.O., D 540/T 9; and for Frances's death, inscr. in ch.
[98] Atkyns, *Glos.* 424.   [99] Glos. R.O., D 936/E 167.
[1] Ibid. D 181/VII/2.   [2] Ibid. D 936/E 71; D 1740/E 37.

[3] Ibid. D 1388/SL 4, no. 80.   [4] Ibid. D 936/E 167.
[5] Hockaday Abs. cxc, note under 1332.
[6] *Dom. Bk.* (Rec. Com.), i. 163v.–4, 167v.
[7] *Tax. Eccl.* (Rec. Com.), 236.
[8] *Inq. Non.* (Rec. Com.), 410.   [9] E 179/113/35A rot. 2A.
[10] E 315/35 no. 249; E 315/37 no. 27; E 315/44 no. 171.
[11] *Cal. Pat.* 1307–13, 372.
[12] Hockaday Abs. cxc, 1539; Glos. R.O., D 540/T 49, lease 1707.
[13] S.C. 2/175/33.
[14] E 315/43 no. 200.   [15] C 139/5 no. 37.
[16] Glos. R.O., Q/RNc 1, pp. 167–8; cf. ibid. D 540/T 19, lease 1705; T 49, lease 1707.
[17] Ibid. Q/RNc 1, pp. 172, 176; E 164/39 f. 7.
[18] Glos. R.O., D 936/E 167.
[19] *Dom. Bk.* (Rec. Com.), i. 163v.–4, 167v.

and half-yardlanders.[20] Abbot's manor had 6 copyhold tenants in the mid 16th century, three of them holding 1½-yardland estates.[21]

Later there was a proliferation of small farms and cottage-tenements, no doubt encouraged partly by the large area of common downland and the allotment of pasture rights to the tenants on a fairly generous scale. In 1717, apart from the occupants of the demesne farms, there were 36 tenants on the Webbs' estate, three of them copyholders and the rest on leases for lives. Two estates of 3½ yardlands and 81 a. respectively, both held by members of the Tuckwell family, were the largest; most of the others were small and several comprised only cottages. In addition there were 11 cottagers who were then excused any rent because of their poverty[22] but in 1723 a few pence in rent was being collected from some of them.[23] In 1769 the parish had a total of 16 landholders. The two big demesne farms and another of 309 a., which included most of the Bedwells' estate, were the largest; there was another of 276 a. and three others of 100–200 a.[24]

In the 13th century Eastleach had two open fields, the north field and the south field[25] (later sometimes called the east and west fields). By the 17th century there was also a third, smaller field called the Wood field, lying between Akeman Street and the Leach.[26] The three fields originally occupied the whole of the parish south of the Leach except for about 60 a. of meadow and pasture lying in ancient closes around the village.[27] Exchanges were made between the Webb and Bedwell estates to inclose part of Wood field in 1723[28] and the Webbs appear to have later made exchanges with some of their tenants,[29] but only about 100 a. had been taken out of the fields[30] by 1772 when 1,574 a. of open-field land remained. The common downland, north of the Leach, covered 865 a. in 1772[31] and provided extensive sheep pasture. Two shepherds were mentioned in 1701[32] and in 1769 the farms of the parish had pasture rights for a total of 3,266 sheep.[33]

The parish was inclosed by Act of Parliament in 1773. In preparation for the inclosure Sir John Webb bought out several of his leaseholders[34] as well as buying the Bedwells' estate and the lease of the rectory.[35] He was awarded 1,751 a. for his freehold and 442 a. for the rectory; 7 of his tenants received allotments of a few acres for their estates. There were also 5 freeholders, among whom only the Revd. Benjamin Boyes with an allotment of 98 a. was of any significance and most of his land was exchanged

with Sir John for some closes in the village and land in Eastleach Martin.[36]

After inclosure Webb's estate was formed into three big farms, comprising 838 a., 862 a., and 597 a. in 1785.[37] They presumably corresponded to those later called Eastleach farm, Macaroni Downs farm, and Macaroni farm. By 1862 Eastleach farm had been enlarged to 1,435 a., while Macaroni farm had 680 a., and Macaroni Downs farm 293 a. Eastleach farm then included the houses and buildings at Eastleach Downs Farm and Manor Farm[38] but later in the century it was farmed as two separate farms and the four farms remained the principal ones in the 20th century. In 1976 Manor farm, which included the Eastleach Martin land of the estate, had c. 652 ha. (c. 1,610 a.), Macaroni farm had c. 202 ha. (c. 500 a.), and the other two had c. 120–40 ha.; there were also two smallholdings on the estate.[39]

Much of the downs was ploughed up after the inclosure[40] and in the 19th century the bulk of the parish was farmed as arable. In 1866 2,027 a. were returned as arable and only 394 a. as permanent grass. Large flocks of sheep, returned at 2,422 in 1866, were still kept and were folded on the turnips and grass leys which with wheat, barley, oats, beans, and peas provided the constituents of the rotation;[41] the farmer at Manor farm was known as a breeder of Oxford Down sheep in 1889.[42] There was the usual shift from arable to grass in the late 19th century and early 20th, and in 1926 1,338 a. of arable and 1,046 a. of permanent grass were returned. Sheep-farming continued on a considerable scale but more cattle were also introduced: 529 cattle, including 108 cows in milk, were returned in 1926[43] compared with 171, including 17 in milk, in 1866.[44] By 1976, however, arable had re-asserted its importance and much of the land was under wheat and barley; sheep and beef cattle were raised in large numbers but there was no dairying.[45]

There is said to have once been a mill in the village on the Leach adjoining Troutbeck Farm.[46] It does not appear to have been in existence in 1823, however, when Coate mill in Eastleach Martin was described as the highest on the river.[47]

Although only a tailor was listed in 1608,[48] the parish was generally fairly well supplied with tradesmen. Nine families were supported by trade in 1831.[49] The recorded history of stone-working in the parish begins with Simon the mason who was mentioned in 1256,[50] and in the late 13th century and early 14th John the mason was one of the

[20] B.L. Eg. Roll 1902.
[21] E 164/39 f. 7.
[22] Glos. R.O., Q/RNc 1, pp. 168–78.
[23] Ibid. 2/4.
[24] Ibid. D 936/E 167.
[25] E 315/32 no. 17; E 315/44 no. 284.
[26] Glos. R.O., D 540/T 7, T 35.
[27] Ibid. D 936/E 165, E 167.
[28] Ibid. D 540/T 20.
[29] Ibid. T 25.
[30] Ibid. D 936/E 165.
[31] Ibid. E 167, inc. Act.
[32] Ibid. P 130/IN 1/1.
[33] Ibid. D 936/E 167.
[34] Ibid. D 540/T 25–6.
[35] Ibid. T 7, T 9.

[36] Ibid. D 181/VII/2; the allotments for the land recently bought by Webb were made to Vct. Montagu for him.
[37] Ibid. D 540/E 6.
[38] Ibid. E 10.
[39] Kelly's Dir. Glos. (1894 and later edns.); ex inf. Smith-Woolley & Co.
[40] Rudge, Hist. of Glos. i. 255.
[41] M.A.F. 68/25/3; M.A.F. 68/26/10.
[42] Kelly's Dir. Glos. (1889), 764.
[43] M.A.F. 68/3295/8.
[44] M.A.F. 68/25/3.
[45] Ex inf. Smith-Woolley & Co.; cf. Agric. Returns 1976.
[46] Ledger, 'Eastleach', 13.
[47] Glos. R.O., D 1388/SL 3, no. 24.
[48] Smith, Men and Armour, 262.
[49] Census, 1831.
[50] E 315/35 no. 71.

leading freeholders in the parish.[51] John was possibly the John the quarryman who was assessed for the subsidy in 1327.[52] Bruern Abbey's manor included a quarry for stone tiles in 1535,[53] and masons and slaters were recorded regularly between the mid 17th and mid 19th centuries.[54] Henry Newport, a smith mentioned in 1702,[55] was followed in the trade by others of the family until at least 1823.[56] A family called Clarke worked as carpenters or wheelwrights between 1669 and 1788,[57] and the village had several carpenters in the earlier 19th century, including one described in 1833 as a chair-mender.[58] A mercer and a weaver were recorded in 1725.[59] There were usually two or three shoemakers in the village in the later 19th century and that trade, together with those of blacksmith and carrier, survived into the 20th century. In the same period the village had several shopkeepers[60] and a single shop remained in 1976.

LOCAL GOVERNMENT.

LOCAL GOVERNMENT. The tenants of the part of Eastleach Turville that was held from the earls of Gloucester attended the view of frankpledge at Fairford.[61] Those from the part held under the Lacys and their successors attended Cirencester Abbey's view for the hundred; in the early 15th century a single tithingman represented the Eastleach tenants and those of 'Esthrop', presumably the associated Williamstrip estate.[62] In 1367 the abbot of Bruern claimed by royal charter the right to a gallows on his manor at Eastleach but the claim was contested by the abbot of Cirencester who caused the gallows to be broken down.[63] Manor court rolls of Abbot's manor survive for 1394, 1407–14, and 1428,[64] and of Paunton's Court manor for 1413–26.[65] Lady Webb was holding a court baron for her manors in 1702[66] and it presumably survived at least until the inclosure.

Of the records of parish government churchwardens' accounts survive from 1754[67] and vestry minutes from 1833.[68] The overseers were using 3 cottages to house paupers in 1785[69] and a parish surgeon was appointed in 1833.[70] The cost of poor-relief showed the usual rise in the late 18th century but in the early 19th, when the population remained static, the parish was able to contain the cost rather better than most of its neighbouring parishes. Fourteen people were receiving permanent relief in 1803 and 19 in 1813.[71] In 1836 Eastleach Turville became part of the Northleach union[72] and it remained in Northleach rural district[73] at the time of the union with Eastleach Martin.

CHURCH.

CHURCH. Eastleach Turville had a church by 1114 when Henry I confirmed it to Tewkesbury Abbey. The abbey had probably been granted it by Robert FitzHamon[74] (d. 1107), overlord of the part of Eastleach attached to Fairford, though a confirmation to the abbey in 1148 ascribed it to the gift of Robert, chaplain to FitzHamon.[75] The abbey, which had a quitclaim of the advowson from Ralph of Leach in 1287,[76] presented rectors to the church[77] until 1500 when it appropriated the rectory.[78] The parish was then served by curates provided by the lessees of the rectory estate[79] until 1762 when augmentation of the living raised its status to that of a perpetual curacy, and from that time the dean and chapter of Gloucester, owners of the rectory estate, kept the advowson in hand.[80] In 1871 the living was united with Eastleach Martin,[81] with which it had long been served, and Southrop was added to the united benefice in 1930.[82]

The rectory was valued at £11 in 1291. Tewkesbury Abbey then had a portion in the tithes worth £1 5s., Gloucester Abbey had a portion worth £1 6s. 8d., and Bruern Abbey had a portion in the small tithes worth 6s. 8d.[83] Gloucester's portion evidently represented part of the tithes from 'Leach in Hatherop' granted to it by the first William Devereux;[84] in a dispute with the rector in 1309 the abbey successfully laid claim to the corn tithes from the former estate of Galiana de Turville, then Bruern Abbey's, and to some of the small tithes from the estate of John Devereux.[85] A plough-land belonging to the rectory in 1291[86] was evidently retained by the rectors after the appropriation, as was the rectory house, which had been enlarged in 1332.[87]

After the appropriation the curates of Eastleach Turville received a stipend from the lessees of the rectory estate.[88] The stipend was £13 in 1650[89] but

[51] E 315/35 no. 180; E 315/44 no. 171; E 315/50 no. 199.
[52] Glos. Subsidy Roll, 1327, 14.
[53] Valor Eccl. (Rec. Com.), ii. 202.
[54] Glos. R.O., D 540/T 17, deed 1702; T 18, deed 1725; T 23, leases 1784, 1791; T 31, deed 1664; T 49, deed 1707; P 130/IN 1/5, 1814, 1823, 1839, 1841, 1855.
[55] Ibid. P 130/IN 1/1.
[56] Ibid. 5, 1816, 1823; D 540/T 22, deed 1784.
[57] Ibid. D 540/T 11, deed 1669; T 16, deed 1702; T 23, lease 1788; P 130/IN 1/1, burials 1701.
[58] Ibid. P 130/IN 1/5.   [59] Ibid. D 540/T 15.
[60] Ibid. P 130/IN 1/5; Kelly's Dir. Glos. (1856 and later edns.).
[61] Cal. Inq. p.m. v, p. 329; ix, p. 332; Glos. R.O., D 1728, Fairford ct. roll 1633.
[62] Ciren. Cart. ii, p. 622.
[63] Cal. Pat. 1367–70, 69.
[64] S.C. 2/175/32–5.   [65] B.L. Eg. Roll 1902.
[66] Glos. R.O., D 540/T 25.
[67] Ibid. P 130/CW 2/1.   [68] Ibid. VE 2/1.
[69] Ibid. D 540/E 6.   [70] Ibid. P 130/VE 2/1.
[71] Poor Law Abstract, 1804, 172–3; 1818, 146–7; Poor Law Returns (1830–1), p. 67; (1835), p. 65.

[72] Poor Law Com. 2nd Rep. p. 523.   [73] Census, 1911.
[74] Reg. Regum Anglo-Norm. ii, no. 1069.
[75] Earldom of Glouc. Charters, p. 161; but a confirmation to Tewkesbury in 1106 of churches formerly Rob. the chaplain's does not include Eastleach: Dugdale, Mon. ii. 66.
[76] C.P. 25(1)/75/34 no. 113.
[77] e.g. Reg. Sede Vacante, 86; Worc. Episc. Reg., Reg. Polton, ff. 5, 142.
[78] Cal. Pat. 1494–1509, 200.
[79] Glos. R.O., D 936/E 71.
[80] See below; Hockaday Abs. cxc. The living was sometimes called a vicarage in the early 19th cent.; Glos. R.O., D 1740/E 37.
[81] Ex inf. the diocesan registrar.
[82] Glouc. Dioc. Yr. Bk. (1976), 66.
[83] Tax. Eccl. (Rec. Com.), 222.
[84] Reg. Regum Anglo-Norm. ii, p. 410; cf. Hist. & Cart. Mon. Glouc. ii. 41.
[85] Glouc. Cath. Libr., Reg. Abb. Froucester B, pp. 184–8.
[86] Inq. Non. (Rec. Com.), 410.   [87] C 143/222/16.
[88] Glos. R.O., D 936/E 71; G.D.R. vol. 397, f. 85.
[89] Trans. B.G.A.S. lxxxiii. 94.

before 1735 the bishop intervened to raise it to £30.[90] Later, however, it fell to £20 and even that sum was not secured to the curates until 1762 when the lessees agreed to confirm it in response to a benefaction of £200 from Queen Anne's Bounty.[91] The lessee was paying a stipend of £21 in 1771 when the dean and chapter and Sir John Webb agreed to raise it to £30 to meet a further grant of £200 from the Bounty. That £200 was assigned to the rectory in return for settlement on the curate of an annual sum equal in value to 28 bushels of wheat, and that sum and the £30 were charged on the rectory estate by the inclosure award of 1772.[92] Further grants from the Bounty, each of £200, followed in 1817, 1825, and 1826[93] and the living was valued at £66 in 1856.[94] There was no residence for the curate in 1750[95] and 1811[96] and probably none was ever provided.

The medieval rectors of Eastleach included Thomas Shiredge who had leave of absence to study at Oxford in 1362.[97] Thomas Wates, who was found unable to repeat the commandments in 1551,[98] was among the curates who served, usually unsatisfactorily, in the 16th century. In 1572 the church lacked Erasmus's *Paraphrases* and the second volume of the homilies and no quarter sermons were preached,[99] and in 1576 the curate was found to have no licence.[1] William Bond in 1593, however, was found a sufficient scholar but not a preacher.[2] Later the poverty of the benefice and lack of a residence meant that the cure was usually served by incumbents or stipendiary clergy from neighbouring parishes. It was being served with Eastleach Martin in 1634 and 1650[3] and with Southrop in 1661 and 1676.[4] John Fifield, vicar of Coln St. Aldwyns, held the cure in 1743[5] and after the augmentation remained perpetual curate until his death in 1775. Under his successors, who included from 1775 to 1787 Hugh Price, also rector of Coln Rogers, and from 1807 Thomas Tracey Coxwell who was living with Sir George Berkeley's family as a tutor in 1813,[6] the cure was left to stipendiary curates who served it with Eastleach Martin. The stipendiary curate R. H. Cooper[7] became perpetual curate in 1851.[8]

The church of *ST. ANDREW*, which bore that dedication by 1282,[9] is built of limestone rubble with ashlar dressings and comprises chancel, nave with north transept and south porch, and west tower. The south wall of the nave is of the mid 12th century and the south doorway has two decorated orders

and a carved tympanum. The chancel arch, though partly renewed c. 1884,[10] is of the late 12th century, as is the north wall of the chancel; a blocked arch of two orders in the wall presumably opened into the chapel of Holy Trinity recorded in 1506.[11] The east wall of the chancel was rebuilt in the 13th century and has 3 lancets within an arcade. Later in the 13th century a north aisle with an arcade of 3 bays, the south porch, and the west tower were added. In the earlier 14th century the north transept, which formed an extension to the easternmost bay of the aisle, was added, and a window with flowing tracery in the south wall of the nave is of the same period.

The removal of the north aisle and the chancel chapel was possibly carried out in the 17th century; the transept walls were extended to meet the easternmost bay of the aisle arcade and the two other bays were blocked and given plain lights with a single mullion. The north and south walls of the chancel may have been altered at that time and repairs to the chancel were carried out in 1776 when the roof had apparently collapsed.[12] In 1825 the east and west walls of the transept were rebuilt, the old lights being reset.[13] The whole church was re-roofed with local elm, given by G. S. Bazley, in 1906.[14]

A window in the transept formerly depicted John of Leach, a priest, and a 14th-century tomb in its north wall had an effigy, perhaps also of one of the Leach family; both glass and effigy had been removed by the 1780s.[15] A reading desk dated 1632 and some old panels, built into the present pulpit, may have once formed part of an old 3-decker pulpit. Some of the pews also have old woodwork, probably from the earlier box-pews. The parish chest of 1678 survives. The carved shaft to the lectern came from Tewkesbury Abbey.[16] The two bells were recast by John Rudhall in 1789.[17] The plate includes a bell-shaped chalice of 1733.[18] In the churchyard is the base of a stone cross. The registers survive only from 1654 and the volume for 1748–79 has been lost.[19]

NONCONFORMITY. A barn in the village registered by a Lechlade minister in 1813 and houses registered in 1824 and 1827[20] were either for the use of Baptists[21] or of Primitive Methodists; the latter sect built a chapel near the western entrance to the village in 1829. In 1851 afternoon and evening congregations of 90 and 110 respectively were claimed for the chapel.[22] In 1870 it was no longer in

[90] G.D.R. vol. 397, f. 85; Hockaday Abs. cxc, 1735.
[91] Glos. R.O., D 936/E 167.
[92] Ibid.; cf. ibid. E 71, lease 1771.
[93] Hodgson, *Queen Anne's Bounty*, p. cclxxxiv.
[94] G.D.R. vol. 384, f. 89.
[95] Ibid. 381A, f. 84.
[96] Hockaday Abs. cxc, 1811.
[97] Worc. Episc. Reg., Reg. Barnet, f. 19.
[98] *E.H.R.* xix. 114.
[99] Hockaday Abs. cxc.
[1] Ibid. xlvii, 1576 visit. f. 61.
[2] Ibid. lii, 1593 state of clergy, f. 9.
[3] G.D.R. vol. 175; *Trans. B.G.A.S.* lxxxiii. 94.
[4] Hockaday Abs. lxviii, 1661 visit. f. 32; cxc, 1676.
[5] G.D.R. vol. 397, f. 85.
[6] Hockaday Abs. cxc; and for Price, cf. ibid. clxvi, 1775.

[7] See above.
[8] G.D.R. vol. 384, f. 89.
[9] *Reg. Giffard*, 166.
[10] Glos. R.O., P 130/VE 2/1.
[11] Hockaday Abs. cxc.
[12] Glos. R.O., D 936/E 165.
[13] Ibid. P 130/CW 2/1.
[14] Ibid. VE 2/1.
[15] Atkyns, *Glos.* 424; Bigland, *Glos.* i. 547.
[16] Glos. Colln. R 119.1, p. 18.
[17] *Glos. Ch. Bells*, 46; cf. Glos. R.O., P 130/CW 2/1.
[18] *Glos. Ch. Plate*, 78.
[19] *B. & G. Par. Rec.* 133.
[20] Hockaday Abs. cxc.
[21] G.D.R. vol. 383 no. xcvii.
[22] H.O. 129/341/1/3/4; O.S. Map 6″, Glos. LIII. NW. (1884 edn.).

use[23] but the congregation had been revived by 1885, when the village also had a Plymouth Brethren chapel.[24] The building of a new Primitive Methodist chapel in the south part of the village was begun in 1900 though it was not opened until 1909.[25] It had gone out of use by 1976 and had been converted to make a house.

EDUCATION. In 1818 there was a single school for both Eastleaches[26] but in 1833 Eastleach Turville had its own parish school, supported by subscriptions and school pence; 30 children attended and there were boys' and girls' Sunday schools associated with it. In the same year a small private school, teaching another 24 children, was started in the village.[27] In 1847 49 children attended the parish school and the schoolroom was said to be virtually secured.[28] The school presumably continued until 1863 when a new National school to serve both Eastleaches was built in Eastleach Martin.[29]

CHARITIES FOR THE POOR. Thomas Howes of Eastleach Turville (d. 1760), a sheep-dealer, left £25 to provide bread for 20 poor people on Easter Sunday.[30] The principal was put out on private security until 1827 when it was deposited in the Cirencester savings bank.[31] In 1970 the charity was amalgamated with the Smith charity for Eastleach Martin and the income was allowed to accumulate to await particular cases of need.[32]

FAIRFORD

FAIRFORD, which grew up at a crossing of the river Coln 13 km. east of Cirencester, was a market town and borough by the 12th century. The town, situated in an area of sheep-farming, prospered in the early 14th century and considerable growth followed a revival of its economic fortunes in the late 15th century. At that time John Tame, a sheep-farmer and wool-merchant, began rebuilding the church, which became famous for its stained-glass windows. Later the town, whose economy depended partly on its position on major routes, was primarily a market and shopping centre of local importance. In the 18th century there was some roadside building east and west of the town which in the 20th century was developed as a residential area.

The ancient parish, which covers 1,624 ha. (4,012 a.) and touches in the south-west the boundary of Wiltshire, is irregular in shape with a peninsulated part extending south-eastwards across flat meadow land near the river Coln. The river bisects the parish from north to south before turning south-eastwards to form part of the southern boundary. Elsewhere the boundaries follow the river and the Droitwich–Lechlade salt-way on part of the north, water-courses on the south and east, and field boundaries.[33] The land falls gently from 122 m. in the north to 76 m. in the south-east. The river valley lies on the Great Oolite or Forest Marble but elsewhere the land is formed by cornbrash or, in the south, by Oxford Clay.[34] The clay is overlaid in places by gravel beds which were used for road repairs by 1770[35] but large-scale excavation did not begin until 1944 when, during the construction of Fairford airfield in Kempsford, pits were opened by the Whelford road.[36]

The river divides the parish into the tithings of Milton End, to the west, and East End, in each of which there were open fields and commons until the inclosures of the 18th century. Meadow land and pasture is found by the river, especially in the south-eastern part, where agricultural land has disappeared since the mid 20th century to make way for the gravel workings which have changed the character of the countryside; some disused workings have been landscaped and adapted for recreation and nature conservation.[37] In the north Lea wood, the principal area of woodland, was mentioned in 1592[38] and covered 65 a. in 1840 when the parish had a total of 148 a. of woods,[39] including later-18th-century plantations in Fairford park immediately north of the town.[40] Andrew Barker inclosed the park around his new manor-house in the late 17th century,[41] and by 1763 an obelisk had been built to terminate a view from the house through a deer-park which had been created in the park-land to the north.[42] In the 1780s the park was landscaped by William Eames[43] and enlarged, after a road diversion east of the river,[44] to include c. 200 a.[45] In the deer-park, which covered 54 a. in 1840,[46] an American Air Force hospital was laid out during the Second World War, after which its buildings housed a centre for Polish refugees.[47] The huts had been demolished by 1977.

The Coln has long been known for its trout.[48] A

[23] Kelly's Dir. Glos. (1870), 541.
[24] Ibid. (1885), 450.
[25] Ledger, 'Eastleach', 77.
[26] Educ. of Poor Digest, 298.
[27] Educ. Enquiry Abstract, 314.
[28] Church School Inquiry, 1846–7, 8–9.
[29] See p. 61.
[30] Glos. R.O., P 130/CW 2/1.   [31] 20th Rep. Com. Char. 18.
[32] Char. Com. Reg.; ex inf. Mrs. M. G. Richardson, of Southrop.
[33] O.S. Area Bk. (1877); Census, 1971. This account was written in 1977.
[34] Geol. Surv. Map 1″, solid, sheet 34 (1857 edn.).
[35] Glos. R.O., D 1728, East End inc. award.

[36] Glos. Countryside, Feb.–Mar. 1961, 20; ex inf. Mrs. P. J. T. Moore, of Thornhill Waters, Fairford.
[37] Glos. Countryside, Feb.–Mar. 1961, 20–1; Glos. Life, Mar. 1970, 33.
[38] Glos. R.O., D 1728, wills.   [39] G.D.R., T 1/81.
[40] Brayley and Britton, Beauties of Eng. and Wales, v. 636.
[41] Glos. R.O., D 674B/P 53.
[42] Ibid. photocopy 64F; Hist. of Fairford Ch. (Ciren. 1763, printed S. Rudder), 16 n.
[43] Verey, Glos. i. 248.   [44] Glos. R.O., Q/SRh 1785 D.
[45] Bigland, Glos. i. 570.   [46] G.D.R., T 1/81.
[47] Glos. Countryside, Aug. 1958, 83; W.I. hist. of Fairford (1959, copy in Glos. Colln.), 2, 5.
[48] Hist. MSS. Com. 29, 13th Rep. II, Portland, ii, p. 299.

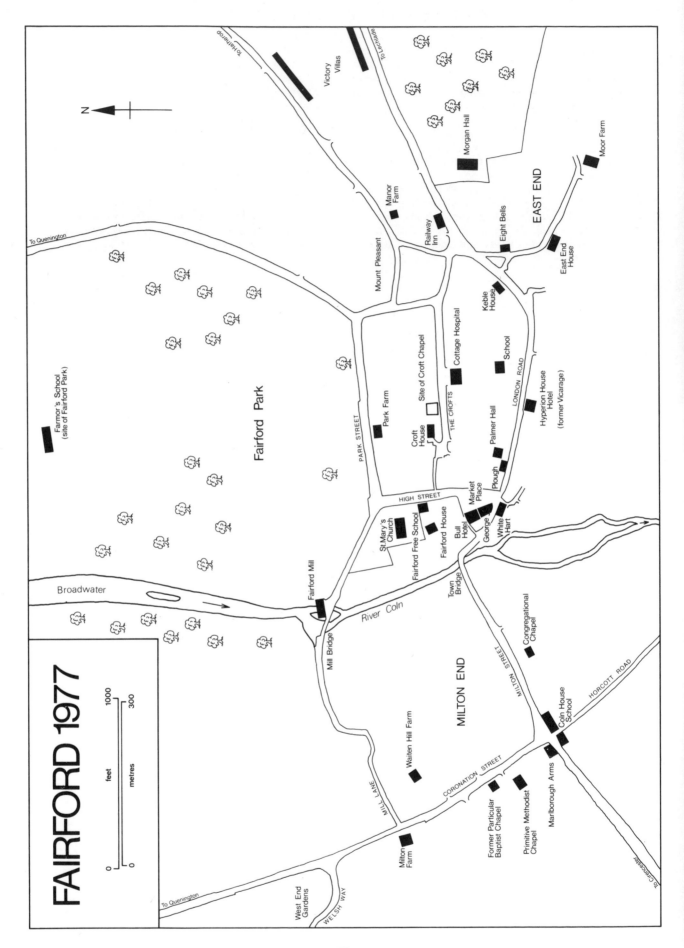

FAIRFORD 1977

N

feet 0 1000
metres 0 300

Broadwater

Fairford Park

Farmor's School
(site of Fairford Park)

Park Street

To Quenington

To Halfacrop

Victory Villas

Morgan Hall

Manor Farm

Mount Pleasant

Railway Inn

EAST END

Eight Bells

Moor Farm

East End House

To Lechlade

Keble House

Cottage Hospital

Site of Croft Chapel

Park Farm

Croft House

THE CROFTS

School

Palmer Hall

London Road

Hyperion House Hotel
(former Vicarage)

High Street

St. Mary's Church

Fairford Free School

Fairford House

Bull Hotel

Market Place

George

White Hart

Plough

Fairford Mill

Mill Bridge

River Coln

Town Bridge

Milton Street

MILTON END

Congregational Chapel

Walten Hill Farm

Mill Lane

Coln House School

Horcott Road

Coronation Street

Marlborough Arms

Former Particular Baptist Chapel

Primitive Methodist Chapel

Milton Farm

West End Gardens

Welsh Way

To Quenington

To Cirencester

70

fisherman lived in Fairford in 1381[49] and an emblem of that trade is carved on the church tower. The fishing rights were let with the demesne from the late 15th century[50] but in the early 17th Fairford inhabitants had by custom a day's fishing at Whitsuntide. In the mid 1680s Viscount Weymouth, lord of Kempsford manor, claimed fishing rights in the river south of the town.[51] By the late 17th century the course of the river above the town took in a mill leat.[52] In the 1780s that stretch of the river was made into a feature of the park, being formed into Broadwater, which contains two islands and is spanned at the southern end by an 18th-century bridge.[53] The cascade feeding it had been constructed by 1757.[54]

The parish is named from a ford across the Coln,[55] which was entered by the Cirencester–London road at a point where a bridge had been built by the late 12th century.[56] The bridge had 4 stone arches when Leland saw it in the early 1540s[57] but has been rebuilt several times.[58] The road, for the repair of which members of the Tame family made bequests in the late 15th and early 16th centuries,[59] was turnpiked between Cirencester and St. John's Bridge in Lechlade in 1727.[60] West of the Coln it was joined by the Gloucester–London road, which remained important in the late 18th century[61] and was known as the Welsh way from the Welsh drovers who followed it. An alternative way into the town from the Gloucester road was provided by Mill Lane which by the early 18th century crossed the river by a substantial bridge.[62] East of the river a road to Eastleach has disappeared since 1770 and the Quenington road[63] was diverted eastwards in 1785.[64]

The town has had an important role in servicing road traffic: in 1699 a stage-coach service to Gloucester called there and in 1713 Cirencester coaches.[65] The town had a post office by 1729. In 1754 a Fairford man started a fortnightly stage-waggon between Gloucester and Oxford with a weekly service to Gloucester, and in 1781 a firm of carriers was operating between Gloucester and London.[66] In the later 18th century coaches running between Cirencester and London and between Bristol and Oxford served the town, on which several other services were based.[67] In 1873 the East Gloucestershire Railway Co. opened a branch line from Witney (Oxon.)[68] to a terminus east of the town.[69] The line closed in 1962.[70]

Early evidence of settlement in the parish is provided by a pagan Saxon cemetery north-west of the town.[71] The town had evidently been established at the river crossing by the mid 9th century[72] and the lords of the land exploited the commercial possibilities offered by that position before a royal grant of markets in the early 12th century.[73] By the end of that century a borough had been laid out east of the crossing[74] where a triangular market-place stretched south of the main road, which originally ran due east from the bridge along the lane called the Crofts. The area of burgages, which numbered 68 in 1307,[75] included a street running ESE. from the southern apex of the market-place and the eastern side of High Street, which ran northwards from the market-place to the church. The market-place was reduced in size by infilling of the western and, to a much lesser degree, eastern parts; that may possibly have occurred during the economic revival of the town which had begun by the late 15th century. Later the main road was diverted along a road from the town bridge to the southern end of the market-place and the road further north disappeared. At the same time the road leading ESE., called Vicarage Street in 1662[76] and later London Road, replaced the Crofts as the through route. Park Street, running eastwards from the northern end of High Street and known until the late 19th century as Calcot Street,[77] was recorded in the later 16th century.[78]

The old part of the town appears to have been largely rebuilt in the later 18th century and the 19th but one house north of London Road contains a 14th-century doorway. South of the market-place the White Hart, with a jettied upper storey, probably dates from the 16th century or earlier. West of the market-place the George, which retains a timber-framed upper storey, is also of an early date, as is the Bull to the north, which has been enlarged at several rebuildings. East of the market-place is a substantial mid-18th-century house. The former free school is also of that date. Seven cottages north of Park Street, which were in ruins by 1754,[79] were evidently replaced by the row built at the end of the 18th century. In High Street, where one building retains some 17th-century features, are two buildings rebuilt in Gothic style, one as a police station and petty sessional court in 1860[80] and the other, a bank, in 1901.[81] Other 19th-century buildings include, south of London Road, the Hyperion House hotel, formerly the vicarage, and,

[49] E 179/113/35A rot. 2.
[50] Cal. Fine R. 1471–85, pp. 157–8; cf. L. & P. Hen. VIII, v, p. 484.   [51] Glos. R.O., D 1728, legal papers.
[52] Ibid. D 674B/P 53; cf. Atkyns, Glos. plate at pp. 430–1.
[53] Verey, Glos. i. 248; cf. Taylor, Map of Glos. (1777); O.S. Map 1", sheet 34 (1828 edn.).
[54] Travels of Dr. Ric. Pococke, ii (Camd. Soc. [N.S.], xliv), 253.
[55] P.N. Glos. (E.P.N.S.), i. 34.
[56] Earldom of Glouc. Charters, ed. R. B. Patterson (Oxford, 1973), pp. 31–2.   [57] Leland, Itin. ed. Toulmin Smith, i, 127–8.
[58] Atkyns, Glos. plate at pp. 430–1; Bodl. MS. Rawl. B. 323, f. 90v.
[59] Prob. 11/12 (P.C.C. 3 Moone); Prob. 11/25 (P.C.C. 17 Hogen); Prob. 11/30 (P.C.C. 45 Pynning).
[60] Cirencester Roads Act, 13 Geo. I, c. 11.
[61] Taylor, Map of Glos. (1777).
[62] Cf. Atkyns, Glos. plate at pp. 430–1.
[63] Glos. R.O., D 1728, East End inc. award.

[64] Ibid. Q/SRh 1785 D.   [65] Sherborne Mun. 117, 95.
[66] Glouc. Jnl. 30 Dec. 1729; 9 Apr. 1754; 5 Feb. 1781.
[67] Ibid. 15 May 1769; 20 Dec. 1784; Univ. Brit. Dir. iii (1794), 94.
[68] E. T. MacDermot, Hist. G.W.R. (1964 edn.), ii. 40.
[69] O.S. Map 6", Glos. LII. SE. (1886 edn.).
[70] Clinker's Reg. of Closed Stations (1971 edn.), 48.
[71] W. M. Wylie, Fairford Graves (Oxford, 1852).
[72] Finberg, Early Charters of W. Midlands, p. 49.
[73] B.L. Harl. MS. 7, f. 17v.
[74] Cf. Earldom of Glouc. Charters, pp. 31–2.
[75] Cal. Inq. p.m. iv, p. 321.
[76] Glos. R.O., D 1070/X/2, p. 14.
[77] O.S. Map 6", Glos. LII. SE. (1886, 1903 edns.).
[78] Glos. R.O., D 1728, Milton End deeds 1590–1760.
[79] Ibid. D 1388, case papers, Fairford chars.
[80] Ibid. D 1070/X/7; W. Beale, Hist. of Fairford (Ciren. 1862), 16: copy in Glos. Colln. 25130 (2).   [81] Date on bldg.

south of Park Street, Park Farm, near which some houses were built in 1977.

South of the church Fairford House, which has a main, late-18th-century, front of five bays with central entrance and pediment, was greatly extended to the north in the 19th century. The other principal residence is Croft House, north of the Crofts. The central portion of the south front is a small three-bay house of the 18th century. Additions made for Jonathan Wane by Richard Pace in 1826 consisted of single-storey bow-fronted extensions to the south elevation and a new staircase hall and service range behind.[82] The house, which was the home of the land-owner Robert S. Mawley in 1851,[83] passed to Albert Iles (d. 1863), whose wife Ellen[84] made it a private asylum for 4 women in 1866 when the bow-fronted extensions were raised to two storeys.[85] It reverted to domestic use in 1893.[86] In a corner of the extensive gardens is an early-18th-century gazebo.

West of the river in Milton End, which was mainly built as a roadside suburb of cottages and small houses in the 18th century and later,[87] the oldest surviving building is a 17th-century house with three gables north of Milton Street, the Cirencester road. A large green, which apparently extended along both sides of the Gloucester road and was part of the Milton End common, was probably used by the Welsh drovers to pasture their cattle when stopping at the town. The green, much of which was evidently inclosed by an agreement of 1633,[88] was represented in 1977 by a small area east of the road. Building along the road had begun by the later 18th century.[89] It was named Coronation Street to commemorate Queen Victoria's coronation.[90] Most buildings in Milton End date from the 19th or early 20th century, including a house in the western angle of Coronation Street and the Cirencester road which was restored by Arthur Charles King-Turner.[91] Milton House, north of Milton Street, which belonged under long lease to William Thomas (d. 1859), Baptist minister of Maiseyhampton,[92] and was the home of professional men in the later 19th century,[93] was demolished after 1911.[94] Milton Farm, north-west of Milton End, dating from a mid-19th-century rebuilding, may occupy the site of the house recorded at Middleton c. 1100.[95] Waiten Hill Farm east of Milton Farm was rebuilt in 1894.[96] At Westend Gardens, which in 1880 included several buildings by the Quenington road,[97] an ornamented wall around a late-19th-century house may have been reset.

East End, a scattered group of houses around a green on the London road, includes substantial dwellings built by the wealthier inhabitants in the 18th century. To the east Morgan Hall, presumably the messuage called Bakers in 1590 and part of a leasehold estate which passed to the Morgan family and was sold by Robert Morgan to John Raymond in 1775,[98] includes a long range with three short western wings. A block of four bays was added to the east in the later 18th century when the older part was refaced.[99] In 1838 the park east of the house, which was then called Fairford Lodge, included c. 16 a.[1] South of the green an early-17th-century house survives in the east wing of Eastend House, the main part of which, added in the late 18th century, has three storeys and a main, south front of three bays. In 1901 a two-storeyed range was added to the west of the main front and behind it a new entrance hall.[2] North of the London road Keble House was built with two storeys and attics in the later 18th century for the Keble family, prominent in local affairs since the late 15th century.[3] From the late 1780s it was the home of John Keble, vicar of Coln St. Aldwyns (d. 1835),[4] whose son John (1792–1866), the Tractarian, lived there in 1838.[5] The house, which by 1840 was occupied by Charles Cornwall, still belonged to the Keble family in 1977 when part was let as a separate dwelling. To the north-east is a substantial 17th-century house with 19th-century bay-windows. By 1840, when it was the Baptist manse, it had been replaced as a farm-house by the 19th-century Manor (formerly Eastend) Farm to the north-east.[6] In the south-east Moor (formerly Beaumoor) Farm dates from the 18th century. A row of cottages built south-west of Keble House c. 1870[7] has the same stucco decoration as cottages north of Eastend House, some of which were derelict in 1977. A pair of estate cottages east of the green was built in 1907.[8]

To the north the area between the Quenington and Hatherop roads was developed from the late 1780s. The main residence, Mount Pleasant House, is an early-19th-century building with a south front of three bays. The original plan of Mount Pleasant Buildings to the east, built in 1835 by Thomas Jones, contained 16 cottages in four identical rows, one of which was rebuilt as three dwellings after 1873.[9] Another row was derelict in 1977. In the 20th century the town has been enlarged considerably by council and private building, particularly between the London and Quenington roads in East End.

[82] Colvin, *Biog. Dict. of Eng. Architects*, 428; cf. Glos. R.O., D 1070/IX/8.
[83] H.O. 107/1968; for the Mawley fam., see below, pp. 122–3.
[84] Mon. in churchyard.
[85] Glos. R.O., D 1070/VII/78; cf. ibid. VI/2.
[86] Cf. *Kelly's Dir. Glos.* (1889), 769; (1894), 152.
[87] Cf. Bodl. MS. Rawl. B.323, f. 90v.; Taylor, *Map of Glos.* (1777).
[88] Glos. R.O., D 1728, Fairford ct. roll; cf. ibid. long leases 1811–83, deed 21 Oct. 1820.
[89] Taylor, *Map of Glos.* (1777). [90] W.I. hist. of Fairford, 2.
[91] Inits. on bldg.; cf. below. The date 1607 may refer to an earlier bldg.
[92] G.D.R., T 1/81; Glos. R.O., D 2823/1.
[93] *Kelly's Dir. Glos.* (1870), 546; (1879), 645; (1894), 152.
[94] Cf. Glos. R.O., SL 234. [95] B.L. Harl. MS. 7, f. 17v.
[96] Glos. R.O., D 1728, scheme 1893.

[97] Cf. O.S. Map 6", Glos. LII. SE. (1886 edn.).
[98] Glos. R.O., D 1728, abs. of title 1772; Morgan fam. est. deeds.
[99] The refacing may have been done for Chas. Tyrell Morgan who carried out improvements c. 1790: Bigland, *Glos.* i. 590.
[1] Glos. R.O., D 1070/IX/8; cf. O.S. Map 6", Glos. LII. SE. (1886 edn.).
[2] Ex inf. Mrs. R. A. Clark, of Eastend Ho.
[3] D.L. 29/638/10362 rot. 9; S.C. 12/8/4 rot. 10d.; Smith, *Men and Armour*, 263.
[4] Hockaday Abs. clxvii; G.D.R. vol. 319; vol. 382, f. 16; inscr. in ch.
[5] *D.N.B.*; Glos. R.O., D 1070/IX/8.
[6] G.D.R., T 1/81; cf. O.S. Map 6", Glos. LII. SE. (1886 edn.).
[7] Glos. R.O., D 1070/III/39, 41. [8] Date and inits. on bldg.
[9] Glos. R.O., D 1728, Mount Pleasant deeds; inscr. on a row of cottages.

Council building, which began there with Victory Villas, completed in 1921, included a few houses built in 1947 nearer the town centre south of London Road. Some private housing had been provided at Westend Gardens by 1959 when it was said that 145 houses had been built recently in the town.[10] In the 1960s private building continued in those three areas and bungalows were built south of Milton Farm.[11]

There are few outlying buildings. At Long Doles in the south-eastern corner of the parish a farmhouse, which had been built by 1770[12] and was part of the leasehold property of Joseph Cripps in 1840,[13] had been destroyed by fire by 1940.[14] The outbuildings of Leafield Farm in the northern part of the parish include a long, early-18th-century range of cartsheds and stables. South-west of the town at Burdocks a cottage, which in 1838 belonged to William Thomas's leasehold estate,[15] was replaced in 1911 by a large house, in the Queen Anne style, designed for J. Reade by Guy Dawber.[16]

In 1327 81 inhabitants were assessed for the subsidy[17] and in 1381 at least 180 for the poll tax.[18] In 1551 c. 260 communicants lived in the parish[19] and although in 1563 there were said to be only 27 households[20] there were 220 communicants in 1603[21] and 100 families in 1650.[22] The population rose from about 660 c. 1710[23] to about 1,200 by c. 1775.[24] From 1,326 in 1801 it increased to 1,859 by 1851 but then fell to 1,654 by 1861, mainly because of the removal of paupers from the private asylum, described below. It had dropped to 1,404 by 1901 and 1,347 by 1921. In 1951, following the establishment of the airfield in Kempsford and the refugee camp in Fairford park, it was at a peak of 2,439. After falling to 1,602 by 1961 it had risen to 1,804 by 1971.[25]

The parish maintained a fire-engine by 1783[26] and for the fire brigade formed in 1867 a second-hand machine was bought.[27] The town was lit by gas supplied by a company established in 1852[28] with works south of the market-place[29] and taken over by the Swindon company in the late 1930s.[30] Electricity, which had been brought to the town by

the Wessex Electricity Co. by 1931,[31] was not applied to street lighting until 1970.[32] A drainage system built for the town centre in 1905 was extended after the Second World War.[33] In 1920 the town's water-supply came from a spring at the old mill north-west of the church[34] but in 1943 the War Department built a new system from the cascade feeding Broadwater.[35] A cottage hospital which opened in 1867, north of Park Street,[36] moved in 1887 to a new brick building on the site of the parish workhouse in the Crofts.[37]

In 1419 an inn was recorded in Fairford[38] where there were at least three in 1563[39] although only two innkeepers were listed in 1608.[40] By the late 17th century road-traffic was served by several inns around the market-place.[41] Seven innkeepers were licensed in 1755[42] and twelve in 1891.[43] The Swan, which had opened on the east side of the market-place by 1610,[44] was used for assemblies[45] and was the calling place of Cirencester and Gloucester coaches.[46] It closed in the later 18th century after the property had been divided.[47] The Bull, which had opened by the mid 17th century[48] and was used for meetings by 1730, was the chief inn of the town by the late 18th century when it was used for concerts and petty sessions.[49] With the George, recorded from 1634,[50] it catered for coaches[51] and in both inns and in the White Hart, which had opened by 1750,[52] the parish officers met in the later 18th century.[53] The inns remained at the centre of the town's social life well into the 19th century, the George being used for balls in the early 1840s.[54] The Red Lion, north of Milton Street, was recorded in 1740[55] but had closed by 1767.[56] The sites of the Cross Keys, opened by 1754 and rebuilt as a private house c. 1790, and the Hare and Hounds, where the parish officers met from 1777, are not known.[57] East End had the Eight Bells by 1863.[58] The Bull Tap, south-east of the town bridge and recorded in 1876,[59] was rebuilt as a private house in the 1970s.[60] In 1977 the George, Bull, White Hart, and Eight Bells remained open with the Marlborough Arms in the Cirencester road, the Plough inn in London Road, and the Railway inn in East End.

---

[10] O.S. Map 6″, Glos. LII. SE. (1924 edn.); W.I. hist. of Fairford, 2, 6, street map.

[11] Cf. O.S. Map 6″, SU 19 NE. (1960 edn.).

[12] Glos. R.O., D 1728, East End inc. award.

[13] G.D.R., T 1/81; cf. Glos. R.O., D 1388/SL 3, no. 123.

[14] Ex inf. Mrs. Moore.

[15] Greenwood, Map of Glos. (1824); Glos. R.O., D 1070/IX/8; cf. ibid. D 1933.

[16] Verey, Glos. i. 248; Glos. Colln. prints, 122.15.

[17] Glos. Subsidy Roll, 1327, 13.

[18] E 179/113/31A rot. 5; E 179/113/35A rot. 2 and d.

[19] E.H.R. xix. 113.   [20] Bodl. MS. Rawl. C. 790, f. 26.

[21] Eccl. Misc. 94.   [22] Trans. B.G.A.S. lxxxiii. 94.

[23] Atkyns, Glos. 434.   [24] Rudder, Glos. 447.

[25] Census, 1801–1971; W.I. hist. of Fairford, 5.

[26] Glos. R.O., D 1070/IX/4.   [27] Ibid. VII/90.

[28] Kelly's Dir. Glos. (1856), 285; cf. Glos. R.O., D 1070/V/5–12.

[29] O.S. Map 6″, Glos. LII. SE. (1886 edn.).

[30] Cf. Kelly's Dir. Glos. (1935), 166; (1939), 166.

[31] Cf. ibid. (1931), 165.

[32] J. R. Lewis, in Cotswold Life, Nov. 1970, 29.

[33] Payne, Glos. Survey, 234.

[34] Richardson, Wells and Springs of Glos. 92.

[35] Payne, Glos. Survey, 215.

[36] Kelly's Dir. Glos. (1885), 445; O.S. Map 6″, Glos. LII. SE. (1886 edn.).

[37] Glos. R.O., D 1070/VII/91; cf. G.D.R., T 1/81; O.S. Map 6″, Glos. LII. SE. (1903 edn.).

[38] Reg. Sede Vacante, 400.   [39] Hockaday Abs. cxciv.

[40] Smith, Men and Armour, 263.

[41] Hist. MSS. Com. 29, 13th Rep. II, Portland, ii, p. 299.

[42] Glos. R.O., Q/AV 2, rot. 3.

[43] Licensed Houses in Glos. 1891, 71–2.

[44] Glos. R.O., D 1070/III/7.   [45] Cf. ibid. D 1728, legal papers.

[46] Sherborne Mun. 95, 117.   [47] Glos. R.O., D 1070/III/7.

[48] Ibid. D 1728, Fairford man. deeds.

[49] Glouc. Jnl. 19 May 1730; 3 Jan. 1785; Glos. R.O., Q/SM 3/1; Kelly's Dir. Glos. (1856), 285.

[50] Sherborne Mun. 114.   [51] Univ. Brit. Dir. iii (1794), 94.

[52] Glos. R.O., Q/RSf 2.   [53] Ibid. D 1070/IX/11.

[54] See below; Glos. R.O., photocopy 955.

[55] Glos. R.O., D 1070/IX/10.

[56] Ibid. D 1728, Milton End inc. award; D 1437, Kingsley fam., deeds 1792–1823, deed 22 Oct. 1792.

[57] Ibid. D 182/III/113; D 1070/IX/11.

[58] Hist. of Fairford Ch. (1863), 13: copy in Glos. Colln. 25130 (3).

[59] O.S. Map 1/2,500, Glos. LII. 12 (1st edn.).

[60] Cf. Cotswold Life, Nov. 1970, 31.

Parish friendly societies were recorded between 1750 and 1906.[61] A mechanics' institute with reading-rooms, founded by 1856, has not been traced after 1863[62] but in the late 1930s there was a reading-room, situated next to the George.[63] In the mid 19th century Croft Hall was built south of the Crofts for public meetings[64] but in the early 20th it became a private house.[65] Another building at the west end of the town was used for concerts at the end of the 19th century.[66] Palmer Hall, the gift of Col. A. J. Palmer, opened in London Road in 1936 and became the chief centre for social events.[67] There were several printers in the town in the later 19th century[68] and in 1877 the *Fairford Herald* was being published.[69]

An annual carnival, inaugurated in the 1890s to raise money for the cottage hospital,[70] was held until c. 1936.[71] By the late 1960s a traction engine rally had been started.[72] A cricket club had been formed by 1902 with grounds in the park at the eastern end of Park Street,[73] and a bowling club by 1935 with a green east of Eastend House.[74] Fishing, sailing, and water-skiing clubs made use of the old gravel pits in 1977.

Alexander Iles, who was caring for insane people by 1821, founded the Retreat, a private asylum in Milton End, the following year.[75] It was extended in 1829 when it had 20 patients and the number increased considerably, mainly by the admission of paupers, some of whom were employed on the Iles family's farm or in gardening or housework.[76] There were 187 patients in 1851,[77] but 104 were transferred to the Wiltshire and Worcestershire county asylums the following year and 21 to the Gloucestershire asylum in 1859. The Retreat, which had 42 patients in 1872,[78] was sold to A. C. King-Turner in 1901[79] and closed c. 1944.[80] The buildings housed a riding school until bought by the county council, which in 1949 opened Coln House School there for educationally subnormal children.[81]

Royal visitors to Fairford have included Edward I in 1276[82] and Henry VIII in 1520.[83] In 1830 agricultural labourers rioting in the surrounding countryside destroyed threshing-machines on the premises of two Fairford machine-makers.[84]

The politician Wills Hill, earl of Hillsborough (1718–93), was born at Fairford and took the name of the town for his viscounty in 1772.[85] Also born in Fairford were the missionaries John Thomas (1757–1801) and Abraham Cowley (1816–?87).[86]

MANORS AND OTHER ESTATES. Gloucester Abbey apparently had an estate at Fairford when it granted ten 'cassati' of land there to Burgred, king of the Mercians 852–74, in return for certain liberties.[87] Before the Conquest the manor of *FAIRFORD*, which comprised 21 hides, including land in Eastleach Turville, was held by Brictric son of Algar. It was granted to the Conqueror's queen Maud, at whose death in 1083 it passed to the Crown, from whom the Fairford land was held by Humphrey in 1086.[88] The manor, which had been granted to Robert FitzHamon by 1100[89] and was assessed at 1½ knight's fee in the early 14th century,[90] descended with Tewkesbury manor as part of the honor of Gloucester until 1314,[91] except that Hawise, widow of William, earl of Gloucester (d. 1183), retained rights in Fairford where she made a grant of a burgage.[92]

Fairford had passed to Hugh le Despenser in right of his wife Eleanor, sister and coheir of Gilbert de Clare, earl of Gloucester (d. 1314),[93] by 1320 when they granted the manor to the elder Hugh le Despenser.[94] In 1327 the Crown granted it to Alice, widow of Edmund, earl of Arundel, for her maintenance, but it was restored to Eleanor the following year.[95] She retained it until her death in 1337 and her son and heir Hugh le Despenser,[96] Lord le Despenser (d. 1349), was succeeded by his nephew Edward le Despenser, a minor.[97] Edward died in 1375[98] and the manor was held in dower by his wife Elizabeth[99] (d. 1409). Her grandson Richard le Despenser died in 1414 leaving as his heir his sister Isabel, who married first Richard de Beauchamp, earl of Worcester, and second Richard de Beauchamp, earl of Warwick (d. 1439).[1] She settled the manor on feoffees before her death later in 1439 when she was succeeded by her son Henry, earl of Warwick.[2] Henry, created duke of Warwick in 1445, died the

[61] Glos. R.O., Q/RZ 1; F.S. 2/3 nos. 24, 55, 234, 326, 464; F.S. 4/12 no. 549.
[62] *Kelly's Dir. Glos.* (1856), 285; (1863), 266.
[63] Ibid. (1935), 166; (1939), 168; *Cotswold Life*, Nov. 1970, 31.
[64] Beale, *Hist. of Fairford*, 16; O.S. Map 6″, Glos. LII. SE. (1886 edn.).
[65] Cf. Glos. R.O., D 1904.
[66] O.S. Map 1/2,500, Glos. LII. 12 (1903 edn.); *Kelly's Dir. Glos.* (1894), 152; (1902), 158.
[67] *Kelly's Dir. Glos.* (1939), 167; date on bldg.
[68] Glos. Colln. RX 130.2; *Cat. of Glos. Colln.* p. 671.
[69] Glos. R.O., D 1070/IX/5.
[70] *Cotswold Life*, Nov. 1970, 31; cf. Glos. Colln. R 130.18.
[71] *Glos. Life*, Mar. 1970, 33.
[72] *Cotswold Life*, Nov. 1969, 19; Oct. 1974, 37.
[73] *Kelly's Dir. Glos.* (1902), 159; O.S. Map 6″, Glos. LII. SE. (1924 edn.).
[74] *Kelly's Dir. Glos.* (1935), 166.
[75] Par. reg. 1813–54, entry for 1821; Glos. R.O., Q/AL 41/1; D 1070/VII/76; G.D.R., T 1/81.
[76] Glos. R.O., D 1070/VII/76–7.
[77] H.O. 107/1968.
[78] Glos. R.O., D 1070/VII/78.
[79] Ibid. DC/E 91; *Kelly's Dir. Glos.* (1902 and later edns.).

[80] Glos. R.O., Q/AL 51.
[81] Ex inf. the headmaster.
[82] *Sel. Cases in K.B.* (Selden Soc. lxxiv), p. xcvi.
[83] *L. & P. Hen. VIII*, iii (2), p. 1542; *Jnl. Brit. Arch. Assoc.* [1st ser.] xxvii. 32–3.
[84] *Glouc. Jnl.* 4 Dec. 1830; 8 Jan. 1831.
[85] *D.N.B.*; Rudder, *Glos.* 442.
[86] Glos. R.O., D 2864; cf. *Cat. of Glos. Colln.* pp. 924, 1006.
[87] Finberg, *Early Charters of W. Midlands*, pp. 49, 162 n.
[88] *Dom. Bk.* (Rec. Com.), i. 163v.–164.
[89] Cf. Dugdale, *Mon.* ii. 65.
[90] *Feud. Aids*, ii. 247, 280.
[91] *V.C.H. Glos.* viii. 131; cf. *Pipe R.* 1200 (P.R.S. N.S. xii), 127; *Rot. Litt. Claus.* (Rec. Com.), i. 209.
[92] *Earldom of Glouc. Charters*, pp. 31–2.
[93] *Cal. Inq. p.m.* v, p. 326.
[94] *Cal. Pat.* 1317–21, 511, 518.
[95] Ibid. 1327–30, 42, 271.
[96] *Cal. Inq. p.m.* viii, pp. 78–9.
[97] Ibid. ix, pp. 328, 332.
[98] Ibid. xiv, pp. 219–20.
[99] *Cal. Close*, 1374–7, 305–6; cf. *Feud. Aids*, ii. 300.
[1] *Complete Peerage*, iv. 277–8, 282.
[2] C 139/96 no. 49.

following year and Fairford passed with the earldom to his daughter Anne[3] (d. 1449) and then to his sister Anne. After the death of the elder Anne's husband Richard Neville, earl of Warwick, in 1471, Fairford was allotted to George, duke of Clarence, who had married Isabel, one of Warwick's daughters and coheirs. He forfeited his lands upon attainder in 1478[4] and, as his son and heir Edward was a minor, the Crown leased the demesne the following year to John Twyniho and his son-in-law John Tame.[5]

John Tame (d. 1500) continued to farm the demesne after Henry VII's accession[6] when the manor was restored to Anne, dowager countess of Warwick, who made it over to the Crown. She regained some rights from 1489 until her death in 1492.[7] In 1532 John Tame's son Sir Edmund secured a lease of the demesne for 21 years[8] and after his death in 1534 his wife Elizabeth assigned it to his son Edmund,[9] who became a knight and died in 1544. The younger Sir Edmund's widow Catherine[10] married Walter Buckler and in 1547 the Crown granted them the manor in fee as part of an exchange.[11] Walter, later knighted and a privy councillor,[12] was dead by 1554 when Catherine settled the manor on herself and Roger Lygon, her third husband, and granted the reversionary right to her brother Sir Walter Dennis and his heirs.[13] Roger survived Catherine (fl. 1578)[14] and the manor had passed to Sir Walter's grandson Walter Dennis by 1587 when it was settled on his marriage to Alice Grenville. They quitclaimed it in 1590 to Sir Henry Unton and John Croke who sold it the following year to Sir John Tracy of Toddington.[15] Sir John was succeeded later in 1591 by his son John, who became a knight and by 1631 had made over the land to his son Sir Robert.[16] Sir John, who retained the manorial rights,[17] was created Viscount Tracy of Rathcoole in 1643 but his estates were sequestered the following year. Sir Robert, his heir,[18] as a result of a debt incurred for delinquency, sold the manor in 1650 to Andrew Barker.[19]

Andrew (d. 1700)[20] was succeeded by his son Samuel[21] who died in 1708 leaving two daughters, Elizabeth (d. 1727) and Esther. Esther, who married James Lambe of Hackney (Mdx.)[22] (d. 1761),[23] left the estate at her death in 1789 to her nephew John Raymond on condition that he took the additional name of Barker. John (d. 1827) was succeeded by his son Daniel Raymond-Barker who died later that year leaving as his heir his son John Raymond Raymond-Barker (d. 1888). His son Percy Fitzhardinge Raymond-Barker (d. 1895) was succeeded by his son Reginald,[24] whose estate covered over 3,157 a. in 1914.[25] In 1945 his representatives sold the estate of c. 2,400 a. to Ernest Cook who included it in the endowments of the Ernest Cook Trust, an educational charity which he established in 1952. In 1977 the trust owned c. 1,320 ha. (c. 3,263 a.) in Fairford and parishes to the north.[26]

Richard Neville, earl of Warwick (d. 1471), is said to have had a manor-house called Warwick Court north of the church.[27] John Tame and his son Edmund rebuilt the house, which apparently had ranges west and south-west of the church.[28] In 1520 Henry VIII visited the house[29] which was the home of Edmund's wife Elizabeth (d. 1545)[30] and possibly of Sir Robert Tracy in the 1630s.[31] It was partly demolished in the later 17th century.[32] Part called the Old Court, north of the church, included stables in the mid 18th century but was later demolished and the site taken into the churchyard.[33]

The building of Fairford Park was begun for Andrew Barker in 1661 by Valentine Strong (d. 1662) of Taynton (Oxon.) who was probably also the designer.[34] The house, 500 m. north of the town and incorporating masonry from the older house,[35] had main fronts of seven bays to the north and south and was set in extensive formal gardens.[36] It was altered for James Lambe[37] and it was probably for him that the gardens to the north were laid out in 'the wilderness way' with canals and serpentine walks adorned with statues, urns, and grottos east of the river.[38] The gardens were included in William Eames's landscaping of the park in the 1780s and part of the surviving walling is dated 1783. Sir John Soane carried out alterations to the interior of the house in 1789.[39] Some out-buildings to the west were demolished in the late 18th or early 19th century when the house was joined to a reorganized stable court by a two-storeyed range. The attics of

[3] Complete Peerage, xii(2), 383–4; C 139/123 no. 53.
[4] Complete Peerage, xii(2), 384–5, 392–4; cf. C 140/68 no. 19.
[5] Cal. Fine R. 1471–85, pp. 157–8; J. G. Joyce, Fairford Windows (1872), 19–20.
[6] D.L. 29/638/10362 rot. 10; mon. in ch.
[7] Cal. Close, 1485–1500, p. 90; Cal. Pat. 1485–94, 298; Complete Peerage, xii(2), 393.
[8] Trans. B.G.A.S. liii. 91; L. & P. Hen. VIII, v, p. 484.
[9] Prob. 11/25 (P.C.C. 17 Hogen); Glos. R.O., D 1728, Fairford man. deeds.
[10] Prob. 11/30 (P.C.C. 17 Pynning).
[11] L. & P. Hen. VIII, xxi(2), p. 417.
[12] Acts of P.C. 1547–50, 428.
[13] Glos. R.O., D 1728, Fairford man. deeds.
[14] B.L. Eg. Ch. 814; C 2/Eliz. I/F 3/37.
[15] Glos. R.O., D 1728, Fairford man. deeds.
[16] Complete Peerage, xii(2), 1–2; Glos. R.O., D 1728, deeds of J. Betterton's lands sold 1749.
[17] Glos. R.O., D 1728, Fairford ct. roll.
[18] Complete Peerage, xii(2), 2.
[19] Cal. Cttee. for Compounding, iii. 1676; Glos. R.O., D 1728, Fairford man. deeds.
[20] Par. reg. 1679–1788.   [21] Glos. R.O., D 1728, wills.
[22] Ibid. D 1070/X/40; par. reg. 1679–1788.

[23] Rudder, Glos. 443.
[24] Glos. R.O., D 1728, misc. deeds, Esther Lambe's will; Burke, Land. Gent. (1937), 103.
[25] Glos. R.O., D 2299/1431.
[26] Ex inf. the sec., Ernest Cook Trust, est. office, Fairford Pk.
[27] Bodl. MS. Rawl. B.323, f. 91.
[28] Leland, Itin. ed. Toulmin Smith, i. 127; cf. Glos. R.O., D 1070/X/23, deed 18 Dec. 1739.
[29] L. & P. Hen. VIII, iii(2), p. 1542.
[30] C 142/74 no. 86.
[31] Cf. Glos. R.O., D 1728, long leases 1591–1752.
[32] Bodl. MS. Rawl. B.323, f. 91; cf. Cotswold Life, Nov. 1970, 28.
[33] Glos. R.O., D 1728, par. papers, lease 4 Oct. 1743; cf. Atkyns, Glos. plate at pp. 430–1.
[34] Colvin, Biog. Dict. of Eng. Architects, 576–8; cf. Hist. MSS. Com. 29, 13th Rep. II, Portland, ii, p. 299.
[35] Bigland, Glos. i. 570.
[36] Atkyns, Glos. plate at pp. 430–1, reproduced as frontispiece to this volume; Glos. R.O., D 674B/P 53.
[37] Rudder, Glos. 442.
[38] Travels of Dr. Ric. Pococke, ii, 252–3; Hist. of Fairford Ch. (1763), 16 n.
[39] Verey, Glos. i. 248.

the main block were possibly converted as a full third storey at that time. The house was empty for some time before 1889[40] when it was let to tenants and in the early 20th century Col. Albert John Palmer lived there.[41] It was demolished in 1955, and in 1977 the stable court was used by the estate for offices and labourers' cottages. Of the lodges one at the west end of Park Street dates from the 19th century[42] but another, by the Quenington road west of the river, has been demolished.[43]

By 1216 Hugh de Chaworth had granted 1 hide of land in Milton End, held from Fairford manor, to Bradenstoke Priory (Wilts).[44] The priory's property, which after the Dissolution was called *HYDECOURT* manor,[45] was granted in 1545 to John D'Oyley and John Scudamore.[46] They sold it to Sir Walter Buckler and his wife Catherine in 1548,[47] after which it passed with Fairford manor.[48]

By 1506 the Knights Hospitallers held property in Fairford as an adjunct of Quenington Preceptory.[49] The property of Studley Priory (Oxon.), granted to John Croke in 1540,[50] has not been identified but it may have been united with Fairford manor in 1590.

By 1291 Tewkesbury Abbey held rents of assize in Fairford,[51] and land which escheated to the abbey at the death of Sir John Worthe in the early 15th century probably became part of the vicar's glebe.[52] The abbey's rectory estate, comprising the grain tithes, was leased in 1533 for 21 years to Sir Edmund Tame, his wife Elizabeth, and son Edmund.[53] In 1541 it was granted to the dean and chapter of Gloucester cathedral[54] who c. 1550 leased it for 90 years to William Thomas. He granted the lease c. 1558 to Roger Lygon and his wife Catherine, and Roger conveyed it to his nephew George Lygon. After George's death action was taken in 1594 against his brother and executor, Henry, to secure the lease for George's grandson Robert Oldisworth, a minor,[55] but the estate was being farmed by Richard Lygon in 1603.[56] William Oldisworth, described in 1660 as the impropriator,[57] took a lease for 21 years the following year. Thereafter the estate was leased to him and his successors, the lease being renewed every few years. William died in 1680 and James Oldisworth (d. 1722), rector of Kencot (Oxon.), was succeeded by his daughter Muriel Loggan (d. 1754).[58] The lease was then held by trustees under her will[59] until 1781 when John

Oldisworth came of age.[60] He sold the lease to John Raymond-Barker in 1794 and it then passed with Fairford manor.[61] In 1840 the rectorial tithes were commuted for a corn-rent-charge of £513 10s.[62] and the Ecclesiastical Commissioners, who acquired the freehold in 1855,[63] sold it to the trustees of the Fairford estate in 1858.[64]

ECONOMIC HISTORY: AGRICULTURE. The demesne of Fairford manor, which was given over to corn production in the late 1230s,[65] included 610 a. of arable, 70 a. of meadow, and 6 several pastures in 1307.[66] By c. 1327 the arable land in hand had been reduced to 574 a. and there were over 105 a. of meadow in demesne.[67] The lord's stock in the 1320s included 3 ploughs and 100 qr. of barley, 30 qr. of wheat, 14 qr. of oats, and some hay. He also owned at least 226 sheep there,[68] and in 1381 several shepherds lived in the town.[69] In the late 15th century the manorial demesne was farmed by John Tame, who employed at least four shepherds on his estates,[70] and his son and apparent successor as demesne farmer, Sir Edmund, owned at least 500 sheep at his death in 1534.[71] Bradenstoke Priory's property, which in 1291 included two plough-lands,[72] had been leased to the younger Edmund Tame by 1538.[73]

In 1066 Fairford manor, including part of Eastleach Turville, supported 56 *villani* and 9 bordars with 30 plough-teams.[74] About 1100 Robert FitzHamon granted a tenement by the service of supplying fowls.[75] In 1307 when 2 plough-lands were held by that service there were 30 other free tenants outside the borough holding by cash rent. Three held yardlands and six had small, unspecified holdings; the other tenements varied in size and included a water-mill and a weir.[76] In the late 15th and early 16th centuries a freehold estate of over 66 a., apparently acquired by John Langley of Sidding-ton in the early 1440s, was held under the manor.[77] In 1307 there were c. 75 customary tenants including 41 yardlanders, c. 10 half yardlanders, and 11 tenants with 6 a. each. Each yardland owed 4 week-works, ploughing- and harrowing-services, and 8 bedreaps. There were also 13 cottagers owing cash rent, and the customary tenants paid £8 for tallage, and cash or kind for other customary payments.[78] By

[40] Glos. R.O., D 674B/B 2, f. 29.
[41] *Kelly's Dir. Glos.* (1889 and later edns.).
[42] *Glos. and Avon Life*, Jan. 1975, 19; Verey, *Glos.* i. 248.
[43] Greenwood, *Map of Glos.* (1824); G.D.R., T 1/81.
[44] *Cal. Chart. R.* 1226–57, 161; *Earldom of Glouc. Charters*, p. 36.
[45] Cf. *Valor Eccl.* (Rec. Com.), ii. 125; Dugdale, *Mon.* vi (1), 340.
[46] *L. & P. Hen. VIII*, xx(1), p. 528.
[47] *Cal. Pat.* 1547–8, 372.
[48] Glos. R.O., D 1728, Fairford man. deeds.
[49] S.C. 11/831 rot. 3d.
[50] *L. & P. Hen. VIII*, xv, p. 115.
[51] *Tax. Eccl.* (Rec. Com.), 234.
[52] *Cal. Pat.* 1494–1509, 101.
[53] Glos. R.O., P 329/MI 1, rot. 41d.
[54] *L. & P. Hen. VIII*, xvi, pp. 572–3.
[55] C 3/246/40.
[56] *Eccl. Misc.* 94.
[57] *Wood's Life and Times*, i (Oxford Hist. Soc. xix), 323.
[58] Glos. R.O., D 936/E 72; Bigland, *Glos.* i. 572.
[59] Cf. G.D.R. wills 1755/15.

[60] Glos. R.O., D 936/E 72, E 168.
[61] Ibid. D 1728, Fairford rectory deeds; D 936/E 72; E 119/13, 20, 27, 37, 44, 51.
[62] G.D.R., T 1/81.
[63] Kirby, *Cat. of Glouc. Dioc. Rec.* ii, p. xiii.
[64] Glos. R.O., D 1740/T 43.
[65] S.C. 6/1109/6 rott. 3–4; S.C. 6/1109/7 rott. 1–5.
[66] C 133/129 no. 47.
[67] S.C. 11/236.
[68] E 142/34.
[69] E 179/113/31A rot. 5; E 179/113/35A rot. 2d.
[70] D.L. 29/638/10362 rot. 10; Prob. 11/12 (P.C.C. 3 Moone).
[71] Prob. 11/25 (P.C.C. 17 Hogen).
[72] *Tax. Eccl.* (Rec. Com.), 237.
[73] S.C. 6/Hen. VIII/3985 rot. 61.
[74] *Dom. Bk.* (Rec. Com.), i. 163v.
[75] B.L. Harl. MS. 7, f. 17v.
[76] C 133/129 no. 47.
[77] C.P. 25(1)/79/90 nos. 89 and 93; *Cal. Inq. p.m. Hen. VII*, ii, pp. 374–5; cf. C 142/74 no. 83.
[78] C 133/129 no. 47.

KEMPSFORD: St. Anne's chapel, Whelford

HATHEROP CHURCH: the south chapel with the tomb of Lady de Mauley (d.1844)

LECHLADE CHURCH from the south-east

KEMPSFORD CHURCH from the north

1314 the yardlander's week-work had been increased to 5 days, excepting feast days and the weeks of the three main festivals.[79] About 1327, although the demesne arable had been reduced, 42 yardlanders owed week-work but gave cash for their bedrepes. There were also 9 half-yardlanders and 16 cottagers.[80]

There is evidence in the collection of rents of a general impoverishment among the manor's free and customary tenants before 1482, and the large amount of land apparently occupied by tenants at will in the later 1480s, when they paid £17 5s. 6d., suggests a difficulty in getting long-term customary tenants. The free rents collected outside the borough then comprised 14s. 4d., including 4s. for land in Chedworth.[81] In the later 16th century Roger Lygon and his wife Catherine created several copyholds and after Roger's death the tenants initiated a Chancery suit to establish their rights.[82] From 1590 the lords of the manor granted leases, some of large holdings, for terms of up to 2,000 years under which much property in the parish was held,[83] but some copyholds remained in 1633.[84]

In 1375 a third of the arable demesne lay fallow, suggesting a three-field system.[85] By the 17th century there were two open fields each in East End and Milton End tithings which were not, however, completely distinct agrarian units, for Milton End property included common rights in East End.[86] East End in 1597 had a home and a further field, the latter on the boundary with Hatherop,[87] and Milton End in 1610 a north field and a field on the boundary with Maiseyhampton,[88] presumably the south field mentioned later.[89] Meadow land and pasture lay near the river and more especially towards Long Doles in the south-eastern corner of the parish[90] where a lot meadow, possibly that recorded in 1597,[91] lay across the Whelford road at the parish boundary.[92] Other meadows lay west of the river above the town bridge.

The two principal commons were at opposite ends of the town.[93] The Moor, recorded in 1610[94] and possibly where meadow land had been granted c. 1100,[95] was bounded by the Coln south-east of the town.[96] To the east and south-east were commons called the Horse common, the Lower common, and the Cow common.[97] The Milton End common, parts of which, including the great green, were inclosed by Sir Robert Tracy under an agreement of 1633,[98] was represented in the mid 18th century by the Cow

common, north of the Cirencester road, and a small area of waste land to the west. The latter was divided into small parcels in which some commoners had several rights to wood and furze. Milton End was finally inclosed in 1755 by agreement between James and Esther Lambe, who held 737 a. of open-field land, and their leasehold tenants, who held the remaining 73 a. Under the agreement one tenant was allotted a small piece of the green and 11 others 97 a. in the south field for their open-field and waste land and common rights.[99] East End was inclosed in 1770 by agreement between Esther Lambe, the vicar, the other landowners, and leaseholders. Under the agreement, which affected 1,657 a., Esther Lambe received 742 a. and the vicar 28 a. for his glebe and common rights. Elizabeth Morgan, Henry Brown, Sarah Brown, and Thomas Cripps received 511 a., 150 a., 75 a., and 59 a. respectively. Twelve others were allotted up to 14 a. each. There were left as commons 12 a. of the Moor, 14 a. of the Cow common, and a ground called the Crofts[1] which had evidently been inclosed by 1828.[2]

In 1831 labour was employed by ten of twelve farmers in the parish[3] where the largest farms had been formed on the Fairford estate. In 1840 when 691 a., including land farmed from Park farm, were in hand there were farms of 1,040 a. (corresponding to those later called Milton and Farhill farms), 555 a. (Manor farm), 383 a. (Leafield farm), 357 a. (Waitenhill farm), 171 a. (Moor farm), and 96 a. based on Waitenhills Barn.[4] In 1914 there were seven farms on the estate, namely Manor (631 a.), Milton (569 a.), Waitenhill (522 a.), Park (483 a.), Farhill (387 a.), Leafield (376 a.), and Moor (189 a.).[5] Park and Farhill were farmed together in the early 20th century.[6] Several of the 29 farmers returned in the parish in 1896[7] worked smallholdings and nearly half of the 23 farmers returned in 1926 had less than 20 a.[8] In 1976 five smallholdings of under 20 ha. (50 a.), worked on a part-time basis, were returned together with seven larger farms of which two had over 300 ha. (741 a.).[9]

Corn and sheep husbandry were dominant after inclosure. In 1781 cereal crops were grown on 1,052½ a.[10] and by 1807 the flock of sheep on the home farm of the Fairford estate had been improved by the introduction of the new Leicester breed.[11] Arable land predominated over grassland in the mid 19th century; in 1866 2,137 a., cropped with cereals, roots, and grass seeds, were returned compared with

[79] C 134/42 no. 17.
[80] S.C. 11/236.
[81] D.L. 29/638/10362 rot. 9 and d.
[82] C 2/Eliz. I/F 3/37.
[83] C 3/266/2; cf. Glos. R.O., D 1728, abs. of title 1772; Betterton deeds 1660–1743; long leases 1591–1753.
[84] Glos. R.O., D 1728, Fairford ct. roll.
[85] C 135/253 no. 1.
[86] Glos. R.O., D 1728, Milton End deeds 1660–1743, deed endorsed 16 Feb. 1689.
[87] Ibid. D 185/IV/23.
[88] Ibid. D 1728, Milton End deeds 1660–1743, deed endorsed 16 Feb. 1689.
[89] Ibid. Milton End inc. award.
[90] Cf. Cal. Inq. p.m. v, p. 329.
[91] Glos. R.O., D 185/IV/23.
[92] Cf. ibid. D 1728, East End inc. award; G.D.R., T 1/81.

[93] Bodl. MS. Top. Glouc. c. 3, f. 156.
[94] Glos. R.O., D 1070/III/7, deed 7 May 1631.
[95] B.L. Harl. MS. 7, f. 17v.
[96] Glos. R.O., D 1728, legal papers.
[97] Ibid. East End inc. award.
[98] Ibid. Fairford ct. roll; cf. ibid. long leases 1591–1752.
[99] Ibid. Milton End inc. award.
[1] Ibid. East End inc. award.
[2] G.D.R., V 5/130T4.
[3] Census, 1831.
[4] G.D.R., T 1/81.
[5] Glos. R.O., D 2299/1431.
[6] Ibid.; Kelly's Dir. Glos. (1902–35 edns.).
[7] M.A.F. 68/1609/9.
[8] M.A.F. 68/3295/8.
[9] Agric. Returns 1976.
[10] Glos. R.O., D 936/E 168.
[11] Rudge, Agric. of Glos. 307.

495 a. of permanent grassland.[12] Large flocks, numbering at least 2,727 sheep, were kept then and the rich meadow land made cattle-raising and dairying a significant part of local farming; a total of 357 cattle, including 44 milk cows, was returned. Pig-raising was also important then.[13] By 1863 allotment gardens had been laid out south of the Lechlade road[14] and in the later 19th century a market gardener lived in the parish.[15] In the later 19th century and early 20th the area returned as under cereal crops fell slightly but the area of recorded permanent grassland nearly trebled. The later 19th century saw an expansion in sheep-farming and dairying but in the early 20th more beef, as well as dairy, cattle were introduced; 581, including 151 milk cows, were returned in 1926.[16] In the mid 1970s four of the main farms were devoted principally to cereal production, chiefly barley and wheat, and two others to dairying. Cattle-raising remained an important part of local farming but sheep-farming and pig-rearing had ceased to be significant.[17]

MILLS. The three mills belonging to Fairford manor in 1066[18] presumably occupied the site of the mill in which c. 1100 Robert FitzHamon granted his fowler the same liberty as he enjoyed.[19] In 1296 the site included a fulling-mill[20] but in 1307 there were apparently only corn-mills, two in demesne and one, with the suit of Milton End, held at fee farm.[21] From the late 17th century a mill was recorded where Mill Lane crossed the Coln.[22] In the mid 19th century it was worked by members of the Tovey family.[23] It went out of use shortly after 1910[24] and was converted to domestic use. The building, which dates from the 17th century, incorporates a wing dated 1827 and alterations made in 1841.[25]

TRADE AND INDUSTRY. By 1135 a market town had been created at Fairford, which thrived later as a centre for retailers and craftsmen. In the 14th century the town, in an important wool-growing region, enjoyed considerable prosperity. In 1307 there were 68 burgages[26] and about twenty years later the borough rents were worth £5 12s. 2½d.;[27] in 1334 Fairford had a higher assessment for tax than Lechlade or Tetbury.[28] The wealthier inhabitants in 1327 included a baker, a chapman, a skinner, a smith, and a wool-monger, while Robert Hitchman and William Sparks, apparently the two wealthiest, were possibly merchants.[29] Thomas Hitchman and Robert Sparks were among at least four merchants living in the parish in 1381 when there were several butchers, a cobbler, a tailor, a tanner, a tiler, and a smith. The presence then of at least two hostelers is early evidence for the town's role in servicing road traffic.[30] By the 1480s, when the free borough rents realized only £2 0s. 9d. and the lord of Fairford retained several burgages in hand because of a lack of tenants, the town had suffered a decline, the reversal of which was apparently stimulated by the activities of members of the Tame family,[31] presumably descendants of that John Tame of Fairford appointed in 1416 to collect a subsidy in the county.[32] John Tame (d. 1500), the principal inhabitant in the later 15th century, who had inherited several burgages from his father, also John, acquired and rented much property in the town[33] and surrounding countryside[34] where he became a sheep-farmer on a considerable scale. Although he had property in Cirencester, he centred his business on Fairford where he rebuilt the church, and his son Edmund, who completed that work, became sheriff for the county three times and was knighted in 1516.[35]

In the late 13th century Fairford had a woollen textile industry based on one of its mills but cloth manufacture was never of great significance although Daniel Defoe described Fairford as one of the county's principal clothing towns in the early 18th century.[36] Edward Byget from Picardy, who was living in the town in 1436, may have worked in the cloth industry or wool trade[37] and later-15th-century inhabitants may have included a fuller and a weaver,[38] but the cloth industry, represented by two weavers in 1608, was evidently small in scale.[39] A cloth worker was recorded in 1693[40] and weavers were living in the parish in the early 19th century.[41] In the late 18th and early 19th centuries a few inhabitants following the trade of wool-stapler employed combers and spinners.[42] A flax-dresser lived in the town in the early 1790s.[43]

By 1608, when 26 tradesmen were recorded in Fairford compared with 28 men employed in agriculture, the town was primarily a centre for

[12] G.D.R., T 1/81; M.A.F. 68/26/10.
[13] M.A.F. 68/25/3.
[14] Glos. R.O., Q/RUm 322; cf. O.S. Map 6", Glos. LII. SE. (1924 edn.).
[15] Kelly's Dir. Glos. (1889), 770; (1897), 155.
[16] M.A.F. 68/1609/9; M.A.F. 68/3295/8.
[17] Agric. Returns 1976; ex inf. the sec., Ernest Cook Trust.
[18] Dom. Bk. (Rec. Com.), i. 163v.
[19] B.L. Harl. MS. 7, f. 17v.
[20] C 133/77 no. 3.
[21] C 133/129 no. 47.
[22] Glos. R.O., D 674B/P 53.
[23] Ibid. D 1070/IX/8; G.D.R., T 1/81; Kelly's Dir. Glos. (1856), 286; (1863), 267.
[24] W.I. hist. of Fairford, 1; cf. Kelly's Dir. Glos. (1910), 163; (1914), 167; O.S. Map 6", Glos. LII. SE. (1924 edn.).
[25] Glos. R.O., photocopy 955.
[26] Cal. Inq. p.m. iv, p. 321.
[27] S.C. 11/236.
[28] Finberg, Glos. Studies, 81.
[29] Glos. Subsidy Roll, 1327, 13.

[30] E 179/113/35A rot. 2 and d.
[31] D.L. 29/638/10362 rott. 9–10; cf. Leland, Itin. ed. Toulmin Smith, i. 127.
[32] Cal. Fine R. 1413–22, 151.
[33] D.L. 29/638/10362 rott. 9–10; S.C. 12/8/4 rot. 10 and d.; Cal. Close, 1468–76, p. 101.
[34] Cf. Cal. Close, 1468–76, p. 132; Cal. Fine R. 1471–85, pp. 157–8; C.P. 25(1)/79/96 no. 32.
[35] Jnl. Brit. Arch. Assoc. [1st ser.] xxvii. 5–33; Prob. 11/12 (P.C.C. 3 Moone); Leland, Itin. ed. Toulmin Smith, i. 127.
[36] D. Defoe, Tour through G.B. (1927 edn.), i. 280.
[37] Cal. Pat. 1429–36, 576.
[38] S.C. 12/8/4 rot. 10.
[39] Smith, Men and Armour, 263.
[40] Glos. R.O., D 1728, abs. of title 1772.
[41] W. R. Hedges, Farmor's School, Fairford (Glouc. 1938), 47; par. reg. 1813–54, entries for 1821, 1839.
[42] Glos. R.O., D 1070/II 2/T 1; III/16; D 1728, long leases 1811–83, deed 4 May 1822; CMS 46/1; Hist. of Fairford Ch. (1863), 4.
[43] Univ. Brit. Dir. iii (1794), 95.

retail and service trades. There were 4 butchers, 4 smiths, 3 tailors, 2 innkeepers, 2 mercers, 2 shoemakers, 2 wheelers, a carpenter, a cutler, a glover and a mason.[44] In the later 17th century the economic life of the town depended considerably on the servicing of road traffic[45] which, with the market and fairs, was its chief support in the early 18th century.[46] The inhabitants included a tobacconist in 1712,[47] a tallow-chandler in 1721,[48] a clock-maker in 1754,[49] a peruke-maker in 1769,[50] and a hairdresser, an iron-monger, and a stationer in the early 1790s.[51] The leather trades were well represented in the 18th century[52] and workers in the clothing trades included a staymaker in 1754.[53] In 1842 the town's tradesmen included 5 cobblers, 3 dressmakers, 2 straw hat makers, 2 chemists, a basket-maker, a wine and spirit merchant, and a coal merchant.[54] In the early 20th century several coal-merchants operated from the railway station[55] on the site of which a member of the Lockwoods Foods Group had a depot in 1977. The craft of blacksmithing survived until c. 1930 and that of wheelwrighting until the Second World War.[56]

Building trades have employed many people in the town, where there was a lime yard in 1590.[57] Glaziers, slaters, and masons were mentioned in the 18th century[58] and building firms from the mid 19th century, including Yells Bros. founded in Milton End by 1914.[59] Bricks, tiles, and drain pipes were made at Waiten Hills, west of the town, by the mid 1870s[60] and in 1977 Portcrete Ltd., a member of the Bath and Portland Group, occupied a site near gravel workings by the Whelford road. Agricultural machinery has been made in the parish since at least the early 19th century when John Savory (d. 1826) was described as a threshing machine maker. His son John[61] and Richard Rose both made machines in Milton End in the middle of the century.[62] In 1842 one inhabitant was described as a tinman.[63] In 1977 the inhabitants worked for local building firms or shops, at the Fairford R.A.F. base in Kempsford, or in Cirencester or Swindon.

A physician may have lived in Fairford in 1500,[64] and in the 18th century the professions were well represented. A Fairford man who took up surgery in 1697 was still in practice in 1735[65] and several inhabitants later that century were surgeons and apothecaries.[66] The residents included an attorney, Alexander Ready (later Colston), in 1734[67] and a land-surveyor in 1770.[68] By 1848 3 surgeons, 3 auctioneers, and a conveyancer were established in the town[69] and there was a bank by 1844.[70]

MARKET AND FAIRS. Robert, earl of Gloucester and lord of Fairford manor, evidently levied tolls and stallage in a market in Fairford before his father Henry I granted their falconer Remphrey a market there on Tuesdays and Fridays.[71] The town was an established market for corn in the 1260s,[72] and the lord of the manor was holding the market and a fair there in 1287.[73] The fair, on the feast of St. James (25 July), was worth 5s. in 1307 when the market tolls were valued at 10s.[74] Their combined value of £2 6s. 8d. c. 1327 compared with the general prosperity of the town at that time indicates a relatively small volume of trade[75] but by 1375 another fair was held on Ascension day.[76]

Leland in the early 1540s described Fairford as a market town[77] but the market had possibly lapsed by 1672 when Andrew Barker had a grant of a Thursday market and fairs on 3 May, 28 July, and 1 November.[78] They were important in the town's commercial life at the beginning of the 18th century[79] but the July fair had been discontinued by 1755. Efforts to revive the market after it had lapsed were twice necessary during that year, providing further evidence of a decline of trade in the mid 18th century.[80] The market, which was mainly for cheese and corn[81] but was not much frequented c. 1775,[82] was held until c. 1860.[83] After the opening of the railway in 1873 a market for cattle was held every second Tuesday[84] but, together with the remaining fairs (held following the calendar change on 14 May and 12 November)[85] was discontinued in the late 1930s.[86]

LOCAL GOVERNMENT. In 1221 Fairford was

[44] Smith, *Men and Armour*, 263.
[45] *Wood's Life and Times*, ii (Oxford Hist. Soc. xxi), 407; Ogilby, *Britannia* (1675), p. 29.
[46] Bodl. MS. Top. Glouc. c. 3, f. 156.
[47] Glos. R.O., D 1728, deeds of land acquired 1831, abs. of title 1831.
[48] Ibid. D 1437, Kingsley fam., deeds 1691–1781.
[49] Ibid. D 182/III/113.   [50] Ibid. D 1070/X/21.
[51] *Univ. Brit. Dir.* iii (1794), 95.
[52] Glos. R.O., D 1070/III/7; D 1437, Kingsley fam., deeds 1744–1820; D 1728, abs. of title 1772.
[53] Ibid. D 182/III/113.
[54] *Pigot's Dir. Glos.* (1842), 105–6.
[55] *Kelly's Dir. Glos.* (1914), 168; cf. ibid. (1927 and later edns.).
[56] Ibid. (1856 and later edns.).
[57] Glos. R.O., D 1728, Milton End deeds 1590–1760.
[58] Ibid. D 182/III/111, 113; D 1070/II 4/T 1; IX/2; X/21; D 1437, Kingsley fam., deeds 1792–1823; CMS 46/1; *Univ. Brit. Dir.* iii (1794), 95.
[59] Glos. R.O., CMS 46/1; *Kelly's Dir. Glos.* (1856 and later edns.); Payne, *Glos. Survey*, 163.
[60] Cf. *Kelly's Dir. Glos.* (1870–1914 edns.); O.S. Map 6", Glos. LII. SE. (1886, 1924 edns.).
[61] Glos. R.O., D 1070/III/25.
[62] Par. reg. 1813–54, entry for 1827; H.O. 107/1968; *Kelly's Dir. Glos.* (1863), 267.
[63] *Pigot's Dir. Glos.* (1842), 106.
[64] Prob. 11/12 (P.C.C. 3 Moone).
[65] Hockaday Abs. cxciv; Finberg, *Glos. Studies*, 192.
[66] Glos. R.O., D 1070/III/19; D 1728, abs. of title 1772.
[67] *Glouc. Jnl.* 22 Jan., 20 Aug. 1734; cf. *V.C.H. Glos.* x. 292.
[68] Glos. R.O., D 1728, East End inc. award.
[69] Ibid. CMS 46/1.   [70] Ibid. photocopy 955.
[71] B.L. Harl. MS. 7, f. 17v.
[72] *Hist. & Cart. Mon. Glouc.* (Rolls Ser.), iii. 199.
[73] *Plac. de Quo Warr.* (Rec. Com.), 253.
[74] C 133/129 no. 47.   [75] S.C. 11/236.
[76] *Cal. Inq. p.m.* xiv, p. 219.
[77] Leland, *Itin.* ed. Toulmin Smith, iii. 39.
[78] Glos. R.O., D 1728, Fairford man. deeds.
[79] Bodl. MS. Top. Glouc. c. 3, f. 156.
[80] *Glouc. Jnl.* 6 May, 4 Nov. 1755.
[81] *Travels of Dr. Ric. Pococke*, ii. 252.
[82] Rudder, *Glos.* 442.
[83] Rudge, *Agric. of Glos.* 339; cf. *Kelly's Dir. Glos.* (1856), 285; (1863), 266.
[84] *Morris's Dir. Glos.* (1876), 256.
[85] *Glouc. Jnl.* 6 May 1755; Rudge, *Agric. of Glos.* 339.
[86] Cf. *Kelly's Dir. Glos.* (1935), 165; (1939), 166–7.

denied its wish to answer the eyre separately from the hundred.[87] The lord of the manor and borough, whose courts in 1246 included some called hundreds[88] and who in 1255 compelled Tewkesbury Abbey to answer at his Fairford court for matters arising in Rendcomb, Ashton Keynes (Wilts.), and elsewhere,[89] claimed view of frankpledge and right of gallows, pillory, and tumbril in 1287.[90] There was a prison at Fairford in 1248.[91]

In the 14th and 15th centuries the view for the manor and borough was held twice a year in their respective courts.[92] The borough had its own bailiff, recorded c. 1400,[93] and the foreign bailiff, mentioned in the later 1480s, possibly administered the rest of the estate, though a single annual account was then rendered for both manor and borough.[94] The lord of the manor exercised the view over several tithings outside the parish; Arlington and Eastleach Turville attended the Fairford court[95] but in the later 1480s separate courts were held in Marston Maisey (Wilts.) and Shorncote in Somerford Keynes (Wilts., later Glos.), the latter evidently also for Siddington and Norcott in Preston.[96] A roll survives for a session in 1633 of a Fairford court in which the view of frankpledge for borough, manor, and 'foreign' (then used to designate the tithings outside the parish), was held with a court baron. The court, which elected a constable and two wardmen for the borough and tithingmen for East End, Milton End, and the other tithings, also appointed a hayward and two surveyors of the fields in Fairford where it dealt with agrarian matters.[97]

The town was policed by two constables in the early 18th century[98] but by only one at the end of the century[99] when it had a crier.[1] A blind-house, the town lock-up, had been built by 1809[2] and in 1838 there were pounds in East End and Milton End.[3] The churchwardens, recorded from the late 1480s,[4] numbered one in 1498[5] but two by 1566.[6] From 1774, when their suviving accounts begin, until 1797 their expenses were ordinarily met by the church or parish lands charity; later they were met by the poor-rate until 1836.[7] The three surveyors of the highways, recorded in 1663,[8] contracted with a local man in the 1840s to repair the roads for periods of three years.[9]

Burdocks Barn south-west of the town was bought with charity money in 1757 for a pest-house.[10] Let from 1836 when it comprised two cottages,[11] it had been demolished by 1905.[12] Three overseers administered poor-relief. Their accounts survive for the period 1774–1809, during which a surgeon and a midwife were retained, although in the early 19th century the former was paid only expenses, which included those of a mass innoculation in 1806. Parishioners were sent to Gloucester Infirmary.[13] In the late 1770s the church house was used as a poorhouse[14] but c. 1787 poorhouses, called Tinkers Row and containing six cottages, were built with charity money. From 1836 they were let.[15] To provide relief the parish purchased and maintained spinning wheels and put men to work digging stones. A salaried overseer was employed from 1788 until 1797 when a parish workhouse was opened in a converted barn south of the Crofts. The house, which had a salaried governor and in which the women spun flax and worsted,[16] had 23 inmates in 1803 when their work produced the sum of £37.[17] It was demolished after 1840[18] and the stone used in the early 1870s for building the infant school.[19] In 1776, when 35 people received regular help,[20] the annual cost of poor-relief stood at £250. It rose to over £1,134 by 1813 but fell to £844 by 1815. In the late 1820s and early 1830s it averaged c. £930. Forty-one people received regular help in 1803, 67 in 1813, and 61 in 1815.[21] In 1849 the vestry agreed to finance the emigration of poor residents out of the poor-rate.[22] Fairford, which became part of the Cirencester union in 1836[23] and remained in Cirencester rural district,[24] was included in Cotswold district in 1974.

CHURCH. There was a priest on the manor before 1086[25] and Fairford church was given by Robert FitzHamon, apparently before 1100, to the church of Tewkesbury.[26] Between 1181 and 1185 Tewkesbury Abbey was licensed to appropriate the benefice but it continued to appoint secular clerks.[27] During a vacancy in the abbey in 1216 the Crown presented to the living.[28] The abbey's licence was renewed in 1221 and 1230[29] but the bishop opposed any

---

[87] *Pleas of the Crown for Glos.* ed. Maitland, p. 42.
[88] *Cal. Pat.* 1364–7, 344.
[89] *Ann. Mon.* (Rolls Ser.), i, 156.
[90] *Plac. de Quo Warr.* (Rec. Com.), 253.
[91] J.I. 1/274 rot. 2.
[92] C 133/129 no. 47; D.L. 29/638/10362 rot. 10.
[93] B.L. Add. MS. 37657, f. 195.
[94] D.L. 29/638/10362 rott. 9–10; D.L. 29/638/10363 rot. 9.
[95] *Plac. de Quo Warr.* (Rec. Com.), 253.
[96] D.L. 29/638/10362 rot. 10; cf. C 139/96 no. 49.
[97] Glos. R.O., D 1728, Fairford ct. roll.
[98] Bodl. MS. Top. Glouc. c. 3, f. 156.
[99] Bigland, *Glos.* i. 570.
[1] Glos. R.O., D 1070/IX/11, p. 95; X/20.
[2] Ibid. IX/12, p. 533.
[3] Ibid. 8.
[4] D.L. 29/638/10362 rot. 9.
[5] Hockaday Abs. xxii, 1498 visit. f. 37.
[6] Ibid. xliii, 1566 visit. f. 23; lxviii, 1661 visit. f. 32.
[7] Glos. R.O., D 1070/IX/4; cf. ibid. mem. dated 12 June 1838.
[8] Ibid. Q/SIb 1, f. 107.
[9] Ibid. D 1070/IX/14; there is an early-19th-cent. surveyors' acct. bk., *penes* Mr. S. Jacques, of Fairford.

[10] Glos. R.O., D 1933.
[11] Ibid. D 1070/IX/4; cf. ibid. 8.
[12] Ibid. D 1933.
[13] Ibid. D 1070/IX/11–12; Isabel Lambe (d. 1789) left £100 to the infirmary: cf. ibid. D 1728, misc. deeds.
[14] Ibid. D 1070/IX/11.
[15] Ibid. 4.
[16] Ibid. 11–12; for the origins of the workho., see ibid. D 269B/F 19.
[17] *Poor Law Abstract, 1804,* 172–3.
[18] Cf. G.D.R., T 1/81.
[19] *Glos. Life,* Mar. 1970, 31.
[20] Glos. R.O., D 1070/IX/11
[21] *Poor Law Abstract, 1804,* 172–3; *1818,* 146–7; *Poor Law Returns* (1830–1), p. 67; (1835), p. 65.
[22] Glos. R.O., D 1070/IX/9.
[23] *Poor Law Com. 2nd Rep.* p. 522.
[24] *Census,* 1961.
[25] *Dom. Bk.* (Rec. Com.), i. 163v.
[26] *Trans. B.G.A.S.* viii. 80; xxv. 89; cf. Dugdale, *Mon.* ii. 65.
[27] *Cal. Papal Reg.* i. 81, 123.
[28] *Rot. Litt. Pat.* (Rec. Com.), 195.
[29] *Cal. Papal Reg.* i. 81, 123.

appropriation of the living[30] until 1333 when a vicarage was ordained.[31] The living has remained a vicarage.[32]

Tewkesbury Abbey held the rectory and the advowson of the vicarage until the Dissolution, and in 1541 the Crown granted them to the dean and chapter of Gloucester cathedral.[33] Under a grant by the assignee of the dean and chapter Roger Lygon and his wife Catherine presented in 1559 and Roger alone in 1560. The dean and chapter presented in 1564 but granted away the next turn in 1576.[34] Roger Lygon was said to be patron in 1584[35] but the patronage was in contention the following year when in the confusion Archbishop Whitgift collated to the living, thereby setting aside the presentation by a patron for the turn. George Lygon, one of the claimants, presented in 1586 and Robert Oldisworth in 1617. After the Restoration the dean and chapter exercised their right of patronage,[36] which they retained in 1977.[37]

The priest mentioned in 1086 held 1 yardland of the manorial demesne.[38] The tithes from 1 hide in Milton End, claimed by Gloucester Abbey for Kempsford church, were awarded between 1198 and 1216 to Fairford in return for two gold coins a year.[39] In 1233 the Crown, which held the manor in ward, granted the mill tithes to Tewkesbury Abbey.[40] In 1291 the abbey had a portion of £3 13s. 4d. for tithes. The rectory was then worth £20.[41]

The vicarage ordained in 1333 comprised the rectory house, ¼ yardland, and some tithes, including those of hay, flax, wool, lambs, and milk.[42] The vicar's glebe, which included 13 a. of arable and 2 a. of meadow in 1535,[43] lay in East End. In 1678 it comprised 14½ a. of open-field land and 8 a. of meadow, part of which had been granted as compensation for the hay tithes of some lot meadows. For the tithes of a corn-mill he received 4 nobles a year.[44] When East End was inclosed in 1770 the vicar was allotted 28 a. south-east of the town for his glebe and common rights[45] save for those in the Crofts, which had been commuted for a small piece of pasture by 1828. By then the glebe had been let out and the lord of the manor was paying the vicar £280 a year for the

tithes on his estate.[46] The vicar's tithes were commuted for a corn-rent-charge of £398 10s. in 1840.[47] The glebe, on which allotments had been laid out by 1863,[48] was excavated following the sale of the gravel rights in 1976.[49]

The vicarage was worth £13 11s. 4d. clear in 1535[50] and £50 in 1650.[51] By 1661 it had been augmented by a stipend of £20 from the rectory estate[52] and from 1739 the vicar also received £40 for sermons.[53] The value of the living rose from £120 in 1750[54] to £505 by 1856.[55]

The vicarage house, which was in ruins by 1569 when the incumbent was non-resident,[56] had 12 bays in 1705.[57] The 18th-century house, south of London Road,[58] was occupied by a curate in the early 1820s;[59] it was rebuilt and enlarged in 1865.[60] It was sold in 1957 when a new vicarage was built in the Crofts.[61]

Ralph de Hengham, royal justice and pluralist, had become rector by 1294[62] but Tewkesbury Abbey was contesting his incumbency in 1298.[63] Ralph had resigned by 1304 and his successor, Stephen Malore[64] (d. by 1323),[65] was licensed to absent himself in 1319.[66] The vicar Thomas Green, who in 1402 was dispensed to let the benefice at farm during any absences in the following ten years, was a pluralist, as were many of his successors.[67] Thomas Taylor, vicar by 1550,[68] lived in Oxford[69] and in 1551, when he could neither repeat the Commandments nor prove the Articles, was also rector of North Cerney.[70] John Strange, who held other livings including Maiseyhampton, became vicar in 1559 but resigned the following year.[71] Nathaniel Harford, non-resident vicar from 1564,[72] also held Hatherop until c. 1572[73] and then another living.[74] He had not preached for over a year in 1576 when he was apparently dispossessed.[75] His successor William Salwey,[76] a non-graduate, was another pluralist.[77] In 1585 Henry Dunne became vicar but following confusion over the patronage was made curate later that year.[78]

Edmund James, who held the living from 1586 until 1589 with Hatherop,[79] was described as a quarreller in 1593.[80] Christopher Nicholson, who

[30] *Ann. Mon.* (Rolls Ser.), i. 82; Hockaday Abs. ccclxviii, 1314; *Reg. Cobham*, 151.
[31] Worc. Episc. Reg., Reg. Orleton, ii, ff. 54v.–55.
[32] *Glouc. Dioc. Yr. Bk.* (1977), 33.
[33] *L. & P. Hen. VIII*, xvi, pp. 572–3.
[34] Hockaday Abs. cxciv.
[35] Ibid. xlix, state of clergy 1584, f. 22.
[36] Ibid. cxciv.
[37] *Glouc. Dioc. Yr. Bk.* (1977), 33.
[38] *Dom. Bk.* (Rec. Com.), i. 163v.
[39] *Hist. & Cart. Mon. Glouc.* i. 303.
[40] *Cal. Pat.* 1232–47, 35.
[41] *Tax. Eccl.* (Rec. Com.), 222.
[42] Worc. Episc. Reg., Reg. Orleton, ii, ff. 54v.–55.
[43] *Valor Eccl.* (Rec. Com.), ii. 445.
[44] G.D.R., V 5/130T 1.
[45] Glos. R.O., D 1728, East End inc. award.
[46] G.D.R., V 5/130T 4.
[47] G.D.R., T 1/81.
[48] Glos. R.O., Q/RUm 322.
[49] Ex inf. the vicar, the Revd. D. M. Bell-Richards.
[50] *Valor Eccl.* (Rec. Com.), ii. 445.
[51] *Trans. B.G.A.S.* lxxxiii. 94.
[52] Glos. R.O., D 936/E 72; cf. G.D.R., V 5/130T 4.
[53] Hedges, *Farmor's Sch.* 20; G.D.R., vol. 397, f. 86.
[54] G.D.R. vol. 381A, f. 85.
[55] G.D.R. vol. 384, f. 94.
[56] Hockaday Abs. cxciv.
[57] G.D.R., V 5/130T 3.
[58] G.D.R., T 1/81.
[59] Hockaday Abs. cxciv; G.D.R. vol. 383, no. xcviii.
[60] *B. & G. Par. Rec.* 138; Hockaday Abs. cxciv.
[61] Ex inf. the vicar.
[62] *Sel. Cases in K.B.* (Selden Soc. lv), p. lxxv; cf. *Reg. Giffard*, 550.
[63] Hockaday Abs. cxciv.
[64] *Reg. Ginsborough*, 84.
[65] B.L. Add. Ch. 21742.
[66] *Reg. Cobham*, 254 and n.
[67] *Cal. Papal Reg.* v. 466.
[68] Hockaday Abs. cxciv.
[69] C 2/Eliz. I/T 8/31.
[70] *E.H.R.* xix. 111, 113.
[71] Hockaday Abs. cxciv; cf. *Trans. B.G.A.S.* lx. 110 n.; *V.C.H. Glos.* xi. 254.
[72] Hockaday Abs. cxciv.
[73] Ibid. xliii, 1566 visit. f. 24; ccxxxvii.
[74] Ibid. xlvii, 1576 visit. f. 60.
[75] G.D.R. vol. 40, f. 156.
[76] Hockaday Abs. cxciv.
[77] Ibid. xlix, state of clergy 1584, f. 22.
[78] G.D.R., D 7/1/7; Hockaday Abs. cxciv.
[79] Hockaday Abs. cxciv; ccxxxvii.
[80] Ibid. lii, state of clergy 1593, f. 13.

succeeded him in 1617,[81] was described as a preacher in 1650.[82] The preservation of the church windows during the latter part of his incumbency was possibly due to his curate Robert Clark, whose opposition to dissenters is revealed in a tract written in 1660 following an attack on a Fairford meeting-place.[83] John Shipman, vicar from 1656, was licensed to preach in the church in 1673. Joseph Atwell, vicar 1738–68, employed curates to serve the living, which he held with Oddington from 1739.[84] In 1778 Edward Sparkes, a pluralist and formerly headmaster of the King's School, Gloucester, for 35 years, became vicar of Fairford[85] where he lived and had a curate.[86] He died in 1785 and his successor James Edwards (d. 1804), also a pluralist,[87] was resident.[88] John Mitchell, vicar from 1810, lived in Gloucester and appointed curates.[89] Francis William Rice, his successor from 1828, also employed curates but was usually resident until 1869 when he inherited the barony of Dynevor (Carms.). From then until his death in 1878 estate and parliamentary duties necessitated periods of absence.[90]

Some of the lights mentioned in the parish church in 1432[91] were possibly supported by the guilds of the Virgin Mary and Holy Trinity recorded in the late 1480s and by the fraternity of St. Cross which may have been dissolved by the later date.[92] John Tame by will dated 1497 assigned £240 to found a chantry in Fairford church but he later used the money to buy land in Castle Eaton (Wilts.) for its endowment. After his death there was a dispute over the land[93] but the chantry had apparently been established by 1532.[94] The priest of a free chapel at Kinley in Nympsfield, where the elder Sir Edmund Tame had acquired the manor, was later said to serve it[95] but in 1547 was refusing the daily service that was required from him.[96] The second chaplain recorded in 1532[97] served a chantry in the church founded by Sir Edmund and on which a Wiltshire manor, worth £7 in 1535, was conferred.[98] It was presumably the chantry dedicated to St. Edmund which had been despoiled by 1546.[99]

Elizabeth Farmor's educational bequest to the parish also provided for a salary of up to £40 for a minister, to be chosen by her uncle Samuel Barker and his heirs, preaching in the church on Sunday afternoons.[1] The sermons were given from 1739 by the vicar who received £40 from land in Chaceley

(Worcs., later Glos.).[2] Later he apparently received a larger part of the income from the land but in 1817 the original provisions of the bequest were implemented. The Mercers' Company of London probably paid the salary from 1890[3] but in 1977 there were no Sunday afternoon sermons.[4]

The churchwardens, who owned property in the town by 1487,[5] established the church or parish lands charity in 1564 to maintain the church, the highways, and an alms-house. The charity had an income of £2 4s. 10d. in 1601.[6] In 1648 the feoffees leased a house for 21 years to two glaziers, John Scriven of Burford and his son Edward, by the service of repairing the church masonry, leads, and windows, apart from the chancel,[7] and John was living there in 1662.[8] In 1729 a Fairford man contracted with the churchwardens to maintain the tower leads for 40 years,[9] and between 1774 and 1797 the churchwardens' expenses were met almost wholly by the charity.[10] In 1754 some property was granted under a long lease to James and Esther Lambe in return for an annuity but that lease was set aside following Chancery proceedings brought against the feoffees in 1857. A Scheme of 1859 appointed new trustees and divided the income equally between the church, the highways, and the poor.[11] The income for road repairs was spent irregularly, leading to an accumulation of funds, from which the cost of a church restoration was partly defrayed in 1891.[12] Under a Scheme of 1971 the income of the charity was divided equally between church repairs and the poor, and in 1976 £600 a year was derived from investments and one property.[13]

The church, dedicated to *ST. MARY* by 1432,[14] is built of ashlar and has a chancel with north vestry and north and south chapels, a central tower, and an aisled and clerestoried nave with south porch. Most of the fabric dates from a rebuilding in the late 15th century, at the expense of John Tame and completed by his son Edmund,[15] but the lower part of the tower and the eastern responds of its arcades survive from the 14th-century building, which was cruciform and had an aisled nave. The respond of the north arcade has a 13th-century base and shaft but the capital and arch date from the early 14th century. The south respond which is also of the early 14th century was presumably reconstructed at that time. At the late-

[81] Ibid. cxciv.
[82] *Trans. B.G.A.S.* lxxxiii. 94.
[83] *Walker Revised*, ed. Matthews, 181; cf. R. Clark, *The Lying Wonders* (1660): copy in Glos. Colln. 10952 (15).
[84] Hockaday Abs. cxciv.
[85] *Glouc. Cath. Rec.* iii(2), 228–9; Hockaday Abs. ccxxxiv, Hartpury; cxciv.
[86] G.D.R. vol. 319.
[87] Hockaday Abs. cxciv; civ, Ashleworth.
[88] G.D.R. vol. 382, f. 15.
[89] Hockaday Abs. cxciv; G.D.R. vol. 383, no. xcviii.
[90] Hockaday Abs. cxciv; Burke, *Peerage* (1963), 810–11.
[91] Hockaday Abs. cxciv, 1445.
[92] D.L. 29/638/10362 rot. 9.
[93] Prob. 11/12 (P.C.C. 3 Moone); Joyce, *Fairford Windows*, 24.
[94] Hockaday Abs. xxv, 1532 subsidy, f. 10; *Cal. Pat.* 1572–5, p. 201.
[95] E 301/85; cf. Rudder, *Glos.* 576–7.
[96] Hockaday Abs. cxciv.

[97] Ibid. xxv, 1532 subsidy, f. 10.
[98] *Valor Eccl.* (Rec. Com.), ii. 445.
[99] Hockaday Abs. cxciv; cf. *Trans. B.G.A.S.* xlvii. 12.
[1] Glos. R.O., D 1728, wills.
[2] Hedges, *Farmor's Sch.* 20; cf. G.D.R. vol. 381A, f. 85.
[3] Glos. R.O., D 1070/X/40; ex inf. the clerk, Mercers' Co., London.
[4] Ex inf. the vicar.
[5] D.L. 29/638/10362 rot. 9.
[6] Glos. R.O., D 1070/X/2, pp. 9–11; cf. C 2/Eliz. I/F 3/37.
[7] Glos. R.O., D 1070/X/4.
[8] Ibid. 2, p. 14.
[9] Ibid. IX/3.
[10] Ibid. 4, mem. dated 12 June 1838.
[11] Ibid. D 1388, case papers, Fairford chars.
[12] Ibid. D 1070/X/9.
[13] Ex inf. Mr. M. S. L. Lee-Browne, Wilmot & Co., Fairford.
[14] Hockaday Abs. cxciv, 1445.
[15] Leland, *Itin.* ed. Toulmin Smith, i. 127; see below, plate facing p. 205.

15th-century rebuilding the tower was provided with octagonal angle turrets and a new top stage, some earlier ornaments being reset in the new work. The rest of the church was completely rebuilt in a uniform late-perpendicular style.

The work created large areas of windows which were filled with stained glass representing in the main windows scenes from the Old and New Testaments and in those of the clerestory figures important in the early life of the Church. The designer may have been Barnard Flower, the king's master glass painter.[16] The survival of the windows was celebrated in poetry by Richard Corbet (d. 1635)[17] and they later attracted the attention of antiquaries such as Anthony à Wood and Thomas Hearne.[18] In 1703 two of the western windows were damaged by a storm[19] and Elizabeth Farmor, by will proved 1706, left £200 for repairs and protective wire frames.[20] Because of Chancery proceedings the work had not been carried out by 1717 when it was assigned to a London wireworker and a Fairford glazier.[21] By the mid 19th century the windows had fallen into disrepair and a campaign to preserve them, which had been launched by 1868,[22] led to a considerable literature.[23] Queen Victoria headed the list of subscribers to their restoration during 1889 and 1890[24] when a Birmingham firm provided a copy of that part of the great west window which had been lost during an attempt at restoration in the middle of the century.[25] During the Second World War the glass was removed for safe keeping.[26]

Original fittings which survive include the south door, the rood- and parclose-screens, 14 stalls in the chancel, and the font, the base of which was found in the vicarage garden c. 1920.[27] An altar dated 1626 was moved from the chancel to the south chapel in 1920.[28] Under a bequest by Andrew Barker the church was repewed in 1702,[29] but new seats were installed, probably during restoration work in 1852 when paintings within the tower arches were uncovered.[30]

The north chapel, which housed the chantry-chapel established under John Tame's will and was dedicated to Our Lady by 1534,[31] contains monuments to John Tame, his wife, and several descendants.[32] It was refitted by John Raymond Raymond-Barker before 1862.[33] During 1912 and 1913 William Lygon, Earl Beauchamp, whose putative ancestor Roger Lygon was lord of Fairford in the mid 16th century, provided a reredos designed by Geoffrey Webb.[34] John Tame's will dated 1497 included a bequest for a great fourth bell.[35] The peal, which included bells cast, some by the Rudhall family, in 1678, 1735, 1760, and 1783, numbered six in 1851 when one was replaced by C. & G. Mears of London. Two were added the following year[36] and the peal was recast by John Taylor of Loughborough (Leics.) in 1927.[37] The church has a mazer bowl of c. 1485 and the plate includes a chalice and paten made in 1576, possibly from earlier pieces, a flagon given by Andrew Barker's widow Elizabeth (d. 1704), and a paten of 1702 given by his daughter Mary.[38] The registers survive from 1617.[39] The churchyard has many tomb-chests, including that with rhyming epitaph of the mason Valentine Strong (d. 1662),[40] and a war memorial of 1919 designed by Ernest Gimson.[41]

NONCONFORMITY. The meeting of Baptists recorded in 1653 at Netherton, probably Milton End, was possibly that whose meeting-place was attacked in 1660.[42] Six protestant nonconformists were recorded in Fairford in 1676[43] and the Baptists, who were again recorded in 1685,[44] opened a new chapel south of Milton Street in 1724.[45] By 1743 membership of the meeting had risen to 60.[46] Thomas Davis was minister from 1744 until his death in 1784[47] and the merchant and writer, Anthony Robinson (1762-1827), for a few years in the 1780s.[48] In the late 18th century, when the meeting included members of the Hooke, Thompson, and Wane families, who were important local tradesmen,[49] the chapel was rebuilt and it retains the gallery and panelling which has been reset.[50] The manse in East End was replaced after 1840[51] by the house west of the chapel left by William Hooke (d. 1834).[52] In 1851 the chapel attracted congregations of up to 195.[53] In 1919 the Baptists united with the Congregationalists of the Croft chapel and services were held in the Milton Street chapel which from 1951, when the union was dissolved, was used

[16] Verey, *Glos.* i. 245.
[17] *Glos. N. & Q.* iii. 273–4; *N. & Q.* 4th ser. ii. 269.
[18] *Wood's Life and Times*, i. 323; ii. 407; W. Roper, *Vita D. Thomae Morie*, ed. T. Hearne (Oxford, 1716), 247–78.
[19] *Glos. N. & Q.* ii. 46.
[20] Glos. R.O., D 1728, wills.
[21] Ibid. D 1070/IX/2; cf. Glos. Colln. RF 130.4.
[22] Glos. Colln. R 130.14.
[23] Joyce, *Fairford Windows*; for other works, see *Cat. of Glos. Colln.* pp. 670–2.
[24] *Glos. N. & Q.* iv. 340–2, 495–6, 557–8, 670.
[25] *Memorials of Old Glos.* 208.
[26] Verey, *Glos.* i. 247.
[27] *Trans. B.G.A.S.* xlii. 70.
[28] O. G. Farmer, *Fairford Ch.* (6th edn. 1956), 76–7.
[29] Glos. R.O., D 1070/IX/1; cf. ibid. X/2.
[30] Beale, *Hist. of Fairford*, 9.
[31] Prob. 11/25 (P.C.C. 17 Hogen).
[32] Verey, *Glos.* i. 247.
[33] Beale, *Hist. of Fairford*, 8.
[34] Farmer, *Fairford Ch.* 75; Verey, *Glos.* i. 247.
[35] Prob. 11/12 (P.C.C. 3 Moone).

[36] *Glos. Ch. Bells*, 47.
[37] Inscr. in ch.
[38] *Glos. Ch. Plate*, 82–3; G.D.R., V 5/130T 3; par. reg. 1679–1788.
[39] *B. & G. Par. Rec.* 138.
[40] Colvin, *Biog. Dict. of Eng. Architects*, 578.
[41] Verey, *Glos.* i. 248.
[42] Glos. R.O., D 2052; Clark, *The Lying Wonders*.
[43] Compton Census.
[44] Glos. R.O., D 2052.
[45] Ibid. Q/SO 4; D 1070/II 2/T 1.
[46] G.D.R. vols. 285B, f. 35; 397, f. 86.
[47] Chapel min. bk. 1794–1843, *penes* Mrs. K. B. Law, chapel sec.; *Glouc. Jnl.* 19 July 1784.
[48] *D.N.B.*
[49] Cf. mons. in chapel yard; Glos. R.O., D 1070/II 2/T 1; III/16; D 1437, Kingsley fam., deeds 1757–1855; 1792–1823; D 1728, Milton End deeds 1590–1760.
[50] The date 1853 on the pediment possibly refers to that work.
[51] G.D.R., T 1/81.
[52] Chapel min. bk. 1794–1843; *Kelly's Dir. Glos.* (1885), 455.
[53] H.O. 129/340/3/10/14.

with the manse by the Congregationalists alone.[54] The house was sold in the mid 1960s when the chapel closed for a time. In 1977 the meeting had 13 members.[55]

In 1731 the manor-house was licensed as a meeting-house.[56] Most of the 10 Presbyterians meeting there in 1735 were members of James Lambe's family[57] but by the early 1770s the meeting had evidently united with the Croft chapel.[58] The membership of a meeting of Independents in Fairford rose from 10 in 1735 to 30 by 1743,[59] and the following year a chapel was built north of the Crofts.[60] A manse was built east of the old Gloucester road in the early 19th century[61] and the chapel was enlarged in 1817.[62] In 1820 the minister was described as Congregational.[66] The chapel, minister who espoused the tenets of the Particular Baptists, withdrew, apparently in the early 1830s, to form a separate church.[64] The Croft chapel, which had an average attendance of 60 in 1851,[65] was rebuilt with a schoolroom and vestry in 1862 when it was described as Congregational.[66] The chapel, which after the union with the Baptists was used for various secular purposes, was demolished in the mid 1960s.[67]

The Independents and Baptists who registered a house in the parish in 1834 probably followed the Particular Baptist minister in withdrawing from the Croft chapel.[68] Ebenezer chapel, which the Particular Baptists had built west of Coronation Street by 1862,[69] could seat 100 in 1889.[70] It closed before 1919[71] and had been converted as a doctors' surgery by 1953.[72]

Quakers, one of whom was presented in 1685, built a meeting-place in 1740[73] but no other evidence of the meeting has been found. Primitive Methodists, who were possibly meeting in Fairford by 1862,[74] opened a chapel in converted cottages in Milton Place, west of Coronation Street, in 1867.[75] The chapel, which closed c. 1925,[76] was used by a boy scout troop in 1957[77] but was disused in 1977. Other houses were registered for nonconformist use in 1820, in 1841 by John William Peters, formerly rector of Quenington, and in 1851.[78] There was a small group of Roman Catholics at Fairford in the early 18th century.[79]

EDUCATION. There was an unlicensed teacher in Fairford in 1619.[80] By 1705 a Mr. Smith of London had given a rent-charge of 30s. in Fairford for teaching poor children to read[81] and a schoolmaster was recorded in 1715.[82] The rent-charge has not been traced after 1791[83] and no evidence has been found of the application of a gift of £1 by a Mrs. Morgan for teaching 4 poor girls.[84]

The Fairford free school[85] was founded by Elizabeth Farmor's will, proved 1706, by which she left £1,000 to provide a salary of £10 for a schoolmaster teaching 20 poor children of Fairford;[86] the bequest was used, following Chancery proceedings,[87] to buy land in Chaceley in 1718.[88] The previous year it had been decreed in Chancery that a legacy of £500, left by Mary Barker (d. 1710) for teaching 40 poor children and for religious books, was to benefit Fairford and in 1721 that bequest was used to buy land.[89] A Chancery decree of 1738 combined the bequests and 60 boys aged between 5 and 12 received free education in the school which was built later that year in High Street on land bought with the proceeds of another of Elizabeth's charitable bequests. Part of the latter had been used with charity money for Cricklade (Wilts.) in 1722 to buy land from which half of the rents were assigned to the Fairford schoolmaster. The master, nominated by the lord of the manor, had an assistant or usher who received £10 a year from the endowments[90] which the master administered in the mid 18th century.[91] Elizabeth Farmor's educational bequest also provided for Sunday afternoon sermons in Fairford church and support for widows in Lady Mico's alms-houses in Stepney (Mdx.) but the latter provision was not implemented until 1817. The Mercers' Company of London, which administered the alms-houses, had apparently acquired the Chaceley land by 1890 when it probably became responsible for the payments to the school and preacher. It redeemed the schoolmaster's part on selling the land in 1920.[92]

[54] Chapel min. bk. 1904–67, *penes* Mrs. Law.
[55] Ex inf. Mr. and Mrs. Law.
[56] Hockaday Abs. cxciv.
[57] G.D.R. vols. 285B, f. 35; 397, f. 86.
[58] Glos. R.O., D 2052; *Trans. Cong. Hist. Soc.* v. 217.
[59] G.D.R. vols. 285B, f. 35; 397, f. 86.
[60] Glos. R.O., D 2052; Croft chapel deeds, *penes* Wilmot & Co., Fairford.
[61] Chapel min. bk. 1883–1914, *penes* Mrs. Law; cf. Glos. Colln. RF 130.3; Glos. R.O., D 1728, long leases 1811–83, deed 21 Oct. 1820.
[62] *Glouc. Jnl.* 20 Oct. 1817; *V.C.H. Glos.* xi. 140–1.
[63] Glos. R.O., D 1728, long leases 1811–83.
[64] Chapel min. bk. 1883–1914.
[65] H.O. 129/340/3/10/13.
[66] *Glouc. Jnl.* 9 Aug. 1862.
[67] *Kelly's Dir. Glos.* (1919–35 edns.); ex inf. Miss P. M. Dugdale, of Croft Ho., who bought the chapel in 1965.
[68] Hockaday Abs. cxciv; Croft chapel min. bk. 1883–1914.
[69] Beale, *Hist. of Fairford*, 16; O.S. Map 1/2,500, Glos. LII. 12 (1st edn.).
[70] *Kelly's Dir. Glos.* (1889), 769–70.
[71] Cf. ibid. (1914), 166; (1919), 156.
[72] Ex inf. Miss J. R. Lewis, of Fairford.
[73] Glos. R.O., D 2052.

[74] *Glouc. Jnl.* 9 Aug. 1862; cf. *Kelly's Dir. Glos.* (1863), 266, which mentions a meeting of Wesleyan Methodists.
[75] *Glouc. Jnl.* 16 Mar. 1867; inscr. on bldg.
[76] Cf. *Kelly's Dir. Glos.* (1923), 167; (1927), 174.
[77] Char. Com. Reg.
[78] Hockaday Abs. cxciv; cccxix; Glos. R.O., Q/RZ 1.
[79] Glos. R.O., Q/SO 4; G.D.R. vols. 285B, f. 35; 397, f. 86.
[80] Glos. R.O., D 2052.
[81] G.D.R., V 5/130T 3; his name may have been Thos.: cf. *20th Rep. Com. Char.* 19.
[82] Glos. R.O., Q/SO 4.
[83] Bigland, *Glos.* i. 570; cf. *20th Rep. Com. Char.* 19, in which it is confused with a reserved rent from the Chaceley est.
[84] *20th Rep. Com. Char.* 25.
[85] Briefly discussed in *V.C.H. Glos.* ii. 443.
[86] Glos. R.O., D 1728, wills.
[87] Glos. Colln. RF 130.4.
[88] Glos. R.O., D 1070/X/40; a reserved rent of 25s. from the est. was paid to the sch.: cf. ibid. 39.
[89] Ibid. 23.
[90] *20th Rep. Com. Char.* 18–20; inscr. on bldg.
[91] Hedges, *Farmor's Sch.* 29–30.
[92] Glos. R.O., D 1070/X/40; ex inf. the clerk, Mercers' Co., London.

In 1817, when the curate Thomas Richards was master, the school, which had been enlarged by John Raymond-Barker, became a National school for the children of the town and neighbourhood. Education for 60 boys and 60 girls from the parish was free and the other children paid pence or fees. The Chancery decree of 1817, which authorized spending up to £30 a year on the girls' school, provided for a salary of at least £60 for the master,[93] who taught 101 boys in 1818 when a mistress received £25 for teaching 129 girls. The endowments, to which more land had apparently been added, produced £106 5s.[94] In 1847 the income was made up of £36 2s. from pence and £112 2s. from the endowments[95] which were augmented in 1877 when a Scheme united Lady Mico's apprenticing charity with the school.[96] In 1866 Thomas Morton, the curate, taught in place of the master who was dismissed for neglect,[97] and the school, enlarged in 1873,[98] had an average attendance of 173 in 1889.[99] Called Farmor's Endowed school in 1904,[1] it did not become fully co-educational until 1922[2] and in 1927 131 of the 188 children were aged over ten, many coming from outside the town.[3] New classrooms were opened east of the infant school in London Road in 1955 when both schools were reorganized as a primary school. The building in High Street closed in 1961 and more classrooms were built in London Road between 1966 and 1973. In 1977 Fairford C. of E. Primary school drew 328 children from the town, Horcott, and Fairford R.A.F. base.[4] The Farmor's Endowed Schools Foundation, established under the Scheme of 1877,[5] sold its last remaining land in 1970. In 1976 it had an income from investments of c. £1,400 which was used, under a Scheme of 1973, to provide educational grants for three persons aged under 25 and to cover expenses of the primary and comprehensive schools not met by the county council.[6]

An infant school, begun in 1831, taught 44 children in 1833 when it was supported by fees and subscriptions;[7] it was possibly that recorded in 1838.[8] Fairford C. of E. Infant school, established in 1866, was held in a converted barn and had an average attendance of 72 in 1869 when it was supported by voluntary contributions and pence.[9] In 1873 a new building was opened in London Road.[10] The average attendance, which in 1889 was 65, had risen, after enlargement of the building, to 85 by 1897[11] but fell from 75 in 1910 to 29 by 1936.[12] In 1955 the school became part of the primary school.

A fee-paying boarding and day-school with 67 children in 1833[13] was probably held in Mount Pleasant House, the site of a private school by 1814 and until at least 1863.[14] A private school for girls in High Street, established by 1842,[15] was later held in a cottage north of Mount Pleasant House until at least 1876.[16]

A Sunday school was supported by charity money from the early 1680s.[17] The church Sunday school, to which John Carter (d. 1811) left £50 stock,[18] was evidently that attached to the free school which taught 209 children in 1833,[19] and in 1976 £1.69 was paid for the use of the Sunday school by his charity.[20] The Croft chapel ran a day-school by 1856[21] but it did not have a schoolroom until 1862[22] and has not been traced after 1863.[23]

In 1891 the county council made a grant to a school of science and art in Fairford but no other record of the school has been found.[24] Farmor's School, a secondary modern school, opened in 1962 in a new building on the site of Fairford Park.[25] In 1966 it became a comprehensive school[26] and had 660 children from the south-eastern part of the county on the roll in 1977.[27]

CHARITIES FOR THE POOR. The church or parish lands charity established in 1564 maintained an alms-house which had six occupants in 1662, when it stood north of Park Street.[28] It had been burnt down by c. 1708.[29] The third of the charity's income designated for the poor by the Scheme of 1859 included a subscription of £2 2s. to Gloucester Infirmary or a similar institution for the treatment of patients;[30] it was paid to the infirmary between 1861 and 1868 and to the cottage hospital from 1877. The rest was spent on coal and clothing[31] and in 1970 the charity helped c. 30 people.[32] That half of the income which from 1971 went to the poor was

[93] 20th Rep. Com. Char. 20–2; Glos. R.O., D 1070/X/25; Hockaday Abs. cxciv, 1811.
[94] Educ. of Poor Digest, 299; cf. 20th Rep. Com. Char. 21.
[95] Ed. 7/34/137.
[96] Glos. Colln. RF 130.1.
[97] Glos. R.O., D 1070/X/25; cf. Kelly's Dir. Glos. (1863), 266; (1870), 545.
[98] Hedges, Farmor's Sch. 36–7.
[99] Kelly's Dir. Glos. (1889), 769.
[1] Public Elem. Schs. 1906, 184.
[2] Hedges, Farmor's Sch. 60.
[3] Glos. R.O., D 2864.
[4] Ex inf. the headmaster and county educ. dept.
[5] Glos. Colln. RF 130.1.
[6] Ex inf. Mr. Lee-Browne.
[7] Educ. Enquiry Abstract, 315.
[8] Glos. R.O., D 1070/IX/8; it may have been in the Crofts: cf. ibid. D 1728, long leases 1811–83, deed 1 Mar. 1851.
[9] Ed. 7/34/138.
[10] Glos, R.O., D 1070/X/33; O.S. Map 6", Glos. LII. SE. (1886 edn.).
[11] Kelly's Dir. Glos. (1889), 769; (1897), 154.
[12] Bd. of Educ., List 21, 1911 (H.M.S.O.), 162; ibid. 1936, 121.
[13] Educ. Enquiry Abstract, 315.
[14] Par. reg. 1813–54; G.D.R., T 1/81; Pigot's Dir. Glos. (1842), 105; H.O. 107/1968; Kelly's Dir. Glos. (1863), 266.
[15] Pigot's Dir. Glos. (1842), 105; H.O. 107/1968.
[16] Morris's Dir. Glos. (1876), 257; cf. O.S. Map 6", Glos. LII. SE. (1886 edn.).
[17] G.D.R., V 5/130T 2; Glos. R.O., D 2864.
[18] 20th Rep. Com. Char. 21; par. reg. 1788–1812.
[19] Educ. Enquiry Abstract, 315.
[20] Ex inf. Mr. Lee-Browne.
[21] Kelly's Dir. Glos. (1856), 286.
[22] Glouc. Jnl. 9 Aug. 1862; Croft chapel deeds, plan 1862.
[23] Kelly's Dir. Glos. (1863), 267.
[24] Glos. C.C. Mins. 26 Oct. 1891, p. 174.
[25] Glos. Countryside, April–May 1962, 7.
[26] Glos. Life, Mar. 1970, 29.
[27] Ex inf. Miss Lewis.
[28] Glos. R.O., D 1070/X/2, pp. 9–13; cf. C 2/Eliz. I/F 3/37.
[29] Bodl. MS. Top. Glouc. c.3, f. 156v. cf. Glos. R.O., D 1728, copy ch. lands terrier 1740.
[30] Glos. R.O., D 1070/X/6.
[31] Ibid. 7, 9–11.
[32] Ibid. CH 21.

used in 1976 to provide television sets for the cottage hospital.[33]

Thomas Morgan by will dated 1632 left £100 for the poor. Though £20 lent out c. 1663 was lost, another part, used with a charitable gift of £5 from Morgan Emmot to buy land for Lady Mico's apprenticing charity[34] in 1673, had been repaid by 1688.[35] The funds of the charity, standing at £100, were lent out but in 1757 £30 was spent on the purchase of the pest-house and from that time the overseers distributed £1 10s. a year to the poor. About 1787 the rest of the principal was spent on building Tinkers Row and from then until 1836 the overseers distributed £5 a year to the poor on Good Friday.[36]

By deed of 1670 Andrew Barker gave Jane Mico, Lady Mico, his sister-in-law, a rent-charge of £5 4s. for a weekly distribution of bread to the poor of Fairford; the charity became known as Lady Mico's bread charity.[37] William Butcher by will proved 1715 gave £40 for a weekly bread charity, and from 1757, when it was put towards buying the pest-house, bread worth £2 was provided from the poor-rate.[38] By 1829 the two charities were distributed together every third week[39] and in 1836 33 people received bread.[40] The vicar Frampton Huntingdon (d. 1738) left £10 for a bread charity for 20 poor church-goers.[41] The principal, which was lent to a baker until 1786, was then spent on building Tinkers Row and the overseers distributed 10s. a year in bread on 21 August.[42] Robert Jenner by will dated 1770 left £10 for a distribution to 5 poor widows on Christmas Eve and Alexander Colston (formerly Ready) (d. 1775) left £105 for a distribution to 4 poor widows at Candlemas. Both charities were spent on building Tinkers Row[43] and the overseers distributed 10s. and £5 5s. in cash respectively.[44] Payment for the Jenner charity had stopped by 1829[45] but was resumed following the transfer of Tinkers Row and the pest-house to the churchwardens, who managed the property also for the Morgan, Butcher, Huntingdon, and Colston charities. By the 1850s the churchwardens distributed £5 5s. a year for the Jenner and Colston charities combined.[46]

John Carter (d. 1811) left £300 stock for a distribution to the poor in December[47] and a bequest by Sarah Luckman (d. 1830) for a distribution of cash in February realized £98 by 1836.[48] All the above-mentioned charities, except for the church or parish lands charity, were amalgamated in 1869.[49] John Harvey Ollney by will proved 1836 left £200 to Fairford for a Christmas coal and blanket charity, which was distributed from 1840[50] and added to the combined charities in 1972.[51] In 1976 the income of the combined charities, c. £200, was distributed in vouchers.[52]

A trust fund of £20 established under the will of Elizabeth Cull (d. 1674) had not been claimed by 1681 when it became payable to the poor. Under the will of her trustee, William Oldisworth (d. 1680), it was used to buy 26s. of bread a year for four poor boys attending a Sunday school, the teacher of which received 4s. William's heir James Oldisworth (d. 1722) also paid 40s. interest on the original grant, evidently believing it separate, but from c. 1725 his daughter Muriel Loggan only paid for the bread and the teacher.[53] The charity had been lost by 1829.[54]

Lady Mico by will proved 1671 left £400 for apprenticing four poor boys of the town each year. In 1673 the principal was used with other charity money to buy land, out of the rents of which the borrowed money had been repaid by 1688.[55] From the later 18th century, although boys were sometimes apprenticed as far afield as Gloucester, Kidderminster, Banbury, and London, the difficulty of finding suitable masters led to an accumulation of funds; £120 was lent between 1798 and 1806 to the workhouse and £200 had been invested in stock by 1829. By then to prevent masters from breaking agreements part of the premium was paid at the end of the period of apprenticeship.[56] The charity had over £1,114 stock in 1871 when a Scheme authorized spending £630, from funds and sale of stock, on building the infant school and enlarging the free school, with which the charity was united for educational purposes in 1877.[57]

HATHEROP

THE RURAL PARISH of Hatherop, which included the hamlet of Netherton, lies 13.5 km. ENE. of Cirencester. The ancient parish was irregular in shape, with a peninsulated part extending south-eastwards beyond the Fairford–Southrop road, and an elongated tongue stretching north-eastwards from the river Coln to take in Dean Farm and Dean Camp, an ancient hill fort beyond the river Leach, which had ceased to run there by 1976. The parish enclosed on three sides Williamstrip, a large

[33] Ex inf. Mr. Lee-Browne.
[34] G.D.R., V 5/130T 2.
[35] Glos. R.O., D 1070/X/20.
[36] Ibid. IX/4, 11; 20th Rep. Com. Char. 24.
[37] 20th Rep. Com. Char. 24; Hedges, Farmor's Sch. 21.
[38] Glos. R.O., D 1070/IX/4, 11; Trans. B.G.A.S. lxxxi. 130.
[39] 20th Rep. Com. Char. 24.
[40] Glos. R.O., D 1070/IX/4.
[41] 20th Rep. Com. Char. 25; Bigland, Glos. i. 573.
[42] Glos. R.O., D 1070/IX/4, 11; 20th Rep. Com. Char. 25.
[43] 20th Rep. Com. Char. 25; Glos. R.O., D 1070/IX/4; cf. ibid. III/21.
[44] Glos. R.O., D 1070/IX/11.

[45] 20th Rep. Com. Char. 25.
[46] Glos. R.O., D 1070/IX/4; X/47.
[47] 20th Rep. Com. Char. 21; par. reg. 1788–1812.
[48] Glos. R.O., D 1070/IX/4; mon. in churchyard.
[49] Glos. R.O., CH 21.
[50] Ibid. D 1070/IX/4; V.C.H. Glos. xi. 40.
[51] Glos. R.O., CH 21; Char. Com. Reg.
[52] Ex inf. Mr. Lee-Browne.
[53] G.D.R., V 5/130T 2; Glos. R.O., D 2864.
[54] 20th Rep. Com. Char. 25.
[55] Ibid. 23; Glos. R.O., D 1070/X/20.
[56] Glos. R.O., D 1070/X/21; 20th Rep. Com. Char. 23–4.
[57] Glos. R.O., D 1070/X/22; Glos. Colln. RF 130.1.

detached portion of Coln St. Aldwyns parish[58] represented in 1086 by an estate called Hatherop,[59] probably attached to Coln St. Aldwyns through the grant before 1096 of some of its tithes to Gloucester Abbey.[60] In 1530 tenants of Coln St. Aldwyns were presented in court for driving their animals through Hatherop manor.[61] The boundary with Williamstrip was changed after inclosure, and by an exchange before 1812 61 a. were transferred to Hatherop and 92 a. to Coln St. Aldwyns.[62] In the later 19th century Hatherop parish with an area of 2,124 a. was bounded by the Coln on the west, a salt-way on parts of the south and east, the Burford road and Akeman Street for short sections north-east of Hatherop village, which grew up near the western boundary, and streams and field boundaries elsewhere.[63]

In 1935 the parish was reduced to 1,360 a. (550 ha.). The tongue of land extending beyond the Leach and parts of Williamstrip park north of Hatherop village, a total of 818 a., were exchanged for 57 a. of Coln St. Aldwyns thereby placing the northern boundary of the parish on the roads to Coln St. Aldwyns and Burford. The transfer of 3 a. to Quenington[64] brought the western boundary back into line with the river Coln which between 1862 and 1881 had been diverted eastwards along the race of Netherton mill.[65] The account printed below covers the area included in the parish until 1935 except for those parts in Williamstrip park which are dealt with under Coln St. Aldwyns.

The parish rises from c. 91 m. in the Coln valley and the south to over 122 m. south-west of Dean Farm and over 137 m. north of the Leach which crossed the parish at over 107 m. The land is formed by Forest Marble or the underlying strata of the Great Oolite but there are areas of cornbrash south of the village and in the far south.[66] The area of Dean farm was inclosed earlier than the rest of the parish which mostly lay in open fields and common pasture until parliamentary inclosure in 1766. Arable farming has predominated, there being only a small area of meadow land, and sheep-farming was important by the mid 13th century.

The woodland on the eastern bank of the Coln was depicted in an engraving of c. 1710[67] and was called Netherton coppice.[68] Several coppices recorded by the Leach in 1785[69] had been joined together by 1862 to form Dean Farm covert,[70] and Swanhill covert east of the village was greatly enlarged between 1881 and 1901.[71] In 1901 85¾ a. of the parish comprised woods and plantations.[72]

Hatherop park, created south of the manor-house before c. 1710,[73] was extended to the east and the south-west before 1862,[74] probably in 1848 when several routes there were closed.[75] The park was enlarged to the south-east c. 1870[76] and included 200 a. in 1879.[77] An area east of the Lechlade road was taken in between 1901 and 1920.[78]

The salt-way between Droitwich and Lechlade which crossed the parish[79] was called London way in the southern part in 1628.[80] The section passing along the eastern bank of the Coln above Netherton coppice[81] was closed in 1848 because of the steep gradients.[82] At Netherton near the southern boundary it was joined by a route from Cirencester, crossing the river by Netherton bridge, which needed repairs in 1526,[83] and then continued south-eastwards past Barrow Elm, the meeting-place of the hundred court at the junction of roads from Fairford and Hatherop village.[84] The latter road, possibly the highway out of repair in 1536,[85] was presented in 1757 as being ruinous[86] but the section through the village became part of the route between Coln St. Aldwyns and Burford in 1777. A road leading from the east end of the village northwards through Williamstrip to Akeman Street was then replaced by one leading north-eastwards.[87] A route between Bibury and Dean Farm recorded in the later 18th century[88] had disappeared by 1862.[89]

The name Hatherop may derive from the village's location above the valley of the Coln.[90] The site of Hatherop Castle, the manor-house, overlooking the valley, was occupied by the later 13th century but although the house incorporates an embattled tower and a close to the west was called the Castle by the mid 16th century[91] there is no evidence of a castle there. The church to the east was recorded from the late 11th century. Both manor-house and church were rebuilt in the mid 19th century and stand apart from the village which grew up around a small green, mentioned c. 1290,[92] to the north-east where the base and part of the shaft of an old stone cross survive. Severalls, the former rectory, was built on the south side of the green, from which the village

[58] *O.S. Area Bk.* (1882). This account was written in 1976.
[59] *Dom. Bk.* (Rec. Com.), i. 167v.
[60] *Reg. Regum Anglo-Norm.* ii, p. 410; see above, p. 44.
[61] D.L. 30/127/1907 f. 27v.
[62] Glos. R.O., D 2440, misc. est. papers 1729–1866; cf. *Manual of Glos. Lit.* ii. 207.
[63] *O.S. Area Bk.* (1882).
[64] *Census*, 1931 (pt. ii); 1971; see below.
[65] Glos. R.O., D 540/E 10; O.S. Map 6″, Glos. LII. NE. (1886 edn.).
[66] Geol. Surv. Map 1″, solid, sheets 34, 44 (1856–7 edns.).
[67] Atkyns, *Glos.* plate at pp. 464–5.
[68] Glos. R.O., Q/RNc 1, p. 159.
[69] Ibid. D 540/E 6, P 2.
[70] Ibid. E 10; O.S. Map 6″, Glos. XLIV. SE. (1886 edn.).
[71] O.S. Map 6″, Glos. LII. NE. (1886, 1903 edns.).
[72] Acreage Returns, 1901.
[73] Atkyns, *Glos.* plate at pp. 464–5.
[74] Cf. Greenwood, *Map of Glos.* (1824); Glos. R.O., D 540/E 10.

[75] Glos. R.O., Q/SRh 1848 A/2.
[76] *Kelly's Dir. Glos.* (1870), 578; cf. O.S. Map 6″, Glos. LII. NE. (1886 edn.).
[77] *Kelly's Dir. Glos.* (1879), 681.
[78] O.S. Map 6″, Glos. LII. NE. (1903, 1924 edns.).
[79] Taylor, *Map of Glos.* (1777).
[80] Glos. R.O., D 540/T 34.
[81] Ibid. photocopy 64B.
[82] Ibid. Q/SRh 1848 A/2.
[83] D.L. 30/127/1907 f. 5v.
[84] *P.N. Glos.* (E.P.N.S.), i. 22, 37.
[85] D.L. 30/127/1907 f. 61.
[86] *Glos. Q.S. Archives*, 83.
[87] Glos. R.O., Q/SRh 1777 A/2.
[88] Ibid. D 540/P 2; cf. Glos. R.O., P 96B/SD 1/1.
[89] Ibid. D 540/E 10.
[90] *P.N. Glos.* i. 37.
[91] E 164/39 f. 4v.; cf. Glos. R.O., D 540/T 34.
[92] When people surnamed 'of the green' were recorded: *Wilts. Arch. Mag.* xxxii. 330.

street developed eastwards. At the eastern end, where there were a few cottages east of the Lechlade road by the mid 18th century,[93] Glebe Farm was rebuilt in the mid 19th century. Part of the village was taken into Williamstrip park in the later 18th century. A few early cottages have survived but most of the buildings standing in 1976 date from the later 19th century. In the village street in 1856 A. G. J. Ponsonby built a school and school-house and some estate cottages, including Lechmere which later became the rectory. A row of cottages north of the street was later converted with the insertion of a central arch.[94] More estate cottages, mostly east of the Lechlade road, were built by Thomas Sebastian Bazley in the late 1860s and 1870s.[95] North-east of Severalls a building dated 1909 probably served as a reading-room, and a memorial was built after the First World War.[96] Three bungalows were built east of the Lechlade road in the mid 20th century. In 1976 Hatherop Working Men's Club occupied a wooden hut south of the village street.

A farm-house recorded at the junction of the Eastleach and Lechlade roads south of the village in 1764[97] was called Townsend Farm in the mid 19th century when some cottages stood near by.[98] The farm-house and buildings were demolished c. 1870 and a lodge was built on the site, which had been taken into Hatherop park.[99] Stonyhurst Cottage to the east had been built by 1901.[1]

The hamlet of Netherton grew up in the Coln valley near the crossing-point of the river by a route from Cirencester to the salt-way. A mill had been built at the crossing by the late 11th century and men surnamed of Netherton were recorded from the mid 13th century.[2] The principal street, which ran north-eastwards from the mill, had cottages which were built on waste ground[3] and contained 11 dwellings in 1764.[4] The higher part of the hamlet, which included cottages in Fairford parish,[5] possibly occupied the site called Overthrop from c. 1290.[6] One small cottage there was remodelled and enlarged in the 19th century. During the extension of Hatherop park the cottages in the street were demolished between 1848 and 1862[7] and the remaining buildings in the valley c. 1870 when a lodge was built there. In the higher part a lodge and, to the east, Home Farm are of a similar date,[8] and a house was built south of the road in the mid 20th century.

At Dean Farm a 17th-century farm-house and out-building[9] stand amongst buildings of the 19th and 20th centuries. The farm-house was converted to cottages in 1870 when a new farm-house was built higher up to the west.[10] The site of Upper Moor's Barn had been built on by 1764[11] and Upper Cottages, recorded in 1785,[12] were rebuilt in the later 19th century.

South Farm in the south-east of the parish is a post-inclosure farm-house built by Sir John Webb in 1766.[13] It has extensive buildings of the 19th and 20th centuries including cottages for farm workers. The remaining outlying cottages in the parish were built by T. S. Bazley in the 1870s, Barn Ground Cottages being converted later to a single dwelling. Barrow Elm Cottages were greatly enlarged during a similar conversion in the late 1960s.[14] Barrow Elm Farm, west of Barrow Elm, is a large farm-house of c. 1890 with contemporary farm buildings.[15] By 1976 it was let as a private residence from the Hatherop estate.[16]

In 1086 35 tenants were mentioned in Hatherop.[17] Thirty people were assessed for the subsidy in 1327 and 50 for the poll tax in 1381.[18] In 1551 there were c. 60 communicants in the parish[19] and in 1563 14 households.[20] By 1650 there were 24 families[21] and the population continued to grow in the 18th century. It was estimated at 150 c. 1710[22] and 204 c. 1775[23] and was 247 in 1801. It increased to 375 by 1851 before falling considerably to 283 by 1871. By 1881 it had risen again to 347 but it dropped to 295 by 1901. After an increase to 308 by 1921 it then declined, partly because of boundary changes, and in 1971 was 178.[24]

Two innholders were licensed in 1755.[25] One possibly occupied the Bell at the western end of the village which was not recorded after Sir John Webb conveyed it to Samuel Blackwell of Williamstrip in 1778,[26] the site evidently being taken into Williamstrip park. In 1851 an innkeeper lived in Netherton.[27]

Between the late 17th and early 19th centuries the parish was a centre of Roman Catholicism supported by the Webbs, the leading family. T. S. Bazley, who became the principal landowner in 1867, was responsible for much building in the later 19th century. His descendant's estate in 1976 still included the village and much land.[28]

[93] Cf. Glos. R.O., photocopy 64B.
[94] Date and inits. 'A.G.P.' on bldgs.
[95] Kelly's Dir. Glos. (1870), 578; dates and inits. on bldgs.
[96] O.S. Map 6", Glos. LII. NE. (1924 edn.).
[97] Glos. R.O., photocopy 64B.
[98] Ibid. D 540/P 4.
[99] Cf. ibid. E 10; O.S. Map 6", Glos. LII. NE. (1886 edn.).
[1] O.S. Map 6", Glos. LII. NE. (1903 edn.).
[2] Lacock Abbey Charters, ed. K. H. Rogers (Wilts. Rec. Soc. xxxiv), no. 426; Hist. & Cart. Mon. Glouc. (Rolls Ser.), iii. 197.
[3] Cf. Glos. R.O., Q/RNc 1, p. 166; D 540/E 4.
[4] Ibid. photocopy 64B.
[5] Cf. O.S. Map 6", Glos. LII. NE. (1886 edn.); Glos. R.O., D 540/T 28.
[6] Wilts. Arch. Mag. xxxii. 330–1; cf. E 164/39 f. 5.
[7] Cf. Glos. R.O., Q/SRh 1848 A/2; D 540/E 10.
[8] Cf. ibid. D 540/E 10; O.S. Map 6", Glos. LII. NE. (1886 edn.).
[9] Cf. Glos. R.O., Q/RNc 1, p. 157; photocopy 64B.

[10] Williamstrip Mun., penes Earl St. Aldwyn, Williamstrip Pk., Coln St. Aldwyns, MTC/21/2.
[11] Glos. R.O., photocopy 64B.
[12] Ibid. D 540/P 2.
[13] Inscr. on bldg.; cf. Taylor, Map of Glos. (1777).
[14] Dates and inits. on bldgs.
[15] Cf. Kelly's Dir. Glos. (1894), 205.
[16] Ex. inf. Smith-Woolley & Co., Woodstock, agents to the Hatherop est.
[17] Dom. Bk. (Rec. Com.), i. 169.
[18] Glos. Subsidy Roll, 1327, 14; E 179/113/35A rot. 1d.
[19] E.H.R. xix. 113.
[20] Bodl. MS. Rawl. C.790, f. 26.
[21] Trans. B.G.A.S. lxxxiii. 94.
[22] Atkyns, Glos. 464.
[23] Rudder, Glos. 482.
[24] Census, 1801–1971.
[25] Glos. R.O., Q/AV 2, rot. 3.
[26] Williamstrip Mun. MTD/93/1.
[27] H.O. 107/1968.
[28] Ex inf. Smith-Woolley & Co.

MANOR AND OTHER ESTATES. In 1066 Uluuard held an estate of 7 hides in Hatherop which by 1086 had been acquired by Ernulf of Hesdin.[29] It evidently passed with Ernulf's daughter Maud to Patrick de Chaworth whose daughter Sibyl married Walter of Salisbury. Walter (d. 1147) was succeeded by his son Patrick, created earl of Salisbury by the Empress Maud between 1142 and 1147, and Patrick (d. 1168) by his son William, earl of Salisbury,[30] who apparently granted rents worth 100s. in Hatherop to Bradenstoke Priory (Wilts.).[31] William died in 1196 leaving as his heir his daughter Ela, whose husband William Longespee became earl of Salisbury[32] and held the estate, assessed at $2\frac{1}{4}$ fees, c. 1212.[33] William settled some Carthusian monks at Hatherop in 1222 but after his death in 1226 Ela moved them to Hinton Charterhouse (Som.).[34] Bradenstoke Priory received further grants of property in Hatherop including land worth 100s. from Ela's estate, called *HATHEROP* manor.[35] The priory, which received a rent-charge of 10s. from the manor until 1412,[36] retained its property until the Dissolution.[37]

Ela probably endowed Lacock Abbey (Wilts.) with Hatherop manor in 1231 or 1232.[38] Overlordship of the manor, which was assessed at $\frac{1}{4}$ fee, belonged in 1285 to Henry de Lacy, earl of Lincoln,[39] who had married Margaret, great-granddaughter and heir of Ela (d. 1261). It passed to Margaret's daughter and heir Alice, wife of Thomas, earl of Lancaster (d. 1322), and was acquired from her by Hugh le Despenser in 1325.[40] Later it apparently continued in the duchy of Lancaster, in the name of which courts were held in the early 16th century.[41]

In 1249 Lacock Abbey, of which Ela was then abbess, awarded a life-interest in the manor to her daughter Ela, countess of Warwick,[42] who was granted free warren for life in 1251.[43] In 1284 she granted an estate of 12 yardlands acquired from Sir Ingram Waleys to the abbey[44] to which she relinquished the manor in return for an annuity in 1287.[45] In the mid 14th century until at least 1366 the manor was held from the abbey for a rent of 2s. by John de Haudlo and his descendants with Coln St. Aldwyns manor.[46]

Lacock Abbey retained Hatherop manor until the Dissolution.[47] Sir William Sharington, who was granted Bradenstoke Priory's property in 1542,[48] acquired it in 1548.[49] In 1552 he sold his estate there to William Herbert, earl of Pembroke,[50] who sold it to John Blomer,[51] the lessee of the manor since 1538.[52] John (d. 1558) left the manor to his second son William[53] who bought more land in 1598.[54] William (d. 1613) was succeeded in turn by his sons Sir Henry[55] (d. 1624) and John.[56] After John's death in 1638 the manor passed to his widow Frances (d. 1657),[57] a Roman Catholic whose property was sequestered by 1653,[58] and then in turn to their children John (d. 1685), William (d. 1686), and Mary.[59] Mary, whose husband Sir John Webb, Bt., of Great Canford (Dors.) died in 1700, was succeeded in 1709 by their son John, after whose death in 1745 the estate passed with the baronetcy to his son Thomas (d. 1763). Thomas's son John (d. 1797)[60] left the estate to his granddaughter Lady Barbara Ashley Cooper[61] who in 1814 married William Francis Spenser Ponsonby, created Baron de Mauley in her right in 1838. Lady de Mauley died in 1844 and after her husband's death in 1855 the Hatherop estate passed to their younger son Ashley George John Ponsonby, M.P. for Cirencester, who sold it in 1862 to the Maharajah Duleep Singh of Lahore. In 1867 it was bought by Thomas Sebastian Bazley[62] who in 1885 inherited the baronetcy of Tolmers (Herts.). By 1900 Sir Thomas (d. 1919) had conveyed the estate to his son Gardner Sebastian Bazley, after whose death in 1911[63] South farm was sold to N. H. Geach. Charles White who bought the farm in 1921 sold it in 1939 to Clarence H. S. Townsend and his wife Sophia whose children John and Ann, wife of Mr. D. M. Backhouse, owned it in 1976.[64] G. S. Bazley's trustees retained the Hatherop estate until the mid 1930s when it passed to his son Sir Thomas Stafford Bazley, Bt.[65] In 1934 Sir Thomas sold Dean farm to his brother Anthony Gardner Bazley (d. 1937) who left it to his wife Anne. Anne, who later married Francis Philip Howard, Baron Howard of Penrith, had by 1976 transferred c. 164 ha. (c. 406 a.) to her daughter Susan, wife of Mr. W. Vicary, but retained ownership of c. 101 ha. (c. 250 a.).[66] Sir Thomas Bazley, who sold c. 101 ha.

[29] *Dom. Bk.* (Rec. Com.), i. 169.
[30] *Complete Peerage*, xi. 375–7.
[31] *Cal. Chart. R.* 1226–57, 161.
[32] *Complete Peerage*, xi. 378–9.
[33] *Bk. of Fees*, i. 49.
[34] *V.C.H. Som.* ii. 118–19; *V.C.H. Glos.* ii. 52.
[35] *Cal. Chart. R.* 1226–57, 159–60; *V.C.H. Wilts.* iii. 283; cf. B.L. Cott. MS. Vit. A. xi, f. 53.
[36] *Cal. Pat.* 1408–13, 394.
[37] *Wilts. Arch. Mag.* xxxv. 195, 197, 206; *Valor Eccl.* (Rec. Com.), ii. 125.
[38] *V.C.H. Wilts.* iii. 303; *Wilts. Arch. Mag.* xxxv. 192 and n., 202.
[39] *Feud. Aids*, ii. 237.
[40] *Complete Peerage*, xi. 382–4; vii. 677; *Cal. Pat.* 1324–7, 102.
[41] D.L. 30/127/1907.
[42] C.P. 25(1)/283/12 no. 238; *V.C.H. Wilts.* iii. 304.
[43] *Cal. Chart. R.* 1226–57, 369.
[44] Hockaday Abs. ccxxxvii.
[45] *V.C.H. Wilts.* iii. 308.
[46] *Cal. Inq. p.m.* viii, p. 494; *Inq. p.m. Glos.* 1359–1413, 15; *Cal. Pat.* 1364–7, 276–7; see above.
[47] Dugdale, *Mon.* vi (1), 510.

[48] *L. & P. Hen. VIII*, xvii, p. 631.
[49] *Cal. Pat.* 1547–8, 402.
[50] Ibid. 1550–3, 417–18.
[51] Ibid. 246.
[52] Glos. R.O., D 540/T 30.
[53] C 142/122 no. 64.
[54] Glos. R.O., D 540/T 4, T 6.
[55] C 142/347 no. 62.
[56] C 142/406 no. 50.
[57] *Inq. p.m. Glos.* 1625–42, ii. 50–4; cf. Bigland, *Glos.* ii. 48, which says John died in 1640.
[58] *Cal. Cttee. for Compounding*, i. 87; Glos. R.O., D 540/T 31.
[59] Bigland, *Glos.* ii. 48; cf. Glos. R.O., D 540/T 6, T 30, T 32.
[60] Glos. R.O., D 540/F 3; cf. ibid. E 4; Burke, *Land. Gent.* (1898), ii. 1561.
[61] Glos. R.O., D 540/F 2.
[62] Burke, *Peerage* (1963), 691; *Glos. Life* (Apr. 1973), 47; cf. *Who Was Who*, 1916–28, 308, s.v. Duleep Singh.
[63] Burke, *Peerage* (1963), 187–8; Williamstrip Mun. MTC/21/2; cf. *Kelly's Dir. Glos.* (1902), 210.
[64] Ex inf. Mrs. Sophia Townsend.
[65] Burke, *Peerage* (1963), 187–8; *Kelly's Dir. Glos.* (1914 and later edns.).
[66] Burke, *Peerage* (1963), 187; ex inf. Lord Howard.

in Hatherop and Quenington to the Ernest Cook Trust in 1975, retained over 283 ha. (700 a.) in the parish in 1976.[67]

The manor-house occupies a site on which buildings were recorded from the later 13th century.[68] That the house was already of considerable size is suggested by the number of hearths, 25, taxed in 1672,[69] and Kip's view shows it in the early 18th century as having a long north front of two storeys with gabled attics and a central porch with hall and parlour to the west and what were presumably service rooms extending to the churchyard on the east. Behind the hall and parlour an embattled tower, probably of medieval origin, rose above the roofs.[70] In 1715 Jacobite sympathisers apparently assembled at the house, from which Sir John Webb's son-in-law James Radclyffe, earl of Derwentwater, left to join the rising.[71] The house, which contained a Roman Catholic chapel, was occupied by Sir John Webb in 1764[72] but later he lived elsewhere and neglected the house.[73] Known as Hatherop Castle by 1848[74] it was rebuilt between 1850 and 1856 to designs by Henry Clutton.[75] He preserved the basic plan of the tower and the rooms behind the north front but added new ranges on the west and south and completely rebuilt the kitchen and service quarters. His exteriors are in a large-scale version of the local early-17th-century style, his interiors in a richly decorated Jacobean style. The Maharajah Duleep Singh lived there in the mid 1860s[76] and after T. S. Bazley bought the estate further work, not now identifiable, was carried out.[77] In the 1920s it was the home of G. S. Bazley's widow Ruth Evelyn, who married Francis Charles Cadogan.[78] From 1946 Sir Thomas Bazley leased the house to Owlstone Croft School, a girls' public school later called Hatherop Castle School, the trustees of which bought the house and c. 15 a. in 1972. In 1976 the school had c. 100 pupils.[79] Of the three lodges built c. 1870 that opposite the Eastleach road replaced one to the south. The other two in Netherton, one in the valley and the other higher up,[80] were rebuilt in 1886 and 1890 respectively.[81]

The Knights Hospitallers held land in Hatherop from the manor at the Dissolution when it was leased with their property in North Cerney, an adjunct of Quenington Preceptory, to Sir Edmund Tame.[82] The endowments of a chantry-chapel in Coln St. Aldwyns included a close in Netherton, to which a customary yardland, called St. Mary land c. 1539, had once been attached.[83] A mill and land in Netherton owned by Gloucester Abbey passed with Coln St. Aldwyns manor until the mid 19th century and is dealt with below.

ECONOMIC HISTORY. In 1086 the manor, which had risen in value from £8 in 1066 to £12, had 16 plough-lands of which 6 were in demesne and worked by 12 *servi*.[84] In 1220 the estate comprised 20 plough-lands[85] but in 1291 Lacock Abbey was said to have only one.[86] In 1249 the manor was let at farm for a term of 7 years, at the end of which the demesne was to include 233 a. prepared for tillage and the abbey was to receive 16 oxen, 4 cows, and 200 sheep, or the value in cash.[87] The demesne was let at farm for £9 a year from 1533.[88] In 1535 Bradenstoke Priory was receiving 43s. 4d. in rents[89] and in 1537 its property was let at farm for 60 years for that sum.[90]

In 1086 there were 23 *villani* with 10 ploughs on the manor.[91] A custumal of c. 1290 lists 34 varied tenements held from the manor. The three largest, one of 1½ hide and two of ½ hide each, were held by service, presumably military, due to the Crown. Two holdings of a yardland, from one of which bedrepes were owed, and one of 12 a. were held for cash rents. The tenant of a two-yardland tenement, held for cash rent and bedrepes, was liable for service as reeve. The customary tenements comprised 8 yardlands and one half-yardland. The service owed from a yardland included work on each weekday except Saturday at the usual agricultural tasks and carrying, five bedrepes (the fifth to be at the lady's cost), and 43 eggs at Lent. The ploughing of 14¾ a. by all 9 tenants was counted as a week's work. Of 15 smallholders, 8 owed labour-services on Mondays and some boon-works, 4 cash rent and bedrepes, and 3, including a smith, cash rent. The tenants who mowed were feasted by the lady, a custom called *medsep*. For another tenement a miller owed a bedrepe, and the demesne shepherd held 10 a. by his service. The tenant of a 5-acre holding was required to perform bedrepes and either to serve as demesne swineherd or provide a hayward.[92] In 1291 Lacock Abbey had rents of assize valued at 12s. in Hatherop, the level perhaps indicating the importance of tenant labour-services,[93] but in 1341 2½ yardlands in the parish lay uncultivated by the tenants, who were apparently too few or too impoverished.[94]

About 1539 the farmer of the manor took 15s. in

[67] Ex. inf. Smith-Woolley & Co. and the sec., Ernest Cook Trust, Fairford Pk.
[68] *Plac. de Quo Warr.* (Rec. Com.), 242; *Wilts. Arch. Mag.* xxxii. 330; E 164/39 f. 4v.
[69] E 179/247/14 rot. 4.
[70] Atkyns, *Glos.* plate at pp. 464–5, detail reproduced opposite.
[71] Rudder, *Glos.* proof pages (Glos. Colln.), MS. note on p. 480; Burke, *Land. Gent.* (1898), ii. 1561.
[72] Glos. R.O., Q/RNc 2/22.
[73] Rudder, *Glos.* 480; Bigland, *Glos.* ii. 46–7; Glos. R.O., D 150/3/3.
[74] Glos. R.O., D 2440, est. papers 1814–48.
[75] Verey, *Glos.* i. 272; see below, plate facing p. 92.
[76] *Kelly's Dir. Glos.* (1863), 293.
[77] Ibid. (1870), 578.
[78] Ibid. (1914 and later edns.).; Burke, *Peerage* (1963), 187.
[79] Ex inf. Dr. Pandora Moorhead, principal, Hatherop Castle

Sch.; ex inf. Smith-Woolley & Co.
[80] Cf. Glos. R.O., D 540/E 10; O.S. Map 6″, Glos. LII. NE. (1886 edn.).
[81] Dates on bldgs.
[82] S.C. 6/Hen. VIII/3985 rot. 33.
[83] E 164/39 ff. 4–5; S.C. 6/Hen. VIII/3985 rot. 32d.
[84] *Dom. Bk.* (Rec. Com.), i. 169.
[85] *Bk. of Fees*, i. 312.   [86] *Tax. Eccl.* (Rec. Com.), 237.
[87] *Lacock Abbey Charters*, no. 416.
[88] S.C. 6/Hen. VIII/3985 rott. 32d.–33; cf. Dugdale, *Mon.* vi (1), 510.
[89] *Valor Eccl.* (Rec. Com.), ii. 125.
[90] S.C. 6/Hen. VIII/3985 rott. 60d.–61.
[91] *Dom. Bk.* (Rec. Com.), i. 169.
[92] *Wilts. Arch. Mag.* xxxii. 329–31.
[93] *Tax. Eccl.* (Rec. Com.), 237.
[94] *Inq. Non.* (Rec. Com.), 410.

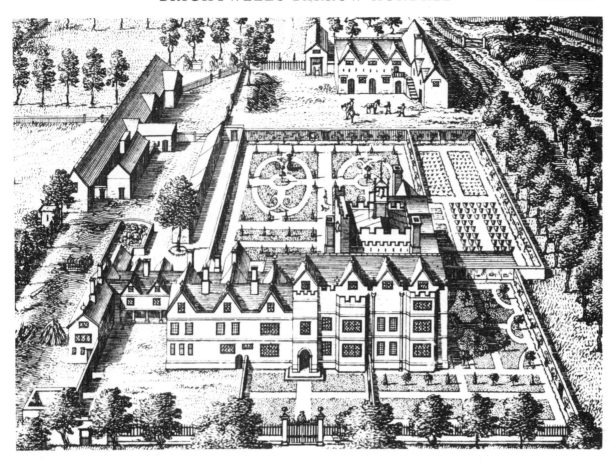

HATHEROP: THE MANOR-HOUSE IN THE EARLY 18TH CENTURY

rents of assize and £4 10s. 2d. and 44s. 2d. in rents from customary tenants and tenants at will respectively.[95] About 1548 Sir William Sharington held the principal farm of 9 yardlands, called North Horns, and there were 5 other free tenants and 9 copyholders holding for cash rents. The customary tenants paid 5s. a year for the right to trade in Cirencester as agreed between Lacock and Cirencester abbeys.[96] Copyhold tenure had mostly been replaced by leases for 99 years or lives by 1717.[97] In 1764 the manor had three farms, including Dean and Downhall farms (partly in Coln St. Aldwyns), a mill, 42 smallholdings, most with cottages, and 16 cottages mostly held by tenants at will.[98]

Two open fields, a south and a home field, were mentioned in 1528.[99] The home field, known also as the north field, covered the area east of the village and the south field lay in the southern part of the parish.[1] They were possibly separated originally by the salt-way. The home field was probably that called the east field in 1563 when a yardland comprised 18 a. in each of the south and east fields.[2] Another field recorded north-east of the village in 1678[3] was evidently included in the home field by 1717.[4] Dean farm, which was not included in the open fields mentioned above, was at least partly inclosed by 1669, when there were closes adjoining a field called the north or Dean field[5] and wholly by 1717.[6] The open fields comprised c. 946 a. in 1766.[7]

By the late 13th century sheep-farming was of importance in the parish economy.[8] The pasturing of sheep and cattle on commonable land was regulated by the manor court in the late 1520s and the 1530s[9] when there was a common called the Downs at the southern end of the parish.[10] Hatherop Downs, the principal common in the mid 18th century, lay between the south and home fields[11] and covered c. 150 a. in 1766.[12] The parish had only a small area of meadow land and the manor included a water-meadow in Kempsford by the mid 16th century[13] and several in Lechlade in the 17th and

[95] S.C. 6/Hen. VIII/3985 rot. 32d.
[96] E 164/39 ff. 4–5; North Horns farm was also recorded in 1628: Glos. R.O., D 540/T 34.
[97] Glos. R.O., Q/RNc 1, pp. 156–66.   [98] Ibid. D 540/E 4.
[99] D.L. 30/127/1907 ff. 13v., 16v.
[1] E 164/39 f. 4v.; Glos. R.O., D 540/T 29; cf. ibid. E 6, P 2.
[2] Glos. R.O., D 540/T 4.
[3] G.D.R., V 5/155T 1.
[4] Glos. R.O., D 540/T 29.

[5] Ibid. T 43.
[6] Ibid. Q/RNc 1, pp. 157–8.
[7] Cf. ibid. D 2440, Acts of Parl.; C.P. 43/734 rott. 24–6.
[8] Wilts. Arch. Mag. xxxii. 330.
[9] D.L. 30/127/1907 ff. 7, 13v., 16v., 46v., 49v.
[10] Ibid. ff. 7, 17–18.
[11] Cf. Glos. R.O., D 540/E 6, P 2.
[12] Ibid. D 2440, Acts of Parl.
[13] E 164/39 f. 4v.; Glos. R.O., D 540/T 49.

early 18th.[14] A lot meadow in the south-eastern corner of the parish became a several meadow between 1717 and 1764.[15]

The parish was inclosed by Act of Parliament in 1766. Sir John Webb was awarded 807 a. and the rector received 329 a., including 52 a. of old inclosures, for the glebe and tithes. A tenant of the lessees of Coln St. Aldwyns manor received an allotment of 12 a. Some minor exchanges of land took place between Webb and the other beneficiaries.[16]

After inclosure Webb's estate was organized as three large farms, Dean farm, Townsend farm, and South farm, which in 1785 respectively comprised 708 a. (partly in Coln St. Aldwyns), 611 a. (partly in Eastleach and Quenington), and 393 a.[17] The farm rents were greatly increased just before 1797.[18] In 1831 five farmers in the parish employed 37 labourers[19] but until the late 19th century there were four principal farms,[20] including Glebe farm which comprised 336 a. in 1850.[21] By 1862 South farm had been enlarged to 440 a. and Townsend farm reduced to 405 a.[22] Townsend farm was farmed with Glebe farm from 1868 but most of its land was later incorporated into Home and Barrow Elm farms which had been created by 1882 and 1889 respectively.[23] From 1923 Barrow Elm farm was farmed with Glebe farm which with Dean and South farms remained the principal ones in the mid 20th century.[24] Dean farm comprised 650 a. in 1957[25] and Glebe farm c. 243 ha. (c. 600 a.) in 1976, when there were also farms in the parish with over 300 ha. (741 a.), 100 ha. (247 a.), and 50 ha. (124 a.) each.[26]

After inclosure the bulk of the parish was farmed as arable[27] and corn and sheep husbandry remained dominant in the 19th century. In 1801 $784\frac{1}{2}$ a. were returned as under crops, growing mainly wheat, oats, barley, and turnips[28] and in 1866 2,038 a. were returned as arable and temporary grass and only 233 a. as permanent grass. Large flocks of sheep, estimated at 1,460 that year, were folded on the turnips and the grass leys which were part of the rotation.[29] In the later 19th century much arable land was laid down as grass and in 1896 943 a. of arable and temporary grass and 875 a. of permanent grass were returned. Sheep-farming became less important in the early 20th century when more cattle were introduced: 333 cattle, including 60 milk cows, were returned in 1926 compared to 213, including 29 milk cows, in 1896. Poultry farming had been introduced by 1926[30] and in 1976 one farm specialized in pig- and poultry-rearing. By then much of the land was given over again to cereal production, mainly barley and wheat, and beef cattle were raised in large numbers. There was then no sheep-farming.[31]

There were evidently three mills on the Coln in Hatherop in 1248 when one, a recently-built fulling-mill, was demolished.[32] Of the others Hatherop mill, west of the manor-house,[33] was apparently a fulling-mill by 1538,[34] but possibly by 1598 and certainly by 1628 the site contained two grist-mills.[35] In the late 18th century a lease of the property was held with the Williamstrip estate.[36] The mill went out of use between 1848[37] and 1862,[38] and a pumping station was built on its site.[39]

Netherton mill lower downstream was probably the mill which belonged to the manor in 1086.[40] It was granted by Ernulf of Hesdin to Gloucester Abbey before 1096[41] and was later held from Coln St. Aldwyns manor.[42] A fulling-mill had been built by 1538 when the copyhold was granted to William Patrick of Cirencester, a tucker,[43] and although the property was described as a grist-mill in 1649[44] it comprised a corn-mill, fulling-mill, and gig-mill in 1753[45] and a grist-mill and cloth-mill in 1774.[46] In 1848 Lord de Mauley acquired the leasehold of the site, a corn-mill[47] known later as Swinnerton mill,[48] and in 1854 the reversion of the freehold from the dean and chapter of Gloucester.[49] The mill was demolished in the late 1860s.[50]

A corn-mill recorded by the Leach at Dean Farm in 1862 has not been traced later.[51]

The inhabitants of Hatherop included a shoemaker and a weaver in the early 13th century,[52] a baker and a smith c. 1290,[53] and a fuller and a tailor in 1381.[54] The tucker listed in 1608[55] presumably worked Netherton mill. A paper-maker lived in Netherton in 1790.[56] Few inhabitants were engaged in trade, which supported only 7 families in 1831 when 65 were supported by agriculture.[57] Members

[14] Glos. R.O., D 540/T 4, T 30.
[15] Ibid. T 29, E 4.
[16] C.P. 43/734 rott. 24–8; Glos. R.O., D 1070/II 4/E 1.
[17] Glos. R.O., D 540/E 6, E 10.
[18] Ibid. D 150/3/2.
[19] Census, 1831.
[20] Glos. R.O., D 540/T 33; G.D.R., V 5/155T 4–5; Kelly's Dir. Glos. (1863 and later edns.).
[21] Glos. R.O., D 540/T 63.
[22] Ibid. D 540/E 10.
[23] Ibid. E 13/1.
[24] Kelly's Dir. Glos. (1923 and later edns.).
[25] Glos. Countryside, June 1957, 197.
[26] Ex inf. Smith-Woolley & Co.; Agric. Returns 1976.
[27] Bigland, Glos. ii. 46.
[28] Acreage Returns, 1801.
[29] M.A.F. 68/26/10; M.A.F. 68/25/3.
[30] M.A.F. 68/1609/9; M.A.F. 68/3295/8.
[31] Agric. Returns 1976.
[32] Lacock Abbey Charters, no. 425.
[33] Wilts. Arch. Mag. xxxii. 330; Glos. R.O., D 540/T 29, E 3, P 2.
[34] S.C. 6/Hen. VIII/3985 rot. 32d.; E 164/39 f. 4.
[35] Glos. R.O., D 540/T 30, T 31; cf. ibid. T 29.

[36] Ibid. E 3, E 6.
[37] Cf. Ibid. Q/SRh 1848 A/2.
[38] Ibid. D 540/E 10.
[39] O.S. Map 6", Glos. LII. NE. (1886 edn.).
[40] Dom. Bk. (Rec. Com.), i. 169.
[41] Hist. & Cart. Mon. Glouc. i. 89; Reg. Regum Anglo-Norm. ii, App., No. LXIA.
[42] Hist. & Cart. Mon. Glouc. iii. 197; Glos. R.O., D 1070/II 4/E 1.
[43] Glouc. Cath. Libr., Reg. Abb. Malvern, ii, f. 160 and v.
[44] Glos. R.O., D 1740/E 1, f. 64v.
[45] Glouc. Jnl. 3 Apr. 1753.
[46] Glos. R.O., D 1070/II 4/E 1.
[47] Ibid. D 2440, est. papers 1814–48.
[48] Ibid. D 936/E 119/50.
[49] Ibid. D 540/E 10.
[50] Kelly's Dir. Glos. (1863), 293; (1870), 578.
[51] Glos. R.O., D 540/E 10; cf. Williamstrip Mun. MTC/21/2.
[52] Lacock Abbey Charters, no. 417.
[53] Wilts. Arch. Mag. xxxii. 330.
[54] E 179/113/35A rot. 1d.
[55] Smith, Men and Armour, 261.
[56] Glos. R.O., D 2440, Quenington deeds 1711–90.
[57] Census, 1831.

LECHLADE MANOR

HATHEROP CASTLE

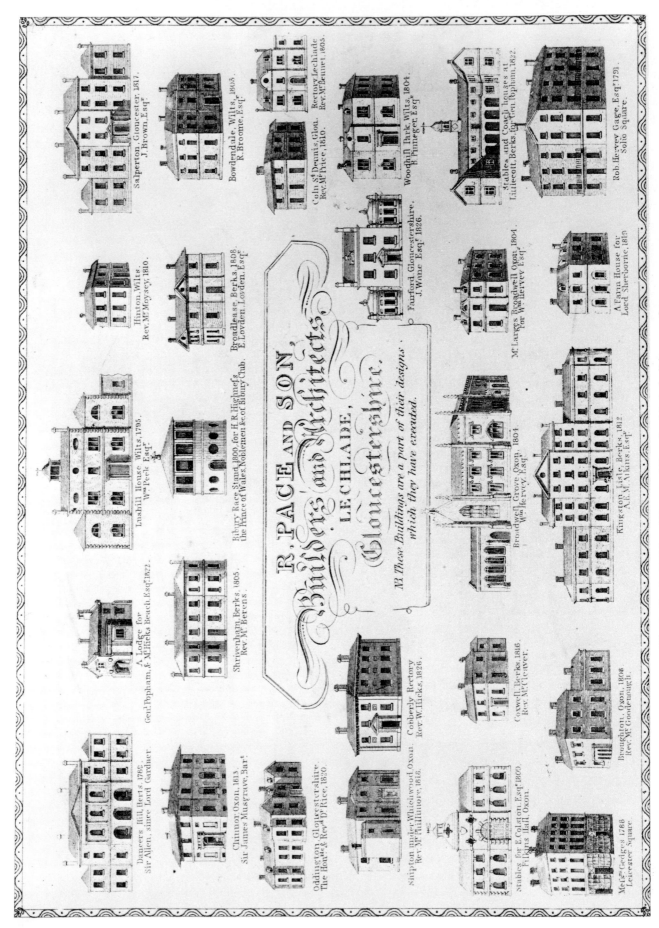

Trade Card of Richard Pace and Son, Lechlade builders, c. 1830

of the Knipe family followed the trade of smith in the 16th[58] and 17th centuries[59] but no blacksmith was recorded in the parish after 1856.[60] Netherton had a carpenter in 1705[61] and Hatherop a joiner in 1711[62] and a carpenter in 1717.[63] There was a shop in the 18th century[64] and in the late 19th century and early 20th there was also a post office. Among the other trades listed then were those of boot and shoemaker, carpenter, dress-maker, draper, plasterer, and mason.[65]

LOCAL GOVERNMENT. Under an agreement made in the 1230s the hundredal bailiffs held the view of frankpledge for Hatherop in the manor court and received 30d. on each lawday from the tithing for the amercements. The lord of the hundred retained jurisdiction over thieves taken there,[66] but in 1287 the countess of Warwick's steward was presented for imprisoning thieves and delivering them upon payment.[67] A book of court records shows that between 1526 and 1538 the view of frankpledge was usually held twice a year with the manor court, which consequently dealt with the assizes of bread and ale, the maintenance of buildings, roads, hedges, and ditches, trespasses, and assaults, besides the usual agrarian and tenurial matters. A tithingman was elected in 1532.[68] In 1533 the lessee of the manor was bound to provide hospitality for the officers of both manor and hundred courts.[69] Leet jurisdiction passed with the manor after the Dissolution.[70] The manor court survived in 1830 when it held a perambulation.[71] Gloucester Abbey's tenants owed suit to Coln St. Aldwyns manor court.[72]

Of the parish officers two churchwardens were recorded from 1498[73] and a constable from 1672.[74] At the latter date there were two overseers of the poor,[75] who in. 1785 held five tenements for the parish.[76] Expenditure on poor-relief rose from £76 in 1776 to an average of £131 c. 1784 but then fell to £97 by 1803 when 10 people received permanent help.[77] By 1813 the cost had more than doubled to £224 with 9 people on permanent and 60 on occasional aid. The numbers had dropped to 5 and 26 respectively by 1815 when £176 was spent.[78] Average annual expenditure rose to £241 in the late 1820s[79] and to £263 in the early 1830s.[80] The parish, which joined the Cirencester poor-law union in 1836,[81] remained in Cirencester rural district[82] until included in Cotswold district in 1974.

CHURCH. The church at Hatherop was granted by Ernulf of Hesdin to Gloucester Abbey before 1096.[83] The living was a rectory in 1248[84] but the incumbent may have served through a chaplain then.[85] About 1281 a vicarage was ordained, probably on account of the non-residence of the rector, who shared with the abbey in the presentation to the vicarage.[86] A plan by the abbey to appropriate the church in 1321[87] was not put into effect and rectors continued to hold the living.[88] They apparently appointed vicars, for the vicarage was recorded in 1341[89] and a perpetual vicar was mentioned in 1493.[90] The vicarage apparently lapsed before the Dissolution.[91] In 1928 the rectory was united with Coln St. Aldwyns and Quenington.[92]

The advowson of the rectory, held by Gloucester Abbey until the Dissolution,[93] was included in 1548 in the grant of the manor[94] with which it then passed,[95] although in 1551 the dean and chapter of Gloucester were named as patrons.[96] Thomas Matthews of Hillesden (Bucks.), who as patron for a turn made a presentation in 1560,[97] was claiming the patronage for a term of years in 1562,[98] but later that year William Blomer sold the next turn to Richard Harford of Bosbury (Herefs.). The Crown presented to the living in 1589 and 1601 when the living was considered vacant by default of the rector. William Dowdeswell, patron in 1680,[99] held a lease of the manor.[1] Sir John Webb presented in 1686.[2] Thereafter the Webbs, a recusant family, retained their title to the patronage,[3] which was the subject of several grants between 1689 and 1710[4] and was exercised in the earlier 18th century by Oxford University.[5] A

---

[58] Hockaday Abs. ccxxxvii, 1577.
[59] Glos. R.O., D 540/T 35, deed 1686.
[60] Kelly's Dir. Glos. (1856), 309; (1863), 293.
[61] Glos. R.O., D 540/T 38.
[62] Ibid. T 49.   [63] Ibid. T 51.
[64] Ibid. Q/RNc 1, p. 163; D 540/E 4.
[65] Kelly's Dir. Glos. (1856 and later edns.).
[66] Dugdale, Mon. vi (1), 507–8; cf. Ciren. Cart. ii, p. 623.
[67] Plac. de Quo Warr. (Rec. Com.), 242.
[68] D.L. 30/127/1907.
[69] S.C. 6/Hen. VIII/3985 rott. 32d.–33.
[70] Glos. R.O., D 540/T 38; Atkyns, Glos. 464.
[71] Glos. R.O., D 2440, est. papers 1760–1843.
[72] Glouc. Cath. Libr., Reg. Abb. Malvern, ii, f. 160 and v.
[73] Hockaday Abs. xxii, 1498 visit. f. 37; G.D.R. vol. 40, f. 157; vol. 319.
[74] E 179/247/14 rot. 4; Glos. R.O., Q/SO 4.
[75] E 179/116/544.   [76] Glos. R.O., D 540/E 6.
[77] Poor Law Abstract, 1804, 172–3.
[78] Ibid. 1818, 146–7.
[79] Poor Law Returns (1830–1), p. 67.
[80] Ibid. (1835), p. 65.
[81] Poor Law Com. 2nd Rep. p. 522.   [82] Census, 1961.
[83] Hist. & Cart. Mon. Glouc. i, p. 89; Reg. Regum Anglo-Norm. ii, App., no. LXIA.
[84] Cal. Papal Regs. i. 245.

[85] Cf. Lacock Abbey Charters, no. 426.
[86] Hist. & Cart. Mon. Glouc. i, p. 328; Hockaday Abs. ccxxxvii; cf. Reg. Giffard, 506.
[87] Cal. Pat. 1317–21, 576.
[88] Reg. Ginsborough, 41; Reg. Wakefeld, p. 153.
[89] Inq. Non. (Rec. Com.), 410.
[90] Hockaday Abs. ccxxxvii, 1494.
[91] Cf. Valor Eccl. (Rec. Com.), ii. 445.
[92] Lond. Gaz. 2 Nov. 1928, pp. 7096–7.
[93] Cal. Pat. 1317–21, 576; Reg. Bransford, pp. 51, 407; Reg. Sede Vacante, 424; Glouc. Cath. Libr., Reg. Abb. Malvern, ii, f. 77 and v.
[94] Cal. Pat. 1547–8, 402.
[95] Ibid. 1550–3, 246; C 142/122 no. 64; Inq. p.m. Glos. 1625–42, ii. 50–4.
[96] E.H.R. xix. 113.
[97] Hockaday Abs. ccxxxvii, 1560.
[98] Glos. R.O., D 540/T 34, lease 13 June 1562.
[99] Hockaday Abs. ccxxxvii.
[1] Glos. R.O., D 540/T 30, lease 1678.
[2] Hockaday Abs. ccxxxvii.
[3] Glos. R.O., Q/RNc 1, pp. 156–7; 2/18; 2/22.
[4] Ibid. D 540/E 4, T 36.
[5] P.R.O. Inst. Bks. 1709, 1710, 1741, 1749, 1783; Hockaday Abs. ccxxxvii, in which Sir John Webb was named as patron in 1710.

term of 99 years or lives granted by Sir Thomas Webb in 1760[6] was, after the relaxation of anti-papist legislation, sold back in 1778 to Sir John Webb[7] who assigned the advowson for 16 years or a life to Mary Smith of Cheltenham,[8] patron in 1783. Although Michael Hicks Beach presented for one turn in 1797 the advowson passed with the manor.[9] In 1976 the patronage of the united benefice was shared by Sir Thomas Bazley, the dean and chapter of Gloucester, and Earl St. Aldwyn.[10]

The endowments assigned to the vicarage c. 1281 included the small tithes and most of the glebe land save for a few buildings.[11] In 1291 the rectory was valued at £12 and the vicarage at £4 6s. 8d.[12] By 1535 the rector was receiving all the tithes, and his glebe included 80 a. of arable.[13] In the late 17th and early 18th centuries the glebe was extended at c. 100 a.[14] The lord of the manor was then taking leases of part of the demesne tithes[15] and in 1745 the rector was said to be receiving £50 and more a year from the manor.[16] The tithes were commuted for c. 280 a. at inclosure in 1766 when the rector was also allotted c. 50 a. for the glebe.[17] In 1776 a private Act of Parliament was secured enabling the rector to consolidate the glebe by exchanging part with Samuel Blackwell for land in Williamstrip.[18] The glebe comprised c. 314 a. in 1828.[19] From 1850 the glebe (then 336 a.) was leased to the Hatherop estate,[20] to which 29 a. north-west of the Hatherop–Burford road were sold in 1870.[21] The glebe, which contained 300 a. in 1927,[22] had been sold to the Hatherop estate by 1976.[23] Glebe Farm with its out-buildings was rebuilt by Lord de Mauley in the mid 19th century.[24]

In 1535 the rectory was worth only £9 13s. 5½d. clear, considerably less than the combined value of rectory and vicarage in 1291. A pension of 6s. 8d. paid to Lacock Abbey in 1535[25] has not been traced after the mid 16th century.[26] The living was worth £80 in 1650,[27] £140 in 1750,[28] and £300 in 1856.[29]

A courtyard and buildings were retained by the rector c. 1281 when three messuages were assigned to the vicarage.[30] The latter presumably occupied the site of the vicarage house mentioned in 1493.[31] In 1377 the rector took a lease of land for the building of a house[32] and the rectory was in disrepair in 1576.[33] The rectory, which in 1672 was assessed on 4 hearths,[34] was too small in the early 19th century and the rector lived elsewhere. It was rebuilt and enlarged between 1833 and 1834 to designs by Richard Pace.[35] The house, later called Severalls, north-east of the church,[36] was sold to G. S. Bazley in 1906. A cottage to the east, later called Lechmere, was converted as the rectory[37] but after 1928 the incumbent lived in Coln St. Aldwyns.[38]

In 1248 Master Palmerius, a clerk of the pope's chamber, was licensed to hold the rectory and another benefice.[39] James Watson, rector from 1533,[40] could reply moderately well to all the articles in 1551.[41] Thomas Anne, rector from 1560,[42] farmed out the church.[43] After his resignation in 1562 uncertainty over the patronage, leading to the institution of Nathaniel Harford in the same year and of William Slessor in the following year, resulted in a decline in the standard of services.[44] William was resident in 1563[45] but by 1566 Nathaniel was holding the rectory with Fairford.[46] After his resignation the living was served in 1572 by an unlicensed curate, George Bath, who became rector later that year.[47] He was presented in 1576 for not having a book of homilies, not teaching the catechism, not keeping hospitality, not preaching quarterly sermons, and for wearing a surplice on perambulations.[48] Edmund James, his successor in 1579,[49] described in 1584 as neither a graduate nor a preacher but a conformist,[50] became vicar of Fairford in 1586.[51] He then neglected Hatherop where he was replaced by Robert Harland, instituted in 1590. The following year Richard Pullen was instituted[52] but Harland, a sufficient scholar but no preacher, was rector in 1593.[53] Pullen compounded for the first-fruits the following year and retained the living until his death in 1604. He was also rector of Stackpole Ellidor (Pemb.) and neglected Hatherop where there was an attempt to replace him in 1601.[54]

In the 17th and 18th centuries the rectory was often held with a near-by living and sometimes served by a curate. John Jones, described in 1650 as

6 Glos. R.O., D 540/T 36.
7 Ibid. D 2440, est. papers 1760–1843, abs. 1790.
8 C.P. 43/780 rot. 65.
9 Hockaday Abs. ccxxxvii; *Kelly's Dir. Glos.* (1906), 213.
10 *Glouc. Dioc. Yr. Bk.* (1976), 66–7.
11 *Hist. & Cart. Mon. Glouc.* i, p. 328.
12 *Tax. Eccl.* (Rec. Com.), 222.
13 *Valor Eccl.* (Rec. Com.), ii. 445.
14 G.D.R., V 5/155T 1, 4; Atkyns, *Glos.* 464.
15 Glos. R.O., D 540/T 35, T 36, T 49.
16 Ibid. Q/RNc 2/18.
17 C.P. 43/734 rott. 24d.–25d.
18 *Manual of Glos. Lit.* ii. 207.
19 G.D.R., V 5/155T 5.
20 Glos. R.O., D 540/T 63, E 10, E 12.
21 Williamstrip Mun. MTD/96.
22 *Kelly's Dir. Glos.* (1927), 232.
23 Ex inf. Smith-Woolley & Co.
24 Glos. R.O., D 540/E 10.
25 *Valor Eccl.* (Rec. Com.), ii. 445; cf. *Tax. Eccl.* (Rec. Com.), 222.
26 S.C. 6/Hen. VIII/3985 rot. 33; *Cal. Pat.* 1547–8, 402; E 164/39 f. 5v.
27 *Trans. B.G.A.S.* lxxxiii. 94.
28 G.D.R. vol. 381A, f. 86.   29 G.D.R. vol. 384, f. 113.

30 *Hist. & Cart. Mon. Glouc.* i, p. 328.
31 Hockaday Abs. ccxxxvii, 1494.
32 Wards 2/27/94B/112.
33 G.D.R. vol. 40, f. 157.   34 E 179/247/14 rot. 4.
35 Hockaday Abs. ccxxxvii; Glos. R.O., D 1388, Hatherop rectory 1833–6.
36 O.S. Map 6", Glos. LII. NE. (1886 edn.).
37 Ibid. (1924 edn.); G.D.R., F 4/6/16.
38 *Kelly's Dir. Glos.* (1939), 228.
39 *Cal. Papal Regs.* i. 245.
40 Glouc. Cath. Libr., Reg. Abb. Malvern, ii, f. 77 and v.
41 *E.H.R.* xix. 113.
42 Hockaday Abs. ccxxxvii.
43 Glos. R.O., D 540/T 34.
44 Hockaday Abs. ccxxxvii, 1562–3.
45 Ibid. xlii, 1563 visit. f. 50.
46 Ibid. xliii, 1566 visit. f. 24; see above.
47 Ibid. xliv, 1572 visit. f. 42; ccxxxvii.
48 G.D.R. vol. 40, f. 157.
49 Hockaday Abs. ccxxxvii.
50 Ibid. xlix, state of clergy 1584, f. 24.
51 Ibid. cxciv.
52 Ibid. ccxxxvii.
53 Ibid. lii, state of clergy 1593, f. 9.
54 Ibid. ccxxxvii; *Eccl. Misc.* 95.

a preaching minister,[55] was dispensed in 1668 to hold Quenington in plurality.[56] He died in 1673[57] and his successors William Wyatt, 1673–80, and John Wyatt, rector of Tormarton, who was imprisoned for debt, appointed curates.[58] John Bradley, vicar of Great Barrington, was rector from 1710 until 1741.[59] Richard Hutchins, rector 1742–9, held Quenington from 1745 and William Sandford, rector 1749–83, Ampney Crucis from 1767. His successor John Weeks Bedwell[60] lived at Prestbury, the living being served by a curate who lived at Bampton (Oxon.) in the 1780s and at Hatherop in 1790.[61] Thomas Pettat, rector 1797–1839, was rector of Quenington 1797–8 and vicar of Stonehouse from 1798 until 1803 when he became rector of Beverstone. He served in person but from 1809 until c. 1835 he lived at Southrop.[62] During much of the rectorship of Sackville Gardiner Bourke, 1839–60, the living was served by stipendiary curates.[63]

The church, dedicated to *ST. NICHOLAS* by 1545[64] but in the 18th and 19th centuries sometimes known as St. Matthew's,[65] is built of ashlar and has a chancel with north vestry and south chapel, a central tower, and an aisled and clerestoried nave with north porch. It was entirely rebuilt between 1854 and 1855 by Lord de Mauley from designs by Henry Clutton and William Burges.[66] Its predecessor was a smaller building with chancel with north vestry, central tower, and nave with north porch.[67] A gallery had been erected by 1825.[68] The main body of the present church is in a mixture of English medieval styles with many of the features carefully observed. The east end is by contrast in a French gothic style and the south chapel, which is a mortuary chapel to Lady de Mauley (d. 1844), is particularly striking.[69] It is tempting to see in this an early work by Burges who was Clutton's assistant.

The monuments include an early-14th-century effigy of a priest, unearthed by the early 18th century,[70] and the tomb of Lady de Mauley of 1848 by Raffaelle Monti.[71] Reset in the chancel are two enriched tablets to the Blomer family of the mid 17th century.[72] The font was given in 1858 as a memorial to Lord de Mauley.[73] The sanctus bell was cast in 1621 by Roger Purdue of Bristol.[74] The tower had

three bells c. 1703[75] but a peal of six cast by Abraham Rudhall was the gift of Sir John Webb in 1715; one was recast in 1852 by C. and G. Mears of London.[76] The plate includes a chalice and paten given in 1599, an alms-dish of 1670 given perhaps by the rector in 1756, a paten of 1789, and a flagon of 1849; there is also a chalice, probably foreign, of medieval design.[77] The registers survive from 1670.[78]

ROMAN CATHOLICISM. Recusants were mentioned in the parish from 1577,[79] their presence probably encouraged by those members of the Blomer family who were also recusants.[80] Nine papists were recorded in 1676[81] and seventeen between 1714 and 1724.[82] A chapel at the manor-house was established, apparently by Lady Webb in the late 17th century. It was served by Robert Bowes (or Lane) from 1698 until shortly before his death in 1735.[83] In that year the parish had 50 papists[84] but by 1743 the number had risen to 70.[85] Francis Lee, chaplain from 1792, had a stipend of £50 with use of the manor-house.[86] The chapel to which 36 Roman Catholics were attached in 1839 was closed after the death of Lady de Mauley in 1844.[87]

PROTESTANT NONCONFORMITY. None known.[88]

EDUCATION. The parish, which had no school in 1818,[89] had two by 1825 when c. 38 children attended one and c. 11 the other, a day-school.[90] In 1833 there was a day-school with 32 children and a Sunday school with 20 boys. Both were supported by pence and by annual subscriptions from W. F. S. Ponsonby and Thomas Pettat, the rector.[91] The schools, which were teaching 50 children by 1846,[92] were probably the two parochial schools mentioned in 1856.[93] Hatherop Memorial C. of E. school at the eastern end of the village[94] was built in 1856 by A. G. J. Ponsonby in memory of his father Lord de Mauley. In 1865 when it was supported by pence

[55] *Trans. B.G.A.S.* lxxxiii. 94.   [56] Hockaday Abs. ccxxxvii.
[57] Bigland, *Glos.* ii. 48.
[58] Hockaday Abs. ccxxxvii; cclxxix, Tormarton, 1680; G.D.R., V 5/155T 1–2.
[59] Hockaday Abs. ccxxxvii; cxiii, Great Barrington, 1710; Bigland, *Glos.* ii. 48.
[60] Hockaday Abs. ccxxxvii; Bigland, *Glos.* ii. 48.
[61] G.D.R. vols. 319; 382, f. 15.
[62] Hockaday Abs. ccxxxvii; cccxix; *V.C.H. Glos.* x. 286.
[63] Hockaday Abs. ccxxxvii.
[64] Ibid.; Rudder, *Glos.* 481; *Kelly's Dir. Glos.* (1889 and later edns.).
[65] Atkyns, *Glos.* 464; H.O. 129/340/3/12/17; *Kelly's Dir. Glos.* (1856–1885 edns.).
[66] Verey, *Glos.* i. 270–1; *Kelly's Dir. Glos.* (1870), 578.
[67] Atkyns, *Glos.* 464 and plate at pp. 464–5.
[68] G.D.R. vol. 383, no. xcix.
[69] See plate facing p. 76
[70] Atkyns, *Glos.* 464; cf. Roper, *Glos. Effigies*, 638–9.
[71] Gunnis, *Dict. of Brit. Sculptors*, 262.
[72] Cf. Bigland, *Glos.* ii. 48.
[73] *Kelly's Dir. Glos.* (1889), 814.
[74] *Glos. Ch. Bells*, 51; *Trans. B.G.A.S.* xli. 83.

[75] Bodl. MS. Rawl. B.323, f. 92.   [76] *Glos. Ch. Bells*, 51.
[77] *Glos. Ch. Plate*, 116–17.   [78] *B. & G. Par. Rec.* 165.
[79] *Trans. B.G.A.S.* v. 235; *Eccl. Misc.* 95; *Cal. S.P. Dom.* 1611–18, 38; 1635–6, 481; Glos. R.O., D 2052.
[80] *Trans. B.G.A.S.* lxxxviii. 19; Glos. R.O., D 2052; *Cal. Cttee. for Compounding*, i. 87; cf. *Cal. S.P. Dom.* 1635–6, 483, 490.
[81] Compton Census.
[82] Glos. R.O., Q/SO 4: the list included Lady Webb (d. 1709).
[83] Langston, 'Cath. Missions', i, p. 10; Glos. R.O., D 150/3/1, 4.
[84] G.D.R. vol. 285B, f. 35.
[85] G.D.R. vol. 397, f. 87.
[86] Glos. R.O., D 150/3/3–4.
[87] Langston, 'Cath. Missions', i, pp. 11–12.
[88] Cf. Compton Census; G.D.R. vol. 383, no. xcix.
[89] *Educ. of Poor Digest*, 301.
[90] G.D.R. vol. 383, no. xcix.
[91] *Educ. Enquiry Abstract*, 317.
[92] *Church School Inquiry*, 1846–7, 10–11.
[93] *Kelly's Dir. Glos.* (1856), 309.
[94] Glos. R.O., D 540/E 10; O.S. Map 6", Glos. LII. NE. (1886 edn.).

and voluntary contributions it had one class with an average attendance of thirty-seven.[95] Attendance had risen to 68 by 1889[96] but then fell to 48 by 1910 when it had mixed and infants' departments.[97] By 1920 the attendance was 60.[98] The infants were transferred to Coln St. Aldwyns in 1929 when the school became the juniors' school for both parishes and Quenington.[99] The attendance in 1936 was 53[1] and in 1976 there were 35 children on the roll.[2]

CHARITIES FOR THE POOR. Sir Henry Blomer (d. 1624) left £100 stock to the church and the poor of Hatherop. By 1683 £20 of the principal had been lost, £10 having been lent out and £10 having been used in casting a bell, and £80 remained in the hands of John Blomer, the interest being paid to the church and the poor then[3] and later.[4] In the mid 18th century £6 a year was paid from the manor[5] and c. 1775 Sir John Webb provided regular doles of bread and money.[6] The charity has not been traced after 1781.[7]

Lady Webb (d. 1709), possibly by a deed of 1701,[8] gave a rent-charge of £18 13s. 4d. from Dean farm to be distributed among the poor by the resident Roman Catholic priest. Other members of the Webb family made bequests and in 1781 the total interest of £12 was said to be used by the priest to provide a bull for the poor of Eastleach Turville and Hatherop and bread and money for the poor of Hatherop.[9] The bequests have not been traced later.

KEMPSFORD

KEMPSFORD, which includes the hamlets of Whelford, Horcott, and Dunfield, occupies a tract of low-lying land by the river Thames 15 km. ESE. of Cirencester. The parish includes 2,009 ha. (4,963 a.)[10] and has its boundaries for the most part on watercourses. The river Coln provides parts of the north-east boundary, though a greater length of the river is within that boundary. The south boundary with Wiltshire is on the Thames and the west boundary, also the county boundary, is marked by the watercourse formerly called the county ditch.[11]

The land is formed mainly by Oxford Clay with tracts of alluvium bordering the Thames and Coln and deposits of gravel, extensively worked in the mid 20th century, near Horcott and east of Whelford.[12] Most of the parish lies very flat at around 80 m., so that even the small hillock called Brazen Church hill (possibly from land once owned by Bradenstoke Priory)[13] forms a landmark. Towards the north there is a gentle rise to c. 90 m. at Furzey hill and Horcott hill. Woodland is limited to a few small copses, though an ancient wood once existed at Dudgrove in the south-east part of the parish.[14] The dominant feature of the landscape for many centuries was the large area of common meadow land lying by the Thames and Coln. The meadows and the open fields, which occupied the centre of the parish, were inclosed in 1801.[15] The parish was drained by a network of ditches and 'carries', some part of which was probably in existence in 1133 when the black dyke was mentioned.[16] In later centuries the system, which was employed each winter to direct floodwater onto the meadows,[17] centred on the Grand Drain, running the width of the parish from Furzey hill across to the Coln. Some additions to the system were made in 1802 following the inclosure.[18] The Thames and Severn canal, crossing the south part of the parish, was opened in 1789 and closed in 1927; there was an agent's house and warehouse where it met the main village street.[19]

In 1976 Kempsford was dominated by the airfield of R.A.F. Fairford with its main runway extending for some 3.7 km. across the centre of the parish. The original airfield was opened in 1944 for use by transport aircraft, which took troops to the D-day and Arnhem operations. After the war it was used intermittently by the R.A.F. until 1950 when it was taken over by the United States Air Force and much enlarged for use as a bomber base; a large staff operated the base during its tenure by the U.S.A.F., accounting presumably for all of the 790 people not in private households enumerated in the 1961 census. Handed back to the R.A.F. in 1964, the base then served a variety of functions but in the early 1970s was for defence purposes maintained only as a reserve airfield; it became widely known at that period, however, from its use by the British Aircraft Corporation for testing the Concorde supersonic airliner. In 1976 B.A.C.

---

[95] Ed. 7/34/158; the sch. has a date-stone of 1856.
[96] Kelly's Dir. Glos. (1889), 814.
[97] Ibid. (1902), 211; Bd. of Educ., List 21, 1911 (H.M.S.O.), 162.
[98] Bd. of Educ., List 21, 1922 (H.M.S.O.), 104.
[99] Glos. R.O., PA 96/1, vols. for 1929–30.
[1] Bd. of Educ., List 21, 1936 (H.M.S.O.), 121.
[2] Ex inf. county educ. dept.
[3] G.D.R., V 5/155T 2.   [4] Ibid. 3.
[5] Glos. R.O., D 540/E 4; Q/RNc 2/18, 22.
[6] Rudder, Glos. 481.
[7] Bigland, Glos. ii. 47, where the bequest was described as a rent-charge of £4.

[8] Glos. R.O., D 150/3/4.
[9] Bigland, Glos. ii. 47.
[10] Census, 1971. This account was written in 1976.
[11] Glos. R.O., TS 182/5.
[12] Geol. Surv. Map 1", solid, sheet 34 (1857 edn.).
[13] Inq. p.m. Glos. 1236–1300, 22.
[14] Longleat Mun. box lxx, bk. 63, pp. 113–14.
[15] Glos. R.O., Q/RI 86.
[16] Hist. & Cart. Mon. Glouc. (Rolls Ser.), i. 344.
[17] Wilts. R.O. 845, man. papers 25, ct. 1707; Glos. R.O., D 1070/III/46.
[18] Glos. R.O., Q/RI 86.
[19] Household, Thames and Severn Canal, 69, 78–9, 194.

employed *c.* 300 people at the airfield and there was a smaller number of R.A.F. personnel and employees.[20]

Kempsford village is named from a ford across the Thames, entered at the point where the moated manor-house was built and left further upstream opposite the church.[21] In the year 800 the earldorman of the Hwicce and his men crossed there and fought a battle with the men of Wiltshire[22] and it was presumably anciently a recognized crossing-point on a route from Fairford and Lechlade towards the Roman road near Cricklade. The ford does not figure to any extent in the later records of Kempsford and all traces of a track connecting with it on the Castle Eaton bank have disappeared. It was apparently a difficult ford to negotiate and flooding of the surrounding land may also have limited its use.[23] The shape of Kempsford village shows that the Cirencester–Highworth road[24] was a more significant factor in its development. That road, which in the west part of the parish has been severed by the airfield, crossed the Thames at Hannington bridge *c.* 1.5 km. downstream of the village. A bridge had been built there by 1439, Kempsford and Hannington being responsible for repairing their respective halves. The bridge was rebuilt in 1647 after being destroyed during the fighting in the Civil War, and it was again rebuilt, as three stone arches, in 1841.[25]

From the manor-house and church at the ford Kempsford village developed along the Cirencester road to form a long street of loosely grouped dwellings, a small green on the south side of the street apparently providing a focal point. The stocks stood at the green until *c.* 1880[26] and in the early 18th century a stone cross stood in the road there;[27] the cross, from which only the base and part of the shaft survive, was later moved to the corner near Reevey Farm[28] and in 1890 was moved again to the new churchyard opposite the church.[29] Opposite the green stood the church house, which was rebuilt after a fire in 1791.[30] In the early 17th century the houses at Kempsford were said to be mostly built of mud walling and thatch.[31] Most were rebuilt of stone in the course of the 18th century, and there is some evidence of building on new sites in the village in the early part of that century.[32] Tuckwell's Farm and Middle Farm are small stone farm-houses of the 18th century and most of the older cottages that survive are from

that period. Council houses were built on the street in the 1920s and later, and in the 1960s and early 1970s its appearance was much altered by the removal of some of the old cottages and the addition of new houses for people working in Swindon.[33] Reevey Farm, west of the village, was named from a late-17th-century tenant;[34] the original small house[35] survives, standing on what was possibly the old course of the Cirencester road, but it was replaced as the farm-house by a larger house built east of it in the mid 19th century. To the north-west is the small hamlet called Dunfield, which comprised 8 houses *c.* 1710.[36] Dunfield House there dates from the late 17th century as does the older part of Poplar House, which was enlarged and remodelled in 1817.[37]

Whelford hamlet takes its name from the crossing of the river Coln by the road from Lechlade to Kempsford. A mill had been built beside the ford by the beginning of the 12th century[38] and a bridge had probably been built by 1283.[39] A new two-arch bridge was built in 1851.[40] The hamlet, which comprised 20 houses by the early 18th century,[41] forms a loose collection of farm-houses and cottages lying west of the crossing. Whelford Little Farm and College Farm and a few cottages date from the 17th century and a greater number of houses were added in the early 19th. A chapel of ease and a school were built in the mid 19th century.

Horcott in the north of the parish takes its name from a dwelling in a muddy place[42] and the first record of it also concerns a mill on the Coln in the early 12th century,[43] perhaps standing by another minor crossing. The hamlet contained 7 houses *c.* 1710[44] and comprised a small compact group of farm-houses close to the river at the place that was called Horcott Street in 1801.[45] A 17th-century cottage survives there together with Horcott Farm and Horcott House, small farm-houses of the 18th century; both farm-houses were given new Tudor-style windows in the 19th century and Horcott House was enlarged by extensions to the rear. There was some later development to the north-west on the Whelford–Fairford road. A row of labourers' cottages was built on the north-east side close to the parish boundary in the early 19th century and in the middle of that century the Catholic church, presbytery, and school, forming a Gothic group further south, were built. In the mid

[20] Ex inf. Sqn.Ldr. B. L. Kerr, of R.A.F. Fairford; *Census,* 1961.
[21] *Trans. B.G.A.S.* lvii. 192–3, in a detailed article on Kempsford by the Revd. A. B. Mynors. *P.N. Glos.* (E.P.N.S.), i. 38, suggests that the name was taken from a ford where the village street crosses a watercourse, but the watercourse was apparently made only in the 1780s as a canal feeder: Glos. R.O., TS 182/5; cf. Atkyns, *Glos.* plate at pp. 489–90.
[22] Earle and Plummer, *Two Saxon Chronicles,* i (1892), 58.
[23] *Trans. B.G.A.S.* lvii. 192–3; O.S. Map 1/2,500, Glos. LX.8 (1877 edn.). By 1976 dredging of the river bottom had destroyed the ford: ex inf. the vicar, the Revd. D. Watson.
[24] Wilts. R.O. 845, man. papers 25, ct. 1713.
[25] C. B. Fry, *Hannington* (Glouc. 1935), 58–63.
[26] *Trans. B.G.A.S.* lvii. 223; O.S. Map 1/2,500, Glos. LX. 8 (1877 edn.).
[27] Atkyns, *Glos.* plate at pp. 489–90.
[28] O.S. Map 1/2,500, Glos. LX.8 (1877 edn.).
[29] *Trans. B.G.A.S.* lvii. 232.
[30] Ibid. 223; Wilts. R.O. 845, Glos. est. papers 14, f. 23.
[31] Longleat Mun. box lvii, no. 2624.
[32] Wilts. R.O. 845, Glos. est. papers 14, f. 23; vol. 4, pp. 23, 83.
[33] Ex inf. the vicar and Brig. J. M. Northen, of Kempsford.
[34] Wilts. R.O. 845, Glos. est. papers 13; 14, f. 7.
[35] Cf. Glos. R.O., Q/RI 86.
[36] Atkyns, *Glos.* 492.
[37] Date on bldg.
[38] *Hist. & Cart. Mon. Glouc.* i. 340.   [39] J.I. 1/278 rot. 51d.
[40] *Trans. B.G.A.S.* lvii. 224.
[41] Atkyns, *Glos.* 492.
[42] *P.N. Glos.* i. 39.
[43] *Hist. & Cart. Mon. Glouc.* i. 340.
[44] Atkyns, *Glos.* 492.
[45] Glos. R.O., Q/RI 86.

20th century Horcott was much enlarged by council and private housing built at various dates on the south-west side of the road.

There are two outlying farmsteads. Dudgrove Farm was built in 1692[46] in the meadows in the south-east part of the parish and the south range of the house survives from that period, though the windows have been renewed. Later additions at the rear included a long cheese-barn, which was converted and taken into the house in the mid 20th century.[47] Furzey Hill Farm in the north-west corner of the parish, a substantial farm-house with mullioned and transomed windows, was built in the early 18th century, probably c. 1708.[48]

In 1086 62 inhabitants of Kempsford were recorded.[49] Seventy-four people were assessed for the subsidy in 1327[50] and 157 for the poll-tax in 1381.[51] There were said to be c. 240 communicants in 1551[52] and 24 households in 1563;[53] the latter figure looks too small to be accurate. The population was estimated at 60 families in 1650[54] and c. 340 inhabitants in 66 houses c. 1710,[55] and the early part of the 18th century apparently saw a considerable expansion, with a figure of 100 houses given in 1743.[56] There were said to be 493 inhabitants in 104 houses c. 1775[57] and 656 people were enumerated in 1801. The population then rose steadily to 1,007 in 1861 but fell during the later 19th century to 711 in 1901 and fluctuated in the early 20th century. In 1951 there were 860 in private households, and new building had raised that figure to 1,333 by 1971.[58]

Two innholders were recorded in the parish in 1755.[59] In 1856 the George on the south side of the street was apparently the only inn in Kempsford village[60] but by 1891 there were also the Axe and Compasses at the west end and the Cross Tree[61] near the green;[62] the last closed in the 1940s but the other two remained in 1976. The Queen's Head inn opened at the south end of Whelford in the earlier 19th century, before 1844, and was demolished during the extensions to the airfield in 1950.[63] The Carrier's Arms at Horcott had opened by 1891.[64] A friendly society met at the George in Kempsford in 1866[65] and reading-rooms had been opened in the village by 1879.[66] A village hall was built on the south side of the street in 1932.[67]

Edward I made at least four visits to Kempsford in the course of his reign, the last in 1305[68] when his nephew Henry of Lancaster held the manor. The ownership of Kempsford by the earls of Lancaster in the early 14th century has given rise to a number of local legends, including some fanciful attempts to connect Kempsford with John of Gaunt and his family,[69] though Gaunt himself never owned the manor. A more tangible connexion with a great family was that with the Thynnes of Longleat, who had a residence at Kempsford in the 17th century.

MANOR AND OTHER ESTATES. The estate later called the manor of *KEMPSFORD* was held by Osgod from Earl Harold before the Conquest. In 1086, assessed at 21 hides, it was held by Ernulf of Hesdin,[70] who was succeeded before 1096 by Patrick de Chaworth, evidently his son-in-law.[71] The manor, which was the head of a reputed barony comprising a group of manors mainly in Wiltshire,[72] was retained by Patrick until at least 1133.[73] It then apparently passed to his son Patrick and to Patrick's son Pain,[74] also called Pain de Mundubleil, who had succeeded by 1155.[75] Pain's brother Hugh may have had an interest in Kempsford manor but Pain's son Patrick de Chaworth (fl. 1199) later succeeded.[76] Patrick was succeeded by Pain de Chaworth, who retained the manor in 1236 and was succeeded before 1243 by his son Patrick.[77] In 1254 Patrick redeemed an annuity of £7 granted out of the manor by his father to Tironneau Abbey (Sarthe) in 1236.[78] Patrick died c. 1258 and the manor passed to his son Pain[79] (d. c. 1279) and then to Pain's brother Patrick[80] (d. c. 1283), who left an infant daughter, Maud, as his heir.[81] Rents in the manor were granted in dower to Isabel, widow of the last Patrick.[82]

The manor passed to Henry of Lancaster,[83] later earl of Lancaster, on his marriage to Maud de Chaworth before 1297. Henry (d. 1345) was succeeded by his son Henry, created duke of Lancaster in 1351.[84] In 1355 the duke granted the manor, together with the neighbouring manors of Inglesham and Hannington (both Wilts.) to the hospital of the Annunciation at Leicester (called

46 Wilts. R.O. 845, Glos. est. papers 22.
47 Ex inf. the owner, Mr. J. G. Peel.
48 Wilts. R.O. 845, Glos. est. papers 14, f. 3v.; vol. 4, p. 19.
49 *Dom. Bk.* (Rec. Com.), i. 169.
50 *Glos. Subsidy Roll, 1327,* 13.
51 E 179/113/35A rot. 2A; E 179/113/31A rot. 5.
52 *E.H.R.* xix. 114.
53 Bodl. MS. Rawl. C. 790, f. 26v.
54 *Trans. B.G.A.S.* lxxxiii. 94.
55 Atkyns, *Glos.* 492.
56 G.D.R. vol. 397, f. 87.
57 Rudder, *Glos.* 511.
58 *Census,* 1801–1971.
59 Glos. R.O., Q/AV 2, rot. 3.
60 *Kelly's Dir. Glos.* (1856), 315.
61 *Licensed Houses in Glos. 1891,* 72.
62 *Trans. B.G.A.S.* lvii. 223, 232.
63 Glos. R.O., D 1070/III/49; O.S. Map 1/2,500, Glos. LX.4 (1877 edn.); ex inf. Brig. Northen.
64 *Licensed Houses in Glos. 1891,* 72.
65 F.S. 2/3 no. 879.
66 *Kelly's Dir. Glos.* (1879), 690.

67 Date on bldg.
68 *Cal. Fine R. 1272–1307,* 39; *Cal. Close, 1272–9,* 269; *1288–96,* 184; *1302–7,* 357–9.
69 *Trans. B.G.A.S.* lvii. 199–204.
70 *Dom. Bk.* (Rec. Com.), i. 169.
71 *Reg. Regum Anglo-Norm.* ii, p. 410; *Hist. & Cart. Mon. Glouc.* i. 340; cf. *Trans. B.G.A.S.* iv. 174–5.
72 *Cal. Inq. p.m.* i, pp. 113–14; ii, p. 288; Sanders, *Eng. Baronies,* 125.
73 *Hist. & Cart. Mon. Glouc.* i. 344–5.
74 Ibid. 341–3.
75 Sanders, *Eng. Baronies,* 125; *Ancient Charters* (P.R.S. x), 56.
76 *Hist. & Cart. Mon. Glouc.* i. 341–3; *Pipe R. 1199* (P.R.S. N.S. x), 34.
77 *Cal. Chart. R. 1226–57,* 221–2; *Bk. of Fees,* ii. 728, 742.
78 B.L. Campb. Ch. vii. 2; xxiii. 8.
79 *Cal. Inq. p.m.* i, p. 113.
80 *Cal. Fine R. 1272–1307,* 117.
81 *Cal. Inq. p.m.* ii, p. 288.
82 *Cal. Close, 1279–88,* 220.
83 *Feud. Aids,* ii. 247.
84 *Complete Peerage,* vii. 400–2.

the Newark), which he elevated into a collegiate church.[85] The college, which had grants of free warren and protection in the manor in 1356 and 1361 respectively,[86] held the manor until its suppression in 1548.[87]

In 1549 the manor was granted to Sir John Thynne[88] (d. 1580) and it passed to his son John,[89] whose son Sir Thomas was lord in 1608.[90] Sir Thomas (d. 1639) was succeeded at Kempsford by his son by his second marriage, Henry Frederick Thynne,[91] who was made a baronet in 1641 and suffered heavy sequestration fines after the Civil War.[92] From Sir Henry (d. 1680) the manor passed to his son Sir Thomas,[93] who was created Viscount Weymouth in 1682, in which year he succeeded to Longleat House and the main family estates. Viscount Weymouth (d. 1714) was succeeded in his estates and title by his great-nephew Thomas[94] (d. 1751), who gave Kempsford to his second son, Henry Frederick Thynne. Henry sold it in 1767 to Gabriel Hanger, Lord Coleraine[95] (d. 1773), whose widow Elizabeth apparently held it until her death in 1780.[96] It passed in turn to his three sons and successors to the title, John (d. 1794), William (d. 1814), and George (d. 1824). George, Lord Coleraine, a former companion of the Prince Regent, used the manor in his dealings with his creditors, who included his nephew and successor at Kempsford, Arthur Vansittart of Shottesbrook (Berks.).[97]

Arthur Vansittart sold part of the estate, comprising Manor and Dudgrove farms, to his brother Robert (d. 1838). The rest passed at his death in 1829 to his son Arthur.[98] The younger Arthur sold it in 1841 to Sir Gilbert East, Bt., who bought in the other part of the estate in 1844. Sir Gilbert (d. 1866) was succeeded by his son Sir Gilbert Augustus Clayton East, who sold the estate, comprising 8 farms and 3,085 a., to William Carey Faulkner in 1871. William (d. 1883) left his estates to his three sons, John, James, and Thomas, who made a division of them in 1889 when John's share included the manor and most of the land and James's included Dudgrove farm.[99] John Faulkner held his estate until his death in 1941[1] and his trustees offered it for sale in 1953, when it comprised 2,320 a.[2] The estate was then split up, several of the tenants buying their farms.[3]

The belief that there was a castle at Kempsford, recorded in the late 18th century,[4] probably derived merely from the existence of a large moated manor-house and from Kempsford's status as the head of a reputed barony. In an extent of 1258 only a manor-house, with a hall, kitchen, gatehouse, and other rooms, was recorded on the manor.[5] It evidently stood close to the river south of the church where part of the moat, recorded in 1801,[6] could still be seen in 1976. In the early 16th century the site of the manor included buildings in an inner and outer court, the former presumably those within the moat. The buildings of the inner court were known as the provost's lodgings from their use by the official of Leicester college who administered the manor, and they were reserved to the college in a lease of 1532.[7] In the late 16th century the manor-house was the home of Francis Thynne, second son of Sir John Thynne.[8] Part of it may have still been standing in 1705 when the buildings of the home farm included one called the porter's lodge.[9]

Sir Thomas Thynne built a large new manor-house at Kempsford between the church and the river, apparently completing it only shortly before his death in 1639.[10] Sir Henry Frederick Thynne was assessed on 44 hearths at Kempsford in 1672.[11] The house was ranged around a courtyard and had a walled garden,[12] known as the provost's garden,[13] on the north and a terrace walk beside the river. The terrace, which survived in 1976 together with the ruins of one of the summer-houses that stood at each end, acquired the name Lady Maud's Walk in the 19th century from a supposed connexion with the daughter of Henry, duke of Lancaster.[14] Of the farm buildings which stood south of the house in the early 18th century two barns and a building which became the back range of Manor Farm still survived in 1976. Kempsford was the chief residence of Sir Henry Frederick Thynne[15] but the house was probably used only occasionally by the family after 1682. In the 1770s it stood uninhabited and ruinous[16] and it was demolished before 1784,[17] some of the materials supposedly going to build Buscot Park (Berks.).[18] An 18th-century house south of the village street later became known as the Manor House[19] but in 1846 Sir Gilbert East built Manor Farm as the new manor-house, adding to an older building a new front range in the

[85] Cal. Pat. 1354–8, 184, 186; V.C.H. Leics. ii. 48.
[86] Cal. Chart. R. 1341–1417, 148; Cal. Pat. 1361–4, 25.
[87] V.C.H. Leics. ii. 50–1.
[88] Cal. Pat. 1548–9, 329; for the Thynnes, see Burke, Peerage (1963), 182–3.   [89] C 142/195 no. 118.
[90] Smith, Men and Armour, 264.
[91] Inq. p.m. Glos. 1625–42, iii. 161–4.
[92] Cal. Cttee. for Compounding, ii. 910–14.
[93] Atkyns, Glos. 491.
[94] Wilts. R.O. 845, man. papers 25.
[95] Glos. R.O., D 1070/III/45; Wilts. R.O. 845, Glos. est. papers 16, partics. of rectory 1797.
[96] Complete Peerage, iii. 367–8; Rudder, Glos. 511.
[97] Complete Peerage, iii. 368–9; Glos. R.O., D 2025, Vansittart fam., deeds 1774–1838; D 182/III/105.
[98] Glos. R.O., D 1388, est. maps; Burke, Land. Gent. (1898), 1512–13.
[99] Glos. R.O., D 3006, Faulkner fam., deeds 1865–89.
[1] Inscr. in ch.
[2] Glos. R.O., SL 563.

[3] Ex inf. Brig. Northen.   [4] Bigland, Glos. ii. 121.
[5] Inq. p.m. Glos. 1236–1300, 21.
[6] Glos. R.O., Q/RI 86.
[7] Longleat Mun. box lxx, bk. 63, pp. 116, 170; cf. V.C.H. Leics. ii. 49.
[8] Longleat Mun. box lv, no. 2535.
[9] Wilts. R.O. 845, Glos. est. papers 14, f. 10v.
[10] S.P. 16/468 no. 90.
[11] E 179/247/14 rot. 4.
[12] Atkyns, Glos. plate at pp. 490–1 (detail reproduced on p. 101).
[13] G.D.R., V 5/176T 1; Glos. R.O., Q/RI 86.
[14] O.S. Map 1/2,500, Glos. LX. 8 (1877 edn.); Trans. B.G.A.S. lvii. 204.
[15] Burke, Peerage (1963), 182; he was buried at Kempsford: Bigland, Glos. ii. 123.
[16] Rudder, Glos. 510.
[17] Bigland, Glos. ii. 121.
[18] Trans. B.G.A.S. lvii. 207.
[19] Glos. R.O., D 1388/SL 5, no. 43.

revived 17th-century style.[20] John Faulkner lived at Benbow House and later at Dunfield House.[21]

Gloucester Abbey, which was granted Kempsford church by Ernulf of Hesdin, also received various lands at Kempsford by gift of the first Patrick de Chaworth and his wife Maud, including $\frac{1}{2}$ hide, 1 yardland, and a mill at Horcott.[22] At the Dissolution most of the land was administered with Coln St. Aldwyns manor[23] and remained part of that manor after it was granted to the dean and chapter of Gloucester in 1541.[24] In 1649 it was a part of the demesne of Coln St. Aldwyns manor,[25] but later most of it formed a copyhold based on College Farm at Whelford. After the inclosure College farm comprised 99 a. while another 15 a. were leased separately with a cottage at Horcott.[26] In 1857 the Ecclesiastical Commissioners sold College farm to Richard Iles,[27] and Augustine Iles sold it in 1923 to the lord of the manor, John Faulkner.[28]

The rectory estate, leased from Gloucester Abbey in the early 16th century, comprised the parsonage barn, the tithes of corn and hay, and 3 a. of land assigned in composition for the tithes of a meadow.[29] It was granted in 1541 to the bishop of Gloucester.[30] The bishop granted an 89-year lease to the Crown before 1585[31] but in 1646 the lessee was the lord of the manor, Sir Henry Frederick Thynne, who was required to grant the rectory as an augmentation of the living of Cirencester.[32] Viscount Weymouth was the lessee c. 1710, when the rectory was said to be worth £100.[33] In 1723 it was leased for lives to Algernon Seymour, Lord Percy, and William Greville, Lord Brooke. Their interest was acquired before 1743 by Viscount Weymouth, and his eldest son Thomas, later marquess of Bath (d. 1796), and Thomas's son and heir Thomas succeeded as lessees.[34] At inclosure in 1801, when the rectory was valued at £236 net,[35] the marquess was awarded 318 a. based on Furzey Hill Farm for it. He sold the lease the same year to John Hewer of Maiseyhampton.[36] It was bought from the Hewer family in 1838 by Col. William Pearce of Cheltenham, who bought the freehold from the bishop in 1854 and sold the estate to Edward Fletcher Booker in 1860. Booker and his mortgagees sold it in 1868 to Richard Rickards,[37] whose family owned and farmed Furzey Hill until the mid 20th century.[38]

Bradenstoke Priory (Wilts.) in 1258[39] and Lacock Abbey (Wilts.) in 1315[40] owned lands in Kempsford. Those lands were evidently the parcels of meadow which continued to descend with Hatherop after the Dissolution; they had presumably become attached to Hatherop in the late 11th and early 12th centuries when it was in the same ownership as Kempsford.[41]

ECONOMIC HISTORY. In 1086 Kempsford manor had 6 teams in demesne and employed 14 *servi*. There was a sheepfold on the manor, the flock being apparently valued principally as a means of producing cheese.[42] In 1258 the demesne of the manor comprised $832\frac{1}{2}$ a. of arable, $156\frac{1}{2}$ a. of meadow, a pasture sufficient to support 24 oxen, and a grove with pasture for 40 cows;[43] the last was presumably Dudgrove, where the manor sheep-house stood in 1517. Most of the demesne land was leased during the 16th century to the Hitchman family,[44] which held 14 yardlands in 1587.[45]

The tenants in 1086 were 38 *villani*, 9 bordars, and a radknight, with 18 teams between them.[46] In 1258 there were 37 yardlands held in villeinage; their value to the lord was then realized mainly in cash rents and aids and from each was owed only 5 days' labour in the year. There were also 66 cottagers, owing rent and 2 days' reaping each, and a number of free tenants.[47]

All or most of the tenant land was copyhold until 1673 when Sir Henry Frederick Thynne apparently ended that form of tenure on the manor.[48] Later the tenant holdings, which numbered more than 60 in 1710, were mostly held on leases for lives owing heriots and reliefs; quite a high number were held by non-parishioners, possibly attracted by the valuable meadow rights attached to the holdings, while among the Kempsford holders the families of Pope, Jenner, Iles, and Packer were prominent.[49] Three larger farms on the estate were held on short leases for years in the 18th century:[50] they were the home farm, which probably had its farm-house at the old site of the manor, Dudgrove farm in the south-east part of the parish,[51] which was apparently established in the late 17th century,[52] and Furzey Hill farm, established in the early 18th

[20] Inscr. on bldg.
[21] *Kelly's Dir. Glos.* (1889 and later edns.).
[22] *Hist. & Cart. Mon. Glouc.* i. 340–1.
[23] *Valor Eccl.* (Rec. Com.), ii. 410.
[24] *L. & P. Hen. VIII*, xvi, p. 572.
[25] Glos. R.O., D 1740/E 1, f. 64 and v.
[26] Ibid. E 2; D 936/E 160.
[27] Ibid. SL 239.
[28] Ibid. SL 563.
[29] Glouc. Cath. Libr., Reg. Abb. Braunche, pp. 88–9; Reg. Abb. Malvern, i, f. 92 and v.; ii, f. 61.
[30] *L. & P. Hen. VIII*, xvi, p. 572.
[31] Hist. MSS. Com. 23, *12th Rep. I, Cowper*, p. 40.
[32] *Cal. Cttee. for Compounding*, ii. 910.
[33] Atkyns, *Glos.* 491.
[34] Glos. Colln. RZ 176.2.
[35] Wilts. R.O. 845, Glos. est. papers 16.
[36] Glos. Colln. RZ 176.2.
[37] Glos. R.O., D 1388, sale papers, Kempsford 1847–68.

[38] *Kelly's Dir. Glos.* (1870 and later edns.).
[39] *Inq. p.m. Glos. 1236–1300*, 22.
[40] *Lacock Abbey Charters*, ed. K. H. Rogers (Wilts. Rec. Soc. xxxiv), no. 410.
[41] Glos. R.O., D 540/T 49; see above.
[42] *Dom. Bk.* (Rec. Com.), i. 169.
[43] *Inq. p.m. Glos. 1236–1300*, 21.
[44] Longleat Mun. box lxx, bk. 63, pp. 113–19; box lv, no. 2525.
[45] Ibid. box liii, no. 2485.
[46] *Dom. Bk.* (Rec. Com.), i. 169.
[47] *Inq. p.m. Glos. 1236–1300*, 22.
[48] A draft deed for that purpose survives in Longleat Mun. box lvii, no. 2597.
[49] Wilts. R.O. 845, Glos. est. papers 14, ff. 1–23v.; cf. Glos. R.O., Q/RI 86.
[50] Cf. Wilts. R.O. 845, Glos. est. papers 16.
[51] Ibid. 14, ff. 8v., 10v.
[52] Ibid. 22.

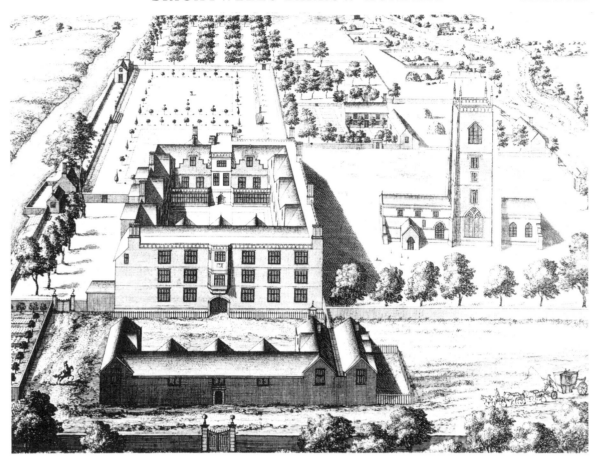

KEMPSFORD: THE MANOR-HOUSE AND CHURCH IN THE EARLY 18TH CENTURY
WITH THE RIVER THAMES ON THE LEFT

century on rough grazing land in the north-west corner of the parish.[53]

The tenants in Kempsford village had their arable in Town field, lying immediately north of the village street, in Upper Moor field, lying beyond Town field, and in Upper and Lower Ham fields, lying east of the village between the Thames and the Grand Drain. Dunfield field lay north of the hamlet of that name and Honey field lay east of Furzey hill. Whelford had a great field and a little field, both lying north of the hamlet, and West Horcott field lay west of Horcott.[54] A rotation of two crops and a fallow was apparently the practice in most of the parish until inclosure[55] but at Dunfield a part of the open fields, called a hitching, was cultivated every year in the late 17th century and until 1727, when it was included again in the usual rotation.[56]

The rich meadow land of the manor by the Thames and Coln was valued at £9 in 1086[57] and in later centuries occupied more than 1,000 a., most of it common meadow held on the lot system. The largest common meadow, Kempsford meadow, occupied the south-east corner of the parish;

Whelford meadow and Bowmoor lay between the Coln and the north-east boundary; and there were several smaller meadows, including one at Dunfield.[58] The practice of 'drowning' the meadows, flooding them in winter to warm the land and bring on early grass, was recorded from 1707, when the costs of the operation were shared among the occupiers.[59] The owners of several upland estates in the neighbourhood owned and used parcels of meadow in Kempsford in connexion with their estates. In 1267 one of Gloucester Abbey's tenants at Coln St. Aldwyns had the duty of carrying hay from Kempsford,[60] and meadow land at Kempsford belonging to the abbey remained attached in later centuries to its manors of Coln, Aldsworth,[61] and Eastleach Martin.[62] Other parcels of meadow were attached to the manors of Hatherop and Southrop,[63] which had both at different times been in the same ownership as Kempsford.

The parish once had a large common pasture called the Moors, lying between the Grand Drain and the Kempsford–Whelford road. It was inclosed by private agreement in the later 17th century,

[53] Ibid. vol. 4, p. 19; Glos. est. papers 14, f. 3v.; cf. ibid. 13.
[54] Ibid. Glos. est. papers 14, ff. 1v., 3v.; 19; Glos. R.O., Q/RI 86.
[55] Wilts. R.O. 845, Glos. est. papers 16, partics. of rectory 1797.
[56] Ibid. man. papers 25, cts. 1689, 1713, 1727; cf. Rudder, *Glos.* 22.   [57] *Dom. Bk.* (Rec. Com.), i. 169.
[58] Glos. R.O., Q/RI 86; Wilts. R.O. 845, Glos. est. papers 16.

[59] Wilts. R.O. 845, man. papers 25; cf. Rudder, *Glos.* 418–19.
[60] *Hist. & Cart. Mon. Glouc.* iii. 200.
[61] Glouc. Cath. Libr., Reg. Abb. Braunche, pp. 122–4; Reg. Abb. Newton, ff. 69–70v.; Glos. R.O., D 1740/E 1, f. 64; D 678, Aldsworth par. 1, 16; Q/RI 86.
[62] Glos. R.O., D 1740/E 1, f. 73v.; Glos. Colln. RF 119.1.
[63] D.L. 42/116 f. 83v.; Glos. R.O., D 540/T 49; Q/RI 86.

before 1677, and divided into small closes which were assigned to the various tenements on the manor.[64] There remained the common pasture rights in the open fields and meadows: in 1682 the stint was 20 sheep, 7 beasts, and 2 horses to the yardland in the fields and 4 beasts to the yardland in the meadows.[65] In 1587 a total of 5,447 sheep and 884 cattle was kept in the parish; the largest flock of sheep, numbering 460, was kept by James Dolle in Whelford while Robert Hitchman, the farmer of the demesne, had 390.[66]

Inclosure by Act of Parliament in 1801 dealt with 2,224 a. of open field and common meadow as well as re-allotting some old inclosures that were inconveniently situated for the farm-houses to which they were attached. The bulk of the allotments was assigned to Lord Coleraine or his life-tenants but whereas he had previously owned almost all the parish, the small estate of the dean and chapter being the main exception, several substantial freeholds were created as a result of the inclosure. Two of them were those given for the tithes of the rectory and vicarage respectively while the sale of a considerable acreage to meet the expenses of the inclosure enabled several people to acquire estates, in particular Mary Jenner, Thomas Pope of Whelford, and Thomas Packer Butt who became owner of Reevey farm.[67]

Following the inclosure several large farms were formed. Two on the manor estate covered 653 a. and 628 a. respectively in 1815.[68] The estate had a total of 8 farms in 1870, the largest being Dudgrove farm with 767 a. and Manor farm with 607 a.; the others were two at Whelford with 472 a. and 200 a. respectively, two at Horcott with 310 a. and 227 a. respectively, Dunfield farm with 297 a., and Tuckwell's farm in Kempsford village with 96 a.[69] There were altogether c. 22 separate holdings in the parish in the 19th century,[70] Furzey Hill farm, comprising 317 a. in 1860, being the largest outside the manor estate.[71] In 1926, however, as many as 31 separate holdings were returned, of which 9 were of over 150 a. and 7 of 50–150 a.[72] The smaller holdings had mostly gone by 1976 when a total of 15 farms was returned, 7 of them of over 100 ha. (247 a.).[73]

Arable land predominated over grassland in the 19th century in spite of the extensive meadow land: in 1866 2,835 a., cropped mainly with wheat, barley, turnips, beans, and grass-seeds, were returned compared with 1,545 a. of permanent grassland.[74] The decline in arable farming in the later 19th century was not so marked as in the upland parishes of the neighbourhood with only wheat suffering a severe reduction in acreage.[75] The rich meadow land naturally made cattle-raising and dairying a significant part of local farming. Cheese-production was no doubt also encouraged by the proximity of Lechlade with its facilities for marketing cheese and shipping it to London; Cobbett in 1826 noted one Kempsford farm with a dairy herd of 60–80 and a cheese-loft containing many hundreds of cheeses.[76] In 1866 a total of 624 cattle, including 165 milk cows, was returned on the farms of the parish[77] and in the earlier 20th century even more farms appear to have concentrated on beef and dairy cattle; 828, including 257 milk cows, were returned in 1926.[78] Sheep were still pastured in large numbers in 1866 when 2,583 were returned,[79] but none were returned in 1976. In 1976 the amount of arable returned was up again to the mid-19th-century level, for although much of the old arable had been lost to the airfield most of the old meadow land was then under the plough; the arable was then almost entirely under wheat and barley. Dairying had declined to some extent in recent years, though 4 of the main farms still specialized in that branch, while 3 were mainly devoted to cereals, 2 mainly to cattle-raising, 1 to poultry, and 1 to mixed farming.[80]

Four mills were recorded on Kempsford manor in 1086.[81] One at Horcott was granted to Gloucester Abbey by the first Patrick de Chaworth, who also gave the abbey the tithes from two at Whelford.[82] The abbey's Horcott mill was again recorded in 1225[83] and may have been working in 1556;[84] no later record of it has been found[85] but a side-channel of the Coln survives at Horcott, presumably the mill-leat. The two Whelford mills were again recorded on the manor estate in 1258[86] and in 1532, when there were two mills under one roof.[87] They were presumably at the site of Whelford mill, on the Coln north of the hamlet. In 1710 Whelford mill was worked in conjunction with a malt-house.[88] By 1732 the tenant was John Edmonds,[89] whose family continued as millers there until the Second World War.[90] The buildings were remodelled and extended in the mid 20th century to form a substantial residence. A derelict windmill standing by the Thames in Kempsford parish was depicted in an undated print;[91] no other

---

[64] Wilts. R.O. 845, Glos. est. papers 16; G.D.R., V 5/176T 1; cf. Glos. R.O., Q/RI 86.
[65] Wilts. R.O. 845, man. papers 25.
[66] Longleat Mun. box liii, no. 2485.
[67] Glos. R.O., Q/RI 86; some of the sale allotments were set out in 1802 under an amendment to the original award.
[68] Ibid. D 2025, Vansittart fam. deeds 1774–1838.
[69] Ibid. D 1388/SL 5, no. 43.
[70] Census, 1831; M.A.F. 68/1609/8.
[71] Glos. R.O., D 1388, sale papers, Kempsford 1847–68.
[72] M.A.F. 68/3295/8.
[73] Agric. Returns 1976.
[74] M.A.F. 68/26/10.
[75] M.A.F. 68/1609/8.
[76] Cobbett, Rural Rides (Everyman edn. 1957), ii. 132.
[77] M.A.F. 68/25/3.
[78] M.A.F. 68/3295/8.
[79] M.A.F. 68/25/3.
[80] Agric. Returns 1976; ex inf. Brig. Northen.
[81] Dom. Bk. (Rec. Com.), i. 169.
[82] Hist. & Cart. Mon. Glouc. i. 340.
[83] C.P. 25(1)/73/7 no. 84.
[84] Hockaday Abs. cxciv.
[85] Taylor, Map of Glos. (1777) marks a mill there but possibly in error for Whelford mill.
[86] Inq. p.m. Glos. 1236–1300, 21.
[87] Longleat Mun. box lxx, bk. 63, p. 113.
[88] Wilts. R.O. 845, Glos. est. papers 14, f. 17.
[89] Ibid. 15.
[90] Glos. R.O., Q/RI 86; Kelly's Dir. Glos. (1856 and later edns.).
[91] Glos. Colln. prints 164.4.

record of it has been found but it is thought to have stood in the meadows downstream of Hannington bridge.[92]

In 1243 Patrick de Chaworth had a grant of a Tuesday market and an annual fair at the Nativity of the Virgin on his manor of Kempsford,[93] and in 1267 his son had a grant of a Friday market and a fair at St. Bartholomew.[94] The alteration of the dates may reflect conflict with markets held at Lechlade and Fairford, though the new market day would still have conflicted with one of the Fairford markets. It seems unlikely that the market and fair ever prospered in such close proximity to the two towns; nothing about their later fortunes has been found.

Henry the walker who was drowned in one of the mill-ponds before 1287[95] was probably plying his trade there. In 1327 2 fishermen were recorded in the parish,[96] presumably lessees or employees under the manor, which enjoyed rights in both the Thames and Coln.[97] Three tailors and a weaver were the only tradesmen listed in 1608[98] and later references found are all to the usual village craftsmen. In 1831 27 families in the parish were supported by trade compared with 142 supported by agriculture.[99] In the 19th century the traditional craftsmen were joined by a number of shopkeepers and by others—in 1856 a timber-merchant, a coal-merchant, and a corn-dealer—whose business was probably connected with the canal trade[1] but the numbers engaged in trade were not large in proportion to the total population and the parish presumably looked to the neighbouring market towns for some of its needs.

LOCAL GOVERNMENT. By an arrangement which was apparently in force by 1258[2] view of frankpledge was held at Kempsford twice a year before the bailiffs of the abbot of Cirencester, lord of the hundred. The bailiffs were dined at the lord of the manor's expense and at one of the views took 5s. and any goods of fugitives and felons; the remaining profits went to the lord of the manor.[3] The lord of the manor's court exercised view of frankpledge in the post-medieval period. Rolls of the court survive for some years in the 14th century[4] and for most years between 1568 and 1646,[5] and there are draft rolls and court papers for 1682–1735. The court appointed a constable, a tithingman for Kempsford, whose bailiwick also

included Dunfield, and a tithingman for Whelford with Horcott. Haywards were appointed for the same two divisions as the tithingmen and in their regulation of common rights were assisted by tellers; from 1692 a parish wonter (mole-catcher) was also appointed. In the 1630s the court still heard occasional pleas of debt and trespass but from the late 17th century it dealt only with agricultural and estate matters, including the upkeep of the system of drainage. It was also at particular pains to enforce the statutory labour on the roads and in 1682 the parish surveyors were apparently appointed in the court.[6] The court continued to be held until 1851.[7]

The old church house was used as a poorhouse in the 18th century.[8] In 1772 the vestry introduced the roundsman system for pauper girls and it adopted the Speenhamland plan in 1795. A parish surgeon was retained from 1797.[9] In the early 19th century expenditure on relief was generally high, sometimes higher than in the two neighbouring towns; 57 people were on permanent relief in 1803 and 72 in 1813.[10] By 1833 a deputy overseer was being retained and in that year employment was encouraged by the offer of a bonus of 2s. to employers for each man taken on at 7s. a week.[11] The parish became part of the Cirencester union in 1836[12] and was later in Cirencester rural district,[13] becoming part of Cotswold district in 1974.

CHURCHES. Kempsford had a church by the late 11th century when Ernulf of Hesdin granted it with the tithes and the land of the priest to Gloucester Abbey; the tithes were confirmed to the abbey by Patrick de Chaworth and his wife Maud.[14] A vicarage had been ordained in the church by 1198[15] and the living has remained a vicarage. It was united with Castle Eaton (Wilts.) in 1974.[16] The advowson of the vicarage, retained by Gloucester Abbey until the Dissolution, was granted in 1541 to the bishop of Gloucester,[17] who remained patron in 1976. In 1422 the living was described as the vicarage of Whelford and Kempsford[18] and the rectory estate was later usually called the rectory of Kempsford and Whelford,[19] but no evidence of an ancient church or chapel at Whelford has been found.

In 1291 the living was valued at £14 13s. 4d. while Gloucester Abbey's rectory estate, held in commendam by Walter of Barton, was valued at £7

[92] Ex inf. Brig. Northen.
[93] D.L. 10/82.
[94] Cal. Chart. R. 1257–1300, 79.
[95] J.I. 1/278 rot. 51d.
[96] Glos. Subsidy Roll, 1327, 13.
[97] Inq. p.m. Glos. 1236–1300, 21.
[98] Smith, Men and Armour, 265.
[99] Census, 1831.
[1] Kelly's Dir. Glos. (1856 and later edns.).
[2] Inq. p.m. Glos. 1236–1300, 22.
[3] Ciren. Cart. ii, p. 623.
[4] Those and other medieval records for Kempsford in the Longleat Mun. were not seen for this article.
[5] Longleat Mun. box liv, bks. 1–4; box lv, bks. 5–7; box lvi, bks. 8–14.
[6] Wilts. R.O. 845, man. papers 25.

[7] Trans. B.G.A.S. lvii. 209. [8] Ibid. lvii. 223.
[9] Ibid. 220, 222, 226, citing vestry min. bks. from 1770, which with churchwardens' accts. for 1807–87 have been lost since 1935.
[10] Poor Law Abstract, 1804, 172–3; 1818, 146–7; Poor Law Returns (1830–1), p. 67; (1835), p. 65.
[11] Trans. B.G.A.S. lvii. 226.
[12] Poor Law Com. 2nd Rep. p. 522.
[13] Census, 1911.
[14] Hist. & Cart. Mon. Glouc. i. 340.
[15] Ibid. 346.
[16] Glouc. Dioc. Yr. Bk. (1976), 66.
[17] L. & P. Hen. VIII, xvi, p. 572.
[18] Worc. Episc. Reg., Reg. Morgan, ii, f. 13.
[19] Glouc. Cath. Libr., Reg. Abb. Braunche, pp. 88–9; Glos. Colln. RZ 176.1–2.

6s. 8d. The abbey also received a payment of 4 marks[20] out of the vicarage, granted to it c. 1197,[21] presumably because the original portion settled on the vicar was thought over-generous. The payment continued to be made by the vicar to the lessees of the rectory after the Dissolution.[22]

In 1677 the vicar's glebe comprised 41 a. in the open fields, 34 a. of pasture and meadow, and 9 'yards' of lot meadow. He then received all the small tithes of the parish and the corn and hay tithes of certain lands,[23] the latter granted in part as compensation for his loss of small tithes by the inclosure of the Moors. Lands known as the demesne meadows but including a large part of the common and lot meadows were claimed to be tithe free at the time of the inclosure in 1801, a claim not accepted by the vicar.[24] The lord of the manor usually paid a composition for the tithes of the home farm and some of the other larger farms on his estate.[25] The tithes were commuted for land at the inclosure, giving the vicar a total estate of 522 a.[26] The vicarage house, standing north of the church, includes a range built c. 1664;[27] additions were made on the north of that range in the 18th century, and c. 1856 there was a general remodelling of the house.[28]

The vicarage was valued at £19 clear in 1535[29] and at £80 in 1650.[30] It was said to be worth £100 at the beginning of the 18th century[31] and £220 in 1750, when the profits included a rent-charge of £20 given by Lord Weymouth in 1709.[32] In 1856 it was worth £604[33] but declined in value in the later 19th century and was worth only £160 in 1910;[34] in 1901 it was said to be held at a loss.[35]

Humphrey Gallimore, instituted to Kempsford vicarage in 1538, was dispensed for plurality in 1550,[36] and in 1559 leased the vicarage to Sir John Thynne, who was to make provision for serving the cure;[37] in 1563 it was served by the rector of Bagendon.[38] Gallimore was apparently in danger of losing the benefice in 1564, when it was said in his support that he was a 'favourer of true religion' who had formerly enjoyed the patronage of Bishop Latimer. In 1569 he was declared contumacious and barred from entering the church and in 1572 he was ejected for not subscribing to the Articles.[39] In 1639 the bishop, Godfrey Goodman, presented himself to the vicarage. He was succeeded in 1643 by Edward Hitchman[40] who remained vicar until his death in 1672, when he also held a prebend of Wells cathedral.[41] William Price, vicar 1761–98,[42] was living at Epsom (Surr.) in 1784 when Kempsford was served by a curate who lived at Fairford.[43] Thomas Huntingford, vicar 1810–55, held the living with the vicarage of Dormington (Herefs.) from 1826 and with the rectory of Weston under Penyard (Herefs.) from 1831.[44] His successor, James Russell Woodford, later bishop of Ely,[45] introduced daily services and weekly communions.[46]

The parish church of ST. MARY[47] is built predominantly of ashlar and has a chancel with south chapel, a tall central tower, and clerestoried nave with north and south porches.

Most of the Norman nave survives and it retains its north and south doorways and four original windows. The present chancel was built in the 13th century and the existence of a central tower by that time can be inferred. A south porch, used as a vestry from 1855,[48] was added in the 13th century. Early in the 14th century new windows were put into the west wall of the nave and the north wall of the chancel. In the 15th century there was a major reconstruction when a clerestory and new roof were added to the nave, new windows were put into the east end of its side walls, and the tower was rebuilt. The massive tower has a lofty, vaulted lower stage and very large windows in its north and south walls.[49] Although the north porch incorporates an earlier ogee-headed recess it too was probably an addition of the 15th century. The church was restored in 1858 under G. E. Street when a south chapel was added to the chancel and the nave was reseated.[50] A west gallery was removed in 1866[51] and some further restoration was carried out in the 1880s.[52]

Few of the early furnishings or fittings survive. The stone pulpit, made in 1862, was designed by G. E. Street as were the choir-stalls. A new font was made in 1868,[53] replacing an old octagonal one.[54] Three of the stained glass windows were painted by the curate H. F. St. John,[55] who with Vernon Benbow was also responsible for painting the bosses and heraldic shields of the tower vault in 1862.[56] A 15th-century canopied tomb with the effigy of a priest survives in the chancel[57] together

[20] Tax. Eccl. (Rec. Com.), 222; cf. Reg. Giffard, 550.
[21] Hist. & Cart. Mon. Glouc. i. 346.
[22] Bodl. MS. Rawl. B.323, f. 92v.
[23] G.D.R., V 5/176T 1.
[24] Wilts. R.O. 845, Glos. est. papers 16.
[25] Ibid. 13, 15–16.
[26] Glos. R.O., Q/RI 86.
[27] Longleat Mun. box liii, no. 2476.
[28] Glos. R.O., D 1381/96.
[29] Valor Eccl. (Rec. Com.), ii. 446.
[30] Trans. B.G.A.S. lxxxiii. 94.
[31] Atkyns, Glos. 489.
[32] G.D.R. vol. 381A, f. 86; Rudder, Glos. 511.
[33] G.D.R. vol. 384, f. 126.
[34] Kelly's Dir. Glos. (1910), 228.
[35] Trans. B.G.A.S. lvii. 233.
[36] Hockaday Abs. ccli.
[37] Longleat Mun. box lix, no. 2679.
[38] Hockaday Abs. cxi.
[39] Ibid. ccli.
[40] Ibid.
[41] Bigland, Glos. ii. 123.
[42] Hockaday Abs. ccli.
[43] G.D.R. vol. 319.
[44] Hockaday Abs. ccli.
[45] D.N.B.
[46] Notes in par. reg. 1813–40.
[47] The dedication is recorded from the early 18th century (Bodl. MS. Rawl. B.323, f. 92v.) but in 1856 it was said to be to St. John the Evangelist: Kelly's Dir. Glos. (1856), 315.
[48] Note in par. reg. 1813–40.
[49] See plate facing p. 77.
[50] Press cutting in par. reg. 1813–40.
[51] Note in par. reg. 1841–68.
[52] Kelly's Dir. Glos. (1914), 234.
[53] Notes in par. reg. 1841–68; Verey, Glos. i. 285.
[54] Glos. Ch. Notes, 110.
[55] Notes in par. reg. 1841–68; cf. Kelly's Dir. Glos. (1863), 299.
[56] Verey, Glos. i. 285.
[57] Roper, Glos. Effigies, 640–1.

with a brass to Walter Hitchman (d. 1521),[58] who was lessee of the manorial demesne and of the rectory and possibly also a wool-merchant.[59] The church had a peal of 6 bells by the early 18th century[60] and in the late 19th century they were as follows: (i) 1739, by Henry Bagley; (ii) 1700, by Abraham Rudhall; (iii and iv) 1678, stamped with the arms of Sir Henry Frederick Thynne and his wife; (v) 1846, by C. & G. Mears; (vi) 1830, by John Rudhall.[61] The plate includes a chalice and paten cover of 1660,[62] presumably those given by Sir Henry Frederick Thynne and his wife, who also gave two silver flagons.[63] The churchyard contains a number of carved chest-tombs to members of the Iles and other 18th-century tenant families, and on the south side of the church is a group in a uniform style to members of the Arkell family, prominent farmers in the 19th century. The parish registers survive from 1573.[64]

At Whelford, where services were held in a granary from 1860, a chapel of ease, dedicated to *ST. ANNE*, was built and consecrated in 1864. Designed by G. E. Street,[65] it comprised nave with bellcot and apsidal chancel. A south transept was added in 1898.[66]

ROMAN CATHOLICISM. A small Roman Catholic church was built at Horcott in 1845[67] to take the place of the chapel that had formerly been in use at Hatherop Castle.[68] The Horcott church had an average congregation of 60 in 1851.[69] In 1976 it served a parish which included Lechlade, Fairford, and eleven surrounding villages.[70]

PROTESTANT NONCONFORMITY. Five Anabaptists were recorded at Kempsford in 1735.[71] Baptists registered a house at Whelford in 1799 and a group attached to the Fairford chapel was meeting in the parish in 1836.[72] A Baptist mission hall was built in 1879.[73] Independents registered a chapel at Whelford in 1820,[74] and there was a village station attached to the Congregational church at Fairford in 1858.[75] Other meeting-places recorded in the 1840s included a chapel at Horcott, belonging to John Kent, registered in 1841, and a house at Dunfield, registered for use by Primitive Methodists in 1844.[76]

EDUCATION. In 1693 Lord Weymouth was paying a schoolmaster £5 a year to teach children at Kempsford,[77] and a building called the school house, though possibly not then used for that purpose, was mentioned in 1706.[78] In 1709 Lord Weymouth settled £10 a year, payable out of estates in Ross-on-Wye and Weobley (both Herefs.), to pay a schoolmaster.[79] The master recorded at Kempsford in 1715[80] was presumably employed by the charity, which in 1735 was teaching poor children to read free of charge and to write for a payment of 2d. a week, while the children from wealthier families paid 1d. for reading and 4d. for writing.[81] In 1750 a new building for the school, paid for by a subscription among the inhabitants, was put up on the south side of the village street on land given by Lord Weymouth.[82] In 1787 the school was said to be supported by Lord Coleraine,[83] who was presumably meeting the costs not covered by the endowment and pence.

By 1818 60–70 children, all the poor children of the parish, were attending the charity school, and a Sunday school supported by the vicar Thomas Huntingford had been started in a cottage adjoining the vicarage.[84] A new school building was built in 1855 adjoining the old one. In 1869 the school, called Kempsford C. of E. school, was supported by voluntary contributions, pence, and the endowment and had an average attendance of 80.[85] The average attendance remained at much the same figure in 1904;[86] it fell during the next 20 years but then recovered and was 81 again in 1936.[87] In 1976 there were 89 children on the roll.[88]

A church school for infants had been started at Whelford by 1867 when it taught c. 25 children and was supported by voluntary contributions and pence.[89] It was held in a cottage until 1874 when a new building was provided.[90] The attendance rose to 50 by 1885, when older children were also taken,[91] but fell to 20 by 1904[92] and remained at c. 25 during the earlier 20th century.[93] By 1949 only 11 children remained on the register and the school was closed.[94] A Roman Catholic school was built at Horcott in 1852 and in 1885 had an average attendance of 36.[95] It was apparently closed in 1888.[96]

CHARITIES FOR THE POOR. John Hampson Jones by will proved 1892 gave £1,000 for the poor, and £1,000 stock was given in memory of William Battersby in 1926. In the mid 1970s the income from the two charities, c. £120, was distributed in cash among the old-age pensioners of the parish.[97]

[58] Davis, *Glos. Brasses*, 126–7.
[59] Longleat Mun. box lxx, bk. 63, pp. 113–19; Glouc. Cath. Libr., Reg. Abb. Malvern, i, f. 92 and v. The brass includes a merchant's mark.   [60] Bodl. MS. Rawl. B 323, f. 92v.
[61] *Glos. Ch. Bells*, 53 and plate X; cf. Burke, *Peerage* (1963), 182.   [62] *Glos. Ch. Plate*, 128.
[63] G.D.R., V 5/176T 2.   [64] *B. & G. Par. Rec.* 175.
[65] *Trans. B.G.A.S.* lvii. 227; see above, plate facing p. 76.
[66] Verey, *Glos.* i. 470.   [67] Date on window in ch.
[68] Langston, 'Cath. Missions', i, p. 12.   [69] H.O. 129/340/3/9/11.
[70] Ex inf. the par. priest, Fr. J. A. Coghlan.
[71] G.D.R. vol. 285B, f. 35.   [72] Hockaday Abs. ccli.
[73] *Kelly's Dir. Glos.* (1910), 228.
[74] Hockaday Abs. ccli.   [75] *Cong. Yr. Bk.* (1859–60), 91.
[76] Hockaday Abs. ccli; Glos. R.O., Q/RZ 1; H.O. 129/340/3/9/10.

[77] Wilts. R.O. 845, Glos. est. papers 22.   [78] Ibid. 14, f. 2.
[79] Rudder, *Glos.* 511.   [80] Glos. R.O., Q/SO 4.
[81] *Trans. B.G.A.S.* lvii. 229.   [82] Inscr. on bldg.
[83] *Glouc. Jnl.* 17 Dec. 1787.
[84] *Educ. of Poor Digest*, 302; note in par. reg. 1813–40.
[85] Ed. 7/34/181.   [86] *Public Elem. Schs.* 1906, 185.
[87] *Bd. of Educ., List 21, 1911* (H.M.S.O.), 163; *1922*, 105; *1932*, 115; *1936*, 121.
[88] Ex inf. county educ. dept.
[89] *Rep. Com. Agric. Employment*, p. 105.
[90] Ed. 7/34/182.   [91] *Kelly's Dir. Glos.* (1885), 510.
[92] *Public Elem. Schs.* 1906, 185.
[93] *Bd. of Educ., List 21, 1911* (H.M.S.O.), 163; *1922*, 105; *1932*, 115; *1936*, 121.
[94] Glos. R.O., S 189A.   [95] *Kelly's Dir. Glos.* (1885), 510.
[96] Ex inf. Miss C. A. Willant, of Fairford.   [97] Ex inf. the vicar.

LECHLADE

LECHLADE is situated 19 km. east of Cirencester in the Thames-side meadow land on the east boundary of the county. A borough and market town from the early 13th century, it later played some part in the Cotswold wool trade. Its chief function, however, was as a staging-post for goods and passenger traffic, for it stood at the head of the navigable Thames and at the entrance into Gloucestershire of a major road route from London. By the late 17th century large quantities of cheese were being shipped down river from Lechlade and after the opening of the Thames and Severn canal in 1789 the inhabitants also traded in coal. From the late 19th century the river played a new role, attracting visitors to the town for fishing and boating.

The boundaries of the ancient parish, which touched those of the counties of Wiltshire, Berkshire, and Oxfordshire, were mainly on rivers and watercourses, the river Thames supplying much of the south boundary and the Coln and Leach, which meet the Thames in the parish, parts of the other boundaries. South of the town the county and parish boundary diverges from the Thames to follow Murdock ditch,[98] presumably the original course of the river. A reference to the old Coln in 1627[99] suggests that it too has been diverted within the parish. North of the old parish Lemhill, comprising 245 a. with a single farm-house, was a detached part of Broughton Poggs (Oxon.). It was added to Lechlade in 1886, increasing the area of the parish to 3,870 a. (1,566 ha.).[1] The history of Lemhill is included in this account.

The south part of the parish lies on alluvium and the north part on Oxford Clay with surface deposits of gravel or cornbrash.[2] The land is low and flat, mainly lying at about 70 m., and meadow land intersected by willow-lined watercourses and drainage channels provides the main feature of the landscape. There has never been much woodland apart from that in small copses and brakes in the north-west part of the parish and that in the park formed around the manor-house, north-east of the town, in the 19th century. In the mid 20th century gravel and sand workings transformed the appearance of the north-east part of the parish.

The crossing of the Thames near its confluence with the Leach has played a major role in the history of Lechlade and probably gave the parish its name;[3] a piece of land at the crossing was known as the Lade in 1246.[4] St. John's bridge, built at the crossing

by 1228, carried the main road connecting mid Gloucestershire with London. Traffic was channelled into Lechlade and the bridge from Cirencester, from Gloucester by the Welsh way which met the Cirencester road at Fairford,[5] and from the north part of the Cotswolds by the Droitwich salt-way through Hatherop.[6] It was presumably to succour sick and poor travellers using the road that the owners of Lechlade manor, Isabel de Mortimer and her second husband Peter FitzHerbert, built the hospital or priory of St. John the Baptist on the north side of the bridge before 1228.[7] The hospital was dissolved in 1472, and c. 1520 part of the buildings was pulled down and the material used to repair the bridge,[8] but Leland some years later reported seeing a chapel and large enclosures of stone walls.[9] There was some effort to preserve the foundations when the site was used for building a parish workhouse in 1763,[10] but they were disturbed on more than one occasion subsequently.[11] In 1977 the site was used as a permanent caravan park.

The hospital had responsibility for the repair of St. John's bridge, for which the prior had grants of pontage in 1338, 1341, and 1388.[12] Later the bridge comprised two large and two small arches and there was a long causeway of more than 20 arches crossing the meadows on the Buscot side of the river.[13] A gateway to the bridge was built by Peter FitzHerbert in 1228[14] and possibly survived as the building on it that was known as Noah's Ark in 1716.[15] By 1831 the bridge was dilapidated and a dispute over the liability to repair it arose between the county and the occupiers of the former hospital lands. In spite of the seemingly clear historical evidence of the liability of the latter the suit was inconclusive[16] and the county later accepted responsibility, employing a local builder, Peter Cox, to rebuild the bridge as a single arch.[17] An ancient right of taking toll from barges passing under the bridge, with which went the obligation of penning back the water to create a 'flash' to enable them to pass, was claimed by the lords of Lechlade manor as owners of the hospital estate.[18] In the late 17th century and early 18th the right to take toll was disputed by the bargemen and in the time of Sir Thomas Cutler led on one occasion to the bridge being chained up.[19] In 1791, however, the difficulties of passing the bridge were avoided when the navigation commissioners for the upper Thames by-passed it with a short new cut and a lock.[20]

[98] Glos. R.O., D 1388, sale papers, Lechlade 1870–94, sale partics. 1890. This account was written in 1977.
[99] *Inq. p.m. Glos.* 1625–42, i. 57.   [1] *Census*, 1891.
[2] Geol. Surv. Map 1", solid, sheet 34 (1857 edn.).
[3] *P.N. Glos.* (E.P.N.S.), i. 40–1.
[4] *Cal. Chart. R.* 1226–57, 296.
[5] Ogilby, *Britannia* (1675), p. 29.
[6] Taylor, *Map. of Glos.* (1777).
[7] *Close R.* 1227–31, 82, an earlier reference than was found for the account of the hosp. in *V.C.H. Glos.* ii. 125–6.
[8] Glos. R.O., D 527/6.
[9] Leland, *Itin.* ed. Toulmin Smith, i. 126.
[10] Glos. R.O., P 197/OV 7/1.
[11] *Univ. Brit. Dir.* iii (1794), 532; Glos. R.O., D 527/6, marginal note added to depositions 1549.

[12] *Cal. Pat.* 1338–40, 57; 1340–3, 291; 1385–9, 409.
[13] Glos. R.O., D 1388, Milward fam., Lechlade man., judge's summing up 1831; cf. ibid. D 527/6.
[14] *Close R.* 1227–31, 82.
[15] Glos. R.O., D 1388, sale papers, Lechlade 1870–94, abs. of title of Sam. Churchill.
[16] Ibid. Milward fam., Lechlade man., judge's summing up 1831; cf. ibid. Q/SO 1, f. 208.
[17] A. Williams, *Hist. of Lechlade* (1888), 21–2, a short but informative hist. of the town.
[18] Glos. R.O., D 1388, Milward fam., Lechlade man., judge's summing up 1831.
[19] Ibid. Q/SO 3, Ep., East. 1703; E 134/5 Geo. I Hil./25.
[20] Household, *Thames and Severn Canal*, 24, 70, 73; cf. *Glouc. Jnl.* 24 Aug. 1789.

The road from Cirencester to St. John's bridge was turnpiked in 1727.[21] The other main route through the parish, from Burford to Highworth and Swindon, was probably not of much importance until 1792. Under a turnpike Act of that year[22] a new bridge,[23] known as Halfpenny bridge from the tolls that were charged to pedestrians until 1839, was built over the Thames south of the town with a new stretch of road leading from it in Inglesham parish. There was formerly a ferry over the river south of the town,[24] and also a ford,[25] but it seems that before 1792 most traffic using the route had to go out to St. John's bridge and then follow Lamborne Lane which crossed Buscot parish to Lynt bridge.[26]

Road transport played an important part in the life of the town, which had several substantial inns. In 1794 an Oxford mail coach passed through the town twice daily and the London coaches from Cirencester passed back and forth three times a week. There was also a considerable traffic of stage-wagons, particularly those carrying cloth from the Stroud region.[27] Entries in the parish registers reflect the number of vagrants and travelling people, such as strolling players and licensed hawkers, passing through the town.[28] The easy connexions with London by road and river meant that the capital exerted a particularly strong attraction and numerous examples of natives of Lechlade who left to work in London are recorded.[29]

The Thames and Severn canal from Stroud to Lechlade was opened in 1789, the junction with the Thames being 1 km. SW. of the town where a circular watchman's house was built. The canal was closed in 1927.[30] After the opening of the Great Western railway in 1840 Lechlade was served by coaches and carriers from Faringdon Road station near Challow (Berks.).[31] In 1873 the East Gloucestershire railway from Witney to Fairford was opened[32] with a station for Lechlade on the Burford road north of the town. The line was closed in 1962.[33]

The place-name Lechlade probably refers to the vicinity of St. John's bridge, and the possibility that the original settlement was there cannot be entirely discounted, though rendered unlikely by the liability of flooding in the area. It is more likely that the Saxon settlement, first recorded in Domesday Book,[34] was at the present site on better-drained ground 1 km. NW. of the bridge near a lesser crossing of the Thames and that it was enlarged by Isabel de Mortimer when she founded a borough in the early 13th century. She obtained a grant of a market in 1210[35] and c. 1230 Lechlade was referred to as her 'new market town'.[36] The rents from the burgages produced £3 16s. 8d. by 1275[37] and £4 13s. 5½d. by 1326.[38] Some 40 houses in the town were classed as burgages in the late 16th century.[39]

The town is based on a reversed **L** shape formed by High Street, on the main Cirencester–London road, on the south side and Burford Street, probably that called Pipemore Street in 1490,[40] on the east side; at the angle formed by the two streets are the parish church and the market-place.[41] Originally, and probably until 1774, the Cirencester road entered the town from the west side by way of the hamlet of Little London,[42] skirting north of the close called All Court[43] which was doubtless the site of the capital messuage owned by Peter atte Hall before 1326.[44] The continuous property boundary at the back of the burgage plots on the north side of High Street may represent an ancient course of the road, aligning with St. John's Street (so called by 1580)[45] by which it leaves the town on the east. Possibly High Street was created when the borough was founded, causing the main road, having passed Little London, to veer southwards to meet it. Sherborne Street, formerly known alternatively as Pudding Lane,[46] is a back lane linking High Street and Burford Street, and the only other ancient streets were those which ran southwards from the town to the wharves on the river. Bell Lane, which ran down to the old crossing-point of the river,[47] was the most important of those until 1792 when Thames Street, leading to the new bridge, became the main road out of the town to Highworth and Swindon. Thames Street probably existed before 1792 as the Red Lion Street mentioned in 1730.[48] Wharf Lane running southwards from St. John's Street to Old Wharf was presumably built with the wharf in the mid 17th century.[49]

A small house on the east side of Burford Street has a 16th-century carved doorway, which is, however, reset and was presumably brought from a larger house. One or two gabled 17th-century houses survive in the town but most of it was rebuilt in the

[21] Cirencester Roads Act, 13 Geo. I, c. 11.
[22] Burford and Swindon Roads Act, 32 Geo. III, c. 153.
[23] See plate facing p. 124.
[24] Williams, *Lechlade*, 22.
[25] The ford, at the bottom of Bell Lane (sometimes called Tidford Lane), was destroyed by dredging in the 1960s: ex inf. Mr. A. J. Baxter, of Lechlade.
[26] Williams, *Lechlade*, 22; W.I. hist. of Lechlade (1959, TS. in Glos. Colln.), 2.
[27] *Univ. Brit. Dir.* iii (1794), 531.
[28] Glos. R.O., P 197/IN 1/3–4.
[29] e.g. ibid. D 1070/III/51; D 1388/III/141, 143; P 197/IN 1/2, burials 1765; 3, burials 1773, 1792; Hockaday Abs. cclvii, 1618.
[30] Household, *Thames and Severn Canal*, 69, 194.
[31] *Kelly's Dir. Glos.* (1856), 318; E. T. MacDermot, *Hist. G.W.R.* (1964), i. 54.
[32] MacDermot, *Hist. G.W.R.* ii. 15.
[33] *Clinker's Reg. of Closed Stations* (1971 edn.), 75.
[34] *Dom. Bk.* (Rec. Com.), i. 163.
[35] *Cal. Pat.* 1396–9, 384–5.
[36] *Ciren. Cart.* i, pp. 220–1.
[37] *Inq. p.m. Glos.* 1236–1300, 102.
[38] C 145/103 no. 17.
[39] C 142/253 no. 71.
[40] S.C. 6/Hen. VII/210; cf. the mention of Pipemoorend Green in Glos. R.O., D 2957/183.3.
[41] Cf. Glos. R.O., D 527/19.
[42] Williams, *Lechlade*, 12.
[43] G.D.R., T 1/113.
[44] C 145/103 no. 17.
[45] Glos. R.O., D 527/8.
[46] Ibid. D 81/T 1; Hockaday Abs. cclvii, 1817.
[47] Williams, *Lechlade*, 22.
[48] Glos. R.O., P 197/CH 3.
[49] E 134/5 Geo. I Hil./25.

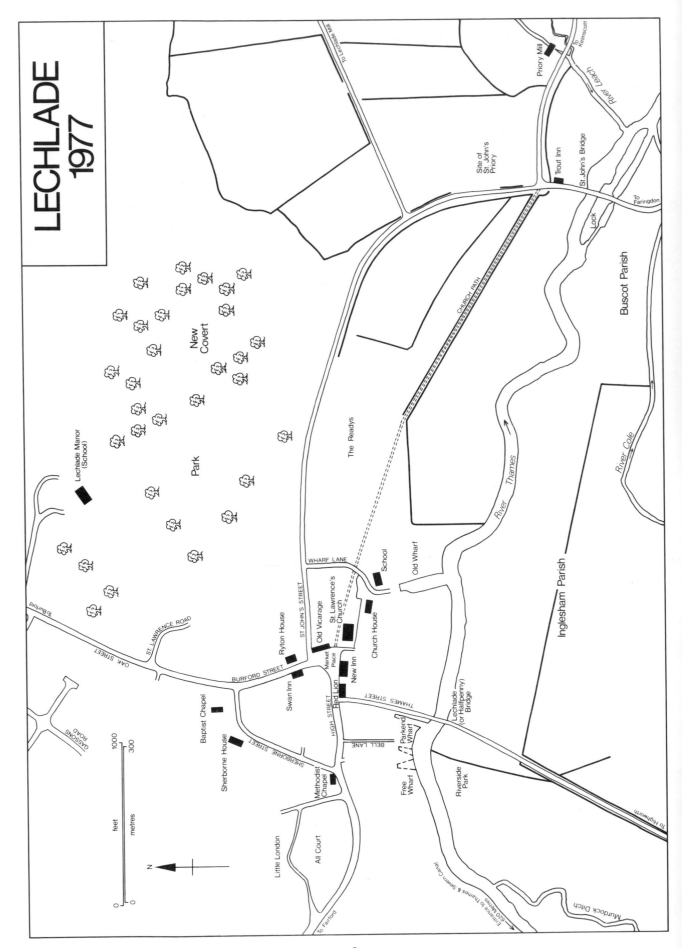

LECHLADE 1977

Priory Mill

To Kemscott

River Leach

St. John's Bridge

Trout Inn

Site of St. John's Priory

To Lechlade Mill

To Faringdon

Lock

Buscot Parish

Church Path

New Covert

The Readys

Park

River Thames

River Cole

Inglesham Parish

Lechlade Manor (School)

Old Wharf

School

WHARF LANE

St. John's Street

Old Vicarage

St. Lawrence's Church

Church House

To Burford

St. Lawrence Road

Ryton House

Market Place

New Inn

OAK STREET

BURFORD STREET

Swan Inn

Red Lion

HIGH STREET

THAMES STREET

Lechlade (or Halfpenny) Bridge

GASSONS ROAD

Baptist Chapel

SHERBORNE STREET

BELL LANE

Parkend Wharf

Sherborne House

Methodist Chapel

Free Wharf

Riverside Park

To Highworth

Little London

All Court

To Fairford

Entrance to Thames & Severn Canal (620 Metres)

Murdock Ditch

N

feet   1000
               300
metres

0   0

very late 17th century and in the 18th when the river trade and the growth of road transport brought it modest prosperity. The principal residences of that period include Church House,[50] on the south side of the churchyard, which was the home of the Ainge family of wharfingers who traded from Old Wharf at the end of the garden; John Ainge settled there in the later 17th century and was followed by his son Richard[51] (d. 1730)[52] and by another Richard (d. 1778).[53] It is a small 17th-century house that was refronted and partly refitted in the early 18th century and extended to east and west in the early 20th. An extensive formal garden laid out in the early 18th century includes a short canal, a brick summer-house, and a gazebo built into the churchyard wall. The gazebo is a feature repeated at other houses in the town, including Grey Gables on Wharf Lane and Sherborne House[54] which stands at the angle of Sherborne Street. The latter is an early-17th-century house which was remodelled late in that century, being given a principal front of 5 bays with mullioned and transomed windows and a doorway with a segmental pediment. In the 18th century the windows were altered to sashes and there was some internal redecoration. The house is traditionally associated with a branch of the Dutton family of Sherborne, but in the 18th century it was the home of a branch of the prominent Lechlade family of Loder.[55] Another of the larger residences is Ryton House on the east side of Burford Street; it was rebuilt early in the 18th century by a wealthy mercer, John Ward (d. 1721 or 1722), and from 1755 was the home of Charles Loder (d. 1803).[56]

There are other small but good-quality 18th-century houses, including some on the south side of High Street which were probably built for wharfingers and maltsters. Other houses reflect the continuing prosperity of the early years of the 19th century when it was said that the appearance of the town was much improved by the work of the local architect and builder Richard Pace.[57] Examples of his work may include the ogee porches added to Grey Gables and to a house at Downington, and the two-storey semicircular bays on a house in St. John's Street and on the house, apparently Pace's own,[58] north of the Swan inn in Burford Street. After 1792 a terrace of cottages was built on Thames Street, and such development as there was in the 19th century was mainly in the form of cottages or small houses in the minor streets, including some in St. John's Street, Sherborne Street, and Oak Street

(the northern continuation of Burford Street presumably named from the Royal Oak inn). Most of the 20th-century development occurred on the north side of the town around Hambidge Lane, the name given to the old salt-way where it meets the Burford road. The building of the Gassons council estate, south of the lane, had begun by 1933[59] and more houses were added to it in the 1960s and 1970s, when a private housing estate was also built north of the lane. Another private estate was being built east of Burford Street on part of the manor-house park in 1977.

There are two small roadside hamlets on the west side of the town. Little London on the old Cirencester road is a small group of cottages, some possibly dating from the 17th century. Downington is a late-17th-century suburb comprising several substantial detached houses of that date.[60] Butler's Court, beyond Downington, is the only outlying farmstead recorded from medieval times apart from Great Lemhill Farm in the detached part of Broughton Poggs. Ruffords Farm, later called Green Farm,[61] on the opposite side of the road to Butler's Court was recorded from 1597 when the lord of the manor Edward Dodge left it to his niece Elizabeth Heylyn;[62] the house was rebuilt in the 19th century.

Most of the outlying farms of the parish date from the dismemberment of the manor estate in the late 17th and early 18th centuries. Clayhill (later called Claydon House) on the north side of the Cirencester road, is a substantial 17th-century gabled house,[63] apparently built by Robert Bathurst (d. 1692), a son of the lord of the manor Sir Edward Bathurst; his family lived there until the 1760s.[64] The house was remodelled and enlarged in the 19th century by the owner G. A. Robbins[65] (d. 1887),[66] and further alterations were made in 1896 when the west front was cased.[67] Thornhill Farm on the west boundary was built for an estate acquired from the manor by the university of Oxford in 1670.[68] The farm-house was refronted in the 19th century but may be late-17th-century in origin. Downs Farm, further north, was built on an estate which passed from the manor to the mortgagee John Chaunler in 1707[69] and it later descended with Stanford Farm in Southrop.[70] The farm-house, which was occupied as cottages in the 19th century,[71] was demolished c. 1961.[72] Warren's Cross, standing on the south side of the Cirencester road, possibly near the site of a wayside cross mentioned in 1458,[73] is a small farmhouse built in the early 18th century, before 1724,[74]

[50] See plate facing p. 125.
[51] E 134/5 Geo. I Hil./25; cf. Williams, *Lechlade*, 63.
[52] Prob. 11/642 (P.C.C. 23 Isham).
[53] Rudder, *Glos.* proof pages (Glos. Colln.), MS. note on p. 520; cf. *Glouc. Jnl.* 20 July 1778.
[54] See plate facing p. 125.
[55] Williams, *Lechlade*, 59; Taylor, *Map of Glos.* (1777).
[56] Glos. R.O., D 1388, Cole fam., Lechlade deeds 1702–1814; cf. G.D.R. wills 1722/211.
[57] Fosbrooke, *Glos.* ii. 456–7.
[58] G.D.R., T 1/113.
[59] Glos. R.O., P 197A/PC 1/2.
[60] One of them, Bridge Ho., has a datestone 1633, but that was moved from a bldg. in the garden: ex inf. Mr. Baxter.
[61] Glos. R.O., D 333/Z 9.

[62] C 142/253 no. 71.
[63] Cf. Bodl. MS. Rawl. B.323, f. 93v.
[64] *Visit. Glos. 1682–3*, 12–13; Bigland, *Glos.* ii. 144; *Glouc. Jnl.* 24 June 1765.
[65] Williams, *Lechlade*, 57.   [66] Inscr. in ch.
[67] Glos. R.O., D 2593, Lechlade.
[68] Oxford Univ. Archives, S.E.P./X/3–5; cf. G.D.R., T 1/113.
[69] Glos. R.O., D 2440, Downs fm. deeds 1708–1826; D 467. Chaunler acquired one moiety then, the other being secured by his son Jas. a few years later.
[70] See below.
[71] Glos. R.O., D 2440, Stanford fm. papers 1821–67.
[72] Ex inf. Mr. R. W. Hinton, of Stanford Fm., Southrop.
[73] Hockaday Abs. cclvii.
[74] G.D.R. wills 1727/209.

and Trouthouse Farm near by is of a similar date. Chipley House, formerly called Little Clayhill (or Claydon) Farm, was probably the new farm-house near Clay hill mentioned in 1764;[75] it was remodelled and a new wing added in the 19th century. In the 19th century several pairs of farm cottages were built along the Cirencester road for the farms in that area of the parish.

In the east part of the parish Leaze Farm was built, probably in the late 17th century, to serve an estate which had passed to a branch of the Loder family by 1673,[76] and Paradise Farm near by had been established by 1788,[77] though apparently rebuilt later. A few small, mostly late, farm-houses in the north part of the parish include Manor Farm (formerly Red Barn Farm), Roughground Farm, and Little Lemhill Farm.[78]

Fifty-three inhabitants of Lechlade were recorded in 1086.[79] Fifty-nine were assessed for the subsidy in 1327[80] and c. 138 for the poll tax of 1381.[81] Estimates of c. 200 communicants and 65 households were made in the middle of the 16th century,[82] of 96 families in 1650,[83] and of c. 500 inhabitants about 1710.[84] The prosperous years of the 18th century contributed to a considerable increase in population, though Rudder's figure of 925 in the 1770s[85] was an over-estimate according to the curate who counted 845 inhabitants in 1789[86] In 1801 the parish had 917 inhabitants and there was a gradual rise to 1,373 by 1851. The population then fell slowly to 989 by 1931. New housing development later boosted it to 1,134 by 1961 and 1,689 by 1971.[87]

In a town with so much passing trade inns naturally played an important role. There were at least 10 innkeepers in the parish at the beginning of the 18th century[88] and 11 were licensed in 1755.[89] The Swan in Burford Street is apparently one of the earliest, for an inn of that name was mentioned in 1513.[90] In 1588 an inn called the George, apparently on the north side of St. John's Street, was mentioned.[91] The other chief inns were in High Street and included the Red Lion on the south side which was presumably the inn called the Lion in 1592,[92] the Crown which had opened on the north side by 1696,[93] and the Bell at the head of Bell Lane which was recorded from 1719.[94] Shortly before 1754 the large New Inn was built on the south side

of the market-place[95] and apparently became the principal inn of the town. The four inns in High Street were evidently suffering from the decline in coaching in 1856 when their landlords all pursued additional callings.[96] Nevertheless there were 15 public houses in the parish in 1891[97] and the numbers of summer visitors and growth of motor traffic in the 20th century helped to give the older inns of the town a new lease of life; the New Inn, Red Lion, Crown, and Swan all survived in 1977.

By 1692 there was an inn at St. John's bridge named the Baptist's Head[98] after St. John's hospital. It was part of the manor estate until c. 1800 when it was sold together with the manorial fishing rights in the Thames. Renamed the Trout before 1831,[99] it became a favourite resort of fishermen and boating parties in the later 19th century and in 1890 included a detached summer-house for picnics.[1]

A friendly society, the 'Old Club', was founded at Lechlade in 1766[2] and several others functioned in the 19th century.[3] In 1870 the town had a reading-room supported by subscriptions,[4] and a working men's club with coffee-house and reading-room was opened in 1880 under the patronage of local gentry but by 1888 was suffering from lack of members.[5] The Victoria Memorial Hall in Oak Street, apparently built by the lord of the manor to mark the Jubilee of 1897, was given to the town in 1919[6] and a recreation ground on the Gassons near by was acquired in 1958.[7] In 1839 horse-races were run on Town East meadow[8] and in the 20th century a cricket club, with a pitch in the manor-house park, was strongly supported. Annual social events in the early 20th century included a flower show,[9] and a water carnival was held between 1903 and 1936.[10] In 1977 the Thames with its facilities for boating continued to attract many visitors to the town during the summer months and the south bank (in Inglesham parish) had been made a riverside park with access for cars.

Water was laid on to Lechlade c. 1888 from a works built north of the town by the rural sanitary authority after the wells were found to be contaminated.[11] The town had a fire-engine by 1845 and from the following year it was housed in the old blind-house[12] adjoining Ryton House.[13] A new fire brigade, formed in 1895 and disbanded in 1936,

[75] *Glouc. Jnl.* 9 Apr. 1764.
[76] Glos. R.O., D 1388/III/140; cf. Bodl. MS. Ch. Glouc. c. 2, no. 194.
[77] Glos. R.O., EL 134, p. 114; cf. G.D.R., T 1/113.
[78] G.D.R., T 1/113.
[79] *Dom. Bk.* (Rec. Com.), i. 163.
[80] *Glos. Subsidy Roll, 1327,* 13.
[81] E 179/113/35A rot. 2; E 179/113/31A rot. 5.
[82] *E.H.R.* xix. 114; Bodl. MS. Rawl. C.790, f. 26.
[83] *Trans. B.G.A.S.* lxxxiii. 94.
[84] Atkyns, *Glos.* 536.
[85] Rudder, *Glos.* 520.
[86] Glos. R.O., P 197/IN 1/3.
[87] *Census,* 1801–1971.
[88] Glos. R.O., P 197/IN 1/1.
[89] Ibid. Q/AV 2, rot. 3.
[90] Hockaday Abs. clv.
[91] Glos. R.O., D 1388, Cole fam., Lechlade deeds 1702–1814.
[92] Ibid. D 527/11.   [93] Ibid. D 1388/III/41.
[94] E 134/5 Geo. I Hil./25; cf. G.D.R., T 1/113.

[95] *Glouc. Jnl.* 20 Aug. 1754; the bldg. was refronted in the 19th cent.
[96] *Kelly's Dir. Glos.* (1856), 318.
[97] *Licensed Houses in Glos. 1891,* 74.
[98] B.L. Harl. MS. 4716, f. 8b.
[99] Glos. R.O., D 1388, Milward fam., Lechlade man., judge's summing up 1831.
[1] Ibid. sale papers, Lechlade 1870–94.
[2] Williams, *Lechlade,* 7.
[3] F.S. 2/3 nos. 408, 454, 462, 887.
[4] *Kelly's Dir. Glos.* (1870), 588.
[5] Williams, *Lechlade,* 10.   [6] Ex inf. Mr. Baxter.
[7] Glos. R.O., P 197A/PC 1/3.
[8] Williams, *Lechlade,* 13.
[9] W.I. hist. of Lechlade, 6; Glos. R.O., SL 254.
[10] 'Calendar of Events in Lechlade' (on sale in ch. 1977).
[11] Williams, *Lechlade,* 23; *Kelly's Dir. Glos.* (1894), 222.
[12] Notes on vestry min. bk. by Mr. F. C. Innocent, of Lechlade.
[13] Glos. R.O., D 1388, Cole fam., Lechlade deeds 1702–1814.

was one of the responsibilities of the Lechlade parish council, an active body which also managed the street-lighting, installed by 1895, and a cemetery, opened north of Downington *c.* 1913.[14] Electricity was supplied to the town by the Lechlade Electric Light and Power Co., formed in 1909 and later absorbed by the Wessex Electricity Co.,[15] and gas was laid on by the Swindon Gas Co. in 1937.[16]

Henry III passed through Lechlade in 1229 and 1258[17] and Edward I in 1279 and 1281.[18] In the Civil War the town, which lay in debatable ground, saw several troop movements[19] and, in November 1645, a minor skirmish when a small parliamentary force sent to fortify it drove off a royalist attack;[20] the town was still garrisoned for parliament the following April.[21] Natives of the town have included Thomas Prence (1600–73) who became governor of Massachusetts, and Thomas Coxeter (1689–1747) who followed literary and antiquarian pursuits.[22] One of Shelley's poems was inspired by a visit to Lechlade churchyard in 1815.[23]

MANORS AND OTHER ESTATES. In 1066 the 15-hide manor of *LECHLADE* was held by Siward, apparently Siward Barn, a great-nephew of Edward the Confessor, who joined the rebellion against the Conqueror in 1071. By 1086 the manor was held by Henry de Ferrers[24] and it probably descended with Oakham (Rut.) to his son William and to William's son Henry. Henry's son Waukelin de Ferrers (d. 1201)[25] held Lechlade in 1185[26] and later gave it to his son Hugh[27] (d. 1204). Hugh's heir was apparently his elder brother Henry whose forfeiture of his English estates on the loss of Normandy[28] led to the Crown taking possession of Lechlade. The Crown granted the manor in 1204 for life to Hugh's sister Isabel, wife of Roger de Mortimer[29] (d. 1214).[30] Isabel married secondly Peter FitzHerbert (d. 1235)[31] and died in 1252. At her death the manor reverted to the Crown[32] whose right was disputed by Isabel's grandson Roger de Mortimer until 1263 when he abandoned his claim in return for a grant of other property.[33]

In 1252 Henry III granted the manor to his brother Richard, earl of Cornwall,[34] (d. 1272), whose son Edmund succeeded and granted it in 1300 to Hailes Abbey to hold for a fee-farm rent of 100 marks. When Edmund's estates passed to the Crown on his death the same year the rent was raised to £100.[35] Half of the rent was granted to Queen Margaret in 1307 but later there were conflicting grants to her and to Peter Gavaston until the queen's moiety was confirmed with arrears after Gavaston's death.[36] The rent was later settled on Queen Isabella and her children John and Eleanor.[37] Hailes Abbey held the manor until 1318 when in exchange for Siddington it granted it to the elder Hugh le Despenser,[38] who had quittance of the fee-farm rent in 1324.[39] From that time, except that Geoffrey de Mortimer held it briefly in 1330,[40] Lechlade manor descended with Barnsley until 1548.[41]

In 1550 the Crown granted the manor to Denis Toppes and his wife Dorothy.[42] Denis (d. 1578) was succeeded by his son Thomas[43] but by 1581 the manor was in the possession of Nicholas and George Rainton, London haberdashers. They sold it that year to two other London tradesmen, Benedict Bartholomew and John Weaver,[44] but before the sale the Raintons had made acknowledgement of a large debt as a result of which Lechlade was seized by the sheriff in 1587 and granted the following year to their creditor Thomas Riggs to hold until he had recouped his money. Bartholomew and Weaver retained a reversionary right to the manor and sold it in 1588 to Edward Dodge and Peter Houghton[45] who had a quitclaim from Thomas Toppes in 1591.[46] Dodge bought out Houghton in 1595 and died, apparently with an unencumbered title to the manor, in 1597. He left it to his nephew Robert Bathurst[47] (d. 1623), whose eldest son Robert[48] died a minor in 1627 and was succeeded by his brother Edward.[49] Edward Bathurst was made a knight and baronet in 1643,[50] though later under threat of sequestration he claimed that any support he gave to the royalist cause in the war was given under duress.[51] Sir Edward died in 1674 but made the manor over to his son Laurence before 1668.[52] Laurence (d. 1670) left the manor to his wife Susanna to hold during the minority of his son Edward.[53] Edward

[14] Ibid. P 197A/PC 1/1–2.
[15] Ex inf. Mr. Baxter.
[16] Glos. R.O., P 197A/PC 1/2.
[17] *Close R.* 1227–31, 189; 1256–9, 271.
[18] *Cal. Close,* 1272–9, 525; *Cal. Fine R.* 1272–1307, 109, 143.
[19] *Cal. S.P. Dom.* 1644–5, 476, 621; *Bibliotheca Glos.* i. 135.
[20] Hist. MSS. Com. 29, *13th Rep. I, Portland,* i, p. 316.
[21] *Cal. S.P. Dom.* 1645–7, 406.
[22] *D.N.B.*
[23] *Glos. N. & Q.* iv. 73 4.
[24] *Dom. Bk.* (Rec. Com.), i. 163; Taylor, *Dom. Glos.* 160.
[25] *V.C.H. Rut.* ii. 11.
[26] *Pipe R.* 1185 (P.R.S. xxxiv), 147.
[27] *Rot. de Ob. et Fin.* (Rec. Com.), 209.
[28] *V.C.H. Rut.* ii. 11.
[29] *Abbrev. Plac.* (Rec. Com.), 145–6; *Rot. de Ob. et Fin.* (Rec. Com.), 209.
[30] *Complete Peerage,* ix. 272–3; *Bk. of Fees,* i. 50.
[31] *Close R.* 1234–7, 102.
[32] Ibid. 1251–3, 82–3.

[33] *Abbrev. Plac.* (Rec. Com.), 145–6; *Cal. Pat.* 1258–66, 302–3.
[34] *Cal. Chart. R.* 1226–57, 392.
[35] Ibid. 1300–26, 2–3.
[36] *Cal. Pat.* 1301–7, 505; 1307–13, 9, 187, 218; 1313–17, 111–12, 121–2; *Cal. Close,* 1307–13, 183.
[37] *Cal. Pat.* 1317–21, 116, 222, 453.
[38] Ibid. 212.   [39] Ibid. 1324–7, 27.
[40] *Cal. Chart. R.* 1327–41, 4.
[41] See above.
[42] *Cal. Pat.* 1549–51, 434.
[43] C 142/185 no. 88.   [44] Glos. R.O., D 527/11.
[45] Ibid. 12.
[46] *Trans. B.G.A.S.* xvii. 134.
[47] Glos. R.O., D 527/12.
[48] C 142/398 no. 106.
[49] *Inq. p.m. Glos.* 1625–42, i. 56–60.
[50] For the Bathursts, see *Visit. Glos.* 1682–3, 12–13.
[51] *Cal. Cttee. for Compounding,* v. 3267.
[52] Glos. R.O., D 467.
[53] Prob. 11/338 (P.C.C. 10 Eure).

died under age in 1677 and Susanna, who was married twice more, to Sir John Fettiplace, Bt., and to Sir Thomas Cutler, then held the manor during the minority of Edward's sisters and heirs, Ann and Mary.[54]

In 1686 Ann and Mary Bathurst married respectively John Greening and George Coxeter,[55] and they made a partition of the manor in 1690. After the deaths of Ann and John their moiety passed to John's niece Elizabeth Greening, who married Nicholas Harding in 1695. Nicholas died in 1736 and his wife the following year. In 1718 the Hardings had granted the moiety to trustees in preparation for a settlement which had never been enacted. After their deaths Sir Francis Page, the surviving trustee, took possession of the estate, notwithstanding the claim of Richard Burgess, cousin and heir-at-law of Elizabeth. Page devised the estate on his death in 1741 to Sir George Wheate, Bt., who defended his claim against Burgess's heirs. The litigation was finally concluded in 1754 with a judgement that Page had had a just title to the estate and that even if he had not Burgess's claim could not have been substantiated.[56] Sir George Wheate had died in 1752 and his son and heir Sir George died under age in 1760 to be succeeded by his brother Sir Jacob Wheate.[57]

The moiety of George and Mary Coxeter was retained by Mary after her husband's death in 1702[58] and was heavily mortgaged by 1721 when she made it over to her son Thomas so that he might clear it from incumbrances. After a suit by the mortgagee the estate was contracted to be sold in 1724 to the trustees of the will of Edward Colston, though the actual conveyance to them was not made by Thomas Coxeter until 1741. The estate was divided among various beneficiaries under Colston's will. Sarah Edwards, the daughter of one of them, married John Pullen who acquired the rights of the other beneficiaries and died in 1769. He was succeeded by his son John who sold the moiety to Sir Jacob Wheate in 1775,[59] thus re-uniting the manor.

Sir Jacob died in 1783 leaving the manor heavily mortgaged. In 1794 his trustees, his brother and heir Sir John Thomas Wheate, and the mortgagees agreed on a sale to Samuel Churchill of Deddington (Oxon.).[60] Churchill sold in 1807 to William Fox,[61] the founder of the Sunday School Society, who may have sold the manor before his death in 1826.[62] It passed to George Milward (d. 1838). The manor,

to which 348 a. of land was then attached, passed in succession to Milward's son George (d. 1871) and grandson George.[63] In 1895 it was bought by H. W. Prior-Wandesforde, from whom it passed to James Jones (d. 1910). Jones's trustees offered the estate for sale in 1921.[64] The manor-house and park were acquired in 1939 by the nuns of St. Clotilde, a Catholic teaching order, who used the house for a girls' boarding school.[65]

The manor-house of Lechlade was recorded from 1270 and was used by the earls of Cornwall on occasion in the 13th century.[66] About 1500 the hall of the manor-house was dismantled and moved to Barnsley[67] but in the late 16th century there was a manor-house at Lechlade, known as the Place.[68] At the partition of the manor it seems to have been included in the Coxeters' moiety[69] and so was presumably the house north-east of the town later occupied by the Pullens.[70] In 1695 the other moiety included a newly-built house, probably built by John Greening,[71] and that was presumably a house by the river south-west of the town where Sir Jacob Wheate lived in the mid 1770s.[72] After he re-united the manor Sir Jacob pulled down both houses and built a new one[73] by the Burford road near the site of the Pullens' house;[74] a square three-storey building with sash windows, it was extended by lower, flanking wings in the early 19th century.[75] It was replaced in 1873 by George Milward who built a new house on a site to the north-east and laid out parkland around it. The new house, a substantial mansion in Jacobean style, was designed by J. L. Pearson.[76] New school buildings were put up adjoining it in the 1970s.

The site and lands of the hospital of St. John at Lechlade were used by its patron Cecily, duchess of York, to endow a chantry in Lechlade church in 1472.[77] In 1508 the chantry was dissolved and its estate granted to the college of St. Nicholas in Wallingford castle.[78] In 1572 the estate, sometimes known as the manor of *ST. JOHN*, was granted by the Crown to Denis Toppes and it descended with Lechlade manor.[79]

LEMHILL, the detached part of Broughton Poggs north of Lechlade, formed a separate manor held from Broughton manor. It belonged in the 14th century to Robert Murdock, possibly the same who died c. 1369. Murdock was succeeded by his nephew Robert Lemhill. The manor later passed to Robert Lemhill's great-niece Margaret, daughter of John Querndon or Lemhill, and her cousin and heir

[54] E 134/5 Geo. I Hil./25; cf. Glos. R.O., D 467.
[55] Hockaday Abs. cclvii.
[56] Glos. R.O., D 467.
[57] Ibid. D 1388, sale papers, Lechlade 1870–94, abs. of title of Sam. Churchill, which gives wrong dates of death for the two Sir Georges: Burke, *Ext. & Dorm. Baronetcies* (1844), 562–3.
[58] Bigland, *Glos.* ii. 145.
[59] Glos. R.O., D 1388, sale papers, Lechlade 1870–94, abs. of title of Sam. Churchill.
[60] Ibid.
[61] Ibid. D 182/III/87.
[62] *D.N.B.*
[63] Glos. R.O., D 1388, sale papers, Lechlade 1870–94, abs. of title 1888; G.D.R., T 1/113.
[64] Glos. R.O., SL 254.
[65] Langston, 'Cath. Missions', iv.

[66] S.C. 6/958/19; S.C. 6/1095/8.
[67] S.C. 6/Hen. VII/210; S.C. 6/Hen. VII/219.
[68] Glos. R.O., D 527/12.
[69] Ibid. D 1388, sale papers, Lechlade 1870–94, abs. of title of Sam. Churchill; cf. Atkyns, *Glos.* 535.
[70] Taylor, *Map of Glos.* (1777).
[71] Glos. R.O., D 467.
[72] Taylor, *Map of Glos.* (1777).
[73] Bigland, *Glos.* ii. 142; *Glouc. Jnl.* 9 Aug. 1784.
[74] Glos. R.O., D 1388, Milward fam., Lechlade man., judge's summing up 1831; cf. G.D.R., T 1/113.
[75] Photog. *penes* Mr. Innocent.
[76] Glos. R.O., SL 254; see above, plate facing p. 92.
[77] *V.C.H. Glos.* ii. 126.
[78] *Cal. Pat.* 1494–1509, 577.
[79] Ibid. 1569–72, p. 361; *Inq. p.m. Glos.* 1625–42, i. 56.

Henry Spicer of Burford held it in 1437.[80] Thomas Dawes (d. *c.* 1554) was a later owner or lessee of the estate[81] and in 1577 it was sold by John Dynham to George Fettiplace of Coln St. Aldwyns, who died that year. George's widow Cecily held it for life and it passed to his son John[82] (d. 1636), who was succeeded by his brother Sir Giles Fettiplace.[83] Sir Giles (d. 1641) was succeeded by his nephew John Fettiplace.[84] In 1713 Lemhill belonged to Elizabeth and Katherine, daughters and coheirs of Henry Sackville of Bibury, and was awarded to Katherine at a partition of Henry's estates.[85] Katherine (d. 1760) was succeeded by her great-nephew Estcourt Cresswell who sold the estate to Michael Hicks Beach of Williamstrip in 1806.[86] Lemhill was sold by the Hicks Beaches in or before 1849 and was later owned by J. T. Tombs (d. by 1888). In 1884 the estate comprised Great Lemhill Farm and 236 a.[87] In 1977 it was owned by R. Hinton and Sons and farmed in association with their land in Southrop. A former kitchen at Great Lemhill Farm may survive from a late-16th-century house, the rest of which appears to have been demolished and replaced by a new house in the late 17th century. The new house, which had a front to the south-east, was enlarged in the later 19th century when gabled additions were made on the south-west.

The manor later called *BUTLER'S COURT* was evidently the 4-yardland estate that John de Bellew granted to John Butler in 1304.[88] Butler or an heir of the same name held it in 1326.[89] John Twyniho of Cirencester was lord of Butler's Court in 1479[90] and died *c.* 1486.[91] His heir was Dorothy Moreton and the manor passed to her son Robert Moreton[92] (d. 1514). Robert's son William[93] died a minor in 1522 when his heirs were his sisters Dorothy and Elizabeth.[94] In 1581 Margaret, widow of Thomas Dutton of Sherborne, granted the manor to Thomas Meysey. Meysey's interest passed to William Dutton, who sold the manor to John Gearing, a London grocer, in 1614. Gearing settled it on the marriage of his son John, also a London grocer, in 1627 and the son or another John Gearing sold it in 1660 to Robert Oatridge. Robert was dead by 1680 when a moiety of the estate was assigned to his widow Miriam for life with reversion to her son Robert, who succeeded to the other moiety.[95] The estate later passed to Anne Oatridge (d. 1722 or 1723) who devised it to a kinsman Henry Oatridge (d. 1758). Henry had settled it on his wife Sarah and devised the reversion to his brother Daniel, whose son Thomas succeeded on Sarah's death *c.* 1772. Thomas (d. 1789) devised it to his wife Ann with

reversion to his brother Simon Oatridge of Doughton, Tetbury. Simon (d. *c.* 1801) devised the estate to his sister Ann Matthews with reversion to his niece Mary Matthews[96] who married John Paul Paul (d. 1828) of Highgrove, Tetbury. John's son Walter Matthews Paul sold Butler's Court in 1841 to William Gearing, who had been lessee of the estate since 1806[97] and was also owner of the adjoining Trouthouse farm. Gearing died in 1850 leaving the estate to trustees for a sale and it was bought by his daughters Elizabeth (d. 1866) and Ann Gearing and his son-in-law Matthew Edmonds (d. 1871). Elizabeth devised her share for life to her sister Ann, who bought the third share after the death of John, son of Matthew Edmonds, in 1872. Ann died in 1874 and in 1876 her trustees and those of her sister sold the estate to New College, Oxford.[98] The college later enlarged its estate, adding Green farm in 1969 and another 100 a. in 1970,[99] and it retained the estate in 1977.

Butler's Court is a substantial mid-17th-century gabled farm-house, which was refronted on the east side early in the 18th century when the rooms behind that front were refitted. In the 19th century additions were made to the north-west but those were much altered when the western end of the house was reconstructed after a fire in 1966. The garden formerly extended southwards to the main road where an early-18th-century gazebo remains.

In 1670 an estate in Lechlade, comprising 221 a., two houses, and rights in the meadows, was bought from Laurence Bathurst by Archbishop Gilbert Sheldon, who settled it on Oxford University for the maintenance of the newly built Sheldonian Theatre.[1] Most of the estate was later based on Thornhill Farm at the west boundary of the parish. The farm was sold by the University in 1919.[2] A small estate of *c.* 40 a. in the east part of the parish, later called Paradise farm, was conveyed by George Hill to Brasenose College, Oxford, in 1675.[3]

ECONOMIC HISTORY: AGRICULTURE. In 1086 there were 4 plough-teams and 13 *servi* on the demesne of Lechlade manor.[4] In 1275 the demesne land comprised 518 a. of arable, 667 a. of meadow, and a several pasture.[5] In 1270 a dairy herd, comprising 16 cows, was maintained on the demesne, mainly to produce cheese, and the other livestock included a flock of *c.* 250 sheep. The extensive demesne meadows were a valuable asset: in 1270 the mowing rights in them were sold for £52, providing a third of all the profits of the manor. The farm-servants employed then included 3 ploughmen and

[80] *Cal. Close, 1435–41*, 135; cf. *Cal. Pat. 1367–70*, 229.
[81] Hockaday Abs. cclvii.   [82] C 142/177 no. 86.
[83] C 142/728 no. 26.   [84] C 142/701 no. 17.
[85] *Sherborne Mun.* 95.
[86] Ibid. 101; Glos.R.O., D 2440, deeds of Bibury man. 1712–1806.
[87] Glos. R.O., SL 243.
[88] C.P. 25(1)/75/39 no. 237.
[89] C 145/103 no. 17.
[90] Worc. Episc. Reg., Reg. Alcock, f. 51.
[91] Hockaday Abs. clv.
[92] *Trans. B.G.A.S.* xx. 124.
[93] C 142/29 no. 136.

[94] C 142/40 no. 34.
[95] New Coll., Oxford, Mun. 5732.
[96] Ibid. 5723; and for Thos. Oatridge's death, Bigland, *Glos.* ii. 146.
[97] New Coll. Mun. 5722.
[98] Glos. R.O., D 1388, Gearing fam., Butler's Ct. est. 1836–76, abs. of title.
[99] *Cat. of Archives of New Coll.* (1974), p. 295.
[1] Oxford Univ. Archives, S.E.P./X/3–5.
[2] Ibid. LA/F/GEN/99.
[3] Glos. R.O., EL 134, pp. 105, 114; cf. G.D.R., T 1/113.
[4] *Dom. Bk.* (Rec. Com.), i. 163.
[5] *Inq. p.m. Glos.* 1236–1300, 101–2.

3 drivers of plough-teams, a carter, a shepherd, a cowherd, and a dairyman.[6] An undated account roll of the same period apparently concerns a year in which demesne farming was resumed after being temporarily abandoned, for all the grain and livestock accounted for had been bought in the course of the year.[7] By 1326 the demesne arable in hand had been reduced to 304 a., and 88 a. of former demesne were let to tenants; the meadow land was then extended at 596 a. and there were pasture rights for 27 oxen, 57 cows and calves, and 300 sheep.[8] The whole demesne was let at farm by 1411.[9] In the early 17th century it was represented by numerous closes and meadows,[10] most of which were alienated from the manor before the end of that century.

The tenants on the manor in 1086 were 29 *villani*, 10 bordars, and a Frenchman holding the land of a *villanus*; they worked 16 plough-teams between them.[11] In 1275 there were, besides some free tenancies and the burgages in the town, 25 customary yardlands and 7 cottage-tenements.[12] In 1326 there were some fairly substantial free tenements held from the manor, including John Butler's estate and a two-hide estate formerly belonging to Peter atte Hall but by 1326 divided among a large number of owners. The customary tenants in 1326 were 15 yardlanders, 17 half-yardlanders, 7 monday-men, and 9 cottagers. They were probably already paying cash instead of working in the winter months when in one year 706 works valued at $\frac{1}{2}d$. each were sold,[13] and in 1326, when each yardlander owed 6s. 6d. cash rent, most of their works had apparently been permanently commuted; they no longer worked on a regular weekly basis but owed 42 days in the year on specific tasks, mostly in the hay- and corn-harvests, as well as doing ploughing-service and a few bedrepes. The monday-men still owed their one day a week and worked in the corn-harvest on Fridays as well and some of the cottagers owed bedrepes. A smith held his land in return for shoeing-service and work on the demesne ploughs.[14]

There were open fields at Lechlade in 1326 when 218 a. of the demesne arable lay in them.[15] They were evidently inclosed at a fairly early date, for the only later reference found to them was in 1670 when lands lying by the Fairford road in the west part of the parish were described as former parts of Over and Nether Street fields.[16] The later evidence of field names suggests that the open fields were small and fairly numerous, scattered across the north and west parts of the parish.[17]

The meadow land was very extensive, as the value of £7 7s. put on it in 1086[18] and the evidence for the demesne given above show. It occupied the whole of the east and south parts of the parish. In the east part between the river and the Kelmscott road lay a large common lot meadow called Town East meadow.[19] The rights of the lord of the manor in Town East meadow, comprising the first math (or crop of hay) of 90 a. of the lots and the second math and subsequent pasture rights in the whole 200 a. of meadow, were sold before 1673 and became part of the Leaze estate. In 1860 the meadow was inclosed by Henry Parker, owner of the Leaze, who bought out the other holders of lots.[20] A smaller common meadow called Town Rumsey lay by the parish boundary south-west of the town[21] and was cultivated as such until at least 1859.[22] Eighty-two acres of several meadow by the Thames south-east of the town belonged to the hospital of St. John in the Middle Ages; the lord of the manor sold them with other meadow to William Blomer before 1613[23] and they remained part of the Hatherop estate until the early 20th century.[24]

In the north-west part of the parish lay a tract of pasture called the Downs, covering 190 a.; it belonged to the manor until the beginning of the 18th century and had probably once been open to commoning rights of the tenants.[25] Thorn hill further south, which comprised 91 a. in 1670 when it was alienated from the manor,[26] may have been another common pasture.[27]

The later history of agriculture in Lechlade is the individual history of the various freehold farms, including the ancient estates of Lemhill and Butler's Court and those such as Clayhill, the Leaze, Downs farm, and Thornhill farm which were established on land alienated from the manor in the late 17th and early 18th centuries. Those farms together with Trouthouse and Little Clayhill farms were the principal farms of the parish in the 1830s though most were of modest size, no more than *c.* 200 a. There were also a number of smaller farms, mostly under 100 a., including Little Lemhill, Warren's Cross, and Ploughed Ground farm (later called Roughground farm). The manor estate, to which only 348 a. remained, was then kept in hand by George Milward though a separate farm-house had been built for it at Red Barn Farm (later called Manor Farm).[28] In 1831, when the agricultural workers of the parish outnumbered its tradesmen and shopkeepers, there were 8 farmers employing a total of 97 labourers and 7 employing no labour.[29] The number of smallholdings became a much more

[6] S.C. 6/1095/8.
[7] S.C. 6/958/19.
[8] C 145/103 no. 17.
[9] *Inq. p.m. Glos.* 1359–1413, 260.
[10] Glos. R.O., D 527/12.
[11] *Dom. Bk.* (Rec. Com.), i. 163.
[12] *Inq. p.m. Glos.* 1236–1300, 101–2.
[13] Cf. S.C. 6/958/19.
[14] C 145/103 no. 17; and for the number of yardlanders and other details that are lost, cf. S.C. 11/236, an undated extent which must be for 1326 or 1327.
[15] S.C. 11/236.
[16] Oxford Univ. Archives, S.E.P./X/4/a.

[17] See fields named as Six Acres, Twelve Acres, etc. in G.D.R., T 1/113.
[18] *Dom. Bk.* (Rec. Com.), i. 163.
[19] Cf. G.D.R., T 1/113.
[20] Glos. R.O., D 1388/III/140; cf. ibid. inc., Lechlade.
[21] Oxford Univ. Archives, S.E.P./X/4/a; cf. G.D.R., T 1/113.
[22] Glos. R.O., D 1388/SL 4, no. 52.
[23] *Inq. p.m. Glos.* 1625–42, i. 57; C 142/347 no. 62.
[24] Glos. R.O., SL 247.
[25] Glos. R.O., D 527/12; D 2440, deeds of Downs fm. 1708–1826.
[26] Oxford Univ. Archives, S.E.P./X/3–4.
[27] S.C. 2/175/22.
[28] G.D.R., T 1/113.
[29] *Census,* 1931.

significant feature of the parish in the later 19th century and the early 20th: in 1896 a total of 53 agricultural occupiers was returned[30] and in 1926 a total of 35, 24 of them having less than 50 a. and 10 having less than 5 a.[31] In 1976, however, only 7 smallholdings of under 20 ha. (49 a.), most of them worked on a part-time basis, were returned, together with 8 larger farms of between 20 ha. and 200 ha. (494 a.).[32]

In spite of the extensive meadows arable land predominated over permanent grassland in the 19th century: in 1838 there were 1,810 a. of the former to 1,440 a. of the latter[33] and the equivalent amounts returned in 1896 (when Lemhill had been added to the parish) were 1,910 to 1,596. The maintenance of the level of arable cultivation to the end of the century may reflect the pattern of holdings in the parish, with small mainly family-run farms being better able to withstand the slump in prices. In the 19th century the farms grew mainly wheat, barley, and roots and raised sheep, of which 2,985 were returned for the parish in 1866. Cheese-making had presumably played a significant role in local farming in the past but in 1866 only a modest number of milk cows, 76 in all, were returned; the increase to 190 by 1896 was probably the result of the growth of a liquid milk trade, made possible by the railway.[34] In the 20th century dairying remained important and local farming was further diversified by the introduction of more pigs and poultry, returned at 770 and 9,114 respectively in 1926,[35] and, in the case of several of the smallholdings, by specialisation in market-garden produce.[36] Sheep-farming declined and no sheep were returned in 1976. Of the full-time farms in 1976 4 specialised in dairying and 3 in pigs and poultry, while another was devoted to general horticulture and another mainly to cereal crops.[37]

MILLS. There were three mills on Lechlade manor in 1086.[38] One, called Lade mill, was granted by Isabel de Mortimer to St. John's hospital before 1246[39] and the other two, later known as West mill and At (or Act) mill, remained part of the manor estate.[40] West mill was a ruin by 1527[41] though there was still at least a dwelling of that name in 1627.[42] It stood in the meadows south-west of the town[43] and according to tradition was a windmill.[44] Act mill on the Leach, later called Lechlade mill, remained part of the manor until at least 1754.[45] It continued to work until c. 1930.[46] Lade mill, later called St. John's or Priory mill, stood further down the Leach near the site of the hospital, with which it passed to the

manor.[47] It was alienated from the manor by John Greening in 1694 and continued to work until the beginning of the 20th century. It is probably significant that the owner of Priory mill in 1730 was a Thames barge-master,[48] for the corn trade on the river doubtless provided the two mills on the Leach with much of their business. At both sites there are fairly substantial mill-houses of the late 18th or early 19th century.

TRADE AND INDUSTRY. Lechlade was a borough and market town from the early 13th century and with the advantages of its position at the head of the navigable Thames and on a major road route to London might have been expected to become a significant commercial centre. That it remained small was perhaps due in part to the proximity of another market town at Fairford, only 6.5 km. away. Two inhabitants selling wine, mentioned in 1287,[49] and the surnames of smith, tanner, and tailor among those assessed for the 1327 subsidy[50] are among the earliest evidence of trading activity. In 1381 the town had a fairly substantial body of tradesmen and craftsmen, 44 being included in those assessed for the poll tax, among them 3 merchants, 2 mercers, 2 tanners, a draper, a skinner, a weaver, a spicer, and 15 brewers.[51] Henry Woolmonger was trading in the town in the late 13th century[52] and the merchants of 1381 were perhaps also involved in the wool trade, for the town stood on one of the chief routes for the carriage of Cotswold wool to London. John Townsend, who died in 1458 leaving legacies totalling over £1,800, was a Lechlade wool-merchant,[53] and the rebuilding of the parish church in 1470 suggests that the town had a number of fairly wealthy inhabitants at that period. As a local market centre, however, the town appears to have been in decay in the late 15th century, for 5 selds in the borough belonging to the lord of the manor were untenanted in 1490.[54] In 1608 31 tradesmen, a few more than those engaged in agriculture, were listed. They included 6 weavers, a mercer (one of the Gearing family which was prominent at Lechlade for several centuries), two masons, and a slater.[55]

Most of the town's commercial activity was later connected with the river trade, said to be its chief support in the early 18th century.[56] The use of the river for carriage was no doubt ancient, though the mention of a wharf house in 1639[57] is the earliest evidence found of such activity and, according to the reminiscences of aged inhabitants recorded in 1719, the main wharves and warehouses were all built in

[30] M.A.F. 68/1609/9.
[31] M.A.F. 68/3295/8.
[32] Agric. Returns 1976.
[33] G.D.R., T 1/113.
[34] M.A.F. 68/1609/9; M.A.F. 68/25/3.
[35] M.A.F. 68/3295/8.
[36] Kelly's Dir. Glos. (1931), 241.
[37] Agric. Returns 1976.
[38] Dom. Bk. (Rec. Com.), i. 163.
[39] Cal. Chart. R. 1226–57, 296.
[40] C 145/103 no. 17; S.C. 6/Hen. VII/210.
[41] S.C. 6/Hen. VIII/1042.
[42] Inq. p.m. Glos. 1625–42, i. 58.
[43] Cf. the fields of that name in G.D.R., T 1/113.

[44] Williams, Lechlade, 26.
[45] Glos. R.O., D 467.
[46] Kelly's Dir. Glos. (1856 and later edns.).
[47] Glos. R.O., D 527/7.
[48] Ibid. D 1070/III/51.
[49] J.I. 1/278 rot. 51.
[50] Glos. Subsidy Roll, 1327, 13.
[51] E 179/113/35A rot. 2.
[52] S.C. 6/958/19.
[53] Davis, Glos. Brasses, 52–4; Hockaday Abs. cclvii, 1458.
[54] S.C. 6/Hen. VII/210.
[55] Smith, Men and Armour, 263–4.
[56] Bodl. MS. Top. Glouc. c. 3, f. 155v.
[57] Inq. p.m. Glos. 1625–42, ii. 51.

the middle years of the 17th century. They included the Bell and Red Lion wharves, named from inns in High Street and evidently at the complex of wharves and warehouses immediately south of the town later called the free wharf and Parkend wharf, and a wharf occupied by the Ainge family, evidently that later called Old wharf at the end of Wharf Lane.[58] In 1716 there were also a warehouse and wharf by St. John's bridge,[59] apparently used as a depot by the London cheesemongers.[60] Cheese collected from Gloucestershire and the north part of Wiltshire or carried across from the Severn at Tewkesbury was the principal commodity shipped down river, and there was also some trade in corn and malt.[61] Other wares were brought by road from Gloucester, particularly in wartime when much of the trade down the Severn bound for London was diverted from coasting vessels to that route.[62] In 1758 Richard Ainge and Robert Anderson, Lechlade wharfingers, announced an arrangement with two Gloucester wharfingers for the conveyance of goods[63] and the opportunity brought by war is presumably again reflected in the scheme of another Lechlade man in 1781 to operate weekly stage-wagons between Gloucester and his wharf.[64] Several Thames bargemasters, at least two in 1701[65] and three in 1779,[66] were also based at Lechlade.

The river trade was increased significantly by the opening of the Thames and Severn canal to Lechlade at the end of 1789, though the failure to improve the Thames navigation lessened the opportunities provided by the new waterway.[67] The first cargo through the canal to Lechlade was Staffordshire coal[68] and coal was always the main item in the west-to-east trade, the opening of the canal reducing the price in the Lechlade region by about 8s. a ton. Grain was one of the chief items shipped westwards to Brimscombe Port at Stroud[69] and in 1794 two coal- and corn-merchants and a corn-factor were based at Lechlade. Also trading in the town then was Henry Burden, agent to the London cheesemongers, the trade in cheese retaining its importance.[70] Parkend wharf, occupied by Richard Gearing and then by William Hill, a Cirencester merchant, at the beginning of the 19th century,[71] was bought in 1813 by the canal company which built new warehouses and an agent's house.[72] There were still three

coal merchants trading in the town in 1856 but after the building of the railway only one such business, that of the Hicks family, survived and in the early years of the 20th century was the last representative of Lechlade's involvement in the river trade.[73]

Apart from the wharfingers and the innkeepers who served the road traffic, the principal inhabitants of the town included some fairly substantial shopkeepers, such as mercers and linen-drapers, and a few professional men, represented in 1794 by two surgeons and an attorney.[74] Malting played a quite significant part in the town's economy in the 18th and 19th centuries[75] and a small wool trade, probably an offshoot of that of Cirencester, employed a wool-stapler in 1774, a wool-comber in 1789,[76] and a wool-merchant who went bankrupt in 1821.[77] A family of rope-makers was recorded between 1773 and 1851,[78] the trade being perhaps connected with equipping Thames barges. Masons and slaters were fairly numerous and the building trade, though on a small scale, was a regular source of employment in the 19th and 20th centuries.[79] James Hollingsworth of Lechlade, bankrupted in 1796, was a mason and architect,[80] as was Richard Pace (d. 1838), who had a considerable local practice. Pace's business was continued by his son Richard[81] until at least 1856.[82] There were three other builders apart from the younger Pace in Lechlade in 1851 and it also had 11 masons.[83] A firm of agricultural implement makers and feed suppliers, established by 1879, and the cattle-dealers, corn-dealers, seedsman, hurdle-maker, and plough-maker, recorded during the 19th century, reflect the town's role as a centre for the local farming community.[84]

From the late 19th century others have found employment in catering for those visiting Lechlade for fishing and boating. There was a boat-hirer by 1897 and two boat-builders in 1935,[85] and in 1977, when many private launches were berthed at Lechlade, a ship's chandler had premises at Parkend wharf. Summer visitors also accounted for the several antique shops then open in the town. The building trade and the sand and gravel workings were the main local sources of employment in the mid 20th century[86] but after the Second World War

[58] E 134/5 Geo. I Hil./25; cf. O.S. Map 1/2,500, Glos. LIII. 14 (1899 edn.).
[59] Glos. R.O., D 1388, sale papers, Lechlade 1870–94, abs. of title of Sam. Churchill.
[60] Williams, *Lechlade*, 9.
[61] Bigland, *Glos.* ii. 141; B.L. Harl. MS. 4716, f. 8; E 134/5 Geo. I Hil./25.
[62] Atkyns, *Glos.* 536; *Glouc. Jnl.* 20 July 1778.
[63] *Glouc. Jnl.* 21 Feb. 1758.
[64] Ibid. 9 July 1781.
[65] Glos. R.O., P 197/IN 1/1.
[66] *Glouc. Jnl.* 30 Aug. 1779.
[67] Household, *Thames and Severn Canal*, 23–6, 69.
[68] *Glouc. Jnl.* 4 Jan. 1790.
[69] *Univ. Brit. Dir.* iii (1794), 531; Household, *Thames and Severn Canal*, 70, 96.
[70] *Univ. Brit. Dir.* iii (1794), 531–2; cf. *Glouc. Jnl.* 18 Jan. 1790.
[71] Glos. R.O., D 182/III/87.
[72] Household, *Thames and Severn Canal*, 79.

[73] *Kelly's Dir. Glos.* (1856 and later edns.); W.I. hist. of Lechlade, 3.
[74] e.g. Glos. R.O., P 197/IN 1/1, 3; D 1070/III/55; D 1388/III/143; *Glouc. Jnl.* 13 July 1767; *Univ. Brit. Dir.* iii (1794), 532.
[75] Atkyns, *Glos.* 536; Glos. R.O., D 81/T 1; D 1388/III/141; H.O. 107/1687.
[76] Glos. R.O., P 197/IN 1/3.   [77] Ibid. D 182/V/20.
[78] Ibid. P 197/IN 1/3–4; H.O. 107/1687.
[79] Glos. R.O., P 197/IN 1/3–4; *Kelly's Dir. Glos.* (1856 and later edns.).
[80] *Glouc. Jnl.* 1 Feb. 1796.
[81] Colvin, *Biog. Dict. of Eng. Architects*, 427–8; see above, plate facing p. 93.
[82] *Kelly's Dir. Glos.* (1856), 318.
[83] H.O. 107/1687.
[84] *Kelly's Dir. Glos.* (1870 and later edns.); *Pigot's Dir. Glos.* (1842), 106.
[85] *Kelly's Dir. Glos.* (1897), 226; (1935), 241.
[86] Cf. Payne, *Glos. Survey*, 163–4.

most of the working population travelled to near-by R.A.F. stations or to factories at Swindon and Witney.[87]

MARKET AND FAIRS. In 1210 Roger de Mortimer and Isabel his wife were granted a Tuesday market and an annual fair on St. Lawrence's day (10 August) and the two days following.[88] In 1234 the hospital of St. John was granted the right to hold a fair at St. John's bridge for 5 days around the Decollation of St. John the Baptist (29 August).[89] In 1270 the lord of the manor's tolls from the market produced 18s. 6d.[90] The market was evidently in decline in the later Middle Ages when the reeves' accounts contain no returns for its tolls and, although the charter was confirmed in 1566 and 1664,[91] the market was later of little significance in the economy of the town. It did little business in the 18th century[92] and an attempt to revive it in 1775, when the day was changed to Friday and 3 years' toll-free trading offered,[93] met with little success. In the earlier part of the 19th century it was almost completely disused,[94] but it was revived in 1873, after the building of the railway, and a firm of auctioneers, Innocent & Son, became the lessees before 1888 and conducted a livestock sale on the last Tuesday of each month.[95] In 1928 the firm moved the market from the streets of the town to a new sale yard at the railway station, where it continued to be held until 1959.[96]

The manor fair held at St. Lawrence brought in tolls of 46s. 6d. in 1270 and in another year at the same period 70s. 5d. were received.[97] Business declined in the later Middle Ages and during the 15th century only about 4s.–7s. were received in tolls.[98] The fair was later eclipsed by the success of the other fair, known as the St. John's Bridge fair, which was in the same ownership after 1572.[99] The closeness of the two fair days was probably the reason why the St. Lawrence fair was continued on the original date after the calendar change of 1752 while the other was moved to 9 September.[1] The St. Lawrence fair was still held in the late 18th century, when it dealt mainly in horses and cattle,[2] but it is not recorded later.

St. John's Bridge fair had become a major cheese-fair by the late 17th century.[3] In 1719 various deponents estimated that between 140 and 200 wagon loads of cheese were brought to the fair besides what was carried on horseback, and the lord of the manor needed to set up several pairs of scales at the site for weighing it. Much of the cheese, being destined for the London market, was taken for convenience directly to the wharves and the lord of the manor had to go to law to uphold his right of having scales and levying toll on the cheese sold outside the site.[4] Interference to the fair by flooding caused it to be moved from the meadow by the bridge to the streets of the town in 1776.[5] It still dealt then in large quantities of cheese though the volume was declining.[6] It continued in the 19th century, apparently mainly as a horse-fair, and after the early 1920s was merely a pleasure-fair.[7]

LOCAL GOVERNMENT. Isabel de Mortimer apparently created a borough within her manor of Lechlade soon after securing the right to a market in 1210. There were tenants holding by burgage tenure c. 1230 when an agreement to regulate the jurisdiction over her 'new market town' was made between Isabel and the abbot of Cirencester, lord of the hundred; the abbot granted her the right to have a tumbril and pillory and allowed her to take the profits of the biannual view of frankpledge, which was to be held in her court at Lechlade in the presence of the abbey's bailiffs.[8] The working of this arrangement was upset after the earl of Cornwall became lord of the manor; he apparently claimed to hold the view in his own right, but in 1258 he restored to the abbey its rights of jurisdiction.[9] A further dispute broke out in 1270, however, over the earl's claim to have gallows at Lechlade, a franchise that had formerly been exercised by Peter FitzHerbert,[10] and the disputes continued under the earl's son.[11] The arrangements for holding the view continued in the 15th and early 16th centuries, when separate views were held for the borough and for the manor or 'foreign',[12] a distinction that had apparently been made from the 13th century.[13] In 1550 the borough was administered by a bailiff and the foreign by a reeve,[14] though earlier a single annual account for both was rendered.[15] The view of frankpledge continued to be held in the manor court[16] and was still being held, though only triennially, in the 1850s.[17] Only one court roll, for a session of the court baron in 1546,[18] is known to survive.

Of the records of the parish officers churchwardens' accounts survive for 1567–1677 and from

[87] *Glos. Countryside*, July–Sept. 1951, 417; W.I. hist. of Lechlade, 4.
[88] *Cal. Pat.* 1396–9, 384–5.
[89] *Close R.* 1231–4, 398.   [90] S.C. 6/1095/8.
[91] *Cal. Pat.* 1563–6, pp. 495–6; *Cal. S.P. Dom.* 1663–4, 654.
[92] Rudder, *Glos.* 518.
[93] *Glouc. Jnl.* 13 Feb. 1775.
[94] *Pigot's Dir. Glos.* (1842), 105.
[95] Williams, *Lechlade*, 9; cf. Glos. R.O., SL 254.
[96] Ex inf. Mr. Innocent.
[97] S.C. 6/1095/8; S.C. 6/958/19.
[98] S.C. 6/850/24; S.C. 6/850/26; S.C. 6/Hen. VII/210.
[99] *Cal. Pat.* 1569–72, p. 361.
[1] Cf. *Glouc. Jnl.* 30 July, 27 Aug. 1764.
[2] Rudder, *Glos.* 518; Bigland, *Glos.* ii. 141.
[3] Hist. MSS. Com. 29, *13th Rep. II, Portland*, ii, p. 299.

[4] E 134/5 Geo. I Hil./25.
[5] *Glouc. Jnl.* 29 July 1776.
[6] Rudder, *Glos.* 518.
[7] *Kelly's Dir. Glos.* (1856 and later edns.); W.I. hist. of Lechlade, 5.
[8] *Ciren. Cart.* i, pp. 220–1.
[9] Ibid. ii, p. 548.
[10] Ibid. iii, pp. 847–8.
[11] *Rot. Hund.* (Rec. Com.), i. 177.
[12] *Ciren. Cart.* ii, p. 623; S.C. 6/Hen. VII/210 sqq.
[13] *Ciren. Cart.* ii, p. 548.
[14] *Cal. Pat.* 1549–51, 434.
[15] S.C. 6/Hen. VII/210 sqq.
[16] *Inq. p.m. Glos.* 1625–42, i. 58.
[17] *Kelly's Dir. Glos.* (1856), 317.
[18] S.C. 2/175/22.

1795.[19] The parish had a workhouse by 1735[20] and a new one was later built at the site of St. John's hospital, which was leased to the parish officers in 1763.[21] The workhouse went out of use between 1793[22] and 1803.[23] There was also a pest-house, in the north part of the parish near the Burford road;[24] it was built after 1744 with charity money given to the parish and was also used as a general poorhouse.[25] In 1803 the number of paupers on permanent relief was 69 and the number on occasional relief 180,[26] the latter figure reflecting the volume of travellers and pauper traffic on the main road. By 1813, presumably as a result of deliberate parish policy, the figure for occasional relief was down to 24, while that for permanent relief remained about the same.[27] In 1835 Lechlade became part of the Berkshire poor-law union of Faringdon,[28] an anomaly that was heightened by its inclusion in the Fairford highways district in 1863.[29] It became part of Faringdon rural district after the implementation of the 1894 Act[30] and a plan to include it in a proposed Fairford rural district later in the 1890s met with strong local opposition, led by the parish council which was dissatisfied with the work of the highways board.[31] In 1935 it was transferred from Faringdon to Cirencester rural district,[32] and in 1974 it became part of the new Cotswold district.

CHURCH. No record of Lechlade church has been found before 1254 though by inference it existed in 1210 when a fair was granted on St. Lawrence's day, its patronal feast.[33] In 1254 the king granted the advowson of the church to Richard, earl of Cornwall, having recovered it as an adjunct of the manor against the claim of the hospital of St. John at Lechlade.[34] In 1255, however, at the instance of the earl the king granted the advowson to the hospital. A vicar's portion had already been assigned out of the profits[35] and the grant was presumably made with the intention that the hospital should appropriate the church. The appropriation was carried out then, or at least by 1305,[36] and the rectory descended with the hospital estate[37] until 1670 when Laurence Bathurst devised it to the vicar of Lechlade.[38] Although from that time endowed with all the profits of the church, the living continued to be called a vicarage.

The grant of 1255 reserved the right of presentation to the vicarage to Richard of Cornwall, his wife Sanchia, and the heirs of their bodies.[39] Edmund, earl of Cornwall, presented in 1280[40] and Hailes Abbey in 1307[41] but the claim of the lords of the manor to the advowson was later challenged. In 1341 the hospital, which may have claimed a reversionary right on the failure of Richard's line at Edmund's death, presented and forced the withdrawal of a clerk presented by the Crown by right of the minority of the lord of the manor;[42] the hospital again successfully presented in 1361.[43] The Crown made unsuccessful attempts to present in 1391[44] and 1404, its candidate conceding on the latter occasion to a clerk presented by the countess of Kent, lady of the manor.[45] The countess was said to be seised of the advowson at her death in 1411,[46] and during the 15th century the owners of the manor appear to have exercised it without challenge.[47]

The Crown retained the advowson in hand when it alienated the manor in 1550[48] but included it in the grant of the hospital estate to the lord of the manor in 1572.[49] Edward Yate and George Raleigh respectively presented at the next two vacancies in 1579 and 1618 under grants for one turn[50] but from 1645[51] the advowson was exercised by the lords of the manor. It was divided at the partition of the manor; the Greenings were patrons in 1689 and the Wheates in 1761 while the alternate right was exercised in 1738 by a Mrs. Purcell and in 1774 by John Moreton of Tackley (Oxon.) who had bought that turn from the Pullens.[52] Samuel Churchill presented in 1795 but later the advowson was alienated from the manor. The bishop presented in 1806; Edward Leigh Bennet presented himself in 1832; Henry Grace of Lambeth (Surr.) presented in 1843; and Henry Carnegie Knox presented himself in 1850.[53] In the last year the advowson was bought by Emmanuel College, Cambridge,[54] which remained patron in 1977.

The vicar was given a fairly generous portion of the profits of the church. His portion was valued at £10, the same as that of the rectory, in 1291[55] and it included part of the corn and hay tithes as well as the

---

[19] Glos. R.O., P 197/CW 2/1–2.
[20] G.D.R. vol. 285B, f. 35.
[21] Glos. R.O., P 197/OV 7/1; cf. the name Workhouse Ground in G.D.R., T 1/113.
[22] Glos. R.O., P 197/IN 1/3, baptisms.
[23] *Poor Law Abstract, 1804*, 172–3.
[24] G.D.R., T 1/113.
[25] *20th Rep. Com. Char.* 27; cf. Glos. R.O., D 1388/III/140, will 1742.
[26] *Poor Law Abstract, 1804*, 172–3.
[27] Ibid. *1818*, 146–7.
[28] *Poor Law Com. 2nd Rep.* p. 511.
[29] *Lond. Gaz.* 23 Jan. 1863, p. 400.
[30] Glos. Colln. R 183.1.
[31] Glos. R.O., P 197A/PC 1/1.
[32] *Census, 1931* (pt. ii).
[33] *Cal. Pat.* 1396–9, 384–5.
[34] *Close R.* 1254–6, 5.
[35] Dugdale, *Mon.* vi (2), 684.
[36] *Reg. Ginsborough*, 20; cf. C 145/103 no. 17.
[37] *Valor Eccl.* (Rec. Com.), ii. 445; *Cal. Pat.* 1569–72, p. 361; *Inq. p.m. Glos.* 1625–42, i. 56.

[38] See below.
[39] Dugdale, *Mon.* vi (2), 684.
[40] *Reg. Giffard*, 125.
[41] *Reg. Ginsborough*, 177.
[42] *Reg. Bransford*, p. 367; *Cal. Pat.* 1340–3, 297; 1350–4, 174.
[43] Worc. Episc. Reg., Reg. Brian, i, ff. 34v., 38v.
[44] *Cal. Pat.* 1388–92, 413, 431.
[45] *Cal. Pat.* 1401–5, 451, 457; Worc. Episc. Reg., Reg. Clifford, f. 81v.
[46] *Inq. p.m. Glos.* 1359–1413, 260–1.
[47] Worc. Episc. Reg., Reg. Carpenter, i, ff. 32v., 235.
[48] Hockaday Abs. cclvii, 1554, 1562, 1572.
[49] *Cal. Pat.* 1569–72, p. 361.
[50] Hockaday Abs. cclvii.
[51] Bigland, *Glos.* ii. 143.
[52] Glos. R.O., D 1388, sale papers, Lechlade 1870–94, abs. of title of Sam. Churchill; Hockaday Abs. cclvii, where Sir Geo. Wheate is named as patron at the institution in 1761, the presentation probably having been made in 1753.
[53] Hockaday Abs. cclvii.
[54] Williams, *Lechlade*, 100.
[55] *Tax. Eccl.* (Rec. Com.), 222.

wool tithes and other small tithes.[56] The gift of the rectory under the will of Laurence Bathurst (d. 1670)[57] had evidently not been implemented in 1680 when a terrier still credited the vicar, Thomas Davies, with only a portion of the hay and corn tithes[58] and in 1686 Davies was at law with Sir Thomas Cutler and his wife over the rectory.[59] The rectory had evidently been confirmed to the vicar by 1705 when he was receiving the full tithes.[60] By 1680 the vicar had negotiated compositions with some of the landholders, and for all tithe payers there were moduses for cows and lambs. The former lands of St. John's hospital were tithe-free. There was no glebe attached to the living.[61] In 1838 the vicar was awarded a corn-rent of £710 for his tithes.[62] The vicarage house, recorded from the 1560s,[63] stood on the east side of the market-place.[64] The house remains basically as rebuilt before 1778[65] but it was remodelled to the designs of Richard Pace in 1804–5[66] and again altered later in the 19th century when a castellated porch was added. In 1952 it was replaced as the vicarage by a house in Sherborne Street.[67]

The vicarage was valued at £12 13s. 3½d. in 1535[68] and at £66 7s. in 1650.[69] It was worth c. £200 about 1710 when the endowment of the rectory tithes was said to have added over £140 to the value.[70] Its value had risen to c. £220 by 1738[71] and to c. £300 by the 1770s.[72] In 1856 it was worth £513;[73] either that was a net value or else the value of the tithe corn-rent had already fallen considerably.

The names of the vicars of Lechlade are known from 1255[74] but nothing significant of them until the time of Conrad Nye who promoted the partial rebuilding of the church following his institution in 1468.[75] That was, however, his second incumbency at Lechlade, assuming him to have been the same Conrad Nye who served from 1446 to 1462.[76] Adam Russell, the vicar in 1551, was found to be ignorant of the commandments;[77] he was deprived for being married in 1554. John Golshill, instituted in 1562,[78] was a pluralist[79] and neglected quarter sermons. His successor in 1572, John Dormer,[80] was described as zealous in religion but omitted some of the prescribed readings and employed an illiterate parish clerk in 1576.[81] He was said to be in trouble with the

Commission for Ecclesiastical Causes in 1579 when he resigned, tricked into doing so, it was claimed, by a man who had obtained from him a lease of the vicarage. He was succeeded by Henry Garbett[82] who was living at Oxford in 1584.[83] He was still serving the cure as a sick man of 80 in 1618 when William Phipps was licensed to assist him. It was probably also Garbett's infirmity that prompted John Gearing of London, owner of Butler's Court, to found a Sunday lectureship in the church before 1618 but it is not recorded later and may have lapsed on Garbett's death the same year. He was succeeded by Phipps[84] who held the living until at least 1642.[85] Thomas Davies, described as a preaching minister,[86] served as vicar from 1645 until his death in 1689. John Whitmore, vicar 1738–53, held the living with Fenny Compton rectory (Warws.). John Thomas Wheate (later Sir John) served from 1774 until 1795.[87]

In 1472 a chantry dedicated to St. Mary and served by three chaplains was founded in Lechlade church by Cecily, duchess of York, who endowed it with the possessions of St. John's hospital. At the same time another chantry, dedicated to St. Blaise, was founded by John Twyniho, lord of Butler's Court manor, and was assigned a pension of 10 marks from the hospital estate.[88] St. Mary's chantry was dissolved in 1508 when the three chaplains granted its possessions to the college of St. Nicholas in Wallingford castle.[89] St. Blaise's chantry survived until the dissolution of the chantries.[90] Before 1565, perhaps at the time of the 15th-century alterations to the church, a number of houses and some land were given for the maintenance of the fabric of the church,[91] and Nicholas Rainton gave a rent-charge of £4 for the same purpose in 1586. Part of the rent-charge came from the church house[92] in St. John's Street, which was being used as an alehouse in 1635[93] and was in ruins by 1677.[94]

The church of *ST. LAWRENCE*, which bore that dedication by 1305,[95] is built of ashlar and comprises a chancel with north vestry and north and south chapels, an aisled and clerestoried nave with north porch, and a west tower with a tall spire.[96]

The church was wholly rebuilt in the late Middle Ages. In 1470 the vicar Conrad Nye stated that he

[56] *Valor Eccl.* (Rec. Com.), ii. 445.
[57] Prob. 11/338 (P.C.C. 10 Eure).
[58] G.D.R., V 5/183T 1.
[59] Bodl. MS. Tanner cxlvii, f. 180.
[60] G.D.R., V 5/183T 3.
[61] Ibid. 1.
[62] G.D.R., T 1/113.
[63] Hockaday Abs. cclvii.
[64] Glos. R.O., D 527/19; O.S. Map 1/2,500, Glos. LIII. 14 (1899 edn.).
[65] Partics. of vic. 1778: photocopy *penes* Mr. Innocent.
[66] G.D.R., V 5/183T 4; Colvin, *Biog. Dict. of Eng. Architects*, 427.
[67] Ch. guide (1964), 23.
[68] *Valor Eccl.* (Rec. Com.), ii. 445.
[69] *Trans. B.G.A.S.* lxxxiii. 94.
[70] Atkyns, *Glos.* 535.
[71] Hockaday Abs. cclvii.
[72] Rudder, *Glos.* 520.
[73] G.D.R. vol. 384, f. 131.
[74] *Close R.* 1254–6, 378.
[75] Worc. Episc. Reg., Reg. Carpenter, i, f. 235; ii, f. 9.
[76] Ibid. i, ff. 32v., 174.

[77] *E.H.R.* xix. 114.
[78] Hockaday Abs. cclvii.
[79] Ibid. xliii, 1566 visit. f. 23.
[80] Ibid. cclvii.
[81] Ibid. xlvii, 1576 visit. f. 144; G.D.R. vol. 40, f. 157v.
[82] Hockaday Abs. cclvii; Req. 2/173/8.
[83] Hockaday Abs. xlix, 1584 state of clergy, f. 24.
[84] Ibid. cclvii.
[85] Ibid. lxiv, 1642 visit. f. 17.
[86] *Trans. B.G.A.S.* lxxxiii. 94.
[87] Hockaday Abs. cclvii.
[88] *Cal. Pat.* 1467–77, 361, where the amount of the pension is given incorrectly as £10: cf. the original in C 66/530 m. 29.
[89] *Cal. Pat.* 1494–1509, 577.
[90] *Trans. B.G.A.S.* viii. 278.
[91] Glos. R.O., P 197/CW 2/1; CW 3/1.
[92] Ibid. CH 1; cf. G.D.R., V 5/183T 2.
[93] G.D.R. vol. 175.
[94] Glos. R.O., D 352/T 1.
[95] *Reg. Ginsborough*, 20; *Reg. Bransford*, p. 367. It has often been wrongly stated to have been so dedicated only from the early 16th cent.
[96] See plate facing p. 77.

and the parishioners with other helpers had rebuilt the 'parish church', presumably the nave and aisles, and that with some friends he intended to rebuild the chancel, though responsibility for the latter was shared with Nye by St. John's hospital as rector.[97] The funds used for Nye's rebuilding probably included £120 left to the church by John Townsend in 1458[98] and the north and south chapels, which presumably formed part of the same rebuilding, are likely to have been paid for by the duchess of York and John Twyniho to house the chantries founded in 1472. While the general arrangement of the new building reflects the contemporary fashion for the larger churches in the county much of the detailing is old-fashioned: the window tracery is in a debased early-14th-century style, the window and arcade arches are two-centred, and some of the mouldings could be mistaken for work of a century earlier. Other parts of the church, notably the nave roof and clerestory, the north porch, and the tower and spire, are more characteristically late Perpendicular in style and may be additions of the early 16th century.

A west gallery for the singers was installed in the church in 1740[99] and in 1829–30 Richard Pace was employed to provide new pews and side-galleries;[1] all were replaced at another refitting under Waller & Son in 1882, when the organ, brought from Faringdon church in 1864, was moved from the west gallery to the north chapel.[2] Screens were installed as a memorial to G. A. Robbins of Clayhill in 1887.[3]

Among the features of the 15th-century work are the bosses on the chancel roof which include a set of angels carrying implements of the Passion. They were restored and re-painted in 1938.[4] The bowl of the font is of the 15th century but the ornate pedestal, recorded in the mid 19th century, has been replaced.[5] A new pulpit provided in 1882 stands on an ancient base which was recovered from the vicarage garden.[6] The clerestory windows have some fragments of ancient glass.[7] There is a brass in the south aisle depicting the wool-merchant John Townsend (d. 1458) and his wife,[8] and another in the north aisle, probably to another wool-merchant.[9] A carved wall-monument in the chancel to Ann Simons (d. 1769) is by Nicholas Read.[10] A brass chandelier was given by Richard Ainge in 1730.[11] There are five old bells: (i) 1742 by Abel Rudhall; (ii) 1802 by James Wells of Aldbourn (Wilts.),[12] a recasting of a medieval bell;[13] (iii) 1590 by Joseph Carter of

Reading;[14] (iv) 1635; (v) 1626.[15] A sanctus bell was cast by John Rudhall in 1796[16] and a treble was added when the peal was rehung in 1911.[17] The plate includes a chalice and paten-cover of 1641 and a pair of chalices with paten-covers of 1727 given by Susanna (née Bathurst), widow of Chancellor Richard Parsons.[18] The registers survive only from 1686 and there are gaps in the 18th century;[19] two volumes are said to have been burnt by one of the vicars.[20]

NONCONFORMITY. By 1676 Lechlade had a small group of Quakers, including a tallow-chandler who died in prison in 1683 after refusing to take oaths. The Quakers sought to register a house for their meetings in 1741 but they are not recorded in the town after the late 18th century.[21] Houses registered for worship in 1784, 1802, and 1811 may have been for the Baptists, who under the leadership of William Fox, lord of the manor, built a chapel in Sherborne Street in 1817.[22] The chapel had an evening congregation of 105 in 1851.[23] In 1848 or 1849 a chapel for Congregationalists was built in the Burford road by the Revd. H. J. Crump but his death soon afterwards left it heavily encumbered and, though it had morning and evening congregations of 35 and 80 in 1851, it passed into the hands of the mortgagees and was closed. It was re-opened in 1867 and attempts made to secure it financially[24] but it had closed again by 1888. Shortly before 1888 a Wesleyan chapel was built at the west end of High Street.[25] It and the Baptist chapel remained in use in 1977.

EDUCATION. William Turner (d. 1791) was schoolmaster and parish clerk at Lechlade for 50 years and Alexander Gearing (d. 1827) was schoolmaster there for 56 years[26] but their schools were apparently purely fee-paying as no record of a charity school has been found. In 1818 the town had two fee-paying day-schools with a total of 80 children and a boarding school for children of the wealthier classes.[27] By 1833 another day-school had opened and there were also church and Baptist Sunday schools,[28] the former perhaps in existence since c. 1790.[29] The first parish school was started in cottages in Wharf Lane by the vicar Edward Leigh

[97] Worc. Episc. Reg., Reg. Carpenter, ii, f. 9.
[98] Hockaday Abs. cclvii, 1458.
[99] Ibid. 1741.
[1] Glos. R.O., P 197/CW 3/2.
[2] Glos. N. & Q. iv. 24–5; ch. guide (1964), 13.
[3] Inscr. in ch.
[4] Trans. B.G.A.S. lx. 47–50.
[5] Ibid. xlii. 70–1, 80.
[6] Glos. N. & Q. iv. 25.
[7] Trans. B.G.A.S. xlvii. 326.
[8] Davis, Glos. Brasses, 52–4.
[9] It included a merchant's mark: ibid. 109–10. The brass was identified by Bigland (Glos. ii, plate facing p. 141) as that of John Twyniho but as he was buried at Cirencester that seems unlikely: Hockaday Abs. clv, 1486.
[10] Gunnis, Dict. of Brit. Sculptors, 316.
[11] Trans. B.G.A.S. lxxxi. 122–3.
[12] Glos. Ch. Bells, 53.

[13] Glos. R.O., P 197/CW 2/2, entries for 1801; IN 1/2, note at front.
[14] Trans. B.G.A.S. xx. 229.
[15] Glos. Ch. Bells, 53.
[16] Glos. R.O., P 197/CW 2/2.
[17] Ch. guide (1964), 22.
[18] Glos. Ch. Plate, 133.
[19] B. & G. Par. Rec. 179.
[20] Glos. N. & Q. ii. 161.
[21] Glos. R.O., D 2052; Q/SR 1741 D/1.
[22] Hockaday Abs. cclvii; cf. Williams, Lechlade 10.
[23] H.O. 129/122/2/2/5.
[24] Glouc. Jnl. 4 May, 7 Dec. 1867; H.O. 129/122/2/2/4.
[25] Williams, Lechlade, 11.
[26] Ibid. 10.
[27] Educ. of Poor Digest, 302.
[28] Educ. Enquiry Abstract, 319.
[29] New Coll. Mun. 5723, will of Thos. Oatridge.

Bennett a few years after his institution in 1832.[30] By 1847 the school, then in association with the National Society, was teaching 145 children.[31] The buildings were extended in 1874 to comprise an infants' section with 65 children and a mixed section of 90; finance was from pence, voluntary contributions, and a small endowment,[32] part of the proceeds of the Loder family's charities. In 1885 the school was receiving a part of the income of the parish charities[33] that was assigned to educational purposes by a Scheme of 1882 and that income, constituted as the Lechlade Educational Foundation in 1905,[34] was used mainly for buying equipment for the school in the 1970s.[35] The average attendance at the school rose to 195 by 1885[36] and 219 by 1911, but declined to 95 by 1936.[37] In the 1960s there was rapid expansion due to new housing development in the town[38] and in 1977, when the school was known as St. Lawrence's, attendance was 204.[39]

CHARITIES FOR THE POOR. An ancient charity known as the Maiden Dole, said to have been given by two maiden sisters,[40] comprised 5 bushels of wheat and 5 bushels of barley charged on land. The charity lapsed in the late 16th century but was restored by royal order in 1602 together with the arrears of 21 years,[41] and in 1604 Robert Bathurst charged it on a part of the manor estate.[42] By the early 19th century its cash value was usually distributed. A gift of £5 for the poor was charged on the manor estate by Edward Dodge (d. 1597) and became known as Dodge's Dole.[43] A commission for charitable uses c. 1679 directed Dodge's Dole to educating and apprenticing children[44] but there is no record of it being so used.

Richard Wellman by will dated 1703 gave a rent-charge of 10s. for 10 poor widows at Christmas.

Francis Loder by will dated 1720 gave £100 for the poor, which was used with another £30 to buy land in 1737;[45] Francis's nephew, the Revd. John Loder (d. 1744), left £100 to augment the charity[46] but the parish used the money to build a pest-house on the land bought with Francis's gift. In 1721 Robert Loder gave 20s. to be distributed in bread each year. Ann Simons (d. 1769) gave £200 which was laid out in stock and the interest later distributed with the proceeds of stock bought with £100 given by Elizabeth Underwood.[47] Thomas Oatridge of Butler's Court (d. 1789) left a reversionary interest in £200 stock, which fell in to the parish in 1828, for a distribution to the 12 oldest poor inhabitants.[48] The Revd. John Lifely, owner of Priory mill, gave £100 by will proved 1801 to support an annual sermon and a distribution in bread.[49] Mrs. S. Powell gave £4 interest from stock in 1807.[50] Richard Bowles (d. 1804), a former vicar of Lechlade, and his wife Catherine (d. 1814) gave a total of £1,000 stock.[51] Robert Wace by will proved 1820 gave £500 stock.[52] Lechlade was one of the parishes which benefited under the will of John Harvey Ollney (d. 1836), receiving £200 for coal and blankets at Christmas.[53]

Under a Scheme of the Charity Commissioners in 1882 all the above charities, which then brought in a total sum of c. £125 a year, were consolidated, one half of the income directed to local educational purposes and the other half to general relief schemes.[54] In 1885 the second half of the income was being paid to a provident club,[55] and in 1977 when it amounted to c. £400 a year it was distributed in coal or cash at Christmas. The Scheme did not include the charity of George Milward (d. 1838) who gave £200 for a distribution among 12 people aged over 65; in 1977 the annual income, c. £15, was distributed in cash at Christmas.[56]

QUENINGTON

QUENINGTON is a small rural parish 12 km. ENE. of Cirencester. The ancient parish comprised 1,996 a. and was compact and roughly rectangular in shape. It was bounded on most of the north and east by the river Coln and a tributary stream and a short section of Akeman Street, and elsewhere by field boundaries.[57] In the east where the Coln was diverted between 1862 and 1881[58] the addition in 1935 of 3 a. from Hatherop brought the boundary back in line with the river and gave the parish an area of 1,999 a. (809 ha.).[59]

Above the valley of the Coln which lies at over 91 m. the land rises to over 137 m. in the north-western corner. The land is formed by Forest

[30] Williams, *Lechlade*, 10. At first it was planned to provide a new bldg. on land leased to the par. at a nominal rent by W. F. S. Ponsonby in 1834: Glos. R.O., D 540/T 58.
[31] *Church School Inquiry, 1846–7*, 10–11.
[32] Ed. 7/34/191.
[33] *Kelly's Dir. Glos.* (1885), 514.
[34] Glos. R.O., D 3469/5/89.
[35] Ex inf. Mr. M. Boustead, of Lechlade.
[36] *Kelly's Dir. Glos.* (1885), 514.
[37] *Bd. of Educ., List 21, 1911* (H.M.S.O.), 163; *1922*, 105; *1932*, 116; *1936*, 122.
[38] *Glos. Life*, June 1969, 29.
[39] Ex inf. county educ. dept.   [40] Atkyns, *Glos.* 536.
[41] Glos. R.O., P 197/CH 2.
[42] Ibid. D 527/19; both Bathurst and Wm. Blomer, who was occupier of the land at the time of the 1602 order, have been wrongly credited with founding the char.
[43] *20th Rep. Com. Char.* 26.

[44] Bodl. MS. Rawl. B.323, f. 94.
[45] *20th Rep. Com. Char.* 27.
[46] Glos. R.O., D 1388/III/140.
[47] *20th Rep. Com. Char.* 27–8; and for Ann's death, Bigland, *Glos.* ii. 145.
[48] Glos. R.O., P 197/CH 4; and for his death, ibid. IN 1/3.
[49] Ibid. D 1070/III/51.
[50] *20th Rep. Com. Char.* 29.
[51] Ibid. 28; inscrs. in ch.
[52] Glos. R.O., D 1388, Cole fam., Wace fam. papers.
[53] Ibid. D 3469/5/89.
[54] Ibid.; Williams, *Lechlade*, 117–18.
[55] *Kelly's Dir. Glos.* (1885), 514.
[56] Ex inf. Mr. Boustead; Char. Com. Reg.
[57] *O.S. Area Bk.* (1883). This account was written in 1976.
[58] Glos. R.O., D 540/E 10; O.S. Map 6″, Glos. LII. NE. (1886 edn.).
[59] *Census*, 1931 (pt. ii); 1971.

Marble, with the underlying strata of the Great Oolite outcropping in the valley and in the south-east and south-west, and by cornbrash in the south.[60] Most of the parish was included in the open fields and commonable downland which were finally inclosed in 1754, but there are some water-meadows. Sheep-farming was important by the mid 14th century. No woodland was recorded in 1086[61] but Coneygar wood in the north of the parish was mentioned from 1754.[62] In 1901 the parish had 82¾ a. of woods and plantations,[63] some of it lying on the river bank which remained wooded in parts in 1976. Land in the wide loop described by the river at the north-eastern corner, which Sir John Webb acquired in 1778,[64] had been taken into Hatherop park by 1901.[65]

From Akeman Street, a route used by the Romans to a crossing of the Coln, a road branched eastwards. That road, which at Coneygar wood was crossed by an old route between Arlington Pike and Fairford, became the main route between Cirencester and Quenington village near the eastern boundary. North-west of the village it was crossed by a road between Coln St. Aldwyns and Fairford, on which a bridge had been built over the Coln by 1559, Quenington and Coln St. Aldwyns being responsible for repairing their respective halves.[66] A watering-place was reserved there at inclosure in 1754.[67] The London road mentioned in 1678[68] was possibly the important old route across the south-western corner between Ready Token and Fairford[69] which with all the above-mentioned roads, except Akeman Street, was among those specified in 1754.[70] A private carriage-way between the Cirencester road at Coneygar wood and Williamstrip Park in Coln St. Aldwyns had been built by 1824.[71] Coneygar Lodge, recorded in 1828, was rebuilt in the later 19th century.[72]

The church recorded in Quenington in 1100 presumably occupied the site of the parish church in the valley. In the late 12th century a preceptory of the Knights Hospitallers was founded to the south-west but, although some of its later out-buildings have survived, it had been demolished by the 17th century and Quenington Court was later built on the site. The houses near the church also include the former rectory and a former paper-mill, both dating from the 18th century.

Quenington village grew up on rising ground to the north. Above it to the west a large triangular green, the junction of a road from Poulton with the route between Coln St. Aldwyns and Fairford,[73] comprised 3 a. in 1754 when it was confirmed as common.[74] An 18th-century house stands north-east of Church Road, which links the church and green, but most buildings, including some large houses and a school, are of the 19th century. Quenington House, an early-19th-century two-storey building north of Mawley Road, which descends eastwards from the green, was a farm-house on the Hatherop estate in 1862.[75] Mawley House to the south-east was built as a farm-house c. 1808 by Robert Mawley.[76] The houses in Victoria Road, which runs north-eastwards from the foot of Church Road, include Mawley Farm and its early-19th-century out-buildings at the south-western end, the Long House to the east which was owned in the late 19th century by the builder William Joynes Godwin,[77] and a former corn-mill at the north-eastern end.

There was a smithy at the cross-roads north-west of the village by the late 17th century but the western end of the village was not developed until the later 19th century when estate cottages were built by the green. A factory south-west of the cross-roads established then by W. J. Godwin expanded after 1920.[78] He also built two pairs of cottages south of the Cirencester road in 1899 and 1914 respectively;[79] the former housed offices for the factory in 1976. On land in the north-eastern angle of the cross-roads, given for a cemetery in 1905,[80] a mortuary chapel had been built by 1920.[81] From the 1920s the area near the factory was chosen for council housing development, 14 semi-detached houses being built east of the Fairford road in 1929,[82] 8 north of the Hatherop road, and an estate of 18 south of the green. Modern buildings in 1976 included the village hall, a non-conformist chapel, 8 bungalows for old people on the north-east side of the green, and several large private dwellings west of the Fairford road and in the village.

Honeycomb Leaze Farm, the only building recorded by the road from Fairford to Ready Token in the 1770s,[83] was rebuilt in the early 19th century. To the north-west a house is dated 1931 with the initials of Ernest George Clifford who farmed at Honeycomb Leaze then,[84] and six detached houses north of the road are in the style of the 1930s. Of the other outlying buildings in the parish the barn north-east of Coneygar wood had been built by 1777.[85] To the north Coneygar Farm, which has some cottages near by, dates from the late 1870s[86] as probably do Coneygar Cottages, west of Coneygar Lodge.[87] Crossroads Cottages north of the Poulton road were built as estate

[60] Geol. Surv. Map 1″, solid, sheet 34 (1857 edn.).
[61] Cf. *Dom. Bk.* (Rec. Com.), i. 167v.
[62] Glos. R.O., Q/RI 115; cf. O.S. Map 1″, sheet 34 (1828 edn.).
[63] Acreage Returns, 1901.
[64] Williamstrip Mun., *penes* Earl St. Aldwyn, Williamstrip Pk., Coln St. Aldwyns, MTD/93/7B.
[65] O.S. Map 6″, Glos. LII. NE. (1886, 1903 edns.).
[66] Glos. R.O., D 1375/496, rot. 4d; Atkyns, *Glos.* 364.
[67] Glos. R.O., Q/RI 115.
[68] G.D.R., V 5/244T 2.
[69] Cf. Taylor, *Map of Glos.* (1777).
[70] Glos. R.O., Q/RI 115.
[71] Bryant, *Map of Glos.* (1824).
[72] O.S. Map 1″, sheet 34 (1828 edn.).

[73] Cf. Glos. R.O., photocopy 64H.
[74] Ibid. Q/RI 115.   [75] Ibid. D 540/E 10.
[76] Williamstrip Mun. EM/BP/5/1; EMP/12.
[77] Glos. R.O., D 2315.
[78] O.S. Map 6″, Glos. LII. NE. (1886, 1903, 1924 edns.).
[79] Dates and inits. on bldgs.
[80] Williamstrip Mun. MTD/108/1.
[81] O.S. Map 6″, Glos. LII. NE. (1924 edn.).
[82] Date and inits. 'C.R.D.C.' on one ho.
[83] Glos. R.O., photocopy 64H; Taylor, *Map of Glos.* (1777).
[84] Cf. *Kelly's Dir. Glos.* (1931), 290.
[85] Taylor, *Map of Glos.* (1777); O.S. Map 1″, sheet 34 (1828 edn.).   [86] Cf. Williamstrip Mun. MTD/105/1.
[87] O.S. Map 6″, Glos. LII. NE. (1886 edn.).

cottages on the Williamstrip estate later in the century.[88] Donkeywell Farm to the south-west was built by S. J. Phillips *c.* 1960.[89]

In 1086 43 tenants were recorded in Quenington.[90] Sixteen people including the preceptor were assessed for the subsidy in 1327[91] and 81 for poll tax in 1381.[92] The parish had only *c.* 16 communicants in 1551[93] and 10 households in 1563[94] but by 1650 there were 30 families.[95] From an estimate of 120 *c.* 1710[96] the population increased considerably to 267 by *c.* 1775.[97] From 239 in 1801 it rose to 371 by 1841 and to 438 by 1871. It then fell to 357 by 1901 and, after rising to 388 by 1911, to 322 by 1921. By 1951 it had risen to 486 but by 1971 had dropped to 415.[98]

In 1755 one innholder was licensed[99] and *c.* 1840 the parish had two beerhouses[1] which by 1891 were called the Keeper's Arms and the Earl Grey.[2] The inns, standing in the angle of Church Road and Mawley Road and lower down Church Road respectively, were open in 1976 but a third beerhouse in the village,[3] recorded from 1870[4] and called the Pig and Whistle by 1885,[5] has not been traced after 1939.[6]

A cottage hospital for children, in Victoria Road south-west of the corn-mill,[7] was opened *c.* 1900 by Mrs. Allfrey, the tenant of Williamstrip Park,[8] and it continued with her support until her death in 1911.[9] The village hall south-east of the school in Church Road apparently stands on the site given for a parish institute in 1906.[10]

In the period 1276–90 Edward I was a frequent guest, usually in February or March, at Quenington Preceptory[11] which was consequently furnished with provisions.[12] Several owners of the manor who were figures of national importance, including Michael Edward Hicks Beach, who as Viscount St. Aldwyn provided street lighting in Quenington *c.* 1911,[13] are mentioned under Coln St. Aldwyns.

MANOR AND OTHER ESTATES. Eight hides

of land in Quenington, held as 3 manors by Aluuold and two men called Dodo in 1066,[14] passed to Walter de Lacy[15] (d. 1085), whose son Roger[16] held them in 1086.[17] On Roger's banishment in 1096 the property passed to his brother Hugh (d. by 1115).[18] It then apparently descended to Hugh's granddaughter Agnes, wife of William de Munchensy,[19] probably the Agnes de Lacy who with her daughter Sibyl granted QUENINGTON manor to the Knights Hospitallers in the mid 12th century.[20] The Hospitallers, who established a preceptory at Quenington *c.* 1193[21] and from whom Edmund Tame of Fairford leased land there before 1506,[22] held the manor until the Dissolution[23] and during the short-lived revival of their order in England which ended in 1558.[24]

In August 1545 the Crown granted the manor to Richard Morrison[25] but in the following month it conferred the estate on Sir Anthony Kingston, the lessee of the demesne.[26] After Sir Anthony's death in 1556 the manor passed to his illegitimate son Edmund Kingston[27] (d. 1590) and then in the direct line to Anthony[28] (d. 1591) and William.[29] At William's death in 1614 the manor passed to his widow Mary for life.[30] Mary, who married Sherrington Talbot and granted a lease of the estate in 1649, was evidently succeeded by William Powle of Coln St. Aldwyns who had purchased the reversion in 1648. William, by will proved 1657, left the manor to his nephew Henry Powle[31] with whose Williamstrip estate it then descended.[32] In 1847 the estate owned 790 a. in the parish, where it acquired 225 a. from the Tombs family in 1879[33] and 172 a. from the Mawley family in 1900.[34] In the mid 20th century Earl St. Aldwyn sold off parts of his estate, Donkeywell farm eventually passing in 1954 to S. J. Phillips & Sons (Kemble) Ltd. which bought Mawley (Crossroads) farm (401 a.) from the earl in 1961. After S. J. Phillips's death in 1965 his property was sold to Alexander Black Mitchell[35] (d. 1972) whose widow Violette held it in 1976.[36]

88 Ibid. (1903 edn.).
89 Ex inf. the sec., S. J. Phillips & Sons (Kemble) Ltd., Kemble.
90 *Dom. Bk.* (Rec. Com.), i. 167v.
91 *Glos. Subsidy Roll, 1327*, 14.
92 E 179/113/31A rot. 5; E 179/113/35A rot. 1.
93 *E.H.R.* xix. 113.
94 Bodl. MS. Rawl. C.790, f. 26.
95 *Trans. B.G.A.S.* lxxxiii. 94.
96 Atkyns, *Glos.* 613.
97 Rudder, *Glos.* 619.
98 *Census*, 1801–1971.
99 Glos. R.O., Q/AV 2, rot. 3.
1 Ibid. D 1388, par. val.
2 *Licensed Houses in Glos. 1891*, 74–5; cf. Glos. R.O., D 1070/III/66, 67.
3 Glos. R.O., P 261/OV 1/1, rate 25 Jan. 1872.
4 *Kelly's Dir. Glos.* (1870), 620.
5 Glos. R.O., D 1070/III/66, deed 15 Feb. 1886.
6 *Kelly's Dir. Glos.* (1939), 295.
7 Cf. O.S. Map 6", Glos. LII. NE. (1903 edn.).
8 Cf. *Kelly's Dir. Glos.* (1897), 270; (1902), 273.
9 Ibid. (1910), 283; (1914), 289; Glos. R.O., D 1070/VII/91, rep. Mar. 1912.
10 Char. Com. Reg.; O.S. Map 6", Glos. LII. NE. (1924 edn.).
11 *Cal. Close*, 1272–9, 270–1, 447–9, 492, 524; 1279–88, 2, 41, 148, 179, 388; 1288–96, 71, 150.
12 Ibid. 1272–9, 366, 447, 474, 482.
13 Williamstrip Mun. EMM/13/2.
14 *Dom. Bk.* (Rec. Com.), i. 167v.

15 Cf. *Hist. & Cart. Mon. Glouc.* (Rolls Ser.), i. 85.
16 *V.C.H. Glos.* xi. 65.
17 *Dom. Bk.* (Rec. Com.), i. 167v.
18 Cf. *V.C.H. Glos.* xi. 65; *Hist. & Cart. Mon. Glouc.* i. 109, 123.
19 W. E. Wightman, *Lacy Fam. in Eng. and Normandy 1066–1194* (Oxford, 1966), 176–7.
20 *Rot. Chart.* (Rec. Com), 16; cf. J. Delaville Le Roulx, *Cartulaire Général des Hospitaliers*, iv (Paris, 1906), p. 326.
21 *V.C.H. Glos.* ii. 113.
22 Glos. R.O., photocopy 785.
23 Cf. *Knights Hospitallers in Eng.* (Camd. Soc. [1st ser.] lxv), 28–9; *Valor Eccl.* (Rec. Com.), ii. 462–3.
24 *Glos. Countryside*, Oct.–Nov. 1964, 33; cf. *Cal. Pat. 1557–8*, 313.
25 *L. & P. Hen. VIII*, xx(2), p. 117.
26 Ibid. p. 230; Hockaday Abs. cccxix.
27 Cf. *V.C.H. Glos.* xi. 16, 49–50.
28 C 142/230 no. 45.   29 C 142/231 no. 94.
30 C 142/347 no. 90.
31 Glos. R.O., D 2440, est. papers 1545–1789, abs. of title; *Trans. B.G.A.S.* vi. 292–5; C.P. 25(2)/422/12 Chas. I East. no. 40.
32 Glos. R.O., D 2440, deed 1790.
33 Williamstrip Mun. EMS/19; cf. ibid. MTD/97.
34 Ibid. MTD 104.
35 Ex inf. the sec., S. J. Phillips & Sons.
36 Ex inf. Mr. I. N. Mitchell, Trull Ho., Cherington; cf. *The Guardian*, 24 Aug. 1972.

After the Dissolution the preceptory became a farm-house[37] but the laying-out of ornamental gardens, including water gardens, on the site in the early 17th century[38] suggests that a manor-house had been built there by then. The house, which would have been lived in only for a short time as a manor-house, was presumably the farm-house called the Court c. 1770.[39] Quenington Court which dates from a rebuilding of the 19th century was sold with 19 a. by Earl St. Aldwyn in 1969 to Mr. and Mrs. Frank Gollins.[40] The out-buildings standing in 1976 included to the north a 14th-century gateway, partly reconstructed and extended to the north-west in the early 16th century, and to the north-west a round dovecot, possibly of the 17th century, with a revolving ladder.

There were several smaller estates in the parish in the 18th and 19th centuries.[41] Land held by John Vokins (d. c. 1710) passed in turn to his sons John (d. 1714) and William. After William's death c. 1754 the estate was held by his widow Catherine[42] who was allotted c. 211 a. at inclosure in 1754.[43] Catherine (d. 1768) left it to her nephew Charles Stephens (d. 1781), whose devisee John Wakefield sold it to Estcourt Cresswell of Bibury in 1789.[44] In the early 19th century Estcourt Cresswell and his son Richard Estcourt Cresswell sold parts of the property totalling c. 110 a. to the lord of the manor.[45]

Allotments of 224 a. and 239 a. to John Carey and Thomas Hamblet respectively in 1754[46] comprised land in the southern part of the parish.[47] Part of their property evidently passed to James Haynes whose estate of c. 338 a. was put up for sale in the 1830s after his bankruptcy.[48] Jenkin Thomas, a dissenting minister of Cheltenham, acquired part, and his estate, which c. 1840 comprised c. 297 a.,[49] included land held in the right of his wife Mary Harriet, daughter and heir of James Tombs (d. 1825) and heir to an estate called Godwins in the mid 18th century.[50] Part of Jenkin Thomas's estate was bought in 1847 by Lord de Mauley of Hatherop,[51] whose son Ashley George John Ponsonby acquired most of the rest before 1860.[52] The Hatherop estate, which had acquired c. 62 a. from the lord of

the manor in 1778,[53] included 567 a. in the parish in 1862.[54] The land was sold in the mid 20th century save for c. 80 a. north of the village.[55]

ECONOMIC HISTORY. By 1086 the manor, on which 16 ploughs were recorded, had risen in value from £8 in 1066 to £10 and had a demesne worked by 3 ploughs and 12 servi.[56] In 1338, when the demesne included 644 a. of arable, sheep-farming was important but a flock of 330 was apparently farmed out, possibly for £10 a year. The preceptory did not retain a shepherd but a swineherd was among those receiving stipends.[57] The demesne, which with its tithes was let at farm for £10 by 1535[58] and was farmed for £20 14s. 10½d. by 1541,[59] comprised 609 a. of arable, 205 a. of pasture, and 64 a. of meadow in 1545.[60]

In 1086 the manorial tenants included 20 villani, 7 bordars, and a reeve with 12 ploughs. The estate also supported 2 radknights with one plough and in Gloucester there was a burgess rendering 4 iron ploughshares and a smith paying 2s.[61] The assized rents of all of the preceptory's free and customary tenants were worth £30 in 1338.[62] Those in Quenington were valued at 2s. and £12 9s. 6d. respectively in 1535[63] but in 1541, when two tenements with 3 yardlands and 13 a. of arable were let at farm for 30s., the rents of the customary tenants, holding by copy for terms of lives, were worth £7 1s. 6d. and those of 6 tenants holding at will £3 3s. 5d.[64]

The two open fields recorded from 1624[65] were a north and a south field[66] and in 1753 they included c. 1,304 a.[67] Quenington Downs, the main common in 1507,[68] lay north of the Cirencester road in the north-west corner of the parish[69] and there the manor had common pasture for 400 sheep in 1545.[70] The taking of parts into severalty had begun by 1624[71] and by 1753 only 14 a. remained commonable.[72] The 10 a. of meadow land belonging to the manor in 1086 probably included water-meadows,[73] and c. 1680 Grandage meadow, part of the Williamstrip estate east of Coln bridge, was valued at £90.[74] The Mill Ham north-east of the village between the river and mill leat may have

37 Req. 2/55/71.
38 Trans. B.G.A.S. lxxx. 93–8.
39 Rudder, Glos. 617.
40 Ex inf. Mr. Gollins.
41 Cf. Glos. R.O., Q/RI 115.
42 Ibid. D 2440, deeds 1709–1806.
43 Ibid. Q/RI 115.
44 Ibid. D 2440, deeds 1709–1806; Bigland, Glos. iii, no. 211.
45 Glos. R.O., D 2440, deeds 1712–1806; est. papers 1753–1852.
46 Ibid. Q/RI 115.
47 Ibid. photocopy 64H.
48 Ibid. D 1388, case papers; D 2440, est. papers 1753–1852, plan.
49 Ibid. D 1388, par. val.
50 Ibid. Tovey fam., deeds 1769–1858, 1769–1887.
51 Ibid. D 2440, est. papers 1753–1852; Williamstrip Mun. EMM/13/1.
52 Cf. Williamstrip Mun. EMC/5, letter 7 Feb. 1860.
53 Ibid. MTD/93/7B.
54 Glos. R.O., D 540/E 10.
55 Ex inf. Smith-Woolley & Co., Woodstock, agents to the Hatherop est.

56 Dom. Bk. (Rec. Com.), i. 167v.
57 Knights Hospitallers in Eng. 28–9; Glos. N. & Q. ii. 519–20.
58 Valor Eccl. (Rec. Com.), ii. 462.
59 S.C. 6/Hen. VIII/7262 rot. 1d.
60 Hockaday Abs. cccxix.
61 Dom. Bk. (Rec. Com.), i. 167v.
62 Knights Hospitallers in Eng. 28.
63 Valor Eccl. (Rec. Com.), ii. 462.
64 S.C. 6/Hen. VIII/7262 rot. 1 and d.; cf. Hockaday Abs. cccxix, 1545.
65 G.D.R., V 5/244T 1–2; Glos. R.O., D 2440, deeds 1670–1826, deed 1670.
66 G.D.R., V 5/244T 4.
67 Glos. R.O., D 2440, est. papers 1753.
68 S.C. 11/831 rot. 3.
69 Cf. Glos. R.O., D 540/P 3.
70 Hockaday Abs. cccxix.
71 Cf. G.D.R., V 5/244T 1; cf. Glos. R.O., D 2440, deeds 1670–1826, deed 1670; deeds 1709–1806, John Vokins's will 1709.
72 Glos. R.O., D 2440, est. papers 1753.
73 Dom. Bk. (Rec. Com.), i. 167v.
74 Glos. R.O., D 2134; cf. ibid. Q/RI 115.

WILLIAMSTRIP PARK: the west front

LECHLADE: Lechlade, or Halfpenny, bridge in 1815

LECHLADE: Burford Street on market day, *c.* 1920

LECHLADE: Sherborne House

NORTH CERNEY: the old rectory

LECHLADE: Church House

ELKSTONE: the old rectory

been a common meadow, for in the later 18th and the 19th centuries the glebe included a strip there.[75] Sufficient pasture was needed for sheep, one farmer having a flock of 300 c. 1580,[76] and the use of land in the northern part of the parish by the river as sheep-pastures is indicated by the number of fields there called slaits.[77]

By 1753 at least 159 a. had been inclosed[78] and most of the remaining open and commonable land was inclosed by Act of Parliament the following year under an award which affected 1,306 a. Humphrey Praed, lord of the manor and chief beneficiary, was allotted 362 a. and of four other principal landowners Edmund King 138 a. The rector was awarded 58 a. for his open-field glebe, and 74 a. was contained in allotments to ten small landowners.[79]

In 1831 8 farmers employed 43 labourers.[80] The farms varied considerably in size in the 19th century. On the Williamstrip estate in 1861 Manor (later Court) farm had 601 a. and 109 a. were farmed from Hartwell Farm in Maiseyhampton.[81] The following year the Hatherop estate included a farm of 543 a. and Honeycomb Leaze farm which had 24 a.[82] Two freehold farms of 220 a. and 176 a. respectively in 1871 were later taken into the Williamstrip estate,[83] on which Coneygar farm, comprising 517 a. in Quenington and Bibury, had been created by 1879[84] and Manor farm had been reduced to 263 a. by 1903.[85] In 1926 when 59 agricultural labourers worked in the parish full-time there were 13 farmers. Six of the farmers were smallholders with less than 20 a. each and the other farms were three over 300 a., two of 150–300 a., and two of 20–50 a.[86] Of 10 farms returned for Quenington and Maiseyhampton in 1976 four had less than 20 ha. (50 a.) each, three were of 50–100 ha. (123–247 a.), and the other three each had over 200 ha. (494 a.).[87]

After inclosure the parish was given over to mixed farming[88] and in the 19th century much land was farmed as arable, growing mainly cereals and turnips with some beans and peas.[89] In 1866, 1,578 a. were returned as arable or grass leys and only 139 a. as permanent grass. Large flocks of sheep were kept and then included at least 1,896 animals.[90] In the late 19th century and early 20th

the area of permanent grassland was enlarged but arable farming retained its importance and in 1926 1,287 a. of arable and rotated grass were returned. During that period sheep-farming continued on a large scale and more cattle were introduced; in 1926 355 cattle, including 22 milk cows, were returned,[91] compared to 56 in 1866.[92] In 1880 there was a flock of Hampshire Down sheep and a herd of shorthorn cattle on Manor farm,[93] and between 1889 and 1906 a dairyman lived in the parish.[94] Pig-rearing and poultry-farming were also important in 1926.[95] Arable retained its importance in 1976 when much land was under cereals but several farms in Quenington and Maiseyhampton specialised in dairying. Sheep and beef cattle were also raised then.[96]

The two mills on the manor in 1086[97] presumably occupied the sites of the water-mill and fulling-mill recorded in 1338.[98] In the former, a corn-mill in 1507,[99] Richard Morton had an interest in the early 18th century.[1] Richard Aldridge owned it in 1776[2] and it was bought by Samuel Blackwell in 1783[3] to pass with the manor until 1871[4] when, as part of an exchange, it was transferred to T. S. Bazley's Hatherop estate.[5] The mill, a 19th-century building in Victoria Road, went out of use apparently after 1920.[6]

In the early 18th century the site of the fulling-mill south of the church, which then included a gig-mill and dye-house, was owned by William Thomas and the clothier Richard Pinfold (d. by 1725).[7] Richard's grandson Edward Pinfold sold it in 1731 to Charles Morgan of Fairford who in 1735 conveyed the fulling-mill to his great-nephew Charles Morgan. At his death in 1755 the mill passed to his widow Elizabeth and was sold by his son Robert in 1775 to John Raymond who later inherited Fairford manor.[8] By 1738 the mill had been leased to Joshua Carby for making paper.[9] He died there in 1791[10] and Joshua Carby Radway,[11] who in 1820 was licensed to operate a paper-making machine there,[12] worked it until his death in 1840. The site included a new mill and a rag house in 1830[13] and had four beating engines in 1851. William Alfred West, who was making newspaper from straw by 1860,[14] still worked there in 1876[15] but the mill had apparently gone out of

[75] Ibid. photocopy 64H; D 1388/SL 3, no. 48; D 540/E 10; Q/RUm 293.
[76] Req. 2/55/71.
[77] Glos. R.O., D 540/P 3.
[78] Ibid. D 2440, est. papers 1753.
[79] Ibid. Q/RI 115.
[80] Census, 1831.
[81] Williamstrip Mun. EMS/17.
[82] Glos. R.O., D 540/E 10.
[83] Ibid. P 261OV 1/1; see above p. 123.
[84] Williamstrip Mun. MTD/105/1.
[85] Glos. R.O., D 2440, est. papers 1903–18.
[86] M.A.F. 68/3295/8.
[87] Agric. Returns 1976.
[88] Rudder, Glos. 617; Rudge, Hist. of Glos. i. 266.
[89] Cf. Acreage Returns, 1801.
[90] M.A.F. 68/26/10; M.A.F. 68/25/3.
[91] M.A.F. 68/1609/9; M.A.F. 68/3295/8.
[92] M.A.F. 68/25/3.
[93] Williamstrip Mun. MTC/14/2.
[94] Kelly's Dir. Glos. (1889 and later edns.).
[95] M.A.F. 68/3295/8.
[96] Agric. Returns 1976.
[97] Dom. Bk. (Rec. Com.), i. 167v.
[98] Knights Hospitallers in Eng. 28.
[99] S.C. 11/831 rot. 3.
[1] G.D.R., V 5/244T 5; C.P. 25(2)/926/6 Anne Trin. no. 25; C.P. 25(2)/1015/1 Geo. I Trin. no. 11; C.P. 25(2)/1016/7 Geo. I East. no. 14.
[2] Glos. R.O., D 2440, deed 1790.
[3] Bigland, Glos. iii, no. 211.
[4] Glos. R.O., D 1388, par. val.
[5] Williamstrip Mun. MTD/96.
[6] O.S. Map 6", Glos. LII. NE. (1924 edn.).
[7] Glos. R.O., D 2269/1.
[8] Ibid. D 540/T 61; D 1728, abs. of title 1772.
[9] Ibid. D 540/T 61.
[10] Glouc. Jnl. 14 Feb. 1791.
[11] Cf. Rudge, Hist. of Glos. i. 267; Glos. R.O., D 2315.
[12] Trans. B.G.A.S. xciv. 135.
[13] Glos. R.O., D 1388/III/167.
[14] Trans. B.G.A.S. lxxi. 161; cf. Kelly's Dir. Glos. (1863), 329; (1870), 620.
[15] Morris's Dir. Glos. (1876), 372.

use by 1879.[16] In 1976 an 18th-century mill and mill-house, then called Knight mill, survived at the site.

In 1811 44 families were supported by agriculture and as many as 24 by trade but by 1831 the latter figure had fallen to sixteen.[17] William Godwin, one of two builders mentioned in 1879,[18] was presumably William Joynes Godwin,[19] who was dealing in drain pipes and cisterns among other things by 1894. By 1919 he had been succeeded by Harold J. Godwin and by 1939 the firm of H. J. Godwin Ltd. specialised in pumping-machinery[20] and employed c. 100 people.[21] In 1974, when the firm was no longer owned by the Godwin family, its c. 140 employees made a wide range of pumping equipment.[22] It remained an important employer in 1976.

In 1338 the services of a baker, cook, and laundress were retained for the preceptor, two other knights, and their dependants.[23] Most of the usual village trades have been recorded. The village smithy in the south-eastern angle of the cross-roads north-west of the village was mentioned in 1678.[24] It was worked by one or both smiths mentioned in 1856[25] but was closed shortly after 1920 since when no smith has been recorded in the parish.[26] There were two carpenters in 1856[27] and from 1889 at least one.[28] Masons were recorded from 1608[29] and the parish had a plasterer in 1910.[30] In the later 19th century several lime-kilns, including some at Honeycomb Leaze, were worked.[31] Tailors were mentioned in 1381[32] and the 19th century, and dress-makers between 1897 and 1923.[33] In 1608 there was a shoemaker,[34] a trade followed in the later 19th century. The inhabitants included a butcher in the 1860s and a baker and shopkeepers from the mid 19th century. Among the trades recorded in the later 19th century were those of draper, tea-dealer, and mealman[35] and in the mid 20th century a hurdle-maker lived in the parish.[36] There was a village post office in 1976.

LOCAL GOVERNMENT. The courts of the

Knights Hospitallers mentioned in 1338[37] presumably included the manor court and an annual view of frankpledge held there in 1535.[38] The lord of the manor had leet jurisdiction c. 1710[39] but no later record of that or the manor court has been found.

Two churchwardens were recorded from 1498[40] but there were three in 1683 and 1807[41] and occasionally only one in the later 18th and early 19th centuries.[42] Their accounts survive from 1744 and their expenses between 1802 and 1830 were met out of the poor-rate.[43] There were two overseers of the poor in 1672[44] but only one between 1802 and 1830.[45] The annual cost of poor-relief rose from £67 in 1776 to £180 by 1803, when 18 people were receiving permanent help,[46] and to £343 by 1813 when 20 people were regularly helped. It had dropped to £169 by 1815[47] but in the late 1820s and early 1830s it remained at over £200.[48] In 1836 the parish became part of the Cirencester poor-law union[49] and remained in Cirencester rural district[50] until 1974 when it was included in Cotswold district.

CHURCH. The church at Quenington was presumably served by the priest recorded there in 1086,[51] and in 1100 the bishop of Worcester awarded a pension of 2 marks in it to Gloucester Abbey. The abbey later took a portion of the demesne tithes and held a yardland,[52] and claimed to hold the church by the grant of Hugh de Lacy[53] but the Knights Hospitallers secured their right to the church, those tithes, and that land in the mid 12th century and agreed to pay the abbey the pension, half of which was to come from the living. Payment was in arrears c. 1260.[54] About 1439 the abbey gave up its right to the pension in return for a grant of property in Gloucester from the Hospitallers,[55] who subsequently received the mark from the living.[56] It was being paid to the patron in the later 19th century.[57] The living, which was a rectory in 1287,[58] was united in 1928 with Coln St. Aldwyns and Hatherop.[59]

[16] Cf. *Kelly's Dir. Glos.* (1879), 726; O.S. Map 6″, Glos. LII. NE. (1886, 1903 edns.).
[17] *Census*, 1811, 1831.   [18] *Kelly's Dir. Glos.* (1879), 726.
[19] Cf. Glos. R.O., D 2315, deed 1887.
[20] *Kelly's Dir. Glos.* (1894), 265; (1919), 271; (1939), 295.
[21] Payne, *Glos. Survey*, 163.
[22] *Cotswold Life*, Aug. 1974, 34–5.
[23] *Knights Hospitallers in Eng.* 28–9; *Glos. N. & Q.* ii. 520.
[24] G.D.R., V 5/244T 2; cf. Glos. R.O., Q/RI 115; O.S. Map 6″, Glos. LII. NE. (1886 edn.).
[25] *Kelly's Dir. Glos.* (1856), 345.
[26] O.S. Map 6″, Glos. LII. NE. (1924 edn.); cf. *Kelly's Dir. Glos.* (1919), 271; (1923), 286–7.
[27] *Kelly's Dir. Glos.* (1856), 345.
[28] Ibid. (1889 and later edns.).
[29] Smith, *Men and Armour*, 261; Glos. R.O., D 1070/III/66; D 1388/III/166; sale papers 1819–93; D 1740/T 17.
[30] *Kelly's Dir. Glos.* (1910), 283.
[31] O.S. Map 6″, Glos. LII. NE. (1886 edn.); Glos. R.O., D 1388/SL 5, no. 42; Q/RUm 293.
[32] E 179/113/35A rot. 1.
[33] Glos. R.O., D 2315, deed 1804; *Kelly's Dir. Glos.* (1856 and later edns.).
[34] Smith, *Men and Armour*, 261.
[35] *Kelly's Dir. Glos.* (1856 and later edns.).
[36] *Glos. Countryside*, Dec. 1959, 313–14.
[37] *Knights Hospitallers in Eng.* 28.
[38] *Valor Eccl.* (Rec. Com.), ii. 462.
[39] Atkyns, *Glos.* 613.
[40] Hockaday Abs. xxii, 1498 visit. f. 37; G.D.R. vol. 40, f. 158v.
[41] G.D.R., V 5/244T 3, 6.
[42] Glos R.O., P 261/CW 2/1; G.D.R., V 5/244T 7.
[43] Glos. R.O., P 261/CW 2/1.
[44] E 179/116/544.
[45] Glos. R.O., P 261/CW 2/1.
[46] *Poor Law Abstract, 1804*, 172–3.
[47] Ibid. *1818*, 146–7.
[48] *Poor Law Returns* (1830–1), p. 67; (1835), p. 65.
[49] *Poor Law Com. 2nd. Rep.* p. 522.
[50] *Census*, 1961.
[51] *Dom. Bk.* (Rec. Com.), i. 167v.
[52] *Hist. & Cart. Mon. Glouc.* ii. 41, 93.
[53] Ibid. i. 109; cf. *Reg. Regum Anglo-Norm.* ii, p. 410.
[54] *Hist. & Cart. Mon. Glouc.* ii. 93, 94–6.
[55] *Cal. Pat.* 1436–41, 290.
[56] S.C. 11/831 rot. 2; S.C. 6/Hen. VIII/7262 rot. 1d.
[57] Cf. *L. & P. Hen. VIII*, xx(2), pp. 117, 230; Rudder, *Glos.* 618; Bigland, *Glos.* iii, no. 211.
[58] *Reg. Giffard*, 337.
[59] *Lond. Gaz.* 2 Nov. 1928, pp. 7096–7.

The patronage, which the prior of the Hospital of St. John of Jerusalem in England exercised in 1279,[60] passed with the manor.[61] Presentations were made by Jerome Barnard, patron for the turn, in 1555 and by Henry Banner, after he had relinquished the living, in 1577,[62] and in 1603 Sir Thomas Conway was said to be patron.[63] The patronage for a turn of Sir Lewis Dive was contested in 1636 and the Crown was patron for a turn in 1745.[64] In 1976 the patronage of the united benefice was shared by Earl St. Aldwyn, the dean and chapter of Gloucester, and Sir Thomas Bazley.[65]

The Hospitallers took the demesne tithes and by 1535 had let them at farm with the demesne.[66] After the Dissolution their land, Court farm with 12 yardlands, was described as tithe free since the rector received no tithes from it;[67] its tithes were valued at £30 c. 1710.[68] Old inclosures at Honeycomb Leaze were also tithe free[69] and some of the tithes from them were sold in 1789 by Thomas Hamblet.[70] The rector took all the tithes from the rest of the parish.[71] They had been let at £60 before the inclosure of 1754 when they were commuted for rent-charges totalling £80, increasing after six years to £90.[72] By the mid 19th century they had been converted to corn-rent-charges.[73] Of the glebe, which comprised 100 a. of arable in 1535,[74] 80 a. of open-field land had been let at £14 by 1754 when the rector was allotted 58 a. for them.[75] The glebe contained 62 a. in 1907[76] when 59 a. were sold to Viscount St. Aldwyn.[77] The rectory was valued at £9 6s. 8d. in 1291[78] but only £7 18s. 2d. clear in 1535.[79] Its value had risen to £60 by 1650,[80] £100 by 1750,[81] and £204 by 1856.[82]

The rectory house north-east of the church was a two-storey building of 8 bays with 4 rooms on each floor in 1704.[83] The main south-east front facing the mill leat dates from the 18th century and a large back wing was added before 1807.[84] Since 1928 the incumbent has lived in Coln St. Aldwyns[85] and in 1929 the house was sold to the Hatherop estate[86] and enlarged.[87] It was enlarged again in 1963.[88]

When Ralph de Hokyngton resigned the living in 1309 it was granted *in commendam* for 6 months to Andrew de Tothale,[89] and Andrew, who later also held it with Stondon vicarage (Essex)[90] and was licensed in 1316 to be absent for 2 years,[91] surrendered it to Ralph in 1318 upon an exchange.[92] Between 1378 and 1417 the rectory figured in at least nine exchanges of livings.[93] Anthony Aldwyn, who could not repeat the Commandments in 1551,[94] was deprived in 1555 for being married. Henry Banner, rector from 1558,[95] who also held the adjacent benefice of Coln St. Aldwyns but was resident,[96] was deprived in 1577. His successor Thomas Skinner,[97] who was considered no preacher but a sufficient scholar in 1593,[98] resigned in 1619. George Albert, who became rector in 1636[99] after serving in Germany during the Thirty Years' War,[1] was with Prince Maurice's army in the West Country during the Civil War.[2] Nevertheless he retained the living in 1650, when he was described as a preaching minister,[3] and died in 1668.[4] His successor John Jones (d. 1673) and Richard Hutchins, rector 1745–9, both held the adjacent living of Hatherop.[5] Hutchins's predecessor Henry Allen, rector from 1732, was removed for simony. John Pettat, rector from 1789,[6] lived at Stonehouse, where he was vicar until 1798, and appointed curates to serve Quenington[7] which he resigned in 1797. His son Thomas, who succeeded him and also became rector of Hatherop, resigned Quenington the following year. John apparently became rector again, holding the living until c. 1810 and appointing a curate in 1799.[8] John William Peters, rector 1823–34, was later an active nonconformist in Quenington and Fairford.[9]

The church, which was called St. Mary's in the 12th century,[10] was dedicated to *ST. SWITHIN* by 1735[11] but it bore an invocation to the Holy Rood in the 18th and early 19th centuries.[12] It is built of limestone rubble and ashlar and has a chancel with north vestry and a nave with north and south porches. A central tower with spire, for which there is now no certain architectural

[60] *Reg. Giffard*, 104.
[61] Cf. *L. & P. Hen. VIII*, xx(2), p. 230.
[62] Hockaday Abs. cccxix.
[63] *Eccl. Misc.* 96.
[64] Hockaday Abs. cccxix.
[65] *Glouc. Dioc. Yr. Bk.* (1976), 66–7.
[66] *Valor Eccl.* (Rec. Com.), ii. 462.
[67] G.D.R., V 5/244T 4–6.
[68] Atkyns, *Glos.* 613.
[69] Glos. R.O., P 261/SD 1/2.
[70] C.P. 25(2)/1317/29 Geo. III Mich. no. 19.
[71] *Valor Eccl.* (Rec. Com.), ii. 446; G.D.R., V 5/244T 5.
[72] Glos. R.O., Q/RI 115.
[73] Bigland, *Glos.* iii, no. 211; cf. *Kelly's Dir. Glos.* (1885), 552.
[74] *Valor Eccl.* (Rec. Com.), ii. 446.
[75] Glos. R.O., Q/RI 115.
[76] Ibid. D 2299/515.
[77] Williamstrip Mun. EMM/13/1.
[78] *Tax. Eccl.* (Rec. Com.), 222.
[79] *Valor Eccl.* (Rec. Com.), ii. 446–7.
[80] *Trans. B.G.A.S.* lxxxiii. 94.
[81] G.D.R. vol. 381A, f. 87.
[82] G.D.R. vol. 384, f. 162.
[83] G.D.R., V 5/244T 4.
[84] Ibid. 6.
[85] *Kelly's Dir. Glos.* (1931 and later edns.).
[86] Glos. R.O., D 2299/4230; Williamstrip Mun. PPC/66.
[87] Date on bldg.

[88] Verey, *Glos.* i. 375.
[89] *Reg. Reynolds*, 149.
[90] *Cal. Papal Regs.* ii. 61–2, 86.
[91] Worc. Episc. Reg., Reg. Maidstone, f. 44.
[92] *Reg. Cobham*, 7, 229.
[93] *Cal. Pat.* 1391–6, 200, 328; 1399–1401, 533; *Reg. Wakefeld*, pp. 14, 35, 108–9, 123; Worc. Episc. Reg., Reg. Clifford, f. 87v.; Reg. Peverell, ff. 26, 79v.
[94] *E.H.R.* xix. 113.
[95] Hockaday Abs. cccxix.
[96] Ibid. xlii, 1563 visit. f. 51; clxvii.
[97] G.D.R. vol. 40, f. 158v.; Hockaday Abs. cccxix.
[98] Hockaday Abs. lii, state of clergy 1593, f. 9.
[99] Ibid. cccxix.
[1] Glos. R.O., D 2052.
[2] Ibid. P 261/IN 1/1.
[3] *Trans. B.G.A.S.* lxxxiii. 94.
[4] Bigland, *Glos.* iii, no. 211.
[5] Hockaday Abs. cccxix; ccxxxvii; Bigland, *Glos.* ii. 48.
[6] Hockaday Abs. cccxix.
[7] *V.C.H. Glos.* x. 264, 286; G.D.R. vol. 382, f. 16.
[8] Hockaday Abs. cccxix; ccxxxvii; Bigland, *Glos.* iii, no. 258.
[9] Hockaday Abs. cccxix; cxciv, 1841; cf. *Cat. of Glos. Colln.* p. 1078.
[10] *Hist. & Cart. Mon. Glouc.* ii. 92–3.
[11] G.D.R. vol. 285B, f. 35.
[12] G.D.R. vol. 381A, f. 87; Rudge, *Hist. of Glos.* i. 267.

evidence although it could have arisen from within the east end of the nave, was said to have been removed by the early 18th century.[13] A west tower, not shown in a view of 1790[14] and possibly added shortly before 1825,[15] was demolished in 1882 when the church was extensively restored.[16]

The lower stages of the walls of the nave and chancel are substantially of the later 12th century, having a continuous string-course and flat buttresses, and the north and south doorways are both of three richly decorated orders. That to the north has the Harrowing of Hell on the tympanum[17] and that to the south the Coronation of the Virgin. The only other medieval features to have survived are the windows of the chancel, those to the north and south being of the 13th century and that to the east of the 15th century. The present side windows of the nave are square-headed and probably of the 17th century. At the 19th-century restoration a west window and bellcot, a north porch of open timberwork, and a canopy to the south doorway were added to the nave, and a vestry was added to the chancel. The chancel was also rebuilt, perhaps to a new design. A western gallery, where the organ had stood in 1867, was removed.[18]

Monuments to members of the Powle and Ireton families and to some rectors have been reset in the west end of the nave.[19] The font, which is of the later 16th century, has a hood dated 1662. The central tower and spire were said to have held six bells in the late 16th century but c. 1703 the church had only two.[20] A bell cast by Abel Rudhall in 1757[21] was the only bell in the mid 19th century but another was added at the restoration of 1882.[22] The plate includes a chalice and paten of 1579.[23] The surviving registers begin in 1653[24] and contain entries for Netherton, a hamlet on the boundary of Hatherop and Fairford, in the 19th century.[25]

NONCONFORMITY. Two protestant nonconformists and two papists were recorded in the parish in 1676[26] and one Independent in the mid 18th century.[27] A house occupied by the Revd. W. Lawrie was registered for use by protestant dissenters in 1822[28] but there were no meetings in the parish in 1825.[29]

Premises in Quenington were registered for dissenting worship by Jenkin Thomas, a Baptist minister of Cheltenham and a local landowner,[30] in 1834 and by John William Peters, who resigned that year as rector, in 1835.[31] The latter were probably for the Baptists who in 1838 built a chapel which had attendances of up to 50 in 1851.[32] By 1854, when it had a burial ground, it was in bad repair[33] and the meeting ceased in the early 1880s.[34]

No other record has been found of a house registered in 1851[35] but a meeting of Plymouth Brethren recorded from the early 1880s[36] used a room adjoining the Long House until c. 1900 when it moved to the smithy north-west of the village.[37] It met there until at least 1939.[38] From c. 1880 Congregationalists met in a room adjoining Mawley Farm.[39] The meeting, which had 8 members in 1898 and was connected with the Fairford chapel,[40] ceased after 1939.[41] In 1926 an evangelical congregation bought a small building at the south-western corner of the green and used it until 1961 when a chapel was built south of the green. In 1976 the meeting, which used the name Christian Brethren, had between 20 and 30 members.[42]

EDUCATION. In 1616 Marmaduke Watson was teaching at Quenington without a licence.[43] The poor lacked sufficient means of education in 1818 when only eight girls were taught in a privately supported day-school. There were separate Sunday schools financed by voluntary contributions for 26 boys and 12 girls.[44] A day-school was begun in 1831 and by 1833, when the income was supplied by contributions and pence, it taught 35 children. At that time a Sunday school taught 28.[45] In 1847 a dame school taught 22 children and there were separate Sunday schools for 18 boys and 19 girls.[46]

A church school, which in 1854 had 40 children with more on Sundays, met in a small cottage[47] until 1856 when the National school was built on land belonging to Sir M. E. Hicks Beach[48] south-west of Church Road.[49] It had an average attendance of 42 in 1871 and was supported by voluntary contributions.[50] The average attendance rose to 63 by 1885 and in 1901 61 children were taught in two classes.[51] It was later called Quenington C. of E.

[13] Bodl. MS. Rawl. B.323, f. 118v.; Atkyns, *Glos.* 613.
[14] Glos. Colln. RR 244.1.   [15] Cf. G.D.R. vol. 383, no. ciii.
[16] *Kelly's Dir. Glos.* (1885), 552; for views of ch. before restoration see Glos. R.O., D 2752.
[17] See plate facing p. 141.
[18] *Glos. Ch. Notes*, 138.
[19] Cf. Bigland, *Glos.* iii, no. 211.
[20] Bodl. MS. Rawl. B.323, ff. 118v.–119.
[21] Glos. R.O., P 261/CW 2/1.
[22] *Kelly's Dir. Glos.* (1870 and later edns.); cf. *Trans. B.G.A.S.* xlii. 166.
[23] *Glos. Ch. Plate*, 171.   [24] *B. & G. Par. Rec.* 224.
[25] Glos. R.O., P 261/IN 1/5.
[26] Compton Census.
[27] G.D.R. vols. 285B, f. 35; 381A, f. 87.
[28] Hockaday Abs. cccxix.
[29] G.D.R. vol. 383, no. ciii.
[30] *A New Guide to Cheltenham* [?1824], 15.
[31] Hockaday Abs. cccxix.
[32] H.O. 129/340/3/11/16; cf. Glos. R.O., D 2052, s.v. 1838.
[33] Glos. R.O., D 1388, sale papers 1819–93.

[34] Cf. *Kelly's Dir. Glos.* (1879), 726; (1885), 552.
[35] Glos. R.O., Q/RZ 1.
[36] Cf. *Kelly's Dir. Glos.* (1879), 726; (1885), 552.
[37] Glos. R.O., D 2315; O.S. Map 6″, Glos. LII. NE. (1886, 1903 edns.).
[38] O.S. Map 6″, Glos. LII. NE. (1924 edn.); *Kelly's Dir. Glos.* (1939), 295.
[39] O.S. Map 6″, Glos. LII. NE. (1886 edn.); cf. *Kelly's Dir. Glos.* (1879), 726; (1885), 552.
[40] Glos. R.O., D 2052.
[41] *Kelly's Dir. Glos.* (1939), 295; O.S. Map 6″, Glos. LII. NE. (1924 edn.).
[42] Ex inf. Mr. R. F. Meade, of Quenington.
[43] Glos. R.O., D 2052.   [44] *Educ. of Poor Digest*, 306.
[45] *Educ. Enquiry Abstract*, 324.
[46] *Church School Inquiry, 1846–7*, 14–15.
[47] Glos. R.O., D 1388, sale papers 1819–93, letter 13 Oct. 1854.
[48] Ed. 7/35/264.
[49] O.S. Map 6″, Glos. LII. NE. (1886 edn.).   [50] Ed. 7/35/264.
[51] *Kelly's Dir. Glos.* (1885), 552; (1901), 273.

school; its attendance fell to 43 by 1922[52] and, after the juniors were transferred to Hatherop in 1929,[53] to 15 by 1936.[54] In 1970 the school also became the infants' school for Coln St.Aldwyns and Hatherop and in 1976 there were 20 children on the roll.[55]

CHARITIES FOR THE POOR. Catherine Ireton

by will proved 1715 left a rent-charge of £10 to be distributed, as at Coln St. Aldwyns, among the Protestant poor of the parish annually.[56] By 1748 a coat for a man and a gown for a woman were provided each year.[57] The remaining income was spent on bread.[58] In 1970, under a Scheme of 1907, investments provided an income of £12, used to buy bread.[59]

SOUTHROP

THE SMALL rural parish of Southrop lies on the west side of the river Leach 18 km. east of Cirencester. It was known as Leach after the river in 1086,[60] but from at least 1211 the name Southrop,[61] associating it with the local group of names that includes Hatherop, Botherop (Eastleach Martin), and Williamstrip, was used.

The boundary between Southrop and Eastleach Martin was apparently not fixed until the inclosure of Southrop, completed in 1621.[62] A perambulation of 1591 appears to place the north boundary of Southrop on what was later the boundary between the two Eastleaches, running from Hammersmith Bottom north-eastwards along a straight track to the Leach.[63] It seems that though land belonging to Eastleach Martin, attached to the estates of Coate farm and Prior's Coate, lay south of that boundary it was mostly dispersed within Southrop's open fields; the inclosure apparently gave Eastleach Martin the compact area west of the Leach as well as a detached piece, lying between Southrop and Hatherop,[64] in exchange for those lands and for rights in the downland of Southrop. The east boundary of Southrop followed the Leach, and the south-east boundary, described as a hedge and ditch in 1591, ran from the river to Westwick ford[65] on the stream called the Beast brook.[66] The part of the south-east boundary that divided the parish from Lemhill farm (formerly in Oxfordshire) appears to have been of particular significance, for a low, broad bank was visible along it in 1976. The south-west boundary followed the Beast brook and then an ancient salt-way between Lechlade and Droitwich[67] which gave the names Great and Little Salt hill to two fields beside it in Southrop;[68] the road, which remained a fairly important local route, was called London way in 1591.[69] After the early-17th-century inclosure the parish covered 1,493 a. (604 ha.),[70] to

which the detached part of Eastleach Martin, comprising Homeleaze Farm and 90 a. (36 ha.), was added in 1883.[71]

The land of the parish is mainly flat, lying at about 100 m. with the Leach and the Beast brook forming shallow coombs. The valley of the Beast brook is formed by Forest Marble which in the rest of the parish is overlaid by cornbrash.[72] Since the inclosure the land has been mainly in tillage with some meadow land by the streams. The small plantation called Bee Furlong brake is the only woodland. Near the end of the Second World War a small airfield was laid out in the west part of the parish but it was not used after the war.[73]

Southrop village is sited by a crossing point of the river Leach where a bridge called Vedyng (or Vedhams) bridge was recorded from 1379.[74] The road across the meadows beyond the bridge was causewayed by 1470 but that did not prevent it being flooded.[75] The manor-house and church were built close to the river and the village grew up along the road running westwards and across the end of that road, on the Lechlade–Eastleach road. It consists mainly of cottages and small farm-houses of the 17th and early 18th centuries. The house called the Pines, now much reduced in size, was the only large house apart from the manor-house. Near the Pines a row of labourers' cottages was built shortly before 1840[76] and there are a few other 19th-century cottages. A group of new houses was built in the south part of the village in the 20th century. Some substantial stone farm buildings survive, including a notable range of barns at Manor Farm by the church.

Stanford Hall (formerly Stanford Farm), an outlying farmstead on the south boundary of the parish, was apparently established in the early 18th century,[77] and in the mid 19th century two farm

[52] Bd. of Educ., List 21, 1911 (H.M.S.O.), 166; 1922, 106.
[53] Glos. R.O., PA 96/1, vols. for 1929–30.
[54] Bd. of Educ., List 21, 1932 (H.M.S.O.), 117; 1936, 122.
[55] Ex inf. county educ. dept.
[56] Glos. R.O., D 2440, est. papers 1545–1789, abs. of title.
[57] Ibid. P 261/CW 2/1.
[58] Ibid. D 2440, est. papers 1654–1859, est. partics. 1784; 20th Rep. Com. Char. 29.
[59] Glos. R.O., CH 21.
[60] Dom. Bk. (Rec. Com.), i. 168v. This account was written in 1976.
[61] Bk. of Fees, i. 50.
[62] See below.
[63] D.L. 42/116 f. 82v.; cf. also f. 84v. where Southrop manor's fishery in the Leach was said to extend up to Eastleach Turville.

[64] O.S. Map 6″, Glos. LIII. NW. (1884 edn.).
[65] D.L. 42/116 f. 82v.
[66] Glos. R.O., D 2440, Southrop est. papers 1807–62, sale partics. 1840.
[67] Taylor, Map of Glos. (1777).
[68] Wadham Coll., Oxford, Mun. 35/1.
[69] D.L. 42/116 f. 82v.
[70] O.S. Area Bk. (1882).
[71] Census, 1891; O.S. Area Bk. Eastleach Martin (1882).
[72] Geol. Surv. Map 1″, solid, sheet 34 (1857 edn.).
[73] Ex inf. Mr. R. W. Hinton, of Southrop.
[74] Wadham Coll. Mun. 61/B 1; D.L. 42/116 f. 82v.
[75] Wadham Coll. Mun. 61/B 1.
[76] Glos. R.O., D 2440, Southrop est. papers 1807–62, sale partics. 1840.
[77] Ibid. Southrop est. papers 1704–58, abs. of title 1842.

cottages were built near by.[78] Hook's Farm in the west part of the parish had been built by 1752. It was demolished to make way for the airfield, which also severed Hook's Lane running past the farm to join the Fairford–Burford road. By 1752 there were some outlying cottages west of Southrop village at Tiltup, which was perhaps once the site of a wayside cross, for the name Standing Cross Lane was given to the Fairford–Eastleach road north of the cross-roads there.[79]

In 1086 35 inhabitants of Southrop were recorded.[80] Twenty-two people were assessed for the subsidy in 1327,[81] and 64 for the poll tax in 1381.[82] There were said to be c. 46 communicants in 1551,[83] 12 households in 1563,[84] and 35 families in 1650.[85] The population was estimated at c. 170 about 1710[86] and at 216 c. 1775.[87] In 1801 there were 238 people in the parish and the population had risen to 425 by 1851. The decrease to 362 by 1861 was attributed partly to the departure of one large family but the decline was continued to 259 by 1901 and, with fluctuations, to 205 by 1971.[88]

The Swan inn in the village at the junction with the road from Eastleach had opened by 1843 when there was also the Greyhound near the east end of the village.[89] The latter had closed by 1891[90] and the Swan was the only public house in the village in 1976. An inn was recorded at one of the cottages at Tiltup in 1824[91] but was not mentioned later. A village hall was built c. 1950.[92]

MANOR AND OTHER ESTATES. The estate called Leach owned before the Conquest by Earl Tostig and in 1086 by Walter son of Pons[93] was apparently the later manor of *SOUTHROP*. It evidently passed with Eaton Hastings (Berks.) to the Hastings family[94] and was presumably one of the Gloucestershire fees held by Ralph de Hastings in 1160.[95] John de Hastings held Southrop in 1211[96] but was dead by 1221 when William de Hastings, presumably his son, recognised the right of John's widow Muriel to a third of the manor as dower.[97] In 1236 Maud, widow of William, held the manor as 1 knight's fee[98] but in 1239 she held only part in dower while her son William held the residue.[99] About 1271 William de Hastings (d. c. 1278) granted the manor

to Benet of Blakenham on his marriage to his daughter Joan but in 1273 Benet and Joan granted it back to William for life.[1] In 1285 the manor was held by Benet's heir, a minor,[2] presumably the Benet of Blakenham who in 1297 gave it to Hugh de St. Philibert and his wife.[3] It passed to John de St. Philibert who had a grant of free warren in 1317[4] and died c. 1333 when his widow Ada received the manor as dower. John's son John[5] granted the manor in 1353 to the Crown,[6] which returned it to him and his wife Margaret for their lives,[7] but they surrendered it to the Crown in return for an annuity for Margaret in 1358.[8] The Crown granted the manor for life in 1359 to Peter de Bruges,[9] whose right was acquired by John Short who granted it to William Harvey before 1367.[10] William and his wife Mary had a grant in tail male in 1376[11] and they maintained a household at Southrop in the 1380s.[12] William was dead by 1400 when the Crown granted Mary an unrestricted title to the manor.[13]

A part of the manor, comprising a plough-land and a third of a mill, was granted by William de Hastings to his brother-in-law Walter de Grey in 1239,[14] and Henry de Grey held it at his death c. 1315. Henry's heir was John de Grey, son of John de Grey of Rotherfield Greys (Oxon.), a minor,[15] whose wardship was granted to David Martin, bishop of St. David's.[16] John came of age in 1321[17] and held the estate as ½ fee in 1333.[18] By the beginning of the next century it had been re-united with the other part of the manor.

In 1406 Mary Harvey granted the two parts of the manor, called Philibert's Court and Grey's Court, to the college of St. Mary at Leicester, called the Newark.[19] The college apparently held the manor undisturbed until its dissolution in 1548;[20] in 1472, however, the Crown made a grant of Southrop manor to Roger Horsley,[21] but it confirmed Mary Harvey's grant to the college the following year.[22]

At the dissolution of St. Mary's College the manor was annexed with its other possessions to the duchy of Lancaster[23] and the Crown retained the freehold until the early 17th century. In 1575 the manor was leased to William Yorke and Ankaret his wife and their right later passed to John Watson, bishop of Winchester. In 1586 a 31-year lease in reversion was granted to Thomas Conway who bought out the

[78] Ibid. Stanford fm. papers 1821–67.
[79] Wadham Coll. Mun. 35/1.
[80] *Dom. Bk.* (Rec. Com.), i. 168v.
[81] *Glos. Subsidy Roll, 1327*, 14.
[82] E 179/113/35A rot. 1; E 179/113/31A rot. 5.
[83] *E.H.R.* xix. 114.
[84] Bodl. MS. Rawl. C.790, f. 26v.
[85] *Trans. B.G.A.S.* lxxxiii. 94.
[86] Atkyns, *Glos.* 678.   [87] Rudder, *Glos.* 681.
[88] *Census*, 1801–1971.
[89] G.D.R., T 1/167.
[90] *Licensed Houses in Glos. 1891*, 74.
[91] Bryant, *Map of Glos.* (1824).
[92] Char. Com. Reg.
[93] *Dom. Bk.* (Rec. Com.), i. 168v.
[94] Cf. *V.C.H. Berks.* iv. 528–9.
[95] *Red Bk. Exch.* (Rolls Ser.), i. 24.
[96] *Bk. of Fees*, i. 50.   [97] *Cur. Reg. R.* x. 147–8.
[98] *Bk. of Fees*, i. 438.
[99] C.P. 25(1)/73/12 no. 224.
[1] *Cal. Inq. p.m.* ii, p. 153; C.P. 25(1)/284/20 no. 7.

[2] *Feud. Aids*, ii. 237.   [3] C 145/57 no. 33.
[4] *Feud. Aids*, ii. 272; *Cal. Chart. R.* 1300–26, 335.
[5] *Cal. Inq. p.m.* vii, p. 366; *Cal. Close*, 1333–7, 41.
[6] C.P. 25(1)/287/44 no. 485.
[7] *Cal. Pat.* 1350–4, 478.
[8] C.P. 25(1)/287/45 no. 547; *Cal. Pat.* 1358–61, 49.
[9] *Cal. Pat.* 1358–61, 294.
[10] Ibid. 1364–7, 351.
[11] Ibid. 1374–7, 268.
[12] *Cal. Inq. Misc.* iv, p. 207.
[13] *Cal. Pat.* 1399–1401, 393.
[14] C.P. 25(1)/73/12 no. 224.
[15] *Cal. Inq. p.m.* v, p. 284.
[16] *Cal. Fine R.* 1307–19, 258.
[17] *Cal. Inq. p.m.* vi, pp. 204–5.
[18] Ibid. vii, p. 367.
[19] *Cal. Pat.* 1405–8, 158.
[20] *V.C.H. Leics.* ii. 49–51; *Valor Eccl.* (Rec. Com.), iv. 171.
[21] *Cal. Pat.* 1467–77, 365.
[22] *Rot. Parl.* vi. 48.
[23] Wadham Coll. Mun. 61/A 1; D.L. 42/116 f. 82v.

successors to the bishop's lease the following year. Conway, who was knighted, died in 1605 or 1606 and in 1607 his trustees sold his lease to Eleanor, widow of Sir Richard Berkeley.[24] A grant of the manor in fee to Peter Bradshaw made by the Crown in 1605[25] was apparently not implemented and in 1607 the manor was granted in fee to Robert Cecil, earl of Salisbury, who sold it to Sir Thomas Roe, Lady Berkeley's son, in 1608. In 1612 Sir Thomas and his mother sold the freehold and leasehold to trustees for Dorothy Wadham who assigned the manor as part of the endowment of her foundation at Oxford.[26] Wadham College retained the manor until 1926 when it sold the 1,245-acre estate to a man who was described as a speculator and who apparently immediately re-sold it.[27] In 1931 the manor-house and part of the estate belonged to Francis J. Jones.[28] He sold his estate in 1932 to Capt. Alan Richardson, whose widow Mrs. M. G. Richardson owned 580 a. in 1976 when the manor-house was the home of her son-in-law, Mr. K. C. Combe.[29] Most of the other land in the parish then belonged to R. Hinton & Sons (Farms) Ltd., an associated company of a firm of agricultural merchants based in the village.[30]

From 1800, when he took a lease of the manor-house,[31] Michael Hicks Beach of Williamstrip Park built up a large estate of land held under Wadham College, acquiring in particular 181 a. from John Tuckwell in 1828. In 1840 his grandson Sir Michael Hicks Beach held most of the parish, including leaseholds and copyholds amounting to 875 a. and the Freehold and Stanford farm estates. Sir Michael sold his leaseholds and copyholds in 1842 to Charles Royds Smith, who made his home at the manor-house.[32] Smith sold his rights in the lands back to Wadham College in 1857.[33]

The manor-house of William de Hastings at Southrop was mentioned in 1221.[34] The Greys had a separate house, known as Grey's Court in the early 15th century,[35] for their part of the manor; it had presumably been demolished by 1591 when a close on the demesne was called Grey's Court.[36] Southrop Manor, the surviving manor-house, was always leased out by Wadham College after it acquired the estate, though the warden and fellows reserved the right to use it in time of plague at Oxford.[37] Alterations and additions in the 19th and 20th centuries have obscured some of the earlier history of the house. It seems probable, however, that the 12th-century doorway, now reset as the entrance to the dining-room but formerly at first-floor level, reflects the date of the earliest part of the house, a tower-like

block close to the north-east corner of the church. That may be the only portion surviving of the house that included a hall and kitchen, both greatly decayed, in 1588;[38] the range to the north of it, now kitchens, appears to have been built in the 17th century. Parts of the eastern range may also be of the 17th century, and the north-eastern room, known as the Court Room and presumably once used for meetings of the manor court, seems to be an addition of the early 19th century. Later in the 19th century, perhaps in the time of C. R. Smith, rooms were added on the south-east and the south front was rebuilt in Victorian Cotswold style.[39] Between 1926 and 1939 the south front was remodelled in Georgian style and the principal rooms were refitted, the dining-room to designs of Norman Jewson; 18th-century fireplaces from Lechlade Manor were introduced in other rooms.[40] The outbuildings include stabling of the 17th and early 19th centuries.

Among freehold estates recorded at Southrop in the Middle Ages were $\frac{2}{3}$ hide held by William of Southrop from William the chamberlain in 1227[41] and lands which John, son of Robert Combe, held before 1470.[42] One or both of those estates may have been represented by that later known as the *FREEHOLD* which Thomas West of Testwood (Hants) sold to Henry Keble in 1570 when it comprised 2 houses and c. 60 a.[43] Henry (d. 1603) was succeeded by his son Edmund who in 1610 also had a considerable copyhold estate. Edmund died in 1612, leaving an infant son Thomas,[44] who was the ward of his stepfather Henry Aisgill in 1616.[45] The Freehold estate remained in the family until 1718 when Thomas Keble of Brown's Hill, Bisley, sold it to the Revd. John Powell, who settled it on his wife Elizabeth and his daughter Elizabeth, wife of Charles D'Oyley. D'Oyley was succeeded at his death in 1776 by his son Charles (d. 1802), whose widow Ann held the estate until her death in 1818. Her children sold it in 1819 to John Tuckwell of Eastleach Turville. John (d. 1826) was succeeded by his son John who sold the estate in 1827 to Michael Hicks Beach.[46] It passed with Hicks Beach's leaseholds and copyholds to C. R. Smith[47] who sold most of the land of the estate to Wadham College in 1858.[48] The house belonging to the estate, where the D'Oyleys lived in the later 18th century, stood in the village on the east side of the road to Eastleach.[49] Most of the building was pulled down before 1842,[50] but one wing, incorporating work of the early 17th and the 18th century, survived in 1976 when it was

[24] Wadham Coll. Mun. 61/A 1–8.
[25] *Cal. S.P. Dom.* 1603–10, 224.
[26] Wadham Coll. Mun. 61/A 9–12, A 19–22, A 31.
[27] Ibid. E 31–2.
[28] *Kelly's Dir. Glos.* (1931), 308.
[29] Ex inf. Mrs. Richardson, of Southrop.
[30] Ex inf. Mr. M. J. Hinton, managing director, R. Hinton & Sons, Yarnold & Gale Ltd.
[31] Wadham Coll. Mun. 61/F 28.
[32] Glos. R.O., D 2440, Southrop est. papers 1807–62, 1842–55.
[33] Ibid. Southrop est. papers 1856–7.
[34] *Cur. Reg. R.* x. 147–8.
[35] *Cal. Pat.* 1405–8, 158; Wadham Coll. Mun. 61/B 1, ct. before SS. Simon & Jude.

[36] D.L. 42/116 f. 83v.
[37] Wadham Coll. Mun. 61/F 1–36.
[38] D.L. 44/417.
[39] Drawing *penes* Mrs. Combe, of Southrop Man.
[40] Ex inf. Mrs. Combe.
[41] C.P. 25(1)/73/7 no. 92.
[42] *Cal. Close*, 1476–85, 349–50.
[43] D.L. 42/116 f. 83.
[44] Wadham Coll. Mun. 61/B 1; C 142/328 no. 156.
[45] Wadham Coll. Mun. 61/C 6.
[46] Glos. R.O., D 2440, Southrop est. papers 1715–1841.
[47] Ibid. Southrop est. papers 1807–62, 1842–55.
[48] Ibid. Southrop est. papers 1856–7.
[49] Wadham Coll. Mun. 35/2–3; 61/E 4–5.
[50] Glos. R.O., D 2440, Southrop est. papers 1842–55, copy of deed 1842.

known as the Pines. A large gabled dovecot stands by the house.

In 1745 an estate called *STANFORD FARM* in the south part of the parish comprised a house, then newly built, and *c.* 114 a. and was owned by James Chaunler (d. 1760). After his death the estate was put up for sale for the benefit of his creditors and it was bought in 1763 by Mary Chaunler (d. *c.* 1779) who was succeeded by her son John Chaunler, rector of Coates. John left the estate, with the adjoining Downs farm in Lechlade, to Mary Cripps of Cirencester. She contracted to sell her estate in 1799 to Joseph Pitt, and Pitt soon afterwards contracted to sell it to Michael Hicks Beach who took possession in 1799 but did not secure his title until 1821.[51] Stanford farm remained part of the Williamstrip estate until 1866 when it was sold to the farmer George Beak; it then included 436 a., mostly the Downs farm land in Lechlade.[52] In 1906 it belonged to John Davies[53] and in 1919 to Thomas Freer Meade.[54] About 1936 it was bought by the Hinton family which owned and farmed it in 1976.[55] The house, which became known as Stanford Hall, was rebuilt by George Beak in 1868.[56] By 1976 it had been alienated from the estate, which was farmed from a new farm-house built near by.

The rectory of Southrop, belonging to the Hospitallers, included a plough-land in 1341[57] but it comprised only the corn tithes with a barn and close in 1537 when it was leased at £4 2s. to John Lord, vicar of Southrop, and others.[58] The Crown leased the rectory to William Hearle from 1582[59] and in 1590 granted it to John Wells and Richard Pate.[60] In 1612 William Swayne and his wife Bridget conveyed it to Robert Keble.[61] Robert conveyed it in 1616 to Thomas Tempest[62] and Thomas with others conveyed it to Francis Tubb and Richard Vokins in 1630.[63] In 1664 Thomas Keble acquired a moiety of the rectory from the Tubb family[64] and he settled it on the marriage of his daughter Elizabeth to Richard Eyloe of Shrivenham (Berks.) in 1686.[65] Richard settled it on his son Richard in 1716 and the younger Richard (d. 1750) left it to his wife Mary and after her death to a relation Mary Keble. From after Mary Keble's death Richard granted the moiety to supplement the income of the vicars of Southrop and pay a parish schoolmaster, but those provisions were declared void under the legislation on charitable gifts and on Mary's death in 1790 Richard's heirs Thomas Tyler of Minchinhampton and Sarah, wife of Daniel Mills of Chalford, took possession. They

sold the moiety in 1791 to Mary Jenner but later had to recompense Eleanor, wife of Thomas Hassal, who established her claim as another coheir of Eyloe.[66]

The other moiety of the rectory had passed by 1719 to Robert Jenner of Marston Maisey (Wilts.) who was succeeded at his death in 1742 by his son John (d. 1787). John's daughter and heir Mary re-united the two moieties and sold the rectory in 1802 to John Tuckwell (d. 1826), whose son John[67] sold it in 1833 to Sir Michael Hicks Beach. Sir Michael, who received a rent-charge of £309 for the tithes in 1840, sold the rectory in 1842 to C. R. Smith[68] who sold it to Wadham College in 1858.[69]

ECONOMIC HISTORY. In 1086 Southrop manor had 4 teams in demesne and 12 *servi*; 20 a. of meadow were also recorded.[70] In 1297 the St. Philiberts' part of the manor had in demesne 2 plough-lands, comprising 192 a. in all, and 20 a. of meadow[71] but by 1333 the arable on that estate had been reduced to 100 a. and the meadow to 10 a.[72] The Greys' estate in 1315 had in demesne 160 a. of arable, 8 a. of meadow, and a several pasture.[73] Part, at least, of the demesne land at Southrop was leased out to tenants by 1383, and the former demesne of the Greys' estate was granted on a 70-year lease in 1409.[74] In 1591 the demesne land occupied by the farmer of the manor included 400 a. of open-field land, 65½ a. in closes, and rights in various meadows including 10 a. in Kempsford.[75]

In 1086 the tenants of the manor were 16 *villani* and 6 bordars who, with a priest, shared 8 plough-teams.[76] The St. Philiberts' estate had 16 tenants in 1297, including 8 customary yardlanders each holding 24 a.[77] In 1333 that estate had 3 free tenants, 6 customary tenants whose services had been commuted for cash rents, 6 customary tenants owing works, and 3 cottars.[78] In 1315 on the Greys' estate there were 4 free tenants with a total of 46 a., 11 customary tenants with 276 a., and 4 cottars.[79] By the late 16th century there was only one freehold estate, that owned by the Kebles, a family which was also prominent among the copyholders. In 1591 there were 7 copyholders mostly with fairly large estates, including one of 5 yardlands and another of 4½ yardlands.[80] Copies were granted for 3 lives, and a life could be replaced in return for a fine valued at a year's purchase.[81] By 1608 there were also some parcels of former demesne land held on leases for years and also two cottage tenements.[82]

[51] Ibid. Southrop est. papers 1704–58.
[52] Ibid. Stanford fm. papers 1821–67.
[53] *Kelly's Dir. Glos.* (1906), 296.
[54] Ibid. (1919), 226; cf. Wadham Coll. Mun. 61/E 32.
[55] Ex inf. Mr. R. W. Hinton.
[56] Date and monogram on bldg.
[57] *Inq. Non.* (Rec. Com.), 417.
[58] E 309/Box 1/3 Eliz./1 no. 4.
[59] *Cal. Pat.* 1572–5, pp. 276–7.
[60] C 66/1351 m. 19.
[61] C.P. 25(2)/298/10 Jas. I. Trin. no. 7.
[62] C.P. 25(2)/298/14 Jas. I Mich. no. 41.
[63] C.P. 25(2)/420/5 Chas. I Hil. no. 9.
[64] C.P. 25(2)/656/16 Chas. II Trin. no. 19.
[65] Glos. R.O., D 2440, deeds of Southrop rectory and Lechlade 1683–99.

[66] Ibid. deeds of Southrop rectory and Lechlade 1716–1827.
[67] Ibid. Southrop est. papers 1715–1841, abs. of title 1832.
[68] Ibid. Southrop est. papers 1842–55; G.D.R., T 1/167.
[69] Glos. R.O., D 2440, Southrop est. papers 1856–7.
[70] *Dom. Bk.* (Rec. Com.), i. 168v.
[71] C 145/57 no. 33.
[72] *Inq. p.m. Glos.* 1301–58, 248.
[73] Ibid. 139.
[74] Wadham Coll. Mun. 61/B 1.
[75] D.L. 42/116 f. 83v.
[76] *Dom. Bk.* (Rec. Com.), i. 168v.
[77] C145/57 no. 33.
[78] *Inq. p.m. Glos.* 1301–58, 248.
[79] Ibid. 139–40. [80] D.L. 42/116 f. 83 and v.
[81] Ibid. f. 84; Wadham Coll. Mun. 61/C 10.
[82] Wadham Coll. Mun. 61/C 2.

The parish contained two open fields, the north field lying north-west of the village and the south field to the south; they covered a total of 855 a. in 1615.[83] In the west part of the parish lay the common downs covering 100 a.[84] In the east by the Leach was some rich meadow land; that on the St. Philiberts' estate was valued at 18*d.* per acre in 1297 compared to a value of 3*d.* per acre put on the arable land,[85] and within a few years the value of the meadow on both manor estates had risen to 2*s.* per acre.[86] In 1591 there were 67 a. of common meadow called the Moors lying by the Leach, and the tenants also had pasture rights in certain meadows on the demesne.[87] As in all the surrounding parishes sheep were pastured fairly extensively. There was a sheep-house at the site of the manor in 1588[88] and a shepherd was recorded in the parish in 1608.[89]

The parish was inclosed in the early 17th century under agreements made in the manor court. One of the incentives for the inclosure was probably the need to define more clearly the boundary with Eastleach Martin. The tenants of Eastleach Martin and Southrop intercommoned in the downs in the late 16th century,[90] and the lands of Coate farm, a demesne estate of the dean and chapter of Gloucester in Eastleach, and of Prior's Coate, an estate there formerly belonging to Malvern Priory, apparently lay intermingled with those of the Southrop manor estate.[91] In 1599 the lessee of the manor, Thomas Conway, suggested a limited inclosure to consolidate his demesne estate but the Southrop tenants, whose relationship with Conway had for some time been strained, rejected his proposal.[92] In 1616, however, a complete inclosure of the parish was agreed and in 1618 six arbitrators, two each representing Wadham College, the dean and chapter, and the tenants, were chosen to carry it through. Besides the freeholders (who included John Blomer as owner of Prior's Coate) all the copyholders were party to the agreement and had lands allotted in right of their estates. The inclosure was completed after the harvest of 1621[93] although the division of rights in the meadows between Coate farm and the manorial demesne continued to give difficulty for some years afterwards.[94]

The inclosure of the parish facilitated sub-letting and the emergence of larger farms. The land was held under Wadham by copyhold, leasehold for lives, or 20-year leases renewable after 7 years. By the 18th century, however, the copyholders and leaseholders, mostly members of the Chaunler, Tuckwell, D'Oyley, and Keble families,[95] did not usually farm their land but let it to tenants-at-will. The main farms were made up of land held from two or three different copyholders and lease-holders[96] and by 1842 the complexity of tenures had made the identification of some of the lands named in the original copies and leases a difficult task.[97]

In 1798 the two biggest farms in the parish had 424 a. and 381 a. respectively, two others had *c.* 100 a., and two more *c.* 75 a.; there were also a few smaller holdings.[98] In 1840, when Sir Michael Hicks Beach held most of the parish by various tenures, his estate was organized as three main farms: Manor farm with its farm-house near the church and additional buildings at Hook's Farm in the west part of the parish had 371 a.; 234 a. were farmed from a house in the village later called Southrop Farm; and *c.* 300 a. of the parish were included in Stanford farm.[99] After 1857 when Wadham College bought in the bulk of the leasehold and copyhold land[1] it leased most of the estate in a single large unit. W. J. Edmonds farmed 1,054 a. from the manor-house in 1868,[2] and Stanford farm, which included land in Lechlade, was the only other farm of any size based in the parish.[3] In 1926 Thomas Arkell farmed all but a small part of the manor estate, although it was offered for sale in that year as three separate farms, based on Manor Farm, Southrop Farm, and Hook's Farm.[4] A number of small holdings still remained at that time, seven of under 50 a. being returned in 1926.[5] In 1976 most of the land of the parish belonged either to Manor farm or to Hinton & Sons.

The farms of the parish were predominantly arable.[6] In 1798 the proportion of arable to pasture was 964 a. to 425 a.[7] and in 1840 1,011 a. to 393 a.[8] The soil was generally light and dry and in 1798 a six-field rotation was the general practice in the parish, with wheat, barley, and oats in three of the years, and in the other three presumably roots and grassland leys to provide feed for the sheep.[9] In 1842, however, some heavier soil required a three-course rotation of wheat, beans, and either vetches or a fallow,[10] and some land on Stanford farm was in need of draining in 1857.[11] In parts of the manor estate W. J. Edmonds threw two or three fields together before 1868 to facilitate steam-ploughing.[12] The pattern of agriculture suffered relatively

[83] Ibid. C 4.
[84] D.L. 42/116 f. 84; cf. Wadham Coll. Mun. 35/1.
[85] C 145/57 no. 33.
[86] *Inq. p.m. Glos.* 1301–58, 139, 248.
[87] D.L. 42/116 f. 84; cf. Wadham Coll. Mun. 35/1.
[88] D.L. 44/417.   [89] Smith, *Men and Armour*, 262.
[90] D.L. 42/116 f. 84.
[91] Cf. Glos. R.O., D 540/E 4/3.
[92] Wadham Coll. Mun. 61/C 1; cf. ibid. B 5.
[93] Ibid. C 6; Glos. R.O., D 540/T 29.
[94] Wadham Coll. Mun. 61/C 7.
[95] Ibid E 4–6; Glos. R.O., D 2440, Southrop est. papers 1807–62.
[96] Wadham Coll. Mun. 61/E 5.
[97] Glos. R.O., D 2440, Southrop est. papers 1807–62, letters 11, 13 May 1842.
[98] Wadham Coll. Mun. 61/E 5.

[99] Glos. R.O., D 2440, Southrop est. papers 1807–62; cf. G.D.R., T 1/167.
[1] Glos. R.O., D 2440, Southrop est. papers 1856–7.
[2] Wadham Coll. Mun. 61/E 30.
[3] *Kelly's Dir. Glos.* (1870), 635; Glos. R.O., D 2440, Stanford fm. papers 1821–67.
[4] Wadham Coll. Mun. 61/E 32.
[5] M.A.F. 68/3295/8.
[6] Atkyns, *Glos.* 678; Rudder, *Glos.* 680.
[7] Wadham Coll. Mun. 61/E 5.
[8] G.D.R., T 1/167.
[9] Wadham Coll. Mun. 61/E 5; cf. *Trans. B.G.A.S.* lxviii. 181.
[10] Glos. R.O., D 2440, Southrop est. papers 1807–62, letter 11 May 1842.
[11] Ibid. Stanford fm. papers 1821–67.
[12] Wadham Coll. Mun. 61/E 30.

little alteration until the middle years of the 20th century. The late-19th-century slump brought some decline in cereals but little arable went out of cultivation, largely because of a greater use of leys in the rotation. The number of sheep kept, returned at 1,481 in 1866, was down by only a few hundred in 1896 and 1926, and the number of cattle, between 100 and 200, was not significantly altered during the period.[13] In 1976, however, dairy and beef cattle, of which 682 were returned, were an important element in local farming and arable cultivation was concentrated on wheat and barley; sheep were still kept in considerable numbers[14] and included a well-known flock of Dorset Horn on Manor farm.[15]

The mill on the manor in 1086[16] was presumably the later Southrop mill standing on the Leach at the east end of the village. A third share in the mill belonged to the Greys' estate in the 13th and 14th centuries.[17] The mill remained part of the manor estate later and was never more than a small cornmill,[18] though it had a malt-house attached in 1684.[19] It apparently ceased to grind corn c. 1912,[20] but the wheel was still in use for pumping water to the manor-house in 1926.[21] The 17th-century mill-house and buildings had been restored for use as a private house by 1976.

A weaver, a smith, and a carpenter were the only non-agricultural workers listed in 1608[22] and only the basic village trades are recorded later. In 1831 12 families gained a livelihood by trade as compared to 48 supported by agriculture.[23] In the 19th century the tradesmen usually included at least two shopkeepers, two carpenters, a blacksmith, and a bootmaker, and the last three trades survived until the 1930s. A stonemason worked in the village in 1856 and another inhabitant was employed as a land surveyor.[24] A firm of agricultural merchants, originally established in Eastleach Martin by Robert Hinton, who farmed land in Southrop from 1928, built premises at Southrop Farm in 1953. It took over another business based at Lechlade in 1969, and in 1976, as R. Hinton & Sons, Yarnold & Gale Ltd., its business included the manufacture and distribution of animal feed and the sale of fertilizers and agricultural chemicals.[25]

LOCAL GOVERNMENT. The Southrop manor court also exercised view of frankpledge. The St. Philiberts retained the frankpledge jurisdiction in the 13th and 14th centuries when the Greys apparently held a separate manor court for their estate.[26] The court also administered the assize of ale and in the late 14th and early 15th centuries heard pleas of debt and trespass. It appointed a constable and a tithingman and, in the early 17th century, an ale-taster. In 1606 supervisors of the fields and commons were appointed. With the inclosure and the decline of the frankpledge jurisdiction the court's business became limited to copyhold matters and the care of roads, streams, and ditches. After the early 17th century only one full session of the court a year was held with occasional extra courts for granting new copies. By the early 19th century the court was held less frequently and the last recorded meeting was in 1837.[27]

The parish had two churchwardens and two overseers[28] but no early records of parish government are known to survive. Two surveyors of the highways were appointed in the manor court in the early 17th century. The court also took action to stop any influx of poor people in 1626,[29] but it is unlikely that poor-relief was ever a very serious problem in the parish where proliferation of poor cottagers was restricted by the early inclosure. In the late 18th and early 19th centuries the cost of relief was contained at a reasonable level; there were 14 people on permanent relief in 1803 and only 3 in 1815 though in the latter year there were also 73 people (a large number compared to neighbouring parishes) who received occasional relief.[30] Nine cottages in the village were taken on lease from Wadham College at a nominal rent by the leading inhabitants in 1778 and were apparently used as rent-free accommodation for the poor.[31] In 1836 Southrop became part of the Northleach union[32] and it was in Northleach rural district[33] until the formation of Cotswold district in 1974.

CHURCH. There was a priest at Southrop, and therefore presumably a church, in 1086.[34] Later the church was granted to the Knights Hospitallers and a vicarage had been ordained by 1320.[35] The rectory and the advowson of the vicarage were retained by the Hospitallers,[36] although the bishop collated to the vicarage several times in the 15th century.[37] After the Dissolution the advowson was

[13] M.A.F. 68/25/3; M.A.F. 68/26/10; M.A.F. 68/1609/10; M.A.F. 68/3295/8.
[14] Agric. Returns 1976.   [15] Ex inf. Mrs. Richardson.
[16] Dom. Bk. (Rec. Com.), i. 168v.
[17] C.P. 25(1)/73/12 no. 224; Inq. p.m. Glos. 1301–58, 139.
[18] Wadham Coll. Mun. 61/F 37.
[19] Ibid. E 3.
[20] Kelly's Dir. Glos. (1910 and later edns.).
[21] Wadham Coll. Mun. 61/E 32.
[22] Smith, Men and Armour, 262.
[23] Census, 1831.
[24] G.D.R. Southrop bps. transcr. 1813–24; Kelly's Dir. Glos. (1856 and later edns.).
[25] Ex inf. Mr. M. J. Hinton.
[26] Inq. p.m. Glos. 1301–58, 140, 248.
[27] Ct. rolls survive for 1376–84, 1409, 1425, 1443–4, 1455–6, 1460–1, and 1470–2; for 20 years between 1602 and 1671; for 1681–95; and for 1728–1837: Wadham Coll. Mun. 61/B 1–4, B

[11] There are also rough notes of cts. held in the late 16th and the 17th cents.: ibid. B 5–8.
[28] Hockaday Abs. xliii, 1566 visit. f. 25; Wadham Coll. Mun. 61/F 39.
[29] Wadham Coll. Mun. 61/B 2.
[30] Poor Law Abstract, 1804, 172–3; 1818, 146–7; Poor Law Returns (1830–1), p. 67; (1835), p. 65.
[31] Wadham Coll. Mun. 61/F 39.
[32] Poor Law Com. 2nd Rep. p. 523.
[33] Census, 1911.
[34] Dom. Bk. (Rec. Com.), i. 168v.
[35] Hospitallers in Eng. (Camd. Soc. [1st ser.] lxv), 28; Reg. Cobham, 236. Rudder, Glos. 681, confused the ch. with Souldrop (Beds.) when he stated that it was granted to the Hospitallers by Alice de Clermont; cf. V.C.H. Beds. iii. 95.
[36] Reg. Wakefeld, p. 48; Hockaday Abs. cccxliv, 1498.
[37] Worc. Episc. Reg., Reg. Polton, f. 4v; Reg. Carpenter, i, ff. 145, 181.

kept in hand by the Crown until the early 17th century when it passed with the manor to Wadham College.[38] In 1930 the vicarage was united with the Eastleaches, from which time the advowson of the united benefice alternated between Wadham College, the Lord Chancellor, and the dean and chapter of Gloucester.[39]

The vicarage included the small tithes and 48 a. of arable land in 1535,[40] and in 1738 the glebe totalled 58 a.[41] The vicarage house, recorded from 1584,[42] stands on the main village street west of the church. It apparently dates mainly from a rebuilding of c. 1810 but it was extended to the east in 1882.[43] It was sold after 1930, the incumbent of the united benefice residing at Eastleach Martin. The vicarage was valued at £4 14s. in 1535,[44] at £30 in 1650,[45] and at £50 c. 1710.[46] In 1743 it was valued at only £45,[47] but in the 1770s it was said to be worth £100.[48] The vicar's tithes were commuted at £206 in 1840,[49] and in 1851 the value of the benefice was £253.[50]

The vicar John Lord could not repeat the Commandments in 1551.[51] Rannulph Swetnam, vicar 1564–75, had another benefice and in 1572 his curate had two cures and apparently neglected Southrop. Thomas Houghton, vicar 1587–1604,[52] was described as a sufficient scholar but no preacher.[53] Robert Kitson, the vicar in 1650,[54] subscribed at the Restoration and held the living until his death in 1671.[55] Later the living, a relatively poor one, appears to have usually been left to curates; John Powell served during three incumbencies from 1676 until his death in 1731.[56] John Baldwin, vicar 1776–1812,[57] lived near Tenbury (Worcs.) and in 1784 the curate serving the parish lived at Lechlade.[58] From 1823 until 1825 John Keble served as curate at Southrop and lived in the vicarage house; his brother Thomas succeeded him as curate.[59]

The church of *ST. PETER*[60] is built of limestone rubble with ashlar dressings and comprises chancel and a nave with north porch and south transeptal chapel. The nave is of the 12th century and most of the original walling, with the stones laid herringbone fashion,[61] survives together with two windows and the north doorway, which is of two orders with a lattice-decorated tympanum. The 12th-century chancel arch also survives, but the chancel was rebuilt in the 13th century and has a double-lancet east window with plate tracery and single-lancet windows in the side walls, the westernmost having low-side windows beneath them. The south transept was added in the earlier 14th century and the blocked south doorway is also of that period though probably replacing an earlier doorway in the same position. The nave walls were heightened in the 15th century and the western one largely rebuilt; several new windows were also put in. The original bellcot was incorporated within the new west gable, but in 1858 there was a wooden belfry above the gable.[62] There are three aumbries and two piscinas in the chancel and above the chancel arch is a squint which gave a view of the high altar from the rood loft, recorded in 1563.[63] Other squints on each side of the chancel arch are now entirely of the 19th century but presumably reproduce medieval predecessors.

At a restoration carried out c. 1852[64] the chancel was reroofed and a gallery removed from the south chapel.[65] There was a further restoration in 1895[66] and the new stone bellcot and two Norman-style windows, replacing an original Norman window and a 15th-century window in the nave, were apparently added then.[67]

The richly decorated font dates from the 12th century; the bowl is carved with an arcade filled with figure sculpture showing the Virtues overcoming the Vices.[68] Effigies of Sir Thomas Conway (d. 1605 or 1606) and his wife Elizabeth,[69] originally on a tomb in the south chapel, were moved to the sanctuary in the 19th century and the coat of arms from the same tomb was placed in the chancel.[70] A fragment of glass in a window in the chapel is painted with the arms of Roach,[71] a family not otherwise known to be connected with Southrop. One of the two bells was cast by Thomas Rudhall in 1774.[72] The plate includes an Elizabethan chalice.[73] The parish registers survive from 1656 for marriages and burials and from 1680 for christenings.[74]

NONCONFORMITY. Houses at Southrop were registered by dissenters in 1835[75] and 1849[76] but no later record of any meeting in the parish has been found.

[38] Hockaday Abs. cccxliv.
[39] *Glouc. Dioc. Yr. Bk.* (1976), 66–7.
[40] *Valor Eccl.* (Rec. Com.), ii. 446.
[41] G.D.R., V 5/280T 2.
[42] E178/889.
[43] Glos. R.O., D 1381/143.
[44] *Valor Eccl.* (Rec. Com.), ii. 446.
[45] *Trans. B.G.A.S.* lxxxiii. 94.
[46] Atkyns, *Glos.* 678.
[47] G.D.R. vol. 397, f. 88.
[48] Rudder, *Glos.* 680.
[49] G.D.R., T 1/167.
[50] H.O. 129/341/1/1/1.
[51] *E.H.R.* xix. 114.
[52] Hockaday Abs. cccxliv.
[53] Ibid. lii, 1593 state of clergy, f. 9.
[54] *Trans. B.G.A.S.* lxxxiii. 94.
[55] Hockaday Abs. cccxliv.
[56] Ibid.; Bigland, *Glos.* iii, no. 246.
[57] Hockaday Abs. cccxliv.

[58] G.D.R. vols. 319; 382, f. 16.
[59] Hockaday Abs. cccxliv.
[60] The dedication is recorded from 1743: G.D.R. vol. 397, f. 88.
[61] See plate facing p. 141.
[62] *Glos. Ch. Notes*, 108.
[63] Hockaday Abs. cccxliv.
[64] *Kelly's Dir. Glos.* (1856), 356.
[65] *Glos. Ch. Notes*, 108; Bigland, *Glos.* iii, no. 246.
[66] *Kelly's Dir. Glos.* (1906), 296.
[67] *Trans. B.G.A.S.* xxii. 54.
[68] Ibid. xxxvii. 109–11.
[69] Wadham Coll. Mun. 61/A 6–7.
[70] Roper, *Glos. Effigies*, 647–51.
[71] *Trans. B.G.A.S.* xlvii. 334.
[72] *Glos. Ch. Bells*, 64.
[73] *Glos. Ch. Plate*, 189.
[74] *B. & G. Par. Rec.* 247.
[75] Hockaday Abs. cccxliv.
[76] Glos. R.O., Q/RZ 1.

EDUCATION. After an abortive scheme of Richard Eyloe (d. 1750)[77] it was apparently not until 1827 that any further move was made to provide schooling at Southrop. A day-school started then had 20 children, paid for by their parents, in 1833 when there was also a Sunday school supported by the clergy.[78] Attendance at the day-school had risen to 39 by 1847 when the income was supplemented by subscriptions, but there was no secured schoolroom[79] until one was built on the north side of the village street in 1850. Wadham College, which apparently paid for the building, provided most of the income in 1864, when school pence were also charged. The school, managed by the vicar, then had an average attendance of 50,[80] rising to 80 by 1885.[81] By 1904, however, the attendance was down to 49[82] and it remained at 50–60 during the earlier 20th century.[83] In 1976, when the school also served the Eastleaches, there were 38 children on the roll.[84]

CHARITIES FOR THE POOR. About 1700 a Mr. Bush gave £100 for the poor.[85] The sum was placed out on personal security and was for many years in the hands of James Chaunler (d. 1760). Chaunler was later said to have made no payment in respect of it but in his will he claimed to have paid £5 to the poor each year and he charged his estate with the continuance of the payment. His insolvency led, however, to the loss of part of the principal and what was recovered was invested in stock and left for many years to recover its original value. Payments were not apparently resumed until the 1820s.[86] In 1836 Alexander Townsend of Theescombe, Minchinhampton, left £100 for bread and blankets for the poor at Christmas.[87] The two charities produced an income of £6 14s. in 1856[88] and were regulated by a Scheme of 1969.[89] In the 1970s when the income was c. £3 a year it was used to provide firewood for pensioners or set aside to accumulate to meet particular cases of need.[90]

[77] Ibid. D 2240, deeds of Southrop rectory and Lechlade 1716–1827.
[78] *Educ. Enquiry Abstract*, 326.
[79] *Church School Inquiry, 1846–7*, 16–17.
[80] Ed. 7/35/295.
[81] *Kelly's Dir. Glos.* (1885), 570.
[82] *Public Elem. Schs. 1906*, 189.
[83] *Bd. of Educ., List 21, 1911* (H.M.S.O.), 166; *1922*, 107; *1932*, 118; *1936*, 124.

[84] Ex inf. county educ. dept.
[85] Called Thos. Bush in Atkyns, *Glos.* 678, and John in *20th Rep. Com. Char.* 29.
[86] *20th Rep. Com. Char.* 29–30; Glos. R.O., D 2440, Southrop est. papers 1704–58, abs. of title Jan. 1842.
[87] Bigland, *Glos.* iii, no. 246.
[88] *Kelly's Dir. Glos.* (1856), 356.
[89] Char. Com. Reg.
[90] Ex inf. Mrs. Richardson.

RAPSGATE HUNDRED

RAPSGATE hundred in 1086 comprised Brimpsfield (which then included Cranham), North Cerney, Chedworth, Colesbourne, Cowley, Elkstone, Rendcomb, Syde, most of Coberley, and part of the Duntisbournes, a total of 78 hides and 1 yardland.[1] The Duntisbourne land, which became known as Duntisbourne Leer from the ownership of an estate there by Lire Abbey (Eure),[2] later formed part of Duntisbourne Abbots parish in Crowthorne and Minety hundred but remained in Rapsgate.[3] Part of Coberley, later called Little or Upper Coberley, belonged to Bradley hundred in 1086 as a member of Northleach manor[4] and remained in that hundred.[5] Eycot, later part of Rendcomb parish, was a member of Bibury manor[6] and passed with it into Brightwells Barrow hundred;[7] in the post-medieval period, however, it was not distinguished as part of that hundred, having lost its separate identity within Rendcomb as a manor and hamlet. Upper Coberley and Eycot are both treated below under their respective parishes.

Rapsgate hundred was one of the Seven Hundreds of Cirencester granted to Cirencester Abbey in 1189; their descent and liberties are described in another volume.[8] Among the estates of Rapsgate hundred exemption from the hundredal frankpledge jurisdiction was secured by the 13th century for Rendcomb, where the earls of Gloucester held a court which also had jurisdiction over the tithings of Calmsden and Woodmancote in North Cerney parish, and for Cowley, where Pershore Abbey claimed to hold a view under a charter of 1227. In Cowley the rights of the lord of the hundred were apparently further limited by the lord of the manor's right to use gallows and other instruments of punishment,[9] while at Rendcomb the earls of Gloucester also claimed return of writs.[10] At Brimpsfield by an agreement made in the 1230s the view was held in the manor court by the abbot of Cirencester's bailiffs, the lord of the manor taking the profits and paying an annual composition;[11] the same court also had jurisdiction over Cranham.[12] Chedworth also had a separate view held within the parish, but the profits of that were retained by the abbey. Another separate view was held in the manor of Marsden (in Rendcomb and Chedworth), where the abbey's bailiffs were given hospitality after they had held the hundred view at Rapsgate near by.[13]

The other places in the hundred—Cerney, Coberley, Colesbourne, Duntisbourne Leer, and Elkstone and Syde (which together formed a single tithing)—all attended the hundred view held twice a year at Rapsgate in the south part of Colesbourne parish on an ancient road from Cirencester to Colesbourne.[14] The tithings where the hundred had full rights were also liable to the watching duty known as wardstaff,[15] recorded in 1394 and apparently commuted by the later 16th century for the fine called wake that was paid at the view.[16]

[1] *Dom. Bk.* (Rec. Com.), i. 164 and v., 166, 167v.–168v., 169v.
[2] Ibid. 166, 167v.
[3] *Glos. Subsidy Roll, 1327,* 10; Rudder, *Glos.* 423.
[4] *Dom. Bk.* (Rec. Com.), i. 164v.
[5] *Glos. Subsidy Roll, 1327,* 12; Rudder, *Glos.* 399.
[6] *Dom. Bk.* (Rec. Com.), i. 164v.
[7] *Glos. Subsidy Roll, 1327,* 14.
[8] *V.C.H. Glos.* xi. 152.

[9] *Plac. de Quo Warr.* (Rec. Com.), ii. 253, 259–60.
[10] *Rot. Hund.* (Rec. Com.), i. 181.
[11] *Ciren. Cart.* i, pp. 214–16.
[12] Ibid. ii, p. 620.
[13] Ibid. p. 619.
[14] Ibid. pp. 618–19; C 115/K 2/6683 ff. 268–9.
[15] *Ciren. Cart.* ii, p. 634.
[16] Glos. Colln. JV 1.5.

Rapsgate hundred comprises an area of the Cotswolds extending from the escarpment above Gloucester in the west to the valley of the river Coln in the east. The valley of the river Churn forms the central feature of the landscape but most of the hundred is on the high wolds at 200–300 m. The land is formed mainly by the Great Oolite with the underlying strata of fuller's earth, the Inferior Oolite, and the Lower Lias outcropping in the valleys. There is extensive ancient woodland at both ends of the hundred in Cranham and Chedworth parishes, and landscaping and planting by the landowners along the Churn has given its valley the appearance of a continuous park.

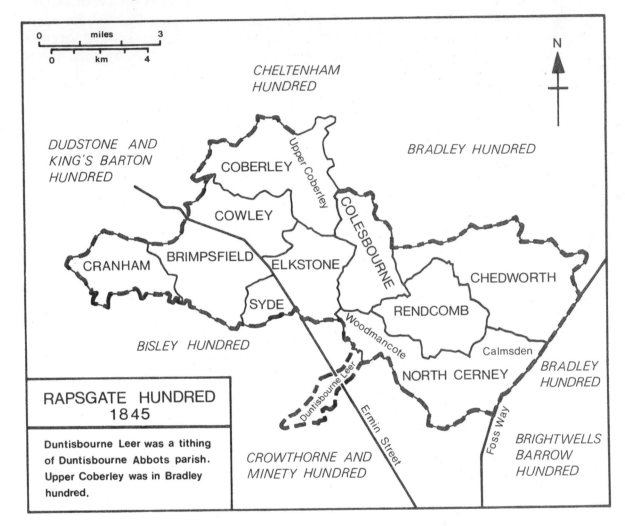

The Foss way provides part of the east boundary of the hundred while Ermin Street from Cirencester to Gloucester crosses the high ground of the west part. The White way, the Calf way, and the Welsh way were among lesser ancient routes which crossed the hills. The era of turnpikes emphasized the importance of the two main Roman roads and of other routes such as the Gloucester–Oxford road by Seven Springs in Coberley parish and the old road from Cheltenham to Cirencester and Tetbury through Elkstone, but the main improvement came in 1825 with the building of the new Cheltenham–Cirencester road along the Churn valley. Only one railway line, the Midland and South Western Junction built through Chedworth in 1891, entered the hundred.

The villages of the hundred, established near crossing-points in the Churn valley or near springs in the coombs of the high wolds, are mainly small nucleated settlements. Cranham, however, is of a more dispersed nature, reflecting its establishment in woodland, and Chedworth was enlarged during the 18th century into a long straggling settlement. Some of the parishes have one or two small hamlets but other hamlets have disappeared, two in Chedworth as a result of agricultural depression in the 14th century and Eycot in Rendcomb and Stockwell in Cowley through the actions of landowners. Most of the villages, which are built of the local oolite, have some cottages and farm-houses of the 17th and 18th centuries, but in several the character is set by 19th-century estate cottages, while the larger houses, notably Rendcomb Park and Cowley Manor, were built by 19th-century landowners.

In the Middle Ages much of the land belonged to monasteries, including Gloucester Abbey, Pershore Abbey, and Llanthony Priory, or to magnates like the earls of Warwick, who held Chedworth, and the Giffards, who had a castle at Brimpsfield. In later centuries lesser local families like the Pooles and Partridges shared the land with more substantial owners like the Guises, Cravens, and Howes. In the mid 19th century a marked feature of the area was the purchase of estates by successful businessmen, including the Lancashire cotton-manufacturers William Hall and Theodore Crewdson and the financiers Sir Francis Goldsmid and James Hutchinson.

Agriculture suffered virtually no challenge from industry as the source of employment in the hundred. Sheep-farming was an important element in local farming from early in the Middle Ages and after the inclosure of the open fields and the introduction of roots and grassland leys was closely integrated with the arable rotation. Following the inclosures much of the land was formed into large farms, some as much as 1,000 a. (405 ha.). The late-19th-century depression brought changes in the pattern of agriculture with much land being taken in hand by the landowners and new enterprises such as dairy-farming being introduced. Some isolated fulling-mills were worked in the Middle Ages and later but the only indigenous industry apart from stoneworking to employ much labour was the potteries established at Cranham in the late 18th century and the 19th. Most of the villages remained essentially estate villages, but Chedworth attracted a considerable population of independent craftsmen and was the only place in the hundred where nonconformity gained a firm footing. In the 1970s most of the villages remained isolated and undeveloped, though many of the old farm-houses and cottages had been modernized and extended.

BRIMPSFIELD

THE RURAL PARISH of Brimpsfield lies above the Cotswold escarpment 10 km. south of Cheltenham. Brimpsfield village, the primary settlement of a manor and ecclesiastical parish which originally included Cranham to the west, was once the site of a castle and a priory. The parish, which also included part of Birdlip village, the hamlet of Caudle Green, and several outlying farmsteads, was approximately diamond-shaped. The boundaries, which contained 2,729 a., were determined by the crest of the escarpment on the north-west and the main Gloucester–Cirencester road, the Roman Ermin Street, on the north-east. In the north that road marked the division of Birdlip village between Brimpsfield and Cowley parishes. Elsewhere the boundaries followed streams and field boundaries. The bank forming part of the south-western boundary[1] probably marked the earlier limit of Hazel Hanger wood. After 121 a. at Birdlip were transferred to Cowley in 1935, the parish covered 2,608 a. (1.055 ha.).[2] The following account concerns the parish as it existed until 1935 and those parts of Birdlip village which lay in Cowley and Great Witcombe.

The parish lies almost entirely above the 183-m. contour and is mainly formed by a plateau of rolling country which rises to over 290 m. near the escarpment where it affords wide views north-westwards across the Vale of Gloucester. Most of the plateau, which is broken by the valleys of several streams draining southwards into the river Frome, lies on the Inferior Oolite, overlaid in places by bands of fuller's earth, but parts, including Brimpsfield village in the centre, are on the Great Oolite. Most of the outlying farmsteads stand near the valleys, the bottoms of which are formed by Midford Sand.[3] A reservoir was built in 1884 to guarantee a regular water-supply for Birdlip.[4]

The parish contains large areas of arable and grassland and, in the valleys, much woodland. Only remnants of the open fields remained in the centre of the parish in 1842 when they were inclosed. The extensive beech woodland, part of the Brimpsfield estate in the later 11th century[5] and subject to common pasture rights by the early 14th,[6] centred on Cranham but included Buckle wood in Brimpsfield.[7] That wood, which covered 109 a. in 1837,[8]

passed with the Cranham property acquired in 1871 by William Frederick Hicks Beach[9] and measured 82 a. c. 1942.[10]

A park had been created in Brimpsfield by 1227.[11] In 1261 the lord of the manor was granted 15 deer to stock it[12] and in the mid 14th century a tenement at Bentham in Badgeworth was held from him by the service of carrying a horn in the park whenever he hunted between the feasts of the Assumption and Nativity of the Virgin (15 Aug.–8 Sept.).[13] The park lay south-east of the village[14] but in 1338 the 200 a. of park-land on the manor also included 100 a. of beeches,[15] possibly at Hazel Hanger wood in the west; that wood had been inclosed by a stone wall by 1379 and was described as a park in 1447.[16] A warren of 60 a. was also mentioned in 1338.[17] In the 15th century the park-land and woodland were administered together.[18] Hazel Hanger wood contained 117 a. in 1807,[19] and in 1901 the parish retained 342¾ a. of woodland,[20] including the small Calley wood in the south which had been granted to the lord of Miserden in 1308.[21] A fishpond created on the south-western boundary near Climperwell in Cranham by 1227,[22] had been filled in by 1807[23] but another pond was created there after 1926.[24]

The lord of the manor's levying of toll at Wortwold, evidently Woodhill green between Buckle and Hazel Hanger woods, in the mid 13th century[25] indicates the importance of a route which crossed the northern part of the parish and was known as Potters or Pothook Lane in 1786 when parts were closed.[26] Ermin Street remained an important thoroughfare[27] and the section from the top of Birdlip hill to Cirencester, which was in a bad state in the late 17th and early 18th centuries,[28] was turnpiked in 1747.[29] As a result of the growing importance of Cheltenham the route from Painswick through Birdlip was turnpiked in 1785.[30] It was straightened south-west of the village the following year but its junction with Ermin Street was moved westwards a few years later.[31] The section from Cranham (formerly Prinknash) Corner in Cranham was included in an Act of 1853 providing an alternative route between Gloucester and the top of Birdlip Hill,[32] and the road joining it in Buckle wood was turnpiked in 1800 as part of a

[1] *O.S. Area Bk.* (1884). This account was written in 1977.
[2] *Census*, 1931 (pt. ii); 1971.
[3] Geol. Surv. Map 1″, solid, sheet 44 (1856 edn.).
[4] 'Birdlip and Brimpsfield. The Story of Two Villages 1850–1957' (W.I. hist. 1959, copy in Glos. R.O. Libr.), 33–4.
[5] *Hist. & Cart. Mon. Glouc.* (Rolls Ser.), i. 63.
[6] *Inq. p.m. Glos.* 1302–58, 275.
[7] *P.N. Glos.* (E.P.N.S.), i. 145.
[8] G.D.R., T 1/38.
[9] Glos. R.O., D 1042, Miserden, Winstone, Brimpsfield, and Cranham deeds 1647–1776; D 2299/2893.
[10] Payne, *Glos. Survey*, 65.
[11] *Flaxley Cart.* ed. A. W. Crawley-Boevey (Exeter, 1887), 74.
[12] *Close R.* 1261–4, 9.
[13] *Cal. Inq. p.m.* ix, p. 163.
[14] Cf. G.D.R., V 5/56T 1.
[15] *Inq. p.m. Glos.* 1302–58, 275.
[16] S.C. 6/850/22; S.C. 6/850/26 rot. 3.
[17] *Inq. p.m. Glos.* 1302–58, 275.

[18] S.C. 6/850/26 rot. 3; *Cal. Pat.* 1467–77, 439; 1476–85, 283.
[19] Brimpsfield and Syde terrier 1807: copy in Glos. Colln. 11922.
[20] Acreage Returns, 1901.
[21] *Cat. Anct. D.* i, A 931.
[22] *Flaxley Cart.* 75; cf. S.C. 6/850/26 rot. 3.
[23] Cf. Brimpsfield and Syde terrier 1807; G.D.R., T 1/38.
[24] Cf. Glos. R.O., D 2299/4104.
[25] *Ciren. Cart.* i, pp. 216–17; cf. Glos. Colln. RQ 56.1; G.D.R., T 1/38.
[26] Glos. R.O., Q/SRh 1786 B.
[27] Ogilby, *Britannia* (1675), p. 29.
[28] Glos. R.O., DC/E 88/1/1, 4; Atkyns, *Glos.* 373.
[29] Cirencester Roads Act, 20 Geo. II, c. 23.
[30] Cheltenham Roads Act, 25 Geo. III, c. 125.
[31] Cf. Glos. R.O., Q/SRh 1786 B; G.D.R., T 1/38.
[32] Upton St. Leonards Roads Act, 16 & 17 Vic. c. 126 (Local and Personal); cf. Glos. R.O., SL 5.

BRIMPSFIELD CHURCH from the south-west

ELKSTONE CHURCH from the south-east

SOUTHROP CHURCH:
herring-bone masonry in the nave

QUENINGTON CHURCH:
the north doorway

ALDSWORTH CHURCH:
14th-century decoration on the north aisle

SYDE CHURCH:
medieval door handle

new Stroud–Cheltenham route.[33]

Brimpsfield village stands 1.5 km. west of Ermin Street. The parish church, which had been built by the 12th century, stands a short distance north-east of the village and overlooks a valley containing the site of an early castle and Brimpsfield Park house. House platforms visible west of the churchyard in 1977 indicate that the village, or much of it, was displaced probably in the 12th century, when a second castle was built to the south. By the mid 13th century there was a priory adjoining the northern side of the churchyard.[34] The ruins of the later castle provided a quarry for buildings in the village, which lies along a street running from north to south with a lane leading westwards on the Knapp. East of the street Brimpsfield House, which dates from the 17th century, was the farm-house of a freehold estate in the early 19th century when a south wing was added.[35] In the early 20th century it became the home of Wilfrid Wait, owner of the Brimpsfield estate,[36] and the east end of the main range was considerably extended and a medieval chimney incorporated in a gable. The field on the opposite side of the street contains traces of a building. On the Knapp the Old Malthouse dates from the early 18th century and an outbuilding is dated 1789.[37] Yew Tree Farm to the north was built in the 19th century. Houses built in the mid 1950s included a council development by the Climperwell road in 1957 when the village had c. 34 houses.[38] A few more houses had been built in the southern part by 1977.

The Romans maintained a settlement on Ermin Street at the top of the escarpment[39] where the village of Birdlip, which had been established by 1221,[40] has continued to serve the needs of travellers. In 1506 two of its inhabitants were presented as brewers in the Cowley frankpledge court,[41] and Thomas Baskerville, a traveller in the early 1680s, noted the entertainment provided by its inns.[42] The only innkeeper listed in Brimpsfield and Cowley parishes in 1608[43] kept an inn at Birdlip which was called the Talbot in 1704[44] and renamed the Red Lion before 1781.[45] It stood east of the Brimpsfield road and was closed after William Metcalfe, rector of Brimpsfield, bought it in 1793. He rebuilt it shortly afterwards as a farm-house, known as Birdlip House, for the freehold

estate which he created.[46] At the top of Birdlip hill stood three inns. The George, so called by 1757,[47] was in the later 19th century the meeting-place of the Cowley frankpledge court[48] and the site of the Cowley pound.[49] The inn, described in 1802 as an old building with four rooms on a floor and stabling,[50] was rebuilt later and by 1897 had been renamed the Royal George hotel.[51] To the south-east the King's Head, described in 1753 as an ancient inn[52] and called the King William in 1837,[53] closed in the late 1860s.[54] It was rebuilt shortly before 1902, when it was a private hotel, and converted c. 1904 as a sanatorium for consumptives.[55] In 1977 it was an antiques shop. The inn with a fine view from its garden in 1796 was probably the Black Horse, west of the Painswick road,[56] where refreshments were being served in a summer-house in 1800[57] and where the Cotteswold Naturalists' Field Club held its first meeting in 1846.[58] It became a temperance hotel in 1890[59] but was leased before 1908 as a private residence.[60]

There were nine houses in Birdlip c. 1710[61] but many buildings, including a school and a former nonconformist chapel, date from the 19th century. Ivy Lodge, which stands south of the Royal George, possibly on the site of cottages called Smiths in 1536,[62] was the farm-house for a small freehold estate from 1614.[63] It was rebuilt in the 19th century, possibly by William Lawrence of Cirencester (d. 1837), who bought the estate from Richard Welch in 1829.[64] Lawrence's initials appear on a barn to the west dated 1829. North of Ermin Street Birdlip Farm, a 17th-century farm-house with later additions, was part of Mary Weedon's Cowley estate in 1848.[65] By 1848 a farm-house to the east had become part of the Ivy Lodge estate, then owned by George Whalley, and was occupied as cottages,[66] later rebuilt. A remodelled 17th-century farm-house stands to the east. At the western end of the village a lodge was built for Witcombe Park in 1845.[67] A police station was built in the late 1940s, and later buildings included a church and a few houses in traditional Cotswold style. In 1957 the village had c. 66 houses.[68] South-west of the village Wood House, a barn on the edge of Buckle wood recorded in 1777, was converted to domestic use in the 19th century.[69]

The buildings on Ermin Street include a group

[33] Lightpill and Birdlip Road Act, 39 & 40 Geo. III, c. 43 (Local and Personal).
[34] Trans. B.G.A.S. lxxxii. 126–42; O.S. Map 6″, Glos. XXXIV. SE. (1903 edn.).
[35] G.D.R., T 1/38.
[36] Cf. Kelly's Dir. Glos. (1906), 49; (1910), 53.
[37] Cf. Glos. R.O., D 2299/4104.
[38] 'Birdlip and Brimpsfield', 71.
[39] R.C.H.M. Glos. i. 39–40.
[40] Cf. Pleas of the Crown for Glos. ed. Maitland, p. 42.
[41] S.C. 2/175/28 rot. 3.
[42] Hist. MSS. Com. 29, 13th Rep. II, Portland, ii, p. 304.
[43] Smith, Men and Armour, 255.
[44] Glos. R.O., D 1866/T 22; D 1229, Brimpsfield deeds 1614–1775.
[45] Ibid. D 150/2.   [46] Ibid. D 2583; G.D.R., T 1/38.
[47] Glos. R.O., DC/E 88/2.   [48] Ibid. 4.
[49] Ibid. D 2440, misc. est. papers 1719–1871, plan 1867.
[50] Ibid. DC/E 88/14.
[51] Kelly's Dir. Glos. (1897), 39.

[52] Glouc. Jnl. 6 Nov. 1753.   [53] G.D.R., T 1/38.
[54] Glos. R.O., D 2440, Brimpsfield and Birdlip papers 1700–1869; Kelly's Dir. Glos. (1870), 474.
[55] Glos. R.O., D 2299/580; ex inf. Miss R. F. Butler, formerly of Birdlip.
[56] Trans. B.G.A.S. xcii. 177; G.D.R., T 1/200.
[57] Glos. N. & Q. i. 346.   [58] Plaque on bldg.
[59] Glos. R.O., D 2440, Great Witcombe, Birdlip, and Brockworth leases 1888–95.
[60] Ibid. est. papers 1908–24.
[61] Atkyns, Glos. 301.   [62] S.C. 11/1022 rot. 1d.
[63] Glos. R.O., D 1229, Brimpsfield deeds 1614–1775.
[64] Ibid. D 2025, Beman fam. deeds; for Wm. Lawrence, see D.N.B., s.v. Chas. Lawrence.
[65] G.D.R., T 1/63.
[66] Ibid.; Glos. R.O., D 2025, Beman fam. deeds.
[67] Susan Hicks Beach, A Cotswold Family: Hicks and Hicks Beach (1909), 365.
[68] 'Birdlip and Brimpsfield', 33, 71, 70.
[69] Taylor, Map of Glos. (1777); G.D.R., T 1/38.

of 19th-century cottages at Parson's Pitch, east of Birdlip. Malthouse Farm, a small farm-house on the road 1 km. north of Brimpsfield village, was destroyed by fire in the early 20th century.[70] Further along the road there was a small settlement at Nettleton by 1777.[71] The Golden Heart inn, which was built there between 1772 and 1796,[72] served Brimpsfield village in 1977.

The hamlet of Caudle Green, in the southern corner of the parish, lies on the side of a valley and is named partly from a source of water.[73] It was apparently settled before 1327, when Thomas of Coldwell was assessed for a subsidy,[74] and there were 15 houses c. 1710[75] and 20 in 1957.[76] Several early cottages have survived. Woodfield House, south-east of the green, dates from the 18th century. Morcombe Farm, higher up to the west, was built in the same century for the Welch family and has a back wing dated 1764 with initials, probably those of William Welch.[77] Caudle Green Farm, north of the green, was built at the end of that century for an estate belonging in turn to the Taylor and Palling families.[78] Below the hamlet to the north-east are a few cottages, including Ostrich Cottage, which as Ham Cottages formerly contained several dwellings.[79]

There was apparently a habitation at Eddington, a farmstead 1 km. NNE. of Caudle Green, by 1241,[80] and in 1706 the lord of Brimpsfield manor sold a messuage there to Matthew Walbank.[81] In the 19th century when it passed with the Syde estate it was known as Hill House Farm but by 1893 it had been abandoned[82] and later the buildings were demolished. At Morcombe, north-west of Caudle Green, a farm-house was built on the Walbank family estate in the mid 18th century.[83] It was used as a cottage by the mid 19th century[84] and was later abandoned. In 1977 the substantial out-buildings, which included a barn dated 1817 with initials acknowledging it as part of William Welch's estate, were derelict.[85]

The tradition that Manless Town, a field north-west of Morcombe recorded in 1622,[86] was once the site of dwellings is supported by archaeological evidence.[87] To the west by the stream Moorhouse, where there was apparently a habitation by 1557,[88]

had become the farm-house for a small freehold estate by the late 18th century.[89] About 1890, after it had been absorbed into the Brimpsfield estate, a small farm-house was built higher to the north-east near the outbuildings. The older house was abandoned in the early 20th century but its overgrown ruins remained visible in 1977.[90] A cottage at Climperwell, to the north-west, was rebuilt as two dwellings after 1837.[91]

The farmstead at Stoneyhill, south-west of Brimpsfield village, includes an early-18th-century farm-house. The farm-house at Blacklains, north-west of the village, was built c. 1820.[92] The house at Watercombe, 1 km. north-east of the village, has been extended and remodelled in the 20th century but the eastern three bays date from the 18th century; the inscription, on a reset plaque above the porch, that William and Mary Barrett built the house in 1712 may record that work. Muzzards across the valley to the south-west dates from 1935.[93]

Some of the 35 tenants recorded on the Brimpsfield estate in 1086 presumably lived on that part which became Cranham.[94] In Brimpsfield 7 people were assessed for the subsidy in 1327[95] and at least 11 for poll tax in 1381.[96] The estimated number of communicants in the parish rose from 77 in 1551[97] to 160 by 1650,[98] and the population from about 200 c. 1710[99] to 283 by c. 1775,[1] to 299 by 1801, and to 443 by 1851. By 1861 it had fallen to 392, and from 425 in 1871 it dropped to 323 by 1901 and to 272 by 1921. By 1931 it had risen to 338, including 73 in the part transferred to Cowley in 1935, and the reduced parish had 219 inhabitants in 1951 and 233 in 1971.[2]

Two friendly societies formed at Birdlip in 1879 and c. 1886 respectively had a total membership of c. 140 in 1957. The assembly room at the Royal George and the summer-house at the Black Horse were used for meetings until c. 1920 when a hut was erected north of the Birdlip school.[3] It was demolished and replaced by a new village hall in 1958.[4] In Brimpsfield a village hall was built north-west of the rectory in the late 1960s.[5]

The achievements of the various landowners are described below. In July 1788 George III rode out to Birdlip from Cheltenham.[6]

[70] 'Birdlip and Brimpsfield', 77.
[71] Taylor, Map of Glos. (1777).
[72] Glos. R.O., 2957/192.165; Glouc. Jnl. 18 Jan. 1796.
[73] P.N. Glos. i. 145.
[74] Glos. Subsidy Roll, 1327, 10.
[75] Atkyns, Glos. 301.
[76] 'Birdlip and Brimpsfield', 81.
[77] Cf. Glos. R.O., D 1229, Brimpsfield deeds 1643–1803.
[78] Ibid. D 1388, Lyon fam., Brimpsfield and Syde papers 1827–30; Bigland, Glos. i. 244; cf. Taylor, Map of Glos. (1777).
[79] O.S. Map 6", Glos. XLII. NE. (1884 edn.).
[80] P.N. Glos. i. 146; cf. E 179/113/31A rot. 2.
[81] Glos. R.O., D 1388, Lyon fam., Brimpsfield papers 1819–29.
[82] Ibid. D 1388/SL 3, no. 113A; Glos. Colln. RX 271.1.
[83] Glos. R.O., D 1388, Lyon fam., Caudle Green papers 1785–1803.
[84] Ibid. sale papers, Brimpsfield 1832–1926; G.D.R., T 1/38.
[85] Cf. Glos. R.O., D 2440, est. papers 1654–1859, est. partics. 1835.
[86] P.N. Glos. i. 147.
[87] Atkyns, Glos. 301; R.C.H.M. Glos. i. 21; Trans. B.G.A.S. xcvi. 79–82.
[88] C.P. 25(2)/71/588 no. 66.
[89] Glos. R.O., D 2440, Brimpsfield and Miserden deeds 1694–1814; G.D.R., T 1/38.
[90] Glos. R.O., D 2299/4104; O.S. Map 6", Glos. XLII. NW. (1885, 1903, 1924 edns.).
[91] G.D.R., T 1/38.
[92] Cf. Bryant, Map of Glos. (1824); Glos. R.O., D 1388/SL 3, no. 31.
[93] 'Birdlip and Brimpsfield', 81.
[94] Dom. Bk. (Rec. Com.), i. 168v.
[95] Glos. Subsidy Roll, 1327, 10.
[96] E 179/113/31A rot. 2.
[97] E.H.R. xix. 115.
[98] Trans. B.G.A.S. lxxxiii. 93.
[99] Atkyns, Glos. 301.
[1] Rudder, Glos. 311.
[2] Census, 1801–1971.
[3] 'Birdlip and Brimpsfield', 47–9, 44.
[4] Ex inf. Miss Butler.
[5] Cf. Char. Com. Reg.
[6] Gent. Mag. lviii (2), 758.

MANOR AND OTHER ESTATES. In 1086 Osbern Giffard held the large manor of *BRIMPSFIELD*, formerly held by Duns from Earl Harold; extended at 9 hides, it included the whole of Cranham.[7] It had passed by 1096 to Ellis Giffard (I)[8] (d. by 1130), and then descended in the direct line to Ellis (II) (d. by 1162), Ellis (III) (d. by 1190) and Ellis (IV), a minor. Ellis (IV) who came of age in 1203 died in 1248 and the Brimpsfield estate, which then included part of Cranham, passed to his son John, a minor who had come of age by 1254.[9]

The manor and castle of Brimpsfield, which John Giffard was said to hold by barony,[10] were assessed at 1 knight's fee in the 14th century.[11] John, a leading figure in the civil disorders of the early 1260s and founder of Gloucester College, Oxford,[12] was granted free warren in 1281.[13] After his death in 1299[14] his wife Margaret was granted custody of the castle during the minority of his son John,[15] who took seisin of the Giffard estates in 1308 when he was still under age.[16] John, who forfeited his lands in 1321 because of his part in the rebellion against Edward II, was executed at Gloucester the following year[17] and his estates were granted to the elder Hugh le Despenser for life.[18] John's widow Avelina received Brimpsfield manor as part of her dower in 1327[19] but died later that year. John's lands were then entrusted to the custody of John Mautravers[20] who was granted them in fee in 1329.[21] The following year Mautravers, to whom John of Kellaways, the heir of the Giffards, had released his right,[22] forfeited his lands because of his part in the death of Edmund, earl of Kent, the king's uncle.[23] Custody of Giffard's lands was granted in 1334 for life to Maurice of Berkeley[24] who in 1339 received a grant of Brimpsfield manor in fee.[25] Maurice (d. 1347) was succeeded by his son Thomas, a minor,[26] but in 1351 the manor was restored to John Mautravers as a reward for service in Flanders.[27] The following year Mautravers granted it to Lionel of Antwerp, the king's son.[28] Lionel, earl of Ulster, was made duke of Clarence in 1362 and died in 1368 leaving as his heir his daughter Philippe, wife of Edmund Mortimer, earl of March.[29] Catherine de la Pole, to whom Lionel had apparently granted some rights in the manor, quitclaimed them to Edmund and Philippe

in 1374.[30] The manor then passed with Edmund's part of Bisley manor until 1548 when, on the death of Catherine Parr,[31] it reverted to Sir John Bridges under a grant of the previous year.[32]

Brimpsfield then descended with Sir John's manor of Coberley to Giles Bridges, Lord Chandos (d. 1594), who was survived by his daughters Elizabeth and Catherine.[33] In 1606 his nephew Grey Bridges, Lord Chandos, provided part of Elizabeth's portion by conveying the estate, called by then the manors of Brimpsfield and Cranham, to trustees including Sir William Sandys of Fladbury (Worcs.).[34] Sir William, who was named as lord of Brimpsfield in 1608,[35] acquired sole interest in 1623. He died in 1641 having outlived his son Sir Miles, whose wife Mary, later Lady Richardson, retained the house and park-land as part of her jointure in 1683. The estate passed with Miserden to Miles Sandys (d. 1697), whose son William (d. 1712) granted it in 1711 to his kinsman Windsor Sandys. Windsor (d. 1729) was succeeded by his son Windsor, who retained the beech woods and common land centred on Cranham after 1740 when Alice and Emm Gilbert foreclosed on a mortgage.[36] Emm (d. 1750) left her share of the estate to her nephew John Gilbert, bishop of Salisbury, who purchased the share of Alice's trustees in 1753. John, who became archbishop of York in 1757, settled the estate in 1761, the year of his death, on the marriage of his daughter Emm and George Edgcumbe, Baron Edgcumbe;[37] some land was sold by the trustees of that settlement in the 1760s.[38] George, who was created Viscount Mount Edgcumbe and Valletort in 1781 and Earl of Mount Edgcumbe in 1789, died in 1795 and was survived by Emm (d. 1807), but his son and heir Richard[39] owned *c.* 768 a. in Brimpsfield parish in 1799.[40]

Joseph Pitt of Cirencester, who bought the estate under an agreement of 1802,[41] enlarged it by several purchases, including in 1807 *c.* 170 a. acquired by Windsor Sandys in 1716. In 1829 he sold it with his Syde property to William Lawrence,[42] an eminent London surgeon.[43] Lawrence owned *c.* 1,119 a. in the parish in 1837[44] and apparently sold his estate in 1847 to John Hall of Bury (Lancs.),[45] a cotton-manufacturer[46] who also acquired the Climperwell

[7] *Dom. Bk.* (Rec. Com.), i. 168v.
[8] *Hist. & Cart. Mon. Glouc.* i. 63.
[9] For the Giffards, see *Trans. B.G.A.S.* lxv. 105–82; Sanders, *Eng. Baronies*, 115–16.
[10] *Feud. Aids*, ii. 239; cf. *Inq. p.m. Glos.* 1302–58, 208.
[11] *Feud. Aids*, ii. 256, 279.
[12] *Trans. B.G.A.S.* lxv. 112–21; *V.C.H. Glos.* ii. 339–40.
[13] *Cal. Chart. R. 1257–1300*, 252.
[14] *Cal. Inq. p.m.* iii, p. 418; *Complete Peerage*, v. 643.
[15] *Cal. Pat. 1292–1301*, 495.   [16] *Cal. Close, 1307–13*, 33.
[17] *Cal. Fine R. 1319–27*, 84; *Trans, B.G.A.S.* lxv. 125–6.
[18] *Cal. Chart. R. 1300–26*, 443–4.
[19] *Cal. Close, 1327–30*, 58.
[20] *Cal. Fine R. 1327–37*, 61, 65.
[21] *Cal. Chart. R. 1327–41*, 116–17.
[22] C.P. 25(1)/286/36 no. 67; *Cal. Close, 1330–3*, 33, 140.
[23] *Complete Peerage*, viii. 583.
[24] *Cal. Pat. 1334–8*, 42.   [25] Ibid. 1338–40, 400.
[26] *Cal. Inq. p.m.* ix, p. 28.
[27] *Cal. Close, 1349–54*, 312.
[28] C.P. 25(1)/77/68 no. 314.
[29] *Complete Peerage*, iii. 257–8 and n.
[30] *Cal. Close, 1374–7*, 96.

[31] *V.C.H. Glos.* xi. 13; *Cal. Pat. 1452–61*, 452; *L. & P. Hen. VIII*, xix(1), p. 82.
[32] Cf. *Cal. Pat. 1547–8*, 115.
[33] C 142/109 no. 70; C 142/163 no. 59; C 142/309 no. 193.
[34] *Complete Peerage*, iii. 127; Glos. R.O., D 2440, Miserden, Cranham, and Brimpsfield papers 1605–1722.
[35] Smith, *Men and Armour*, 255.
[36] Glos. R.O., D 1388, Lyon fam., legal papers 1818; D 1042, Miserden, Winstone, Brimpsfield, and Cranham deeds 1647–1776.
[37] Ibid. D 2440, Cranham, Brimpsfield, and Cowley papers 1715–1924; for Gilbert, see *D.N.B.*
[38] Glos. R.O., D 1388, Lyon fam., Brimpsfield and Syde papers 1827–30; Pitt fam., Brimpsfield deeds 1755–1885.
[39] Burke, *Peerage* (1963), 1743.   [40] Glos. R.O., D 443/2.
[41] Ibid. D 1388, Lyon fam., Brimpsfield and Cranham abstracts 1829, bond of indemnity 25 Dec. 1829; cf. Rudge, *Hist. of Glos.* i. 296.
[42] Glos. R.O., D 1388, Lyon fam., Brimpsfield and Cranham abstracts 1829; cf. ibid. D 1388/SL 3, no. 31.
[43] *D.N.B.*
[44] G.D.R., T 1/38.   [45] Glos. Colln. RX 271.1.
[46] Cf. Glos. R.O., D 480, Lawrence fam., papers 1853–8.

estate.[47] He died in 1870[48] and in 1873 the manor was sold to Thomas Pendlebury.[49] Later, probably in 1880, the manorial rights and some land were acquired by William Killigrew Wait of Clifton, M.P. for Gloucester 1873–80. William and his son and heir Wilfrid built up an estate covering 1,543 a. in Brimpsfield and Cranham in 1926 when it was broken up.[50] Part including Brimpsfield Park house was bought by John Kendall, the owner until 1942. It was then acquired by the Cirencester Conservative Benefit Society and in the late 1950s by Peter Percy. Mrs. L. P. Larthe, who bought the house and 280 a. of farm-land in 1960 and Poston and Syde woods in 1965, owned c. 162 ha. (c. 400 a.) in 1977.[51]

A motte and bailey castle stood on the side of a valley 0.75 km. west of Ermin Street but, further west, a much larger castle had been built overlooking the valley by the mid 12th century; masonry of that date is incorporated in several buildings in the village.[52] The later castle, which was the Giffards' military base[53] until its demolition by royal order in 1322,[54] was partially moated and had an elaborate southern gateway. The outer bailey apparently contained the hall range and stabling, and the inner bailey to the east a square keep and other buildings.[55] Substantial earthworks survived in 1977 but were overgrown.

East of the village a house was built in the park, probably in the early 17th century when it was known as Brimpsfield Lodge.[56] In 1672 Miles Sandys was assessed on 13 hearths for the house,[57] which was in ruins c. 1775.[58] A few years later it was rebuilt as a substantial farm-house,[59] known later as Brimpsfield Park, which was remodelled in the 19th century and again by John Kendall. He also laid out extensive ornamental gardens on the slope east of the house.[60]

Part of the Climperwell estate, which Flaxley Abbey had acquired by 1227,[61] lay in Brimpsfield parish.[62]

St. Bartholomew's Hospital, Gloucester, was granted 2 yardlands in Brimpsfield to sustain a chaplain by Osbert Giffard c. 1227 and land at Groveridge hill in the centre of the parish by Nicholas of Kellaways c. 1260.[63] In 1837 the hospital's trustees, the mayor and corporation of Gloucester, owned c. 82 a. near Stoneyhill.[64] In 1881 part of a near-by field, held by the mayor and

corporation as trustees of a charity established under the will of John Cooke, was added to the hospital's endowments. The hospital land, which was apparently sold to Theodore Crewdson of Syde in 1899,[65] had passed by 1920 to J. D. Crewdson, the owner of over 240 a. in the parish.[66]

At Caudle Green part of the property of the Welch family, settled there by 1629,[67] passed to Jeremiah Hooper[68] who sold his land in 1703 to Matthew Walbank. Matthew, who built up an estate based on WOODFIELD HOUSE,[69] died in 1721.[70] Another Matthew Walbank (d. 1761) left the estate to his second son Abraham, who sold it in 1766 to his elder brother William, rector of Cranham. After William's death in 1784 his wife Hester retained the estate,[71] which comprised c. 163 a. in 1799.[72] It was broken up after her death in 1802; Joseph Pitt bought the house and Eddington farm (c. 123 a.) and Walter Welch the land at Morcombe.[73] The 18th-century house has 19th-century bay-windows and additions. By 1837 it had been acquired by John Biddle Ockwell,[74] and in the early 20th century it was a farm-house until Theodore Crewdson made it his home.[75]

ECONOMIC HISTORY. In 1086 Brimpsfield manor, which then included Cranham, had in demesne 3 plough-teams worked by 8 servi and 4 ancillae.[76] In 1327, when the demesne land comprised 600 a. of arable, 4 a. of meadow, and 24 a. of pasture, some tenants of Gloucester Abbey owed ploughing and harrowing services on the estate.[77] Those services had possibly been retained when land in Cranham had been granted to the abbey. The same tenants owed hoeing-services in the late 14th century.[78] After 1338, when a yardland contained 48 a. and the arable demesne extended to 5 ploughlands (960 a.),[79] there was a change to pastoral farming on the Brimpsfield estate[80] but by 1413 the demesne pastures and meadows were leased.[81]

The tenants on the manor in 1086 were 16 villani, 6 bordars, and a priest, with 12 ploughs between them. There were also 5 burgesses in Gloucester belonging to the manor.[82] In 1327 there were 13 free tenants on the estate, and 21 customary tenants of whom 9 were half-yardlanders, owing money rents and labour-services. Nine cottagers and 34 other

[47] Ibid. D 2440, par., Cranham poor-rate 1860.
[48] Glos. Colln. RX 271.1.
[49] Ex inf. Mrs. L. P. Larthe, of Brimpsfield Pk.; Kelly's Dir. Glos. (1879), 574.
[50] Glos. R.O., D 2299/4104; Kelly's Dir. Glos. (1885 and later edns.); Who's Who in Glos. (Heref. 1934), 224.
[51] Ex inf. Mrs. Larthe.
[52] Cf. Proc. C.N.F.C. xxxiii. 113–16.
[53] Robert of Gloucester, Metrical Chron. (Rolls Ser.), ii. 739–40; Trans. B.G.A.S. lxv. 112–14.
[54] Cal. Pat. 1321–4, 42; Livere de Reis de Brittanie (Rolls Ser.), 339–41.
[55] Proc. C.N.F.C. xxxiii. 114–16; Glos. Colln. RF 56.5.
[56] Inq. p.m. Glos. 1625–42, ii. 171.
[57] E 179/247/14 rot. 6.
[58] Rudder, Glos. 311.   [59] Bigland, Glos. i. 244.
[60] Ex. inf. Mrs. Larthe.
[61] Flaxley Cart. 74–5, 114–15, 132.
[62] See p. 204; cf. Glos. R.O., photocopy 346; G.D.R., T 1/38.
[63] Glouc. Corp. Rec. pp. 119–20, 155.

[64] G.D.R., T 1/38.
[65] Glos. R.O., G.B.R. 3550, deed 21 Dec. 1881; cf. V.C.H. Glos. ii. 344; Kelly's Dir. Glos. (1894), 309.
[66] Glos. R.O., D 2299/2439; G.D.R., T 1/38.
[67] Glos. R.O., D 1229, Brimpsfield deeds 1614–1775.
[68] Ibid. Brimpsfield deeds 1643–1803.
[69] Ibid. D 1388, Lyon fam., Brimpsfield papers 1819–29.
[70] Bigland, Glos. i. 245.
[71] Glos. R.O., D 1388, Lyon fam., Caudle Green papers 1785–1803; Glos. N. & Q. i. 460; Hockaday Abs. clxxiii.
[72] Glos. R.O., D 443/2.
[73] Ibid. D 1388, Lyon fam., Caudle Green papers 1785–1803; Rudge, Hist. of Glos. i 297.
[74] G.D.R., T 1/38.
[75] Kelly's Dir. Glos. (1902–23 edns.).
[76] Dom. Bk. (Rec. Com.), i. 168v.
[77] Inq. p.m. Glos. 1302–58, 208–9.   [78] S.C. 6/850/22.
[79] Inq. p.m. Glos. 1302–58, 275.
[80] S.C. 6/850/22.   [81] S.C. 6/850/23.
[82] Dom. Bk. (Rec. Com.), i. 168v.

tenants owed cash rents.[83] In 1380 one tenant was described as a mondayman.[84] By 1536 some of the holdings had been amalgamated and in Brimpsfield parish there were 7 free tenants, 4 at Brimpsfield, 2 at Birdlip, and 1 at Caudle Green, and 14 customary tenants, 9 (including Sir John Bridges) at Brimpsfield, 3 at Birdlip, and 2 at Caudle Green.[85]

Open-field land recorded in Brimpsfield in 1221[86] had probably been reduced to a relatively small area by 1380 when 301 autumn works were not used, but oats were sown in various parts of the parish.[87] In the later 17th century there were at least four open fields in the parish, a north and a south field (the latter also known as the middle field) on opposite sides of Brimpsfield village, a far field beyond Manless Town, and Caudle Home field west of Caudle Green.[88] In 1788 most of the open-field land was confined to a single area which, when fallow, was open to sheep between 19 April and 5 September. The sheep, which were stinted at two to the acre, were also allowed in with cattle after the harvest.[89] That area, lying south and south-west of the village, and a small area south of the Blacklains, called the Slait common field, comprised 181 a. in 1842 when they were inclosed. Commissioners were appointed in 1838 but agreement between the landowners was delayed mainly by disputes between St. Bartholomew's Hospital and William Lawrence and Joseph Winning, the owner of Stoneyhill farm. Under the award, which concerned 309 a. of open-field land and inclosures, fifteen landowners received allotments. The largest, 57 a., went to William Lawrence, and six other owners each received 20–50 a., the rector 13½ a., and the rest each under 7½ a. A series of exchanges confirmed by the award consolidated the holdings of nine landowners.[90]

There were several areas of common pasture. Buckle wood, the largest, remains uninclosed but Woodhill green to the south-east, which was possibly subject to common rights in the 1230s[91] and was open in 1380 between Whitsun and the feast of the Purification,[92] was finally inclosed by the lord of the manor c. 1786.[93] Two parcels remaining commonable in 1977, the green at Caudle Green and Muzzards common in the valley north-east of Brimpsfield village, were both closed between Candlemas and Whitsun in the mid 1780s.[94]

The importance of sheep-farming by the early 13th century is indicated by a grant to Flaxley Abbey of common rights in Brimpsfield and Cranham for 240 sheep,[95] and in 1327 the person assessed for most tax in the parish was a shepherd.[96] The manor estate, which included a sheepfold in 1327,[97] had been reorganized for large-scale sheep-farming by 1380 when the sale of wool realised nearly six times as much as the sale of corn and timber combined.[98] In 1536 the estate had a sheep-house in Birdlip,[99] and St. Bartholomew's Hospital had one on its estate in the mid 17th century.[1]

In 1801 a relatively low acreage (608½ a.) produced arable crops, mainly cereals with some turnips and peas and small areas of rye, beans, and potatoes.[2] In 1807 most of the farms had a mixed economy with substantial areas of pasture; only one farm was predominantly arable.[3] By 1837, however, the arable land comprised more than half the farmland in the parish[4] and in 1866 1,467 a. were returned as under crops, mainly cereals and roots, or temporary grass, and 881 a. as under permanent grass. By 1896 the area under cereals and roots had decreased by almost 500 a. and permanent grassland accounted for at least 1,052 a.[5] In the late 1880s cheese was produced on Caudle Green farm. Dairying expanded in the 1930s[6] and by then the red poll variety of cattle had been introduced on Brimpsfield Park farm.[7] Sheep-farming remained important throughout the later 19th and early 20th centuries[8] and by the 1930s the Cotswold breed had given way to others.[9] The number of pigs reared dropped in the early 20th century and large-scale poultry-farming had begun by 1926.[10]

In 1807 the farms on the Brimpsfield estate of Joseph Pitt covered 552 a., 171 a., 95 a., and 42 a. Walter Welch's land at Birdlip and Caudle Green (214 a.) was farmed as a unit and another five freehold farms, comprising 179 a., 171 a., 142 a., 139 a., and 128 a., were in hand.[11] In 1831 eight farmers in the parish employed a total of 44 labourers.[12] In 1896 most of the land was rented and cultivated in 22 holdings. In 1926 half of the 16 holdings returned were under 50 a. each but there were 4 farms of 150–300 a. and 21 agricultural labourers found full-time employment in the parish.[13] At that time Park farm (385 a. including Poston and Syde woods), Blacklains farm (280 a.), Yew Tree farm (237 a.), and Moorhouse (35 a.) were part of the Brimpsfield estate[14] but in 1957 most of the 13 farms in the parish were worked by their owners.[15] By 1976, when there were a few smallholdings worked part-time, the production on five larger farms, each of

---

[83] Inq. p.m. Glos. 1302–58, 208–9.
[84] S.C. 6/850/22.
[85] S.C. 11/1022.
[86] Pleas of the Crown for Glos. ed. Maitland, p. 42.
[87] S.C. 6/850/22.
[88] G.D.R., V 5/56T 1, 3, 6; Glos. R.O., D 1229, Brimpsfield deeds 1643–1803, deed 29 Sept. 1693; cf. Cal. Pat. 1549–51, 91; G.D.R., T 1/38.
[89] Glos. R.O., D 1388, Lyon fam., Brimpsfield and Cranham correspondence 1788–1839.
[90] Ibid. Q/RI 29; D 3565.
[91] Ciren. Cart. i, p. 215.
[92] S.C. 6/850/22.
[93] Glos. Colln. RQ 56.1.
[94] Glos. R.O., D 1388, Lyon fam., Brimpsfield and Cranham correspondence 1788–1839; G.D.R., T 1/38.
[95] Flaxley Cart. 74.
[96] Glos. Subsidy Roll, 1327, 10.

[97] Inq. p.m. Glos. 1302–58, 208.
[98] S.C. 6/850/22.
[99] S.C. 11/1022.
[1] Hockaday Abs. cciii, 1655.
[2] Acreage Returns, 1801.
[3] Brimpsfield and Syde terrier 1807.
[4] G.D.R., T 1/38.
[5] M.A.F. 68/26/19; M.A.F. 68/1609/1.
[6] 'Birdlip and Brimpsfield', 19–22.
[7] Kelly's Dir. Glos. (1931), 53; (1935), 54.
[8] M.A.F. 68/25/16; M.A.F. 68/1609/1; M.A.F. 68/3295/5.
[9] 'Birdlip and Brimpsfield', 20; Kelly's Dir. Glos. (1935), 54.
[10] M.A.F. 68/1609/1; M.A.F. 68/3295/5.
[11] Brimpsfield and Syde terrier 1807.
[12] Census, 1831.
[13] M.A.F. 68/1609/1; M.A.F. 68/3295/5.
[14] Glos. R.O., D 2299/4104.
[15] 'Birdlip and Brimpsfield', 75–8.

which was returned as containing over 50 ha. (124 a.), was specialized; two were given over to dairying, one to cereals, one to cattle- and sheep-rearing, and one to poultry-farming.[16]

A windmill, built north of Morcombe by William Welch in 1823,[17] went out of use between 1851 and 1873.[18]

In 1354 Lionel, earl of Ulster, had a grant of a Tuesday market and a two-day fair at Corpus Christi in Brimpsfield.[19] There is no evidence that they were ever held, apart from a statement c. 1775 that they had been long since discontinued.[20] In 1856 a non-statutory fair for sheep and cattle was held in Birdlip on the last Tuesday in April. In the 1860s there was also a similar Tuesday fair at the end of September.[21]

A walker had land in Brimpsfield in 1262[22] but the only cloth-workers found recorded later were members of the Gardner family which owned property at Moorhouse in the 17th century and early 18th.[23] In 1608 3 tailors, 2 badgers, a baker, and an innkeeper were listed in the parish,[24] where 22 families were supported by trade in 1831, as opposed to 44 supported by agriculture.[25] Many of the tradesmen lived in Birdlip, which grew up to serve road traffic and had a smith by 1287.[26] There were several smithies there in the late 17th century and early 18th, when other village trades were represented there,[27] and two smithies closed in the early 20th century. A garage opened in 1922.[28] A clock-maker lived there in the early 19th century[29] and in 1977 the village retained a shop and a saddler. At Wood House, where a wood turner carried on his trade by 1837,[30] a workshop with a new saw-mill was leased in 1895 to James Gastrell of Cranham, a timber-merchant. From 1900 the mill was worked by J. G. Ayers, whose company J. G. Ayers & Sons Ltd. of Pitchcombe[31] employed up to 21 people there in 1907.[32] It closed in or soon after 1922.[33] The sale of faggots in Cheltenham, carried on in the later 19th century by the Driver family of Birdlip, declined in the early 20th.[34] In the early 19th century stone was quarried in Buckle wood.[35] There were important quarries north of Birdlip,[36] where a building firm, established in 1913 by Martin Partridge, employed

c. 60 people in 1957[37] and continued in business in 1977.

Brimpsfield inhabitants included a gunsmith in 1739.[38] Most of the usual village trades were to be found in Brimpsfield village and Caudle Green until the later 19th century and carpenters worked in Caudle Green until the Second World War. In the later 19th century and early 20th carriers connected the three main settlements of the parish with Cheltenham, Gloucester, and Cirencester[39] and by 1957 several residents worked in Cheltenham or Gloucester.[40]

LOCAL GOVERNMENT. Ellis Giffard (IV) raised and used gallows in Brimpsfield but the abbot of Cirencester as lord of the hundred secured their demolition c. 1222.[41] Under an agreement of the 1230s, concerning the liberties of the manor, the abbey's right to try thieves was confirmed and Ellis was to have the amercements from the two views of frankpledge to be held each year in his manor court by the abbey's bailiffs upon payment of 2s. at each view. Ellis was also entitled to pecuniary rights in cases arising from the hue and to strays.[42] A reference to Brimpsfield hundred in 1382[43] presumably relates to the holding of the view, which in the early 15th century was attended by the inhabitants of Birdlip and Cranham.[44] In the early 16th century, however, the Cowley court held view of frankpledge for the Cowley part of Birdlip.[45]

For Brimpsfield manor there is a court roll of 1546 recording tenurial and agrarian matters.[46] By 1788 the court, meeting in October at the King's Head inn, was called a court leet.[47] Presentments to that court survive for the period 1798–1829, during which it still dealt with Cranham matters; the main business was preventing encroachments on commonable land and fencing off quarries, but it elected constables and haywards for both parishes.[48] The court leet had moved by 1869 to the Golden Heart, where in 1875 it appointed a hayward and dealt with the state of a brook.[49]

The parish had two churchwardens from the late 15th century[50] although there may have been only

[16] Agric. Returns 1976.
[17] Glos. R.O., D 1388, Lyon fam., Caudle Green papers 1785–1803, letter 12 Feb. 1823; Greenwood, Map of Glos. (1824); G.D.R., T 1/38.
[18] Glos. R.O., D 1388, sale papers, Brimpsfield 1832–1926; D 2440, Brimpsfield and Cranham papers 1841–1928.
[19] Cal. Chart. R. 1341–1417, 140.
[20] Rudder, Glos. 310.
[21] Kelly's Dir. Glos. (1856), 228; (1870), 474.
[22] Glouc. Corp. Rec. pp. 237–8.
[23] Glos. R.O., D 247/17; D 2440, Brimpsfield and Miserden deeds 1694–1814.
[24] Smith, Men and Armour, 255.
[25] Census, 1831.
[26] J.I. 1/278 rot. 53.
[27] Glos. R.O., D 2440, Birdlip deeds 1658–1861; D 2025, Beman fam. deeds; D 1229, Brimpsfield deeds 1614–1775.
[28] 'Birdlip and Brimpsfield', 24, 41; O.S. Map 6", Glos. XXXIV. SE. (1903, 1924 edns.).
[29] G.D.R. wills, 27 June 1835.
[30] G.D.R., T 1/38; Kelly's Dir. Glos. (1856), 228.
[31] Glos. R.O., D 2440, misc. est. papers 1603–1926; cf. Kelly's Dir. Glos. (1906), 273.

[32] V.C.H. Glos. ii. 200.
[33] Glos. R.O., D 2299/2902; cf. Kelly's Dir. Glos. (1923), 44.
[34] 'Birdlip and Brimpsfield', 26; Kelly's Dir. Glos. (1856–1910 edns.), s.v. Birdlip.
[35] Glos. R.O., D 2440, Brimpsfield and Cranham presentments.
[36] Ibid. DC/E 88/21.
[37] 'Birdlip and Brimpsfield', 28–9.
[38] Glos. R.O., DC/E 88/17.
[39] Kelly's Dir. Glos. (1856 and later edns.).
[40] 'Birdlip and Brimpsfield', 4, 70.
[41] Eyre Rolls, 1221–2 (Selden Soc. lix), pp. 123–6.
[42] Ciren. Cart. i, pp. 214–16.
[43] Cal. Close, 1381–5, 151.
[44] Ciren. Cart. ii, p. 620.
[45] S.C. 2/175/28–30; S.C. 2/176/21.
[46] S.C. 2/175/22.
[47] Glos. R.O., D 1388, Lyon fam., Brimpsfield and Cranham correspondence 1788–1839.
[48] Ibid. D 2440, Brimpsfield and Cranham presentments.
[49] Glos. Colln. RF 56.3.
[50] Hockaday Abs. xxii, 1498 visit. f. 30; xxviii, 1540 visit. f. 46.

one in the early 19th.[51] Their accounts for the period 1703–96 survive.[52] Two surveyors of the highways were recorded from 1786.[53] The cost of poor-relief, which was £50 in 1776, had risen to £133 by 1803 when 20 of the 29 persons being helped received regular aid.[54] The number on occasional relief rose in following years and the cost in 1815 was £232.[55] From 1828 a doctor received expenses for attending the poor; part of the cost of vaccinating 88 children in 1831 was met by the rector, William Moore. By 1835 the number of poor receiving weekly payments had fallen to eight.[56] From 1831 a house north-east of Caudle Green was used as a poorhouse.[57] Brimpsfield parish, which joined the Cirencester poor-law union of 1836,[58] remained in Cirencester rural district. Birdlip was wholly in Cheltenham rural district after the 1935 boundary change[59] and was included in Tewkesbury district in 1974 when the rest of the ancient parish of Brimpsfield became part of Cotswold district.

CHURCHES. The priest recorded on Brimpsfield manor in 1086[60] presumably served in the church which was granted, probably in the 12th century, with some manorial tithes to Fontenay Abbey (Calvados). The abbey endowed a cell, Brimpsfield Priory, with the demesne tithes,[61] and a vicarage, which had been ordained at Brimpsfield by 1230,[62] was in the gift of the priory in 1317.[63] The Crown presented when the priory was in the king's hands during the war with France[64] and after its suppression in 1414,[65] although in 1427 the bishop held an inquiry into the patronage.[66] In 1441 Henry VI granted the advowson with the priory to Eton College[67] but in 1461 the bishop collated to the living[68] and later that year Edward IV revoked his predecessor's grant.[69] By 1465 his mother Cecily, duchess of York and lady of Brimpsfield manor, had secured the patronage of the church, and the demesne tithes had evidently been absorbed into the living, which was then and later called a rectory.[70] In 1798 the living was united with Cranham[71] but the

union was dissolved in 1892.[72] Brimpsfield was united with Elkstone and Syde in 1972.[73]

The patronage of the rectory passed with the manor,[74] although the bishop collated through lapse in 1585, and John Guise of Gloucester and Charles Coxe of Nether Lypiatt were patrons for turns in 1672 and 1726 respectively.[75] The church had the same patron as Cranham when the livings were united.[76] By 1803 the rector, James Pitt, had bought the patronage of the united benefice[77] and after his death in 1806 it belonged to his wife Mary (d. 1836),[78] who left it to William Goodrich (d. 1845). His son James sold it in 1879 to Denne Denne of Canterbury and in 1890 the rector, Richard Henry Denne, acquired it.[79] He sold the patronage of Cranham shortly afterwards[80] but the Denne family retained the patronage of Brimpsfield, in which G. H. Pritchard-Rayner had an interest by 1949,[81] until it was acquired by the bishop c. 1967.[82] In 1977 the patronage of the united benefice belonged in turn to the bishop, Mrs. G. M. Price, and the Diocesan Board of Patronage.[83]

The vicar's portion was presumably included in the valuation of the church at £10 in 1291 when the parish included Cranham. Flaxley Abbey then had a portion, valued at £1 5s., for the Climperwell tithes.[84] Brimpsfield rectory was worth £9 11s. 11d. clear in 1535,[85] but its value had risen to £42 6s. 8d. by 1650[86] and to £70 by 1750.[87] The glebe was extended at c. 33 a. in 1664. In 1680 tithes of cows, calves, sheep, and lambs were paid in kind and nothing was owed for milk and aftermath. For the tithes of Brimpsfield park and the manorial demesne 6s. 8d. and £10 respectively were paid in composition then,[88] but in the early 19th century £9 16s. 11½d. was paid in moduses or in composition for the tithes of over 946 a.[89] It was because of its poverty that the living was united with Cranham in 1798 when the united benefice was valued at £259.[90] The Brimpsfield tithes were commuted in 1838 for a corn-rent-charge of £303 and the Cranham tithes the following year for a corn-rent-charge of £162.[91] In 1856 the living was worth £458.[92] In Brimpsfield,

[51] *20th Rep. Com. Char.* 80.
[52] *Penes* the rector, the Revd. P. Newing.
[53] Glos. R.O., Q/SRh 1786 B; D 2025, Reynard fam. papers.
[54] *Poor Law Abstract, 1804,* 180–1.
[55] Ibid. *1818,* 154–5.
[56] Overseers' acct. bk. 1812–71, *penes* the rector: the vol. includes vestry minutes for the period 1836–56.
[57] Glos. R.O., D 181/III/T 8; G.D.R., T 1/38.
[58] *Poor Law Com. 2nd Rep.* p. 522.
[59] *Census,* 1911; 1931 (pt. ii).
[60] *Dom. Bk.* (Rec. Com.), i. 168v.
[61] *Trans. B.G.A.S.* lxxxii. 127–32; cf. *V.C.H. Glos.* ii. 102–3, where the mother ch. of the priory is mistakenly said to be St. Wandrille (Seine Maritime): *V.C.H. Wilts.* viii. 49 n.
[62] *Trans. B.G.A.S.* lxxxi. 76.
[63] *Reg. Sede Vacante,* 183.
[64] *Reg. Bransford,* p. 105; *Reg. Sede Vacante,* 344; *Cal. Pat.* 1377–81, 457.
[65] *V.C.H. Glos.* ii. 103; Worc. Episc. Reg., Reg. Morgan, i, f. 8v.
[66] *Trans. B.G.A.S.* lxxxi. 90.
[67] Ibid. lxxxii. 134.
[68] Worc. Episc. Reg., Reg. Carpenter, i, f. 157v.
[69] *Trans. B.G.A.S.* lxxxii. 135.
[70] Ibid. lxxxi. 77, 91; *Cal. Pat.* 1452–61, 542; cf. *Valor Eccl.* (Rec. Com.), ii. 496.

[71] G.D.R., D 17/2.
[72] Ex inf. the diocesan registrar.
[73] *Glouc. Dioc. Yr. Bk.* (1977), 32.
[74] *Trans. B.G.A.S.* lxxxi. 92; *Cal. Pat.* 1547–8, 115; *E.H.R.* xix. 115
[75] Hockaday Abs. cxxxiii.
[76] G.D.R., D 17/2.
[77] Rudge, *Hist. of Glos.* i. 297.
[78] Hockaday Abs. cxxxiii; *Glouc. Jnl.* 10 Mar. 1806; 5 Nov. 1836.
[79] G.D.R., D 5/1/10.
[80] Cf. *Kelly's Dir. Glos.* (1894), 130.
[81] *Trans. B.G.A.S.* lxxxi. 96; *Glouc. Dioc. Yr. Bk.* (1962–3), 34–5.
[82] Letter to churchwardens 22 Feb. 1967, *penes* the rector.
[83] *Glouc. Dioc. Yr. Bk.* (1977), 32.
[84] *Tax. Eccl.* (Rec. Com.), 221; cf. *Inq. Non.* (Rec. Com.), 408.
[85] *Valor Eccl.* (Rec. Com.), ii. 496.
[86] *Trans. B.G.A.S.* lxxxiii. 93.
[87] G.D.R. vol. 381A, f. 25.
[88] G.D.R., V 5/56T 1, 3.
[89] G.D.R., T 1/38.
[90] G.D.R., D 17/2.
[91] G.D.R., T 1/38, 64.
[92] G.D.R. vol. 384, f. 29.

where in 1842 the rector had been awarded 13½ a. for his open-field glebe, reduced after exchanges to 9 a.,[93] most of the glebe was sold in 1923.[94] The rector retained 1.6 ha. (4 a.) which was let in 1977.[95]

The rectory house mentioned in 1664 contained four bays in 1680.[96] The house, at the northern end of the village,[97] was considerably enlarged in the 19th century. It had been sold by 1974[98] and a new rectory house to the north was occupied from 1975.[99]

Of the vicars of Brimpsfield William of Cowley, instituted in 1380, and Robert Cranham, apparently his successor in 1382,[1] were probably local men. Thomas Lane, rector by 1540,[2] who was found to be moderately learned in 1551,[3] was resident until he became rector of Cranham in 1565. In 1572, when the chancel and other parts of the church were in disrepair, Brimpsfield was served by a curate shared with Syde.[4] Lane, whose curate in 1576 was absolved from excommunication,[5] was resident in 1584 when he was described as neither a graduate nor a preacher.[6] William Wolley, who in 1636 became rector of both Brimpsfield and Miserden,[7] used curates at Brimpsfield,[8] which he retained in 1664.[9] In the mid 1650s the living was possibly served by Henry Hooke, who was described as rector in the later 1660s,[10] but in 1670 Humphrey Randall, vicar of Down Hatherley, became rector. He also employed a curate and was succeeded in 1672 by Hooke (d. 1710).[11] The rectors between 1726 and 1785 appointed curates; Thomas Chamberlayne Coxe, rector from 1726, was also rector of North Cerney from 1736;[12] John White, rector from 1745, was also rector of Minchinhampton from 1774;[13] and James Parsons, rector from 1777, was also rector of Eastleach Martin[14] but lived in Cirencester.[15] Between 1785 and 1797 the rectory was held in plurality with Cranham by William Metcalfe[16] who resided in Brimpsfield.[17] James Pitt, rector from 1797,[18] was instituted to Cranham the following year when the livings were united.[19] James Phelps, his successor in 1806, lived in Alderley where he was rector.[20] For Brimpsfield with Cranham he employed as curate from 1819 John Davies, owner of the Overtown estate in Cranham, who lived in Painswick and from 1823 William Moore who lived in the Brimpsfield rectory house.

Moore, who succeeded Phelps as rector in 1829,[21] retained the united benefice until 1879 but his successor R. H. Denne (d. 1914) had relinquished Cranham rectory by 1892.[22]

The parish church of *ST. MICHAEL*, so called by 1791[23] although it bore dedications to the Blessed Saviour *c.* 1708[24] and St. Lawrence in the early 1920s,[25] is built of rubble and ashlar and has a chancel, nave with eastern tower, north vestry, and south porch. The nave, which has an undecorated chancel arch and south doorway of the late 11th or early 12th century, is unusually wide for the area and may originally have had arcades.[26] The chancel, which is almost square, and part of the north wall of the nave were rebuilt in the 13th century. During the 14th century new windows were put into the south side of the chancel, the south porch was added, and the lower parts of the tower were built into the east end of the nave. The east and west walls of the tower rest on plain pointed arches, that to the east being beyond the chancel arch; the north and south walls incorporate 13th-century piers and are flanked by small side chapels at the east end of the nave. Later in the 14th century part of the north wall of the nave was rebuilt to incorporate a low window, lighting the adjacent chapel, and a stair which gave access to a rood-loft against the west face of the tower. The rood-screen cut off the side chapels from the nave and narrow openings were made into them through the north and south walls of the tower. In the 15th century the west wall of the nave was rebuilt, new windows were put into the nave, and the top of the tower was added or rebuilt.

A western gallery of 1833 was removed during a restoration of the church in 1883, when the window lighting the gallery was presumably blocked and new pews were installed.[27] The church retains a medieval font and a pulpit dated 1658. The bells include one cast by Robert Norton of Exeter (fl. *c.* 1420–1460) and another by Thomas Gefferies (fl. 1508–46). A third bell dated 1657 was recast in 1904[28] and a fourth was cast in 1910.[29] The church plate includes a late-17th-century chalice and a salver of 1730.[30] The registers survive from 1587.[31]

An altar stone, which before 1937 was used as a stile,[32] has been placed in the north chapel. A few sculptured stones of early medieval date have been

[93] Glos. R.O., Q/RI 29.
[94] Ibid. D 2299/4104.
[95] Ex inf. the rector.
[96] G.D.R., V 5/56⊤ 3.
[97] O.S. Map 6″, Glos. XXXIV. SE. (1883 edn.).
[98] *Glos. Life*, May 1974, 52–3.
[99] Ex inf. the rector.
[1] *Reg. Wakefeld*, pp. 12, 34.
[2] *Trans. B.G.A.S.* lxxxi. 83.   [3] *E.H.R.* xix. 115.
[4] Hockaday Abs. xlii, 1563 visit. f. 20; cxxxiii; clxxiii.
[5] Ibid. xlvii, 1576 visit. f. 102.
[6] Ibid. xlix, state of clergy 1584, f. 32.
[7] Ibid. cxxxiii; *V.C.H. Glos.* xi. 55.
[8] *Glos. N. & Q.* i. 404.
[9] G.D.R., V 5/56⊤ 1.
[10] *Trans. B.G.A.S.* lxxxi. 85; *Glos. N. & Q.* i. 404.
[11] Hockaday Abs. cxxxiii; ccxxxvii.
[12] Ibid. cxxxiii; *Trans. B.G.A.S.* lxxxi. 86.
[13] Hockaday Abs. cxxxiii; G.D.R. vol. 381A, f. 25.
[14] Hockaday Abs. cxxxiii; cxc; *Glos. N. & Q.* i. 460–1.
[15] G.D.R. vol. 319.
[16] Hockaday Abs. cxxxiii; clxxiii; *Glos. N. & Q.* i. 461.
[17] G.D.R. vol. 382, f. 36.   [18] Hockaday Abs. cxxxiii.
[19] Ibid. clxxiii; G.D.R., D 17/2.
[20] Hockaday Abs. cxxxiii; xcviii; G.D.R. vol. 383, no. ccxxiii.
[21] Hockaday Abs. cxxxiii; G.D.R., T 1/64; G.D.R. vol. 384, f. 29.
[22] *Trans. B.G.A.S.* lxxxi. 86–7; G.D.R., D 5/1/10; *Kelly's Dir. Glos.* (1923), 143.
[23] Bigland, *Glos.* i. 243.
[24] Bodl. MS. Top. Glouc. c. 3, f. 214.
[25] *Trans. B.G.A.S.* xliv. 189; xlvi. 131 n.
[26] The width is 7.3 m.; for the smaller 12th cent. churches in the area it is normally between 4.9 m. and 6.1 m. For a view of the ch., see plate facing p. 140.
[27] *Trans. B.G.A.S.* lxxxi. 87; faculty 28 Aug. 1883, *penes* the rector.
[28] *Glos. Ch. Bells*, 34; *Trans. B.G.A.S.* xviii. 237; xli. 66, 67 n.; xlii. 153.
[29] 'Birdlip and Brimpsfield', 6.
[30] *Glos. Ch. Plate*, 28–9.
[31] *B. & G. Par. Rec.* 75.   [32] *Trans. B.G.A.S.* lxxxi. 75.

moved to the chancel from the churchyard, which contains many richly carved, 18th-century monuments.[33]

A church mentioned in Birdlip in 1287 has not been traced.[34] An iron mission church, dedicated to *ST. MARY*, opened there in 1897. The church, built by subscription on land next to the Black Horse provided by W. F. Hicks Beach,[35] was served by the rector of Great Witcombe or lay readers.[36] After the First World War the rector of Brimpsfield took the services[37] and in 1928 the church was included in Brimpsfield ecclesiastical parish.[38] The church was destroyed by fire in 1954, and in 1958 a new church of St. Mary opened by the Brimpsfield road.[39] That church, built of coursed rubble with ashlar dressings, comprises chancel with north vestry, nave, and south porch.

NONCONFORMITY. The nonconformist meeting in Birdlip for which the Stroud Congregationalist minister John Burder registered premises in 1820 and 1821[40] was shortlived,[41] as was that in Caudle Green for which Thomas Davis registered a meeting-place in 1825.[42] Davis, a missionary of the Particular Baptist chapel at Eastcombe, was later minister of Coberley, from where he introduced services to Birdlip in 1833.[43] The Baptists, for whose use the building in Birdlip registered the following year was possibly intended,[44] built a chapel there in 1841 and in 1851 it had congregations of 26 for afternoon and 30 for evening services.[45] The chapel, south of Ermin Street,[46] was a mission of Cambray chapel, Cheltenham, by 1891 and until 1952[47] shortly after which it closed.[48] In 1846 a Cheltenham man registered a house in Caudle Green as a meeting-place.[49]

EDUCATION. In 1818 only *c.* 16 children attended a day-school in the parish[50] but in 1833 there were separate schools, supported by the rector and parents, for 11 boys and 21 girls.[51] In 1841 a National school was built at the northern end of Brimpsfield village.[52] About 1846, when the income came from subscriptions and pence, the boys and girls, who numbered 13 and 20 respectively, were apparently taught separately.[53] In 1867, when there were 40 children on the roll, the average attendance was 20 and the teacher elderly and untrained.[54] The school taught 36 children in 1875[55] and, as Brimpsfield C. of E. school, had an average attendance of 22 in 1936.[56] It closed in 1947, when 12 children were transferred to Birdlip. The building was sold and later demolished.[57]

One of the day-schools recorded for Cowley parish in 1833 was possibly in Birdlip,[58] which apparently had a dame school in the mid 19th century.[59] In 1877 Birdlip C. of E. school opened in a new, small building in simple Gothic style, erected at the eastern end of the village by Robert Richardson-Gardner of Cowley Manor. It had an average attendance of 35 in 1885.[60] After the county council bought the building in 1929 the school was known as Birdlip Council school, which had an average attendance of 28 in 1936,[61] and later as Birdlip County Primary school. In 1977 it taught 67 children from surrounding villages and hamlets.[62]

CHARITIES FOR THE POOR. The parish had £14 stock, arising apparently from gifts by Sir William Sandys and two others, by 1683 when it was lent out and the interest paid to poor people not receiving parish relief.[63] Following a gift of £6, apparently made after 1704, the charity had an income of £1 distributed on Easter Monday. In the later 18th century four legacies of £5 each, another of 2 guineas, and £5, part of a fine, were added to the charity, which was again augmented in 1805 by a legacy of 2 guineas and raised to £50 by adding 12s. of fines and 4s. of gifts. The income of £2 was distributed among 11 people in 1813 and among 35 in 1871.[64] By will proved 1873 Mary Ann Ockwell of Caudle Green left £200 for the poor of the parish.[65] In 1882 her charity was combined with the Easter gift charity, and the combined charities were distributed until 1893 at Christmas in coal for up to 50 persons. From 1895 they gave cash to 40 people but the number of recipients fell in the early 20th century. The charities, which in 1921 paid £2 to the parish nursing fund, benefited 28 people in 1927[66] but in 1970 the income of £6 was shared between two old people living alone.[67]

Thomas Bicknell (d. 1780) left £1 from his estate for the poor but his heirs did not pay the legacy.[68]

[33] *Kelly's Dir. Glos.* (1856), 233; *Trans. B.G.A.S.* xci. 151–2.
[34] J.I. 1/278 rot. 53.
[35] *Kelly's Dir. Glos.* (1902), 39; O.S. Map 6", Glos. XXXIV. SW. (1903 edn.).
[36] 'Birdlip and Brimpsfield', 6.
[37] *Kelly's Dir. Glos.* (1919), 42; (1935), 42.
[38] *Lond. Gaz.* 7 Feb. 1928, pp. 835–7.
[39] 'Birdlip and Brimpsfield', 7; Brimpsfield ch. guide (1966).
[40] Hockaday Abs. cxxxiii; clxxii, Cowley; *V.C.H. Glos.* xi. 140–1.
[41] Cf. G.D.R. vol. 383, nos. ccxxiii, ccxxvi.
[42] Hockaday Abs. cxxxiii.
[43] R. W. Oliver, *Strict Bapt. Chapels of Eng.* v. (1968), 110–13.
[44] Hockaday Abs. cxxxiii.
[45] H.O. 129/340/1/8/9.
[46] O.S. Map 6", Glos. XXXIV. SE. (1883 edn.).
[47] Glos. R.O., D 2766/4/3; D 2766/1/5.
[48] Oliver, *Strict Bapt. Chapels*, v. 113.
[49] Hockaday Abs. cxxxiii.

[50] *Educ. of Poor Digest*, 292.
[51] *Educ. Enquiry Abstract*, 304.
[52] *Kelly's Dir. Glos.* (1885), 373; O.S. Map 6", Glos. XXXIV. SE. (1903 edn.).
[53] *Church School Inquiry, 1846–7*, 4–5.
[54] *Rep. Com. Agric. Employment*, p. 99.
[55] 'Birdlip and Brimpsfield', 11.
[56] *Bd. of Educ., List 21, 1936* (H.M.S.O.), 119.
[57] 'Birdlip and Brimpsfield', 12.
[58] *Educ. Enquiry Abstract*, 312.
[59] 'Birdlip and Brimpsfield', 13.
[60] *Kelly's Dir. Glos.* (1885), 365; Ed. 7/34/96; O.S. Map 6", Glos. XXXIV. SE. (1883 edn.).
[61] *Bd. of Educ., List 21, 1932* (H.M.S.O.), 114; *1936*, 120.
[62] Ex inf. county educ. dept.
[63] G.D.R., V 5/56T 5; cf. ibid. 6.
[64] Overseers' acct. bk. 1812–71; Bigland, *Glos.* i. 244.
[65] G.D.R. wills 1873, f. 114 and v.
[66] Glos. R.O., P 103/CII 1.
[67] Ibid. CH 21.
[68] Bigland, *Glos.* i. 244.

NORTH CERNEY

NORTH CERNEY parish, which includes the hamlets of Woodmancote and Calmsden, lies 6 km. north of Cirencester in the valley of the river Churn, from which river the parish takes its name.[69] The parish boundaries remain substantially those of an estate at Cerney and Calmsden that were described in a charter of 852.[70] Identifiable landmarks in the Saxon perambulation include Bereford, the crossing of the Churn at Perrott's Brook at the south end of the parish; the 'dyke of the spring', part of the Iron Age defences of Bagendon,[71] which still survives on the west boundary; *brihtinc broc*, the brook that provides the boundary in the north-west by Shewel wood; *hrindan broc*, the brook in the valley on the north boundary east of the Churn; a standing stone, which was later known as the Beck stone and still survived in 1660 where the boundary crosses the Roman road called the White way;[72] the 'winter spring', which rises by Rainbow barn; and the Foss way which provides a long stretch of the east boundary. In the later 18th century an exchange of open-field lands involved some re-drawing of the boundary with Rendcomb near Calmsden[73] and in 1935 a strip of land at the north end of the parish was given to Rendcomb when the boundary there was moved from the Churn to the Cirencester–Cheltenham main road.[74] The 1935 alteration reduced the area of the parish from 4,176 a. to 4,156 a. (1,682 ha.).[75]

The river Churn bisects the parish from north to south in a deep valley. From south of North Cerney village to near Perrott's Brook a straight channel was cut in 1824 alongside the original meandering course of the river to supply a newly built cloth-mill[76] but in 1978 the new cut was dry and had been partly filled in. The river valley lies at *c.* 120 m., the land rising on each side to reach *c.* 200 m. in the Calmsden area in the east and over 230 m. near Woodmancote in the north-west; in the Calmsden area the high land is broken through by the shallow valley that gives that hamlet its name[77] and beyond Woodmancote the ground falls towards another valley and is broken into by a short coomb, called Burcombe, probably from a hill-fort which once existed on the high ground to the north.[78] The narrow Churn valley is formed of the successive strata of the Upper Lias, the Inferior Oolite, and fuller's earth, but the high land of the bulk of the parish is on the Great Oolite.[79]

Woodland recorded on Gilbert son of Turold's manor of Cerney in 1086[80] evidently lay in the north-west part of the parish, where Woodmancote hamlet takes its name from a woodman's cottage.[81] Old Park, part of the woodland surviving in that area, was presumably imparked by one of the owners of Rendcomb in the Middle Ages; it belonged to the Rendcomb Park estate in 1837 when it covered 71 a. Shewel wood in the north-west corner then belonged to the Colesbourne estate and covered 61 a.[82] The Woodmancote woods owned by the Coxwells of Ablington in the early 17th century[83] were apparently other woods east of Shewel wood.[84] The eastern part of the parish was probably an area of treeless wolds before the 19th century when several small brakes and fox-coverts were planted. In 1544 the trees growing on Calmsden manor were said to be barely sufficient to maintain the hedges and fences.[85]

The slopes of the Churn valley, above a narrow belt of meadow-land in the valley bottom, and much of the Calmsden area were formerly cultivated as open fields while the high and level ground on the east side of the valley was occupied by extensive downland. In the early 18th century Cerney Downs were said to be famous for hawking, hunting, coursing, and racing[86] and they were long the venue for the annual Cirencester races.[87] The starting-post, apparently adjoining the White way, was mentioned in 1712[88] and the new course in 1756.[89] In the early 19th century the course occupied 49 a. of the south part of the downs by the road from Calmsden to Perrott's Brook[90] with the stand-house,[91] which gave its name to the later Stand plantation, on the east side of the course.

The Welsh way, the old London–Gloucester road, forms part of the south boundary of the parish before crossing the Churn[92] at the place called Bereford in 852. A bridge had been built at the crossing by the mid 13th century[93] and the name, which appears variously as Berrards bridge and Barretts bridge, eventually took the form Perrott's bridge,[94] the surrounding area becoming known as Berrards[95] or Perrott's Brook. The White way running northwards across the east part of the parish was a minor Roman road from Cirencester[96] and remained one of the principal roads through the parish. Until the mid 18th century the White way and a road branching from it apparently

---

[69] *P.N. Glos.* (E.P.N.S.), i. 148. This account was written in 1978.
[70] Grundy, *Saxon Charters*, 56–61.
[71] R.C.H.M. *Glos.* i. 6–9.
[72] Glos. R.O., D 2525, N. Cerney man. 1713–32, draft ct. roll; cf. G.D.R., T 1/45.
[73] Glos. R.O., Q/RI 63.
[74] *Census*, 1931 (pt. ii); cf. O.S. Map 6″, Glos. XLIII. NW. (1884 edn.).
[75] *Census*, 1931, 1951.
[76] Glos. R.O., D 2525, loose deed 1824.
[77] *P.N. Glos.* i. 148.
[78] R.C.H.M. *Glos.* i. 85–6.
[79] Geol. Surv. Map 1″, drift, sheet 235 (1933 edn.).
[80] *Dom. Bk.* (Rec. Com.), i. 168v.
[81] *P.N. Glos.* i. 149.
[82] G.D.R., T 1/45.

[83] *Inq. p.m. Glos.* 1625–42, ii. 120; Glos. R.O., D 269B/T 16.
[84] Cf. Bryant, *Map. of Glos.* (1824).
[85] Hockaday Abs. cxliii.
[86] Bodl. MS. Top. Glouc. c. 3, f. 214.
[87] *Glouc. Jnl.* 5 May 1752; Rudder, *Glos.* 325.
[88] Glos. R.O., D 2525, N. Cerney man. 1713–32.
[89] Ibid. N. Cerney leases 1715–89.
[90] Ibid. N. Cerney draft leases 1790–1833.
[91] Ibid. N. Cerney vals. 1811–55.
[92] Ogilby, *Britannia* (1675), p. 29.
[93] *Lacock Abbey Charters*, ed. K. H. Rogers (Wilts. Rec. Soc. xxxiv), nos. 392–3; S.C. 11/831 rot. 3d.
[94] e.g. Glos. R.O., D 2525, N. Cerney man. 1713–32, draft ct. roll 1660; deed 1731; Ogilby, *Britannia* (1675), p. 29.
[95] e.g. Glos. R.O., D 2525, N. Cerney and Ciren. deeds, deed 1732.
[96] Margary, *Rom. Roads*, i. 133–4.

provided the usual route from Cirencester to North Cerney village but a lower and more direct road to the village, running along the east side of the valley through Sladbottom copse, existed by 1751 when it was described as a new road.[97] The route across the north part of the parish, on which all three of the settlements of the parish stand, was presumably of ancient significance, for it links the Foss way to Ermin Street and, as Burcombe Lane, it marks the parish boundary west of Woodmancote. At Woodmancote it crosses another ancient road which forms a long stretch of the west boundary and was described as the way from Cirencester to Colesbourne in the 13th century.[98] The road through Calmsden down to Perrott's Brook was called Bristol way in the 17th and 18th centuries[99] and presumably formed part of a route which continued across Bagendon and Daglingworth to join the Cotswold ridgeway route at Park Corner in Duntisbourne Rouse parish.

In 1825 the new Cirencester–Cheltenham turnpike, built along the valley bottom on the west side of the Churn,[1] became the principal thoroughfare in the parish. It occasioned the stopping up of several of the old roads,[2] including the Cirencester–Cerney road east of the river, a road from the White way to Rendcomb through Conigree wood which had been built c. 1773,[3] and a road in the west part of the parish which ran by Scrubditch and Old Park and formed part of a hillside route from Perrott's Brook to Colesbourne.

North Cerney village stands in the centre of the parish on the east bank of the river Churn. The church stands by itself on the opposite bank, probably because it was founded by the owner of an estate which passed to the honor of Gloucester and included the land of Woodmancote tithing west of the river, while the village and the land adjoining on the east of the river belonged to a manor held by the archbishops of York. From a crossing-point on the Churn the village developed up the hillside on the road leading up to the White way near Nordown; a small green was formed at the junction with the Calmsden road. The only large house is the former manor-house, Cerney Manor (formerly North Cerney Farm), at the bottom of the village. The village is formed mainly of stone cottages of the late 17th and the 18th centuries, several of which were restored and modernized in the 1960s and 1970s when some new houses in reconstructed stone were built at the top of the village. On the new Cirencester road south of the village a pair of farm labourers' cottages was built beside an older cottage c. 1835 by the tenant of North Cerney farm,[4] and four pairs of

council houses were built further south on the opposite side of the road in the 1920s.[5] The few buildings on the west bank of the river opposite the village include the 18th-century mansion called Cerney House, the former rectory, and a cottage by the churchyard which contains a late-medieval arched-braced roof of four bays and was probably the church house mentioned in 1519.[6]

The hamlet of Calmsden, in an isolated position in the valley in the east part of the parish, had evidently been established by 852.[7] The hamlet was formed around a small green and a spring, from which the two inhabitants surnamed atte well in 1327 were presumably named. Nine people were assessed for the subsidy at Calmsden in that year,[8] and 18 people for the poll-tax in 1381,[9] and the hamlet had its own chapel of ease in the Middle Ages. Calmsden was said to comprise only 6 houses c. 1710[10] and it has remained small, comprising two manor-houses and a few cottages, including a row of 6 with rustic details built in the early 19th century.[11] A medieval stone cross, put up before 1405,[12] still stands above the spring.

Woodmancote hamlet in the west part of the parish was recorded from the beginning of the 13th century[13] and had at least 7 tax-payers in 1327;[14] it too had a medieval chapel. There were 13 houses there c. 1710.[15] The most substantial house is that called the Manor House which may once have belonged to one of the two Woodmancote manors but had been divorced from its estate by the early 19th century.[16] It dates from the 17th century and has a front range with three gables and a short rear wing containing the original kitchen. An addition was made on the north in similar style in the late 19th century and the interior of the house was apparently re-arranged in the 18th, when a new staircase was put in. The hamlet also has some cottages and one or two small farm-houses of the 17th and 18th centuries, a few model cottages built in the mid 1860s for the Rendcomb Park estate,[17] and a group of early-20th-century council houses.

A mansion called Cotswold Park was built in an isolated valley in the north-west corner of the parish in the late 18th century. The few other outlying dwellings of the parish include Scrubditch Farm, built in the late 18th or early 19th century for the Cerney House estate[18] and named from one of the dykes of the Bagendon complex on which it stands, and Downs Farm which was apparently the new house built c. 1755 in connexion with an inclosure made from Cerney Downs.[19]

In 1086 32 inhabitants of North Cerney were recorded and there was an unspecified number of

[97] Glos. R.O., D 2525, N. Cerney leases 1715–89; cf. ibid. Q/SRh 1827 B/1.
[98] Lacock Abbey Charters, no. 387.
[99] G.D.R., V 5/67T 2; Glos. R.O., D 2525, N. Cerney leases 1715–89, lease 1751.
[1] Cirencester Roads Act, 6 Geo. IV, c. 143.
[2] Glos. R.O., Q/SRh 1827 B/1; 1828 B/1–3.
[3] Ibid. D 2525, N. Cerney leases 1744–1844, lease 1785.
[4] Ibid. N. Cerney deeds 1825–55.
[5] Ibid. P 70A/PC 1/1, entry for 1922.
[6] Hockaday Abs. cxliii.
[7] Grundy, Saxon Charters, 56.
[8] Glos. Subsidy Roll, 1327, 10.

[9] E 179/113/35A rot. 13; E 179/113/31A rot. 2.
[10] Atkyns, Glos. 324.
[11] See plate facing p. 45.
[12] Staffs. R.O., D 641/1/4M/2.
[13] Pipe R. 1204 (P.R.S. N.S. xviii), 150.
[14] Glos. Subsidy Roll, 1327, 10, where the list for Rendcomb and its members probably includes other Woodmancote inhabitants. [15] Atkyns, Glos. 323.
[16] G.D.R., T 1/45; the ho. is illustrated above, plate facing p. 45.
[17] Rep. Com. Agric. Employment, 101.
[18] G.D.R., T 1/45.
[19] Glos. R.O., D 2525, N. Cerney leases 1715–89.

other tenants.[20] In 1327 26 people were assessed for the subsidy[21] and in 1381 45 people were assessed for poll-tax in Cerney village and Calmsden.[22] There were said to be c. 145 communicants in the parish in 1551[23] and 18 households in 1563[24] but only 110 communicants were recorded in 1603.[25] Later estimates of the population were 40 families in 1650,[26] about 190 inhabitants in 42 houses c. 1710,[27] and 384 inhabitants c. 1775.[28] In 1801 the population stood at 565. It rose slowly to 692 by 1861 but fell during the remainder of the century, to 529 in 1901. It fluctuated during the first 70 years of the 20th century, the lowest figure reached being 499 in 1951. In 1971 it stood at 545.[29]

An inn built in the parish near Perrott's Brook in 1706[30] was evidently the building on the Welsh way later called Perrott's Brook House. In 1732, when it was sold to Lord Bathurst, the inn was called the New Inn[31] but by 1750 it bore the sign of the Huntsman and Hounds and was advertized as a centre for hunting, a pack being kennelled on the premises.[32] In the late 18th century the inn appears to have been known as the Bear,[33] the sign that was taken later by the near-by inn in Bagendon parish at the junction of the Welsh way and the new Cheltenham–Cirencester turnpike. Perrott's Brook House was used as a farm-house on the Bathurst estate from the early 19th century.[34] The south range facing the Welsh way appears to be the building of 1706, long additions being made to the rear in the 19th century and alterations to the front in the 20th. The Bathurst Arms at the bottom of Cerney village had opened by 1821.[35] By 1837 there was also the Blue Boy on the Cheltenham road south of Old Park; belonging to the Rendcomb Park estate,[36] it was later called the Guise Arms.[37] It closed before 1891.[38]

A friendly society met at the inn at Perrott's Brook in 1775.[39] A friendly society for women was meeting at the church in 1812 and was presumably succeeded by that for women of Cerney, Rendcomb, and Bagendon which was meeting at the rectory in 1835.[40] For most of the 19th century two separate societies for men met at the Bathurst Arms; they were dissolved in 1889 and 1894 respectively.[41] In 1885 Lord Bathurst built premises for a reading-room and coffee-house in North Cerney village[42] and a village hall was built in 1921 as a war memorial. A hall for the inhabitants of Calmsden was provided in 1918 by J. A. K. Falconer as a memorial to his son.[43]

Sir Thomas Viner (1588–1665), a lord mayor of London, was born at North Cerney.[44]

MANORS AND OTHER ESTATES. In 852 Beorhtwulf, king of the Mercians granted to Alfeah 12 hides of land in Cerney and Calmsden, evidently including the whole of the later parish of North Cerney.[45] Part of the estate, extended at 4 hides, later passed to St. Oswald's Priory, Gloucester, and was among the lands of the priory that the archbishop of York held in 1086.[46] That land, known as the manor of NORTH CERNEY, was retained by the archbishop as a member of his barony of Churchdown[47] until 1545 when the manors of the barony were exchanged with the Crown.[48] In 1552 they were granted to Sir Thomas Chamberlayne[49] who sold North Cerney manor in 1556 to William Partridge[50] (d. 1578). William was succeeded by his son Robert[51] (d. 1600) and Robert by his son John Partridge[52] of Syde who sold the manor in 1610 to his brother Anthony, of Wishanger.[53] Anthony Partridge sold it in 1611 to William Poole of Long Newnton (Wilts., later Glos.)[54] (d. 1625 or 1626) who was succeeded by his son Nathaniel[55] (d. 1641).[56] Nathaniel's widow Catherine, who married John Newman, had a life-interest in the site of the manor and some lands and also exercised the manorial rights until her son William Poole came of age c. 1656. William bought out his mother's right in 1659 and later settled the site of the manor and some lands on his wife Elizabeth, who after his death married John Bromwich and died in 1697. William's daughter Eleanor succeeded him in the residue of the manor and died c. 1681.[57]

Eleanor Poole's heirs were her father's sisters Cecily, wife of Simon Oatridge, Elizabeth, wife of Daniel Oatridge, and Anne,[58] widow of John Giles. In 1699 Anne Giles conveyed her third share of the manor to her son Nathaniel who sold it in 1702 to Henry Combes (d. c. 1714). Henry's widow Jane sold that share in 1715 to Allen Bathurst, Lord

[20] Dom. Bk. (Rec. Com.), i. 164v., 168v.
[21] Glos. Subsidy Roll, 1327, 10.
[22] E 179/113/35A rot. 13; E 179/113/31A rot. 2. In the first roll a list which is partly lost but contains at least 19 names is probably that for Woodmancote tithing.
[23] E.H.R. xix. 111.
[24] Bodl. MS. Rawl. C.790, f. 24v.
[25] Eccl. Misc. 95.
[26] Trans. B.G.A.S. lxxxiii. 93.
[27] Atkyns, Glos. 324.
[28] Rudder, Glos. 327.
[29] Census, 1801–1971.
[30] Glos. R.O., D 2525, N. Cerney man. 1685–1713.
[31] Ibid. N. Cerney and Ciren. deeds 1732–54.
[32] Glouc. Jnl. 18 Sept. 1750.
[33] Glos. R.O., Q/RSf 2, 1775.
[34] Glos. R.O., D 1388, tithe papers, N. Cerney, 1818.
[35] F.S. 2/3 no. 198.
[36] G.D.R., T 1/45.
[37] Kelly's Dir. Glos. (1856), 236; cf. Glos. R.O., D 1388/SL 6, no. 52.
[38] Licensed Houses in Glos. 1891, 42.

[39] Glos. R.O., Q/RSf 2.
[40] F.S. 2/3 nos. 115, 394.
[41] F.S. 2/3 nos. 198, 288; F.S. 4/12 nos. 198, 288.
[42] Glos. R.O., D 2525, reading-room papers.
[43] Kelly's Dir. Glos. (1927), 62.
[44] D.N.B.
[45] Grundy, Saxon Charters, 56–61.
[46] Dom. Bk. (Rec. Com.), i. 164v.
[47] Feud. Aids, ii. 239, 299.
[48] L. & P. Hen. VIII, xx (1), p. 214.
[49] Cal. Pat. 1550–3, 357.
[50] Glos. R.O., D 2525, N. Cerney man. 1552–1657.
[51] C 142/185 no. 85.
[52] C 142/268 no. 146.
[53] Glos. R.O., D 2525, N. Cerney man. 1582–1610.
[54] Ibid. N. Cerney man. 1611–20.
[55] Prob. 11/149 (P.C.C. 88 Hele).
[56] Glos. R.O., D 2525, N. Cerney man. 1552–1657, deed 1641.
[57] Ibid. N. Cerney man. 1625–81; cf. ibid. N. Cerney man. 1713–32, ct. rolls; and for Eliz. Bromwich's death, Bigland, Glos. iii, no. 270.
[58] Glos. R.O., D 2525, N. Cerney man, 1625–81, deed 1681.

Bathurst. Simon and Cecily Oatridge were succeeded by Henry Oatridge, and Daniel and Elizabeth Oatridge by their son John. Henry and John sold their shares to Lord Bathurst in 1718, thus reuniting the manor.[59] The manor, or a part of it, was later made over to Lord Bathurst's eldest son Benjamin,[60] who died in 1767 before his father. Subsequently the manor descended with the Bathurst peerage,[61] with which it remained in 1978.

Cerney Manor, at the bottom of North Cerney village, evidently occupies the site of the capital messuage of the manor recorded from the 1550s.[62] For most of its history the house has been used merely as a farm-house; of the lords of the manor only Nathaniel Poole is recorded as being resident at Cerney.[63] The house dates mainly from a rebuilding of c. 1700 and has a main range with a symmetrical front of seven bays and a short rear wing housing a staircase. Additions were made to the north in the later 18th century and to the east in the 19th and 20th.

Another part of North Cerney, extended at 7 hides, was held in 1066 by two thegns, Eilaf and his brother, for a rent of 2 marks and the service of making journeys for the king. In 1086 it was held by Gilbert son of Turold[64] and passed with Rendcomb to the earls of Gloucester. The estate evidently included at Domesday the whole of Woodmancote and Calmsden, over which the earls later exercised frankpledge jurisdiction,[65] but most of the land of those hamlets was apparently subinfeudated with Rendcomb to the de la Mares and had passed to other owners by the early 13th century. Some Cerney lands, however, were retained in demesne by the earls of Gloucester and their successors, following the descent of their small manor in Rendcomb,[66] and by the early 16th century those Cerney lands were regarded as separate manors of *NORTH CERNEY* and *WOODMANCOTE*.[67] The Woodmancote manor, though included in a sale to Thomas Taylor in 1566 and claimed by his successors,[68] may actually have been retained by the Staffords, for Mary, widow of Edward Stafford, Lord Stafford, was named as lady of that hamlet in 1608.[69] Later, however, Woodmancote figures with the Rendcomb and North Cerney manors in the litigation between the Pooles and the Guises,[70] passing with them to the latter family,[71] which owned over 500 a. in Woodmancote tithing as part of its Rendcomb Park estate in 1837.[72]

Sir Thomas Rich, who became lessee of the manors formerly belonging to the earls of Stafford, also acquired a long lease of two farms in Woodmancote tithing called Green's and Viner's which were held from those manors.[73] They apparently formed the basis of the later *CERNEY HOUSE* estate. Sir Thomas granted the lease of the two farms to his son William who died before him in 1639.[74] Sir Thomas at his death in 1647 devised a capital messuage in Woodmancote, where he had been living, and lands to his wife Anne,[75] and his estate, which was presumably converted to freehold, apparently passed to his grandson Thomas Rich (d. 1705). The family was said to have a good house and estate at Cerney c. 1710[76] and in 1719 the owner was Edward Rich,[77] apparently the son of the younger Thomas. Edward Rich died c. 1721 when in financial difficulties[78] and the Cerney House estate later passed to the Revd. Edward Pickering Rich, after whose death in 1761 it was put up for sale.[79] It was bought by Thomas Tyndale (d. 1783), whose son sold the estate c. 1795 to William Kimber.[80] It later passed to Barrington Price but by 1807 the owner was John Hooper Holder, who sold the estate in 1814 to William Croome.[81] The estate, which covered 475 a. in 1837,[82] passed from William Croome (d. 1855) to his son William Fielder Croome (d. 1886). It then passed to the younger William's nephew Thomas Lancelot Croome (d. 1895), and to Thomas's son William Iveson Croome, who was an infant at his father's death. W. I. Croome sold the estate in 1930[83] to Mrs. de la Hey, wife of the rector of North Cerney,[84] and it passed to Capt. R. M. O. de la Hey who put it up for sale in 1953. The farmland of the estate, comprising Scrubditch farm, was then sold to Mr. J. C. Herdman, and Cerney House, sold separately, passed through various owners and belonged in 1978 to Mr. C. P. Francis.[85]

A small block on the north side of Cerney House, which has the remains of two 17th-century windows, survives from the Rich family's house, as do possibly some thick internal walls incorporated into the main block. The main block dates from a rebuilding carried out by Thomas Tyndale, probably soon after 1761.[86] Further alterations were made c. 1800, when semicircular bows were added to the sides and the interior was largely refitted, and the porch to the main front was apparently brought from Driffield Manor in 1803.[87] Additions to the service quarters were made at various times in the

---

[59] Ibid. N. Cerney man. 1685–1713, 1715–18.

[60] Ibid. N. Cerney leases 1715–89; D 182/III/203.

[61] For which, see Burke, *Peerage* (1975), 200–1.

[62] Req. 2/20/168; Glos. R.O., D 2525, N. Cerney man. 1552–1657, lease 1604.

[63] Glos. R.O., D 2525, N. Cerney man. 1625–81.

[64] *Dom. Bk.* (Rec. Com.), i. 168v.

[65] *Plac. de Quo Warr.* (Rec. Com.), 253. [66] See below.

[67] C 142/80 no. 23; *L. & P. Hen. VIII*, v, p. 129.

[68] C 54/721 mm. 40–2; C 107/112.

[69] Smith, *Men and Armour*, 253; cf. *Complete Peerage*, xii (1), 184–5.

[70] Glos. R.O., D 326/L 11–12.

[71] Ibid. T 10; Bigland, *Glos.* i. 285.

[72] G.D.R., T 1/45.

[73] Cf. C 54/721 m. 40; C 3/260/29.

[74] *Inq. p.m. Glos.* 1625–42, ii. 103–4; for the Rich fam., see *Visit. Glos. 1682–3*, 142–4.

[75] Prob. 11/202 (P.C.C. 217 Fines).

[76] Atkyns, *Glos.* 322.

[77] Bodl. MS. Top. Glouc. c. 6, f. 42.

[78] G.D.R. wills 1721/333.

[79] *Manual of Glos. Lit.* ii. 44; Prob. 11/868 (P.C.C. 298 Cheslyn).

[80] Inscr. in ch.; Rudder, *Glos.* proof pages (Glos. Colln.), MS. note on p. 325; Glos. R.O., D 2525, N. Cerney rating val. 1796.

[81] Glos. R.O., D 1388, tithe papers, N. Cerney; *Delineations of Glos.* 98.

[82] G.D.R., T 1/45.

[83] Burke, *Land. Gent.* (1937), 523–4.

[84] Glos. R.O., D 2299/4315; *Kelly's Dir. Glos.* (1935), 60.

[85] Sale partics. *penes.* and ex inf., Mr. Francis.

[86] Rudder, *Glos.* proof pages (Glos. Colln.). MS. note on p. 325. A date in the early 1760s is more likely on archit. grounds than the date 1780 given in *Delineations of Glos.* 98.

[87] Verey, *Glos.* i. 337.

19th century. The small landscaped park around the house was probably the work of Thomas Tyndale, who secured the closure of a road that passed close to the house in 1780.[88] A circular lodge was built at the end of the drive to the Cirencester road in 1914.[89]

Another part of Woodmancote, also called the manor of *WOODMANCOTE*, passed with Rendcomb manor to the de la Mares. In 1204 Robert de la Mare owed a fine to the Crown for the restoration of land at Woodmancote that William Noel had held[90] and the manor later passed to the Leigh family, apparently by the marriage of Mabel de la Mare and William of Leigh.[91] In 1221 Richard Noel quitclaimed half of the manor to Maud of Leigh[92] and in 1233 the manor, extended at 2 plough-lands, belonged to Constance of Leigh, daughter of Mabel and William, and she gave it in that year to the newly founded abbey of Lacock (Wilts.).[93] William de la Mare of Rendcomb released his right to homage as overlord[94] but in 1269 his descendant, also William, was claiming aid from Lacock in respect of the manor.[95] In 1538 the abbey leased the manor for 40 years to Sir Edmund Tame, and the Crown granted the reversion to Giles Poole of Sapperton in 1542.[96] The later descent of the manor has not been traced but it is likely that it was acquired by the owners of the Rendcomb estate.

An estate called the manor of *CALMSDEN* also passed to William of Leigh who granted it in 1190 to the Knights Hospitallers,[97] to whose preceptory of Quenington it was attached until the Dissolution. In 1544 the Crown granted the manor to Thomas Stroud and his partners, who sold it a few days later to Thomas Seymour, Lord Seymour, and Henry Brouncker.[98] Brouncker sold his moiety in 1553 to Catherine Buckler, widow of Sir Walter Buckler and of Sir Edmund Tame, and the same year she bought the other moiety from the Crown, which had taken possession on Seymour's execution for treason in 1549. Richard Buckler, heir to the manor,[99] apparently conveyed his interest to Catherine's third husband Roger Lygon in 1568,[1] and Roger and Catherine held it in 1571.[2]

The sparseness of the evidence for Calmsden in the next two centuries makes it impossible to establish a clear connexion between the two manors that existed there in the Middle Ages and the later estates. It seems most likely, however, that the Lygons' manor was the one that became divided into three parts, one part passing to the Shipside family and being sold c. 1630 to Sir Thomas Crewe.[3] In 1682 the site and one third of Calmsden manor were conveyed to John Vannam,[4] D.D., vicar of Bibury, who claimed two-thirds of the manor at his death in 1721, leaving them to his son John.[5] Dr. Vannam's estate apparently passed eventually to his daughter Elizabeth, wife of Robert Hicks of Coombe, in Wotton under Edge, and then to their daughter Elizabeth, wife of George Somerville of Dinder (Som.). William Somerville, vicar of Bibury, son of George and Elizabeth,[6] claimed to be lord of Calmsden manor in 1785[7] and had a considerable estate there in 1795.[8] After the Revd. William's death in 1803 his widow Jane held the estate[9] and at her death in 1830 it passed to his nephew James Somerville Fownes, who changed his surname to Somerville. James, whose Calmsden estate comprised 580 a. in 1837,[10] was succeeded at his death in 1848 by his son James Curtis Somerville, the owner in 1867.[11] Before 1878 the estate was bought by Sir Francis Goldsmid of Rendcomb and joined to the other Calmsden estate.[12] The Somervilles' estate was based on the small gabled manor-house of the 17th century which survives at the centre of Calmsden.[13]

Another estate in Calmsden, known as the manor of *CALMSDEN* or *BARLEY* and held from the de la Mares,[14] may have been the matter in dispute between Robert of Calmsden and William de la Mare in 1185;[15] Robert or a successor of the same name was recorded in 1231.[16] In 1327 Roger of Barley was given the highest assessment for the subsidy among the inhabitants of Calmsden,[17] and in 1402 John Barley and Isabel his wife held the manor subject to Alice Barley's right to a third as dower.[18] John died c. 1405[19] and the manor passed before 1427 to John Blount of Bitton in right of his wife William. John died in 1444[20] and William in 1454 when she was succeeded by their son Edmund Blount.[21] Edmund apparently sold the manor before his death in 1468, though he retained an estate of a plough-land at Woodmancote[22] that his parents had bought from Richard and Alice Colles.[23] The Blounts' Calmsden manor was presumably that which later belonged to Sir Edmund Tame (d. 1544) who settled it on his wife Catherine, who later owned the other Calmsden manor. The reversion of Tame's manor was assigned to his sister Margaret and her husband Sir Humphrey Stafford,[24] and it was presumably still

[88] Glos. R.O., Q/SRh 1780 C; cf. *Glouc. Jnl.* 1 Sept. 1794.
[89] Date on bldg.
[90] *Pipe R.* 1204 (P.R.S. N.S. xviii), 150.
[91] *Cat. Anct. D.* iv, A 8911.
[92] C.P. 25(1)/73/6 no. 65.
[93] C.P. 25(1)/73/9 no. 139; *Cat. Anct. D.* iv, A 8911.
[94] *Cat. Anct. D.* iv, A 9250.
[95] Ibid. A 9378.
[96] *L. & P. Hen. VIII*, xvii, p. 567.
[97] *Cat. Anct. D.* iv, A 8990.
[98] *L. & P. Hen. VIII*, xix (2), pp. 179, 196.
[99] *Cal. Pat.* 1553, 79–80, 114.
[1] Note (*penes* the editor V.C.H. Glos.) of fine of 10 Eliz. East., the original of which appears to be lost.
[2] *Cal. Pat.* 1569–72, p. 324.
[3] C 3/399/153.
[4] C.P. 25(2)/659/34 Chas. II East. no. 2.
[5] Prob. 11/581 (P.C.C. 154 Buckingham).

[6] For the Somervilles, see Burke, *Land. Gent.* (1846), ii. 1262–3; (1898), ii. 1373.
[7] Glos. R.O., Q/SO 10.
[8] Ibid. Q/RI 63.
[9] Ibid. D 3495, Calmsden and N. Cerney deeds.
[10] G.D.R., T 1/45.
[11] *Rep. Com. Agric. Employment*, 100.
[12] Glos. R.O., D 1388/SL 6, no. 52.
[13] G.D.R., T 1/45.
[14] C 139/114 no. 20B.
[15] *Pipe R.* 1185 (P.R.S. xxxiv), 148.
[16] *Close R.* 1231–4, 14.
[17] *Glos. Subsidy Roll, 1327*, 10.
[18] C.P. 25(2)/290/60 no. 51.
[19] Staffs. R.O., D 641/1/4M/2.
[20] C 260/136 no. 11; C 139/114 no. 20B.
[21] C 139/153 no. 17; *Cal. Fine R.* 1452–61, 118–19.
[22] C 140/30 no. 50.
[23] C 139/153 no. 17.
[24] C 142/71 no. 156; C.P. 40/1134 Carte rot. 2d.

only the reversion that Margaret and her second husband Sir John Cope were dealing with in 1554.[25]

It was apparently Tame's manor that passed to the Berkeleys and then to the Guises but whether by the same descent as his Rendcomb manor is not clear. Dame Eleanor Berkeley was said to be lady of Calmsden in 1608,[26] and Sir John Guise, at the beginning of the 18th century, and Sir William Guise, in the 1770s, claimed manorial rights there.[27] The Guises, however, seem then to have had little or no land at Calmsden; the large farm that was later attached to their Rendcomb Park estate, comprising 634 a. in 1837,[28] was apparently bought c. 1789 from the Cherington family by Shute Barrington.[29] The Calmsden land of the Rendcomb Park estate was later increased by the purchase of the Somervilles' estate and, in 1907, the rector's glebe at Calmsden, and when put up for sale in 1914 it comprised 1,290 a.[30] It was bought then by J. A. K. Falconer[31] (d. 1948)[32] who left it to his daughter Mrs. Eleanor Tufnell (d. 1969); Mrs. Tufnell left the estate in trust for the children of her son, Mr. C. J. R. Tufnell, who farmed the estate in 1978.[33] The house belonging to the Guises' estate in 1837,[34] presumably the home of the Cheringtons in the 18th century,[35] stood at the west side of the hamlet. It was described as an old gabled farm-house in 1914,[36] after which date it became the residence of the owners of the Calmsden estate; it was rebuilt in Cotswold style to the designs of V. A. Lawson in 1924–5.[37]

The *COTSWOLD HOUSE* (later Cotswold Park) estate at the west side of the parish was established by 1781 when it was owned by Samuel Walbank,[38] a former London wine-merchant. It later passed to Grey Jermyn Grove who sold it in 1796 to William Veel. Veel sold the estate in 1808 to Robert Milligan,[39] a prominent London merchant and chief promoter of the building of the West India Docks.[40] Robert (d. 1809) left life-interests in the estate to such of his daughters as remained unmarried, with a reversionary interest to all his children. The immediate beneficiaries were Jean, who married in 1811, Justinia, who died in 1840, and Mary. In 1851 Mary's brother William Milligan bought her interest and the rights of the other heirs and he sold the estate in 1859 to James Bownes (d. 1873), a tobacco-merchant of Mansfield (Notts.). Bownes's trustees sold it in 1879, when it

comprised 202 a. in Cerney, Duntisbourne Abbots, and Winstone, to James Canby Biddle-Cope, who sold it in 1885 to T. T. S. Metcalfe.[41] By 1897 it had passed to the Revd. John Priestley Foster[42] who sold it in 1915 to the Hon. F. W. Stanley;[43] Lt.-Col. Stanley, as he became, remained the owner in 1939.[44] Later the estate was bought by Lt.-Col. A. M. Gibb (d. 1955), and his widow Yoskyl,[45] who afterwards married Malcolm McCorquodale, Lord McCorquodale (d. 1971),[46] retained it in 1978.

Cotswold Park was evidently built shortly before 1781,[47] the original house comprising a narrow range, with a symmetrical west front of 3 storeys and 3 bays, and a rear service wing of 2 storeys. An extension terminating in a semi-octagonal bay was later added to the north end of the main range, presumably part of the recent additions mentioned in 1795,[48] and other additions were made to the south side in the later 19th century. The narrow valley overlooked by the house was formed into a small ornamental park before 1825.[49]

Tewkesbury Abbey owned a small estate at Woodmancote by the mid 13th century, probably granted to it by one of the earls of Gloucester.[50] Comprising 2 houses and 1½ yardland at the Dissolution,[51] it was granted to John Pope and Anthony Foster in 1544.[52] The hospital of St. John at Cirencester had a few acres of land at Calmsden until the earlier 20th century.[53]

ECONOMIC HISTORY. In 1086 there were two plough-teams and a single *servus* on the demesne of the archbishop of York's manor of North Cerney.[54] In 1283 three teams were maintained for Cerney and Compton Abdale, another of the archbishop's manors.[55] The demesne at Cerney was apparently still cultivated for the lord in 1373[56] but by 1401 it was leased. In the latter year it comprised 217 a. of open-held land, 5 a. of several meadow, and a 200-acre pasture called Cerney Mead on the wolds,[57] evidently Cerney Downs, which were presumably as later open to commoning rights of the tenants. In 1657 the land attached to the site of the manor included 160 a. of land in each of the open fields and some meadow closes; extensive rights of sheep-pasture were also used with the demesne in the 17th century, some of them deriving from tenant land that had lapsed to the lord.[58]

The demesne of Gilbert son of Turold's manor in

[25] C.P. 25(2)/71/587 no. 39.
[26] Smith, *Men and Armour*, 252.
[27] Bodl. MS. Top. Glouc. c. 3, f. 214; Rudder, *Glos.* 326.
[28] G.D.R., T 1/45.
[29] Glos. R.O., Q/REl 1, 1788, 1790; cf. *Glouc. Jnl.* 15 Oct. 1751.
[30] Glos. R.O., SL 214.
[31] Ibid. D 2299/1508, 5816.
[32] Tombstone in N. Cerney churchyard.
[33] Ex inf. Mr. Tufnell.   [34] G.D.R., T 1/45.
[35] Bigland, *Glos.* i. 286.
[36] Glos. R.O., SL 214.
[37] Verey, *Glos.* i. 338.
[38] Glos. R.O., D 326/T 97; cf. Rudder, *Glos.* 439.
[39] Glos. R.O., D 1909/1.
[40] *Delineations of Glos.* 99–100.
[41] Glos. R.O., D 1909/1; cf. ibid. D 1388/SL 6, nos. 4, 134 A.
[42] *Kelly's Dir. Glos.* (1897), 54.

[43] Glos. R.O., D 2299/1169.
[44] *Kelly's Dir. Glos.* (1939), 62.
[45] *Who Was Who, 1951–60*, 415–16.
[46] Burke, *Peerage* (1963), 1544–5; tombstone in N. Cerney churchyard.
[47] Cf. *Glouc. Jnl.* 9 July 1787.
[48] Ibid. 28 Sept. 1795.
[49] *Delineations of Glos.* plate facing p. 99.
[50] *Lacock Abbey Charters*, no. 401. It was probably the property at 'Rendcomb' for which the abbey owed suit at the earl's Fairford ct. in 1255: *Ann. Mon.* (Rolls Ser.), i. 156.
[51] Glos. R.O., P 329/MI 1, rot. 41.
[52] *L. & P. Hen. VIII*, xix (2), p. 190.
[53] Glos. R.O., P 86/CH 15/3, 8.
[54] *Dom. Bk.* (Rec. Com.), i. 164v.
[55] *Cal. Chart. R.* 1257–1300, 268.
[56] S.C. 6/1144/10.   [57] Glos. R.O., D 621/M 7.
[58] Ibid. D 2525, N. Cerney man. 1552–1657, 1625–81.

1086 had 4 teams and 6 *servi*.[59] A small part of the Staffords' lands in the parish were originally in demesne but by 1413 were let at farm.[60] The Hospitallers' Calmsden manor had 8 yardlands and a meadow at Perrott's Brook in demesne in the early 16th century.[61] Lacock Abbey had a plough-land in demesne at Woodmancote in 1291.[62] In the early 16th century its manor there was leased in its entirety.[63]

The tenants on the archbishop's manor in 1086 were 6 *villani* and 2 bordars with 5 teams among them, while Gilbert son of Turold's estate had 7 *villani* and 6 bordars with 5 teams among them. There were also 4 knights holding estates under Gilbert which were worked by 7 teams. The total of 23 teams enumerated in 1086[64] and the assessment of the various manors at a total of $24\frac{1}{2}$ plough-lands in 1220[65] show the parish to have been intensively cultivated in the early Middle Ages. The agricultural depression of the earlier 14th century, however, caused depopulation and presumably a sharp contraction in arable farming. In 1341 it was reported that 10 of the tenant holdings had been abandoned since 1291 and that wool-production had suffered severely from murrain and a shortage of grazing.[66] The Black Death presumably caused further depopulation and an account roll for the archbishop's manor in 1401 reflects the general decline. The customary tenants of the manor were then still accounted for at a theoretical strength of 6 yardlanders, 4 half-yardlanders, 3 mondaymen, and 4 cottars but all 11 of the smaller holdings had lapsed to the lord of the manor and one of the yardlands also was given up in the course of the year. Five of the houses belonging to the 11 smaller holdings had been demolished or had fallen down and the lands of those holdings were leased by the year among only 4 tenants. There were then also 3 free tenants holding from the manor.[67]

In the early 16th century some of the copyholds on the archbishop's manor still betrayed their composition from several original holdings; in 1536 one comprised 4 houses and $2\frac{1}{2}$ yardlands and owed 4 heriots.[68] In the late 16th and early 17th centuries much of the tenant land of the manor was leased for lives or for long terms of years[69] but some copyholds remained in 1656. All the tenants held for lives *c.* 1713, most of them presumably, as later in the 18th century, by leases for 99 years or 3 lives. There were 6 large holdings *c.* 1713, ranging from 33 a. to 114 a., and 9 cottage-holdings, most with the statutory 4 a of land.[70]

The bulk of the tenant land of the earl of Stafford's manors in Rendcomb and Cerney lay in Woodmancote tithing. In 1408 six of the seven customary holdings of those manors, ranging in size from a fardel to $1\frac{1}{2}$ yardland, were described as in Woodmancote or Cerney.[71] In 1566 all the tenant land still attached to those manors lay in Woodmancote tithing and comprised four large farms, three of 5 yardlands and the other of 4 yardlands.[72] By the early 17th century most of that land had been alienated or granted on long leases[73] and much of it was later formed into the Cerney House estate. On the Hospitallers' manor of Calmsden the only tenants in 1541 were a free tenant holding $2\frac{1}{2}$ yardlands and a copyholder, whose holding, comprising 3 houses, a cottage, and $3\frac{3}{4}$ yardlands, was evidently made up of several original holdings.[74] The definition of a yardland varied over the centuries: in 1444 a plough-land in Woodmancote contained 60 a.;[75] in 1635 the yardland used in the parish, or at least in Woodmancote and Calmsden tithings, comprised 24 a.;[76] and in 1715 46 a. in Cerney tithing was described as a yardland.[77]

The three tithings, Cerney, Woodmancote, and Calmsden, had their separate open fields. The north and south (or upper and lower) fields of Cerney, which comprised mainly the lands of the archbishop's manor, were recorded from 1401;[78] they occupied the slopes on the east side of the Churn.[79] The two large Calmsden fields lay north and south of that hamlet.[80] Woodmancote tithing appears to have had at least four open fields. Those called Burcombe and Morcombe fields in the 13th century were probably the same as the west and north fields recorded at the same period[81] and presumably lay in the north-western arm of the tithing, while two fields recorded later occupied the slopes of the south part of the tithing, above the Churn.[82]

The small amount of meadow (8 a.) recorded in the parish in 1086[83] and on the archbishop's demesne in 1401 suggests that the possibilities of irrigating the land bordering the Churn were not fully exploited until the post-medieval period. What meadow land existed earlier was certainly highly prized; the 2 a. belonging to an estate at Woodmancote in 1444 was extended at six times the value of its arable land.[84] In later centuries a continuous if narrow strip of meadow, some of it said *c.* 1710 to be among the best in the county,[85] bordered the Churn, and in 1851 one of the farms on the Bathurst estate had 32 a. of rich water meadow.[86] The hatches in the river used for con-

---

[59] *Dom. Bk.* (Rec. Com.), i. 168v.
[60] Staffs. R.O., D 641/1/2/160.
[61] S.C. 11/831 rot. 3d.; S.C. 6/Hen. VIII/7262 rot. 2.
[62] *Tax. Eccl.* (Rec. Com.), 237.
[63] S.C. 6/Hen. VIII/3985.
[64] *Dom. Bk.* (Rec. Com.), i. 164v., 168v.
[65] *Bk. of Fees*, i. 311.
[66] *Inq. Non.* (Rec. Com.), 409.
[67] Glos. R.O., D 621/M 7.
[68] Ibid. M 14.
[69] Ibid. D 2525, N. Cerney man. 1552–1657.
[70] Ibid. N. Cerney man. 1713–32; N. Cerney leases 1715–89.
[71] Staffs. R.O., D 641/1/4M/2.
[72] C 54/721 m. 40.

[73] C 3/260/29; Glos. R.O., D 293/4, transcr. of Chancery proceedings 1614; *Inq. p.m. Glos.* 1625–42, ii, 103–4.
[74] S.C. 6/Hen. VIII/7262 rot. 2; cf. Hockaday Abs. cxliii, 1544.
[75] C 139/114 no. 20B.
[76] G.D.R. V 5/67T 1.
[77] Glos. R.O., D 2525, N. Cerney leases 1715–89.
[78] Ibid. D 621/M 7.
[79] Ibid. D 2525, N. Cerney man. 1713–32, partition 1712.
[80] Ibid. Q/RI 63.
[81] *Lacock Abbey Charters*, nos. 387, 401, 411.
[82] G.D.R., V 5/67T 1–2.
[83] *Dom. Bk.* (Rec. Com.), i. 164v., 168v.
[84] C 139/114 no. 20B.
[85] Glos. R.O., D 2525, N. Cerney man. 1713–32.
[86] Ibid. N. Cerney vals. 1811–55.

trolling the flooding of the meadows that were mentioned in 1824[87] had presumably by then been in use for many years. Some of the meadows by the Churn were cultivated on the lot system in the 17th century and another part, though owned by the lord of the manor formerly the archbishop's, was subject to commoning rights of the tenants; William Poole may have planned to inclose the meadows on that manor in 1656 when he reserved the pasture rights in his copyhold grants.[88] In the 17th century there were also small plots of meadow intermixed with the arable in the open fields.[89]

Above the open fields on the east side of the Churn valley lay the extensive common downland called Cerney Downs and beyond that was a smaller area of downland belonging to Calmsden.[90] In the late Middle Ages the eastern corner of the parish beyond Calmsden hamlet was occupied by a large tract of rough pasture known as Oldgore. It covered 600 a. in the 15th century when two-thirds of it belonged to the Hospitallers' manor and one third to the Blounts' manor.[91] Woodmancote also had an area of common downland, lying north of the hamlet.[92] Cerney Downs and the open fields on the archbishop's manor were stinted at 60 sheep to the yardland in 1540 but in part of the downs the farmer of the demesne had the sole right to the summer pasture.[93] Measures for the regulation of the pasture taken by the tenants of that manor in 1672 included the appointment of sheep-tellers.[94] The stint for sheep on the Staffords' manors was also 60 to the yardland in 1566.[95]

Sheep-farming had become an important element in the husbandry of the parish by the late Middle Ages though it remained inferior in total value to crop-raising in 1535 when the rector's wool and lamb tithes were valued at £6 17s. and his corn tithes at £10 6s.[96] Nicholas Gazard of Calmsden was one of the largest sheep-farmers in the 1430s when he was in constant trouble with the earl of Stafford's manor court for pasturing his flock of 400 where he had no rights.[97] Another flock was kept by the rector William Whitchurch in 1476.[98] The substantial holdings in the parish acquired by the Tame family of Fairford and Rendcomb were no doubt connected with their sheep-farming operations. William Tame acquired a lease of 200 a. of Oldgore from the Hospitallers c. 1485[99] and it was held later by John Tame and his descendants.[1] The younger Sir Edmund Tame (d. 1544) besides owning one of the Calmsden manors and a free tenement on the archbishop's manor[2]

also held on lease the demesne of the Hospitallers' manor,[3] Lacock Abbey's Woodmancote manor,[4] and Tewkesbury Abbey's Woodmancote estate.[5] William Fifield, who farmed the demesne on the manor formerly the archbishop's, had a flock of 460 sheep in 1558[6] and the demesne farm appears to have been exploited for sheep-raising by the Poole family in the earlier 17th century. William Poole, later owner of the manor, took a lease of the farm with pasture for 307 sheep in 1604, and four years later Thomas, one of his sons, took a lease of an additional 340 sheep-pastures. In 1641 820 sheep-pastures were used with the demesne farm, which Nathaniel Poole probably had in hand.[7]

Inclosure of the Cerney fields had begun by the early 18th century, when Henry Combes's portion of the demesne farm included some newly inclosed arable,[8] and was evidently completed by the Bathursts later in the century; new inclosures taken out of the south field were mentioned in 1751. Inclosure of the south part of Cerney Downs was in progress in 1755[9] and by 1807 72 a. in the north part had also been inclosed and ploughed up. The remaining 244 a. of the downs were attached to North Cerney farm in 1807[10] and comprised the land lying east of the White way bounded on the north and south by the roads from Calmsden to North Cerney and from Calmsden to Perrott's Brook. All pasture rights in that land apparently then belonged to the farm but other occupiers had furze-cutting rights. Those rights were apparently extinguished and inclosure of the downs completed by Lord Bathurst in the 1830s.[11]

The two Woodmancote fields in the Churn valley were called Thomas Rich's north and south fields in 1635 and he apparently then held all the land there apart from some belonging to the rector's glebe.[12] Rich made some inclosures from the fields by agreement with his son Samuel, the rector, in the early 1630s,[13] and inclosure of the fields was evidently completed by later agreements between the owners of the Cerney House estate and the rectors; Edward Rich and the Revd. John Coxe made an exchange of lands in the north field in 1719.[14] In 1837 the Cerney House estate included the succession of regular closes lying between the Bagendon boundary and the meadow land by the Churn, evidently representing the south field, and closes called Woodmancote field lying by the road from North Cerney to Woodmancote, evidently former parts of the north field.[15] Part of the open fields of the north-western arm of the tithing

[87] Ibid. loose deed 1824.
[88] Ibid. N. Cerney man. 1611–20, deed 1619; 1713–32, ct. roll 1656.
[89] Ibid. N. Cerney man. 1611–20, deed 1619; 1625–81, deed 1631.
[90] Ibid. Q/RI 63.
[91] C 260/136 no. 11; C 139/114 no. 20B.
[92] Glos. R.O., Q/RI 35.
[93] Ibid. D 621/M 14.
[94] Ibid. D 2525, N. Cerney man. 1713–32.
[95] C 54/721 m. 40.
[96] Valor Eccl. (Rec. Com.), ii. 448.
[97] Staffs. R.O., D 641/1/4M/3–4.
[98] Ibid. 11.
[99] C 1/99 nos. 13–15.
[1] S.C. 11/831 rot. 3d.; S.C. 6/Hen. VIII/7262 rot. 2.

[2] Glos. R.O., D 621/M 14, ct. 12 Apr. 26 Hen. VIII.
[3] S.C. 6/Hen. VIII/7262 rot. 2.
[4] S.C. 6/Hen. VIII/3985.
[5] Glos. R.O., P. 329/MI 1, rot. 41.
[6] Req. 2/20/168.
[7] Glos. R.O., D 2525, N. Cerney man. 1552–1657; cf. Prob. 11/149 (P.C.C. 88 Hele).
[8] Glos. R.O., D 2525, N. Cerney man. 1713–32.
[9] Ibid. N. Cerney leases 1715–89.
[10] Ibid. D 1388, tithe papers, N. Cerney.
[11] Ibid. D 2525, N. Cerney draft leases 1790–1833; cf. ibid. P 70A/PC 1/1, entry for 1898.
[12] G.D.R., V 5/67T 1.
[13] C 107/112.
[14] Bodl. MS. Top. Glouc. c. 6, f. 42.
[15] G.D.R., T 1/45.

survived until at least 1781 when Samuel Walbank of Cotswold House and another owner made exchanges there.[16] Woodmancote Downs, covering 64 a., were inclosed by Act of Parliament in 1855 so that they could be turned over to arable. Most of the land was allotted to Sir John Wright Guise and William Croome of Cerney House, who shared the right of soil and the bulk of the pasture rights; William Milligan of Cotswold House and another occupier received small allotments for pasture rights.[17]

At Calmsden some inclosures were made by private agreement before 1795 but over 1,000 a. of fields and downs remained to be inclosed by Act of Parliament in that year. The bulk of the land went to Shute Barrington and his wife, who received 540 a. for the land and rights belonging to the Rendcomb estate, and the Revd. William Somerville, who received 459 a.; the rector received 47 a. for his glebe in the Calmsden fields.[18]

From the late 18th century most of the land of the parish was consolidated into six or seven large farms. Lord Bathurst's estate was divided between two farms: North Cerney farm based on the manor-house comprised 794 a. in 1796 while another farm of 252 a., later known as Perrott's Brook farm, was formed from the south part of the estate.[19] North Cerney farm was tenanted in the late 18th and early 19th centuries by the prosperous Kimber family who farmed it with other land in the parish which they owned or leased.[20] Perrott's Brook farm, which from the early 19th century had its farm-house at the former inn by the Welsh way,[21] was usually farmed together with North Cerney farm in the later 19th and early 20th centuries but was leased separately again after the Second World War.[22] Calmsden was divided between two big farms, comprising 618 a. and 569 a. in 1796, respectively the Rendcomb Park and Somerville family's estates,[23] and continued as such after the Rendcomb estate became owner of all the land.[24] The two big farms were taken in hand and administered by farm bailiffs for a short period in the 1890s, and from the First World War the owners of Calmsden farmed the estate as a single unit.[25]

In Woodmancote tithing the pattern of holdings was more varied. In 1796 a large part of the land was farmed by William Kimber of North Cerney Farm who owned the Cerney House and another smaller estate there and leased the rector's glebe, while another large farm, of 421 a., was formed mainly of the land belonging to the Rendcomb Park

estate; the Cotswold House estate and two other freeholds made three smaller farms.[26] In 1837 William Croome had part of his Cerney House estate, based on a farm-house at the north end of Woodmancote hamlet, in hand while his son W. F. Croome farmed a larger portion including the farm buildings at Scrubditch. The Rendcombe Park land was then farmed with North Cerney farm by Thomas Kimber,[27] but later in the century it was put with adjoining land in Rendcomb parish to form a large farm, of 681 a. in 1878, for which a new farm-house was built at the south end of Woodmancote.[28] In the 1890s that farm too was farmed for the estate by a bailiff.[29]

Some smaller holdings survived in the parish in the late 19th and early 20th centuries bringing its total of agricultural occupiers up to c. 20; in 1926 10 had under 50 a.[30] By 1976, however, there were only two small holdings (under 10 ha.) run on a part-time basis, and the rest of the land was by then consolidated in five farms, of which the largest were the Calmsden estate and North Cerney farm, which in 1978 had 518 ha. (1,280 a.) and 344 ha. (850 a.) respectively. The farms of the parish gave employment to 38 people in 1976[31] compared with just over 100 in 1831[32] and 1926.[33]

After the inclosures one of the usual Cotswold rotations, involving wheat, barley, oats, turnips, and grass-seeds, the last two mainly to provide sheep-fodder, became the usual pattern of husbandry.[34] The growing of sainfoin on some of the inclosed land as an additional source of fodder is recorded from the early 18th century.[35] Most of the farms were devoted predominantly to the rotation of arable land in 1796, when for example the two big Calmsden farms had only 72 a. and 19½ a. of permanent grassland respectively,[36] and arable cultivation became even more dominant during the next 60 years as former downland was put under the plough. In 1837 the parish contained 2,850 a. of arable compared with 914 a. of permanent pasture and meadow[37] and the comparable figures returned in 1866 were 3,058 to 544. The trend was reversed during the slump of the late 19th century. The acreage of wheat and barley returned in 1896 was down to 660 compared with 1,011 in 1866 and much unwanted arable had been turned to grass;[38] c. 1899 the lease to a new tenant of North Cerney farm made particular allowances in respect of several fields that had degenerated to a foul condition.[39] The farms attempted to mitigate the effects of the slump in cereals by building up their flocks and introducing more beef and dairy cattle:

[16] Glos. R.O., D 326/T 97.
[17] Ibid. Q/RI 35; D 326/E 92.
[18] Ibid. Q/RI 63.
[19] Ibid. D 2525, N. Cerney rating val. 1796.
[20] See below; Glos. R.O., D 1388, tithe papers, N. Cerney 1807, 1818.
[21] Glos. R.O., D 1388, tithe papers, N. Cerney 1818; G.D.R., T 1/45.
[22] Glos. R.O., D 2525, draft deeds 1820–79; ex inf. Lady Langman, of Perrott's Brook Fm.
[23] Glos. R.O., D 2525, N. Cerney rating val. 1796.
[24] Ibid. D 1388/SL 6, no. 52.
[25] Kelly's Dir. Glos. (1894 and later edns.).
[26] Glos. R.O., D 2525, N. Cerney rating val. 1796.
[27] G.D.R., T 1/45.
[28] Glos. R.O., D 1388/SL 6, no. 52; cf. Glos. Colln. RV 248.1.
[29] Kelly's Dir. Glos. (1894), 52.
[30] M.A.F. 68/1609/16; M.A.F. 68/3295/4.
[31] Agric. Returns 1976; ex inf. Mr. Tufnell, and Capt. J. W. H. Goddard, of N. Cerney Man.
[32] Census, 1831.
[33] M.A.F. 68/3295/4.
[34] Cf. Acreage Returns, 1801.
[35] Glos. R.O. D 2525, N. Cerney man. 1713–32, partic of Mr. Combes's third of the man.; Glouc. Jnl. 15 Oct. 1751.
[36] Glos. R.O., D 2525, N. Cerney rating val. 1796.
[37] G.D.R., T 1/45.
[38] M.A.F. 68/26/19; M.A.F. 68/1609/16.
[39] Glos. R.O., D 2299/1585.

3,070 sheep and 303 cattle were returned in 1896 compared with 2,446 and 195 in 1866, and during that period the acreage of turnips showed only a relatively small decrease while rotated grass for grazing or mowing showed a slight increase.[40] Sheep-farming was considerably reduced, however, in the early 20th century, but herds were further increased with 540 cattle being returned in 1926[41] when they included a pedigree Shorthorn herd on the Calmsden estate.[42] Dairying and cattle-raising were still important elements in the agriculture of the parish in the later 1970s, though the number of sheep had increased again to the late-19th-century level and the two big farms, Calmsden and North Cerney, were devoted largely to growing cereal crops.[43]

In 1086 three mills were recorded at North Cerney, one each on the manors owned and held from Gilbert son of Turold and one on the archbishop's manor.[44] No later record of a mill has been found on the several estates which derived from Gilbert's but the archbishop's mill was presumably at the site of North Cerney mill on the Churn below the manor-house. It remained part of Cerney manor[45] and during the 19th century was leased to the tenants of North Cerney farm. Though not listed in the directories after 1897[46] it perhaps continued to operate merely for the use of the farmer, for the machinery was still in place in 1966 when it was removed to Arlington Mill at Bibury.[47] A tucker, who was not the tenant of the manor mill, was recorded at Cerney in 1608,[48] so it is possible that another mill then existed elsewhere on the river.

A new mill built on the Cerney manor estate by Richard Painter c. 1715[49] was probably Perrott's Brook mill c. 600 m. upstream of the Perrott's Brook bridge. In 1799 John Radway, a woolstapler, became lessee of Perrott's Brook mill[50] and he was succeeded there by Giles Radway before 1809, when the mill was described as formerly a grist-mill[51] and had perhaps been converted to cloth-making. In or shortly before 1824 Giles Radway built a new cloth-mill south of the old mill[52] and he was still working it in 1837.[53] In the later 19th century it was used as a corn-mill.[54] Both the old and new mills survived together with some cottages in 1978 when the newer mill was used as a farm building for Perrott's Brook farm, which had its other buildings and its recently built new farmhouse at the site.

Though predominantly agricultural, North Cerney parish usually had a fairly substantial number of tradesmen. Eight tradesmen, including the tucker mentioned above, were listed in 1608 compared with 21 men employed in agriculture,[55] and trade supported 33 families in 1831 compared with 90 supported by agriculture.[56] With the exception of the man described as parchment-maker in 1751 and glue-maker in 1778, the tradesmen found recorded during the 18th and 19th centuries were the usual village craftsmen together with a few small shopkeepers.[57] Carpenters were perhaps represented in more than usual numbers for a rural parish in 1851 when 12 lived in the parish; the 9 slaters and masons formed the next largest group while other trades had only one or two representatives.[58] Weavers are occasionally recorded in the parish[59] and in the early 19th century it presumably had a number of cloth-workers; the increase from 16 to 33 tradesmen families between 1811 and 1831[60] may be partly explained by developments at Perrott's Brook mill. A few crafts survived into the mid 20th century: in 1939 Cerney village still had a boot repairer and Calmsden a blacksmith,[61] and a firm of tailors established at Woodmancote before 1906[62] remained in business in 1978. From 1927 a quarry beside the railway in the east corner of the parish was worked by the Fosse Lime and Limestone Co. which burnt lime for agricultural and building purposes; the firm employed 30 men in 1936 and remained at the site until at least 1959.[63]

LOCAL GOVERNMENT. Frankpledge jurisdiction over the tithings of Calmsden and Woodmancote was exercised by the court held at Rendcomb by the owners of the honor of Gloucester, and the court baron held with the Rendcomb frankpledge court exercised manorial jurisdiction over the Woodmancote and Cerney lands belonging to the owners of the honor.[64] The tenants of the archbishop of York's manor attended the hundred frankpledge court.[65] Manor court rolls for that manor survive for several years in the period 1528–48 when the court was usually held in conjunction with that for the archbishop's manor of Compton Abdale, sometimes at Compton and sometimes at Cerney.[66] There are also draft rolls for 1656 and 1660.[67]

Churchwardens' accounts from 1709[68] are the

[40] M.A.F. 68/25/16; M.A.F. 68/26/19; M.A.F. 68/1609/16.
[41] M.A.F. 68/3295/4.   [42] Glos. R.O., D 2299/3542.
[43] Agric. Returns 1976; local information.
[44] Dom. Bk. (Rec. Com.), i. 164v., 168v.
[45] S.C. 6/1144/5; Glos. R.O., D 2525, N. Cerney man. 1552–1657.
[46] Glos. R.O., D 2525, N. Cerney leases 1733–1888; G.D.R., T 1/45; Kelly's Dir. Glos. (1879 and later edns.).
[47] Verey, Glos. i. 337.
[48] Smith, Men and Armour, 253; cf. Glos. R.O., D 2525, N. Cerney man. 1552–1657, leases 1585, 1612.
[49] Glos. R.O., D 2525, N. Cerney man. 1713–32.
[50] Ibid. D 182/III/203.
[51] Ibid. D 2525, N. Cerney leases 1804–62.
[52] Ibid. loose deed 1824; Bryant, Map of Glos. (1824).
[53] G.D.R., T 1/45.
[54] O.S. Map 6", Glos. XLIII. SE. (1884 edn.).

[55] Smith, Men and Armour, 252–3.
[56] Census, 1831.
[57] Glos. R.O., D 2525, N. Cerney leases 1715–89, 1749–1825; H.O. 107/1968; Kelly's Dir. Glos. (1856 and later edns.).
[58] H.O. 107/1968.
[59] Glos. R.O., D 326/E 25, abs. of title to cott. at Calmsden; Hockaday Abs. cxliii, 1816.
[60] Census, 1811–31.
[61] Kelly's Dir. Glos. (1939), 62.
[62] Ibid. (1906), 55.
[63] Glos. R.O., D 2299/5816; W.I. hist. of Chedworth (1959, TS. in Glos. Colln.), 70.
[64] Plac. de Quo Warr. (Rec. Com.), 253; Staffs. R.O., D 641/1/4M/1–11.   [65] Ciren. Cart., ii, p. 619.
[66] Glos. R.O., D 621/M 3–5, M 14.
[67] Ibid. D 2525, N. Cerney man. 1713–32.
[68] B. & G. Par. Rec. 84.

only early records of parish government known to survive. A parish poorhouse in Cerney village was recorded in 1799.[69] In the early 19th century the number of people receiving permanent relief from the parish was c. 40–60.[70] In 1836 North Cerney became part of the Cirencester poor-law union[71] and it was later in Cirencester rural district,[72] becoming part of the new Cotswold district in 1974.

CHURCH. The church building at North Cerney dates from the 12th century. The living was a rectory in 1306[73] and has remained one. It was united with Bagendon in 1974.[74]

Richard de Clare, earl of Gloucester, held the advowson in 1255[75] and it descended with his manors in Rendcomb and North Cerney to the Staffords.[76] The Crown presented in 1533[77] and Richard Bridges, who had apparently been assigned the right in satisfaction of a debt owed him by Edward, Lord Stafford,[78] presented in 1576.[79] During the 17th and early 18th centuries the ownership of the advowson was in doubt, partly as a result of the uncertainties over the manors formerly belonging to the Staffords.[80] It was later maintained that Richard Poole acquired the advowson from Edward, Lord Stafford, in 1599 when he secured confirmation of his title to the manors, but Edward's son and heir Edward, Lord Stafford, claimed it at his death in 1625.[81] The Crown granted it with the wardship of Lord Stafford's grandson and heir, Henry Stafford, to Thomas Howard, earl of Arundel, who presented Samuel Rich to the rectory in 1630. A rival candidate, William Poole, was presented by Sir William Masters, Edmund Estcourt, and John Bridges, who claimed differing titles to the advowson: Sir William claimed under a grant from one of Richard Poole's creditors; Estcourt under a grant from Sir Valentine Knightley made for the benefit of Poole's father, William Poole of Long Newnton; and Bridges under the title of his father Richard Bridges. The ensuing litigation resulted in the decision of 1637 confirming Samuel Rich in the living but allowing Poole the option of pursuing his claim in the future.[82]

The advowson later featured in the dispute between the Pooles and the Guises over the Stafford manors. Richard Poole of London successfully presented in 1684[83] in the face of opposition from the Guises, and his successor Nathaniel Poole included the advowson in his release to the Guises in 1721. Jane Parry, a later opponent of the Guises' claim to the manors,[84] described herself as undoubted patroness in 1727 when she granted the next turn to Charles Coxe with a promise to sell him the advowson in perpetuity.[85] Some accommodation between the disputing parties had apparently been made by 1736 when Charles Coxe's son, Thomas Chamberlayne Coxe, was instituted on Sir John Guise's presentation,[86] and the parties later resolved the dispute by granting their rights to University College, Oxford.[87] After 1974 the college shared the advowson of the united benefice with Jesus College, Oxford.[88]

The rector owned all the tithes of the parish except those from the demesne of the archbishop of York's manor, which belonged to St. Oswald's Priory and were granted to the dean and chapter of Bristol in 1542.[89] The priory's portion, valued at 6s. 8d. in 1291,[90] was being disputed by the rector in 1306 when the prior was said to have forcibly taken sheaves from the archbishop's barn.[91] By the early 18th century the rector had let all his tithes to the occupiers of the lands, providing him in 1732 with a total rental of £181.[92] The tithes were commuted for a corn-rent-charge of £750 in 1837.[93] The glebe comprised a yardland (24 a.) in each of the two Woodmancote fields and one in each of the two Calmsden fields, together with pasture rights and some pieces of meadow land.[94] In 1837 it covered 106 a.[95] The rectory house, standing west of the church, was recorded from 1479 when the rector Willaim Whitchurch built a conduit from a near-by spring to supply it with water.[96] In the 17th century it was a fairly large house with farm buildings ranged round a courtyard. It was rebuilt by the rector John Coxe before 1705 as a substantial square building with a hipped roof and sash windows.[97] A rounded bow was added to the drawing-room c. 1828 and a kitchen wing c. 1913.[98] The house was sold in the 1970s and a smaller house in the village acquired for the rector.

The living was valued at £18 13s. 4d. in 1291,[99] at £21 10s. 5½d. in 1535,[1] and at £120 in 1650.[2] In 1722 it was worth c. £180[3] and by the 1770s had

[69] Glos. R.O., D 2525, N. Cerney leases 1799–1852.
[70] *Poor Law Abstract, 1804,* 180–1; *1818,* 154–5.
[71] *Poor Law Com. 2nd Rep.* p. 522.
[72] *Census,* 1911.
[73] J.I. 1/286 rot. 6d.
[74] *Glouc. Dioc. Yr. Bk.* (1977), 31.
[75] C.P. 25(1)/74/21 no. 453.
[76] e.g. *Cal. Inq. p.m.* v, p. 342; ix, p. 62; *Reg. Wakefeld,* p. 2; Worc. Episc. Reg., Reg. Morgan, i, f. 16; Reg. Carpenter, i, f. 185v.
[77] *L. & P. Hen. VIII,* vi, pp. 88, 260.
[78] C 107/112.
[79] Hockaday Abs. cxliii.
[80] See p. 221.
[81] C 142/419 no. 72.
[82] C 107/112.
[83] Hockaday Abs. cxliii; G.D.R., D 5/3/8.
[84] Glos. R.O., D 326/L 12.

[85] Glos. Colln. RX 67.1.
[86] Hockaday Abs. cxliii; cf. *V.C.H. Glos.* xi. 244.
[87] Rudder, *Glos.* 326.
[88] *Glouc. Dioc. Yr. Bk.* (1977), 31.
[89] *L. & P. Hen. VIII,* xvii, p. 638.
[90] *Tax. Eccl.* (Rec. Com.), 221–2.
[91] J.I. 1/286 rot. 6d.
[92] Bodl. MS. Top. Glouc. c. 6, f. 43.
[93] G.D.R., T 1/45.
[94] G.D.R. V 5/67T 1.
[95] G.D.R., T 1/45.
[96] Staffs. R.O., D 641/1/4M/11; cf. C 1/909 nos. 1–2.
[97] G.D.R., V 5/67T 1, 3, 5; see above, plate facing p. 125.
[98] Verey, *Glos.* i. 336–7.
[99] *Tax. Eccl.* (Rec. Com.), 221–2.
[1] *Valor Eccl.* (Rec. Com.), ii. 448.
[2] *Trans. B.G.A.S.* lxxxiii. 93.
[3] Hockaday Abs. cxliii.

risen in value to £300.[4] There was evidently a considerable rise in value by the time of the tithe commutation and in 1850 the value was £668.[5]

The living of North Cerney, being a fairly wealthy one, encouraged long incumbencies; there were only five rectors in 200 years after 1533. Thomas Taylor, instituted in 1533, neglected his duties in various ways[6] and was frequently in trouble with the consistory court. In 1551 he declared himself ready to believe whatever was handed down by royal authority, a flexible attitude which no doubt helped his retention of the living through the changes of the mid 16th century; but finally he was deprived of North Cerney and his other rectory at Minchinhampton in 1576.[7] His successor Philip Pritchard[8] was described in 1576 as a poor Latinist but sound in religion,[9] and in 1593 was among those classed as sufficient scholars but no preachers.[10] The two contenders for the rectory after Pritchard's death in 1630 were both from leading local families: William Poole was brother to Nathaniel Poole, lord of one of the manors, and Samuel Rich was a son of Sir Thomas Rich. Rich was briefly ousted by Poole in the mid 1630s but he returned in 1637 and, though apparently again challenged by Poole in the early 1660s,[11] he retained the living until his death in 1683. From 1665 he was also rector of Elkstone.[12] John Coxe, rector 1684–1731, held the living in plurality with Rodmarton from 1722 and Thomas Chamberlayne Coxe (d. 1779), instituted in 1736 after a vacancy due to the dispute over the advowson, held it with the livings of Brimpsfield, Preston, and Avening in succession.[14] Matthew Surtees, rector 1793–1826, was vicar of Swindon (Wilts.) from 1809. Thomas Dawson Allen, 1827–75,[15] was a supporter of the Evangelical party and advertised for a curate of similar views in 1866.[16]

Both Woodmancote and Calmsden had chapels of ease to the parish church in the Middle Ages. That at Woodmancote was said to be still in use and served by a curate in 1563[17] but the information was probably out of date, for the chapel building was already in use as a dwelling by 1548. It was then held as a tenement on the Cerney manor formerly belonging to the archbishop of York,[18] surprisingly in view of the fact that no other land in the Woodmancote part of the parish is recorded as being attached to that manor. The dwelling house (called Chapel House in 1823) which replaced the chapel was apparently Tudor House, standing at the centre of Woodmancote hamlet, opposite the Manor House.[19] The oldest part of Tudor House, though it seems to betray its origins in its alignment, was rebuilt in the 17th century, presumably the reason for the statement c. 1703 that the Woodmancote chapel had been demolished.[20] The chapel at Calmsden was said to be no longer served in 1563[21] and it also became a dwelling. It can apparently be identified with a cottage that stood above the cross and spring in Calmsden hamlet until the mid 19th century,[22] though it had been rebuilt or remodelled by the beginning of the 18th century when the Calmsden chapel, too, was said to have been demolished.[23]

A chantry-chapel was recorded as part of the earl of Stafford's manor of Woodmancote and had presumably been founded by an owner of that manor. By 1402, however, the chantry had evidently lapsed for its property was leased to tenants and the rents were taken by the manor. The profits of the chantry included the herbage of the churchyard[24] and it had no doubt been held in part of the church.

The church of *ALL SAINTS*, recorded by that dedication from 1492,[25] is built of ashlar and rubble and has a chancel, a nave with transeptal chapels, north organ chamber, and south porch, and a west tower with saddle-back roof.

The nave and the base of the tower date from the early 12th century when a new church apparently replaced a smaller building.[26] Early in the 13th century the upper parts of the tower were added and the chancel was rebuilt, almost certainly to a greater length than its predecessor. The tower arch was enlarged in the later 13th century and in the 14th the tall south porch was added. Evidence of a serious fire in the tower and nave has been found and is thought to be the reason for the reconstruction of their roofs and the rebuilding of the north wall of the nave in the mid or late 15th century.[27] Soon afterwards the two transeptal chapels were added; they presumably housed the side-altars of St. Catherine and St. Mary mentioned in 1492,[28] and a window in the northern chapel has an inscription to the rector William Whitchurch, who held the living from 1465 until at least 1479.[29]

The chancel, which was already showing signs of instability in 1576 when it was propped up with a post,[30] had to be largely rebuilt in 1736.[31] The two windows in the south wall of the nave are similar in design to those in the side walls of the chancel and were presumably inserted at the same period. Also in the 18th century a gallery with an outside staircase was added. At a restoration under Waller

[4] Rudder, *Glos.* 326.
[5] G.D.R. vol. 384, f. 50.
[6] *L. & P. Hen. VIII*, vi, p. 260; Hockaday Abs. cxliii, 1542, 1572.
[7] *Trans. B.G.A.S.* lix. 151–3.   [8] Hockaday Abs. cxliii.
[9] Ibid. xlvii, 1576 visit. f. 144.
[10] Ibid. lii, 1593 state of clergy, f. 9.
[11] C 107/112.
[12] Hockaday Abs. cxliii.
[13] Ibid.; notes on rectors in par. reg. 1695–1784.
[14] Hockaday Abs. cviii, cxxxiii, cccxvi.
[15] Ibid. cxliii; notes on rectors in par. reg. 1695–1784.
[16] Glos. R.O., D 1388, Allen.
[17] Bodl. MS. Rawl. C.790, f. 24v.
[18] Glos. R.O., D 621/M 5.

[19] Ibid. D 1070/I/50, abs. of title 1828; cf. G.D.R., T 1/45, Anne Stephens's property.
[20] Bodl. MS. Rawl. B.323, f. 56.
[21] Ibid. C.790, f. 24v.
[22] Glos. R.O., D 326/E 25, abs. of title to cott. at Calmsden; cf. G.D.R., T 1/45, cott. occupied by Thos. Fry.
[23] Bodl. MS. Rawl. B.323, f. 56.
[24] Staffs. R.O., D 641/1/2/156, 160.
[25] Hockaday Abs. cxliii.   [26] Verey, *Glos.* i. 333.
[27] *Trans. B.G.A.S.* lxxxiv. 191–2.
[28] Hockaday Abs. cxliii.
[29] Worc. Episc. Reg., Reg. Carpenter, i, f. 190v.; Staffs. R.O., D 641/1/4M/11.
[30] *Trans. B.G.A.S.* lix. 93 n.
[31] Bodl. MS. Top. Glouc. c. 6, ff. 55–9.

& Son begun in 1876 the east wall of the chancel was rebuilt, the organ chamber added, and the nave repewed.[32]

The pulpit which dates from the late 15th century, is of stone, richly carved, and the font is of similar date. The reading desk is dated 1631 but is made up of woodwork, some of it of the 16th century, from pew-ends or other furnishings. The medieval stone altar slab was found under the floor of the south chapel in 1912 and restored to its original use.[33] A statue of a priest in the south wall of the chancel was removed in 1736[34] but the base of the monument survived and was uncovered in the early 20th century.[35] A brass to the rector Thomas Fereby (d. 1414)[36] has also been lost. There is some medieval glass, including a crucifixion in the east window of the north chapel.[37] Eighteenth-century additions include a chandelier acquired c. 1737,[38] altar-rails, and the font cover. The south chapel has wall monuments to the owners of the Cerney House estate, the earliest a baroque tablet to Sir Thomas Rich (d. 1647).

The present appearance of the interior of the church is largely governed by the lavish furnishing and ornamentation provided in the earlier 20th century by W. I. Croome of Cerney House (d. 1967), who played a leading role in the preservation of ancient churches,[39] and by the rector E. W. M. O. de la Hey. The additions made at that period include the screen to the south chapel and the rood-loft, inserted in 1914 and 1925 respectively and designed on traditional models by F. C. Eden.[40] The plate includes a chalice and paten of 1701, given by Robert Rich,[41] and some pieces of foreign workmanship given in the 20th century.[42] The church had 3 bells[43] before 1714 when a new peal of 5 was cast by Abraham Rudhall; one bell was recast by John Rudhall in 1820 and the peal made up to 6 in 1863.[44] In the churchyard is a medieval cross with a restored head. The parish registers survive, with some gaps, from 1568 for baptisms and from 1574 for marriages and burials.[45]

NONCONFORMITY

NONCONFORMITY. A house at North Cerney was registered for dissenting worship in 1808.[46] The Baptist minister at Eastcombe in Bisley registered a house in 1816[47] and that sect had a meeting-place in the village, with congregations of up to 50, in 1851.[48] The Primitive Methodists opened a chapel at the top of the village in 1891;[49] it remained in use as a Methodist chapel in 1978.

Independents registered a house at Calmsden in 1811. A house at Woodmancote was registered by an unidentified group in 1841[50] and in 1914 the hamlet had a Plymouth Brethren mission hall.[51]

EDUCATION. In or before 1796 a school of industry for girls was started at North Cerney and continued until 1825, teaching spinning and knitting to about 9 girls. It was supported by the subscriptions of the chief landowners and the same fund also supported a Sunday school. From 1808 until 1824 and again from 1827 a separate Sunday school was held at Calmsden and one was opened at Woodmancote in 1828;[52] a total of 78 children were taught in the Cerney and Calmsden schools in 1818. The only day-schools in the early 19th century were paying schools; there were 5 of these with a total of 60 pupils in 1833.[53]

A National school was built in the village in 1844[54] and was supported initially by subscriptions, school pence, and a contribution by the rector.[55] In 1867, when it had an attendance of c. 60, it was receiving an annual government grant but half the cost of running it had still to be supplied by the rector. The boys who attended then usually left at the age of 10 and the master reported that many of the boys in the parish were still illiterate; a night-school established for boys over 12 had been abandoned through lack of support.[56] The average attendance at the National school was 90 in 1885[57] and the building was enlarged by the addition of a new infants' classroom in 1913.[58] The average attendance remained at c. 85 in the earlier part of the 20th century,[59] and in 1978 the numbers on the roll were 52.[60]

CHARITIES FOR THE POOR. In 1683 14½ a. of land belonged to the parish; the income was then said to be distributed by the churchwardens and overseers,[61] so part of it presumably went to the poor. Later, however, the whole income went on church maintenance.[62] Under the Calmsden inclosure of 1795 13 a. of Calmsden Downs were set aside for growing furze as fuel for the poor of the hamlet and the profits of the pasture in the allotment were assigned to be distributed annually amongst the poor.[63] In the 1820s the pasture was let for £7.[64] Management of the allotment was regulated by a Scheme of 1953 and the profits were assigned to the general benefit of the poor.[65]

[32] *Glos. N. & Q.* i. 231–2.
[33] *Trans. B.G.A.S.* lxxxiv. 192.
[34] Atkyns, *Glos.* 323; Bigland, *Glos.* i. 285.
[35] Roper, *Glos. Effigies,* 601.
[36] Bodl. MS. Rawl. B.323, f. 56.
[37] *Trans. B.G.A.S.* xlvii. 301–2.   [38] Ibid. lxxxi. 124.
[39] Inscr. in S. chap.
[40] For the furnishing and ornaments added in the 20th cent., see Verey, *Glos.* i. 335–6; *Trans. B.G.A.S.* lxxxiv. 192–3.
[41] *Glos. Ch. Plate,* 34–5.
[42] *Trans. B.G.A.S.* lxiii. 211–12.
[43] Bodl. MS. Rawl. B.323, f. 56.
[44] *Glos. Ch. Bells,* 39; cf. *Kelly's Dir. Glos.* (1856), 236.
[45] B. & G. Par. Rec. 84.   [46] Hockaday Abs. cxliii.
[47] Ibid.; cf. *V.C.H. Glos.* xi. 37.

[48] H.O. 129/340/1/12/16.
[49] *Kelly's Dir. Glos.* (1894), 52.
[50] Hockaday Abs. cxliii.   [51] *Kelly's Dir. Glos.* (1914), 61.
[52] Glos. R.O., P 95/MI 1.
[53] *Educ. of Poor Digest,* 294; *Educ. Enquiry Abstract,* 309.
[54] *Kelly's Dir. Glos.* (1885), 377.   [55] Ed. 7/35/236.
[56] *Rep. Com. Agric. Employment,* 101.
[57] *Kelly's Dir. Glos.* (1885), 377.   [58] Ibid. (1914), 61.
[59] *Bd. of Educ.,* List 21, 1911 (H.M.S.O.), 165; *1922,* 106; *1932,* 117; *1936,* 123.
[60] Ex inf. county educ. dept.   [61] G.D.R., V 5/67т 4.
[62] Rudder, *Glos.* 326; G.D.R., T 1/45.
[63] Glos. R.O., Q/RI 63.
[64] *20th Rep. Com. Char.* 80–1.
[65] Glos. R.O., D 3469/5/113.

CHEDWORTH

CHEDWORTH, one of the more populous Cotswold parishes, lies 10.5 km. NNE. of Cirencester and covers 1,935 ha. (4,781 a.).[66] It is bounded on the south-east by the Foss way and on the east and north-east by the river Coln and is fairly compact in shape except for a peninsula in the north-west extending down to the river Churn.

Much of the parish lies on the high Cotswolds at 180–250 m. but a broad valley, formed by a tributary of the river Coln, is its central feature and on the north and east the land falls fairly steeply to the Coln. The bottom of the Marsden valley in the north-west peninsula is on the Upper Lias, which is overlaid in the rest of the parish by successive strata of the Inferior Oolite, fuller's earth, and the Great Oolite; along the valley sides the fuller's earth forces out numerous springs which have contributed to the dispersed nature of the scttlement.[67] The high ground on each side of the central valley was once farmed as large open fields, which, together with Chedworth Downs in the north part of the parish, were inclosed in 1803.[68] An airfield was laid out on the former downs in 1940; intended originally for fighters, it was later used mainly by aircraft engaged in bombing practice over the Severn estuary.[69] It reverted to farm-land after the war and some of its buildings were used for pig- and poultry-farming.[70]

A broad belt of woodland, occupying the slopes in the north-east and north, has long been a major feature of the landscape. It is likely, however, that parts of it, lying above the Coln opposite Yanworth parish, were temporarily cleared for cultivation during the period of pressure on land in the early Middle Ages, when a small hamlet called Gothurst probably existed by the river in that area.[71] The names Wheatley, Peasley, and Chedworth Long Acres, later given to parts of the woodland there,[72] suggest that, as does the comparatively small acreage of woodland, 240 a., recorded on the two parts of the manor in the early 14th century.[73] The woods were evidently a valuable asset in 1398 when a grant or mortgage of them was supported by a bond for £400;[74] in the late 15th century, when the annual profits were c. £10, they were carefully managed for the manor with a regular policy of replanting and protecting the young trees.[75] During the 15th century and the early 16th the office of keeper of the woods was sometimes used to reward royal servants.[76] In 1618 there were 629 a. of woodland on the manor, including the 60-a. Dean's wood[77] near the north boundary which had been acquired by the lord in 1611, having belonged to the part of the manor held by the dean and canons of St. Mary's College, Leicester, in the late Middle Ages.[78] The woods, extended at 801 a. in 1842,[79] all remained with the manor until 1923 when those adjoining the Coln passed with Stowell Park to the Vestey family and those in the north part of the parish became divided between the Chedworth Manor farm, Woodlands farm, and Cassey Compton estates.[80] The effect of extensive felling during the two world wars[81] was repaired by replanting, and the woods retained their former extent in 1978, when those on the Stowell Park estate were still much used for rearing game.

Chedworth is widely known for its Roman villa, one of the most extensive to be uncovered in England. The villa, which is situated in the woods in the north-east part of the parish, was found in 1864 and exposed by James Farrer, whose nephew Lord Eldon, the owner of the land, roofed over some of the remains and built a museum[82] and later employed a caretaker for the site.[83] The villa was transferred to the National Trust in 1924.[84] The parish has several other Roman sites, including a temple downstream from the villa and another villa in Listercombe discovered c. 1760;[85] another site is presumably recalled by the name Chestells given to part of a former open field north of Longfurlong Farm.[86]

The Foss way, turnpiked in 1755,[87] has always been the main thoroughfare touching the parish, and a lesser Roman road from Cirencester, the White way, crosses the high downland of the north part of the parish before descending to the Coln as Tunway Lane.[88] On the downs, where a hand-and-post stood in 1803, the White way met a number of local roads (some of which were partly obliterated by the airfield),[89] and the downs appear to have once been a focal point for traffic in that part of the Cotswolds. The name Newport given to a house near by has suggested the existence of a wayside market in the Middle Ages,[90] and a beacon stood close by in 1623.[91] Further south-east a clump of trees called St. John's Ashes, one of the few landmarks included by Saxton on his map of the county in 1577,[92] evidently marked the site of a medieval chapel; some carved stonework was excavated at the site in 1852[93] but no documentary record of the chapel has been found before the early 18th century when some ruins were apparently still visible.[94] The position seems an

---

[66] *Census*, 1971. This account was written in 1978.
[67] Geol. Surv. Map 1″, drift, sheet 235 (1933 edn.).
[68] Glos. R.O., Q/RI 39.
[69] Ex inf. Mr. J. D. F. Green, of the Man., Chedworth.
[70] W.I. hist. of Chedworth (1959, TS. in Glos. Colln.), 7, 38.
[71] See below.
[72] Wilts. R.O., 753/1, f. 237; cf. Glos. R.O., Q/RI 39. Open-field land lying 'on Gothurst' was mentioned in the 13th cent.: C 115/K2/6683 f. 267 and v.
[73] *Inq. p.m. Glos.* 1301–58, 159, 216.
[74] *Cat. Anct. D.* iv, A 6289.
[75] D.L. 29/638/10364; D.L. 29/638/10369.
[76] *Cal. Pat.* 1441–6, 434; 1476–85, 103; 1485–94, 225, 408–9; *L. & P. Hen. VIII,* iv (3), p. 2710; x, p. 358.
[77] Wilts. R.O., 753/1, f. 237 and v.
[78] Glos. R.O., D 1878, Chedworth deeds 1606–52.

[79] G.D.R., T 1/50.
[80] Glos. R.O., D 2299/5018.
[81] W.I. hist. of Chedworth, 15–17.
[82] R.C.H.M. *Glos.* i. 24.
[83] *Kelly's Dir. Glos.* (1894), 58.
[84] *Trans. B.G.A.S.* xlvi. 35–8.
[85] R.C.H.M. *Glos.* i. 28–9; Rudder, *Glos.* 334.
[86] G.D.R., T 1/50.
[87] Glos. and Warws. Roads Act, 28 Geo. II, c. 47.
[88] Margary, *Rom. Roads,* i. 133–4.
[89] Glos. R.O., Q/RI 39.
[90] Finberg, *Glos. Studies,* 62.
[91] G.D.R., V 5/73T 1.
[92] *Glos. and Bristol Atlas* (B.G.A.S. 1961).
[93] *Trans. B.G.A.S.* xli. 159.
[94] Bodl. MS. Rawl. B.323, f. 46v.

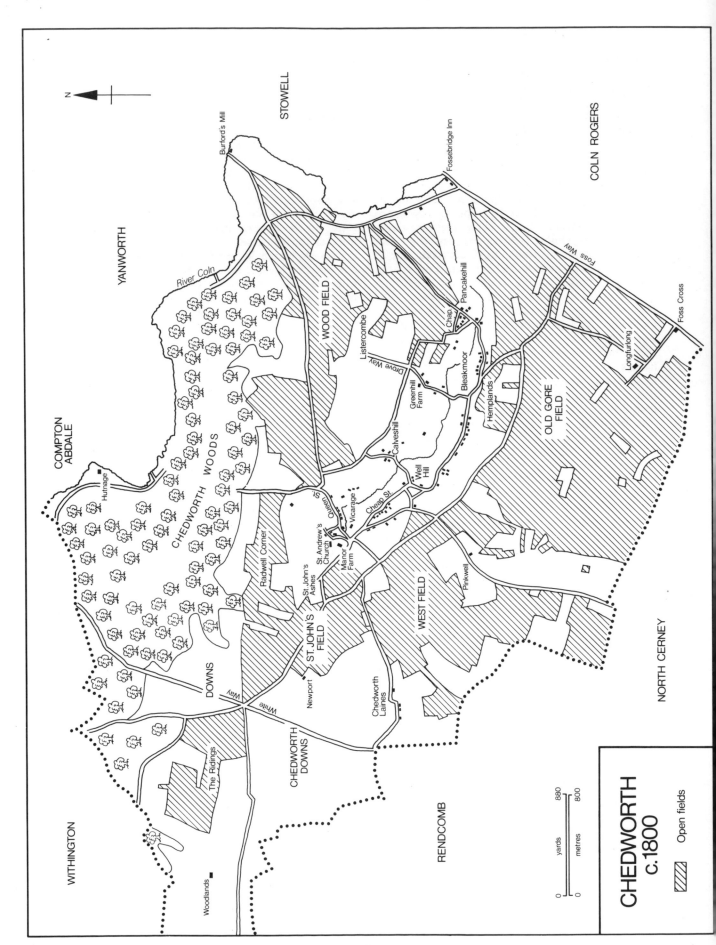

CHEDWORTH
c.1800

Open fields

STOWELL

COLN ROGERS

YANWORTH

COMPTON
ABDALE

Burford's Mill

River Coln

Fossebridge Inn

Foss Way

Foss Cross

WOOD FIELD

Pancakehill

Chap.

Listercombe

Drove Way

Bleakmoor

Longfurlong

Greenhill
Farm

Hemplands

OLD GORE
FIELD

Calveshill

Well
Hill

CHEDWORTH WOODS

Hutnage

Cheap St.

Vicarage

Queen St.

St. Andrew's
Church

Radwell Corner

St. John's
Ashes

Manor
Farm

WEST FIELD

Pinkwell

Newport

ST. JOHN'S
FIELD

DOWNS

White Way

Chedworth
Laines

NORTH CERNEY

The Ridings

CHEDWORTH
DOWNS

RENDCOMB

WITHINGTON

Woodlands

yards   880

metres   800

0

0

unlikely one for a chapel of ease, though the fact that the site was part of the vicar's glebe in 1623 may suggest that;[95] the chapel is more likely to have been built to serve travellers. Although the ash trees at the site had long since disappeared, a line of tall beeches standing along the road to the west still made that high point of the Cotswolds a significant landmark in 1978.

In the southern half of the parish the road-pattern is fairly complex as a result of the sprawling nature of the village. The road by Pinkwell towards Calmsden was one of the more important, being the main route from the village towards Cirencester in 1623, and another road mentioned in 1623 was that called the port way,[96] running through the open fields by Pinkwell and Longfurlong to form the road junction at Foss Cross. The port way, which was still in use in 1777[97] but in 1978 survived only in short stretches, was presumably part of a route from Chedworth Downs towards Fairford and Lechlade. Also recorded in the early 17th century and apparently still in use in the early 19th was Listercombe drove-way which crossed the valley of that name to a landmark called Horsley's Ash above Greenhill Farm,[98] where it survived in 1978 as a wide green lane. The significance of the drove-way is not clear but it may have formed part of a route linking the White way in Compton Abdale to the Welsh way at Barnsley or Ready Token; it presumably continued across the Chedworth valley by the lane called Green Lane[99] and met the port way at Longfurlong.

The Midland and South Western Junction railway, providing a rail link between Cirencester and Cheltenham, was built across the parish in 1891 with stations in the village and near Foss Cross. The line was closed in 1961.[1]

Chedworth village was established at the head of the central valley where the church and manor-house stand on the hillside by a copious spring. The village was probably confined in early times to the area that was later distinguished as Upper End,[2] based on Queen Street (formerly Blackwell's Lane)[3] and Cheap Street.[4] The former runs across the valley below the church and originally continued over the hill to provide access to outlying settlements in the Coln valley, while the latter runs southwards along the west side of the central valley. Both those streets are fairly closely built up with cottages, though none now apparently older than the late 17th century. During the late 17th century and the 18th the village developed in a sprawling fashion along the valley for c. 2 km. with scattered cottages and small farm-houses on the north-east side and a more continuous belt of houses along the road on the south-west side. At the far end at Pancakehill where the valley narrows again the village ends in a more concentrated group of cottages with a Congregational chapel established in the mid 18th century. Most of the houses along the valley are stone-built cottages and small farm-houses of the 18th century and early 19th but there are a few farm-houses of slightly earlier date, including Old Farm, a substantial gabled house of the 17th century near the south end of Cheap Street, and Greenhill Farm, a house of c. 1700 on the opposite side of the valley. On the south-west side there was some infilling with modern houses in the mid 20th century and many of the cottages of the village were restored and enlarged at that period, in some cases by taking in former outbuildings.

In early medieval times there were a number of outlying dwellings in the woodland area of the north part of the parish, most of which were abandoned during the period of general contraction in land use in the earlier 14th century. In 1341 it was reported that 16 tenants in Woodlands and Gothurst had left their holdings.[5] Woodlands was evidently a small hamlet in the north-western peninsula of the parish; its inhabitants were presumably tenants on the Woodlands estate, the capital messuage of which was the only dwelling that survived into modern times. The name Gothurst does not survive but its probable location was beside the river Coln in the north-east part of the parish, near the Roman temple site. Edric's Mead in Gothurst, a meadow that was sold to Winchcombe Abbey in 1265,[6] has been identified, on what evidence is not known, with the meadow below the temple[7] and the name Gothurst survived until at least the 16th century for a water-mill,[8] which may have stood at the end of the straight, and probably man-made, stretch of river there. Further upstream the late-19th-century cottage called Hutnage is probably on the site of another ancient dwelling, for a family surnamed de Hodeknasse was recorded in 1236 and later in the Middle Ages.[9]

At Fossebridge on the east side of the parish the earliest dwelling recorded on the Chedworth side of the Foss way was a capital messuage owned and occupied by a branch of the Dutton family in 1634[10] and until at least 1672.[11] It is possible that the house later became the inn, though the present substantial inn building dates from the late 18th century. The inn had opened by 1759 and was then known as the Lord Chedworth's Arms,[12] changing its name to the Fossebridge inn in the early 19th century.[13] Adjoining the inn are a small farm-house and some cottages and there are a few dwellings, mainly of the 20th century, on Raybrook Lane, leading north-westwards from Fossebridge.

[95] G.D.R., V 5/73T 1; cf. Glos. R.O., Q/RI 39.
[96] G.D.R., V 5/73T 1; cf. field name NW. of Longfurlong: Glos. R.O., Q/RI 39.
[97] Taylor, Map. of Glos. (1777).
[98] G.D.R., V 5/73T 1; Glos. R.O., Q/RI 39.
[99] O.S. Map 6″, Glos. XLIII. NE. (1884 edn.).
[1] C. G. Maggs, The Midland and SW. Junction Rly. (Newton Abbot, 1967), 43, 90.
[2] Glos. R.O., P 77A/OV 2/3.   [3] Ibid. D 182/III/54.
[4] Ibid. D 3495, Chedworth deeds, Beech ho. and lands, deed 1727.

[5] Inq. Non. (Rec. Com.), 409.
[6] Reg. Mon. Winch. ii, pp. 365, 375–6.
[7] Trans. B.G.A.S. lii. 255.
[8] C 115/K2/6683 ff. 265 v.–8; L. & P. Hen. VIII, xiv (1), p. 532.
[9] C.P. 25(1)/73/10 no. 157; Inq. p.m. Glos. 1236–1300, 199; Ciren. Cart. ii, p. 630.
[10] Glos. R.O., D 674B/E 67, f. 78.
[11] E 179/247/13 rot. 29.
[12] Glos. R.O., Q/RZ 1.
[13] Ibid. Q/RI 39; D 1878, Chedworth deeds, sale bill 1819.

In the south and west parts of the parish a few scattered dwellings were built in the 18th century on inclosures from the open fields. Longfurlong (or Newman's) Farm, a substantial farm-house on the port way near Foss Cross, was built on one such inclosure before 1751[14] and the establishment of the small roadside group of cottages at Chedworth Laines, south of Chedworth Downs, had begun by 1746.[15] Pinkwell, on the Calmsden road, and Fields Farm, north of Longfurlong, were also built before the general inclosure of the open fields in 1803.[16] Setts Farm, built before 1824,[17] was apparently the only farm-house established as a result of the inclosure. In the mid 20th century part of Fields Road running above the village on the south-west side of the valley was developed with bungalows, and a few groups of council houses were built in the same area of the parish, the largest group standing near the junction of Fields Road and the road up from the valley.

Thirty inhabitants of Chedworth were enumerated in 1086.[18] Thirty-one people were assessed for the subsidy in 1327[19] and at least 72 for the poll tax in 1381.[20] There were said to be c. 160 communicants in the parish in 1551,[21] 40 households in 1563,[22] 200 communicants in 1603,[23] and 100 families in 1650.[24] About 1710 the population was estimated at c. 500 inhabitants in 150 houses[25] and c. 1775 the figure of 787 inhabitants in 181 families, presumably drawn from a fairly careful local census, was given.[26] In 1801 there were 848 people in 191 houses and by 1831 the population had risen to 1,026. During the remainder of the century there were small fluctuations but with a general downward trend; there were 962 people in 1871 and 885 in 1901. In the first 30 years of the 20th century there was a more rapid and consistent decline, reaching 614 in 1931. New building brought about some recovery after the Second World War and the population stood at 708 in 1971.[27]

Besides the Fossebridge inn there was also the Hare and Hounds on the Foss way at Foss Cross which had opened by 1835[28] and possibly by 1777.[29] By 1891 there were also three public houses in Chedworth village, of which only the Seven Tuns,[30] below the church, survived in 1978. A friendly society met at the Fossebridge inn in 1759[31] and there were two in the parish during the middle years of the 19th century.[32] Plans to establish a village reading-room were made in 1913[33] and from that time or soon afterwards the old Sunday school building near the church was used for that purpose.[34] A building transferred from the disused airfield at Rendcomb was opened as a village hall, affiliated to the Y.M.C.A., in 1920[35] and in 1976 a large new hall was built above the village by Fields Road.[36] In the later 19th century Chedworth supported two separate village bands, one of them attached to the Primitive Methodist chapel. They were replaced in 1905 by a single band which, as the Chedworth silver band, later became well known in the district.[37] An annual horticultural show had been started by 1896.[38]

MANORS AND OTHER ESTATES. Between 779 and 790 Aldred, under-king of the Hwicce, granted 15 cassati at Chedworth to Gloucester Abbey. The grant was confirmed by King Burgred of Mercia in 872[39] but the land had been lost to the abbey by the reign of Edward the Confessor when it was held by one Wulward. After the Conquest it was probably granted to William FitzOsbern (d. 1071), earl of Hereford, whose foundation Lire Abbey (Eure) in Normandy became owner of the church. William's son Roger de Breteuil owned the manor of CHEDWORTH until his rebellion in 1075, and in 1086 the Crown held it.[40] It may have been granted to Henry de Beaumont, created earl of Warwick in 1088,[41] and was certainly held by Henry's son Roger (d. 1153), who gave land in the parish at Marsden to Bruern Abbey (Oxon.).[42] Roger's son William (d. 1184) succeeded to Chedworth[43] but it was later taken by the Crown, from which William Turpin held it at farm between 1194 and 1200.[44] Waleran, earl of Warwick, owned the manor, however, at his death in 1203 or 1204 and it was retained in dower by his widow Alice,[45] passing later to their son Henry (d. 1229).[46]

During the remainder of the 13th century the history of the descent of the manor is complicated by the apparently conflicting dower rights awarded to successive countesses of Warwick. Richard Siward, who married Philippe, widow of Earl Henry, held the manor before 1233 when Henry III granted it during pleasure to two of his crossbowmen, but soon afterwards the king gave full seisin instead to Henry's son Thomas.[47] At Earl Thomas's death in 1242, however, Siward, whose marriage to Philippe was annulled that year, was said to hold Chedworth for life as 1 knight's fee[48] and in the same year he had a grant of free warren in the manor.[49] In 1261

[14] Ibid. D 1350.
[15] Ibid. D 1395/II/3ᵀ6.
[16] Ibid. Q/RI 39.
[17] Bryant, Map of Glos. (1824).
[18] Dom. Bk. (Rec. Com.), i. 164.
[19] Glos. Subsidy Roll, 1327, 10.
[20] E 179/113/35A rot. 13, where part of the list is lost.
[21] E.H.R. xix. 112.
[22] Bodl. MS. Rawl. C.790, f. 24.
[23] Eccl. Misc. 97.
[24] Trans. B.G.A.S. lxxxiii. 93.
[25] Atkyns, Glos. 331.
[26] Rudder, Glos. 334.
[27] Census, 1801–1971.
[28] F.S. 2/3 no. 393.
[29] Taylor, Map of Glos. (1777).
[30] Licensed Houses in Glos. 1891, 160.
[31] Glos. R.O., Q/RZ 1.
[32] F.S. 2/3 nos. 393, 398; F.S. 4/12 nos. 393, 398.
[33] Glos. R.O., P 77A/PC 1/1.
[34] Ibid. D 2299/5018.
[35] W.I. hist. of Chedworth, 114.
[36] Date on bldg.
[37] W.I. hist. of Chedworth, 114; Glos. Countryside, Oct.–Dec. 1955, 11–12.
[38] Glos. R.O., P 77A/PC 1/1.
[39] Cart. Sax. ed. Birch, ii, pp. 151–3; Finberg, Early Charters of W. Midlands, p. 40.
[40] Dom. Bk. (Rec. Com.), i. 164; Complete Peerage, vi. 447–50.
[41] For the earls of Warwick, see Complete Peerage, xii (2), 357–400.
[42] Cal. Chart. R. 1341–1417, 221.
[43] Pipe R. 1198 (P.R.S. N.S. ix), 7–8.
[44] Ibid. 1194 (P.R.S. N.S. v), 3; 1200 (P.R.S. N.S. xii), 121.
[45] Cur. Reg. R. iv. 216.
[46] Bk. of Fees, i. 49.
[47] Close R. 1231–4, 328, 335.
[48] Cal. Inq. p.m. i, p. 3.
[49] Cal. Pat. 1232–47, 315.

Philippe claimed two-thirds of the manor as dower against John du Plessis, earl of Warwick, who conceded her right and agreed to hold her share from her at an annual rent of £10. Under the agreement the two-thirds should at John's death in 1263 have reverted to Philippe,[50] who died in 1265. The other third was apparently held in dower by Ela, widow of Earl Thomas: she had a grant of free warren at Chedworth in 1251[51] and in 1265 she and her husband Philip Bassett had life-grants of her third of the manor from William Mauduit, earl of Warwick,[52] who had presumably succeeded to the rest of the manor on Philippe's death. Mauduit died seised of the manor in 1268[53] and his widow Alice was conceded it in dower by the heir to the earldom, William de Beauchamp,[54] who held it in 1285.[55] Ela, whose right was confirmed by the Crown in 1269,[56] may, however, have retained her third until her death in 1298 a few months before William de Beauchamp.[57]

During the next 150 years the manor descended in direct line with the earldom of Warwick,[58] except that between 1317[59] and 1326[60] it was held by Hugh le Despenser the elder during the minority of Thomas de Beauchamp, earl of Warwick, and between 1397 and 1399 during the forfeiture of Thomas, the next earl, it was held by John Montagu, earl of Salisbury.[61] Henry, duke of Warwick (d. 1446), settled the manor in dower on his wife Cecily,[62] on whose death in 1450 it passed to Richard Neville[63] (d. 1471), earl of Warwick. George, duke of Clarence, Richard's son-in-law, held Chedworth at his death in 1478.[64] Richard's widow Anne was restored to the family estates in 1487 but regranted them to the Crown.[65] In 1489, however, Chedworth was among manors granted to Anne for life.[66]

The Crown retained Chedworth manor from Anne's death in 1492 until 1547 when it was granted to John Dudley, newly created earl of Warwick.[67] Dudley, later duke of Northumberland, settled it on his son John and his wife Anne, but it was forfeited to the Crown after the events of 1553. Anne was later restored to the manor and in 1560 her second husband Sir Edward Unton was granted title to the manor in his own right from her death.[68] He conveyed the manor in 1569 to John Tracy of Toddington[69] but the conveyance may only have transferred the reversion after Anne's death, which occurred in 1588 when she had been a lunatic for some years.[70] John Tracy, who was knighted, was succeeded at his death in 1591 by his son, also Sir John,[71] who in 1608 sold the manor-house and demesne land to John Bridges, William Bridges, and Thomas Howse and the manor to William Higgs of London. Higgs (d. 1612) was succeeded by his son Thomas Higgs of Colesbourne. The three owners of the demesne sold it in 1616 to Sir Richard Grobham of Great Wishford (Wilts.)[72] who bought the manor in 1618 from Thomas Higgs and a group of Londoners, apparently Higgs's creditors.[73]

Sir Richard Grobham (d. 1629) settled Chedworth on his wife Margaret with reversion to a nephew George Grobham,[74] but the manor apparently passed before 1652 to another of his nephews John Howe, who was made a baronet in 1660.[75] Sir John's son Sir Richard Grobham Howe owned Chedworth in 1672[76] and was succeeded at his death in 1703 by his son Sir Richard Howe[77] (d. 1730). It passed to Sir Richard's cousin John Howe of Stowell[78] who was created Lord Chedworth in 1741 and died in 1742. The manor and title descended successively to John's sons John Thynne Howe (d. 1762) and Henry Frederick Howe (d. 1781) and to their nephew John Howe (d. 1804). The last Lord Chedworth devised his estates to trustees for sale,[79] and Chedworth together with Stowell and other adjoining manors was bought in 1812 by the judge Sir William Scott.[80]

Sir William was created Lord Stowell in 1821 and died in 1836 when his estates passed to his daughter Marianne, wife of Henry Addington, Viscount Sidmouth. The viscountess (d. 1842) was succeeded by her cousin John Scott, 2nd earl of Eldon.[81] The estate in Chedworth then comprised 1,973 a.,[82] to which the earl added another 280 a. by purchase from William Dyer in 1846;[83] Dyer had bought part of his estate in 1812 from Lord Chedworth's trustees and another part in 1813 from Joseph Pitt who had amassed it by a series of small purchases between 1802 and 1808.[84] The earl (d. 1854) was succeeded by his son John,[85] who put Chedworth up for sale with the rest of his Stowell Park estate in 1923. The smaller farms were all bought then by their tenants but 578 a., mostly woodland, were bought with Stowell by Samuel Vestey, heir to Lord

[50] Close R. 1259–61, 472; C.P. 25(1)/74/26 no. 595.
[51] Cal. Chart. R. 1226–57, 369.
[52] Ibid. 1257–1300, 133.
[53] Cal. Inq. p.m. i, p. 212.
[54] Close R. 1264–8, 515.
[55] Feud. Aids, ii. 239.
[56] Cal. Chart. R. 1257–1300, 133.
[57] Cal. Inq. p.m. iii, p. 375.
[58] Ibid. v, p. 401; xii, p. 310; Inq. p.m. Glos. 1359–1413, 227–8; C 139/94 no. 54.
[59] Cal. Pat. 1313–17, 667.
[60] E 142/34.
[61] Cal. Pat. 1396–9, 213–14.
[62] Ibid. 1446–52, 37–8.
[63] Cal. Fine R. 1452–61, 268.
[64] C 140/68 no. 47.
[65] Cal. Close, 1485–1500, p. 90.
[66] Cal. Pat. 1485–94, 298.
[67] Ibid. 1547–8, 252.
[68] Ibid. 1560–3, 9–10.

[69] Ibid. 1566–9, p. 418.
[70] Cf. C 142/196 no. 45.
[71] Rudder, Glos. 771.
[72] Glos. R.O., D 1878, Chedworth deeds 1609–17; C 142/336 no. 45.
[73] Wilts. R.O., 753/1, ff. 236–241v.   [74] C 142/460 no. 53.
[75] C.P. 25(2)/616/Mich. 1652 no. 26; for the Howes, see Burke, Ext. & Dorm. Baronetcies (1844), 271.
[76] E 179/247/13 rot. 29.
[77] Atkyns, Glos. 331.
[78] Cf. Rudder, Glos. 708 n.
[79] Glos. R.O., D 1878, Chedworth deeds 1776–1846, abs. of title.
[80] Ibid. title deeds 1812–18.
[81] Burke, Peerage (1935), 884; Prob. 11/1859 (P.C.C. 190 Stowell).
[82] G.D.R., T 1/50.
[83] Glos. R.O., D 1878, Chedworth deed.
[84] Ibid. Chedworth deeds 1776–1846, abs. of title.
[85] Burke, Peerage (1935), 885.

Vestey, and 850 a., comprising Chedworth Manor farm and another large tract of woodland,[86] was bought by the Revd. John Green (d. 1944). The Revd. John was succeeded by his brother Capt. Henry Green, who had farmed the estate for some years, and Capt. Henry's son, Mr. J. D. F. Green, owned and farmed Manor farm in 1978.[87]

The ancient manor-house of Chedworth, recorded from 1268,[88] was at Manor Farm beside the church. The small central range of the present house retains one upper cruck truss and probably formed part of a medieval hall. To that range adjoins a large 17th-century kitchen with some additional 19th-century service rooms and, on the south-east, a long cross-range of c. 1700, incorporating some older walling. The relatively small size of the house reflects the fact that for most of its history it was used as a farm-house. Hugh Westwood, the lessee of the site and demesne of the manor from 1521,[89] who was usually styled of Chedworth, presumably lived in the manor-house,[90] but the only lord of the manor recorded as resident was Sir Richard Grobham Howe who appears to have used the house for a period in the late 17th century.[91] From the middle of that century, however, the lords were usually resident locally at Cassey Compton (in Withington) or at Stowell Park.

A third part of the manor of Chedworth[92] was given by William de Beauchamp, earl of Warwick, to his daughter Isabel on her marriage to Patrick de Chaworth (d. c. 1283). Their daughter Maud married Henry of Lancaster[93] who gave the estate for life to his brother Thomas, earl of Lancaster. On Thomas's execution in 1322 it was briefly forfeited before being restored to Henry,[94] who succeeded to the earldom and died in 1345. Henry's son Henry, duke of Lancaster, gave the estate in 1355 to the hospital of St. Mary at Leicester,[95] which he raised to the status of a collegiate church. At the dissolution of the college in 1548[96] the manorial rights over the estate and the bulk of the land were re-united with the other part of the manor by a grant to John Dudley, earl of Warwick.[97]

The estate called *WOODLANDS* in the north-west part of the parish was probably that which Richard Atwood (de Bosco) held from the earl of Warwick in 1268 by the serjeanty of service in the earl's pantry.[98] The serjeanty estate, comprising a plough-land, was held by another Richard Atwood in 1315[99] and John Atwood held an estate at Woodlands in 1386.[1] The latter was apparently the John Atwood of Gloucestershire who suffered

oppression at the hands of Anselm Guise and James Clifford, his estates being forcibly occupied by Guise for some seven years. John recovered his estates in 1402 but in 1405 he was murdered by an assassin hired by Clifford.[2] In the early 15th century Woodlands seems to have been held by William Daffy.[3] About 1486 the owner of the manor took possession of the estate on the ground of a supposed reversionary interest[4] but Sir Walter Dennis later proved his title and recovered the estate in 1496.[5] Woodlands, or part of it, was later acquired by the younger Sir Edmund Tame, presumably by his marriage to Catherine Dennis.[6] It was retained by Catherine after Sir Edmund's death 1544, the reversion being settled on his sister Margaret and her husband Sir Humphrey Stafford,[7] and it apparently passed with Rendcomb manor to Sir Richard Berkeley.[8] In 1612, however, Woodlands was owned by Jasper Meyrick of Wick Rissington who then made a settlement for the benefit of his children, and in 1647 the estate was settled on trustees to provide for the maintenance of William Clent of Gloucester and Bridget his wife.[9]

By 1682 the Woodlands estate had passed to James Mitchell of Harescombe and Bridget his wife who settled it from after their deaths on the marriage of their son James (d. by 1704). The estate was partitioned among the three daughters of the younger James, Mary who married George Small of Nailsworth, clothier, Elizabeth who married Jacob Eltom of Bristol, merchant, and Bridget who married Samuel Clutterbuck of Brimscombe, clothier. Jacob and Elizabeth sold their third share in 1711 to George Small (d. c. 1736) who devised his two-thirds to a kinsman John Small, who was succeeded before 1749 by his brother Richard.[10] Richard Small sold his share in 1752 to Henry Tuffley, who bought the other third the following year from William Clutterbuck of Bristol, merchant, son of Samuel. Henry Tuffley's mortgagee, Edward Wilbraham,[11] a Cirencester wool-stapler, was in possession of Woodlands by 1756 and was succeeded at his death before 1782 by his son Edward[12] (d. 1830); the younger Edward was succeeded by his son Edward Wilbraham of Horsley (d. 1859).[13] The estate, which comprised 378 a. after the inclosure of 1803,[14] was sold by the last Edward's trustees in 1861 to two men who were apparently acting for the earl of Eldon.[15] Woodlands was included in the sale of the earl's estates in 1923 and was bought then by H. H. Stephens who sold the house and farm-land to his tenant C. F. Finch in

[86] Glos. R.O., D 2299/5018.
[87] Ibid. 7796; ex inf. Mr. Green.
[88] C 132/35 no. 13.
[89] L. & P. Hen. VIII, iii (1), p. 480; v, p. 483.
[90] Trans. B.G.A.S. liv. 92; Req. 2/48/28.
[91] E 179/247/13 rot. 29; B.L. Harl. MS. 4716, f. 6v.
[92] Inq. p.m. Glos. 1305–58, 216.
[93] Cal. Inq. p.m. ii, p. 288; Complete Peerage, vii. 400.
[94] Cal. Inq. p.m. vii, p. 62; S.C. 6/1147/12.
[95] Cal. Pat. 1354–8, 184.
[96] V.C.H. Leics. ii. 48, 50–1.
[97] Cal. Pat. 1548–9, 29–30.
[98] C 132/35 no. 13, where the statement that the service was owed to the king is presumably a clerical error: cf. Inq. p.m. Glos. 1301–58, 159.
[99] Inq. p.m. Glos. 1301–58, 159.

[1] Glos. R.O., EL 196.
[2] Select Cases before the King's Council (Selden Soc. xxxv), 86–92, civ–vi.
[3] Ciren. Cart. ii, p. 630.
[4] D.L. 29/638/10364.
[5] D.L. 29/638/10369.
[6] Cf. Glos. R.O., D 1728, Fairford man. deeds.
[7] C.P. 40/1134 Carte rot. 2d.; Glos. R.O., D 326/T 100.
[8] C 142/285 no. 150.
[9] Glos. R.O., D 2009.
[10] Ibid. D 36/T 61.
[11] Ibid. D 2957/73.1–11.
[12] Ibid. D 1878, Woodlands est. 1756–1805.
[13] Ibid. Woodlands est. abs. of title 1861.
[14] Ibid. Q/RI 39.
[15] Ibid. D 1878, Woodlands est. deed 1861.

1931, retaining the woodland of the estate.[16] The Finch family still owned and farmed Woodlands in 1978. The farm-house was rebuilt or extensively remodelled in 1854.[17]

The land at Chedworth given to Bruern Abbey by Roger, earl of Warwick, in the 12th century occupied the end of the north-west peninsula of the parish. It was farmed from the adjoining Marsden Farm in Rendcomb and passed into the Rendcomb Park estate; it comprised 291 a. in 1803.[18]

William (d. 1184), earl of Warwick, granted land at Chedworth to Roger son of Warin, who had a confirmatory grant c. 1198 from William Turpin by which he was to hold it as $\frac{1}{5}$ knight's fee.[19] It was presumably the estate held at that assessment by Robert de Camera in 1268,[20] by Richard de Anneford in 1303, and by another Richard de Anneford in 1346.[21] It has not been found recorded later, unless it was the estate at Chedworth that the Cassey family of Cassey Compton held in the 15th century and the early 16th.[22]

The rectory of Chedworth was owned by Lire Abbey[23] until the dispossession of the alien houses in 1414 when it was granted with the abbey's other possessions to Henry V's foundation, Sheen Priory (Surr.).[24] Sir Edmund Tame and his son Sir Edmund were lessees under Sheen in the early 16th century and the younger Sir Edmund devised the lease to Hugh Westwood.[25] In 1545 Westwood bought the freehold of the rectory from two speculators,[26] who had just acquired it from the Crown,[27] and at his death in 1559[28] he devised it for the foundation of a grammar school at Northleach. The new school was not, however, secured in possession of the estate until 1606, partly because of an attempt by Westwood's heir, Robert Westwood, to upset the will.[29] The rectory estate was worth £80 a year c. 1710.[30] It comprised glebe land, which after the inclosure of 1803 covered 118 a.,[31] and two-thirds of the tithes, for which the master and usher of the school were awarded a corn-rent-charge of £591 in 1842.[32]

An estate called Hillwalls, comprising a house and 2 yardlands, was held from Lire Abbey, to which it escheated on the death of a tenant without heirs before 1317.[33] It then appears to have descended as part of the rectory estate, Hugh Westwood including it in his endowment of the Northleach school.[34] Another estate, comprising a house and 1 yardland, was forfeited to the Crown after Lire Abbey acquired it without licence. Although for some years

in the 15th century placed in the custody of Sheen Priory,[35] it was retained by the Crown until 1545 when it was sold with the rectory to Hugh Westwood.[36]

ECONOMIC HISTORY. In 1066 the demesne of Chedworth manor was worked by 7 teams.[37] In 1298, when two-thirds of the manor were described, Isabel de Chaworth's portion having been severed from it, the demesne comprised 200 a. of arable, 5 a. of meadow, and rights in a common pasture;[38] the amount of arable remained unchanged in 1315.[39] The earl of Lancaster's third of the manor had 100 a. of arable and 6 a. of meadow in demesne in 1327.[40] By 1490 the demesne land was leased, the farmer also filling the office of reeve of the manor. A sheep-house was then included in the lease and a later farmer, Hugh Westwood, who held the demesne from 1521,[41] is said to have had a flock of c. 600 sheep at Chedworth.[42] In 1608 the demesne farm of the manor comprised 5 yardlands in the open fields, 85 a. of pasture and meadow in closes, and pasture rights for 300 sheep and other beasts.[43]

In 1066 the tenantry on the manor were 16 *villani* and 3 bordars with 6 teams between them. Before 1086 the sheriff of the county as part of an attempt to increase the value of the manor settled on it an additional 8 *villani* and 3 bordars with a total of 4 teams.[44] In 1268 the manor had 8 free tenements and $21\frac{2}{3}$ yardlands held in villeinage.[45] In 1298 on the reduced manor estate there were 10 free tenants, 14 yardlanders, who owed 4 days' work a week and cash-rents, and 8 tenants holding 7 a. each, who owed only cash-rents.[46] By 1315 the works of one of the yardlanders had been wholly commuted and from the others less was apparently required for the works at some seasons, lower values being placed on them. A larger number of lesser tenants, 14 described as cottars holding $2\frac{1}{2}$ yardlands between them, were listed in 1315 and they then owed some bedrepes as well as cash-rents.[47] In 1327 the tenants on the earl of Lancaster's part of the manor were 11 yardlanders and 18 cottars; all held by cash-rents alone and the tenants were then farming the rents together with the profits of court from the earl.[48] During the early 14th century the number of tenants in Chedworth declined as a result of the slump in arable farming and the effect on sheep-farming of murrain and the failure of pasture: by 1341 16 tenants in the outlying hamlets of

---

[16] Ibid. D 2299/5018.
[17] Date on bldg.
[18] See below, Rendcomb; Glos. R.O., Q/RI 39.
[19] *Pipe R.* 1198 (P.R.S. n.s. ix), 7–8.
[20] *Cal. Inq. p.m.* i, p. 212.
[21] *Feud. Aids,* ii. 247, 280.
[22] *Cal. Close,* 1435–41, 100–1; C 142/24 no. 50.
[23] *Reg. Bransford,* pp. 36–7.
[24] *V.C.H. Surr.* ii. 89.
[25] Hockaday Abs. cxciv, 1533; cccxxii, 1544.
[26] Glos. R.O., D 2478.
[27] *L. & P. Hen. VIII,* xx (1), p. 666.
[28] *Trans. B.G.A.S.* liv. 104; Glos. R.O., P 44A/CH 1.
[29] *V.C.H. Glos.* ii. 436; cf. C 142/265 no. 59.
[30] Atkyns, *Glos.* 331.
[31] Glos. R.O., Q/RI 39.
[32] G.D.R., T 1/50.

[33] *Cal. Inq. Misc.* ii, p. 67; *Ciren. Cart.* ii, p. 631.
[34] *Trans. B.G.A.S.* liv. 94.
[35] *Cal. Fine R.* 1445–52, 260; 1471–85, p. 247; 1485–1509, p. 115.
[36] *L. & P. Hen. VIII,* xx (1), p. 666.
[37] *Dom. Bk.* (Rec. Com.), i. 164.
[38] *Inq. p.m. Glos.* 1236–1300, 198.
[39] Ibid. 1301–58, 159.
[40] Ibid. 216.
[41] D.L. 29/638/10364; S.C. 6/Hen. VIII/1017.
[42] Req. 2/48/28.
[43] Glos. R.O., D 1878, Chedworth deeds 1609–17.
[44] *Dom. Bk.* (Rec. Com.), i. 164.
[45] C 132/35 no. 13.
[46] *Inq. p.m. Glos.* 1236–1300, 198–200.
[47] Ibid. 1301–58, 159–60.
[48] Ibid. 216–17.

Woodlands and Gothurst had abandoned their holdings.[49] In 1490 on the manor estate 12 yardland tenements and 12 smaller holdings, most described as a 'hunche' of land, were occupied, but it was evidently not a profitable period for the manor, for the tenants' rents had been considerably reduced in recent years and there were some other tenements for which no tenants could be found.[50] In 1584 the Leicester college estate, then about to be reunited with the manor, had 12 tenants.[51]

Seven tenements were alienated from the manor by Thomas Higgs,[52] who was in financial difficulties, but another 17, ranging in size from ¾ to 2½ yardlands, appear to have remained with the manor when it was sold by Higgs in 1618.[53] More of the tenant land was probably alienated later, for in the 18th century the number of small freehold farms and cottage-tenements was a major feature of the parish. The number of small freeholds was somewhat reduced at the end of the 18th century by the Ballinger family, which bought 7 holdings and added them to a farm which they already owned,[54] and at the beginning of the 19th by Joseph Pitt, who bought out another 6 owners.[55] At inclosure in 1803 there were 110 owners of freehold land in the parish, 80 of them having (after the inclosure had been carried through) under 10 a., 18 having 10–50 a., and 12 having larger estates. The larger estates included the manor, which had over 900 a. of agricultural land, the Woodlands estate, the Rendcomb estate's Marsden land, John Ballinger's 301 a., Joseph Pitt's 199 a., two estates of 215 a. and 167 a. owned by members of the Radway family, and the rectory and vicarage estates.[56]

The parish had four extensive open fields: Wood field occupied the area between the central valley and the woodland, St. John's field occupied the high ground at the head of the valley, West field (formerly Chittle Grove field) lay between the valley and the Rendcomb boundary, and Old Gore field occupied the whole of the south part of the parish. Another area of open-field arable called the Ridings lay east of Woodlands Farm[57] and was no doubt formed of assarts made from the woodland before 1329 when open-field land lying east of Marsden field was mentioned.[58] If the Marsden field recorded then was an open field it seems to have been inclosed at an early date.

An area of common downland, covering 260 a. before inclosure in 1803, lay by the White way between St. John's field and the Ridings.[59] At least part of the woodland was once also open to rights of common: the 200 a. of wood recorded on the manor in 1315[60] was commonable and the tenants may still have had rights in the woods in 1543 when a lease of the demesne required that measures be taken to preserve the young trees against grazing animals.[61] Later the lords held all the woodland in severalty. The meadow land of the parish was limited to a narrow strip in the central valley and in some small stretches by the Coln on the north boundary.

Consolidation of holdings of open-field land, presumably as a prelude to private inclosures, occurred fairly regularly in the course of the 18th century.[62] In 1757 Edward Wilbraham exchanged land in Wood field for land in the Ridings near his farm-house at Woodlands[63] and Charles Ballinger made exchanges to consolidate his open-field land in the early 1790s.[64] Inclosures from Wood field had begun by 1739[65] and by 1803 a considerable area had been taken out of that field near Listercombe and out of St. John's field near St. John's Ashes. The open fields still remained extensive, however, in 1803 when together with the downs they were inclosed by Act of Parliament. Most of the land went to the manor and to the larger estates mentioned above, though not to the Marsden estate which was already all inclosed. Many small owners also received allotments for their few strips of open-field land or for commoning rights, and 12 a. near Chedworth Laines were assigned to the poor in general for furze-gathering. In all 56 people received allotments.[66] Twenty-five of them, three of them fairly substantial owners and the rest cottagers, expressed opposition to the inclosure in a notice in the newspapers.[67]

After the inclosure some large farms were formed from the main estates. In 1805 John Radway farmed 976 a., including his own land, the Ballinger estate, and a large part of the manor estate; another farm on the manor estate comprised 387 a.; the Woodlands estate formed a single farm of 378 a.; Francis Radway farmed 318 a. of his own and Joseph Pitt's land; and another farm of 275 a. included the two glebe estates.[68] In 1842 Manor farm with 472 a. was the main farm on the manor estate, which also included Greenhill farm with 242 a. and another with 192 a. The Ballinger estate was then farmed with Longfurlong farm by James Newman, the owner of the latter, making 421 a. in all; Woodlands Farm had 289 a.; and Setts farm with 171 a. and a farm with 126 a., based on a house in Queen Street, were among the other more considerable holdings.[69] There remained many small freehold farms: in 1831 the parish contained 16 farmers who employed labour and 17 who did not,[70] and there were over 40 agricultural occupiers in the parish in the late 19th and early 20th centuries, more than half of those returned in 1926 having under 20 a.[71] By the 1970s much of the land had been absorbed into a few very large farms but some small farms survived, 9 part-

[49] Inq. Non. (Rec. Com.), 409.
[50] D.L. 29/638/10364.   [51] E 315/68 f. 385.
[52] Wilts. R.O., 753/1, f. 238.
[53] Glos. R.O., D 1878, Chedworth deeds 1609–17.
[54] Ibid. D 1388/III/51.
[55] Ibid. D 1878, Chedworth deeds 1776–1846, abs. of title.
[56] Ibid. Q/RI 39.
[57] Ibid.; and for Chittle Grove field, G.D.R., V 5/73T 1–2.
[58] Glos. R.O., D 326/T 110.
[59] Ibid. Q/RI 39.
[60] Inq. p.m. Glos. 1301–58, 159.

[61] L. & P. Hen. VIII, xviii (1), p. 198.
[62] e.g. Glos. R.O., D 1350; D 1388/III/52; D 3495, Chedworth deeds 1750–69.
[63] Ibid. D 1878, Woodlands est. 1756–1805.
[64] Ibid. D 1388/III/51.
[65] Ibid. D 3495, Chedworth deeds, Beech ho. and lands.
[66] Ibid. Q/RI 39.
[67] Glouc. Jnl. 11 Oct. 1802.
[68] Glos. R.O., P 77A/VE 1/1.
[69] G.D.R., T 1/50.   [70] Census, 1831.
[71] M.A.F. 68/1609/2; M.A.F. 68/3295/17.

time agriculturalists being returned for Chedworth and Yanworth parishes in 1976.[72]

The usual sheep and corn husbandry of the Cotswolds remained dominant at Chedworth during the 19th century with a five-course rotation of grass-seeds for mowing, wheat, turnips, barley and oats, and grass-seeds for grazing by sheep the usual practice.[73] As many as 8 parishioners were employed full-time as shepherds in 1851.[74] In 1866 2,729 a. were returned as under cereal crops, roots, and rotated grassland compared with only 358 a. of permanent grass, but by 1896 the decline in profitability of arable farming had reduced the acreage of cereals and roots by about 600 a., much of which was laid down as permanent grassland. That trend continued in the early 20th century[75] when agriculture in the parish was diversified, particularly by the introduction of dairy and beef cattle; the first large dairy herd was brought into the parish in 1919.[76] In 1926 the number of cattle returned for the parish was 446 compared with 247 in 1896, while the number of sheep was down to 1,261 compared with 2,185 in 1896.[77] Dairy-farming remained important in 1976 but sheep-raising had recovered its prominence and at least one of the larger farms was mainly concerned with cereal crops.[78]

There were three mills on Chedworth manor in 1066[79] and there were two on the earl of Warwick's manor in 1298, when one was used as a fulling-mill and held from the lord by all the customary tenants in common.[80] A mill called Gothurst mill, probably on the Coln in the north-east part of the parish, was granted to Llanthony Priory in 1279 by Miles of Stowell, who reserved life-interests for himself and his wife. Soon afterwards the priory alienated the mill to Thomas of Gothurst at a quit rent of 10s.,[81] which it was still receiving at the Dissolution.[82] The mill passed to the manor before 1490[83] and is last found recorded in 1539.[84] Another mill stood on the Coln where the road to Stowell crossed out of the parish. It was called Burford's mill in 1803, when it remained part of the manor estate,[85] but later in the 19th century it was usually called Stowell mill. It was working until the 1930s.[86] There were possibly other mills in the parish in the 19th century, for two other millers as well as the miller of Stowell mill lived there in 1851; one lived at Gadbridge[87] which appears to have been where the road crossed the central stream of the parish

below Pancakehill,[88] though no signs of a mill were visible there in 1978.

The name Newport given to a house on Chedworth Downs has prompted the suggestion that an unofficial wayside market was once held near by where the White way meets a number of lesser roads.[89] It is possible that the right claimed by the lord of the manor in 1490 to levy toll on certain goods within 7 leagues of Chedworth[90] was connected with such a market and the name Cheap Street may also derive from it, either because that street in the village leads towards the downs or because the market was later moved to the street itself. The surviving records, however, provide no indication, beyond the existence of the fulling-mill in 1298, that Chedworth was anything more than an agricultural village in the Middle Ages; two tailors are the only tradesmen who appear on the incomplete poll-tax assessment of 1381.[91] It was in more modern times that the village became a minor local centre, providing crafts and other services to the much smaller estate villages which surrounded it. It already had a fairly substantial body of tradesmen in 1608 when 16 were among those listed for militia service,[92] and the pattern of land-holding created by the sale of much of the tenant land of the manor was later a factor in the growth of a large population of tradesmen. Many of the tradesmen in the 18th century owned and farmed small holdings of land.[93]

The stoneworking trades were particularly strong at Chedworth. Among the numerous masons of the parish the families of Smith, Robins, and Bridges were represented for several generations[94] and the trade of slater employed at least 10 men from another family, the Wilsons, between 1698 and 1851.[95] In 1851 the parish had a total of 15 masons and 4 slaters.[96] Several of the small quarries that were worked on the high ground of the parish also had lime-kilns,[97] and lime-burning supported a few men full-time in the 18th century.[98] Shoemaking and woodworking were among other village trades well represented in the 18th and 19th centuries and there were also some tradesmen less usual to a village, including a mercer in 1730, two clockmakers later in the 18th century,[99] a pawnbroker in 1823,[1] and three land-surveyors, all of the same family, in 1851.[2] In 1831 54 families were supported by trade compared with

[72] Agric. Returns 1976.
[73] W.I. hist. of Chedworth, 34.
[74] H.O. 107/1969.
[75] M.A.F. 68/26/12; M.A.F. 68/1609/2; M.A.F. 68/3295/17.
[76] W.I. hist. of Chedworth, 35–6.
[77] M.A.F. 68/1609/2; M.A.F. 68/3295/17.
[78] Agric. Returns 1976.
[79] Dom. Bk. (Rec. Com.), i. 164.
[80] Inq. p.m. Glos. 1236–1300, 199.
[81] C 115/K2/6683 ff. 266, 268.
[82] S.C. 6/Hen. VIII/1224 m.15d.
[83] D.L. 29/638/10364.
[84] L. & P. Hen. VIII, xiv (1), p. 532.
[85] Glos. R.O., Q/RI 39.
[86] O.S. Map 6", Glos. XXXVI. SW. (1883 edn.); ex. inf. Mr. Green.
[87] H.O. 107/1969.
[88] See the field-name Garbage close in Glos. R.O., Q/RI 39.
[89] Finberg, Glos. Studies, 62.

[90] D.L. 29/638/10364.
[91] E 179/113/35A rot. 13.
[92] Smith, Men and Armour, 254.
[93] e.g. Glos. R.O., D 1350; D 1388/III/51–3; D 3495, Chedworth deeds 1750–69; Chedworth deeds, Midwinter est.; deeds 1681–1732; G.D.R. wills 1714/41; 1730/341.
[94] Glos. R.O., D 182/III/53–4; D 1878, Chedworth deeds 1681–1732; D 1350; G.D.R. wills 1764/91; 1778/137; 1797/149; 1798/149; H.O. 107/1969.
[95] Glos. R.O., D 182/III/52; D 1350; D 2957/73.18; D 3495, Chedworth deeds 1750–69; Chedworth deeds, Midwinter est.; H.O. 107/1969.
[96] H.O. 107/1969.
[97] W.I. hist. of Chedworth, 69–70; G.D.R. wills 1730/341.
[98] Glos. R.O., D 1350, deed 1799; D 3495, Chedworth deeds 1750–69, deed of exchange 1755.
[99] Glos. R.O., D 1388/III/53–4.
[1] Ibid. D 1395/II/3T 6.
[2] H.O. 107/1969.

131 supported by agriculture[3] and in 1851 there were more than 70 inhabitants employed in non-agricultural pursuits. At the latter date 12 carpenters and 8 shoemakers formed the largest groups after the masons, and 3 grocers, 3 butchers, and 3 other shopkeepers indicate that the village also had a role as a minor retailing centre. The woodlands of the Stowell Park estate gave employment to 5 woodmen and 3 gamekeepers in 1851[4] and the estate had a foreman of trades in 1885.[5] The woods provided the material for hurdle-making which employed several parishioners in the days when the folding of sheep on the arable was an important element in local agriculture.[6] Some of the traditional village trades, including those of blacksmith, wheelwright, and slater, survived into the middle years of the 20th century at Chedworth,[7] where more modern business activities were represented by the coal-merchants who traded from Foss Cross station after the opening of the railway[8] and a bus proprietor who operated from 1928.[9]

LOCAL GOVERNMENT. In the early 15th century the abbot of Cirencester as lord of the hundred retained frankpledge jurisdiction in Chedworth and all profits from it, though the view was held in Chedworth itself; it met twice a year on an outdoor site,[10] possibly the road junction on Chedworth Downs which had been the focal point of the parish before the depopulation of its northern hamlets. By 1490, however, the lady of the manor was claiming the right to hold the view together with her manor court.[11] A court roll of 1505 is the only one known to survive,[12] though the court leet continued to be held until the First World War, when it met at the Fossebridge inn.[13]

The surviving records of parish government include churchwardens' accounts from 1645, a vestry order book for 1823–94,[14] and overseers' accounts for 1762–1835.[15] The cost of poor-relief rose from under £100 in the mid 1760s, when c. 13 people were on permanent relief,[16] to sometimes as high as £800 in the second decade of the 19th century when 50–60 people received regular relief.[17] Its large population gave Chedworth by far the highest figures for poor-relief among surrounding parishes. From the mid 18th century cottages belonging to the parish were being used as poorhouses.[18]

In 1830 some paupers were being employed on road-work and in 1831 and 1832 families were helped to emigrate to America.[19] Chedworth became part of the Northleach union in 1836[20] and was later in Northleach rural district[21] until the formation of the new Cotswold district in 1974.

CHURCH. Chedworth church was probably founded before or immediately following the Conquest, for it was presumably William FitzOsbern (d. 1071) who granted it to Lire Abbey, which he founded.[22] The church was appropriated and a vicarage ordained before 1291,[23] and the living remained a vicarage. It was united with the livings of Yanworth and Stowell in 1964[24] and Coln Rogers and Coln St. Dennis were added to the united benefice in 1975.[25]

The advowson of the vicarage was retained with the rectory by Lire Abbey[26] but in the 14th century was usually exercised by the Crown because of the war with France.[27] It passed to Sheen Priory in 1414[28] and was included in the sales of the rectory in 1545.[29] In 1580, however, Justinian Bracegirdle presented, presumably under a grant for one turn, and the Crown presented at the next vacancy in 1602, though a rival unsuccessful presentation was made then by Corpus Christi College and St. Edmund Hall, Oxford. The advowson had, however, probably been intended as part of Hugh Westwood's endowment of Northleach school, for from 1659 it was exercised by Queen's College, Oxford,[30] which had been appointed patron of the school in 1606.[31] In 1978 the college shared the advowson of the united benefice by alternation with the dean and chapter of Gloucester and the Lord Chancellor.[32]

The portion assigned to the vicar was valued at £5 in 1291 compared with the rectory portion valued at £16 13s. 4d.[33] The vicar's portion included a third of all the tithes of the parish, for which he received a corn-rent-charge of £296 at commutation in 1842.[34] In 1623 his glebe comprised a few acres in closes, 2½ yardlands of open-field land, and sheep-pastures,[35] and after inclosure in 1803 it comprised 110 a.[36] In the mid 16th century an additional payment of £1 6s. 8d. was made to the vicar out of the rectory estate[37] and it was still being made in 1807, though at some time previously a Chancery decree had been needed to enforce it.[38] The vicarage house, on the north-east side of Cheap Street, was described as a convenient

3 Census, 1831.
4 H.O. 107/1969.
5 Kelly's Dir. Glos. (1885), 382.
6 W.I. hist. of Chedworth, 67.
7 Ibid. 69; Glos. Countryside, Oct.–Dec. 1955, 11.
8 Kelly's Dir. Glos. (1906 and later edns.).
9 W.I. hist. of Chedworth, 84–5.
10 Ciren. Cart. ii, p. 619.
11 D.L. 29/638/10364.
12 D.L. 30/77/984.
13 W.I. hist. of Chedworth, 131; ex inf. Mr. Green.
14 Penes the vicar, the Revd. A. W. Dodds.
15 Glos. R.O., P 77A/OV 2/1–4.
16 Ibid. 1.
17 Poor Law Abstract, 1818, 154–5.
18 G.D.R. vol. 397, f. 78; Glos. R.O., P 77A/OV 2/1–3.
19 Vestry order bk. 1823–94.
20 Poor Law Com. 2nd Rep. p. 523.

21 Census, 1911.
22 Complete Peerage, vi. 447–8.
23 Tax. Eccl. (Rec. Com.), 222.
24 Glouc. Dioc. Yr. Bk. (1974), 56.
25 Ibid. (1977), 33.
26 Reg. Reynolds, 148.
27 Reg. Sede Vacante, 235, 337.
28 Cf. Worc. Episc. Reg., Reg. Morgan, ii, f. 31v.
29 L. & P. Hen. VIII, xx (1), p. 666; Glos. R.O., D 2478.
30 Hockaday Abs. cl.
31 V.C.H. Glos. ii. 436.
32 Glouc. Dioc. Yr. Bk. (1977), 33.
33 Tax. Eccl. (Rec. Com.), 222.
34 G.D.R., T 1/50.
35 G.D.R., V 5/73T 1.
36 Glos. R.O., Q/RI 39.
37 E 318/11/535 rot. 23.
38 G.D.R., V 5/73T 6.

mansion in 1623;[39] it was rebuilt by the vicar James Rawes *c.* 1770[40] and was extended by a lower range to the north-west in the early 19th century. It was sold *c.* 1976 and another house near by in Cheap Street was acquired as the vicarage.[41] The living was valued at £7 8s. 2d. in 1535,[42] £50 in 1650,[43] £70 in 1750,[44] £276 in 1813,[45] and £302 in 1863.[46]

Sixteenth-century vicars of Chedworth included, from 1527, Gilbert Jobburne,[47] who was found only partly satisfactory in theological knowledge in 1551,[48] and Richard Woodward (d. 1580), probably a former monk of Hailes Abbey,[49] who was said in 1576 to preach only once or twice a year and read the commination only once a year.[50] Edmund Bracegirdle, vicar 1580–1602, was challenged in his tenure of the living in 1599 on the grounds that he also held the rectories of Stowell and Hampnett. He was succeeded by Nathaniel Aldworth[51] who held the living until at least 1642.[52] Robert Sawyer, described as a preaching minister, held it in 1650,[53] and in 1659 John Cudworth was instituted, remaining vicar after the Restoration.[54] Geoffrey Wall served a long incumbency from 1682 until his death in 1743.[55] He and his successors in the 18th century appear to have been resident until the time of Benjamin Grisdale, vicar 1785–1828,[56] who was living at Tooting (Surr.) in 1789.[57] Arthur Gibson, vicar 1828–78, served a curacy at Norwood (Surr.) in the early years of his incumbency.[58]

The church of *ST. ANDREW*, which bore that dedication by 1425,[59] is built of rubble and ashlar and has a chancel with north vestry, a nave with north aisle and south porch, and a west tower. By the mid 12th century there was apparently a substantial church on the site, from which only part of the nave walling survives. The lower stage of the tower and a north aisle were added in the late 12th century, the three-bay north arcade formed by cutting through the existing nave wall. The chancel arch was enlarged and the chancel extended or rebuilt early in the 13th century and at the same period the upper stage of the tower and the porch were added. Except for a 14th-century window in the chancel there appears to have been little work done later until the mid 15th century when the south wall of the nave was rebuilt with five large windows;[60] one of the buttresses bears an inscription to Richard Sly (d. 1461), perhaps the benefactor responsible for the work, and the rood-stair turret at the end of the wall bears the date 1485. Other work done in the 15th century included the tower parapet, a new window in the chancel, and the renewal of the doorway to the porch. In 1883 under Waller & Son the north aisle was rebuilt, the vestry added, and church restored and reseated.[61]

The church has a Norman tub-shaped font[62] and a 15th-century carved stone pulpit. The early-17th-century lectern was a gift to the church in 1927.[63] There are some fragments of early painted glass in a chancel window.[64] There are five bells cast by Abraham Rudhall, four in 1717 and the other in 1719; a sixth was added by John Rudhall in 1831.[65] The plate includes a chalice and paten-cover of 1684.[66] The parish registers survive from 1653.[67]

NONCONFORMITY. The Congregational interest at Chedworth, which with its large body of independent craftsmen was favourable to the establishment of nonconformity, is said to have been founded as a result of the preaching of George Whitefield there.[68] Congregationalists presumably formed the group led by a minister, Joseph Humphreys, who registered his house for worship in 1743. About 1750 the Congregationalists built a chapel at Pancakehill (then called Limekiln hill) at the south-east end of the village,[69] and the chapel was rebuilt in 1804, when the group was styled Independent. In 1851 the average congregations at morning, afternoon, and evening services were 130, 206, and 80 respectively,[70] and another congregation of *c.* 70 under the same minister used a building in the upper part of the village, opened in 1847.[71] The chapel ceased to have a resident minister in 1950, and in 1957 it was amalgamated with the chapel at Dyer Street in Cirencester.[72]

A Primitive Methodist chapel was built in Cheap Street in 1861 and was in use until the early 1940s.[73] In 1949 it was acquired by the Chedworth silver band as a practice-room.[74]

EDUCATION. In the earlier 19th century dame schools, of which there were three in 1818 teaching a total of 36 children, provided the only weekday education at Chedworth. A church Sunday school was attended by 130 children in 1818 and by 1833 there was also a Sunday school attached to the

[39] Ibid. 1.
[40] Rudder, *Glos.* 333; cf. Hockaday Abs. cl, 1765.
[41] Ex inf. the vicar.
[42] *Valor Eccl.* (Rec. Com.), ii. 449.
[43] *Trans. B.G.A.S.* lxxxiii. 93.
[44] G.D.R. vol. 381A, f. 78.
[45] Ibid. 382, f. 7.
[46] *Kelly's Dir. Glos.* (1863), 217.
[47] Worc. Episc. Reg., Reg. Ghinucci, f. 29v.
[48] *E.H.R.* xix. 112.
[49] Bodl. MS. Rawl. C.790, f. 24; *Trans. B.G.A.S.* xlix. 90.
[50] G.D.R. vol. 40, f. 154v.
[51] Hockaday Abs. cl.
[52] Ibid. lxiv, 1642 visit. f. 20.
[53] *Trans. B.G.A.S.* lxxxiii. 93.
[54] Hockaday Abs. cl.
[55] Atkyns, *Glos.* 331; Rudder, *Glos.* 333.
[56] Hockaday Abs. cl.
[57] G.D.R. vol. 382, f. 7.
[58] Hockaday Abs. cl; W.I. hist. of Chedworth, 91.
[59] Worc. Episc. Reg., Reg. Morgan, ii, f. 31v.
[60] See plate facing p. 29.
[61] *Kelly's Dir. Glos.* (1885), 382.
[62] *Trans. B.G.A.S.* xxxvi. 175.
[63] *Kelly's Dir. Glos.* (1931), 66.
[64] *Trans. B.G.A.S.* xlvii, 303.
[65] *Glos. Ch. Bells*, 41; *Glos. N. & Q.* ix. 63.
[66] *Glos. Ch. Plate*, 38.
[67] *B. & G. Par. Rec.* 89.
[68] *Glouc. Jnl.* 27 May 1848.
[69] Hockaday Abs. cl; the new bldg. was registered in 1750 but its date is given as 1752 in an inscr. on the present chap.
[70] Hockaday Abs. cl; H.O. 129/341/2/4/8.
[71] H.O. 129/341/2/4/7.
[72] W.I. hist. of Chedworth, 92.
[73] Ibid. 92–3.
[74] *Glos. Countryside*, Apr.–June 1949, 224.

Independent chapel.[75] The church Sunday school, held in a building near the church,[76] was affiliated to the National Society by 1847.[77] A National day-school was started before 1863[78] and in 1873 moved into a new building west of Cheap Street.[79] The average attendance was 90 in 1885[80] and 110 in 1910 but fell to 53 by 1932.[81] In 1978 the number on the roll was 46.[82]

CHARITIES FOR THE POOR. Land given, it was said, in Richard II's reign for the repair of the church and relief of the poor was alleged in 1601 to have been appropriated by the trustees to their own use when a Chancery decree was obtained placing the land under the management of the churchwardens.[83] The land was later let on 99-year leases with the result that in 1743 it brought in a rent of only 54s. though said to be worth £10 a year; there was also, however, a rent of £3 received from the parish for cottages built on part of the land and then used as poorhouses.[84] The land, which after the inclosure comprised 21 a., brought in a rent of £27 in the mid 1820s when all of it was apparently being applied to the church.[85] The income of the charity was about the same in 1896 when a Scheme divided the profits equally into separate charities for the church and the poor.[86] In 1978 the poor's part of the charity was distributed in cash at Christmas.[87]

Hugh Westwood (d. 1559) charged his rectory estate with 13s. 4d. a year for the poor.[88] The sum was being distributed by the tenant of the rectory land to poor widows in the 1820s[89] and later in the 19th century was received from the governors of Northleach grammar school and distributed by the vicar.[90] Charles Ballinger of Chalford (d. 1798), who owned an estate in the parish,[91] gave a third of the proceeds of two shares in the Stroudwater canal to buy cloth for the poor of Chedworth. About £14 a year was received from that source in 1827[92] but the profits fell to £3 by 1896[93] and by 1930 no dividends were produced by the shares.[94]

COBERLEY

THE RURAL PARISH of Coberley lies above the Cotswold escarpment 6.5 km. south of Cheltenham. The parish, which is irregular in shape with an area of 1,437 ha. (3,639 a.), includes in the eastern part the hamlet of Upper Coberley,[95] formerly called Little Coberley, Over Coberley, or Pinswell.[96] Upper Coberley was part of Bradley hundred and was assessed for poll tax in 1381 with part of Northleach, with which it was connected tenurially.[97] For poor-law purposes Upper Coberley was, at least before the later 18th century, part of the Eastington tithing of Northleach[98] but in the 19th century Coberley, although divided between two hundreds, was accounted a single civil parish.[99]

Except where it passes south-east of Leckhampton hill the boundary of the parish on the north and north-west follows the crest of the escarpment from Wistley hill in the north-east to the promontory formed by Crickley hill in the west, where the rector of Coberley erected a stone on the boundary with Cowley in 1690.[1] Part of the eastern boundary follows an ancient route across Wistley hill, recorded by that name in a description of the boundaries of a Dowdeswell estate in 759,[2] and in Chescombe bottom in the south the boundary follows a tributary stream of the river Churn. The Churn and another tributary running along Coldwell bottom mark much of the southern boundary. Elsewhere the boundaries follow old field boundaries.[3] The parish lies almost exclusively above the 183-m. contour and outside the valleys of the Churn and its tributaries rises to over 290 m. at Wistley hill and to over 274 m. at Upper Coberley, South hill in the south-west, and Hartley hill in the north. The valleys, including one running eastwards from Ullenwood, formerly called Hallingwood,[4] in the western part, lie on Midford Sand; the higher land is formed mainly by the Inferior Oolite but Upper Lias clay is exposed in the Churn valley and above the escarpment near Ullenwood.[5] Many springs rise in the parish. In the north a group called Seven Springs forms the source of the Churn and has sometimes been considered that of the Thames of which the Churn is a tributary.[6] On the summit of Crickley hill fortifications and archaeological evidence indicate an interrupted series of occupations from the

[75] Educ. of Poor Digest, 294; Educ. Enquiry Abstract, 310.
[76] G.D.R., T 1/50.
[77] Church School Inquiry, 1846–7, 6–7.
[78] Kelly's Dir. Glos. (1863), 217.
[79] Ed. 7/34/70; Glos. R.O., P 77A/SC 1/1.
[80] Kelly's Dir. Glos. (1885), 382.
[81] Bd. of Educ., List 21, 1911 (H.M.S.O.), 160; 1922, 103; 1932, 113.
[82] Ex inf. county educ. dept.
[83] 21st Rep. Com. Char. 166–7.
[84] G.D.R. vol. 397, f. 78.
[85] 21st Rep. Com. Char. 167.
[86] Glos. R.O., D 3469/5/31.
[87] Ex inf. the vicar.
[88] Trans. B.G.A.S. liv. 103–4.
[89] 21st Rep. Com. Char. 168.
[90] Glos. R.O., D 3469/5/31, letter 1971.
[91] Ibid. D 1388/III/51.
[92] 21st Rep. Com. Char. 168.
[93] Kelly's Dir. Glos. (1897), 60.
[94] Ibid. (1931), 67; cf. Glos. R.O., D 3469/5/31, letter 1971.
[95] O.S. Area Bk. (1886); Census, 1971. This account was written in 1978.
[96] Hist. & Cart. Mon. Glouc. (Rolls Ser.), i. 233–5; Hockaday Abs. clxiv, 1594; Rudder, Glos. 399.
[97] Dom. Bk. (Rec. Com.), i. 164v., 168; E 179/113/31A rot. 3.
[98] Rudder, Glos. 399, 580.
[99] Census, 1801–1901.
[1] Glos. R.O., DC/E 88/2, ct. 2 May 1757.
[2] Grundy, Saxon Charters, 114.
[3] O.S. Area Bk. (1886).
[4] Glos. R.O., D 1388/SL 4, no. 83.
[5] Geol. Surv. Map 1″, solid, sheet 44 (1856 edn.).
[6] Hist. MSS. Com. 29, 13th Rep. II, Portland, ii, p. 296; Atkyns, Glos. 378.

Neolithic period. There was also Romano-British occupation of the area to the north-east which is now covered by Short wood.[7]

The woodland which measured 3 furlongs by 2 furlongs in 1086[8] was represented later by Short wood and Ullen wood in the west, which were both recorded in 1601.[9] The principal wood in the east, probably that recorded in 1182,[10] was Chatcombe wood, in which Gloucester Abbey reserved 300 oaks and ashes for building repairs in 1524.[11] The woodland of the parish, which measured 615 a. in 1901,[12] included areas of park-land and plantation created in the later 19th century. On the southern boundary an area east of Cowley village was taken into the park of Cowley Manor in the late 1850s.[13] Hartley bottom west of Seven Springs was sparsely wooded[14] until it was laid out and planted before 1894 as grounds for Seven Springs House,[15] and a park was created at Ullenwood Manor in the late 19th century.[16] In the early 20th century a few plantations were laid out on the Colesbourne estate in the south-east.[17]

There was a rifle range west of Chatcombe wood by 1897[18] and after the Second World War the area between Ullenwood and Hartley bottom was made into a golf-course. The National Trust acquired the eastern part of the Crickley hill area, known as the Scrubbs, in 1935.[19] In the later 17th century there were fishponds at Seven Springs, Conygree pool lower downstream, the manor-house east of the river, and Ullenwood.[20] Conygree pool, the largest, had been drained by 1838[21] but had been refilled by 1894 as part of the pleasure grounds for Seven Springs House.[22]

Several early tracks crossed the parish, including the green way which ascended the escarpment from Shurdington.[23] The section of the Gloucester–Oxford road which runs from Crickley hill by Seven Springs towards Frogmill was turnpiked in 1751.[24] A road from Cheltenham, which ran southwards to the Churn, where it crossed into Elkstone at Cockleford, was turnpiked as part of the Cheltenham–Cirencester and Cheltenham–Tetbury routes in 1756.[25] Its course across the escarpment was moved to the east in 1825 when it became part of the new Cheltenham–Cirencester road built along the Churn

valley.[26] A small brick parcel office, which had been built at its junction with the Gloucester–Oxford road east of Seven Springs by 1894,[27] was derelict in 1978. In the west a road from Stroud to Cheltenham by way of Leckhampton hill was out of repair in 1661[28] and was included in the Painswick–Cheltenham road turnpiked in 1785.[29]

Coberley church, situated east of a crossing of the Churn, had been built by the 12th century. Next to it stood the medieval manor-house, later incorporated in Coberley Court, which was demolished in 1790;[30] the farm-house north of the church, which had also formed part of Coberley Court, was rebuilt soon afterwards.[31] A house lower down the river was formerly a mill. Earthworks, possibly house-platforms, were visible north-west of the church in a field across the river in 1978 but Coberley village, the main settlement of the parish, grew up further north-west around a green,[32] on which a sundial was erected in 1902 as a memorial to Queen Victoria.[33] The village, which in 1838 contained only eight buildings, has remained small.[34] The oldest surviving houses, including the rectory, date from the early 19th century. The school and most of the cottages were built later that century and some council houses were put up in the northern part in the 20th century. South-west of the village there was evidently a house at Close Farm by 1777[35] but the present farm-house dates from the 19th century. To the north-west Dowman's Farm, which probably dates from the 17th or 18th century, has been altered and enlarged considerably.[36] Booker's Cottage to the west has been converted from an early-18th-century row of dwellings.[37]

By the later 18th century farmsteads had been established at Ullenwood[38] and on Hartley hill[39] where the northern end of Hartley House probably dates from that century and the southern end from the 19th. In the later 19th century three mansions were built in the parish. Seven Springs House at Seven Springs and Salterley Grange near the crest of the escarpment to the west date from c. 1860[40] and Ullenwood Manor was built south of the Ullenwood farm-house several years later.[41] All three were converted to institutional use in the 20th century. Other buildings put up in the later 19th century included estate cottages in the western part of the parish and

[7] R.C.H.M. *Glos.* i. 33–4; Glos. R.O., AR 82.
[8] *Dom. Bk.* (Rec. Com.), i. 168.   [9] Req. 2/398/15.
[10] *Hist. & Cart. Mon. Glouc.* i. 234–5.
[11] Glouc. Cath. Libr., Reg. Abb. Malvern, i, ff. 220–1.
[12] Acreage Returns, 1901.
[13] Glos. R.O., D 1388/SL 5, no. 84.
[14] Bryant, *Map of Glos.* (1824).
[15] Cf. Glos. R.O., D 1388/SL 8, no. 7.
[16] O.S. Map 6", Glos. XXXIV. NE. (1883 and 1903 edns.).
[17] Ibid. XXXV. NW. and SW. (1903 and 1924 edns.); cf. H. J. Elwes, 'Colesborne Estate Hist.' (TS. *penes* Mr. H. W. G. Elwes, of Colesbourne Pk.)
[18] S. S. Buckman, *Chelt. as a Holiday Resort* (Chelt. 1897), 23, 97.
[19] *Properties of the National Trust* (1969), 78.
[20] Glos. R.O., D 2134, sale partics.
[21] G.D.R., T 1/58.
[22] Cf. O.S. Map 6", Glos. XXXIV. NE. (1883 edn.); Glos. R.O., D 1388/SL 8, no. 7.
[23] *Trans. B.G.A.S.* liii. 117, 130.
[24] Gloucester and Oxford Road Act, 24 Geo. II, c. 28.

[25] Tewkesbury and Cheltenham Roads Act, 29 Geo. II, c. 51.
[26] Cirencester Roads Act, 6 Geo. IV, c. 143; cf. Glos. R.O., Q/RUm 96.
[27] Glos. R.O., D 1388/SL 8, no. 7.
[28] Ibid. Q/SIb 1, f. 14.
[29] Cheltenham Roads Act, 25 Geo. III, c. 125.
[30] *The Topographer*, iv. 176.
[31] Cf. Glos. R.O., D 1388/SL 3, no. 20.
[32] Taylor, *Map of Glos.* (1777).
[33] Glos. R.O., P 105/IN 4/3.
[34] G.D.R., T 1/58.
[35] Taylor, *Map of Glos.* (1777).
[36] Glos. R.O., D 1388/SL 8, no. 7.
[37] Cf. ibid. D 443/1.
[38] Taylor, *Map of Glos.* (1777).
[39] Cf. Glos. R.O., D 269B/F 13.
[40] *Kelly's Dir. Glos.* (1856), 275; (1863), 256; *Chelt. Examiner*, 5 Oct. 1870.
[41] Cf. Glos. R.O., D 1388/SL 4, no. 83; terrier of J. Hampson's est. 1875 with churchwardens' acct. bk. 1779–1892, *penes* the rector, the Revd. S. I. Pulford.

farm-houses at Seven Springs and on South hill; the latter had been replaced by Cuckoopen Barn by the early 1880s.[42] North-west of Ullenwood a group of huts, built as a hospital during the Second World War, was later an American Army camp but by 1978 some huts had been demolished and the remainder had a variety of uses, including storage of commercial goods.[43] In the mid 20th century two farm-houses were built near Ullenwood.

The eastern part of the parish has remained sparsely settled but there were several dwellings there in the mid 12th century.[44] Upper Coberley, the principal settlement there, contained two farmsteads by the early 18th century.[45] Lower Farm is of various dates of the 18th and 19th centuries and Upper Coberley Farm to the east is presumably the farm-house built there not long before 1807.[46] By the Churn the buildings of a former mill belonging to the settlement of Lower Cockleford stand in Coberley parish.

Twelve people were assessed under Coberley for the subsidy in 1327 and 4 under Upper Coberley.[47] In 1381 at least 42 people outside Upper Coberley were assessed for poll tax in the parish.[48] The number of communicants in the parish was estimated at 69 in 1548[49] and at 50 in 1551[50] and there were said to be 11 households in 1563,[51] 66 communicants in 1603,[52] and 14 families in 1650.[53] The same number of families was estimated in the early 18th century when 14 houses in the parish were occupied by c. 80 people.[54] The population was estimated at 178 c. 1775[55] but in 1801 it was 161. It increased rapidly to 237 in 1821 and, after falling away, had recovered by 1851, and by 1861 there had been a considerable increase to 343. During the following century the population fluctuated, never falling below 306 and reaching a peak of 376 in 1911, but by 1971 it had declined to 268.[56]

On 17 October 1278 Edward I was in Coberley, which has had other royal visits. Elizabeth, wife of Henry VII, stayed at Coberley Court on 4 August 1502[57] and Charles I on the nights of 6 November 1643 and 12 July 1644.[58]

MANORS AND OTHER ESTATES. An estate of 10 hides in Coberley, held at the Conquest by Dena, had been granted by 1086 to Roger of Berkeley[59] and

descended to his grandson Roger of Berkeley (III) (d. 1170). At that time the estate, assessed at 1 knight's fee, was subinfeudated and obtained by a kinsman William of Berkeley.[60] Overlordship of the estate, called the manor of COBERLEY, passed to Roger's descendants, the Berkeleys of Dursley.[61] A rent of £4 from the manor was settled with Siston manor on the marriage of Isabel, daughter of Roger of Berkeley (IV), lord of Dursley, and Thomas of Rochford (d. 1205). Isabel later married William Walrond who unsuccessfully claimed Coberley manor by right of escheat in 1224. Alice, Isabel's daughter by Thomas,[62] granted the rent for a term of years to her half-brother Robert Walrond (d. 1273), and in 1309 the reversionary right belonged to her grandson Alan de Plucknett (d. 1325).[63] Alan's widow Sibyl, who married Henry of Pembridge, sought dower in Coberley manor.[64]

The William of Berkeley who acquired Coberley manor was either the founder of Kingswood Abbey or his son.[65] The younger William, who was patron of Coberley church c. 1188,[66] was succeeded in turn by his sons Robert (d. by 1224)[67] and Giles (d. by 1242). Giles's son Nicholas, who apparently came of age in 1257, died in 1263 and, although he had a posthumous daughter by his wife Alice, the manor passed to his brother Giles, sheriff of Herefordshire between 1275 and 1280. Giles (d. 1294) was succeeded by his son Thomas, a minor, who submitted in 1322 after joining the rebellion against Edward II. In 1364, shortly before his death, Thomas settled the manor on himself with remainder to Thomas, his son[68] by his second wife Joan, later wife of William of Whittington. The younger Thomas, who came of age in 1372,[69] died in 1405. His heirs were his daughters Margaret, wife of Nicholas Matson, and Alice (d. 1414), wife of Thomas Bridges (d. 1408) and later of John Browning.[70] Nicholas Matson, who was possibly also called Nicholas Droys,[71] survived his wife and died in 1435. Margaret's half share of the manor then presumably passed to their son Robert (d. 1458) who was evidently succeeded by Alice's son and heir Giles Bridges.[72]

Giles Bridges died seised of the whole manor in 1467 and his son and heir Thomas[73] (d. 1493) was succeeded by his son Giles.[74] Giles, later knighted, was succeeded at his death in 1511 by his son John.[75]

[42] Cf. G.D.R., T 1/58; Glos. R.O., D 1388/SL 4, no. 83; O.S. Map 6″, Glos. XXXIV. NE. (1883 edn.).
[43] Local information.
[44] Hist. & Cart. Mon. Glouc. i. 235.
[45] Bodl. MS. Rawl. B.323, f. 198; Rudder, Glos. 399.
[46] Glos. R.O., D 1388/SL 3, no. 20.
[47] Glos. Subsidy Roll, 1327, 10, 12.
[48] E 179/113/35A rot. 13d.; cf. ibid. rot. 12.
[49] Trans. B.G.A.S. viii. 275.
[50] E.H.R. xix. 115.
[51] Bodl. MS. Rawl. C.790, f. 9v.
[52] Eccl. Misc. 80.
[53] Trans. B.G.A.S. lxxxiii. 93.
[54] Atkyns, Glos. 378.
[55] Rudder, Glos. 399.
[56] Census, 1801–1971.
[57] Trans. B.G.A.S. xvii. 107; vii. 274.
[58] Bigland, Glos. i. 405 n.
[59] Dom. Bk. (Rec. Com.), i. 168.
[60] Trans. B.G.A.S. xvii. 96–7; V.C.H. Glos. x. 259.
[61] V.C.H. Glos. x. 259–60; Inq. p.m. Glos. 1359–1413, 238; Glos. Colln. RX 98.2.

[62] Trans. B.G.A.S. xvii. 100–2; Rot. Litt. Claus. (Rec. Com.), i. 615.
[63] Cal. Inq. p.m. v, pp. 72–7; Sanders, Eng. Baronies, 73; by virtue of the rent the man. was sometimes said to be held of Robert's heirs: Feud. Aids, ii. 239; Cal. Inq. p.m. iv, p. 343; Cal. Inq. p.m. Hen. VII, i, p. 367.
[64] C.P. 40/275 rot. 316d.
[65] For the Berkeleys of Coberley, see Trans. B.G.A.S. xvii. 96–125.
[66] Ibid. xliv. 266–7.
[67] Cf. Rot. Litt. Claus. (Rec. Com.), i. 615; Close R. 1227–31, 426.
[68] C.P. 25(1)/288/47 no. 639; cf. Cal. Close, 1364–8, 157.
[69] Cal. Inq. p.m. xiii, p. 256; cf. Reg. Bransford, p. 142.
[70] Inq. p.m. Glos. 1359–1413, 238, 248; V.C.H. Glos. x. 193.
[71] Worc. Episc. Reg., Reg. Morgan, i, f. 5v.
[72] Cf. V.C.H. Glos. viii. 12.
[73] C 140/23 no. 15.
[74] Cal. Inq. p.m. Hen. VII, i, pp. 366–7.
[75] C 142/26 no. 22.

John, who was created Baron Chandos of Sudeley in 1554, died in 1557 when the manor passed with the title to his son Edmund (d. 1572). Edmund's son and heir Giles died in 1594 leaving two daughters, Elizabeth and Catherine,[76] but by 1601 his wife Frances held the manor in dower.[77] She was named as lady of Coberley in 1608[78] but by 1618 the manor had been acquired by William Dutton of Sherborne, owner of a manorial estate in Upper Coberley. William was succeeded that year by his son John[79] who evidently settled the Coberley lands on the marriage of his daughter Lucy (d. 1656) and Thomas Pope, earl of Downe (d. 1660),[80] for Thomas sold them shortly before his death to Paul Castleman.[81] Paul (d. 1678) left as his heir his son Jonathan, a minor,[82] who sold the estate to John Grobham Howe of Stowell in 1720.[83] John (d. 1721) was succeeded by his son John,[84] who in 1724 settled the Coberley manors on himself and his wife Dorothy.[85] John, who was created Baron Chedworth in 1741, died in 1742[86] and although Dorothy was alive in 1771[87] their son Henry Frederick Howe,

Lord Chedworth, was evidently in possession of the estate by 1769.[88] It then passed with the title to John Howe (d. 1804). He devised his estates to trustees for sale[89] and in 1807, following a Chancery suit, they were auctioned in lots and the Coberley estate was divided.[90]

Coberley Court, incorporating the Berkeleys' manor-house,[91] was neglected by the Howe family for some time before it was demolished in 1790.[92] The house, for which Paul Castleman was assessed on 26 hearths in 1672,[93] was an extensive building enclosing three open courts. The range containing the hall and other principal rooms divided the southern from the central court, and the parish church was part of the northern dividing range. The northernmost range included a farm-house, a gatehouse, and farm buildings. There were extensive formal gardens to the south and west and a kitchen garden and orchard to the east. Along the southern side of the gardens a canal was crossed by a bridge which led to the avenues of a park.[94]

At the auction of 1807 the manorial rights and

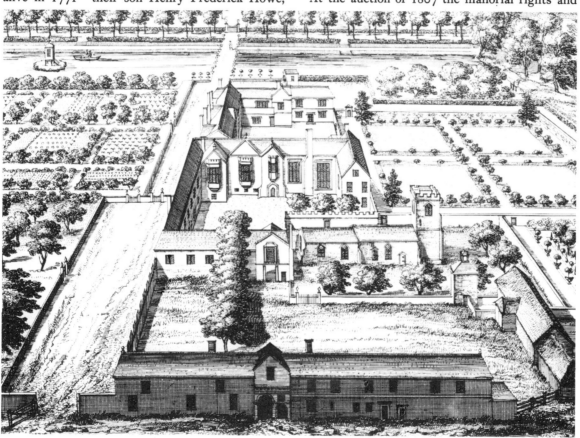

COBERLEY COURT AND THE PARISH CHURCH IN THE EARLY 18TH CENTURY

[76] *Complete Peerage*, iii. 126–7; C 142/109 no. 70; C 142/163 no. 59; C 142/309 no. 193.
[77] Req. 2/398/15; Fosbrooke, *Glos.* ii. 523.
[78] Smith, *Men and Armour*, 255, 257, where her lordships of Cowley and Coberley are interchanged.
[79] C 142/378 no. 107.
[80] Cf. *Complete Peerage*, iv. 450.
[81] Bodl. MS. Rawl. B.323, f. 198; Bigland, *Glos.* i. 405.
[82] *Visit. Glos. 1682–3*, 36.
[83] Glos. R.O., D 480, Castleman and Howe fams., deeds 1711–1808; par. reg. 1695–1779.
[84] Bigland, *Glos.* iii, no. 259; Burke, *Peerage* (1935), 1288.

[85] Glos. R.O., D 480, Castleman and Howe fams., deeds 1711–1808. [86] Burke, *Dorm. & Ext. Peerages* (1883), 288.
[87] Hockaday Abs. clxiv. [88] Glos. R.O., D 182/III/98.
[89] Ibid. D 480, misc. papers 1807–57, abs. of title; Burke, *Dorm. & Ext. Peerages* (1883), 288.
[90] Glos. R.O., D 1388/SL 3, no. 20.
[91] Cf. *Cal. Inq. p.m.* v, p. 164; xiii, p. 256; Leland, *Itin.* ed. Toulmin Smith, i. 130.
[92] Bigland, *Glos.* i. 405; *The Topographer*, iv. 176.
[93] E 179/247/13 rot. 29.
[94] Hist. MSS. Com. 29, *13th Rep. II, Portland*, ii, p. 296; Atkyns, *Glos.* plate at pp. 376–7, detail reproduced above.

over 1,400 a. in the eastern part of the parish were bought by John Elwes[95] and then descended with his Colesbourne estate.[96] In the 20th century much of the Coberley land, including c. 680 a. acquired by John Hamilton Waterston in 1959,[97] was sold but the estate retained land in the parish in 1978.[98]

In 1807 the purchaser of the western part of the Coberley estate, amounting to almost 1,700 a., was William Lawrence of Shurdington.[99] William (d. 1820)[1] was succeeded by his son William Edwards Lawrence, a minor.[2] He died in 1857 and the following year c. 850 a. at Ullenwood was sold to John Gay Attwater, the tenant there, and c. 800 a. to the east to William Hall of Bury (Lancs.), a cotton-manufacturer.[3] Hall, who bought Ullenwood from Attwater in 1863,[4] died in 1872[5] and the estate passed to his daughter Sarah, wife of John Hampson[6] (d. 1876).[7] By 1885 Sarah had married Henry Bubb and had sold the eastern half of the estate, including Seven Springs House, to Samuel Peters.[8] He owned over 800 a in 1894[9] when he sold part with the house to Hamilton Fane Gladwin, who died in 1913.[10] Capt. Alan Richardson owned that part until the later 1930s when much of the land was possibly bought by Mrs. Wills-Goldingham.[11] Seven Springs House, which was evidently built by William Hall in the late 1850s,[12] was tenanted in 1875[13] and was unoccupied in 1934.[14] In 1938 the trustees of Barnwood House Hospital bought the house with 76½ a. but at the outbreak of the Second World War Cheltenham Ladies' College took over the building. In 1948 the trustees sold the house, which was a girls' preparatory school from 1945[15] until the mid 1960s when Gloucestershire county council bought it.[16] The stable block had been converted and enlarged to provide classrooms by 1978 when the house was used by Sandford School, which then taught 93 maladjusted children.[17]

Henry and Sarah Bubb retained the rest of the estate which was based on Ullenwood Manor. Henry, a leading member of the Spiritualist church in Cheltenham, survived his wife and died in 1931.[18]

His representatives agreed to sell the estate, which covered c. 985 a., to Thomas Place of Northallerton (Yorks. N.R.) and in 1934 he sold it in lots,[19] the house and some land being acquired by Mrs. Wills-Goldingham.[20] Ullenwood Manor, a symmetrically fronted house in an Elizabethan style, was built c. 1870[21] and additions were made on the east c. 1895. The late-19th-century out-buildings include a number of lodges.[22] After the Second World War the house was in turn an American officers' hostel, a country club, and a boys' public school. In 1967 the house, with c. 30 a., became a residential school for the National Star Centre for Disabled Youth, which later bought the property. Extensive new buildings, including residential blocks, had been put up to the west by 1978 when the centre had 92 students.[23]

Between 735 and 767 St. Peter's Abbey, Gloucester, acquired an estate of 20 'cassati' at PINSWELL for a sheep-walk.[24] That property was presumably represented by the hide of land in Upper Coberley belonging to Northleach manor, one of the abbey's estates held in 1066 by Eldred, archbishop of York, and in 1086 by his successor Thomas.[25] In 1095 those estates were given back to the abbey, which acquired more land in Coberley, including some held from Foxcote in Withington,[26] and was granted free warren there in 1354.[27] The Pinswell estate, described as a manor in the mid 13th century[28] and as Upper Coberley manor in 1524,[29] was granted by the Crown in 1595 to John Wells and Henry Best[30] and was later acquired, evidently before 1606, by William Dutton.[31] Dutton later acquired Coberley manor, with which the Pinswell estate was merged.[32]

An estate called HARTLEY FARM, which Henry Norwood owned in 1779,[33] comprised 319 a. and descended as part of his Leckhampton estate to Henry Norwood Trye (d. 1854).[34] By 1865 the farm had been acquired by Henry Camps[35] of Cheltenham, who in 1858 had bought 50 a. to the south-west, formerly part of W. E. Lawrence's estate.[36] Camps sold his estate in 1870 to Lt.-Col.

[95] Glos. R.O., D 1388/SL 3, no. 20; deed 1808, penes Mr. H. W. G. Elwes.
[96] See below; G.D.R., T 1/58, 59; Kelly's Dir. Glos. (1897), 133.
[97] Glos. R.O., D 2299/4451; D 2582/8; SL 456.
[98] Ex inf. Mr. Elwes.
[99] Glos. R.O., D 1388/SL 3, no. 20; D 480, Lawrence fam., papers 1738–1846, deed 1808.
[1] Glouc. Jnl. 30 Oct. 1820.
[2] Glos. R.O., D 361/T 5.
[3] Ibid. D 480, Lawrence fam., papers 1828–58, 1851–7, 1853–8.
[4] Ibid. D 1388/SL 4, no. 83; D 2299/277.
[5] Chelt. Examiner, 4 Dec. 1872.
[6] Chelt. Chron. 14 Mar. 1931; terrier of J. Hampson's est.
[7] G.D.R. wills 1876, ff. 345–346v.
[8] Cf. Kelly's Dir. Glos. (1879), 628; (1885), 438.
[9] Glos. R.O., D 1388/SL 8, no. 7.
[10] Chelt. Chron. 27 Dec. 1913.
[11] Who's Who in Glos. (Heref. 1934), 187; Kelly's Dir. Glos. (1914 and later edns.).
[12] Cf. Kelly's Dir. Glos. (1856), 275; (1863), 256; as Hall's residence it was called Hartley Ho. in 1859: deed penes the rector.
[13] Terrier of J. Hampson's est.
[14] Kelly's Dir. Glos. (1935), 140.
[15] Ex inf. the sec., Barnwood House Trust; cf. Glos. R.O., D 2299/7810.
[16] The Times, 20 July 1964; 29 Mar. 1965.
[17] Ex inf. county educ. dept.
[18] Chelt. Chron. 14 Mar. 1931.
[19] Glos. R.O., D 2299/277; Kelly's Dir. Glos. (1935), 140.
[20] Ex inf. Mr. E. V. Clark, remedial tutor, National Star Centre, Ullenwood Man.
[21] Cf. Glos. R.O., D 1388/SL 4, no. 83; terrier of J. Hampson's est.
[22] O.S. Map 6″, Glos. XXXIV. NE. (1883 edn.).
[23] Ex inf. Mr. Clark.
[24] Hist. & Cart. Mon. Glouc. i, p. lxxii; Finberg, Glos. Studies, 12.
[25] Dom. Bk. (Rec. Com.), i. 164v.
[26] Hist. & Cart. Mon. Glouc. i. 11, 233–5.
[27] Cal. Chart. R. 1341–1417, 142.
[28] Hist. & Cart. Mon. Glouc. i. 70.
[29] Glouc. Cath. Libr., Reg. Abb. Malvern, i, f. 220.
[30] C 66/1435 mm. 37–46.
[31] Trans. B.G.A.S. xvii. 230; cf. Smith, Men and Armour, 268.
[32] Cf. Glos. R.O., D 1388/SL 3, no. 20.   [33] Ibid. D 2698/F 47.
[34] G.D.R., T 1/58; D. Lysons, Life of Chas. Brandon Trye (Glouc. 1812), 8; Glos. R.O., D 1809/F 1/11.
[35] Glos. R.O., P 125/IN 4/3.
[36] Ibid. D 480, misc. papers 1767–1858.

Charles Prevost[37] who sold it to Theodore Ellis Williams in 1878. In 1907 it was bought from Williams by Birmingham city corporation which sold the farm and farm-house in 1951.[38] Salterley Grange, which Henry Camps built on his estate c. 1860,[39] was converted by Birmingham city corporation as a municipal sanatorium for the treatment of tuberculosis, and chalets were built in its grounds. The sanatorium, which opened in 1908,[40] became a chest hospital in the 1960s. It closed in the early 1970s and by 1978 the chalets had been converted and sold as private dwellings.[41]

ECONOMIC HISTORY. In 1086 there were 4 *servi* working 2 plough-teams on the demesne of Coberley manor. The estate included 5 a. of meadow land and its appreciation in the previous twenty years may have resulted from an extension of the cultivated area.[42] The demesne was organized in part for sheep-farming by the late 13th century[43] and a shepherd lived in Coberley in 1381.[44] In the early 15th century the flock on John Browning's part of the manor included 400 ewes.[45] Sir John Bridges, who took leases of sheep-pastures in several Cotswold parishes in 1539, was evidently an active sheep-farmer.[46] Sheep-farming was especially important in the eastern part of the parish where Gloucester Abbey had acquired land for a sheep-walk,[47] and by 1504 a flock of 320 ewes from the abbey's estate in Sandhurst had summer pasture there.[48] In 1524 the abbey granted a lease of its demesne and the common pasture used by its sheep for a term of 61 years or four lives.[49]

The tenants recorded on Coberley manor in 1086 were 19 *villani* and 4 bordars working 5 plough-teams.[50] Twenty-three customary tenants were recorded on Gloucester Abbey's estate in the mid 1260s. Three were yardlanders but another 5 yard-lands, which had fragmented, supported 13 tenants. Each yardland, which comprised 72 a., had to provide 5 week-works and 3 men performing 4 bedrepes during the harvest. Extra services were owed for ploughing, harrowing, and shearing and washing sheep, and there was a duty to mow in Gloucester for 4 days. A quarter yardland, including a mill, was held for cash rent. The other customary tenants had smaller holdings. One was held for 1 week-work, including the carriage of poultry, eggs, and cheese to Gloucester, and 3 bedrepes; three for

works during the harvest; one for cash; and one for cash or the service of repairing demesne ploughs.[51] By 1548 the land belonging to the Coberley chantry-chapel included six tenements, mainly arable with pasture and some meadow land; a yardland there contained c. 25 a.[52] In the later 17th century there were six farms held for terms of lives on the Coberley estate.[53]

Although there were open fields in the eastern part of the parish in the late 12th century[54] there is not much later evidence of open-field cultivation in the parish. In the later 17th century the demesne of the Coberley estate did not include open-field land,[55] but there may have been some in 1705 when part of the glebe lay in a south field.[56] At least part of the woodland on the Pinswell estate may have been open to rights of common before 1182 when the lord of Coberley manor renounced pasture rights in woodland in Upper Coberley, probably Chatcombe wood.[57] A common in the parish had been stinted by 1303.[58] The parish contained extensive sheep-pastures including in 1601 land at Ullenwood.[59] Later in the century there was a pasture covering 471½ a. on Monday hill, south-east of Upper Coberley, and some of the large fields recorded then in the eastern half of the parish may have been sheep-pastures. There was also a common pasture, which was stinted for at least 400 sheep[60] and may have been in the area north of Seven Springs called Coberley Downs in the early 18th century.[61] In the later 13th century the men of Coberley manor had common rights in a field in Cowley.[62]

A sheepfold was mentioned in 1705[63] and there were some good pastures at that time but most of the land was then devoted to arable husbandry.[64] In 1801 1,076 a. were returned as producing arable crops, mainly cereals but including 90 a. of turnips and smaller areas of peas and potatoes,[65] and almost two-thirds of the land (2,370 a.) were given over to arable in 1838, when grassland covered 774 a.[66] By the end of the century the area returned as under cereals and roots had fallen by over half and more land was under permanent grass. In 1896 there were 135 a. of heath used for grazing.[67] Sheep-farming was on a large scale in 1866 when at least 1,811 sheep were kept in the parish. Fewer were returned in 1896 but sheep-farming and stock-rearing became relatively more important in the later 19th century and early 20th. There was also some dairying and pig-rearing then.[68]

[37] Ibid. D 1388/SL 5, no. 47; *Chelt. Examiner*, 5 Oct. 1870; for Prevost, see Burke, *Peerage* (1935), 1945.
[38] Sched. of title deeds, *penes* the city solicitor, Birmingham.
[39] Inits. on ho.; cf. *Kelly's Dir. Glos.* (1856), 275; (1863), 256.
[40] *V.C.H. Warws.* vii. 345; *Kelly's Dir. Glos.* (1910), 139.
[41] Local information.
[42] *Dom. Bk.* (Rec. Com.), i. 168.
[43] Cf. *Reg. Giffard*, 450; *Cal. Close*, 1349–54, 341.
[44] E 179/113/35A rot. 13d.
[45] Hockaday Abs. clxiv, 1416.
[46] Ibid. clxx, Condicote; cxc, Eastleach Turville; ccxxvii, Lower Guiting.
[47] Finberg, *Glos. Studies*, 12.
[48] Glouc. Cath. Libr., Reg. Abb. Braunche, p. 109; cf. *Hist. & Cart. Mon. Glouc.* iii. 291–3; Glos. R.O., D 1740/E 15.
[49] Glouc. Cath. Libr., Reg. Abb. Malvern, i, ff. 220–1.
[50] *Dom. Bk.* (Rec. Com.), i. 168.
[51] *Hist. & Cart. Mon. Glouc.* iii. 211–13.

[52] Hockaday Abs. clxiv.
[53] Glos. R.O., D 2134, sale partics.
[54] *Hist. & Cart. Mon. Glouc.* i. 233–4.
[55] Glos. R.O., D 2134, sale partics.
[56] G.D.R., V 5/98T 2.
[57] *Hist. & Cart. Mon. Glouc.* i. 234–5.
[58] *Trans. B.G.A.S.* xxxviii. 30.
[59] Req. 2/398/15.
[60] Glos. R.O., D 2134, sale partics.; G.D.R., T 1/58.
[61] Bodl. MS. Top. Glouc. c.3, f. 214.
[62] E 315/61 f. 26.
[63] G.D.R., V 5/98T 2.
[64] Atkyns, *Glos.* 378.
[65] Acreage Returns, 1801.
[66] G.D.R., T 1/58.
[67] M.A.F. 68/26/17; M.A.F. 68/1609/1; Acreage Returns, 1901.
[68] M.A.F. 68/28/8; M.A.F. 68/1609/1; M.A.F. 68/3295/3.

In 1838 most of the agricultural land was included in six principal farms which covered 775 a., 646 a., 564 a., 558 a., 319 a., and 209 a.[69] There were eight farmers in 1896 but in 1926, when 50 agricultural labourers worked in the parish full-time, there were thirteen: five of the farmers in 1926 were smallholders with less than 20 a. each and the other farms were four of over 300 a., two of 150–300 a., and two of 50–150 a.[70] In 1976 about half of the land in the parish was worked in four farms, each with over 100 ha. (247 a.), and six of the remaining eight farms had less than 20 ha. (50 a.) each. One farm specialized in dairying and two were devoted mainly to cereal production, but sheep-farming and stock-rearing remained important.[71]

Two mills have been recorded on the Churn in Coberley parish. Coberley mill, a corn-mill SSW. of the church, had possibly been established by the later 17th century[72] and was let with a bakehouse by the later 19th century.[73] The mill, which was on that part of the Coberley estate eventually acquired by Samuel Peters,[74] stopped working in the 1930s and the building, mainly of the 19th century, was converted to domestic use.[75]

Cockleford mill, at Lower Cockleford in the south-eastern corner of the parish, was possibly the mill recorded on Gloucester Abbey's estate in the mid 1260s.[76] It was probably a cloth-mill by the later 17th century, when Tuck Mill mead was recorded,[77] and was acquired, evidently from Thomas Gibbons in 1701, by Matthew Walbank. It then passed with his Caudle Green property to Abraham Walbank who sold the mill in 1764 to James Bidmead.[78] It remained a cloth-mill in 1788[79] but for much of the 19th century was owned and worked as a corn-mill by Edward Williams[80] (d. 1870).[81] It apparently went out of use in the late 1880s.[82] In 1978 the mill-house, dating from the 18th century with stabling of the 19th, was a substantial residence.

A fuller lived in the parish in the mid 13th century and a walker in the mid 14th, but the cloth industry, based presumably on local mills, was evidently small in scale.[83] The character of employment in the parish has remained principally agrarian and few trades have been recorded. In 1831 only 4 of 37 families depended solely on trades for a livelihood.[84] Coberley residents included a millward in 1347[85] and

a smith in 1381.[86] There was a smith on Gloucester Abbey's estate in the mid 13th century and early 14th.[87] In the later 19th century a carpenter and a shoemaker lived in the parish. The stonemason recorded at the end of the century[88] probably worked stone quarried in the parish, especially in the western part near Crickley hill.[89] A timber-merchant lived in Coberley in 1817.[90] The parish usually had at least two shops in the later 19th century and early 20th[91] and the village retained a post office in 1978.

LOCAL GOVERNMENT. In the early 15th century the view of frankpledge for most of the parish was held in the hundred court but Upper Coberley as part of the foreign tithing of Northleach attended the view held in Bradley hundred court.[92] Gloucester Abbey's Upper Coberley halimote was recorded from 1287[93] and the lessee of the abbey's demesne from 1524 had to provide hospitality for its steward.[94]

Proctors of the church accounted in 1351 for repairs to the church,[95] a duty that later passed to the churchwardens. Two churchwardens were recorded from 1498[96] but in the 18th and 19th centuries there was frequently only one. Their surviving accounts begin in 1779.[97] Other parish officers included a surveyor of the highways, whose accounts survive for the period 1783–1838.[98] The cost of poor-relief in Coberley was exceptionally high in 1776 when £172 was spent, and had risen to £205 by c. 1784.[99] In the early 1780s 74 inhabitants, between a third and half of the population, were listed as poor[1] but only 19 people received regular help in 1803 and the cost had fallen by then to £164.[2] Each year during the period 1798–1836 two overseers of the poor were elected but only one accounted. The parish then had a workhouse which from c. 1808 was at Booker's Cottage, one of several dwellings in Coberley and Leckhampton rented for the poor in the early 1830s. In addition to cash payments the parish provided clothing, fuel, and medical care, some inhabitants being sent to Gloucester Infirmary.[3] Expenditure was £218 in 1813, when 15 people received regular help and 31 occasional,[4] but was considerably less in the late 1820s and early 1830s.[5] Coberley, which became part of the Cheltenham poor-law union in

[69] G.D.R., T 1/58.
[70] M.A.F. 68/1609/1; M.A.F. 68/3295/3.
[71] Agric. Returns 1976.
[72] Glos. R.O., D 2134, sale partics.; Rudder, Glos. 398; Bryant, Map of Glos. (1824).
[73] Kelly's Dir. Glos. (1863 and later edns.); Glos. R.O., D 1388/SL 8, no. 7.
[74] Glos. R.O., SL 346.
[75] Kelly's Dir. Glos. (1931 and later edns.).
[76] Hist. & Cart. Mon. Glouc. iii. 211.
[77] Glos. R.O., D 2134, sale partics.; cf. Taylor, Map of Glos. (1777).
[78] Glos. R.O., D 2025, Mrs. Williams's papers 1868–82; cf. ibid. D 1388, Lyon fam., Caudle Green papers 1785–1803.
[79] Ibid. D 443/1.
[80] Ibid. D 2025, Mrs. Williams's papers 1868–82; G.D.R., T 1/58.
[81] Inscr. in churchyard.
[82] Cf. Kelly's Dir. Glos. (1885), 438; (1889), 751.
[83] E 315/61 f. 26; Reg. Bransford, p. 41.
[84] Census, 1831.
[85] Reg. Bransford, p. 140.
[86] E 179/113/35A rot. 13d.
[87] Hist. & Cart. Mon. Glouc. iii. 213; Trans. B.G.A.S. xxxviii. 34–5.
[88] Kelly's Dir. Glos. (1856–1902 edns.).
[89] Cf. Glos. R.O., D 1388/SL 4, no. 83; DC/E 88/2, ct. 14 Oct. 1788.
[90] Lease of Chatcombe wood, penes Mr. Elwes.
[91] Kelly's Dir. Glos. (1856 and later edns.).
[92] Ciren. Cart. ii, pp. 619, 621.
[93] Trans. B.G.A.S. xxxviii. 29–35.
[94] Glouc. Cath. Libr., Reg. Abb. Malvern, i, f. 220v.
[95] Cal. Inq. p.m. xiii, p. 256.
[96] Hockaday Abs. xxii, 1498 visit. f. 28; cf. ibid. xxix, 1543 subsidy, f. 10; xlvii, 1576 visit. f. 98.
[97] G.D.R., V 5/98T 2; churchwardens' acct. bk. 1779–1892.
[98] Glos. R.O., D 443/1.
[99] Poor Law Abstract, 1804, 180–1.
[1] Glos. R.O., D 269B/F 47.
[2] Poor Law Abstract, 1804, 180–1.
[3] Overseers' acct. bk. 1798–1836, penes the rector.
[4] Poor Law Abstract, 1818, 154–5.
[5] Poor Law Returns (1830–1), p. 70; (1835), p. 69.

1835,[6] remained in Cheltenham rural district[7] and in 1974 was included in Tewkesbury district.

CHURCH. Coberley church was evidently granted to Leonard Stanley Priory, which Roger of Berkeley (II) founded c. 1131 and which became a cell of Gloucester Abbey in 1146,[8] but c. 1188 the abbey and priory surrendered their rights in the advowson to William of Berkeley.[9] The living, recorded as a rectory from 1274,[10] was united with Colesbourne in 1868[11] but the union did not take effect until 1871.[12] In 1937 Cowley was joined to the united benefice,[13] but Colesbourne became a separate living in 1954.[14]

From the late 12th century the advowson usually followed the descent of Coberley manor.[15] In 1270 Giles of Berkeley granted Walter Helion and his wife Alice, widow of Nicholas of Berkeley, an alternate right of presentation during her life-time.[16] Alice unsuccessfully claimed the advowson in 1307 when it was adjudged to belong to the Crown, which held the manor in ward.[17] The holders of the two halves of the manor in the early 15th century probably had alternate rights of presentation.[18] John Cary and William Beauvoir presented to the living in 1657[19] and Dorothy, widow of John Howe, Lord Chedworth (d. 1742), in 1771.[20] The church had the same patron as Colesbourne when the benefices were united but after the union with Cowley the Lord Chancellor had the right to present at every third vacancy.[21] In 1978 the executors of Henry Cecil Elwes and the Lord Chancellor had alternate rights of appointment.[22]

Leonard Stanley Priory received a pension of 5s. from the church until c. 1188 when it was granted half the tithes of William of Berkeley's demesne land and cottage tenants. Soon afterwards Gloucester Abbey granted those tithes for life to Robert the clerk for ½ mark yearly paid to the priory.[23] In 1291 the priory and abbey had tithe portions valued at 13s. 4d. and 3s. 4d. respectively.[24] The priory's portion later lapsed and the abbey, which in 1504 evidently accused a former rector of appropriating some of its tithes,[25] was receiving a pension of 13s. 4d. at the Dissolution.[26] The rector, who in 1451 had been disputing some tithes with the rector of Leckhampton,[27] later took all the tithes in kind.[28] In 1705, when tithes of lambs were paid on 3 May and of cheese during the summer, he received 1d. per sheep at shearing.[29] Charles Coxwell, rector 1778–82, received fixed cash payments, and in 1782 Henry Norwood was arrested for non-payment.[30] The tithes were commuted for a corn-rent-charge of £470 in 1838.[31] In 1342 the rector had 1 plough-land in demesne[32] but the glebe was extended at c. 8 a. in 1705 and c. 17 a. in the 19th century.[33] It was sold c. 1916.[34] In 1291 the living was worth £10[35] but in 1535 only £9 14s. 7d. clear.[36] The value was reckoned to be £75 in 1650[37] and £180 in 1750,[38] and in 1787 the rector received £190.[39] In 1856 the living was worth £326.[40]

The three hearths on which the rector was assessed in 1672[41] presumably represented the rectory house which was described in 1705 as a building of seven bays with a barn of three bays.[42] The house, which stood east of the village green,[43] was rebuilt on a large scale to a design by Richard Pace in 1825 and 1826.[44]

Philip of Coberley, rector from 1270, was licensed in 1274 to study for 2 years and to farm out the church during that period.[45] Edward Heydon, rector by 1542, who was dispensed to hold two benefices in 1546,[46] was non-resident and employed curates. The latter included John Phillips who, although found ignorant on some points of doctrine in 1551,[47] had become rector by 1553.[48] Phillips, who was probably a cripple, also held Sudeley from 1565 and Maisey-hampton by 1572.[49] At Coberley, where he was suspended in 1570 for not preaching and instructing the young,[50] he may have employed Thomas Greise, a preacher who was found in 1581 to have forged his licence.[51]

The living has had several incumbents notable for their longevity. Lewis Jones, rector from 1599,[52] who employed a curate described as a preaching minister in 1650,[53] was reputed to be 105 years old

[6] Poor Law Com. 2nd Rep. p. 522.
[7] Census, 1971.
[8] V.C.H. Glos. ii. 72–3.
[9] Trans. B.G.A.S. xliv. 234, 266–7.
[10] Reg. Giffard, 58.
[11] G.D.R. vol. 385, p. 69.
[12] Kelly's Dir. Glos. (1870), 531; (1885), 434.
[13] Kelly's Dir. Glos. (1931 and later edns.), s.v. Colesborne, Cowley, and Cubberley; cf. Lond. Gaz. 7 Feb. 1928, pp. 835–6.
[14] Glouc. Dioc. Yr. Bk. (1978), 29.
[15] Inq. p.m. Glos. 1359–1413, 238; C 142/378 no. 107.
[16] C.P. 25(1)/74/29 no. 667; Trans. B.G.A.S. xvii. 106.
[17] Reg. Sede Vacante, 83–4.
[18] Cf. Worc. Episc. Reg., Reg. Morgan, i, f. 5v.; Reg. Sede Vacante, 410.
[19] Hockaday Abs. clxiv; Complete Peerage, iii. 127.
[20] Hockaday Abs. clxiv; Burke, Dorm & Ext. Peerages (1883), 288.
[21] Cf. Kelly's Dir. Glos. (1870), 530–1; (1939), 140.
[22] Glouc. Dioc. Yr. Bk. (1978), 29.
[23] Trans. B.G.A.S. xliv. 266–9.
[24] Tax. Eccl. (Rec. Com.), 221.
[25] Glouc. Cath. Libr., Reg. Abb. Braunche, pp. 85–6.
[26] Valor Eccl. (Rec. Com.), ii. 496.
[27] Cal. Papal Reg. x. 105.
[28] Glos. R.O., D 1388/SL 3, no. 20.
[29] G.D.R., V 5/98T 2.
[30] Glos. R.O., D 269B/F 13, F 47.
[31] G.D.R., T 1/58.
[32] Inq. Non. (Rec. Com.), 408.
[33] G.D.R., V 5/98T 2–3; T 1/58; Kelly's Dir. Glos. (1856–1914 edns.).
[34] Cf. Kelly's Dir. Glos. (1914), 143; (1919), 133.
[35] Tax. Eccl. (Rec. Com.), 221.
[36] Valor Eccl. (Rec. Com.), ii. 496.
[37] Trans. B.G.A.S. lxxxiii. 93.
[38] G.D.R. vol. 381A, f. 25.
[39] Rudder, Glos. proof pages (Glos. Colln.), MS. note on p. 399.
[40] G.D.R. vol. 384, f. 66.
[41] E 179/247/13 rot. 29.
[42] G.D.R., V 5/98T 2.
[43] Taylor, Map of Glos. (1777).
[44] G.D.R. vol. 383, no. ccxxvii; Verey, Glos. i. 191.
[45] Reg. Giffard, 40, 58.
[46] Hockaday Abs. clxiv.
[47] Ibid. xxx, 1544 stipendiaries, f. 14; E.H.R. xix. 115.
[48] Hockaday Abs. clxiv.
[49] Ibid. xlvii, 1576 visit. f. 98; xliv, 1572 visit. f. 52.
[50] Ibid. clxiv.
[51] Trans. B.G.A.S. lix. 154–5.
[52] Hockaday Abs. clxiv.
[53] Trans. B.G.A.S. lxxxiii. 93.

when he died the following year.[54] Robert Rowden, who had apparently been ejected from Notgrove in 1654,[55] was presented to Coberley in 1657 but was not admitted for two years. Both Rowden (d. 1712) and his successor John Brown (d. 1754), also vicar of Longdon (Worcs.), employed curates in their later years. John Arnold, rector 1771–8, held Coberley in plurality with Dowdeswell.[56] His successor Charles Coxwell, rector until 1782, was also rector of Barnsley. At Coberley he employed as curate Thomas Nash, D.D.,[57] rector of Great Witcombe, who also served Cowley.[58] Nash continued for a time as curate to Coxwell's successor William Wright,[59] who was said in 1807 to be a lunatic.[60] From 1816 Coberley was held by William Hicks, also rector of Whittington[61] where he lived until he had rebuilt Coberley rectory.[62] From 1853 he appointed curates who lived in or near Cheltenham[63] and was succeeded at his death in 1866 by Charles Wilson, who was rector of the united benefice of Coberley with Colesbourne from 1871 until c. 1912.[64]

In 1270 Geoffrey of Coberley built a chantry-chapel dedicated to Holy Trinity on a tenement held from the Berkeleys' manor but its later history is not known.[65] Thomas of Berkeley founded a chantry dedicated to Our Lady in Coberley church in 1337 when he granted it 2 tofts, 4 yardlands, and rents totalling 2 marks a year. The foundation was confirmed in 1340 but was superseded in 1347 when Thomas founded another chantry, dedicated to Holy Trinity, Our Lady, and St. Giles. That chantry, which he endowed with 13 messuages, 2 tofts, and 36 yardlands, including 2 of woodland, was to be served by three priests, including a warden, who were to live in a house called Beauvalley.[66] The chantry was known as Beauvalley in the late 14th century and the 15th when the warden was presented by the rector.[67] By 1532 it was served by a stipendiary priest[68] whose salary at the dissolution of the chantries was £6 13s. 4d.[69] In 1548 the endowments, which included c. 374 a., were bought by Sir John Bridges[70] (d. 1557). He devised the land, called Beauvalley farm, to Elizabeth Clarke for life with remainder to her daughter Anne[71] but it was later merged with his Coberley manor.[72]

Clerk's Patch, part of a small plantation south of the Coberley-Ullenwood road, was vested in the parish clerk but by 1857 he had exchanged it for the use of 1¾ a. in a field belonging to W. E. Lawrence.[73] That exchange was evidently temporary for under a charitable Scheme of 1932 the income derived from Clerk's Patch was confirmed to the parish clerk.[74]

The parish church, which had been dedicated to *ST. GILES* by 1294,[75] is built of coursed rubble and rusticated ashlar and has a chancel with south chapel, nave with south porch, and west tower. The walls incorporate 12th-century fragments but the church was extensively rebuilt and enlarged in the mid 14th century[76] and the earliest features *in situ*, the south doorway and porch, are of that date. The chapel, which was built to house the chantry founded in 1347,[77] presumably formed part of the same rebuilding, which was evidently paid for by Thomas of Berkeley. The tower, which may have been added then, has a sundial dated 1693. With the exception of the porch and tower the church was largely rebuilt between 1868 and 1871[78] to designs by John Middleton of Cheltenham,[79] and while some parts of the old building, like the chapel, appear to have been faithfully reproduced that was not generally so in the chancel and nave, between which a chancel arch was inserted.[80]

In the church are several ancient monuments but by the early 18th century some had been defaced, including that on the south wall of the chapel to Sir Giles Bridges (d. 1511) and his wife Isabel.[81] On the south wall of the chancel is a small monument to Giles of Berkeley (d. 1294), whose heart was buried in the chancel.[82] That monument was moved from the north wall of the chancel during the rebuilding when two large recumbent effigies, believed to be of Thomas of Berkeley (d. c. 1365) and one of his wives, and a much smaller one, perhaps a daughter, were moved from the chancel to the chapel. Also in the chapel, in a recess on the south wall, is a recumbent effigy of a young man.[83] Of the three bells recorded in 1681[84] one had been cast or recast by Edward Neale of Burford in 1661. The other two were medieval, but one was recast by John Warner in 1870.[85] The church plate includes a paten given in 1835 when two chalices were fashioned from a flagon given by Jonathan Castleman and a chalice stolen and damaged earlier that year.[86] The registers begin in 1539.[87]

An ancient stone cross discovered during the

[54] Bigland, *Glos.* i. 406.
[55] *Walker Revised*, ed. Matthews, 177.
[56] Hockaday Abs. clxiv; Bigland, *Glos.* i. 406–7, 486.
[57] Hockaday Abs. clxiv; Glos. R.O., D 269B/F 13.
[58] Bigland, *Glos.* iii, no. 304; G.D.R., V 1/76.
[59] Hockaday Abs. clxiv; G.D.R. vol. 319; cf. ibid. vol. 382, ff. 33–4; ibid. V 1/76.
[60] Glos. R.O., D 1388/SL 3, no. 20.
[61] Hockaday Abs. clxiv, cccxcvi.
[62] Cf. G.D.R. vol. 382, f. 33; vol. 383, no. ccxxvii; *Kelly's Dir. Glos.* (1856), 275.
[63] Hockaday Abs. clxiv.
[64] *Glos. N. & Q.* iv. 135; *Kelly's Dir. Glos.* (1885), 434, 438; (1914), 143.
[65] *Reg. Giffard*, 40; C.P. 25(1)/74/29 no. 669.
[66] *Reg. Bransford*, pp. 41–2, 140–4.
[67] *Reg. Wakefeld*, pp. 29, 77; Worc. Episc. Reg., Reg. Carpenter, i, f. 185.
[68] Hockaday Abs. xxv, 1532 subsidy, f. 15; xxvi, 1534 subsidy, f. 13.

[69] *Trans. B.G.A.S.* viii. 275.
[70] Hockaday Abs. clxiv; *Cal. Pat.* 1547–8, 313.
[71] Hockaday Abs. ccclxi, Sudeley.
[72] Cf. C 142/309 no. 193.
[73] Glos. R.O., D 1388/SL 4, no. 83; D 480, Lawrence fam., papers 1853–8.
[74] Ibid. D 3469/5/43; Char. Com. Reg.
[75] *Reg. Giffard*, 449.
[76] *Cal. Inq. p.m.* xiii, p. 254; Bigland, *Glos.* i. 405.
[77] *Reg. Bransford*, p. 141.
[78] Glos. R.O., P. 105/CW 4/2–3; IN 4/3.
[79] Verey, *Glos.* i. 190, 35.
[80] Cf. *Glos. Ch. Notes*, 124–5; Glos. Colln. JR 4.21.
[81] Bodl. MS. Rawl. B.323, f. 198; Bigland, *Glos.* i. 405–6.
[82] *Reg. Giffard*, 449; *Cal. Inq. p.m.* iv, p. 343.
[83] Roper, *Glos. Effigies*, 375–83.
[84] G.D.R., V 5/98T 1.
[85] *Glos. Ch. Bells*, 44.
[86] *Glos. Ch. Plate*, 59.
[87] *B. & G. Par. Rec.* 106.

rebuilding of the chapel was not preserved[88] but the base of a medieval cross stands in the churchyard.[89]

NONCONFORMITY. Particular Baptists, for whom Henry Hawkins, minister of Eastcombe, registered a meeting-place in Coberley in 1822,[90] built a chapel in the village the following year. The chapel, which later controlled meeting-places in the surrounding countryside, had Thomas Davis as minister from 1832[91] and claimed congregations of up to 130 in 1851.[92] It remained open until 1939 or later,[93] and was converted as a house in 1966.[94]

In the late 1880s and early 1890s there was a meeting of Plymouth Brethren in the parish.[95]

EDUCATION. In 1818 30 children attended a Sunday school in Coberley,[96] and in 1833 a church Sunday school, begun in 1823, and a chapel Sunday school taught 20 and 30 children respectively.[97] About 1846 a dame school taught 11 children[98] and by 1856 the rector was supporting a day-school.[99] During 1859 and 1860 a National school with a school-house was built in the village. It was supported by voluntary contributions and pence, and in 1860 evening classes were being held twice a week.[1] The school had average attendances of 60 in 1885[2] and 47 in 1904, when it was called Coberley C. of E. school.[3] A temporary classroom had been erected by 1978 when 32 children from several Churn valley villages attended the school.[4]

CHARITIES FOR THE POOR. The congregation of the Baptist chapel shared in a charity founded in 1856 by Thomas Davis.[5] Hamilton Fane Gladwin by will proved 1914 left money to be invested in stock to produce an annual income of £5 for the poor of the parish at Christmas.[6]

COLESBOURNE

COLESBOURNE, a small rural parish lying 12 km. SSW. of Cheltenham, covers 890 ha. (2,198 a.) and is irregular in shape.[7] The river Churn runs across the middle of the parish before turning southwards to form part of the eastern boundary, the rest of which is formed by Hilcot brook, a tributary called Lyde brook in the 18th century and early 19th;[8] in a Saxon survey of an estate in Withington the river above the confluence was apparently called the Colesbourne, the name Churn being used for Hilcot brook.[9] On the west the parish is bounded by the river and streams but elsewhere by field boundaries.[10]

The Churn valley forms the major feature of the landscape. Above it the parish takes in high wolds rising to 271 m. in the north-western corner near Pinswell and to 267 m. in the southern part on Pen hill, called Grove hill c. 1703 when Colesbourne Pen, a group of trees forming a landmark on the summit, was recorded.[11] Most of the high ground is on the Inferior Oolite, which in the southern part is overlaid by fuller's earth and the Great Oolite, and the valleys of the Churn and its tributaries lie on Midford Sand.[12] The high land was once cultivated as open fields but some had been laid down as pasture by the later 18th century. The parish is extensively wooded. Woods planted c. 1800 included the Forest in the north-west, Cocklar plantation, then a small area on the southern side of the Churn valley, and Harp plantation, a triangular area in a road junction to the east.[13] Nevertheless in 1839 there were still only 194 a. of woodland in the parish, confined mainly to the south-west.[14] Most of the woodland was created in the early 20th century by Henry John Elwes, who planted a large part of the Colesbourne estate, including the Hilcot brook valley and the area east of Pen hill.[15] In 1979 plantations on the estate covered 283.3 ha. (700 a.) of Colesbourne and adjoining parishes.[16]

By 1770 an area of park-land called Rapsgate or Rendon park had been laid out on the southern boundary of the parish.[17] The park, which was let with other farm-land in the early 19th century, covered 64 a. in Colesbourne and North Cerney[18] and had been disparked by 1839.[19] By 1820 a deer-park comprising 61 a. had been created for the Elwes family's manor-house in the angle of the Churn and Hilcot brook.[20] The park, which had been enlarged by the early 1880s,[21] was developed as an arboretum by H. J. Elwes, who planted rare

[88] Glos. R.O., D 1715; PA 105/1.
[89] Verey, Glos. i. 191.
[90] Hockaday Abs. clxiv; V.C.H. Glos. xi. 37.
[91] R. W. Oliver, Strict Bapt. Chapels of Eng. v (1968), 111; Kelly's Dir. Glos. (1894), 131; O.S. Map 6", Glos. XXXIV. NE. (1883 edn.).
[92] H.O. 129/344/1/6/9.
[93] Kelly's Dir. Glos. (1939), 140.   [94] Glos. R.O., PA 105/2.
[95] Kelly's Dir. Glos. (1889), 751; (1894), 131.
[96] Educ. of Poor Digest, 295.
[97] Educ. Enquiry Abstract, 312.
[98] Church School Inquiry, 1846–7, 8–9.
[99] Kelly's Dir. Glos. (1856), 275.   [1] Ed. 7/3/99.
[2] Kelly's Dir. Glos. (1885), 438.
[3] Public Elem. Schs. 1906, 183.
[4] Ex inf. county educ. dept.
[5] V.C.H. Glos. xi. 40.   [6] Glos. R.O., D 1715; CH 21.

[7] O.S. Area Bk. (1884); Census, 1971. This account was written in 1979.
[8] Rudder, Glos. 383; Glos. R.O., Q/RI 48.
[9] Grundy, Saxon Charters, 265.   [10] O.S. Area Bk. (1884).
[11] Bodl. MS. Rawl. B. 323, f. 220; cf. Taylor, Map of Glos. (1777); Bryant, Map of Glos. (1824).
[12] Geol. Surv. Map 1", solid, sheet 44 (1856 edn.).
[13] Glos. R.O., photocopies 264, 263.   [14] G.D.R., T 1/59.
[15] H. J. Elwes, 'Colesborne Estate Hist.' (TS. penes Mr. H. W. G. Elwes, of Colesbourne Pk.).
[16] Ex inf. Mr. Elwes.
[17] Glos. R.O., photocopy 593; cf. Taylor, Map of Glos. (1777).
[18] Glos. Colln. RF 87.1; Glos. R.O., photocopy 263.
[19] G.D.R., T 1/59.
[20] Glos. R.O., photocopy 263.
[21] Cf. G.D.R., T 1/59; O.S. Map 6", Glos. XXXV. SW. (1883 edn.).

specimens collected from many parts of the world, especially Asia.[22] Hilcot brook on reaching the north-eastern corner of the parish opens into an elongated lake, formed by 1820.[23] Downstream, just above the confluence with the Churn, another lake was formed in 1925 as part of the pleasure grounds of Colesbourne Park.[24]

An old road from Gloucester to Northleach ran eastwards by way of High Cross in Elkstone to a crossing of the Churn at its confluence with Hilcot brook.[25] The crossing, which was a ford at the time of the Saxon survey of Withington,[26] had probably been bridged by the mid 13th century. From the southern boundary a route from Cirencester which passed Rapsgate,[27] the meeting-place of the hundred court,[28] ran NNE. and, on the north-eastern side of Pen hill, crossed an old route between High Cross and Rendcomb. North of the river it continued towards Hilcot in Withington and was known as Winchcombe way in 1680.[29] A road to Cheltenham, which led north-westwards from Colesbourne church in the angle of the Churn and Hilcot brook, followed two routes south-east of Pinswell.[30] By 1824 it had become a private carriage-way from the manor-house to the cross-roads east of Seven Springs in Coberley,[31] and later, possibly before 1839, the Elwes family built a toll-house at Pinswell to collect toll from others using that route.[32] In 1825 the new Cheltenham–Cirencester road along the bottom of the Churn valley became the main road through the parish.[33] The section of the road from High Cross to Rendcomb running through the parish was closed in 1827[34] and by 1838 the old Cirencester road had become a private carriage-way for much of its length.[35]

Colesbourne village grew up beside the Churn near the Gloucester–Northleach and Cirencester–Winchcombe routes, but there had been earlier settlements in the parish, including Norbury Camp, a hill fort near Pinswell, and, in the south-western corner, a Roman villa[36] which Samuel Lysons excavated in the later 18th century.[37] Around Colesbourne church, which had been built by the end of the 11th century, the settlement included a manor-house and the rectory, both of which were demolished in the mid 19th century. Some way south-west on the other side of the river Old Farm, a farm-house, was apparently rebuilt c. 1790[38] and has a 19th-century addition.

Among the out-buildings is a barn dated 1789 and enlarged in the 19th century. There was an area of cottage development to the west along a lane leading northwards from the old Gloucester–Northleach road, and a 17th-century cottage built on that road survives. Further west the Colesbourne inn, which was built soon after the completion in 1825 of the new Cheltenham–Cirencester road,[39] was enlarged in the later 19th century. The enlargement was presumably financed by John Henry Elwes, who then built or rebuilt many of the cottages on his estate.[40] The new cottages were possibly designed by David Brandon, whom Elwes employed in the early 1850s when he restored the church and built Colesbourne Park, near the site of the former manor-house, and a school and school-house by the main road south-west of Old Farm. In the later 1860s Elwes extended the school-house westwards to make it a residence suitable for the rector and put up stabling to the west behind the 17th-century cottage.[41]

On the old Gloucester road some distance west of the village a small cottage settlement had been established at a cross-roads by 1820.[42] Some of the cottages recorded there in 1839 were later rebuilt and others demolished.[43] Penhill Farm, to the west, was rebuilt in the early 19th century by the Elwes family, which acquired it in 1790.[44] Either that house, which is on a site once the property of Llanthony Priory, or Old Farm may have been the ancient farm-house with an adjoining chapel called the Priory in the early 18th century.[45] On the old Rendcomb road south of Penhill Farm three cottages had been built by 1820[46] but two had been demolished by 1979. By the main road north-east of Penhill Farm J. H. Elwes built two pairs of estate cottages in 1857 and 1883 respectively.[47] East of the Hilcot road at Southbury a lodge, built in the 1790s,[48] was evidently rebuilt in the early 19th century as a farm-house.[49] Two pairs of council houses were built west of the road in the mid 20th century.

By c. 1770 a farmstead had been established at Pinswell[50] where the farm-house was a private residence in 1979.[51] In the north-eastern corner of the parish Lyde Cottage, which had been built by 1820,[52] was converted in the 19th century as a summer-house for the Elwes family by the addition of a verandah.[53]

Those inhabitants of Colesbourne who were

[22] *Country Life*, 16 May 1974, 1211–12.
[23] Glos. R.O., photocopy 263.
[24] Ex inf. Mr. Elwes.
[25] Glos. R.O., photocopy 264; Glos. R.O., Q/SIb 1, f. 158.
[26] Grundy, *Saxon Charters*, 266.
[27] C 115/K 2/6683 ff. 253v., 268–9.
[28] *Ciren. Cart.* ii, p. 618.
[29] Glos. R.O., photocopy 264; G.D.R., V 5/87T 3.
[30] Glos. R.O., photocopy 264.
[31] Bryant, *Map of Glos.* (1824).
[32] G.D.R., T 1/59; ex inf. Mr. Elwes.
[33] Cirencester Roads Act, 6 Geo. IV, c. 143.
[34] Glos. R.O., Q/SRh 1827 B/3.
[35] Ibid. Q/RI 48.
[36] R.C.H.M. *Glos.* i. 34–6.
[37] *Archaeologia*, ix. 319–22; xviii. 112–25.
[38] Partics. of Colesborne mans. c. 1790, *penes* Mr. Elwes.

[39] Cf. Glos. R.O., Q/RI 48.
[40] Dates and inits. on bldgs.; cf. *Rep. Com. Agric. Employment*, p. 99.
[41] Docs. *penes* Mr. Elwes; Verey, *Glos.* i. 194–5.
[42] Glos. R.O., photocopy 263.
[43] G.D.R., T 1/59.
[44] Deeds *penes* Mr. Elwes; cf. Glos. R.O., Q/RI 48.
[45] G.D.R., T 1/59; Atkyns, *Glos.* 363.
[46] Glos. R.O., photocopy 263.
[47] Dates and inits. on bldgs.
[48] Cf. Glos. R.O., photocopy 264; Glos. Colln. RF 87.1; O.S. Map 1", sheet 44 (1828 edn.).
[49] Cf. Glos. R.O., photocopy 263.
[50] Ibid. photocopy 593.
[51] Ex inf. Mr. Elwes.
[52] Glos. R.O., photocopy 263.
[53] Ex inf. Mr Elwes.

described as of the coomb in the 13th century and early 14th[54] apparently lived in the south-western part of the parish in the deep valley forming the boundary with Elkstone near the hamlet of Combend in that parish.[55] By 1838 there were several cottages in that valley for labourers on the Combend estate.[56] To the south-east the hamlet of Rapsgate, below the old Cirencester road, comprised a large house, Rapsgate Park, and a few cottages in 1979. Rapsgate Park, an 18th-century farm-house set in an area of park-land c. 1770,[57] may have been adapted by Francis Eyre, owner of the Colesbourne estate, as his residence[58] but it was a farm-house c. 1790.[59] In 1903 the interior was remodelled and out-buildings to the east were incorporated in the house,[60] which later was either let as a gentleman's residence or used by the Elwes family.[61] A pair of late-19th-century cottages among the farm-buildings 800 m. to the north-east was converted as a farm-house in the mid 20th century.[62]

In 1086 26 tenants were mentioned on two estates in Colesbourne,[63] and 13 people were assessed for the subsidy in 1327[64] and at least 6 for the poll tax in 1381.[65] In 1551 there were said to be c. 60 communicants in the parish[66] and 18 households were recorded there in 1563.[67] The parish had 67 communicants in 1603[68] and the population was estimated at 34 families in 1650[69] and at 120 people living in 30 houses c. 1710.[70] It had risen to 254 by c. 1775.[71] In 1801 it was 231 and, apart from a slight fall in the 1850s, it rose slowly to a peak of 286 in 1881. It had fallen to 204 by 1901 and then, after a slight rise over the next two decades, to 142 by 1961. In 1971 153 people lived in the parish.[72]

The Elwes family has been the leading influence in the parish since c. 1790 when it acquired most of the land. H. J. Elwes (d. 1922), the naturalist and traveller, collaborated with the botanist Augustine Henry in writing *The Trees of Great Britain and Ireland*, published between 1906 and 1913.[73]

MANORS AND OTHER ESTATES. Colesbourne became a possession of the bishopric of

Worcester before 822. Bishop Denebeorht leased 9 'manentes' there to a priest, Balthun, for three lives and in 840 Beorhtwulf, king of the Mercians, exempted the bishop's estate from certain dues.[74] Before the Conquest the estate, comprising 8 hides, was held from the bishop by Sweyn but by 1086 the tenant was Walter son of Roger,[75] better known as Walter of Gloucester, who in 1095 granted two-thirds of the Colesbourne tithes to the church of St. Owen in Gloucester.[76] By the later 12th century two separate estates of 4 hides each were held in Colesbourne under Walter's descendants[77] and together were assessed for 2 knights' fees in the late 13th and early 14th centuries.[78]

Walter of Gloucester's son and heir Miles, the founder of Llanthony Priory, was created earl of Hereford in 1141 and died in 1143. His estates passed in turn to his four sons, the last of whom, Mahel,[79] died in 1165. Mahel's English possessions were divided between his sisters Margaret, wife of Humphrey de Bohun, and Lucy, wife of Herbert FitzHerbert,[80] but evidence for the descent of the intermediate lordship of the two Colesbourne estates is contradictory. Margaret, who c. 1178 confirmed grants of land to Bruern Abbey (Oxon.),[81] held it in the later 12th century[82] but Herbert's son Peter (d. 1235)[83] confirmed a grant of land to Llanthony Priory[84] and his son Reynold held the 2 fees under the bishop of Worcester in 1285.[85] Reynold's interest passed with Barnsley manor, from which land in Colesbourne was held in the early 15th century.[86] Nevertheless in the later 13th century Margaret de Bohun's descendants, the earls of Hereford, held Colesbourne with Southam from the bishop's manor of Bishop's Cleeve.[87] Southam passed with the earldom to the Crown[88] and in 1508 a Colesbourne estate was held from Henry VII's mother Margaret, countess of Richmond.[89] The superior overlordship of the bishop of Worcester was recorded in 1613 when the same estate was held from his manor of Withington.[90]

By c. 1140 all or part of the Colesbourne estate was evidently held in demesne by Ellis Loholt.[91] Ellis and his son Walter granted land there to Bruern Abbey[92] and Walter later held part of the

[54] C 115/K 2/6683 ff. 257v.–258; *Glouc. Corp. Rec.* p. 295; *Glos. Subsidy Roll, 1327*, 10.
[55] Bryant, *Map of Glos.* (1824).
[56] Glos. R.O., Q/RI 48; G.D.R., T 1/59.
[57] Glos. R.O., photocopy 593.
[58] Cf. Bigland, *Glos.* i. 408.
[59] Partics. of Colesborne mans. c. 1790; G.D.R., T 1/59; *Kelly's Dir. Glos.* (1856–94 edns.).
[60] Glos. R.O., D 2593.
[61] Ibid. D 2299/4451; *Kelly's Dir. Glos.* (1914–39 edns.).
[62] G.D.R., T 1/59; O.S. Map 6″, Glos. XLIII. NW. (1884 edn.); ex inf. Mr. Elwes.
[63] *Dom. Bk.* (Rec. Com.), i. 164v., 169v.
[64] *Glos. Subsidy Roll, 1327*, 10.
[65] E 179/113/31A rot. 2.
[66] *E.H.R.* xix. 106.
[67] Bodl. MS. Rawl. C.790, f. 21v.   [68] *Eccl. Misc.* 76.
[69] *Trans. B.G.A.S.* lxxxiii. 93.
[70] Atkyns, *Glos.* 363.
[71] Rudder, *Glos.* 384.   [72] *Census*, 1801–1971.
[73] *D.N.B.* 1922–30; cf. H. J. Elwes, *Memoirs of Travel, Sport, and Natural Hist.* (1930).

[74] Finberg, *Early Charters of W. Midlands*, pp. 44, 46.
[75] *Dom. Bk.* (Rec. Com.), i. 164v.; the Colesbourne property held in 1086 from the bishop's man. of Withington by Anschitel was at Little Colesbourne in Withington par.: ibid. 164v.–165.
[76] *Camd. Misc.* xxii (Camd. 4th ser. i), pp. 37 n., 38.
[77] *Trans. B.G.A.S.* lxxix. 201; *Red Bk. of Worc.* 437.
[78] *Feud. Aids*, ii. 239, 247.
[79] *Complete Peerage*, vi. 451–7; Dugdale, *Mon.* vi (1), 136.
[80] *Trans. B.G.A.S.* lxxix. 175, 192–3.
[81] E 315/52 no. 29.
[82] *Red Bk. of Worc.* 437.
[83] For the FitzHerberts, see *Trans. B.G.A.S.* xix. 295.
[84] Ibid. lxxix. 201.
[85] *Feud. Aids*, ii. 239.
[86] *Cal. Inq. p.m.* vii, p. 228; x, p. 51; *Cal. Close, 1349–54*, 553; *Inq. p.m. Glos.* 1359–1413, 260.
[87] *Cal. Inq. p.m.* ii, p. 71; *Red Bk. of Worc.* 328.
[88] *V.C.H. Glos.* viii. 9–10.
[89] *Cal. Inq. p.m. Hen. VII*, iii, pp. 269–70.
[90] C 142/336 no. 45.
[91] Dugdale, *Mon.* vi (1), 136.
[92] E 315/52 no. 29.

estate.[93] That part, which was assessed at 1 knight's fee in the 13th and 14th centuries[94] and was known as the manor of *COLESBOURNE* by the mid 14th,[95] was held by Walter's descendants, including Walter Loholt (fl. 1260) who made a grant of the advowson, Ellis Loholt who was involved in a dispute over tithes in 1283,[96] and Walter Loholt who was described as lord of Colesbourne in 1316.[97] In 1341 John Loholt conveyed the manor to John Coggeshall and his wife Elizabeth.[98]

The descent of the manor following that conveyance is not clear. In 1396 Walter Catewy made a grant of a reversion of it[99] and the following year half of the manor was held under John Wotton of Kemble and his wife Isabel by John Mene in right of his wife Joan,[1] who had evidently married Thomas Attwater by 1407 and Simon Raleigh by 1422.[2] The other half of the manor may have been held in the early 15th century by Robert Gifford in right of his wife Elizabeth,[3] though in 1402 John Mene was assessed on 1 knight's fee, evidently for the whole manor.[4] Joan Raleigh's half of the manor reverted after her death by 1435 to John Vampage, who then apparently acquired the other half.[5] The following year he settled the whole manor on the marriage of his son John but retained life-interests for himself and his wife Elizabeth.[6] Colesbourne manor passed to the younger John Vampage's son, also John[7] (d. 1502), who was succeeded by his son Robert.[8] After Robert's death in 1516 the manor was held by his wife Eleanor, later passing to his son John.[9] John, who settled the manor on himself and his wife Anne for their lives, died without issue in 1548. He left the reversion of the manor and property in Withington to his sister Dorothy and her husband Thomas Winchcombe with remainder to John Higford, Dorothy's son by an earlier marriage.[10] Anne Vampage married Sir Thomas Baskerville[11] but the descent of the manor after 1548 is not clear. John Higford owned it in 1571[12] and Edmund Harewell of Besford (Worcs.), John Vampage's nephew and coheir, was in possession by 1586 when he granted a lease of the manor-house.[13]

Edmund Harewell's son Edmund[14] sold the manor in 1602 to William Higgs, the owner of another estate in the parish.[15] William (d. 1612) was succeeded by his son Thomas,[16] who settled the Colesbourne estate the following year on his marriage to Elizabeth Bludder.[17] Thomas, who bought more land in Colesbourne and Withington in 1624,[18] was dead by 1649 and was survived by Elizabeth.[19] The estate passed to their son Thomas who conveyed it in 1672 to Samuel Sheppard.[20] Samuel died the following year and his son Philip, lord of Avening and Minchinhampton manors,[21] owned the Colesbourne estate in 1680.[22] By c. 1710 Philip had conveyed Colesbourne to his younger son Philip[23] (d. 1738).[24] John Sheppard, who apparently sold the estate to Francis Eyre in 1770,[25] possibly lived in the manor-house until his death in 1791.[26]

Francis Eyre, who became M.P. for Grimsby in 1780,[27] sold the estate, covering 1,515 a.,[28] to John Elwes[29] soon after the latter had purchased a smaller estate in the parish in 1790, when he was described as of St. Marylebone (Mdx.).[30] John, who became High Sheriff of Gloucestershire in 1799,[31] enlarged the estate to c. 6,000 a. mainly by purchases in Coberley and Withington parishes.[32] He died in 1817 and the estate then passed in the direct line to Henry (d. 1851),[33] John Henry (d. 1891), Henry John (d. 1922), and Henry Cecil (d. 1950). The last was succeeded by his grandson Mr. H. W. G. Elwes,[34] who sold parts of the estate in the 1950s to meet death duties and retained 1,011.7 ha. (2,500 a.) in Colesbourne and adjoining parishes in 1979.[35]

In 1586 Edmund Harewell leased the manor-house to John Stone, who was involved in two lawsuits against William Higgs in 1605.[36] In 1672 the house had 11 hearths.[37] In 1786 the house, standing north of the church, was said to have been recently modernized[38] and in the early 19th century it had a symmetrical eastern elevation of mid-18th-century date.[39] It was demolished in the early 1850s and replaced by Colesbourne Park, built a little to the north-east in 1854 to the designs of David Brandon. That house was demolished in the late

[93] *Red Bk. of Worc.* 437.
[94] C 115/K 2/6683 f. 254 and v.; *Feud. Aids*, ii. 247, 280.
[95] C.P. 25(1)/77/63 no. 199.
[96] C 115/K 2/6683 ff. 249, 268–9, 261 and v.
[97] *Feud. Aids*, ii. 271.
[98] C.P. 25(1)/77/63 no. 199.
[99] *Cat. Anct. D.* i, C 467.
[1] *Trans. B.G.A.S.* lxii. 164.
[2] C.P. 25(1)/290/61 no. 113; C.P. 25(1)/79/86 no. 26.
[3] *Inq. p.m. Glos.* 1359–1413, 260.
[4] *Feud. Aids*, ii. 299.
[5] C.P. 25(1)/79/88 no. 34; C.P. 25(1)/79/89 no. 59.
[6] *Cat. Anct. D.* i, C 1747.
[7] For the Vampages, see *Visit. Worcs. 1569* (Harl. Soc. xxvii), 69–70.
[8] *Cal. Inq. p.m. Hen. VII*, iii, pp. 269–70.
[9] C 142/31 no. 104; C 1/586 no. 60.
[10] C 142/86 no. 91; Hockaday Abs. clxv, 1549.
[11] *V.C.H. Worcs.* iv. 73.
[12] C.P. 25(2)/259/13 Eliz. Hil. no. 12.
[13] C 142/86 no. 91; Req. 2/308/38.
[14] Cf. *V.C.H. Worcs.* iv. 21.
[15] Glos. R.O., D 1878, Chedworth deeds 1609–17, deed 1613.
[16] C 142/336 no. 45.

[17] Glos. R.O., D 1878, Chedworth deeds 1609–17, deed 1613.
[18] Ibid. D 2612/T 4.
[19] Hockaday Abs. clxv.
[20] *Visit. Glos. 1623*, 81; C.P. 25(2)/658/23 & 24 Chas. II Hil. no. 15.
[21] *Visit. Glos. 1682–3*, 167; *V.C.H. Glos.* xi. 157, 190 and n.
[22] G.D.R., V 5/87T 3.
[23] Atkyns, *Glos.* 363.
[24] Par. reg. 1729–95, *penes* Mr. Elwes.
[25] Glos. Colln. RF 87.1; Bigland, *Glos.* i. 408.
[26] Glos. R.O., photocopy 593; *Glouc. Jnl.* 8 Aug. 1791.
[27] Rudder, *Glos.* proof pages (Glos. Colln.), MS. note on p. 384.
[28] Glos. R.O., photocopy 264; cf. *Glouc. Jnl.* 24 July 1786.
[29] *Delineations of Glos.* 101; cf. Glos. Colln. RF 87.1.
[30] Deeds *penes* Mr. Elwes.
[31] *Glos. N. & Q.* iii. 414.
[32] Deeds *penes* Mr. Elwes.
[33] Par. reg. 1795–1812, *penes* Mr. Elwes; cf. G.D.R., T 1/59.
[34] For the Elwes fam., see Burke, *Land. Gent.* (1965), i. 232.
[35] Ex inf. Mr. Elwes.
[36] Req. 2/308/38; Req. 2/406/84.
[37] E 179/247/13 rot. 28d.
[38] *Glouc. Jnl.* 24 July 1786.
[39] *Delineations of Glos.* plate facing p. 101.

1950s save for the dining-room, around which a smaller house was built.[40] West of the church, on the site of the former rectory, stabling and coach-houses occupy three sides of a courtyard; two of the ranges are dated 1842 and 1859 respectively.[41]

Maud de Wateville, who granted land in Colesbourne to Bruern Abbey c. 1160,[42] was related to William le Poer, who held the other part of the Colesbourne estate in demesne in the later 12th century.[43] That part was also assessed at 1 knight's fee in the 13th and 14th centuries.[44] William le Poer was succeeded by his son William, who granted half of his Colesbourne property to his sister Hawise de Wateville in free marriage for life. She conveyed that part to Llanthony Priory before 1235 and William's son Roger confirmed her grant. By 1260 Walter le Poer held the rest of the property[45] which apparently passed to John of Morton and his wife Elizabeth, evidently in her right, before 1303 when they were assessed for 1 knight's fee.[46] It may have been held later by Walter Cokey but by 1346 it had apparently been taken into Llanthony Priory's estate.[47]

At its foundation Llanthony Priory had been endowed with those Colesbourne tithes which had been granted to St. Owen's church,[48] and in 1291 its portion in Colesbourne church was valued at £2 6s. 8d.[49] In the 13th century the priory acquired land in the parish, including ½ hide from Joseph Marsh and his wife,[50] and in 1291 was granted free warren.[51] The priory retained its enlarged estate, later known as COLESBOURNE LLANTHONY manor, until the Dissolution.[52] In 1540 Henry VIII granted the estate for life to his servant Thomas Guise.[53] Under grants of 1542 a sheep-pasture passed to the Porter family after Guise's death[54] and the rest of the estate to the Crown. In 1551 the king, who was entitled to the greater part of the tithes, was called rector.[55] In 1564 the Crown granted the manor to Thomas Reeve, William Ryvett, and William Hutchins.[56] Ryvett, who presented to the rectory in 1570,[57] conveyed the manor and tithes to John Robinson in 1589,[58] and Robinson, a London mercer, sold them in 1595 to William Higgs.[59]

In 1602 Higgs bought the other Colesbourne manor, thus creating the Colesbourne estate which passed to the Elwes family. The estate included

two-thirds of the Colesbourne tithes but c. 385 a. in the parish, which had belonged to the priory, were exempt from tithes and were described as tithe-free.[60] In the late 17th century and the 18th owners of the Combend estate, based in Elkstone, took or claimed two-thirds of the tithes from their land in Colesbourne[61] but in the later 18th century owners of the Colesbourne estate took all the tithes of the parish and paid the rector a modus for his share.[62] In the early 19th century Henry Elwes took two-thirds of the tithes, except those of the glebe and 66 a. of woodland on the Combend estate, and in 1839 his tithes were commuted for a corn-rent-charge of £242 14s.[63] The Combend estate, which had acquired part of the Colesbourne estate by 1680[64] included 237 a. in the south-western corner of the parish in the early 19th century, mainly former Llanthony Priory land.[65]

In Edward the Confessor's reign Eluuin held an estate of 1½ hide in Colesbourne as a manor. After the Conquest it was granted with Elkstone to Ansfrid de Cormeilles. The Colesbourne land, which was held under him by a knight in 1086,[66] presumably descended as part of the Elkstone estate and in 1166 was evidently held under Richard de Cormeilles by William of Colesbourne, a tenant by knight service.[67]

Bruern Abbey, which acquired land in Colesbourne piecemeal from the mid 12th century,[68] was granted free warren there in 1366.[69] In 1543, after the Dissolution, the Crown granted the abbey's lands in Colesbourne and Little Colesbourne in Withington to Edmund Harman and his wife Agnes.[70] The following year Edmund granted them to Thomas Preedon,[71] who died in 1558 leaving as his heir his son Richard.[72] In 1624 Thomas's property was sold by Sir Egremont Thynne and Arthur Lowe to Thomas Higgs.[73]

In the mid 18th century George Weare of Cirencester owned an estate which included the western part of Colesbourne by the Churn. It had been divided among his four daughters, Anne, Elizabeth, Mary, and another, by 1754 when Anne's share was settled on her husband Thomas Chamberlayne Coxe, rector of North Cerney. Coxe later acquired Mary's share and part of Elizabeth's[74] and at his death in 1779 left land in Colesbourne and Elkstone to trustees for sale. Part

[40] Verey, *Glos.* i. 195; docs. and plans, *penes* Mr. Elwes.
[41] Cf. Glos. R.O., photocopy 263.
[42] B.L. Add. Ch. 20394.   [43] *Red Bk. of Worc.* 437.
[44] *Feud. Aids,* ii. 239, 247.
[45] C 115/K 2/6683 ff. 251v.–252v., 268–9.
[46] *Feud. Aids,* ii. 239, 247; cf. C.P. 25(1)/75/40 no. 274.
[47] *Feud. Aids,* ii. 280.
[48] Dugdale, *Mon.* vi (1), 136.
[49] *Tax. Eccl.* (Rec. Com.), 223.
[50] C 115/K 2/6683 ff. 249v.–261; cf. *Tax. Eccl.* (Rec. Com.), 232.
[51] *Cal. Chart. R.* 1257–1300, 428.
[52] Dugdale, *Mon.* vi (1), 140; *Glouc. Jnl.* 24 July 1786.
[53] *L. & P. Hen. VIII,* xvi, p. 715.
[54] Ibid. xvii, pp. 157, 212; cf. C 142/253 no. 97.
[55] *E.H.R.* xix. 106.
[56] *Cal. Pat.* 1563–6, p. 12.
[57] Hockaday Abs. clxv.
[58] *Trans. B.G.A.S.* xvii. 130.
[59] Glos. R.O., D 1878, Chedworth deeds 1609–17, deed 1613.

[60] Ibid.; G.D.R., T 1/59.
[61] G.D.R., V 5/87T 3, 5; C.P. 25(2)/1316/16 Geo. III no. 8; Glos. R.O., D 1386.
[62] Glos. R.O., photocopy 593; partics. of Colesborne mans. c. 1790.
[63] G.D.R., T 1/59.   [64] G.D.R., V 5/87T 3.
[65] G.D.R., T 1/59; Glos. R.O., D 1388/SL 3, no. 116.
[66] *Dom. Bk.* (Rec. Com.), i. 169v.
[67] *Red Bk. Exch.* (Rolls Ser.), i. 285.
[68] *Cal. Chart. R.* 1341–1417, 221; E 315/52 no. 29; cf. E 315/48 no. 258; E 315/49 no. 313; E 315/50 no. 196; *Ciren. Cart.* i, p. 221.
[69] *Cal. Chart. R.* 1341–1417, 196.
[70] *L. & P. Hen. VIII,* xviii (2), p. 241.
[71] Ibid. xix (2), p. 321.   [72] C 142/274 no. 39.
[73] Glos. R.O., D 2612/T 4; the Preedon fam. retained land in Colesbourne in the mid 18th cent.: ibid. D 2025, deed 1750; Glos. Colln. RF 87.1.
[74] Glos. R.O., D 2525, Ciren. deeds 1716–55; cf. ibid. photocopy 264.

of the land had been sold by 1790 when the remainder, *c.* 320 a. mainly in Colesbourne, was bought by John Elwes.[75]

In 1668 Thomas Higgs granted 2 yardlands of his Colesbourne estate to Richard Sollace, already a landowner in the parish. In 1679 Sollace settled his land on the marriage of his daughter Mary and Anthony Edwards but retained life-interests for himself (d. 1702) and his wife Jane (d. 1705). Anthony granted the land in 1711 to his second son Richard (d. 1743) and it had passed to another Anthony Edwards by 1744 when Sir John Guise, lord of Rendcomb, bought it.[76] In the 19th century the Rendcomb estate included almost 100 a. in the south-eastern corner of Colesbourne.[77]

St. Bartholomew's Hospital, Gloucester, which was granted ½ yardland in Colesbourne in the mid 13th century,[78] retained 22 a. there until 1819 when it was exchanged with Henry Elwes for land in Withington.[79] In 1574 land in Colesbourne which had supported a lamp or lights in Cheltenham church was sold by the Crown.[80]

ECONOMIC HISTORY. Some land on the bishop of Worcester's Colesbourne estate may have fallen out of cultivation between 1066 and 1086 when the estate was halved in value. Of the six ploughs on it at the latter date only one was used on the demesne, which had two *servi*. The demesne on the Colesbourne manor then held under Ansfrid de Cormeilles comprised ½ plough-land.[81] In 1291 there were 2 plough-lands in demesne on Llanthony Priory's estate.[82] In 1537 the priory granted a lease of its demesne together with the rent from a sheep-pasture.[83]

Among the tenants of the bishop's estate in 1086 were 18 *villani* and 2 bordars who between them worked 5 ploughs. On the manor held under Ansfrid de Cormeilles the tenants were 2 *villani* and 2 bordars with 1 plough.[84] Llanthony Priory received assized rents valued at 22s. in 1291[85] and at £1 15s. 5d. in 1539 when the rents of its customary tenants were worth £2 1s. 3d.[86] No further evidence of tenurial history has been found before the mid 17th century when tenants on the Colesbourne estate held by copy.[87] Much of the copyhold land was probably converted to leasehold during the creation of large farms.[88] On the Colesbourne estate *c.* 1790 were farms of 500 a., 470 a., 340 a., and 170 a., and the smaller tenements were a mill estate held by copy and several

cottages.[89] In 1820 995 a. of the estate in Colesbourne were in hand, and farms based on Penhill Farm and Rapsgate Park covered 532½ a. and 325 a. respectively.[90]

Some commons, including one called Lammas Grounds, were recorded in the early 18th century[91] but much of the higher land in the parish was included in two extensive open fields, a north and a south field on opposite sides of the Churn valley, recorded from the mid 13th century.[92] In the mid 18th century the pasture rights in those fields were used primarily for sheep.[93] The estate of 22 a. owned by St. Bartholomew's Hospital lay scattered throughout the fields in 52 pieces in 1819.[94] The owners of the Colesbourne estate, to which most of the open-field land belonged, had begun inclosing land by the early 18th century[95] and in the mid 1780s 195 a. south of Pen hill were inclosed.[96] In 1838 the north field covered 533 a. in an area extending from the Cheltenham–Cirencester road and Southbury north-eastwards almost to Hilcot brook, and the south field covered 317 a. in an area south of the old Rendcomb road and extending eastwards from Pen hill to the Churn.[97] By the later 18th century the open-field land of the Colesbourne estate had been arranged in compact holdings attached to the large farms of the estate. One farm included 158 a. on Pen hill which had been laid down as a sheep-pasture but was still regarded as commonable.[98] The open fields were inclosed in 1838 when Henry Elwes was allotted 812 a. and the rector 48 a. for his glebe, but the award was not finalized until 1849 when Elwes had bought out the only other owner of open-field land.[99]

After inclosure Elwes retained 295 a. of woodland and pasture in hand and the rest of his estate in Colesbourne was organized as four farms, comprising 505 a., 480 a., 359 a., and 150 a. in 1839 and based on the farmsteads at Southbury, Penhill Farm, Rapsgate Park, and Pinswell respectively. Other land in the parish was farmed at that time from Combend in Elkstone or Marsden in Rendcomb.[1] From the late 1870s when arable farming became unprofitable the farms on the Colesbourne estate were taken in hand and by the mid 1880s H. J. Elwes was farming *c.* 2,500 a. for his father.[2] The letting of parts of the estate had been resumed by 1889[3] and in 1926 there were four farms in the parish, three with over 150 a. each and one with over 100 a. They provided full-time employment for only 14 labourers.[4]

In 1839 1,473 a. were given over to arable and

[75] Deeds 1790, *penes* Mr. Elwes.
[76] Glos. R.O., D 326/T 112; Bigland, *Glos.* i. 116–17.
[77] G.D.R., T 1/59; Glos. R.O., D 1388/SL 6, no. 52.
[78] *Glouc. Corp. Rec.* p. 177.
[79] Glos. R.O., Q/RI 162.
[80] *Cal. Pat.* 1572–5, p. 324.
[81] *Dom. Bk.* (Rec. Com.), i. 164v., 169v.
[82] *Tax. Eccl.* (Rec. Com.), 232.
[83] Glos. R.O., D 184/T 35.
[84] *Dom. Bk.* (Rec. Com.), i. 164v., 169v.
[85] *Tax. Eccl.* (Rec. Com.), 232.
[86] Dugdale, *Mon.* vi (1), 140.
[87] Glos. R.O., D 326/T 112, deed 1668.
[88] Cf. ibid. photocopy 593.
[89] Partics. of Colesborne mans. *c.* 1790.

[90] Glos. R.O., photocopy 263.
[91] Bodl. MS. Rawl. B.323, f. 219v.
[92] C 115/K 2/6683 f. 249; Glos. R.O., Q/RI 48.
[93] Glos. R.O., D 2025, deed 1750.
[94] Ibid. Q/RI 162.
[95] G.D.R., V 5/87T 5.
[96] Map of Colesborne est. *c.* 1790, *penes* Mr. Elwes; Glos. R.O., photocopy 264.
[97] Glos. R.O., Q/RI 48.
[98] Ibid. photocopies 593, 264.
[99] Ibid. Q/RI 48.
[1] G.D.R., T 1/59.
[2] Elwes, *Memoirs*, 278–9, 289.
[3] *Kelly's Dir. Glos.* (1885 and later edns.).
[4] M.A.F. 68/3295/4.

CHEDWORTH: the northern end of the village from the east

NORTH CERNEY: the village from the west

CRANHAM: the village from the north, with Cranham common beyond

CRANHAM: the 'Swiss cottages' at the retreat in Cranham woods, *c.* 1835

525 a. to pasture[5] and in the mid 19th century the parish was devoted mainly to sheep and corn husbandry. In 1866 the area returned as under crops or temporary grass was 1,104 a. and that under permanent grass 391 a. The sheep, then returned at 941, were folded on turnips, mangolds, and grass leys. The other crops in the rotation were wheat, barley, oats, peas, and potatoes. Other livestock returned then included 119 cattle of which 24 were kept for dairying.[6] There was a considerable shift from arable after 1879 as land on the Colesbourne estate was allowed to revert to grass,[7] and 1,399 a. in the parish were returned in 1896 as permanent grass and only 352½ a. as arable or temporary grass.[8] From 1882 H. J. Elwes made silage in place of hay[9] and by 1885 there were seven silos on the estate.[10] Elwes improved the quality of the estate's flock of Cotswold sheep in the early 1880s by selective breeding but by the 1890s sheep-farming had become less important.[11] To make the estate profitable he developed some parts as rabbit warrens and in the early 20th century planted large areas.[12] The area returned as permanent grass had been reduced to 466½ a. by 1926 when another 157 a. were used for rough grazing. The number of cattle returned then was 158, including 36 milk cows. At least 511½ a. were farmed as arable then.[13]

After 1950 most of the land was kept in hand by the Colesbourne estate and by 1979 only 242.8 ha. (600 a.), farmed from Rapsgate Farm and Lower Hilcot Farm in Withington, were worked by tenants. Elsewhere in Colesbourne in 1976 were three farms with less than 30 ha. (74 a.) each. In the later 1970s local farming was largely based on sheep and corn husbandry but pig- and cattle-rearing were also significant. In 1979 the home farm of the Colesbourne estate, managed from 1967 by a company, included 404.7 ha. (1,000 a.) of farm-land, most of which was worked as arable with a six-year rotation, and it had a flock of 700 ewes. The woodland on the estate was managed separately.[14]

Several mills were recorded in Colesbourne in the Middle Ages. In 1086 there were two on the bishop of Worcester's estate and one on the manor held under Ansfrid de Cormeilles.[15] William le Poer's property in the early 13th century included a mill.[16] Another mill was granted by William Marsh to Llanthony Priory, which alienated it in 1272 to

Walter Loholt the younger.[17] At the Dissolution a fulling-mill in Colesbourne was held from the priory together with a small estate in Chedworth.[18] In 1661 Thomas Higgs conveyed two water-mills in Colesbourne and Chedworth to John Hicks[19] but they were bought in again by Philip Sheppard in 1713.[20] One of those mills probably stood on the Churn south-west of Colesbourne church where a grist-mill was recorded c. 1770.[21] It had evidently stopped working by 1820 when it was called the old mill.[22] By the middle of the century a saw-mill had begun operating a little to the west.[23] Its water-wheel was scrapped in the late 1950s[24] but the timber-yard remained open in 1979.

In 1831 29 families were supported by agriculture and 13 by trades[25] but in the mid 1860s, a time of agricultural prosperity, there were not enough resident labourers to work the farms of the Colesbourne estate, for most of the cottages were occupied by small tradesmen and servants.[26] A smith lived in the parish in the early 13th century[27] and the blacksmith recorded in 1641[28] may have worked the smithy recorded west of Old Farm in 1845.[29] Inhabitants included a butcher and a shoemaker in 1327[30] and possibly a walker in 1381.[31] A dyer lived in the parish in the early 13th century[32] and there is evidence of a small cloth industry in 1608 when a tucker and a weaver were among the inhabitants. A mason also lived in Colesbourne then[33] and a number of masons and slaters in the 19th century.[34] Many of the usual village trades died out from the end of the 19th century but the village still had a blacksmith in 1939[35] and a gate- and hurdle-maker in 1940.[36] In 1979 the village had a post office and a small garage, which had opened in 1919.[37]

LOCAL GOVERNMENT. The view of frankpledge for Colesbourne was held in the hundred court but by the early 15th century some of Bruern Abbey's tenants may have attended the view held by the lord of the hundred's steward on the abbey's manor of Marsden.[38] In the early 13th century courts were held by the Loholt and le Poer families for their parts of Colesbourne.[39] Llanthony Priory agreed, probably in the mid 13th century, to do suit every three weeks to Cirencester Abbey's foreign court at Cirencester for property in

[5] G.D.R., T 1/59.
[6] M.A.F. 68/26/19; M.A.F. 68/25/16.
[7] Elwes, Memoirs, 280.
[8] M.A.F. 68/1609/16.
[9] Elwes, Memoirs, 280.
[10] Kelly's Dir. Glos. (1885), 434.   [11] Elwes, Memoirs, 281–5.
[12] Elwes, 'Colesborne Estate Hist.'
[13] M.A.F. 68/3294/4.
[14] Agric. Returns 1976; ex inf. Mr. Elwes.
[15] Dom. Bk. (Rec. Com.), i. 164v., 169v.
[16] C 115/K 2/6683 f. 251v.   [17] Ibid. ff. 256, 253v.
[18] S.C. 6/Hen. VIII/1224 m.15d.
[19] C.P. 25(2)/656/13 Chas. II Trin. no. 30.
[20] C.P. 25(2)/927/12 Anne Hil. no. 24.
[21] Glos. R.O., photocopy 593; Taylor, Map of Glos. (1777).
[22] Glos. R.O., photocopy 263.
[23] Ibid. Q/SRh 1855 A/2; O.S. map 6", Glos. XXXV. SW. (1883 edn.).

[24] Ex inf. Mr. Elwes.
[25] Census, 1831.
[26] Rep. Com. Agric. Employment, p. 99.
[27] C 115/K 2/6683 f. 252 and v.
[28] Hockaday Abs. clxv.
[29] Glos. R.O., Q/RUm 210; O.S. Map 6", Glos. XXXV. SW. (1924 edn.).
[30] Glos. Subsidy Roll, 1327, 10.
[31] E. 179/113/31A rot. 2; cf. Cat. Anct. D. iii, D 736.
[32] C 115/K 2/6683 ff. 252v.–253.
[33] Smith, Men and Armour, 256–7.
[34] Par. reg. 1813–80, penes Mr. Elwes; Kelly's Dir. Glos. (1863–1902 edns.).
[35] Kelly's Dir. Glos. (1856 and later edns.).
[36] Payne, Glos. Survey, 171.
[37] Ex inf. Mr. Elwes.
[38] Ciren Cart. ii, p. 619; cf. ibid. i, p. 221.
[39] C 115/K 2/6683 ff. 250 and v., 251v.

Colesbourne,[40] and profits of court were received for the priory's Colesbourne manor in 1539.[41]

The parish was served by two churchwardens, recorded from 1548,[42] but in the 19th century there was sometimes only one. Their accounts survive from 1754.[43] There were two overseers of the poor in 1718 when the parish apprenticed a boy.[44] The cost of poor-relief, which was £93 in 1776, had risen to £164 by 1803 when 17 people received regular help and 19 occasional but the numbers had dropped to 14 and 2 respectively by 1813. The cost that year was pushed up to £201 by an expenditure of £38 on lawsuits but had fallen to £110 by 1815[45] and in the late 1820s and early 1830s varied between £116 and £154.[46] By 1820 the parish rented as a poorhouse a cottage on the old Rendcomb road south of Penhill Farm.[47] Colesbourne, which became part of the Cirencester poor-law union of 1836,[48] was included in Cirencester rural district until 1974[49] and then in Cotswold district.

CHURCH. A church had evidently been built at Colesbourne by 1095 when Walter of Gloucester granted two-thirds of the tithes, which were collected in two courts, to the church of St. Owen, Gloucester.[50] The living was a rectory in 1260[51] and remained one, though the incumbent was styled vicar in 1551, presumably because he received only part of the tithes.[52] The rectory was united, under an order of 1868,[53] with Coberley in 1871,[54] and Cowley was added to the united benefice in 1937.[55] In 1954 Colesbourne again became a separate living, described as a vicarage or perpetual curacy, but a vacancy in 1975 was left unfilled and the rector of Coberley and Cowley was appointed priest-in-charge.[56]

In the mid 13th century Walter Loholt granted the advowson of the church to Llanthony Priory,[57] which presented to the living of 1266[58] and retained the patronage until the Dissolution.[59] The Crown, which exercised the advowson in 1542,[60] granted it to George Huntley in 1564[61] but it evidently passed with the priory's Colesbourne estate the same year, for William Ryvett was patron in 1570.[62] In 1578 Tobias Damforde was patron for a turn and in 1665 the bishop presented through lapse.[63] Colesbourne and Coberley churches had the same patron when the benefices were united, but after the union with Cowley the Lord Chancellor had the right to present at every third vacancy.[64] Mr. H. W. G. Elwes was patron of Colesbourne in 1979.[65]

Colesbourne was a poor living because the rector took only a third of the tithes.[66] In the later 13th century Llanthony Priory was in dispute with the rector, who had been taking its tithes before 1283, and in 1301 it granted its share of the hay tithes to another rector for the duration of his incumbency.[67] The rector had ceased to receive his part of the tithes from the priory's estate by 1407[68] and in 1680 Thomas Horton was withholding his share in those from some woodland on the Combend estate.[69] In the later 18th century owners of the Colesbourne estate took all the tithes of the parish and paid the rector £50 a year as a modus for his share.[70] The rector's tithes, including those from 66 a. of woodland on the Combend estate, were commuted in 1839 for a corn-rent-charge of £122 10s.[71]

The rector's glebe measured 24 a. in 1535,[72] 2 yardlands in 1572, and c. 44 a. in 1680.[73] Two awards of £200 each, made by Queen Anne's Bounty in 1809 and 1812 to meet benefactions by the patron of £200 and £300 respectively,[74] had been used by 1827 by buy 27 a. and 4 dilapidated cottages in Withington.[75] The glebe, which was enlarged slightly by an exchange with Henry Elwes at inclosure in 1838[76] and by a gift from J. H. Elwes in 1869,[77] covered c. 85 a. at the end of the century and was sold c. 1916.[78] The living was worth £4 6s. 8d. in 1291[79] and £5 6s. 9½d. clear in 1535.[80] The value had risen to £26 by 1650,[81] and to £43 by 1750.[82] The living was worth £130 in 1856.[83]

The rectory house, which was ruinous in 1569,[84] had three hearths in 1672[85] and comprised three bays in 1680.[86] The house, standing west of the churchyard,[87] was described as unfit for a residence

[40] *Ciren. Cart.* iii, pp. 843–5.
[41] Dugdale, *Mon.* vi (1), 140.
[42] Hockaday Abs. xxxi, 1548 visit. f. 48; xliii, 1566 visit. f. 3; lxviii, 1661 visit. f. 12; G.D.R., V 5/87T 5.
[43] Churchwardens' acct. bk. 1754–1894, *penes* Mr. Elwes.
[44] Glos. R.O., D 2565.
[45] *Poor Law Abstract, 1804*, 180–1; *1818*, 154–5.
[46] *Poor Law Returns* (1830–1), p. 70; (1835), p. 69.
[47] Glos. R.O., photocopy 263; Q/SRh 1827 B/3.
[48] *Poor Law Com. 2nd Rep.* p. 522.   [49] *Census*, 1971.
[50] *Camd. Misc.* xxii, pp. 37 n., 38.
[51] C 115/K 2/6683 f. 268.
[52] *E.H.R.* xix. 106.   [53] G.D.R. vol. 385, p. 71.
[54] *Kelly's Dir. Glos.* (1885), 434, 438.
[55] *Kelly's Dir. Glos.* (1931 and later edns.), s.v. Colesborne, Cowley, and Cubberley; cf. *Lond. Gaz.* 7 Feb. 1928, pp. 835–6.
[56] *Glouc. Dioc. Yr. Bk.* (1978), 29.
[57] C 115/K 2/6683 f. 249.
[58] *Reg. Giffard*, 361.
[59] *Reg. Wakefeld*, p. 89; Worc. Episc. Reg., Reg. Carpenter, i, f. 36v.
[60] Hockaday Abs. clxv.
[61] *Cal. Pat.* 1563–6, p. 153.
[62] Ibid. p. 12; Hockaday Abs. clxv.
[63] Hockaday Abs. clxv.
[64] Cf. *Kelly's Dir. Glos.* (1870), 530–1; (1939), 135.
[65] *Glouc. Dioc. Yr. Bk.* (1979), 55.
[66] Cf. Glos. R.O., D 184/T 35; Rudder, *Glos.* 384.
[67] C 115/K 2/6683 ff. 261–262v.
[68] *Trans. B.G.A.S.* lxiii. 127.   [69] G.D.R., V 5/87T 3, 5.
[70] Glos. R.O., photocopy 593; partics. of Colesborne mans. c. 1790.
[71] G.D.R., T 1/59.
[72] *Valor Eccl.* (Rec. Com.), ii. 442.
[73] G.D.R., V 5/87T 1, 3.
[74] Hodgson, *Queen Anne's Bounty*, p. cclxxxiv.
[75] Agreement 12 Apr. 1827, *penes* Mr. Elwes; G.D.R., V 5/87T 6.
[76] Glos. R.O., Q/RI 48.
[77] Copy of deed 21 June 1869, *penes* Mr. Elwes.
[78] *Kelly's Dir. Glos.* (1856–1919 edns.).
[79] *Tax. Eccl.* (Rec. Com.), 223.
[80] *Valor Eccl.* (Rec. Com.), ii. 442.
[81] *Trans. B.G.A.S.* lxxxiii. 93.
[82] G.D.R. vol. 381A, f. 25.
[83] G.D.R. vol. 384, f. 67.   [84] Hockaday Abs. clxv.
[85] E 179/247/13 rot. 28d.
[86] G.D.R., V 5/87T 3.
[87] Glos. R.O., photocopy 263.

in 1838[88] when it was part of the property exchanged with Henry Elwes.[89] It had been demolished by 1842.[90] The school-house, which J. H. Elwes gave to the rector for a parsonage in 1869,[91] became the home of curates.[92]

In 1269 the rector, William of Thornbury, was dispensed to stay in Rome for a year on business concerning the church.[93] In 1306 the rector Ranulph White, who purged himself of homicide and other crimes, was licensed to let the church at farm for three years to pay debts incurred during his imprisonment.[94] He was granted leave of absence for part of 1310.[95] In 1331 the rector, John of London, was licensed to be absent for study.[96] William Vance, instituted in 1465, was the bishop's chancellor.[97] Richard Hawker, who became rector in 1542,[98] was unable to prove the Articles in 1551.[99] By 1563 he was non-resident and employed curates, including in 1566 one who was not in orders.[1] In 1569 the rector, who had been non-resident for two years, was said to have erased passages in the Bible. Humphrey Horton, rector from 1570,[2] also held the livings of Rendcomb and Tetbury. He was non-resident in 1576 but may have served for a while earlier, for he was presented for wearing a cope during communion.[3]

Thomas Freeman, who became rector in 1637 or 1638[4] and was described as a preaching minister in 1650,[5] retained the living until his death c. 1665. Joseph Wilkes was rector from 1668 to 1713[6] but in 1672 a Mr. Haigh, who was living in the parsonage, was described as rector.[7] William Alexander, rector 1713–29,[8] taught at Cheltenham grammar school until 1718 when he became headmaster of the King's School, Gloucester.[9] George White, his successor at Colesbourne, was also rector of Rendcomb.[10] John Raffles became rector in 1780 but was deprived soon afterwards for forging his letters of ordination.[11] John de la Bere, rector from 1782,[12] lived in Cheltenham and employed curates.[13] His successor James Holmes, rector, 1789–1837,[14] lived in Suffolk[15] but moved to Colesbourne in 1806.[16] After he became perpetual curate of Compton Abdale in 1824[17] Colesbourne had only one service each Sunday.[18] Frederick

Hohler, who became rector in 1837, lived in Winstone where he was curate and later rector. He employed curates at Colesbourne from 1855 and the church was also served by curates after the union with Coberley.[19] When Colesbourne became a separate living in 1954 it was served in plurality with Rendcomb until 1973.[20]

Land, which brought in an income of 20d. in 1548 for two lights and a lamp in the church,[21] was sold by the Crown the following year.[22] Although no evidence has been found of a chantry-chapel in Colesbourne, the Crown acquired land in Colesbourne at the dissolution of the chantries and sold it in 1568.[23] By 1683 the income from some land had been assigned to providing two bell-ropes or repairing the church.[24] That land has not been traced after c. 1775.[25]

The church, which had apparently been dedicated to St. Samson by c. 1140[26] but bore a dedication to *ST. JAMES* by 1743,[27] is mostly built of rubble and has a chancel, a nave with transeptal north and south chapels and south porch, and a west tower. The nave was probably built in the 12th century but the only obvious features of that date are the jambs of the chancel arch and the lower parts of a blocked north doorway. The chancel arch and the south doorway were rebuilt in the 13th century and the chancel in the 14th, during which the porch and south chapel were added. During the 15th century the tower and north chapel were added, the nave walls were heightened to take a roof of lower pitch, and new windows were put into the north and south walls.

An early-19th-century view suggests that the church had a west gallery lit by a window in the south wall.[28] In 1851 and 1852 the church was extensively restored by J. H. Elwes to designs by David Brandon.[29] The north chapel was rebuilt, the nave walls were reduced in height, and the roof was returned to its original pitch. In the churchyard a chapel over the Elwes family vault north of the chancel was demolished and several memorial plaques to members of the family were placed in the chancel. The organ was given in 1919.[30] The font and stone pulpit date from the 15th century.

[88] Hockaday Abs. clxv.
[89] Glos. R.O., Q/RI 48.
[90] Date on range of stabling on site.
[91] Letters and copy of deed 21 June 1869, *penes* Mr. Elwes.
[92] O.S. Map 6″, Glos. XXXV. SW. (1883 and 1924 edns.); *Kelly's Dir. Glos.* (1870 and later edns.).
[93] *Reg. Giffard*, 29.
[94] *Reg. Ginsborough*, 28, 162; *Cal. Close*, 1302–7, 400.
[95] *Reg. Reynolds*, 87.
[96] Worc. Episc. Reg., Reg. Orleton, ii, f. 12v.
[97] Ibid. Reg. Carpenter, i, f. 187v.
[98] Hockaday Abs. clxv.
[99] *E.H.R.* xix. 106.
[1] Hockaday Abs. xlii, 1563 visit. f. 41; xliii, 1566 visit. ff. 3, 32.
[2] Ibid. clxv.
[3] G.D.R. vol. 40, f. 37.
[4] Par. reg. 1632–1729, *penes* Mr. Elwes.
[5] *Trans. B.G.A.S.* lxxxiii. 93.
[6] Hockaday Abs. clxv; par. reg. 1632–1729.
[7] E 179/247/13 rot. 28d.; E 179/116/544.
[8] Hockaday Abs. clxv.
[9] A. Bell, *Tudor Foundation* (Chalfont St. Giles, 1974), 768; D. Robertson, *King's School, Glouc.* (1974), 76, 80–1.

[10] Hockaday Abs. clxv, cccxxii.
[11] Ibid. clxv; Rudder, *Glos.* proof pages (Glos. Colln.), MS. note on p. 384.
[12] Hockaday Abs. clxv.
[13] G.D.R. vol. 319; par. reg. 1754–1812, *penes* Mr. Elwes.
[14] Hockaday Abs. clxv.
[15] G.D.R. vol. 382, f. 44.
[16] Par. reg. 1795–1812, mem.
[17] Hockaday Abs. clxviii.
[18] G.D.R. vol. 383, nos. li, ccxci.
[19] Hockaday Abs. clxv; *Kelly's Dir. Glos.* (1856 and later edns.).
[20] *Glouc. Dioc. Yr. Bk.* (1956–7 and later edns. to 1974).
[21] *Trans. B.G.A.S.* viii. 300; E 301/23 no. 91.
[22] *Cal. Pat.* 1549–51, 98.
[23] Ibid. 1566–9, p. 225.
[24] G.D.R., V 5/87T 4.
[25] G.D.R. vol. 397, f. 25; Rudder, *Glos*, 384.
[26] Dugdale, *Mon.* vi(1), 136; *Reg. Giffard*, 406.
[27] G.D.R. vol. 397, f. 25.
[28] Water-colour by Geo. Shepheard dated 1801, *penes* Mr. Elwes.
[29] Verey, *Glos.* i. 194; *Kelly's Dir. Glos.* (1856), 272.
[30] Cf. Glos. R.O., PA 94/1.

The bells which were apparently recast in 1679[31] numbered two[32] and were replaced by a ring of five cast by Abraham Rudhall in 1719.[33] The plate includes a chalice and paten-cover of 1576.[34] The parish registers survive from 1632.[35]

NONCONFORMITY. Colesbourne had three non-conformists in 1676[36] and Joshua Head (d. 1719), a Baptist, preached there.[37] In 1816 and 1819 Henry Hawkins, Particular Baptist minister of Eastcombe, registered meeting-places in the parish[38] but in 1825 there were said to be no dissenting meetings.[39] Cheltenham men registered houses as meeting-places in 1831 and 1846,[40] and there was a Baptist meeting in 1851 with attendances of up to 40.[41]

EDUCATION. In 1818 a Miss Hamond, a relation of Henry Elwes, supported a Sunday school in Colesbourne which taught 55 children.[42] In 1825 10 children attended a day-school,[43] and a day-school, opened in 1831 and supported by Elwes and the rector, taught 15 children in 1833.[44] In 1847 a day-school with 36 children was supported by subscriptions and pence and had 2 teachers but no schoolroom.[45] J. H. Elwes opened a school in a new building by the Cheltenham–Cirencester road[46] in 1852. It had become a National school by 1866, when the income was derived from voluntary contributions and pence,[47] and the following year it had an average attendance of 30. A night-school held twice a week then taught 9 boys.[48] The school building was enlarged in 1879 and the day-school had an average attendance of 50 in 1885 and of 33 in 1889, when the infants were taught separately.[49] Later and until the mid 20th century the average attendance was usually over 40 but it fell as low as 25 in 1936.[50] The school closed in 1965 and the building became the village hall.[51]

CHARITIES FOR THE POOR. None known.

COWLEY

COWLEY is a rural parish lying above the Cotswold escarpment 8 km. south of Cheltenham. The ancient parish, which contained 1,898 a., was irregular in shape and included in the western corner part of Birdlip village.[52] The boundaries, which those of Cowley manor described in 1757 closely followed, included the main Gloucester–Cirencester road, the Roman Ermin Street, on the south-west, the river Churn, then called Cockleford's brook, on the east, and tributary streams on part of the north in Coldwell bottom, then known as Goldwell bottom, and on the south-east.[53] The north-western boundary, which followed the crest of the escarpment, including a short spur called the Peak, was defined where it ran across common land north of Birdlip in 1869 following an encroachment by Lady Cromie, owner of the Witcombe estate.[54] In 1935 the parish was enlarged to 2,019 a. (817 ha.) by the transfer of 121 a. at Birdlip from Brimpsfield.[55] The following account relates to the ancient parish except that Birdlip village is treated wholly under Brimpsfield.

Above the valleys of the boundary streams the parish occupies a plateau of rolling country lying at over 244 m. and reaching over 290 m. in the west, where there are extensive views north-westwards across the Vale of Gloucester. The valley bottoms lie on Midford Sand while the plateau is formed by the Inferior Oolite, overlaid in places by fuller's earth, or on some higher land by the Great Oolite.[56] Open fields and commons occupied much of the parish until the 18th century. Barrow Wake, a small common at the top of the escarpment, remained uninclosed in 1978.[57]

In 1086 the Cowley estate included woodland measuring three furlongs by one,[58] presumably in the south-east[59] at Cowley wood, also called Norgrave in 1652.[60] In the later 17th century copyholders could take sticks for wattle in the wood.[61] A view aligned on the manor-house had been cleared by 1778[62] and by 1874, when the wood comprised 90 a., two fishponds had been created at its north-eastern corner.[63] Harcombe bottom to the north and an area south-east of the Peak were planted later that century[64] and in 1901 woodland and plantations accounted for 157 a.[65] East of Cowley

31 Ibid. D 2052.
32 G.D.R., V 5/87 T 4.   33 *Glos. Ch. Bells*, 43.
34 *Glos. Ch. Plate*, 61.
35 *B. & G. Par. Rec.* 107.   36 Compton Census.
37 *Calamy Revised*, ed. Matthews, 255; cf. *V.C.H. Glos.* vi. 47, 133.
38 Hockaday Abs. clxv; *V.C.H. Glos.* xi. 37.
39 G.D.R. vol. 383, no. ccxci.   40 Hockaday Abs. clxv.
41 H.O. 129/340/1/10/13.
42 *Educ. of Poor Digest*, 296; Burke, *Land. Gent.* (1965), i. 232.
43 G.D.R. vol. 383, no. ccxci.   44 *Educ. Enquiry Abstract*, 311.
45 *Church School Inquiry, 1846–7*, 6–7.
46 *Kelly's Dir. Glos.* (1856), 272; O.S. Map 6", Glos. XXXV. SW. (1883 edn.).
47 Ed. 7/34/88.
48 *Rep. Com. Agric. Employment*, pp. 98–9.
49 *Kelly's Dir. Glos.* (1885), 434; (1889), 748.
50 Ibid. (1894–1914 edns.); *Bd. of Educ., List 21, 1922* (H.M.S.O.), 103; *1932*, 114; *1936*, 120; Glos. R.O., PA 102/1.
51 Glos. R.O., PA 94/1.
52 *O.S. Area Bk.* (1884). This account was written in 1978.
53 Glos. R.O., DC/E 88/2.
54 Ibid. D 2440, est. papers 1777–1875.
55 *Census*, 1931 (pt. ii); 1971.
56 Geol. Surv. Map 1", solid, sheet 44 (1856 edn.).
57 Cf. Glos. Colln. RV 95.2.
58 *Dom. Bk.* (Rec. Com.), i. 166.
59 Cf. *Cat. Anct. D.* iii, D 181.   60 C 54/3672 no. 19.
61 Glos. R.O., DC/E 88/1/1.
62 Ibid. D 1388/SL 3, no. 12.
63 G.D.R., T 1/63; Glos. R.O., D 1388/SL 5, no. 84.
64 G.D.R., T 1/63; O.S. Map 6", Glos. XXXIV. SE. and SW. (1883 and 1903 edns.).
65 Acreage Returns, 1901.

village a small deer-park was laid out on either side of the Churn in the mid 1850s and two lakes with small islands were then formed in the river as part of the pleasure grounds of Cowley Manor.[66] In the later 1890s the park was enlarged[67] and a third lake created downstream.[68] The Churnside Schools Camp and Adventure Centre north of the village opened in 1962,[69] and the Gloucestershire Girl Guides Association built its headquarters in the park on land leased to it in 1968.[70] Birdlip radio station on Shab hill in the western part of the parish was established by the Air Ministry early in the Second World War. It was later used for air traffic control but from 1977 provided only cover for VHF radio.[71]

One of the early tracks crossing the parish ran near the top of the escarpment,[72] where late Iron Age finds, including the 'Birdlip Mirror' discovered on Barrow Wake in 1879, and Roman finds provide evidence of early occupation.[73] Ermin Street, which remained an important thoroughfare,[74] was turnpiked between Birdlip and Cirencester in 1747.[75] The Painswick–Cheltenham road turnpiked in 1785 included the route running north-eastwards from Birdlip across Barrow Wake.[76] A green way recorded in the north-eastern part of the parish from the later 13th century was possibly part of a route ascending the escarpment from Shurdington and leading to the village.[77]

The settlement at Cowley is a small estate village dominated by Cowley Manor, a substantial 19th-century mansion beside the Churn. The church stands east of the house and in its grounds. Manor Farm, an 18th-century house to the north-west, ceased to be a farm-house in the early 1930s.[78] The village grew up a little way to the west around the junction of several local routes where an ancient stone cross, recorded in 1713, stands;[79] the head of the cross dates from the 19th century.[80] The village spread westwards along the lane rising from the cross, and in that part, known as the west end in 1537,[81] the most substantial house is a farm-house, the former rectory, which stands a little way south of the lane.[82] North of the lane a cottage, which was part of the glebe and was occupied by the parish clerk in 1848, has been rebuilt.[83] In the early 19th

century a row of three cottages was built north of the road to the church[84] but most buildings in the village, including a school and school-house west of the cross, were put up or remodelled by owners of Cowley Manor later that century. One pair of estate cottages was built in 1888 by William Baring-Bingham and five more pairs were built in 1897 and 1898 by James Horlick[85] who also provided the village with a water-supply.[86] In 1904 Horlick built a pair of houses and stabling some distance north-east of Manor Farm.[87] The former school had been adapted as a village hall by 1951.[88]

Stockwell, 2.5 km. west of the village, was recorded from the early 13th century when land there was incorporated into the manor estate.[89] The settlement, which grew up around a green[90] and contained 10 houses c. 1710,[91] was evidently depopulated during the inclosure of the open fields there in the late 1780s and early 1790s, for in 1802 several tenements were derelict and there was only one farmstead. Stockwell Farm[92] appears to have been rebuilt in the late 19th century but a back wing may incorporate the earlier house. To the south-east is a 17th-century out-building and a pair of 19th-century cottages. There are several outlying post-inclosure barns,[93] of which one, south-west of Cowley wood and called Wood Barn in 1802,[94] had been converted as cottages by 1857.[95] Hill Barn by the road from the village to Stockwell and a pair of cottages to the north were built in the mid 19th century. On Ermin Street the settlements at Parson's Pitch and Nettleton included houses in Cowley parish.[96]

At the junction of the Gloucester–Oxford and Painswick–Cheltenham roads in the northern corner of the parish an inn opened shortly before 1777[97] in a building which appears to have been a pair of cottages.[98] It was known as the Balloon by 1796[99] and later as the Air Balloon.[1] There was a tavern in Cowley in 1284[2] but the village, which had a beer-house in the 1870s, had no inn in 1978.[3]

Twenty tenants were recorded on the Cowley estate in 1086[4] and in 1327 only 2 people in Cowley were assessed for the subsidy and 8 in Stockwell.[5] More than 14 in both settlements were assessed for the poll tax in 1381.[6] There were said to be c. 50

[66] G.D.R., T 1/63; Glos. R.O., DC/E 88/26; Glos. Colln. (H)G 4.2.

[67] *Country Life*, 4 Aug. 1906, 164.

[68] O.S. Map 6″, Glos. XXXIV. SE. (1903 edn.).

[69] Ex inf. county land agent and valuer.

[70] Char. Com. Reg.

[71] Ex inf. Mr. G. T. Elmer, officer-in-charge, Winstone radio station.

[72] *Trans. B.G.A.S.* liii. 117, 130.

[73] R.C.H.M. *Glos.* i. 39–40.

[74] Ogilby, *Britannia* (1675), p. 29.

[75] Cirencester Roads Act, 20 Geo. II, c. 23.

[76] Cheltenham Roads Act, 25 Geo. III, c. 125.

[77] E 315/61 f. 26; S.C. 2/175/29 f. 2.

[78] *Kelly's Dir. Glos.* (1931), 140; (1935), 138.

[79] Glos. R.O., DC/E 88/2; O.S. Map 6″, Glos. XXXIV. SE. (1883 edn.).

[80] Verey, *Glos.* i. 203.

[81] S.C. 2/210/94.

[82] Bryant, *Map of Glos.* (1824); Glos. R.O., D 2820.

[83] G.D.R., T 1/63.

[84] Cf. Glos. R.O., DC/E 88/21; G.D.R., T 1/63.

[85] Dates and inits. on bldgs.

[86] Richardson, *Wells and Springs of Glos.* 78.

[87] Date and inits. on bldgs.

[88] Glos. R.O., PA 102/1.

[89] E 315/61 f. 25.

[90] Glos. R.O., DC/E 88/1/18; the man described as of the green in 1676 probably lived in Stockwell: cf. par. reg. 1676–1768; Glos. R.O., DC/E 88/18/1.

[91] Atkyns, *Glos.* 373.

[92] Glos. R.O., DC/E 88/14.

[93] Cf. Bryant, *Map of Glos.* (1824); O.S. Map 1″, sheet 44 (1828 edn.).

[94] Glos. R.O., DC/E 88/14, 21.

[95] Ibid. 26; cf. O.S. Map 6″, Glos. XXXIV. SE. (1924 edn.).

[96] G.D.R., T 1/63; O.S. Map 6″, Glos. XXXIV. SE. (1883 edn.).

[97] Glos. R.O., DC/E 88/13.

[98] Cf. ibid. 14.

[99] *Trans. B.G.A.S.* xcii. 177.

[1] O.S. Map 1″, sheet 44 (1828 edn.); *Licensed Houses in Glos. 1903*, 34–5.

[2] J.I. 1/278 rot. 53.

[3] Glos. R.O., D 1388/SL 5, no. 84; *Kelly's Dir. Glos.* (1870), 530; (1879), 627.

[4] *Dom. Bk.* (Rec. Com.), i. 166.

[5] *Glos. Subsidy Roll, 1327*, 10.

[6] E 179/113/31A rot. 2; E 179/113/35A rot. 13.

communicants in 1551[7] and 14 households in 1563,[8] but 95 communicants were recorded in 1603.[9] In 1650 there were said to be 67 families.[10] The population, which was estimated as 160 *c.* 1710,[11] had risen to 268 by *c.* 1775[12] and was 251 in 1801. By 1831 it had increased to 323 but it then fell to 293 by 1871 and to 269 by 1901. By 1911 it had risen to 317 but had dropped again to 221 by 1931. Aided by the addition in 1935 of part of Birdlip and by the use of Cowley Manor as a conference centre, it had reached a peak of 361 by 1951 but had fallen to 280 by 1971.[13]

MANOR. Pershore Abbey, which by 1086 held an estate comprising 5 hides at Cowley[14] and was granted free warren there in 1251,[15] retained the manor of *COWLEY* until the Dissolution.[16] In 1542 Cowley was granted with the abbey's property in Longney to the dean and chapter of Westminster[17] but William Blomer, to whom the abbey had granted a lease of that estate in 1538,[18] held Cowley until his death in 1554. William left the lease to his brother-in-law William Colley of Buscot (Berks.)[19] but in 1576 a member of the Blomer family farmed the manor.[20] In 1608, although Giles Blomer maintained a large household in Cowley, the lessee was apparently Frances (d. 1623), widow of Giles Bridges, Lord Chandos.[21]

In 1630 the dean and chapter granted the manor for three lives to Henry Brett,[22] a royalist who was fined for his sympathies.[23] In 1673 he took another lease for three lives, including that of his grandson Henry Brett,[24] who succeeded him as lord farmer of the manor at his death the following year[25] and was granted a similar lease in 1695 or 1696.[26] The younger Henry, who built residences at Cowley and Sandywell in Dowdeswell[27] and was a bell-ringing enthusiast, fell heavily into debt.[28] In return for an annuity and the payment of his debts he conveyed Cowley in 1721 to his son-in-law William Henry Morgan of Bristol[29] but was described as lord of the manor when he died in 1724.[30] The

following year the dean and chapter leased the manor for 21 years to his mortgagee, James Jennings. That lease was surrendered in 1727 in favour of Morgan who took another, for a similar term.[31] Morgan, who also fell into debt, sold that lease to Samuel Hawker of Rodborough, a clothier, in 1736,[32] and thereafter the dean and chapter renewed the lease every seven years.[33] Samuel (d. 1760)[34] was succeeded by his son George (d. 1786). George left the lease to his illegitimate son Joseph Hawker or Ockford who surrendered it in 1787 in favour of the mortgagee Thomas Arundell. Arundell sold the lease the following year to Theyer Townsend of Steanbridge House, Painswick (d. 1801), who left it to his brother Charles,[35] a gunpowder merchant living in Hackney (Mdx.). Charles (d. 1803) left it to a cousin, William Lawrence of Shurdington[36] (d. 1820),[37] whose son and heir, William Edwards Lawrence, was a minor. In 1829, following a Chancery suit, the trustees sold the lease to Lindsey Winterbotham and Edward Weedon, both then of Tewkesbury.[38] Winterbotham, a solicitor later involved in banking,[39] acquired sole interest in the lease in 1830[40] but the following year granted Weedon some copyhold land for three lives. In 1842, after Weedon's death, that land passed in freebench to his wife Mary who was said to own *c.* 545 a. in 1848. In 1853 the land was surrendered to James Hutchinson who had become lord farmer of the manor after Winterbotham *c.* 1852.[41]

Hutchinson, a London stock-broker, purchased the freehold from the dean and chapter in 1860 and enlarged the estate by purchasing the Cowley part (105 a.) of the Ivy Lodge estate (in Brimpsfield) in 1866 and land in Elkstone and Coberley.[42] He died in 1873[43] and the following year the estate of 1,870 a. was sold to Robert Richardson-Gardner, M.P. for Windsor (Berks.).[44] In 1882 it was bought by William Baring-Bingham[45] and in 1895 by James Horlick[46] (cr. Bt. 1914, d. 1921), the founder of the Horlick's Malted Milk Co. Horlick was succeeded by his son Sir Ernest Burford Horlick[47] who owned *c.* 2,920 a. in 1928 when the break-up of the estate

[7] *E.H.R.* xix. 114.
[8] Bodl. MS. Rawl. C.790, f. 10.
[9] *Eccl. Misc.* 81.
[10] *Trans. B.G.A.S.* lxxxiii. 93.
[11] Atkyns, *Glos.* 373.
[12] Rudder, *Glos.* 395.
[13] *Census*, 1801–1971.
[14] *Dom. Bk.* (Rec. Com.), i. 166.
[15] *Cal. Chart. R.* 1226–57, 365.
[16] *Valor Eccl.* (Rec. Com.), iii. 260.
[17] *L. & P. Hen. VIII*, xvii, p. 392; cf. *Cal. Pat.* 1555–7, 348–9; 1558–60, 397–8.
[18] S.C. 6/Hen. VIII/4057 rot. 6.
[19] C 142/106 no. 76; Hockaday Abs. cxc, Eastleach Martin 1554.
[20] G.D.R. vol. 40, f. 190.
[21] Smith, *Men and Armour*, 255, 257, where her lordships of Cowley and Coberley are interchanged; *Complete Peerage*, iii. 126–7.
[22] Westm. Abb. Mun. 8393.
[23] *Cal. Cttee. for Compounding*, ii. 1447–8; cf. Bigland, *Glos.* i. 493.
[24] Glos. R.O., DC/E 88/16.
[25] Bigland, *Glos.* i. 432; cf. Glos. R.O., DC/E 88/1/1–2.
[26] Glos. R.O., DC/E 88/16, deed 16 June 1725; 17, deed 10 Mar. 1721.
[27] Bigland, *Glos.* i. 484.
[28] Rudder, *Glos.* 394.
[29] Glos. R.O., DC/E 88/17; Wm. had married Henry's daughter Henrietta Brownlowe (d. 1718): inscr. in ch.
[30] G.D.R., V 1/76.
[31] Glos. R.O., DC/E 88/16–17.
[32] Westm. Abb. Mun. 55189–91; Glos. R.O., DC/E 88/17.
[33] Glos. R.O., DC/E 88/16.
[34] Bigland, *Glos.* iii, no. 219.
[35] Glos. R.O., DC/E 88/16–17; Rudge, *Hist. of Glos.* i. 301.
[36] Glos. Colln. SA 21.7; Glos. R.O., DC/E 88/17.
[37] *Glouc. Jnl.* 30 Oct. 1820.
[38] Glos. R.O., D 361/T 5; cf. ibid. DC/E 88/21.
[39] J. Stratford, *Glos. Biog. Notes* (Glouc. 1887), 288.
[40] Glos. R.O., D 361/T 4.
[41] Ibid. DC/E 88/4; G.D.R., T 1/63.
[42] Cf. Glos. Colln. (H)G 4.3; Glos. R.O., D 1388/SL 5, no. 84.
[43] Glos. R.O., DC/E 88, newspaper cutting of advert. dated 2 Feb. 1874.
[44] *Glouc. Jnl.* 13 June 1874.
[45] Cf. *Kelly's Dir. Glos.* (1879), 627; (1885), 437; Glos. Colln. RV 95.2.
[46] *Manual of Glos. Lit.* ii. 168.
[47] *Who Was Who, 1916–28*, 516; Burke, *Peerage* (1963), 1252.

began.[48] The house and some land, which were purchased by Sidney Allen,[49] had passed to Cyril Heber-Percy by 1937.[50] Gloucestershire county council bought the house with c. 618 a. in 1946 and retained 101.5 ha. (251 a.) in 1978.[51]

The footings, and possibly some of the outer walls, of the house built by Henry Brett in 1695[52] survive beneath the main block of Cowley Manor, an Italianate house which James Hutchinson built to the designs of G. Somers Clarke c. 1855.[53] That house, like its predecessor, had main fronts of five bays and was three storeys high.[54] There was a covered colonnade on the south which extended beyond the house along the front and side of a conservatory on the east and along part of the front of a two-storeyed wing on the west. North of the wing were service quarters, partly of three storeys.[55] In the late 1890s James Horlick demolished the two-storeyed range, extended the earlier house westwards by six bays, and enlarged the service wing. R. A. Briggs was the architect for that work and the interiors were lavishly panelled with hardwoods and the main ceilings were richly decorated.[56] About 1930 Sidney Allen created a new entrance hall, removing Horlick's staircase and replacing it with one in mid-18th-century style, but by 1934 the house was unoccupied.[57] Cyril Heber-Percy, who c. 1937 refitted some of the rooms, his additions including a glass-walled bathroom in the 'modern' style, was probably responsible for removing most of the decorated ceilings. The house, which was leased to Cheltenham Ladies' College during the Second World War,[58] was used by the county council as a conference centre and for social events in 1978.[59] The pleasure grounds laid out by Hutchinson south of the house included a terrace and an ornamental pond linked to the Churn below by a cascade.[60]

Land in Cowley granted c. 1240 to St. Bartholomew's Hospital, Gloucester, has not been traced.[61]

ECONOMIC HISTORY. In 1086 the demesne of Cowley manor supported 5 *servi* working 2 plough-teams.[62] One of the two people assessed for tax in Cowley in 1327 was a cowherd[63] and in the mid 14th century ploughmen and drivers of plough-teams, shepherds, and a dairymaid earned wages on the estate. In October 1349 three shepherds received allowances of corn but the account for that year recorded no sheep in stock.[64] The inhabitants of Cowley and Stockwell in 1381 included a cowherd and a shepherd.[65] Pershore Abbey had let the demesne by 1422.[66]

The tenants recorded at Cowley in 1086 were 14 *villani* and a bordar working 7 ploughs[67] and in the early 13th century they included a shepherd at Stockwell, who owed labour-services at the usual agricultural tasks.[68] From 1360 a tenement was held by the annual service of providing an arrow.[69] Copyhold tenure was recorded in the early 16th century,[70] and the 13 husbandmen listed in the parish in 1608 probably included tenants holding by copy.[71] In 1713 there were 21 copyhold tenements, 16 of which comprised 1 yardland or less and the largest 4½ yardlands.[72] Those tenements were granted by the lord farmer for terms of three lives. In the 18th century large copyhold estates were built up by James Pitt of Gloucester and his son John, and by the Revd. Thomas Baghot (d. 1762), who became rector of Naunton and Dumbleton.[73] In 1778 copyhold land covered 898 a., of which 132 a. were in hand and the remainder in 17 holdings ranging in size from one of 13 perches to one of 342 a. held by John Pitt with other copyholds of 95 a. and 4 a. Thomas Baghot held 222 a. and four other tenants 20–25 a. each. The demesne, which covered 652 a., included a farm of 513 a. let to the Humphris family. Cottages and a mill were part of 39 a. held on leases for lives.[74]

An agreement of c. 1268 allowed intensive cultivation by Pershore Abbey of part of an arable field, called Nether Cowley, north of Cowley village. Under the agreement the abbey retained the right to inclose a third of the field when fallow temporarily in an 'inhook' for its own use and granted Giles of Berkeley, lord of Coberley manor, and his men common rights in the other two-thirds.[75] That grant might be the reason why in 1848 three small areas of land by the Churn were said to be open.[76] Outside the valley, open fields and commons occupied much of the land. In the mid 13th century there were a south and a west field.[77] In 1673 the open-field land was contained in five areas, a north and a south field at Cowley, a north and a south field at Stockwell, and a field north of Birdlip. The pasture rights in those fields, which were stinted, were used primarily for sheep,[78] and

---

[48] Glos. R.O., DC/E 88/23; *Glouc. Jnl.* 27 Oct. 1928.
[49] *Kelly's Dir. Glos.* (1931), 140.
[50] Burke, *Land. Gent.* (1937), 1792.
[51] Ex inf. county land agent and valuer.
[52] Par. reg. 1676–1768.
[53] Verey, *Glos.* i 203; watercolour impression of Cowley Man., apparently from Clarke's plans, by Thomas Shotter Boys: Glos. R.O., PA 102/7, pp. 29, 46–7.
[54] Cf. Bodl. MS. Top. Glouc. c. 3, f. 214v.; Glos. R.O., DC/E 88/11, 13.
[55] Glos. R.O., D 1388/SL 5, no. 84; Glos. Colln. (H)G 4.2–3.
[56] *Country Life*, 4 Aug. 1906, 164–9; undated print, *penes* the warden, Cowley Man., reproduced below, plate facing p. 204.
[57] *Kelly's Dir. Glos.* (1935), 138.
[58] Glos. R.O., DC/E 88/29; *Glos. and Avon Life*, Feb. 1975, 29.
[59] Ex inf. the warden.   [60] Glos. R.O., D 1388/SL 5, no. 84.

[61] *Glouc. Corp. Rec.* p. 172.
[62] *Dom. Bk.* (Rec. Com.), i. 166.
[63] *Glos. Subsidy Roll, 1327*, 10.
[64] S.C. 6/853/13; S.C. 6/853/14.
[65] E 179/113/31A rot. 2.
[66] S.C. 6/853/15; cf. S.C. 6/853/31; S.C. 6/Hen. VII/240.
[67] *Dom. Bk.* (Rec. Com.), i. 166.
[68] *Cat. Anct. D.* iii, D 209.
[69] Dugdale, *Mon.* ii. 422.
[70] S.C. 2/175/29 f. 2.
[71] Smith, *Men armour*, 255.
[72] Glos. R.O., DC/E 88/22.
[73] Ibid. 2, 10; for the Baghots, see *Visit. Glos. 1682–3*, 6.
[74] Glos. R.O., D 1388/SL 3, no. 12.
[75] E 315/61 f. 26; cf. J.I. 1/275 rot. 8.
[76] G.D.R., T 1/63.   [77] E 315/61 f. 26.
[78] Glos. R.O., DC/E 88/1/1.

court rolls contain evidence of sheep-farming in the early 16th century when two sheep-houses were mentioned.[79] In 1652 Cowley Downs, the main common pasture, lay in two parts, the lower and the upper downs, north and south of Cowley wood respectively.[80] In the early 18th century that common was opened on 14 May[81] and was grazed by cows and sheep in alternate years. In 1736 its area was 121 a.[82] Another common pasture recorded in 1652 was Conygers hill in the southeast,[83] and in the later 17th century at least three tenants apparently shared common rights in the Ox Pasture, south-west of Cowley wood, and the Moors, which were opened by agreement.[84] In 1762 there were in the parish six common pastures, including two quarries, covering 39 a. The largest, Barrow Wake, then called the Woolpits, comprised 26 a. and a small common called Yew Tree bank, at the top of Birdlip hill, 2 a.[85]

Some inclosure took place in the 1720s and early 1730s when the lord farmer was consolidating the demesne and laying it down as pasture.[86] In 1727 the rector granted him the open-field land belonging to the glebe for a term in return for a piece of land north of the village. Cowley Downs and the remainder of the two Cowley fields were inclosed in 1739 by agreement between the lord farmer and seven copyholders. The lord farmer took the downs in severalty while the largest allotment (230 a.) in the fields went to the Revd. Thomas Baghot. Thomas Welles, rector of Cowley, received 44 a. for copyhold land and four tenants 27 a., 23 a., 10 a., and 3 a. respectively. The seventh allotment, 2½ a. of pasture in the lower downs,[87] was surrendered the following year.[88] The Stockwell and Birdlip open fields, which provided common pasture for sheep until at least 1787, were inclosed by the lord farmer following the surrender of much of the copyhold land there in the late 1780s and early 1790s.[89] A small area north of Birdlip Farm in Birdlip remained uninclosed in 1828[90] but by 1848 the parish had been completely inclosed apart from the commons at Barrow Wake and the top of Birdlip hill and the three small areas by the Churn.[91]

At the inclosure of the Stockwell and Birdlip open fields the lord farmer created consolidated farms[92] but the land remained copyhold until 1875 when 976 a. were enfranchised.[93] The principal farms on the Cowley estate in 1802 covered 470 a., 419 a., 284 a., 154 a., and 83 a.,[94] and in 1828 723 a., 345 a., 285 a., and 157 a.[95] In the later 19th century most of the parish, apart from land farmed from Highgate Farm in Elkstone, was included in three large farms, Manor, Stockwell, and Birdlip farms. Respectively they comprised 511 a., 471 a., and 311 a. in 1859,[96] and 489 a., 484 a., and 416 a. in 1881.[97] From the later 1890s they were taken in hand but were let again after the First World War.[98] In 1926, when 24 agricultural labourers found full-time employment in the parish, there was another farm of over 150 a. and five smallholdings with less than 20 a. each.[99] Manor farm was broken up during the sale of the estate in the later 1920s.[1]

In the early 18th century the land was chiefly in tillage[2] but in the 1720s and early 1730s some was converted to pasture[3] and large herds of cattle were kept. Tillage still predominated, however, c. 1775,[4] and in 1839 there was a flock of c. 400 sheep on Stockwell farm.[5] In 1848 arable covered 1,128 a. and meadow and pasture 520 a.,[6] but in the later 19th century and early 20th the area returned as under crops, mainly cereals and roots, decreased by over 300 a. and the area of recorded permanent grassland rose from 472 a. in 1866 to 998 a. in 1926.[7] Many sheep were kept in the later 19th century[8] and James Horlick established a flock of Oxford Down sheep and also introduced a herd of shorthorn cattle.[9] The number of dairy cattle returned for the parish increased from 141 in 1896 to 350 in 1926.[10] In 1976 dairying was important on three of the four farms returned for the enlarged parish.[11]

There was a mill at Cowley in 1086.[12] In the mid 13th century a corn- and fulling-mill, apparently on the Churn, was granted by Pershore Abbey, with the suit of mill owed by the Cowley inhabitants, to a Coberley fuller for 12s. a year,[13] and the abbey recovered it from the widow of a walker in 1325.[14] A corn-mill working in the parish in the early 16th century[15] was presumably on the site of the mill recorded south of the church on a short tributary of the Churn in 1777.[16] That mill, which had a bakehouse among its out-buildings in 1793,[17] was in use in 1848[18] but was demolished in the mid 1850s during the landscaping of the grounds of Cowley Manor.[19]

[79] S.C. 2/175/28 rot. 2; S.C. 2/176/21.
[80] C 54/3672 no. 19; G.D.R., T 1/63.
[81] Glos. R.O., DC/E 88/2.   [82] Ibid. 22.
[83] C 54/3672 no. 19.
[84] Glos. R.O., DC/E 88/1/18; E 88/2; G.D.R., T 1/63.
[85] Glos. R.O., DC/E 88/10; 17, deed 29 Sept. 1829; G.D.R., T 1/63.
[86] C 78/1778 no. 6.
[87] Glos. R.O., DC/E 88/17.
[88] Ibid. E 88/18/13.   [89] Ibid. E 88/2.
[90] Ibid. 21.
[91] G.D.R., T 1/63.
[92] Glos. R.O., DC/E 88/14.
[93] Ibid. 4; D 1388/SL 5, no. 84.
[94] Ibid. DC/E 88/14.
[95] Ibid. 21.   [96] Ibid. 27.
[97] Glos. Colln. (H)G 4.2.
[98] Kelly's Dir. Glos. (1894 and later edns.), s.v. Birdlip and Cowley.

[99] M.A.F. 68/3295/3.
[1] Cf. Glos. R.O., DC/E 88/23.
[2] Atkyns, Glos. 373.   [3] C 78/1778 no. 6.
[4] Rudder, Glos. 394.
[5] Glos. R.O., D 2202.   [6] G.D.R., T 1/63.
[7] M.A.F. 68/25/17; M.A.F. 68/1609/1; M.A.F. 68/3295/3.
[8] M.A.F. 68/25/8; M.A.F. 68/1609/1.
[9] Country Life, 4 Aug. 1906, 168; Glos. Colln. RV 95.2; ibid. cuttings of obituaries 1917–55, entry 14 May 1921.
[10] M.A.F. 68/1609/1; M.A.F. 68/3295/3.
[11] Agric. Returns 1976.   [12] Dom. Bk. (Rec. Com.), i. 166.
[13] E 315/61 f. 26.
[14] C.P. 40/268 rot. 17d.
[15] S.C. 2/175/28 rott. 2–4; cf. Glos. R.O., DC/E 88/22.
[16] Taylor, Map of Glos. (1777); cf. Richardson, Wells and Springs of Glos. 79.
[17] Glouc. Jnl. 10 June 1793.
[18] G.D.R., T 1/63.
[19] Glos. R.O., DC/E 88/4.

There was possibly a small cloth industry in Cowley in the 14th century when several inhabitants were surnamed walker.[20] By 1478 a tenement had been called Tuckers[21] and a weaver was listed in Cowley in 1608 when four badgers, a tailor, and a mason, some of whom probably lived in Birdlip, also carried on their trades in the parish.[22] In 1978 the sites of several quarries were visible near the top of the escarpment, where stone was being quarried by the mid 18th century[23] and where the main 19th-century quarries were located.[24] One at the top of Birdlip Hill was worked by Henry Arkell in 1828[25] and closed c. 1908.[26] There were limekilns on Barrow Wake in the later 19th century.[27]

In 1831 58 families in the parish were supported by agriculture and 11 by trade.[28] Outside Birdlip the trades followed were those usual for a rural parish[29] but they died out in the later 19th century.[30] Estate workshops in the northern part of Cowley village in the 1920s included a smithy and a saw-mill.[31] In the early 20th century the village usually had a bakery and a post office.[32]

LOCAL GOVERNMENT. View of frankpledge was exercised at Pershore Abbey's court in Cowley under a charter of 1227, which also granted the abbey and its estates exemption from hundred and shire courts, certain pleas including *murdrum*, and tallages, but in 1287 the abbey used instruments of punishment belonging to the lord of the hundred at Cirencester.[33] In the early 16th century the Cowley frankpledge court, which appointed a tithingman and a constable and also acted as a court baron, dealt with assaults, affrays, strays, the state of roads, the sale of meat and victuals, the brewing of ale, and the levying of toll at the mill.[34] By the late 17th century the lord farmer held the full court in October and convened separate courts baron when required. In 1703 a deodand was presented in the frankpledge court,[35] which appointed separate overseers of the commons for Cowley with Birdlip and for Stockwell in 1673[36] and sheep-tellers for the Stockwell and Birdlip fields from the 1730s. The court, which from 1757 periodically recorded the manor's boundaries, appointed a constable and a hayward in the 19th century, when it dealt mainly with tenurial matters and quarrying on common land. In 1875 it met at the George in Birdlip[37] which had probably been its meeting-place in 1785.[38] Court rolls survive for 1501–12[39] and 1526–37;[40] there are draft court rolls from 1673[41] and court books covering the period 1703–1875.[42]

By 1498 the parish was served by two churchwardens[43] but in the early 19th century there was only one. Their accounts survive for the period 1745–1839 and there are overseers' accounts for the years 1737–40 and 1742. In those years seven or eight people received regular help and in 1742 a woman was paid £1 for being overseer for a year. There were two overseers in 1770.[44] Expenditure on poor-relief fell from £84 in 1776 to c. £75 by 1784, but £214, a high figure for the size of the parish, was spent in 1803 when 13 people received regular and 10 occasional help. By 1813, when all but two of the 35 people relieved received regular aid, the cost was £361 but two years later it had almost returned to the level of 1803 although the numbers were virtually unchanged.[45] In the late 1820s, when the overseers rented some accommodation for the poor,[46] the average annual cost of relief was £156 but in the early 1830s it rose to £215.[47] Cowley became part of the Cheltenham poor-law union in 1835[48] and was later in Cheltenham rural district.[49] In 1974 it was included in Tewkesbury district.

CHURCH. The fabric of Cowley church dates from the early 13th century and its priest was recorded c. 1242.[50] In 1291 the living was in the gift of Pershore Abbey.[51] The abbey was later licensed to appropriate the church[52] but the living was a rectory in 1342 and has remained one.[53] Cowley was joined, under an order of 1928, to the united benefice of Coberley with Colesbourne in 1937[54] but Colesbourne was detached from the living in 1954.[55]

Pershore Abbey retained the patronage of Cowley rectory until the Dissolution and in 1542 William Clark and Nicholas Butler were patrons for one turn under a grant from the abbey. Later

[20] C.P. 40/268 rot. 17d.; S.C. 6/853/14; E 179/113/31A rot. 2.
[21] S.C. 6/853/32.
[22] Smith, *Men and Armour*, 255.
[23] Glos. R.O., DC/E 88/2, ct. 27 Oct. 1772; E 88/10.
[24] Ibid. 17, deed 29 Sept. 1829; O.S. Map 6″, Glos. XXXIV. NE. and SW. (1883 edns.).
[25] Glos. R.O., DC/E 88/21; cf. ibid. 27.
[26] Cf. O.S. Map 6″, Glos. XXXIV. SW. (1903 and 1924 edns.); *Kelly's Dir. Glos.* (1906), 134; (1910), 138.
[27] Glos. R.O., DC/E 88/27; D 1388/SL 5, no. 84.
[28] *Census*, 1831.
[29] Glos. R.O., DC/E 88/18/5, 14; E 88/14; par. reg. of baptisms from 1813.
[30] *Kelly's Dir. Glos.* (1856–89 edns.).
[31] O.S. Map 6″, Glos. XXXIV. SE. (1924 edn.); Glos. R.O., D 2299/1109; DC/E 88/23.
[32] *Kelly's Dir. Glos.* (1889 and later edns.); Glos. R.O., PA 102/1.
[33] *Plac. de Quo Warr.* (Rec. Com.), 259–60.
[34] S.C. 2/175/28–9.
[35] Glos. R.O., DC/E 88/1–2.
[36] Ibid. 1/1.

[37] Ibid. E 88/2–4.
[38] Ibid. 9.
[39] S.C. 2/175/28–9; S.C. 2/176/21; S.C. 2/214/69.
[40] S.C. 2/175/30; S.C. 2/210/87–91; S.C. 2/210/94.
[41] Glos. R.O., DC/E 88/1.
[42] Ibid. 2–4.
[43] Hockaday Abs. xxii, 1498 visit. f. 29; xlvii, 1576 visit. f. 98; G.D.R., V 5/95T 1.
[44] Churchwardens' acct. bk. 1745–1839, *penes* the rector, the Revd. S. I. Pulford.
[45] *Poor Law Abstract, 1804*, 180–1; *1818*, 154–5.
[46] Glos. R.O., DC/E 88/21.
[47] *Poor Law Returns* (1830–1), p. 70; (1835), p. 69.
[48] *Poor Law Com. 2nd Rep.* p. 522.   [49] *Census*, 1971.
[50] *Cat. Anct. D.* iii, D 209; *V.C.H. Worcs.* ii. 136.
[51] *Reg. Giffard*, 382.
[52] *Cal. Papal Regs.* v. 118; C 143/432 no. 2.
[53] *Inq. Non.* (Rec. Com.), 408; *Reg. Bransford*, p. 93; Worc. Episc. Reg., Reg. Peverell, f. 71.
[54] *Lond. Gaz.* 7 Feb. 1928, pp. 835–6; *Kelly's Dir. Glos.* (1931 and later edns.), s.v. Colesborne, Cowley, and Cubberley.
[55] *Glouc. Dioc. Yr. Bk.* (1978), 29.

presentations were made by the Crown. Frances Bridges, Lady Chandos, presented to the living in 1619 but her presentee was evidently dispossessed soon afterwards. By the mid 18th century the Crown appointed through the Lord Chancellor,[56] who under the order of 1928 had the right to present at every third vacancy in the united benefice[57] and after 1954 at every other turn.[58]

In 1291 Pershore Abbey had a portion valued at £1 2s. 6d. in the Cowley tithes[59] but later the rector took all the tithes.[60] In 1739 the lord farmer of the manor took a lease of most of the tithes,[61] and in 1797 the rector received £206 2s. a year in composition for all save the wood tithes, which were worth £2 to him.[62] The tithes were commuted in 1848 for a corn-rent-charge of £310.[63] In 1729 the rector consolidated the glebe for the remainder of his incumbency by exchanging 19 pieces in the open fields for 64½ a. north of the village, and that exchange was evidently made permanent by the inclosure of 1739.[64] The glebe, which was rented by neighbouring farmers by the later 18th century,[65] comprised c. 78½ a., including a cottage, in 1848.[66] James Horlick bought 65½ a. in 1900[67] and Sidney Allen most of the remainder in 1932.[68] The living was worth £5 in 1291[69] and £8 7s. 9d. in 1535,[70] but the value was reckoned to be £60 in 1650 when a union with Coberley rectory was recommended.[71] In 1750 the living was worth £140[72] and by 1856 the value had risen to £322.[73]

The rectory house, which was out of repair in 1690,[74] was evidently derelict in 1742 when the site was given to the lord farmer as part of an exchange. The rector was allowed to remove material for building a new rectory.[75] The new house, south-west of the cross, was enlarged by James Commeline in 1797.[76] Between 1822 and 1870 it was occupied by curates[77] but it had fallen into such disrepair by 1838 that alterations were needed to render it habitable.[78] It was sold to Sidney Allen in 1932 and became the farm-house for Manor farm.[79] The rector then lived in Colesbourne[80] but by 1978 the incumbent of the united benefice had moved to Coberley rectory.

John Rivet, rector 1453–61, was a doctor of laws.[81] William Compton, rector from 1530,[82] employed curates, including a former Franciscan[83] whom John Bromwich, rector from 1542, retained for a few years. Bromwich, who was also rector of Abberton (Worcs.),[84] was non-resident and his curates included one who could not repeat the Ten Commandments[85] and another who in 1572 also served Elkstone.[86] Bromwich, who had become rector of Rous Lench (Worcs.) by 1576,[87] was succeeded at Cowley in 1582 by Thomas Paine, who lived in Syde where he was also rector.[88] In 1588 the uncertain circumstances of Paine's resignation delayed the induction of his successor. James Ingram, D.D., who held Cowley in plurality with Whittington from 1639, had been ejected by 1652 when his curate apparently succeeded to the rectory. Ingram had been reinstated by 1662.[89] Nathanial Lye, rector from 1673, became rector of Kemerton in 1675 but served Cowley in person for a time.[90] Later Lye employed a curate[91] and resigned Cowley in 1717, a few years after his appointment as archdeacon of Gloucester and rector of Dursley.[92] Thomas Welles, rector 1724–63, lived in Prestbury but served in person. Other 18th-century incumbents usually held livings some distance from Cowley and appointed curates. Between 1776 and 1796 the cure was served for several rectors by Thomas Nash, D.D.,[93] rector of Great Witcombe[94] and for much of that time also curate of Coberley.[95] James Commeline, rector from 1796, served in person until 1800 when he became rector of Redmarley D'Abitot (Worcs., later Glos.).[96] His successor Robert Smith, rector 1837–70, lived in or near Gloucester and employed curates.[97]

The church of *ST. MARY*, so called by 1743[98] although it bore a dedication to St. Michael c. 1708,[99] is built partly of ashlar and partly of rubble and has a chancel, nave with south porch, and west tower. The font is of the 12th century but the earliest parts of the building are the nave and the third bay of the chancel, which date from the early 13th century and retain most of their lancet

[56] Hockaday Abs. clxxii; G.D.R. vol. 397, f. 25; 384, f. 72.
[57] *Lond. Gaz.* 7 Feb. 1928, p. 836; *Kelly's Dir. Glos.* (1939), 139.
[58] *Glouc. Dioc. Yr. Bk.* (1978), 29.
[59] *Tax. Eccl.* (Rec. Com.), 221.
[60] *Valor Eccl.* (Rec. Com.), ii. 496; cf. ibid. iii. 260.
[61] Glos. R.O., D 361/T 5.
[62] Hockaday Abs. clxxii.
[63] G.D.R., T 1/63.
[64] Glos. R.O., DC/E 88/17; cf. ibid. 10; G.D.R., T 1/63.
[65] Churchwardens' acct. bk. 1745–1839; Glos. R.O., D 1347, Cowley deed; D 1381/49; Glos. Colln. (H)G 4.3.
[66] G.D.R., T 1/63.
[67] Glos. Colln. RV 95.2.
[68] Glos. R.O., D 2299/4035, 4734.
[69] *Tax. Eccl.* (Rec. Com.), 221.
[70] *Valor Eccl.* (Rec. Com.), ii. 496.
[71] *Trans. B.G.A.S.* lxxxiii. 93.
[72] G.D.R. vol. 381A, f. 25.
[73] G.D.R. vol. 384, f. 72.
[74] Glos. R.O., DC/E 88/1/14.
[75] Ibid. E 88/17.
[76] Hockaday Abs. clxxii; Bryant, *Map of Glos.* (1824).
[77] Hockaday Abs. clxxii; *Kelly's Dir. Glos.* (1856–79 edns.).
[78] G.D.R., F 4/1.
[79] Glos. R.O., D 2299/4035; D 2820.

[80] *Kelly's Dir. Glos.* (1935–9 edns.), s.v. Colesborne and Cowley.
[81] Worc. Episc. Reg., Reg. Carpenter, i, ff. 112v., 159v.
[82] Ibid. Reg. Ghinucci, f. 44.
[83] Hockaday Abs. xxv, 1532 subsidy, f. 15; xxviii, 1540 visit. f. 47; *Trans. B.G.A.S.* xlix. 96.
[84] Hockaday Abs. xxx, 1544 stipendiaries, f. 15; clxxii.
[85] *E.H.R.* xix. 114.
[86] Hockaday Abs. clxxii, in which Cowley has several times been confused with Coaley.
[87] Ibid. xlvii, 1576 visit. f. 98; G.D.R. vol. 40, f. 190.
[88] Hockaday Abs. clxxii; xlix, state of clergy 1584, f. 29.
[89] Ibid. clxxii; *Walker Revised*, ed. Matthews, 175.
[90] Hockaday Abs. clxxii; G.D.R., V 1/76.
[91] Par. reg. 1676–1768.
[92] Kirby, *Cat. of Glouc. Dioc. Rec.* i. 132; Bigland, *Glos.* i. 515.
[93] Hockaday Abs. clxxii; G.D.R., V 1/76; Glos. R.O., DC/E 88/17.
[94] Bigland, *Glos.* iii, no. 304.
[95] Glos. R.O., D 269B/F 13.
[96] Hockaday Abs. clxxii; G.D.R., V 1/76; G.D.R. vol. 383, no. ccxxvi.
[97] Hockaday Abs. clxxii; G.D.R. vol. 384, f. 72; *Kelly's Dir. Glos.* (1856–79 edns.).
[98] G.D.R. vol. 397, f. 25.
[99] Bodl. MS. Top. Glouc. c.3, f. 214.

windows. The first two bays of the chancel and the lower stages of the tower are a little later in date. There is no chancel arch and it may be that the chancel was extended or rebuilt so that it encroached on the former first bay of the nave. The porch was added in the 15th century as were a rood-stair in the north wall and a window in the west wall of the nave. The upper stages of the tower and the stair turret against the north side were added in the late 15th or early 16th century. The nave was probably reroofed in the 17th century but the chancel was reroofed in 1872 when the church was restored to designs by Albert Hartshorne.[1]

The church has the bowl of a Norman font on a modern base, and a late medieval carved stone pulpit. The most notable monument is an early-14th-century effigy of a priest in a recess on the north wall of the chancel.[2] There were three bells before Henry Brett added three cast by Abraham Rudhall in 1697. Of the original bells one was recast by Rudhall in 1707, another by John Rudhall in 1812, and the third by C. & G. Mears of London in 1857.[3] The plate includes a chalice of 1607 and a paten of 1699.[4] The surviving registers begin in 1676.[5]

NONCONFORMITY. A house in Cowley parish was registered by protestant dissenters in 1741[6] and a Quaker lived in the parish in 1762.[7] A house registered by John Moss of Cheltenham in 1831[8] was for Baptists[9] whose Easter meeting in 1851 had an attendance of 41.[10]

EDUCATION. A school-house was recorded in 1777[11] but a day-school and a Sunday school, which were supported by voluntary contributions, had closed by 1818 because parents failed to send their children.[12] In 1825 40 children in the parish attended a school.[13] A day-school, begun in 1831 and supported partly by the principal landholder, possibly Lindsey Winterbotham, and the rector, taught 15–20 children in 1833. At that date another day-school, possibly in Birdlip, teaching 10–20 children depended for financial support solely on the parents.[14] In 1847 a dame-school in Cowley, supported by pence, was attended by 16 children.[15]

Cowley Parochial school, established in 1873, derived an income from voluntary contributions and pence and had an average attendance of 33 the following year. It met in the cottage belonging to the rector's glebe[16] until 1875 when it moved to a new building erected with a school-house by Robert Richardson-Gardner. The school, rebuilt by James Horlick in 1900,[17] had 30 pupils c. 1910 when it was called Cowley C. of E. school. It closed in 1920[18] and the children were transferred to Coberley.[19] The school building later became the village hall.[20]

CHARITIES FOR THE POOR. Theyer Townsend by will proved 1802 left £100 stock for a distribution of bread in Cowley on St. Thomas's day.[21] The rector, who distributed the charity in food, fuel, or clothing in the early 19th century, bought woollen stockings for children attending Sunday school in 1827[22] but by 1856 the income was distributed in cash.[23] James Hutchinson by will proved 1873 left £200 for the poor.[24] The incomes of the two charities were £6 and £8 respectively in 1971. By then their trustees had established a reserve fund for use in emergencies[25] and by 1978 the number of old-age pensioners receiving cash payments had fallen to three.[26]

CRANHAM

CRANHAM, a rural parish with extensive woodland and scattered settlement, lies 9 km. south-east of Gloucester and has in the 20th century become a residential area for people working in near-by towns. The ancient parish, once part of Brimpsfield, was irregular in shape and included the sources of the Painswick stream and the Overtown brook, which flow south-westwards in deep narrow valleys. The valley of the Painswick stream, the head of which was known as Ladlecombe by 1539,[27] was called Ledecome in a description of the boundaries of an estate to the north-west in 1121 and the stream, below its confluence with the brook, was possibly the Salcumesbroca of the perambulation. Cranham's northern boundary followed the crest of the Cotswold escarpment, part of which was called Witcombe's edge or hedge in 1121, and a track across a spur at High Brotheridge in the northern corner, and it then included three landmarks:[28] a beech tree, a place of execution, was

[1] Verey, Glos. i. 202; Kelly's Dir. Glos. (1885), 437.
[2] Roper, Glos. Effigies, 384–5.
[3] Bodl. MS. Top. Glouc. c.3, f. 214v.; Glos. Ch. Bells, 43, s.v. Coaley.
[4] Glos. Ch. Plate, 65.
[5] B. & G. Par. Rec. 112.
[6] Hockaday Abs. clxxii.
[7] Glos. R.O., DC/E 88/10.   [8] Hockaday Abs. clxxii.
[9] Cf. ibid. clxxiii, Cranham 1840; H.O. 129/338/2/6/13.
[10] H.O. 129/344/1/7/11.
[11] Glos. R.O., DC/E 88/13.
[12] Educ. of Poor Digest, 296.
[13] G.D.R. vol. 383, no. ccxxvi.
[14] Educ. Enquiry Abstract, 312.

[15] Church School Inquiry, 1846–7, 8–9.
[16] Ed. 7/37/95.
[17] Kelly's Dir. Glos. (1889), 750; (1906), 134; O.S. Map 6″, Glos. XXXIV. SE. (1883 edn.).
[18] Bd. of Educ., List 21, 1911 (H.M.S.O.), 160; 1922, 103.
[19] Kelly's Dir. Glos. (1923), 142; (1927), 148.
[20] Glos. R.O., PA 102/1.
[21] Glos. R.O., DC/E 88/17.
[22] 21st Rep. Com. Char. 168.
[23] Kelly's Dir. Glos. (1856), 274.
[24] Ibid. (1879), 627; Char. Com. Reg.
[25] Glos. R.O., CH 21.   [26] Ex inf. the rector.
[27] S.C. 11/1022 rot. 2. This account was written in 1978.
[28] Hist. & Cart. Mon. Glouc. (Rolls Ser.), i. 205.

probably by that track; the tree called Prinknash[29] was probably at the road junction called Prinknash Cross or Prinknash (later Cranham) Corner;[30] and *Idel Berge*, a barrow of which no trace is visible, was at the north-western corner. The northern boundary was the subject of a perambulation, requested in 1254, between a Cranham estate and Philip of Matson's land, presumably Pope's wood, now in Upton St. Leonards but formerly part of Matson.[31] The bank forming part of the eastern boundary of the parish probably marked the earlier limit of Hazel Hanger wood in Brimpsfield. Elsewhere the Cranham boundaries followed field boundaries and streams, including in the south-east a tributary of the river Frome.

The parish comprised 1,856 a.[32] in area after 1882 when Cranham absorbed a small detached part of Painswick in the south-west, where an open field had been shared by the two parishes.[33] In 1885 detached portions of Miserden and Bisley, containing 55 a. at Wateredge to the south-east and 3 a. east of Wateredge, were added to Cranham,[34] which retained 774 ha. (1,914 a.) in 1978.[35] The following description refers to the ancient parish as it was before 1882.

Outside the valleys the parish lies almost exclusively above the 152-m. contour on ground rising to over 274 m. at High Brotheridge and in the eastern part and to over 259 m. at Saltridge hill in the south-western corner. Most of the high land is on the Inferior Oolite but in places there are deposits of fuller's earth and the Great Oolite. The valley bottoms lie on Midford Sand, from the base of which issue many springs, but in those of the Painswick stream and the Overtown brook Upper Lias clay is exposed.[36]

Beech woods form the major feature of the landscape especially on the steep slopes in the north but the land on the high south-eastern plateau is suited to arable, and in the south-western part, an area of early inclosure, meadow land and pasture predominate. The extensive woodland recorded as Buckholt from the late 11th century extends into adjacent parishes[37] and includes large tracts subject by 1338 to common pasture rights.[38] The woods on the Brimpsfield estate, from which 76 trees were sold in the year 1379–80,[39] were a regular source of firewood for St. Sepulchre's Hospital, Gloucester, from the later 12th century[40] and Llanthony Priory from 1477.[41] In the mid 16th century a Gloucester tanner felled trees in Climperwell wood, lying partly in Brimpsfield on the south-eastern boundary.[42] Later that century copyhold tenants on the dean and chapter's estate were using oaks, ashes, and elms to repair houses, ploughs, and fences or, if the trees were dead, as firewood.[43] In the later 18th century the woods supplied timber for gun-stocks sold in Birmingham and for charcoal;[44] charcoal-burning continued in the later 19th century.[45] In 1901 c. 628 a., about a third of the parish, was covered by woodland and plantations[46] which provided much timber during the Second World War.[47]

The common woodland included those areas which became Cranham common in the centre of the parish, Saltridge common wood in the south, Cranham wood in the east, and Buckholt wood in the north (also known in the north-western corner as Short wood).[48] In the mid 17th century common rights in Buckholt wood were enjoyed by the inhabitants of Cranham, Brimpsfield, Birdlip, Brockworth, Upton St. Leonards, and Witcombe.[49] The common woods and the common that had been left when the woodland had been cleared were guarded against encroachments during the 19th century. In 1868 the commoners demolished several walls, erected during Robert Bartholomew Lawes's rebuilding of Cranham Lodge near the eastern boundary, as the area inclosed was larger than that which had been agreed.[50] Cranham common retained c. 105 a. in 1921[51] and in all c. 453 a. of the parish were commonable in the mid 20th century.[52]

The Port way from Gloucester ascended the escarpment to Cranham Corner where several routes branched off across the parish. That to Birdlip became part of the route between Painswick and Cheltenham which was turnpiked in 1785.[53] The section between Painswick and Cranham Corner was moved to the south-east shortly before 1820[54] when the new road from Cranham Corner through Shurdington to Cheltenham was completed.[55] The junction with the Port way was moved south-westwards shortly before 1853[56] when the Gloucester–Birdlip road through Cranham Corner was included in a turnpike.[57] At Cranham Lodge that route's course was diverted to the north in 1889.[58] A road in the south-eastern

[29] *P.N. Glos.* (E.P.N.S.), ii. 170.
[30] *Cal. Pat.* 1377–81, 547; O.S. Map 6″, Glos. XXXIV. SW. (1924 edn.).
[31] *Close R.* 1253–4, 121; Glos. R.O., Q/SRh 1787 C/2.
[32] *O.S. Area Bk.* (1885).
[33] *Census*, 1891; cf. G.D.R., T 1/64; *Inq. p.m. Glos.* 1625–42, i. 71.
[34] *Census*, 1891; cf. *O.S. Area Bk.* Miserden (1885); Bisley (1885).
[35] *Census*, 1971.
[36] Geol. Surv. Map 1″, solid, sheet 44 (1856 edn.).
[37] *Hist. & Cart. Mon. Glouc.* i. 63, 196, 205, 244.
[38] *Inq. p.m. Glos.* 1302–58, 275.
[39] S.C. 6/850/22.
[40] *Glouc. Corp. Rec.* pp. 71, 432.
[41] *Trans. B.G.A.S.* lxiii. 123; *Cal. Pat.* 1476–85, 44.
[42] Req. 2/20/117.
[43] Glos. R.O., D 936/M 4.

[44] Rudder, *Glos.* 396.
[45] *Kelly's Dir. Glos.* (1863), 255; (1870), 244.
[46] Acreage Returns, 1901.
[47] Glos. R.O., PA 103/2.
[48] Ibid. D 1388/SL 4, nos. 68, 103; cf. ibid. D 1740/E 3, f. 93.
[49] Ibid. D 1740/E 1, f. 20.
[50] Cf. ibid. D 2440, Brimpsfield and Cranham presentments; est. papers 1868.
[51] Ibid. D 2299/5151.
[52] Payne, *Glos. Survey*, 65.
[53] Cheltenham Roads Act, 25 Geo. III, c. 125.
[54] Glos. R.O., Q/RUm 63; cf. *V.C.H. Glos.* xi. 57.
[55] Painswick and Cheltenham Road Act, 1 Geo. IV, c. 16 (Local and Personal).
[56] Cf. Glos. R.O., Q/RUm 238.
[57] Upton St. Leonards Roads Act, 16 & 17 Vic. c. 126 (Local and Personal).
[58] Glos. R.O., Q/SRh 1889 A.

part of the parish, part of the old Calf way route from Chalford to Birdlip,[59] was turnpiked as the Stroud–Cheltenham road in 1800.[60]

Cranham church stands on a ridge south of the Painswick stream and its isolated position suggests that when it was built, probably as a chapel before the late 12th century, settlement in the area was dispersed and confined to clearings from the woodland. Cranham village, the main settlement, grew up by the stream 1 km. to the north-east on a road leading from the Calf way to meet the Port way route at the top of the escarpment. In the eastern part the Old House, which has a doorway dated 1687 and 1727, is a late-17th-century gabled structure but most of the houses in the village date from the 19th century. Cranham House was the home of a curate c. 1880.[61] The pound at the eastern end of the village had been constructed by 1838.[62] Higher up and east of the village is the Knoll, a settlement which was enlarged considerably after the Second World War. Knoll House, the principal building, dates from the conversion in 1845 of an earlier dwelling as the residence of Peter Horlick.[63] During the 19th century a school and school-house were built by the road from the church and in the 1950s many houses were put up in the area of the church and school, including both private houses and an estate of 12 council houses. The playing field south-east of the church was opened in 1953.[64]

In the western part of the parish are scattered houses which belonged to small estates, farms, and mills.[65] North-east of the church Simmonds Hall Farm is an 18th-century farm-house with later additions. Brook Farm, by the Overtown brook, was rebuilt c. 1945.[66] The main range at Haregrove, lower down the valley, retains a medieval fireplace and blocked doorway which are probably *in situ*. The house appears to have been remodelled at various times and c. 1790 the south end was extended westwards and refronted; in the mid 19th century it belonged to the Pinchin family.[67] Further south-west Hazelhanger (formerly Woodlands Farm)[68] was a small farm-house on the Trotman family estate in the mid 19th century.[69] It was converted as a private residence after the land had been sold in the early 20th century.[70] Batch Farm, further west, may be of medieval origin but the house, which was possibly part of the property in

Cranham and Painswick granted to Walter Tocknell in 1589,[71] was remodelled probably c. 1600[72] and in the 19th century when the walls were heightened. To the north Mann's Court, which belonged to William Mann (d. 1766) and was acquired by the Frankiss family in 1790, was rebuilt in the 19th century.[73]

There were probably dwellings at Cranham (formerly Prinknash) Corner by 1381 when several people surnamed Nash lived in Cranham.[74] Four houses south of the road to the village were built in the 1920s. Further east stands Woodside Farm, a symmetrical early-18th-century house; it belonged to a small copyhold estate farmed by the Sadler family until the mid 19th century.[75] In 1918 the farm-house was bought by James Herbert Edwards[76] who built Woodside, to the west, as his residence. He rebuilt that house c. 1929 and laid out formal gardens to the south including a pond on the Painswick stream.[77] The area south of Cranham Corner also included Fream's Farm and several other farm-houses belonging to copyhold estates. The small house at Greenhill is dated 1698. Yewricks was originally the farm-house for a smallholding called Rises in 1743[78] but by 1838 it was occupied as two dwellings[79] and it was later rebuilt.

There are few houses in the wooded northern part of the parish, where earthworks provide evidence of an early occupation of High Brotheridge.[80] Brotheridge Farm, a modern farm-house on the eastern side, occupies a site recorded in the mid 18th century.[81] The Buckholt, by the Birdlip road, dates from the 19th century. There was a dwelling at Crayfield Cottage on the northern boundary in 1728 when it belonged to a copyhold. The house, which was possibly in ruins in 1838, was rebuilt later that century. The barn to the south-east is on the site of a farmstead which was part of a copyhold estate acquired by the Haviland family in 1776.[82] Settlement in the eastern part of the parish is sparse. Bramble Cottage, south-east of the Knoll, dates from the mid 19th century. At Dunley to the east a few cottages of similar date were demolished in the early 20th century[83] and by 1935 a substantial house and cottage had been built there.[84] Upper Cranham, recorded in 1543,[85] was possibly located to the south-west at Overtown where there were several dwellings in the 17th

[59] *V.C.H. Glos.* xi. 5.
[60] Lightpill and Birdlip Road Act, 39 & 40 Geo. III, c. 43 (Local and Personal).
[61] *Kelly's Dir. Glos.* (1879), 627; O.S. Map 1/2,500, Glos. XXXIV. 13 (1884 edn.).
[62] G.D.R., T 1/64.
[63] Date and inits. on porch; cf. Glos. R.O., D 1297, deeds 1767–1864, deed 21 Nov. 1844.
[64] W.I. hist. of Cranham, *penes* Mrs. A. D. Whitaker, of Overtown Fm., 11, 33.
[65] Cf. G.D.R., T 1/64; Glos. R.O., D 2440, par., Cranham highway-rate 1866.
[66] W.I. booklet for archit. heritage year (1975), *penes* Mrs. Whitaker.
[67] G.D.R., T 1/64.
[68] W.I. booklet; O.S. Map 6″, Glos. XXXIV. SW. (1883 edn.).
[69] G.D.R., T 1/64.
[70] Cf. W.I. hist. of Cranham, 23.

[71] C.P. 25(2)/144/1878 no. 10; cf. *V.C.H. Glos.* xi. 72.
[72] The fire-place in the west room has a scratch date 1614.
[73] Glos. R.O., D 1388, maps and plans, misc. est. maps; G.D.R. wills 1766/175.
[74] E 179/113/31A rot. 2; E 179/113/35A rot. 13d.
[75] Glos. R.O., D 1740/E 3, f. 95; P 2; *Glouc. Jnl.* 29 July 1848.
[76] Glos. R.O., SL 607.
[77] W.I. hist. of Cranham, 110, 130.
[78] Glos. R.O., D 936/M 1/1; D 1740/E 3, f. 94; P 2.
[79] G.D.R., T 1/64.
[80] R.C.H.M. *Glos.* i. 40–1.
[81] Glos. R.O., D 1740/P 2.
[82] Ibid. D 936/M 1/1; D 1740/E 3, f. 96; P 2; G.D.R., T 1/64.
[83] G.D.R., T 1/64; O.S. Map 6″, Glos. XXXIV. SW. (1883, 1903, 1924 edns.).
[84] *Kelly's Dir. Glos.* (1931), 140–1; (1935), 139.
[85] *L. & P. Hen. VIII*, xviii(1), p. 536.

century[86] and one substantial house in 1978. There was a dwelling near the south-eastern boundary at Climperwell (called Habewoldesham in the late 12th century) by 1227 when a man was described as of Climperwell.[87] At the parish boundary south-west of Climperwell there was a small settlement at Foston's Ash on the Calf way in 1777.[88]

Ladlecombe, east of Cranham village, included fishponds when it was taken into the grounds of a summer retreat built c. 1821 for William Todd, a timber-merchant. The retreat, which stood in a glade by the Birdlip road, comprised several thatched buildings with verandahs, sometimes described as Swiss cottages[89] or villas. One contained the principal rooms, and another the service accommodation and kitchens. Sporting facilities were housed in the other buildings, including a billiard room. The retreat was known as Cranham Lodge by the late 1830s,[90] when it was retained in hand by the Revd. Edward Reed,[91] and it had fallen into disuse by 1861.[92] In 1866 R. B. Lawes rebuilt the two main buildings as a single residence,[93] which in 1872 was bought by the tenant, the Revd. Arthur Armitage of Cheltenham. He enlarged the house and in 1878 sold it back to William Frederick Hicks Beach,[94] who lived there for a time[95] before altering it in the later 1880s.[96]

In 1898 Cranham Lodge became part of the Cotswold Sanatorium, a private hospital begun that year for the treatment of tubercular diseases. The sanatorium, which also occupied a group of buildings, including chalets, to the west, had c. 32 patients by early 1901,[97] but the number rose considerably[98] and additional chalets were built in the 1920s.[99] In 1949 Eric Blair, better known as George Orwell, finished his last articles in the sanatorium.[1] It closed in 1956[2] and most of the buildings were demolished. In 1978 Cranham Lodge, which was in a dilapidated state, was used for agricultural storage and the forecourt for a timber-yard. The Red House, to the west, was built c. 1910 and later became the home of the Hoffman family, which ran the sanatorium for many years.[3]

In Cranham 14 people were assessed for the subsidy in 1327[4] and 53 for the poll tax in 1381.[5] There were said to be 24 households in 1563,[6] 93 communicants in 1603,[7] and 26 families in 1650.[8] The population, which was estimated at 170 c. 1710 and was said to be nearly the same c. 1775,[9] had reached 250 by 1801 and 428 by 1841. It had dropped to 354 by 1851 but had recovered by the 1860s when a recession in local employment led to another though less sharp fall. The population declined further in the 1880s, although a farmhouse was included in the area added to the parish then, and by 1911 it had dropped to 282. A rise to 441 by 1921 was accounted for by an increase in the number of patients in the sanatorium but after the Second World War the parish was favoured as a residential area and by 1971 the population had reached 476.[10]

In 1619 a weaver kept a victualling house in Cranham.[11] In 1788 the parish had two alehouses[12] and in 1838 a public house and three beer shops,[13] one of which was possibly the Potters Arms recorded in 1851.[14] In Cranham village the Black Horse inn, recorded in 1787,[15] had moved to a pair of cottages south-west of Cranham House by 1856.[16] Foston's Ash inn, which may have opened soon after 1800 when Foston's Ash became the junction of turnpike roads from Stroud and Chalford to Cheltenham, was mentioned in 1833.[17] The building dates from the 19th century and has been enlarged. On the Painswick–Cheltenham road the Royal William inn south-west of Cranham Corner was probably built shortly before 1837 when it was called the King William. The inn, part of the Sadler family's copyhold estate, was a local meeting-place[18] and in the mid 19th century two friendly societies met there.[19] The building was altered between 1904 and 1915.[20]

In Cranham village a disused pottery north-west of the Painswick stream was converted as a village institute in 1922 but since 1947 it has been the headquarters of the Gloucestershire Scout Association.[21] At the eastern end of the village a pottery, which had been converted as a nonconformist chapel, became the village hall in 1977.[22] The Cranham feast, which c. 1703 was held on the

---

[86] *Inq. p.m. Glos.* 1625–42, i. 71; Glos. R.O., D 3704/T 3.

[87] *Flaxley Cart.* ed. A. W. Crawley-Boevey (Exeter, 1887), 74–5.

[88] Taylor, *Map of Glos.* (1777).

[89] Glos. R.O., D 2440, Brimpsfield and Cranham presentments; H. Davies, *Stranger's Guide through Chelt.* (2nd edn. 1834), 187–8; *Diary of a Cotswold Parson*, ed. D. Verey (Dursley, 1978), 50–1; see above, plate facing p. 189.

[90] Glos. R.O., A 103/2; D 1388/SL 3, no. 59.

[91] G.D.R., T 1/64.   [92] Glos. R.O., D 1388/SL 4, no. 68.

[93] Ibid. Lyon fam., legal papers, Atkyns v. Lawes 1862–8.

[94] Ibid. D 2440, est. papers 1878–1933.

[95] *Kelly's Dir. Glos.* (1879), 627.

[96] Glos. R.O., D 2953.

[97] Ibid. D 2440, est. papers 1878–1933; O.S. Map 6″, Glos. XXXIV. SW. (1903 edn.).

[98] *Census*, 1921.

[99] Glos. R.O., D 2299/4522.

[1] *D.N.B.* 1941–50; G. Orwell, *Collected Essays, Journalism, and Letters,* iv (1968), 460–506, 520–1.

[2] W.I. hist. of Cranham, 141.

[3] Glos. R.O., D 2299/4522; D 2440, est. papers 1911–16; Glos. Colln. R 96.1.

[4] *Glos. Subsidy Roll. 1327*, 10.

[5] E 179/113/31A rot. 2; E 179/113/35A rot. 13d.

[6] Bodl. MS. Rawl. C.790, f. 9.

[7] *Eccl. Misc.* 82.

[8] *Trans. B.G.A.S.* lxxxiii. 93.

[9] Atkyns, *Glos.* 375; Rudder, *Glos.* 396.

[10] *Census*, 1801–1971.

[11] Glos. R.O., EL 315.

[12] *Glouc. Jnl.* 25 Aug. 1788.

[13] *Rep. Com. Handloom Weavers*, pt. v [220], p. 471, H.C. (1840), xxiv.

[14] H.O. 107/1964.

[15] Notes taken from newspaper cuttings, *penes* Mr. B. Frith, of Tuffley, Glouc.

[16] Glos. R.O., D 1815, deeds 1830–45; *Kelly's Dir. Glos.* (1856 and later edns.).

[17] Glos. R.O., D 2440, Brimpsfield and Cranham presentments.

[18] G.D.R., T 1/64; cf. *Glouc. Jnl.* 29 July 1848.

[19] F.S. 2/3 nos. 438, 648.

[20] Glos. R.O., D 2299/311, 1277.

[21] W.I. hist. of Cranham, 111; Glos. Colln. R 96.3.

[22] Ex inf. Mrs. Whitaker.

Sunday after the feast of St. James (25 July), was evidently an ancient event in honour of the patron saint of the parish church.[23] It lapsed during the Second World War and from its revival in 1951 was held on the day after the second Sunday in August.[24]

MANORS AND OTHER ESTATES. In 1086 Cranham was part of Osbern Giffard's large Brimpsfield estate,[25] but his successors had granted the area north-east of the Painswick stream to Gloucester Abbey by 1121,[26] and land at Climperwell had passed to Flaxley Abbey by 1227.[27] From the later 16th century that part of Cranham remaining in the Brimpsfield manorial estate was distinguished as the manor of *CRANHAM*.[28] In 1740, when the manors of Brimpsfield and Cranham passed to Alice and Emm Gilbert,[29] Windsor Sandys retained c. 398 a., comprising the common and common woodland in Cranham and Brimpsfield.[30] That land passed with the Miserden estate, which he inherited in 1745, to Sir Edwin Bayntun Sandys[31] while the manorial rights passed with Brimpsfield to Joseph Pitt.[32] Sir Edwin disputed Pitt's title,[33] but Pitt claimed the woodland and common[34] and was said in 1838 to own all save c. 17 a. at Ladlecombe.[35] The dispute was resolved in 1840 when Pitt sold Cranham manor to James Wittit Lyon.[36] It was bought in 1862 by Robert Bartholomew Lawes and in 1869 by Richard Mullings of Stratton.[37] He sold it in 1871 to William Frederick Hicks Beach,[38] heir to the Witcombe estate,[39] with which the Cranham property descended to William Whitehead Hicks Beach (d. 1975). His widow Diana retained the estate but gave the woodland to her son Mr. Mark Hicks Beach.[40]

In 1096 Ellis Giffard (I) gave Gloucester Abbey part of the woodland called Buckholt with 3 bordars. That land was presumably included in the grant, made to the abbey in 1121, of that heavily wooded part of the Brimpsfield estate north-west of the Painswick stream. When Ellis Giffard (II) became a monk of the abbey after 1148 he granted it his remaining property in Cranham, except for part of the woodland,[41] but that gift was set aside in 1167 in exchange for land belonging to the

Giffards in Ullingswick (Herefs.).[42] In the early 14th century the abbey was apparently dispossessed by John Giffard but in 1343 Maurice of Berkeley, lord of Brimpsfield, acknowledged the abbey's right.[43]

The abbey's property was known as the manor of *CRANHAM* in 1541 when it was granted to the dean and chapter of Gloucester cathedral,[44] and it was held with Barnwood and Wotton manors under the dean and chapter by c. 1547 when a lease was apparently granted to Sir Thomas Seymour. The lease had passed to Thomas Winston of King's Stanley by 1550 when a lease in reversion was granted to Thomas Ellill of Northleach. The later lease passed to Edward Stephens (d. 1587) who devised it to his son Thomas, later of Over Lypiatt, whose title was contested by the dean and chapter in 1597. Thomas's grandson, Thomas Stephens of Sodbury,[45] took a lease of Barnwood and Cranham manors for a term of 21 years in 1661. Thereafter the estate was held under leases renewed every few years. In 1674 a lease was granted to George Johnson of Bowden Park near Chippenham (Wilts.) and from 1687 William Johnson was lessee. In 1713 Mary Wright of Gloucester was granted a lease but William's son William, a Bristol merchant, was lessee from 1715 until his death in 1750. Leases were then granted in turn to his father-in-law, Anthony Edwards of Little Shurdington (d. 1760), and his wife, Elizabeth Johnson (d. 1773).[46] Elizabeth was succeeded by her three daughters, Elizabeth wife of John Jones, Hester wife of William Walbank, rector of Cranham, and Sarah Wyatt,[47] but in 1783 the dean and chapter took the demesne and manorial rights in hand.[48] The following year they granted a lease of the demesne, which comprised woodland, to John Morris of Gloucester[49] but retained the manorial rights until the mid 1850s when they passed to the Ecclesiastical Commissioners.[50] The farm-land (c. 275 a.) continued to be held by copy after 1783 but about half was enfranchised in 1799[51] and the remainder in the later 19th century.[52]

About 1799 the dean and chapter sold the woodland to the lessee, Robert Morris. He sold it to Thomas Jeffreys but by 1803 the woods had been bought by David Whatley.[53] Samuel Lediard

[23] Bodl. MS. Rawl. B.323, f. 197v.
[24] Glos. R.O., PA 103/1.
[25] *Dom. Bk.* (Rec. Com.), i. 168v.
[26] *Hist. & Cart. Mon. Glouc.* i. 205.
[27] *Flaxley Cart.* 114–15.
[28] C 142/163 no. 59; *Inq. p.m. Glos. 1625–42*, ii. 170–2.
[29] See above; Glos. R.O., D 2440, Cranham, Brimpsfield, and Cowley papers 1715–1924.
[30] Cf. ibid. D 1042, Miserden, Winstone, Brimpsfield, and Cranham deeds 1647–1776; D 1388/SL 3, no. 59.
[31] *V.C.H. Glos.* xi. 50; Bigland, *Glos.* i. 433.
[32] Glos. R.O., D 1388/SL 3, no. 38; D 2440, Brimpsfield and Cranham presentments.
[33] Ibid. D 1388, Lyon fam., legal papers, Pitt *v.* Sandys 1818, 1819–27.
[34] Ibid. Brimpsfield and Cranham papers 1788–1839, draft agreement Mar. 1839.
[35] G.D.R., T 1/64.
[36] Glos. R.O., D 1388, Lyon fam., Cranham man. papers 1753–1840.

[37] Ibid. D 2440, Cranham deeds 1862–71.
[38] Ibid. Cranham papers 1878–1933.
[39] Burke, *Peerage* (1935), 2077; cf. Glos. R.O., D 2299/5151.
[40] Ex inf. Mrs. Hicks Beach, of Witcombe Pk., Great Witcombe.
[41] *Hist. & Cart. Mon. Glouc.* i. 63, 205, 244–5.
[42] Ibid. 117.
[43] Ibid. iii. 247–8.
[44] *L. & P. Hen. VIII*, xvi, p. 572.
[45] Req. 2/162/119; for the Stephenses, see *Visit. Glos. 1682–3*, 174–7.
[46] Glos. R.O., D 936/E 17; Bigland, *Glos.* i. 131, 118.
[47] Glos. R.O., D 936/E 18.
[48] Cf. ibid. M 1/2.
[49] Ibid. E 18.
[50] Rudge, *Hist. of Glos.* i. 302; Glos. R.O., D 936/M 1/2–3; cf. Kirby, *Cat. of Glouc. Dioc. Rec.* ii, p. xiii.
[51] Glos. R.O., D 1740/E 3, ff. 93–6.
[52] Ibid. D 2440, est. papers 1605–1891, 1869–96.
[53] Rudge, *Hist. of Glos.* i. 302; Glos. R.O., D 936/E 18–19.

owned them in 1838[54] and Mary Croft Lediard sold them in 1862 to M. R. Griffin and J. Gardner.[55] The property, called Buckholt manor in 1866,[56] was purchased about that time by John Dearman Birchall of Upton St. Leonards (d. 1897).[57] His son and heir John, knighted in 1929, died in 1941. The woodland then passed in turn to his wife Adela (d. 1965) and son Maj. P. D. Birchall who owned c. 250 a. in Buckholt wood in 1978.[58]

In the late 12th century Llanthony Priory granted a yardland at CLIMPERWELL, formerly part of the Brimpsfield estate, to Dore Abbey (Herefs.) for a rent of 3s. Dore Abbey conveyed it to Flaxley Abbey which by 1227 had acquired more land there and at Bidfield in Bisley.[59] The abbey's Climperwell estate, which at the Dissolution was valued with property in Arlingham,[60] was described as a manor or grange in 1537 when the Crown granted it to Sir William Kingston (d. 1540). He was succeeded by his son Sir Anthony[61] (d. 1556), whose illegitimate son Edmund had licence in 1565 to grant it with Bidfield manor to his brother-in-law Edward Barnard.[62] Edward (d. 1570) left Climperwell to Edmund's son Anthony Kingston (d. 1591), whose son William was seised of it at his death in 1614.[63] In 1617 Charles and Anthony Kingston granted the estate for life to William's widow Mary, who had married Sherrington Talbot.[64] By 1762 Climperwell had been acquired by Samuel Hayward[65] (d. 1790), who was succeeded by his son-in-law Walter Wilkins,[66] M.P. for Radnorshire.[67] Walter Hayward Wilkins de Winton owned it in 1838 when it comprised c. 290 a. in Cranham and Brimpsfield,[68] but by 1860 it was part of John Hall's Brimpsfield estate[69] with which it passed.[70] By 1951 the farm-house, which dates from a late-19th-century rebuilding, had been acquired with c. 620 a., mostly in Brimpsfield, by Albert Broadstock.[71]

Evidence that Henry I granted Cirencester Abbey land in Cranham was apparently forged but in the 12th or early 13th century the abbey acquired 1 hide of land there from the Brimpsfield estate.[72] The land, which at the Dissolution was administered with the abbey's manor of Througham in Bisley and included property in Upper Cranham, was granted by the Crown in 1543 to Richard Andrews and Nicholas Temple. The following year they conveyed it to John Robins[73] of Matson whose son Thomas inherited it in 1564.[74]

Richard Davies, who purchased land in Cranham in 1624,[75] was a member of a family whose OVERTOWN estate was settled in 1658, on the marriage of John Davies. John's son John enlarged the estate by several purchases, including one from a branch of the Cowles family in 1714. After his death before 1728 the estate passed in turn to his wife Abigail and son Halliday[76] who conveyed part in 1738 to his eldest brother John, a doctor.[77] By 1771 John had apparently acquired much more of the estate from Halliday[78] (d. 1783),[79] who in 1779 purchased from Samuel Sandys a substantial holding bought by Windsor Sandys in 1721.[80] By 1838 the Overtown estate (c. 395 a.) had passed to the Revd. John Davies[81] (d. 1870), but by 1860 his sister Martha was in possession. Martha (d. 1871)[82] left it to the Revd. William Henry Temple.[83] His successor Reginald Willock Temple[84] sold it in 1922 to Henry Workman,[85] owner of the Ebworth estate in Painswick. Henry (d. 1924)[86] was succeeded by his nephew F. E. Workman (d. 1962) and by 1978 the Cranham woodland had been divided between Mr. John Workman, his son, and Mrs. D. D. Walmsley, one of his daughters. They owned the Cranham farm-land jointly but c. 1966 the house had been sold to Mr. P. G. Meigh.[87] Old Overtown House, a small house of the early 17th century, had a short south wing added at the eastern end by John Davies in 1660[88] when it was known as Colliers.[89] A barn which abuts the western gable was incorporated in the house in the 20th century. East of the house farm-buildings, used as service rooms in the 19th century, may have been built as a house in the 17th century.

Part of a large estate owned by George Cowles (d. 1627)[90] had been sold by 1660 to Sylvanus Wood,[91] owner of the Ebworth estate[92] which in 1838

54 G.D.R., T 1/64.
55 Glos. R.O., D 2440, est. papers 1605–1891.
56 Ibid. D 1388/SL 4, no. 103.
57 Kelly's Dir. Glos. (1889), 750–1; Glouc. Jnl. 12 June 1897.
58 Kelly's Dir. Glos. (1939), 139; Who Was Who, 1941–50, 103; ex inf. Maj. Birchall, of Cotswold Fm., Duntisbourne Abbots.
59 Flaxley Cart. 114–15, 132.
60 Valor Eccl. (Rec. Com.), ii. 486.
61 L. & P. Hen. VIII, xii(1), p. 353; for the Kingstons, see Trans. B.G.A.S. vi. 292–3.
62 Cal. Pat. 1563–6, pp. 284–5; cf. V.C.H. Glos. xi. 16.
63 C 142/231 no. 94; C 142/347 no. 90.
64 C.P. 25(2)/289/15 Jas. I Mich. no. 47.
65 C.P. 25(2)/1314/2 Geo. III Trin. no. 10; cf. Glos. R.O., D 626.
66 Rudge, Hist. of Glos. i. 302; ii. 156; Glos. R.O., photocopy 346.
67 For the Wilkins fam., see Burke, Land. Gent. (1898), i. 400–1.
68 Glos. R.O., Q/RI 29; G.D.R., T 1/38, 64.
69 Glos. R.O., D 2440, par., Cranham poor-rate 1860.
70 Cf. ibid. D 2299/4104.
71 'Birdlip and Brimpsfield. The Story of Two Villages 1850–1957' (W.I. hist. 1959, copy in Glos. R.O. Libr.), 72.

72 Ciren. Cart. i, pp. 22, 217–18.
73 L. & P. Hen. VIII, xviii (1), p. 536; xix (1), p. 283; V.C.H. Glos. xi. 14.
74 Trans. B.G.A.S. xlvi. 331.
75 Glos. R.O., D 3704/T 1.
76 Ibid. T 3, T 7–8; G.D.R. wills 1728/422; Bigland, Glos. i. 433, gives 1595 as the year in which the Davies fam. acquired the est.
77 Glos. R.O., D 3704/T 8.
78 Cf. ibid. D 626; D 3704/T 5.   79 Bigland, Glos. i. 434.
80 Glos. R.O., D 3704/T 9.
81 G.D.R., T 1/64.
82 Mon. in ch.; Glos. R.O., D 2240, par., Cranham poor-rate 1860.
83 Glos. R.O., D 3704/F 3.
84 Kelly's Dir. Glos. (1879–1919 edns.).
85 Glos. R.O., D 2299/6050; 2893, letter 26 July 1922.
86 V.C.H. Glos. xi. 67, 301.
87 Ex inf. Mr. Workman, of Far End, Sheepscombe, Painswick.
88 Date and inits. on doorway.
89 Glos. R.O., D 3704/T 3, T 5.
90 Inq. p.m. Glos. 1625–42, i. 70–1.
91 Cf. Glos. R.O., D 2957/96. 3–4, 19, 22–3, 26–9.
92 V.C.H. Glos. xi. 67.

RENDCOMB PARK

COWLEY MANOR: the south front after the alterations of the 1890s

FAIRFORD CHURCH from the north

RENDCOMB CHURCH from the south

included *c.* 145 a. in Cranham.[93] In the early 20th century the land was divided between Henry Workman[94] and Robert Preston (d. 1933); Preston built up an estate of 160 a. in the parish.[95]

In 1650 two copyholds were held by Thomas Fream[96] (d. 1663).[97] The Fream family's holding, which was farmed from *FREAM'S FARM* and comprised *c.* 91 a. in 1750,[98] passed in 1786 to William Hinton[99] and was enfranchised in 1799.[1] The Hinton family built up an estate which from 1804 included the small copyhold called Rises[2] and covered *c.* 272 a. in 1838.[3] In the late 1850s it belonged to Robert Hinton[4] and later passed through several owners[5] before William Sadler Hall acquired part with the farm-house. In 1918, following his death, his estate, which covered 435 a. in Cranham, Brockworth, and Upton St. Leonards, was broken up.[6] The farm-house, known in the late 19th century as Woodside,[7] is a tall gabled building of the 17th century. A two-storey wing added on the south-east is dated 1676 with the initials 'W.F.', presumably those of William Fream (fl. 1679).[8]

ECONOMIC HISTORY. On the Brimpsfield estate in Cranham in 1536 two free tenements were recorded and there had been some amalgamation of its customary tenements, which included at least 7 half yardlands and 4 fardels and were held by 8 people for cash rent and customary payments. There was also a payment of 11*s.* for part of Hazel Hanger park,[9] presumably in the area of Brimpsfield where land was claimed for Cranham in 1838.[10] The rents of Cirencester Abbey's customary tenants were worth £1 13*s.* 4*d.* at the Dissolution.[11] Little is known about the demesnes of the various estates in Cranham but that on Flaxley Abbey's Climperwell estate included 3 plough-lands in 1291.[12]

In the 1260s the tenants listed on Gloucester Abbey's estate, which also included most of Barnwood parish, were unfree and owed aid and other customary payments. The customary tenements comprised 3 yardlands each held by a single tenant and 8 yardlands each held jointly by 2 tenants. The service owed from the full yardland, which was held with one or two acres of meadow land, included work on 4 days of the week with extra work on ploughing, harrowing, mowing, and haymaking. The ploughing-services included *benerthe*,

the ploughing of an acre which was sown with the tenant's seed. During the busy months of August and September week-work was increased to 5 days, including reaping with 2 men, and bedrepes were performed. The cash rent owed from 24 smaller holdings, including 10 Cranham fardels, possibly represented commuted labour-services, for the tenants owed only bedrepes. There were also 19 or 20 mondaymen holding a few acres by a day's week-work, which was doubled during August and September, and tasks at mowing and haymaking.[13] In 1650 the farm-land on the Cranham part of the estate was divided among 7 copyhold tenements held for terms of one or more lives. Apart from a mill the holdings ranged from *c.* 20 a. to *c.* 54 a. and included small areas of meadow land and pasture.[14] A century later 13 copyhold tenants held between them *c.* 275 a., in Cranham parish and a cottage in Brockworth. About half of that land was enfranchised in 1799[15] and in 1826 7 copyhold tenements accounted for *c.* 137 a.[16] In 1894 the Ecclesiastical Commissioners retained only a few acres of former copyhold land near the northern boundary.[17]

In 1261 Cranham had at least two open fields, an east and a west field.[18] In the western part of the parish much of the farm-land, including arable, was inclosed early[19] though, west of Batch Farm, Haw field, an open field which had been partly inclosed by 1596,[20] was shared with Painswick parish until the early 19th century.[21] Buckholt and Sowdley fields were other areas of open-field land in the early 17th century.[22] Buckholt field, also called the Downs by 1740, lay south-east of the Knoll,[23] and Sowdley (or Town) field[24] was possibly the south field where John Davies and Samuel Hayward consolidated their holdings by the Birdlip–Bisley road in 1771.[25] The remaining part of that field, over 110 a., and an area of 76 a. east of Dunley were inclosed in the early 19th century.[26] Since then the common in the centre of the parish has been the principal common pasture.

By the early 13th century, when Flaxley Abbey was granted common rights in Brimpsfield and Cranham,[27] sheep-farming was important in the south-eastern part of the parish where the Climperwell estate was described as a sheep-walk in the late 16th century.[28] In 1381 the inhabitants included a shepherd,[29] and copyholders on the dean

[93] G.D.R., T 1/64.
[94] Cf. *Kelly's Dir. Glos.* (1910–19 edns.).
[95] Glos. R.O., SL 91.
[96] Ibid. D 1740/E 1, f. 18.
[97] Bigland, *Glos.* i. 434.
[98] Glos. R.O., D 1740/E 3, f. 93; P 2.
[99] Ibid. D 936/M 1/2.
[1] Ibid. D 1740/E 3, f. 93.
[2] Cf. ibid. D 936/M 1/2, cts. 22 Oct. 1799, 5 Nov. 1801, 23 Nov. 1804.
[3] G.D.R., T 1/64.
[4] Cf. *Kelly's Dir. Glos.* (1856), 274.
[5] Glos. R.O., D 2440, par., Cranham poor-rate 1860, highway-rate 1866; est. papers 1868–1927, list of freeholders 1868.
[6] Ibid. D 2299/1561.
[7] O.S. Map 6″, Glos. XXXIV. SW. (1883 edn.).
[8] G.D.R., V 5/96T 1.
[9] S.C. 11/1022 rott. 1d.–2.

[10] Glos. R.O., P 103/VE 1/1.
[11] Dugdale, *Mon.* vi (1), 179.
[12] *Tax. Eccl.* (Rec. Com.), 235.
[13] *Hist. & Cart. Mon. Glouc.* iii. 120–6.
[14] Glos. R.O., D 1740/E 1, ff. 17v.–19.
[15] Ibid. E 3, ff. 93–6.
[16] Ibid. D 936/E 143.
[17] Ibid. D 2440, est. papers 1869–96.
[18] C.P. 25(1)/74/26 no. 587.
[19] Cf. Glos. R.O., D 1740/E 1, ff. 17v.–19.
[20] Ibid. D 2957/96. 9; Taylor, *Map of Glos.* (1777).
[21] *Inq. p.m. Glos.* 1625–42, i. 71; *V.C.H. Glos.* xi. 71.
[22] *Inq. p.m. Glos.* 1625–42, i. 71.
[23] Glos. R.O., D 2957/96. 13; G.D.R., T 1/64.
[24] Glos. R.O., D 127/211.
[25] Ibid. D 626.
[26] Glos. Colln. RF 96.1; G.D.R., T 1/64.
[27] *Flaxley Cart.* 74.
[28] C 142/231 no. 94.   [29] *Glos. N. & Q.* iii. 278.

and chapter's estate in the north-western part of the parish in the mid 17th century enjoyed common rights for up to 100 sheep for each yardland held.[30] Many pigs were fed in the extensive beech woodland. In the late 16th century the rector kept swine[31] and customary tenants on the dean and chapter's estate paid pannage for rights in Buckholt wood.[32]

Arable farming occupied most of the land outside the woods and common in the 18th century[33] but in 1801 only 398 a. were said to be under crops, mainly wheat and barley with some oats, turnips, and peas.[34] In 1838 arable occupied 688 a. and meadow land and pasture only 215 a.,[35] and in 1866 777 a. were returned as under crops, mainly cereals and roots, or temporary grass compared with 290 a. under permanent grass. Later that century the area under cereals and roots declined and that of recorded permanent grassland increased considerably.[36] Most of the 198 cattle returned for Cranham in 1866 were kept for dairying but dairy cows accounted for less than a quarter of those returned in 1926 when permanent grassland covered at least 762 a. and rough grazing 104 a.[37] The number of sheep returned declined from 964 in 1896 to 668 in 1926.[38] In the mid 20th century large flocks were kept in the eastern part of the parish but the numbers of cattle and pigs and the area given over to cereals increased.[39] By the 1950s most farms included dairy herds[40] and by 1976, when dairying and cereal production remained important, especially on the larger farms, the level of sheep-farming had been reduced.[41] Orchards accounted for at least 31 a. in 1926 and cider was produced at Mann's Court. Poultry-farming had been introduced by then[42] but fewer birds were reared after the Second World War.[43]

Agriculture was the chief source of employment in 1831 when there were 11 farms employing 43 labourers between them and 4 family-run farms.[44] There were two large farms in the eastern part of the parish: in 1838 Overtown covered 380 a. and Climperwell, lying partly in Brimpsfield, 259 a. Elsewhere the farms were much smaller: in 1838 Fream's comprised 185 a. but another eight ranged in size from 10 a. to 87 a.[45] In the later 19th century

Woodside farm was evidently farmed with Fream's.[46] Several farms in the south-western part were being worked together by the early 20th century when the Woodlands farm-house was detached from its lands.[47] In the later 19th century the smaller farms were worked on a part-time basis, one farmer finding additional work drilling seed for his neighbours.[48] The number of full-time agricultural labourers had dropped to 22 by 1926 when half of the 20 holdings listed in the parish comprised 20 a. or less. Three farms included 150 a. or more.[49] In 1958 seven farms, Climperwell (240 a.) and six ranging from 25 a. to 94 a., were owner-occupied, and Woodside (70 a.) was worked by a bailiff. The other principal farms, Overtown (350 a.) and Mann's Court (30 a.), had tenants.[50] Small farms worked on a part-time basis remained a feature in 1976 when 10 of the 15 farms returned for the parish had less than 30 ha. (75 a.) each.[51]

The two mills recorded on the Brimpsfield estate in 1086[52] were probably in Cranham, where the estate retained two mills in 1536.[53] In 1608 two millers were listed in the parish[54] and by the early 18th century four corn-mills were working there.[55]

Three were on the Painswick stream.[56] Cranham mill, north-west of the church, was owned by the Walker family in 1750[57] and by Thomas Sadler in the mid 19th century.[58] It went out of use c. 1900[59] and the building, which is largely of the 19th century, had been converted to domestic use by 1978. Sutton's mill, the next downstream, evidently belonged to Robert Bliss of Painswick, a baker, in the later 17th century[60] and to John Sutton by the end of the 18th.[61] It fell into disuse in the 1860s.[62] The mill buildings comprise a 17th-century house with a later mill, driven by an overshot wheel, at the western end. A range of out-buildings to the west had been converted to domestic use by 1978. Eddell's mill, near the boundary with Painswick, may have been the mill granted to Gloucester Abbey in 1121.[63] As a grist-mill, it was held by copy in 1650.[64] In 1731 the copyhold was granted to John King of Gloucester, a dyer, who devised it by will proved 1743 to his wife Mary. The copyhold was granted in 1783 to George Birch,[65] owner of Oliver's mill in Painswick,[66] and in 1797

[30] Glos. R.O., D 1740/E 1, ff. 17v.–20.
[31] Hockaday Abs. clxxiii, 1572.
[32] Glos. R.O., D 936/M 4.
[33] Atkyns, Glos. 375; Rudge, Hist. of Glos. i. 301.
[34] Acreage Returns, 1801.
[35] G.D.R., T 1/64.
[36] M.A.F. 68/26/13; M.A.F. 68/1609/17.
[37] M.A.F. 68/25/5; M.A.F. 68/3295/20.
[38] M.A.F. 68/1609/17; M.A.F. 68/3295/20.
[39] 'Birdlip and Brimpsfield', 72; W.I. hist. of Cranham, 23–8.
[40] Glos. R.O., PA 103/1.
[41] Agric. Returns 1976.
[42] M.A.F. 68/3295/20; W.I. hist. of Cranham, 24.
[43] W.I. hist. of Cranham, 28; Agric. Returns 1976.
[44] Census, 1831.
[45] G.D.R., T 1/64, 38.
[46] W.I. hist. of Cranham, 24; cf. O.S. Map 6", Glos. XXXIII. SE. (1884 and 1903 edns.).
[47] Kelly's Dir. Glos. (1897–1931 edns.); W.I. hist. of Cranham, 23.
[48] Kelly's Dir. Glos. (1856–94 edns.); W.I. hist. of Cranham, 25.

[49] M.A.F. 68/3295/20.
[50] W.I. hist. of Cranham, 27.
[51] Agric. Returns 1976.
[52] Dom. Bk. (Rec. Com.), i. 168v.
[53] S.C. 11/1022 rot. 2; cf. Cal. Pat. 1547–8, 115.
[54] Smith, Men and Armour, 252.
[55] G.D.R., V 5/96T 3; Atkyns, Glos. 375.
[56] O.S. Map 6", Glos. XXXIV. SW. (1883 edn.).
[57] Glos. R.O., D 1740/P 2.
[58] G.D.R., T 1/64; Glouc. Jnl. 29 July 1848.
[59] W.I. hist. of Cranham, 18; Kelly's Dir. Glos. (1879–1902 edns.).
[60] Glos. R.O., D 1297, deeds 1767–1864, sched.; cf. C.P. 25(2)/834/12 Wm. III Trin. no. 31.
[61] Glos. R.O., D 443/2.
[62] Cf. Kelly's Dir. Glos. (1863), 255; (1870), 530; photog. dated 1868, penes Mr. E. R. Myatt, of Sutton's mill.
[63] Hist. & Cart. Mon. Glouc. i. 205; cf. ibid. iii. 121.
[64] Glos. R.O., D 1740/E 1, f. 18v.
[65] Ibid. D 936/M 1/1, cts. 31 Aug. 1731, 29 Apr. 1745, 3 June 1783; G.D.R. wills 1742/5.
[66] V.C.H. Glos. xi. 72.

to Thomas Eddells of Minchinhampton, a clothier.[67] The mill had been enfranchised by 1805 and was then worked as a cloth-mill under Eddells, who had gone bankrupt, by Benjamin Wood.[68] It was later worked as a corn-mill[69] but went out of use in the late 1860s.[70] The 19th-century building was extensively restored as a house in 1926.[71]

The fourth mill was on the Overtown brook south of Haregrove.[72] It was idle in the 1860s[73] but a new wheel was installed in 1869.[74] The mill was then worked by William Gardiner until the early 1890s[75] when it went out of use.[76] The building, which fell into ruins after the Second World War had been demolished by 1978.[77]

There are few references to trades in Cranham before the later 18th century. Cranham had a smith in 1327[78] and in 1381 when a tailor and several brewers also lived there.[79] The only tradesmen listed in 1608 were a tailor and a weaver,[80] but a tucker lived in the parish in 1651. In the late 17th century and early 18th members of the Baylis family of clothiers lived in the parish[81] where another clothier was recorded in the middle of the 18th.[82]

By the later 18th century some inhabitants were employed in trades exploiting the natural resources of the parish and in 1831 31 families were supported by trade compared with 42 supported by agriculture.[83] A mason lived in Cranham in 1797[84] and the sites of quarries were discernible in the northern and eastern parts of the parish in 1978. Timber-merchants are recorded from the later 18th century.[85] In the mid 19th century there were timber-yards near the Knoll and at Greenhill[86] and several inhabitants were sawyers.[87] In the mid 20th century the woodland provided seasonal employment.[88]

By 1779, when John Weeks followed the trade of potter,[89] pottery was being made from clay found by the Painswick stream and in 1823 the Brimpsfield court leet prohibited the digging of clay and fuller's earth unless the pits were filled in immediately and levelled.[90] In the 19th century Cranham had several potteries producing chimney pots and rough earthenware suitable for horticultural or domestic use.[91] The potteries were small and sometimes short-lived,[92] but nevertheless provided much employment. A recession in the trade contributed to a fall in the population of Cranham and Miserden in the 1860s.[93]

John Weeks's pottery, which was at the east end of Cranham village,[94] was worked in the early 19th century by Joseph Lovegrove, who was also a timber-merchant.[95] William Moulton, who worked the pottery by 1851[96] and claimed the patronage of Queen Adelaide (d. 1849),[97] bought it in 1872. He died in 1884 and his son Edward[98] went bankrupt in 1886.[99] Later Charles Stirling included ornamental ware among his products there but the pottery closed in 1906.[1] Thomas Richings, who bought a pottery in the village north-west of the stream in the mid 1860s,[2] was also a grocer and postmaster but enjoyed a wide reputation as a craftsman. Production at the pottery stopped shortly after his death in 1909.[3]

Apart from the usual village tradesmen the inhabitants included three shopkeepers in 1856 and two castrators in the early 20th century.[4] A brewery at the Royal William by 1838[5] closed between 1904 and 1915.[6] The malt-houses on the opposite side of the Painswick–Cheltenham road were demolished later.[7] From the Second World War many parishioners worked in neighbouring towns.[8]

LOCAL GOVERNMENT. An agreement reached in the 1230s about the liberties of Brimpsfield manor[9] evidently concerned Cranham, for in the early 15th century the view of frankpledge for Cranham was held in the Brimpsfield manor court. Cirencester Abbey then received the amercements of its tenants.[10] Encroachments on common land, the cutting of turf, and the fencing off of quarries in Cranham, as well as the election of officers, provided the bulk of the business of the Brimpsfield

[67] Glos. R.O., D 936/M 1/2, ct. 2 Aug. 1797.
[68] *Glouc. Jnl.* 28 Jan. 1805.
[69] G.D.R., T 1/64; *Kelly's Dir. Glos.* (1856), 275.
[70] Glos. R.O., D 2440, est. papers 1868–1927, list of freeholders 1868; *Kelly's Dir. Glos.* (1870), 530.
[71] W.I. hist. of Cranham, 133.
[72] G.D.R., T 1/64.
[73] Glos. R.O., D 2440, par., Cranham poor-rate 1860; est. papers 1868–1927, list of freeholders 1868.
[74] W.I. hist. of Cranham, 18.
[75] *Kelly's Dir. Glos.* (1870–94 edns.).
[76] O.S. Map 6″, Glos. XXXIV. SW. (1903 edn.).
[77] W.I. hist. of Cranham, 18, 146.
[78] *Glos. Subsidy Roll, 1327*, 10.
[79] *Glos. N. & Q.* iii. 278.
[80] Smith, *Men and Armour*, 252.
[81] Glos. R.O., D 3704/T 2; T 8, deed 1702.
[82] G.D.R. wills 1759/175.
[83] *Census*, 1831.
[84] Glos. R.O., D 1347, Cranham deeds 1797–1804.
[85] Ibid. D 1042, misc. papers, declaration 30 Jan. 1839; P 103/IN 1/7; *Kelly's Dir. Glos.* (1856 and later edns.).
[86] G.D.R., T 1/64.
[87] Glos. R.O., P 103/IN 1/7.
[88] Ibid. PA 103/2.
[89] Ibid. D 127/210.

[90] Ibid. D 2440, Brimpsfield and Cranham presentments.
[91] *Kelly's Dir. Glos.* (1856–1919 edns.); Glos. Colln. RR 96.1.
[92] Cf. *Glouc. Jnl.* 29 July 1848; Glos. R.O., D 2440, par., Cranham poor-rate 1860.
[93] *Census*, 1871.
[94] Cf. Glos. R.O., D 182/III/102; D 1297, deeds 1767–1864.
[95] Ibid. D 127/213–15; G.D.R., T 1/64; *Diary of a Cotswold Parson*, 98.
[96] H.O. 107/1964; Glos. R.O., D 2440, par., Cranham poor-rate 1860.
[97] *Kelly's Dir. Glos.* (1863), 255.
[98] W.I. hist. of Cranham, 115, 15.
[99] *Glouc. Jnl.* 13 Feb. 1886.
[1] *Kelly's Dir. Glos.* (1906), 135; *V.C.H. Glos.* ii. 214 n.
[2] *Kelly's Dir. Glos.* (1863), 255; Glos. R.O., D 2440, est. papers 1868–1927, list of freeholders 1868; O.S. Map 6″, Glos. XXXIV. SW. (1883 edn.).
[3] *Kelly's Dir. Glos.* (1870–1919 edns.); *Glouc. Jnl.* 27 Feb. 1909.
[4] *Kelly's Dir. Glos.* (1856 and later edns.).
[5] G.D.R., T 1/64.
[6] Glos. R.O., D 2299/1277.
[7] Cf. O.S. Map 6″, Glos. XXXIV. SW. (1924 edn.).
[8] Glos. R.O., PA 103/2.
[9] *Ciren. Cart.* i, pp. 214–16.
[10] Ibid. ii, p. 620.

court leet until 1829 and of the separate court leet for Cranham held from 1830 by Joseph Pitt. The court, which was meeting yearly at Foston's Ash inn by 1833, dealt with the state of a bridge in 1840. After 1847 it was convened less frequently but presentments survive until 1866 when it met at the Royal William.[11]

In 1546 the Brimpsfield manor court dealt with agrarian and tenurial matters for part of Cranham.[12] For the court of the dean and chapter's manors of Cranham, Barnwood, and Wotton, which the lessees held at will by 1650[13] and until 1783, there are court books for 1726–47 and 1774–1867 and a roll of a court of survey in 1796. It was almost exclusively concerned with tenurial matters.[14]

The parish had two churchwardens by 1498[15] and their accounts, which survive from 1790, include vestry minutes for the period 1822–1930.[16] Two overseers of the poor were recorded in 1677.[17] Annual expenditure on poor-relief rose from £30 in 1776 to £75 in 1803, when regular help was provided for 13 of the 25 persons given aid.[18] Expenditure remained relatively low in the early 19th century when many parishioners found employment outside agriculture. It had reached £148 by 1814, when half of the 36 relieved received regular aid,[19] but averaged £67 in the late 1820s and rose to £103 by 1833.[20] In 1819 some poorhouses known later as the Row were built in the eastern part of the village.[21] The parish, which in 1836 joined the Stroud poor-law union[22] and was later part of Stroud rural district,[23] was included in 1974 in the new Stroud district.

CHURCH. Cranham remained part of Brimpsfield parish in 1342[24] but architectural evidence suggests that there was a chapel on the site of Cranham church by the late 12th century. The chapel, which may have been that recorded on Cirencester Abbey's property in 1261,[25] had evidently been assigned parochial rights by 1455 when it was in the gift of the lord of Brimpsfield, Richard, duke of York.[26] The living, which in 1486 was a rectory,[27] was united with Brimpsfield in 1798.[28] That union

was dissolved in 1892[29] and Cranham remained a separate living until 1976 when it was added to the united benefice of Miserden with Edgeworth.[30]

The advowsons of Cranham and Brimpsfield rectories shared the same descent until the late 19th century.[31] For Cranham William Sandys of Painswick made an unsuccessful presentation in 1663. In 1673 Kenneth Freeman of Gloucester was patron for a turn and in 1739 the bishop presented through lapse.[32] In the early 1890s Richard Henry Denne sold the patronage of Cranham to Thomas Dyer-Edwardes of Prinknash Park,[33] who became a Roman Catholic shortly before his death in 1926,[34] and by 1927 it belonged to Athelstan Riley.[35] In 1978 Mr. Q. T. P. M. Riley was joint patron of the united benefice.[36]

Cranham rectory was worth £6 4s. 7d. in 1535[37] and £30 in 1650.[38] There was no glebe. Tithes of corn, hay, and wool were paid either in kind or cash by 1679 when the rector received no tithes from 10 a. belonging to the Ebworth estate;[39] by 1705 that estate paid a modus of £1 18s. for tithes.[40] In 1772 the rector disputed a claim by Samuel Sandys, Samuel Hayward, and William Hinton that their beech woods had always been exempt from tithes.[41] The living, valued at £50 in 1750,[42] was allotted £200 by Queen Anne's Bounty in 1793[43] but because of its poverty was later united with Brimpsfield.[44] In 1895, after the dissolution of that union, Queen Anne's Bounty awarded Cranham rectory £200 to meet a gift of £120 and land adjoining the rectory house.[45]

The rectory house north-east of the church is probably on the same site as that recorded in 1563.[46] The west wall includes an early window, possibly of the 16th century, on the first floor. In 1679 the two-storey building was said to have six rooms and there was a barn to the west of five bays.[47] The barn was demolished in 1845 and the site taken into the churchyard in 1868.[48] From the later 18th century rectors were non-resident; in 1835 the house was occupied by the parish clerk[49] and later by the schoolmistress.[50] It was repaired and extended to the north in 1892 when it became the rectory house again.[51] It was sold in 1977.[52]

Walter Bidfield, rector from 1486, was pre-

[11] Glos. R.O., D 2440, Brimpsfield and Cranham presentments.
[12] S.C. 2/175/22.
[13] Glos. R.O., D 1740/E 1, f. 20.
[14] Ibid. D 936/M 1/1–3; M 5.
[15] Hockaday Abs. xxii, 1498 visit. f. 30; lxiv, 1642 visit. f. 27.
[16] Glos. R.O., P 103/CW 2/1.
[17] Ibid. Q/SO 1, f. 157v.
[18] Poor Law Abstract, 1804, 180–1.
[19] Ibid. 1818, 154–5.
[20] Poor Law Returns (1830–1), p. 70; (1835), p. 69.
[21] Plaque on bldg.; G.D.R., T 1/64; W.I. booklet.
[22] Poor Law Com. 2nd Rep. p. 523.
[23] Census, 1961.
[24] Inq. Non. (Rec. Com.), 408.
[25] C.P. 25(1)/74/26 no. 587.
[26] Worc. Episc. Reg., Reg. Carpenter, i, f. 130v.; cf. Cal. Pat. 1452–61, 542.
[27] Worc. Episc. Reg., Reg. Alcock, f. 161v.
[28] G.D.R., D 17/2.
[29] Ex inf. the diocesan registrar.
[30] Glouc. Dioc. Yr. Bk. (1978), 19.
[31] Trans. B.G.A.S. lxxxi. 91; Worc. Episc. Reg., Reg. Alcock, f. 161v.; Hockaday Abs. cxxxiii, clxxiii.

[32] Hockaday Abs. clxxiii.
[33] Cf. G.D.R., D 5/1/10; Kelly's Dir. Glos. (1894), 130.
[34] Glouc. Jnl. 13 Feb. 1926.
[35] Kelly's Dir. Glos. (1927), 148.
[36] Glouc. Dioc. Yr. Bk. (1978), 19.
[37] Valor Eccl. (Rec. Com.), ii. 496.
[38] Trans. B.G.A.S. lxxxiii. 93.
[39] G.D.R., V 5/96T 1; V.C.H. Glos. xi. 67.
[40] G.D.R., V 5/96T 3.
[41] E 126/13/Trin. 1775 no. 7.
[42] G.D.R. vol. 381A, f. 25.
[43] Hodgson, Queen Anne's Bounty, p. cclxxxiv.
[44] G.D.R., D 17/2.
[45] Glos. R.O., P 103/IN 3/1.
[46] Bodl. MS. Rawl. C.790, f. 9.
[47] G.D.R., V 5/96T 1; G.D.R., T 1/64.
[48] Glos. R.O., P 103/CW 4/1; 3/1.
[49] G.D.R., V 5/56T 8.
[50] H.O. 129/338/2/6/12; Glos. R.O., D 1381/24.
[51] Cf. W.I. hist. of Cranham, 66.
[52] Ex inf. the Revd. J. Harper, rector of Miserden with Edgeworth and Cranham.

sumably a local man.[53] In 1551 the rector, John Sewen, was found to be unlearned on some points of doctrine,[54] and in 1563 it was said that there had been no sermons for two years. Thomas Lane, who held Cranham from 1565 in plurality with Brimpsfield, was resident in 1570[55] but later a curate served Cranham[56] and by 1584 Lane lived in Brimpsfield.[57] Thomas Wynell, rector from 1642, preached against Baptists and was ejected by the county committee before 1650[58] when James Cleyland, described as a preaching minister, held the living.[59] Charles Stock, who subscribed in 1662 as curate of Great Witcombe and Cranham, was presented to Cranham the following year, when he was rector of Aston Ingham (Herefs.), but evidently failed to secure the living. In 1664 he subscribed as curate of Cranham and Upton St. Leonards and in 1667 Edward Jackson became rector. In 1669 Stock, by then rector of King's Stanley, was licensed to hold Cranham in plurality, but Brian Parry succeeded Jackson in 1670. Edward Hales, rector from 1673, also held Condicote from 1675.[60] William Hatton, rector from 1677, was suspended in 1688 for adultery[61] and was succeeded the following year by his curate, Obadiah Done (d. 1738).[62] Samuel Ridler, Done's successor, was also rector of Edgeworth[63] and a curate served Cranham.[64] Ridler's successor William Walbank, rector 1750–84,[65] served in person but lived in Brimpsfield[66] where he became a landowner in 1766.[67] William Metcalfe, rector 1785–97, was also rector of Brimpsfield from where he served in person. The livings were united in 1798 after James Pitt had become rector of both parishes[68] but from 1874 a curate was employed at Cranham. Henry Rastrick Hanson, rector of Cranham 1892–1924,[69] introduced High Church ritual.[70]

The church, which apparently was called ST. JAMES c. 1703,[71] is built of ashlar and has a chancel with north vestry and south chapel, aisled nave with north porch, and west tower. The chancel arch was probably of the late 12th century before its restoration in the late 19th century,[72] and there is a reset lancet window in the west wall of the south aisle and a 12th-century voussoir set over the north doorway. The only parts of the structure which have survived later restorations without

being rebuilt are the late-15th- or early-16th-century tower, the south arcade, and parts of the south aisle including a window. The rood-screen is contemporary with those late medieval additions but the figures surmounting it were added in 1911.[73]

The church, which in the mid 19th century had a chancel, nave with south aisle, and west tower,[74] was restored between 1861 and 1862 by subscription, Martha Davies being the principal contributor.[75] Between 1894 and 1895 it was rebuilt, apart from the tower and aisle, and enlarged, chiefly at the expense of Thomas Dyer-Edwardes, to designs by Sidney Gambier Parry.[76] The chancel monuments were removed to the south aisle and the original east window, which had been inserted as a memorial to Mary Reynolds (d. 1852), to the west wall of the new north aisle. An altar stone was brought from Prinknash Park[77] and in 1915 Dyer-Edwardes gave some altar fittings, including a triptych of 16th-century paintings.[78] There were five bells c. 1703[79] but in the mid 19th century the peal comprised three bells cast or recast by Abraham Rudhall in 1708 and one cast by John Rudhall in 1800.[80] One of the older bells was recast in 1887 when two by Mears and Stainbank were added, one being the gift of Joseph Alexander Horlick.[81] Four were recast in 1947 by Gillett and Johnston of Croydon (Surr.).[82] The plate includes a chalice of 1716.[83] The earliest surviving parish register, which begins in 1666, contains entries for Prinknash.[84] The lych-gate was built as a memorial to men of Cranham and Prinknash killed in the First World War.[85]

NONCONFORMITY. In 1642 a Baptist preacher serving a meeting at Whaddon was active in Cranham[86] and, although no nonconformists were recorded there in 1676,[87] 12 people were presented in 1682 for not receiving the sacrament.[88] A group of Presbyterians, numbering 10 in 1735, has not been traced after 1750,[89] and there were a few, evidently shortlived, meetings in the late 18th and early 19th centuries.[90] In 1839 Particular Baptists built a chapel in the eastern part of the village. The meeting was too poor to employ a minister in 1851

[53] Worc. Episc. Reg., Reg. Alcock, f. 161v.
[54] E.H.R. xix. 115.
[55] Hockaday Abs. clxxiii, cxxxiii.
[56] G.D.R. vol. 40, f. 198v.
[57] Hockaday Abs. xlix, state of clergy 1584, f. 32.
[58] Walker Revised, ed. Matthews, 179; Hockaday Abs. lxiv, 1642 visit. f. 27.
[59] Trans. B.G.A.S. lxxxiii. 93.
[60] Hockaday Abs. clxxiii, cccxlvii.
[61] Ibid. clxxiii; G.D.R. vol. 259, f. 68, where his forename is given as Ric.
[62] Hockaday Abs. clxxiii; Glos. R.O., P 103/IN 1/1–2; cf. mon. in ch.
[63] Hockaday Abs. clxxiii, cxci.
[64] Glos. R.O., P 103/IN 1/2.
[65] Hockaday Abs. clxxiii.   [66] G.D.R. vol. 319.
[67] Glos. R.O., D 1388, Lyon fam., Caudle Green papers 1785–1803.
[68] Hockaday Abs. clxxiii, cxxxiii; G.D.R. vol. 382, f. 36.
[69] Glos. R.O., P 103/IN 1/7; Kelly's Dir. Glos. (1879–1927 edns.).

[70] Glos. R.O., P 103/CW 2/1.
[71] Bodl. MS. Rawl. B.323, f. 197v.; G.D.R. vol. 397, f. 25.
[72] Water-colour in base of tower.
[73] Glos. R.O., P 103/CW 4/1; inscr. in ch.
[74] Glos. Ch. Notes, 6–7.
[75] Glos. R.O., P 103/CW 2/2.
[76] Ibid. CW 4/1; Kelly's Dir. Glos. (1897), 132.
[77] W.I. hist. of Cranham, 62, 67.
[78] Glos. R.O., P 103/CW 2/1.
[79] Bodl. MS. Rawl. B.323, f. 197v.
[80] Glos. Ch. Bells, 44.
[81] Glos. R.O., P 103/CW 2/4; cf. ibid. 2/1; Kelly's Dir. Glos. (1889 edn.), 948.
[82] Chart in base of tower.
[83] Glos. Ch. Plate, 65.
[84] B. & G. Par. Rec. 113; Glos. R.O., P 103/IN 1/1.
[85] Inscr. on gate.
[86] Glos. R.O., D 2052.
[87] Compton Census.   [88] Glos. R.O., D 2052.
[89] G.D.R. vols. 285B, f. 17; 381A, f. 25.
[90] Hockaday Abs. clxxiii; Glos. R.O., D 2052.

when the average attendance was ten.[91] Services were still held in the early 1880s but the building was demolished at the end of the century.[92] Congregationalists were meeting in the parish by 1899[93] and in 1930 they converted the pottery at the east end of the village as a chapel,[94] for which furniture and fittings were made by Peter Waals.[95] The meeting had seven members in 1965.[96] The chapel was closed in the mid 1970s and adapted as a village hall.[97]

EDUCATION. In 1818 there were dame schools in Cranham teaching a total of *c.* 25 children.[98] A day-school begun in 1827 taught 55 children, including infants, in 1833 when it was supported by a private benefactor.[99] It was held in the rectory barn until 1845[1] when a National school, known later as Cranham C. of E. school, opened in a new building on the road from the church to the village.[2] The income was supplied in part by subscriptions and pence and at first the boys and girls, who *c.* 1846 numbered 18 and 19 respectively, were taught separately.[3] A school-house was built *c.* 1883.[4] The average attendance at the school, which Thomas Dyer-Edwardes enlarged in 1894, was 70 in 1897[5] but had fallen to 27 by 1936.[6] In 1948 there were 11 children on the roll but by 1958 that number had risen to 34[7] and in 1978 the attendance was 40.[8]

CHARITIES FOR THE POOR. In 1868 George Jones of Upton St. Leonards gave a pair of cottages in Cranham village with £162 7s. 7d. stock to provide rent-free accommodation for widows or, in default, widowers. In 1900, when one cottage was empty and the other let, a Scheme included unmarried people among the beneficiaries.[9] In the early 1970s, when the charity's income was made up of donations and *c.* £3 from investments, one cottage remained empty because of failure to meet local authority building regulations.[10]

ELKSTONE

THE PARISH of Elkstone is situated on one of the highest points of the Cotswolds, 10.5 km. south of Cheltenham. It covers 856 ha. (2,116 a.)[11] and its boundaries include on the south-west the Roman road, Ermin Street, on part of the north the old Gloucester–Northleach road, on the north-east the river Churn, and on the south and part of the east two brooks which combine to form the Bagendon brook.

The high ground of the parish lies at over 270 m. On the north-east the land falls steeply to the Churn and from the south it is broken into by a system of coombs, including the long central coomb at the head of which Elkstone village stands. Most of the parish lies on the Great Oolite, while fuller's earth and the Inferior Oolite outcrop on the slopes and Cotswold Sands form the base of the Churn valley.[12] The high ground was once almost all farmed as open fields, of which the still substantial remains were inclosed in 1835, and the slopes mostly as sheep-runs. Ward's wood at the north end of the parish, covering 14 a. in 1630,[13] is the only significant piece of woodland, though the inclusion of a wood measuring a half by a quarter league in the description of the manor in 1086[14] suggests that woodland once claimed more of the slopes.

The most significant thoroughfare in Elkstone was that crossing the parish from Cockleford in the north to Beechpike, formerly called Combend Beeches, on Ermin Street in the south. It was mentioned as Cheltenham way in 1680[15] and served as the main Cheltenham–Cirencester road until 1825 when the new Churn valley road was built, in part to avoid the obstacle posed to travellers by Cockleford hill on the old road.[16] The original course through the centre of the parish was presumably along the road, later partly closed, on which Elkstone village grew up; from High Cross, at the junction with the Gloucester–Northleach road at the top of Cockleford hill, that road ran due south into the north part of the village and continued east of the church and manor-house to take a curving course through the head of the coomb and meet the present road *c.* 1 km. due south of the church.[17] The higher and easier course running from High Cross west of the church is presumably later and may have been built only in the mid 18th

[91] H.O. 129/338/2/6/13; O.S. Map 6″, Glos. XXXIV. SW. (1883 edn.).
[92] W.I. hist. of Cranham, 80; cf. O.S. Map 6″, Glos. XXXIV. SW. (1903 edn.).
[93] Glos. R.O., D 2052.
[94] W.I. hist. of Cranham, 78. Plans for a chapel *c.* 1910 were not realized: cf. ibid.; *Kelly's Dir. Glos.* (1910), 138; (1914), 142.
[95] Glos. R.O., D 2876, p. 61.
[96] W.I. scrap-book for 1965, *penes* Mrs. Whitaker.
[97] Cf. Glos. Colln. RR 96.1.   [98] *Educ. of Poor Digest*, 296.
[99] *Educ. Enquiry Abstract*, 312.
[1] Cf. G.D.R., V 5/56T 8–9.
[2] Ed. 7/34/96; O.S. Map 6″, Glos. XXXIV. SW. (1883 edn.).
[3] *Church School Inquiry, 1846–7*, 4–5.

[4] W.I. hist. of Cranham, 96; cf. *B. & G. Par. Rec.* 113.
[5] *Kelly's Dir. Glos.* (1897), 132; (1910), 138.
[6] *Public Elem. Schs. 1906*, 183; *Bd. of Educ., List 21, 1936* (H.M.S.O.), 120.
[7] W.I. hist. of Cranham, 88–92.
[8] Ex inf. county educ. dept.
[9] Glos. R.O., D 3469/5/44; D 1297, Geo. Jones char. deeds.
[10] Ibid. CH 22.
[11] *Census*, 1971. This account was written in 1979.
[12] Geol. Surv. Map 1″, drift, sheet 235 (1933 edn.).
[13] Glos. R.O., D 184/M 24, p. 184.
[14] *Dom. Bk.* (Rec. Comm.), i. 169v.
[15] G.D.R., V 5/125T 1.
[16] Rudder, *Glos.* 439.
[17] Glos. R.O., D 184/P 1, plan of Elkstone.

century as the result of the establishment of a new turnpike route between Cheltenham and Tetbury. The Act for that route in 1756 apparently included the stretch from High Cross to the west side of the church, where the route branched away to Smith's Cross on Ermin Street to connect with the old ridgeway and salt-way by Winstone and Park Corner.[18] Possibly at the same time the road was continued southwards from the church to meet the old village road and provide an easier route for the Cirencester traffic; certainly the whole of the western road existed by 1769.[19] After 1774 the Tetbury and Cirencester routes through the parish were the same, for the former was switched in that year from Smith's Cross to Beechpike.[20] The old village road, bypassed by the improvements, was truncated in 1834 when its northern part, between High Cross and the village, and its southern part, leading into the Beechpike road, were closed.[21]

Ermin Street, which was usually known as the foss way[22] before the 19th century, was turnpiked in 1747.[23] Minor roads leading from it through the parish included the old Gloucester–Northleach road by way of High Cross and Colesbourne, the Gloucester–Rendcomb road branching away near Sparrowthorn,[24] and the road, recorded in 1612, from Beechpike to Colesbourne.[25] The last probably once followed the track and footpath passing close to Combend Manor before being diverted northwards away from the house, causing the sharp bend at the point where it meets the parish boundary.[26]

Elkstone village grew up on the old road running east of the church and formed two separate groups of buildings, which were of similar size[27] until the mid 19th century when the southern group, lying around the church, manor-house, and rectory, was reduced in size and the northern group, lying around the junction with a lane called Cock Lane,[28] was enlarged. The southern group once included dwellings east of the church and further south where the old road crossed the coomb. Two houses described as in Elkstone coomb in 1433[29] probably stood in the latter area and three houses there mentioned in 1707 included one long held by the family of Baldwin or Combe, whose alternative surname doubtless derived from the location of the house.[30] In 1769 most of the cottages on the manor estate were in the southern group while the northern comprised mainly the old tenant farm-houses in their home closes.[31] The pulling down of almost all the cottages in the south part of the village and the removal of some of the old farm-

houses in the north part and the building of new cottages there appears to have been the work of the lord of the manor William Hall; he was said to have pulled down c. 12 cottages in the 1860s and to have built almost as many new ones.[32]

The oldest house surviving in the village is the former church house, at the south-east corner of the churchyard, which was probably built in the 15th century. It comprised a main range of two storeys with a small staircase projection at the north-east corner. The principal room, on the first floor, could be entered direct from the churchyard and had a fire-place at the east end and an open arched-braced roof. The lower floor may always have been in two rooms, the eastern one having a large fire-place. By 1589 the building was let as a cottage,[33] and its roof was reconstructed in the 17th century. Later it was divided into two dwellings, a new chimney being built at the west end, but by 1979 it had been restored and enlarged as a single dwelling. The fact that the church house was singled out by the description of a 'fair house of stone' in a survey of the manor in 1630[34] suggests that the other dwellings of the village were at that date still built mainly of other materials.

In the north part of the village two or three of the old farm-houses survive; one of them (called Elkstone Court in 1979) dates from the 17th century but has a 20th-century addition on the north. Otherwise most of the houses are the plain stone cottages built by William Hall, and there are also a pair of cottages built by the Revd. R. H. M. Bouth in 1902[35] and two pairs of mid-20th-century council houses. Ivy Cottage Farm is a small 19th-century farm-house on the turnpike west of the village and a few houses were built on that road further north in the 20th century. The 19th-century school building in the north part of the village became the village hall in 1961.[36]

Where the central coomb meets the east boundary of the parish a small hamlet called Combend existed by 1630 when it was referred to as a 'town'.[37] The hamlet, grouped around the Beechpike–Colesbourne road, comprised only 4 houses c. 1710 but appears to have been somewhat larger by the early 19th century.[38] All but one of the houses were pulled down before 1883.[39] The house called Combend Manor, on the hillside to the south-west, was established by the early 16th century and from 1612 was the centre of a large freehold estate.

At Cockleford on the north boundary where the Cheltenham road crossed the Churn there was a

[18] Tewkesbury and Cheltenham Roads Act, 29 Geo. II, c.51; notes on Glos. turnpikes by Mr. A. Cossons, *penes* the editor, V.C.H. Glos.; cf. Bryant, *Map of Glos.* (1824).
[19] Glos. R.O., D 184/P 1, plan of Elkstone.
[20] Cheltenham Roads Act, 14 Geo. III, c.111.
[21] Glos. R.O., Q/SRh 1834 B/5.
[22] e.g. ibid. D 184/T 37, deed 1612; T 39, lease 1589.
[23] Cirencester Roads Act, 20 Geo. II, c.23.
[24] G.D.R., V 5/125T 1; Glos. R.O., D 444/T 18, mortgage 1610; cf. ibid. Q/SIb 1, f. 158.
[25] Glos. R.O., D 184/T 37.
[26] Cf. Bryant, *Map of Glos.* (1824).
[27] Glos. R.O., D 184/P 1, plan of Elkstone; G.D.R., T 1/76.

[28] Glos. R.O., D 184/T 37, lease 1617; P 1, f. 90.
[29] Ibid. M 6.
[30] Ibid. T 40; cf. ibid. P 1, ff. 85, 92; *Cal. Pat.* 1553–4, 449.
[31] Glos. R.O., D 184/P 1, ff. 85–101.
[32] *Rep. Com. Agric. Employment*, pp. 98–9; cf. O.S. Map 6", Glos. XXXIV. SE. (1883 edn.).
[33] Glos. R.O., D 184/T 39; cf. ibid. M 24, p. 181.
[34] Ibid. M 24, p. 181.
[35] Date and init. on bldg.
[36] Char. Com. Reg.
[37] Glos. R.O., D 184/M 24, p. 171.
[38] Bryant, *Map of Glos.* (1824); Atkyns, *Glos.* 428.
[39] O.S. Map 6", Glos. XXXV. SW. (1883 edn.).

group of three houses *c.* 1710.[40] Among them was the early-17th-century house which had been opened as an inn by 1675, the only one found recorded in the parish. It was known as the Cockleford inn or the Green Dragon[41] and remained open under the latter sign in 1979.

An early outlying dwelling appears to have existed at Oldbury close, lying in the angle of the Beechpike–Colesbourne road and the Gloucester–Rendcomb road.[42] Adam of Oldbury, mentioned in 1327, presumably had a dwelling there[43] and in 1537 the close was the site of the manor sheep-house.[44] The name may derive from the Roman site which has been discovered beneath the farm buildings at Slutswell at the north-west corner of the close[45] but as two other closes on the north side of the Gloucester–Rendcomb road, one and probably both inclosed from the open fields, were known as Clay Oldbury and Green Oldbury[46] there may also have been some earlier fortification which enclosed the whole of the end of the ridge.

Butler's Farm, in the Churn valley near the east corner of the parish, was built before 1671 on a small estate which passed from the manor to the Rogers family of Sandywell Park, Dowdeswell, at the beginning of the 17th century.[47] Highgate Farm, another outlying farmstead, in the opposite corner of the parish by Ermin Street, was built shortly before 1729 by Thomas Hamlett, a stone-cutter,[48] who presumably worked one of the near-by quarries. The house was rebuilt or remodelled in the later 19th century when it was a farm-house on the Cowley estate.[49]

Nineteen inhabitants of Elkstone were recorded in 1086.[50] Fourteen people were assessed for the subsidy in 1327[51] and 29 for the poll tax in 1381.[52] There were said to be *c.* 56 communicants in 1551,[53] 10 households in 1563,[54] and 24 families in 1650.[55] The population was estimated at *c.* 160 about 1710[56] and at 178 inhabitants about 1775.[57] The latter figure was probably an underestimate as 299 people were enumerated in 1801. There was virtually no change during the next 30 years and then a slight increase brought the numbers up to 336 by 1851. The population then went into a decline, which quickened with the period of agricultural depression: between 1871 and 1891 it fell from 302 to 199. There was a slight recovery before 1901, when another decline set in, bringing the population down to 140 by 1971.[58]

MANORS AND OTHER ESTATES.

In Edward the Confessor's reign Elkstone was held as two separate manors by two men called Lewin. After the Conquest the whole of Elkstone was granted to Ansfrid de Cormeilles, though in 1086 a knight held half of it from him.[59] The manor of *ELKSTONE* then descended with the honor of Cormeilles and after the death of Walter de Cormeilles (fl. 1211) passed to his daughter Aubrey who married Richard le Brun. John le Brun, son of Richard and Aubrey,[60] who was presumably the John of Elkstone who was in the king's wardship in 1221,[61] held Elkstone as 2 knights' fees from the honor of Cormeilles in 1236.[62] John le Brun died *c.* 1266 and was succeeded by another John le Brun,[63] who in 1303 settled the manor from after his death on John son of John of Acton.[64]

The younger John of Acton had succeeded to the manor by 1316[65] but in 1322 it was in the king's hands[66] because of John's involvement in the rebellion.[67] It was later granted to Hugh le Despenser, earl of Winchester,[68] executed in 1326. By the following year the same or another John of Acton had recovered possession of the manor.[69] John of Acton (d. *c.* 1362) was succeeded, under the terms of an agreement of 1343, by John Poyntz[70] (d. 1375). During the minority of John Poyntz's son Robert[71] the manor was held by John Cousin[72] of Cirencester, and in 1381 when Robert had come of age he granted it to Cousin and his wife Joan for their lives.[73] Cousin died in 1403[74] and the manor had reverted to Robert Poyntz by 1411 when he made it over to his son Nicholas,[75] who was succeeded at his death before 1460 by his son Humphrey.[76] Humphrey (d. 1487) was succeeded by his son Nicholas,[77] and the manor later passed to Robert Poyntz (d. *c.* 1521) and then in succession to Robert's sons Sir Francis[78] (d. 1528) and Sir Anthony.[79] In 1539 it belonged to Sir Nicholas Poyntz of Iron Acton who sold it that year to John Huntley of Standish.[80]

In 1542 John Huntley made the manor over to

[40] Atkyns, *Glos.* 428.
[41] Glos. R.O., Q/SO 1, f. 91v.; G.D.R. wills 1704/33; *Glouc. Jnl.* 7 May 1781.
[42] Glos. R.O., D 184/P 1, f. 89.
[43] *Glos. Subsidy Roll, 1327,* 10.
[44] Glos. R.O., D 184/T 38.
[45] *Trans. B.G.A.S.* xcvi. 85.
[46] Glos. R.O., D 184/P 1, f. 89; T 36, mortgage 1610.
[47] Ibid. T 36; D 444/T 19.
[48] Ibid. D 361/T 5.
[49] Ibid. D 1388/SL 5, no. 84.
[50] *Dom. Bk.* (Rec. Com.), i. 169v.
[51] *Glos. Subsidy Roll, 1327,* 10.
[52] E 179/113/35A rot. 14A; E 179/113/31A rot. 2.
[53] *E.H.R.* xix. 114.
[54] Bodl. MS. Rawl. C. 790, f. 9v.
[55] *Trans. B.G.A.S.* lxxxiii. 93.
[56] Atkyns, *Glos.* 428.
[57] Rudder, *Glos.* 439.
[58] *Census,* 1801–1971.
[59] *Dom. Bk.* (Rec. Com.), i. 169v.
[60] *Bk. of Fees,* i. 50; *Trans. B.G.A.S.* xiii. 33.

[61] *Bk. of Fees,* ii. 1338.
[62] Ibid. i. 440.
[63] *Cal. Inq. p.m.* i, p. 201.
[64] C.P. 25(1)/75/39 no. 231.
[65] *Feud. Aids,* ii. 271, where John Giffard is given as joint ld. of the man. but by what right has not been discovered.
[66] *Cal. Fine R.* 1319–27, 96.
[67] E 142/31 rot. 5.
[68] *Cal. Inq. p.m.* vi, p. 423; E 142/34.
[69] *Glos. Subsidy Roll, 1327,* 10; *Cal. Pat.* 1327–30, 285.
[70] *Cal. Close,* 1360–4, 317–18; *Cal. Pat.* 1343–5, 52.
[71] *Cal. Inq. p.m.* xiv, pp. 303–4.
[72] *Cal. Fine R.* 1368–77, 345.
[73] *Cal. Pat.* 1377–81, 616.
[74] Hockaday Abs. clv.
[75] *Cal. Pat.* 1408–13, 297–8.
[76] *Cal. Close,* 1454–61, 465.
[77] *Cal. Inq. p.m. Hen. VII,* i. pp. 133–4; *Cal. Fine R.* 1485–1509, p. 84.
[78] C 142/35 no. 8.
[79] C 142/50 no. 9°.
[80] Glos. R.O., D 184/T 35.

his son George and George's wife Catherine.[81] George died in 1580 and was survived by Catherine; later the manor passed to their son James who was, however, described as farmer of the manor until the mid 1590s and so presumably then held it on lease from his mother.[82] James Huntley died in 1611, having a few days earlier granted a 900-year lease of the manor to his sons Edmund and John, excepting the site and demesne lands which he devised to another son, Henry. Henry was joined by his brothers in a sale of a large part of the demesne land to Sir John Horton in 1612, and the site and residue of the demesne were acquired by Edmund Huntley who sold them in 1613 to his cousin Sir George Huntley of Frocester. In 1614 Edmund, having acquired his brother John's interest in 1612, sold the manor to Sir George.[83] Sir George (d. 1622) was succeeded by his son William[84] who sold Elkstone in 1623 to Dame Elizabeth Craven and her son William.[85]

William Craven, who was created Lord Craven in 1627 and earl of Craven in 1665, died in 1697 and the manor followed the descent of the Craven barony,[86] passing to another William Craven (d. 1711), to his sons William (d. 1739) and Fulwar (d. 1764), to their cousin William Craven (d. 1769), and to William's nephew William Craven (d. 1791). The last-mentioned William, Lord Craven, devised the manor to his second son Henry Augustus Berkeley Craven[87] (d. 1836) who was succeeded by his brother Richard Keppel Craven (d. 1851). On Richard's death or soon afterwards the manor reverted to the representative of the main line, William Craven, earl of Craven,[88] who sold the 1,040-acre estate in 1858 to William Hall, later of Seven Springs, Coberley.[89] Hall died in 1872 and his daughter Mrs. Sarah Bubb of Ullenwood[90] owned the manor in 1885. By 1889 it had passed to a Mrs. Bouth, and R. H. M. Bouth, rector of Elkstone, owned it in 1902. Before 1919 it was acquired by Sir James Horlick, Bt.[91] (d. 1921), of Cowley Manor, whose son Sir Ernest put it up for sale in 1928.[92] It was bought c. 1930 by John Pearce Pope, auctioneer of Gloucester, members of whose family had farmed Manor farm and Combend farm during the late 19th and early 20th centuries. The Pope family sold the estate, comprising Manor farm, in 1954 to the tenant Mrs. G. M. Price, who retained it in 1979.[93]

The manor-house of Elkstone, which comprised a hall and other buildings in 1537,[94] stood south of the church. After the early 17th century it was used as the farm-house of the manor farm,[95] none of the lords of the manor apparently living at Elkstone. In the mid 19th century the house was demolished and replaced by new farm buildings, and a new house, called Elkstone Manor, was built on the opposite side of the road.[96]

The sale by the Huntleys to Sir John Horton in 1612 created the separate *COMBEND* estate. Included in the sale were the mansion at Combend and 544 a. of land, comprising all the closes south of the Beechpike–Colesbourne road and a substantial acreage of open-field land.[97] Sir John Horton (d. 1667) was succeeded by his son Thomas[98] (d. 1693) and Thomas by his grandson Thomas Horton, who was a lunatic by 1722[99] and died in 1727.[1] The last Thomas was succeeded by his son Thomas Horton of Wotton, Gloucester, who was declared a lunatic in 1746 and his estates placed in the custody of his brothers-in-law. Although by a will made in 1735 Thomas had devised his estates to members of the Brereton family, in 1739 he settled them on his sisters Eleanor, wife of Richard Roberts, and Elizabeth, wife of William Blanch, and after Thomas's death in 1755 the interested parties disputed the estates; in 1758 an agreement was reached for a threefold partition and in 1763 the Gloucestershire lands were confirmed as the share of William Blanch, son of William and Elizabeth.[2] William died in 1766 leaving Combend for life to his widow Anne, who married Samuel Walbank, with reversion to James Rogers of Gloucester.[3] The estate was later sold, apparently in 1778 by the Walbanks and Rogers's heirs, to Samuel Bowyer,[4] an Exchequer official. Samuel's son Samuel sold the estate, which with adjoining land in Colesbourne amounted to 860 a., to William Robinson in 1797.[5] In 1841 the estate belonged to the same or another William Robinson[6] and by 1856 it had passed to Thomas Dunn (d. 1894).[7] It was acquired before 1897 by C. F. Greathead of Kirkham Abbey (Yorks. E.R.), who held it until c. 1919 when it was acquired by G. R. P. Llewellyn.[8] Llewellyn offered it for sale in 1923[9] and it was bought then or soon afterwards by Asa Lingard[10] (d. 1957), whose executors sold it to Capt. P. H. Gibbs. Capt. Gibbs owned the estate in 1979 when it comprised 486 ha. (1,200 a.) in Elkstone and adjoining parishes.[11]

[81] Ibid.
[82] C 142/194 no. 16; Glos. R.O., D 184/M 7.
[83] C 142/322 no. 154; Glos. R.O., D 184/T 37.
[84] C 142/394 no. 57.   [85] Glos. R.O., D 184/T 37.
[86] For the Cravens, see Burke, *Peerage* (1935), 651–2.
[87] Glos. Colln. JF 22.5.
[88] Glos. R.O., D 184/T 54.
[89] Ibid. D 2622.
[90] *Chelt. Examiner*, 4 Dec. 1872; *Chelt. Chron.* 14 Mar. 1931.
[91] *Kelly's Dir. Glos.* (1885 and later edns.).
[92] Burke, *Peerage* (1935), 1275; *Glouc. Jnl.* 27 Oct. 1928.
[93] *Kelly's Dir. Glos.* (1870 and later edns.); ex inf. Mr. C. Pope, of J. Pearce Pope & Sons, Gloucester.
[94] Glos. R.O., D 184/T 38.   [95] Ibid. T 37.
[96] G.D.R., T 1/76; O.S. Map 6″, Glos. XXXIV. SE. (1883 edn.).

[97] Glos. R.O., D 184/T 37.
[98] *Wilts. Arch. Mag.* xli. 255, 259; and for the Hortons, cf. *Visit. Glos. 1682–3*, 93–4.
[99] *Wilts. Arch. Mag.* v. 325; Glos. R.O., P 135/IN 1/2.
[1] Bigland, *Glos.* i. 559.
[2] *Wilts. Arch. Mag.* v. 325–7; xli. 262.
[3] Prob. 11/918 (P.C.C. 167 Tyndal).
[4] Bigland, *Glos.* i. 558; cf. C.P. 25(2)/1316/16 Geo. III Hil. no. 8.
[5] Glos. R.O., D 1386; *Glouc. Jnl.* 9 Nov. 1795.
[6] G.D.R., T 1/76.
[7] *Kelly's Dir. Glos.* (1856), 284; Glos. R.O., SL 414.
[8] *Kelly's Dir. Glos.* (1897 and later edns.); T. S. Tonkinson, *Elkstone, Its Manors, Church and Registers* (Chelt. 1919), 11.
[9] Glos. R.O., D 2582/11.
[10] Ibid. D 930.
[11] Ex inf. Capt. Gibbs.

Architectural evidence shows that there was a house on the site of Combend Manor some 100 years before the beginning of the 17th century when James Huntley, lord of Elkstone manor, lived there.[12] Sir John Horton lived there or at his manor-house at Broughton Gifford (Wilts.),[13] and his son, who was assessed on 12 hearths in 1672,[14] and his great-grandson also used Combend.[15] By 1735, however, the house had fallen into disrepair[16] and about 1780 it was said to have been demolished.[17] In 1795 the property included a farm-house, occupied by the tenant of the estate, and a newly-built dwelling-house,[18] and it was presumably the latter that was destroyed by fire in 1807.[19] Alterations carried out in the 20th century, however, make the documentary evidence difficult to relate to the surviving buildings. A two-storey building of the early 16th century at the north end of the site, used as a barn in 1979, is presumably a remnant of the original house. South-east of it another range of buildings incorporates on the north a barn of the 16th or 17th century and on the south a domestic building which may be of the 17th century. That range was transformed in 1921 to the designs of Sidney Barnsley when part of the barn was taken into the house.[20]

An estate at Elkstone, assessed at ¼ knight's fee, was held in 1303 (and probably by 1285) by Thomas de Gardino. The same or another Thomas held it in 1346 and John Mene held it in 1402.[21] It was evidently that estate which was later accounted a manor and in 1431 was held with part of Colesbourne,[22] descending with it to John Vampage (d. 1548).[23] The estate, then comprising two houses and 4 yardlands, was divided among three coheirs of Vampage. Vampage's nephews Edmund Harewell and John Higford sold their shares to George Huntley, lord of Elkstone, in 1556 and 1564 respectively;[24] the third share has not been traced.

Before 1285 William de Sollers gave 1 yardland and 4 a. at Cockleford in Elkstone to Llanthony Priory which received two other gifts at the same period, 1 yardland and 6 a. from William Atwood (de Bosco) and ½ yardland from William of Oldbury.[25] The land was presumably retained by the priory until the Dissolution as part of its manor of Colesbourne.[26]

ECONOMIC HISTORY. In 1086 each half of the manor had two plough-teams working the demesne land, and that half kept in hand by Ansfrid de Cormeilles had 4 *servi.*[27] In 1376 the demesne of the manor comprised 2 plough-lands, 12 a. of meadow, and 10 a. of several pasture.[28] At the beginning of the 17th century, when several former freehold tenements had been absorbed into it, the demesne was very extensive, including more than two-thirds of the parish. Even after the sale of 424 a. in closes, 120 a. of open-field land, and 300 sheep-pastures to Sir John Horton in 1612[29] there remained 880 a. of land on the manor demesne, including c. 350 a. of open-field land and the large slaits, or sheep-runs, which occupied the hillsides of the parish.[30] The whole 880 a. was on lease with the manor-house as a single unit in 1665.[31]

In 1086 each half of the manor supported 5 *villani* and 2 bordars, on one half working 3½ plough-teams between them and on the other 3 plough-teams.[32] In 1376 the manor had villein and free tenants paying a total rent of 40s.[33] and in 1415 28 tenants held from the manor.[34] The number of separate holdings in the parish was reduced by the Huntleys who bought in some free tenements in the 1540s[35] and the Vampage estate later. Some tenements were held on leases for years in 1433 but by the end of that century the same tenements were held as copyholds.[36] From the later 16th century leases for lives became the usual form of tenure[37] and had all but ousted copyholds by 1630. There were eight main holdings on the manor in 1630, ranging in size from 23 a. to 79 a., and a few cottage holdings.[38]

The high ground of the parish was originally in open fields, while the coombs and hillsides provided pasture closes and large sheep-runs and the valley bottoms by the Churn and the streams in the Combend area some inclosed meadow land. A three-field rotation was the practice in the parish in 1376[39] but in the post-medieval period it had only two large open fields, the north field, extending across north of the village and along the spur of high ground as far as Slutswell, and the south (or Combend)[40] field, which appears originally to have occupied the whole of the west side of the parish bordering Ermin Street. Uncomb common, 11 a. of rough grazing lying above Lower Cockleford, was the only common pasture by the late 18th century,[41] though earlier there had been others: common rights in Comb Green, adjoining Combend Manor, and in the woods of the manor were reserved in copyholds granted in the 1570s

---

[12] Glos. R.O., D 184/T 37, deed 1612.
[13] *Wilts. Arch. Mag.* xli. 252–9.
[14] E 179/247/14 rot. 6.
[15] Glos. R.O., P 135/IN 1/2; Atkyns, *Glos.* 428; cf. *Wilts. Arch. Mag.* v. 324–5, which apparently confuses Elkstone with Elston (Wilts.), another possession of the Hortons.
[16] *Wilts. Arch. Mag.* v. 325.
[17] Bigland, *Glos.* i. 558.
[18] *Glouc. Jnl.* 9 Nov. 1795. [19] Ibid. 6 Apr. 1807.
[20] Verey, *Glos.* i. 241; Glos. R.O., D 2299/3681.
[21] *Feud. Aids*, ii. 239, 247, 280, 299.
[22] C.P. 25(1)/79/88 no. 34.
[23] C 142/86 no. 91.
[24] Glos. R.O., D 444/T 18.
[25] C 115/K 2/6683 ff. 256v.–7, 263 and v., 270.
[26] Cf. S.C. 6/Hen. VIII/1224 m. 15d., which includes only a free rent owed from land in Elkstone; other Elkstone land was

perhaps held by the customary tenants whose holdings are not described.
[27] *Dom. Bk.* (Rec. Com.), i. 169v.
[28] E 149/41 no. 18.
[29] Glos. R.O., D 184/T 37.
[30] Ibid. M 24, p. 184.
[31] Ibid. T 38.
[32] *Dom. Bk.* (Rec. Com.), i. 169v.
[33] E 149/41 no. 18.
[34] Glos. R.O., D 184/M 6.
[35] Ibid. T 35.
[36] Ibid. M 6.
[37] Ibid. T 40.
[38] Ibid. M 24, pp. 165–83.
[39] E 149/41 no. 18.
[40] Glos. R.O., D 184/T 40, lease 1707.
[41] Ibid. P 1, f. 101.

and later.[42] In the open fields pasture was stinted at 3 sheep to the acre in 1707.[43] Some flocks belonging to non-parishioners were apparently pastured regularly in Elkstone in the late 16th century[44] and the tithing customs recorded in 1705 covered both the wintering and summering of sheep by outsiders.[45]

Some considerable inclosures from the open fields were made by James Huntley and his tenants in 1594;[46] Sir George Huntley exchanged land in the north field with the rector in 1621;[47] and William Huntley inclosed a large area of the north field by agreement with nine of his tenants in 1622.[48] One motive for those inclosures was evidently the provision of additional permanent sheep-pasture: New field, a 160-acre sheep-pasture included in the sale of Combend in 1612, was evidently formed of land taken out of the south end of the south field,[49] and Clay Oldbury, inclosed out of the east of the north field,[50] had been turned to pasture by 1630.[51] About 520 a. of open-field land remained on the manor estate in 1630[52] and inclosure presumably continued in a piecemeal fashion during the next 150 years, for by 1775 only 263 a. remained on that estate, the two fields being limited by then to an area in the immediate vicinity of the village.[53] The remaining open-field land was inclosed by Act of Parliament in 1835, when the lord of the manor received the bulk of it and the rector was the only other substantial recipient.[54]

The pattern of holdings on the manor estate had altered considerably by the later 18th century, most of the old tenant holdings having been absorbed into larger units. In 1775 there were five main farms. The manor-house, part of the demesne land, and a former tenant holding made a farm of 601 a., and another of 260 a., with farm buildings at Slutswell, comprised a further part of the demesne and a former holding. Two other former holdings, 74 a. in all, were leased to the rector Humphrey Lloyd, who perhaps farmed them with the glebe, and there was a farm of 50 a. in the west corner of the parish, presumably farmed from Highgate Farm though the house itself was not part of the manor estate. Another farm of 35 a. was the only one to survive from those described in 1630 and was still in the possession of the family of the rector William Poole, who had been the tenant in 1630. Five other tenants held small pieces of land in 1775 and there were 14 cottagers.[55] Most of the remainder of the parish was included in the Combend estate, which

after the early 18th century appears to have been farmed by lessees as a single unit.[56] The only substantial farm independent of the two big estates in the 18th century was Butler's farm covering c. 90 a. in the Churn valley.[57]

After the parliamentary inclosure most of the manor estate was farmed as a single unit, Manor farm, which comprised 1,065 a. in 1841. William Proctor, who farmed it together with the rector's glebe and some land of his own,[58] employed 45 labourers in 1851 and almost as many worked on Combend farm, which comprised 998 a.[59] Butler's farm, lately bought by the lord of the manor, had had other land added to it by the 1850s to make a farm of 177 a.,[60] and the only other substantial farm based in the parish after the mid 19th century was Highgate farm, which had most of its land in Cowley, to which estate it belonged.[61] Various small holdings brought the total of agricultural units in the parish up to 9 in 1896[62] and 15 in 1926, when the 11 smaller ones were all under 50 a.[63] Most of those small holdings had gone by the 1970s[64] when the Manor farm and Combend estates still divided most of the parish between them.

In the later 18th century the parish was predominantly arable,[65] the land under the plough including the former demesne sheep-pastures of Cockleford slait and North slait, on the hillsides above the Churn, and Home slait and Walling slait, in the central coomb.[66] The Combend estate, however, had 260 a. of permanent meadow and pasture in 1795, which was then said to be an unusual amount for a hill estate.[67] The high and exposed situation of Elkstone, which made the harvest one of the latest in the county,[68] did not encourage agricultural innovation; in 1773 the inclosed land of the manor estate was managed on a three-course rotation with a fallow or else clover and grass-seeds in the third year, while the open-field land was still cropped and fallowed in alternate years.[69] Turnips had been introduced on at least some farms by 1801,[70] however, and in the mid 19th century the arable was evidently managed on the usual four- or five-course rotation of the region, comprising turnips, barley and oats, seeds in one or two years, and wheat.[71] In 1841 1,372 a. were under the plough and 576 a. were permanent meadow and pasture.[72] With the agricultural depression of the later 19th century the acreage of wheat and barley slumped. That was offset to some

[42] Ibid. M 7; cf. G.D.R., T 1/76.
[43] Glos. R.O., D 184/T 40.
[44] Ibid. M 7.
[45] G.D.R., V 5/125T 4.
[46] Glos. R.O., D 184/M 7.
[47] Ibid. T 37.
[48] Ibid. M 8.
[49] Ibid. T 37; cf. G.D.R., T 1/76.
[50] Glos. R.O., D 184/T 36, mortgage 1610; cf. ibid. P 1, f. 89.
[51] Ibid. M 24, p. 178.   [52] Ibid. pp. 165–85.
[53] Ibid. P 1, ff. 85–101.
[54] Ibid. Q/RI 62.
[55] Ibid. D 184/P 1, ff. 85–101; and for the Poole holding, cf. ibid. M 24, p. 176; T 48.
[56] Ibid. P 135/IN 1/2, entry for Apr. 1710.
[57] Ibid. D 181/III/T 39.

[58] G.D.R., T 1/76.
[59] H.O. 107/1968.
[60] Glos. R.O., D 2622.
[61] Ibid. D 1388/SL 5, no. 84.
[62] M.A.F. 68/1609/1.
[63] M.A.F. 68/3295/5.
[64] Agric. Returns 1976.
[65] Rudder, Glos. 438; Bigland, Glos. i. 558.
[66] Glos. R.O., D 184/T 37; cf. ibid. P 1, ff. 85, 89.
[67] Glouc. Jnl. 9 Nov. 1795.
[68] Rudder, Glos. 438.
[69] Glos. R.O., D 184/T 37.
[70] Acreage Returns, 1801.
[71] M.A.F. 68/26/19; cf. Rep. Com. Agric. Employment, p. 100.
[72] G.D.R., T 1/76.

extent, however, by an increase in oats, of which 128 a. were returned in 1866 and 322 a. in 1896, and turnips and temporary grassland were little affected, the number of sheep showing a considerable increase in the period.[73] In the early 20th century, however, arable farming suffered a severe reduction, with only 708 a. being returned as under the plough in 1926 when the bulk of the parish was classed as permanent grassland, including 511 a. described as rough grazing.[74] The farms came to concentrate mainly on cattle, of which 242, including 31 milk cows, were returned in 1896, and 366, including 84 milk cows, in 1926.[75] In 1906 one of the farmers and the landlord of the Green Dragon both had cattle-dealing as a sideline,[76] and W. H. Hitch, who farmed Combend in the 1920s and early 1930s, built up a pedigree herd of dairy shorthorns.[77] In 1979 Manor farm specialized in dairying while Combend was used mainly for cereals.

A mill called Badnams mill was sold by the lord of the manor, George Huntley, to William Bayly of Wheatenhurst in 1549.[78] John Bayly sold it in 1570, when it comprised a fulling-mill and a corn-mill, to Thomas Pleydell of Shrivenham (Berks.), whose son George succeeded to it before 1594.[79] In 1630 Edward Pleydell was paying rent for right of access through North slait to his mill,[80] so it was presumably located at Lower Cockleford. A mill at Lower Cockleford in Elkstone was sold by Lord Chedworth's trustees to John Elwes of Colesbourne in 1808[81] but may have been demolished by the 1840s when the only mill there was apparently one in Coberley parish.[82]

Another corn- and fulling-mill was built c. 1582 by William Gibbons[83] on the Churn 600 m. below Lower Cockleford at the point where the river is joined by the small stream called the Wash brook. It was being worked as a fulling-mill by Samuel Gibbons in 1612 and Richard Gibbons in 1636 but Anthony Gibbons, who renewed the lease of the site from the lord of the manor in 1671, was described as a yeoman of Miserden.[84] The mill had apparently been demolished by 1775 when the site was called Old Mill close.[85] In the late 19th century and the early 20th a small mill called Bone mill stood on the Watercombe brook on the Combend estate.[86]

Nathaniel Poole was trading as a clothier at Elkstone in 1677[87] as was Robert Bompass in 1818,[88] but they are the only representatives of the cloth industry found recorded apart from the fullers in the late 16th century and the early 17th. Otherwise Elkstone had only a few of the usual village tradesmen. Five were listed in 1608[89] and in 1831 only 4 families were supported by trade.[90] Two masons, one of whom was the lessee of Brimspits quarry by Ermin Street,[91] were among the tradesmen listed in 1608, and the stoneworking trades, including masons, slaters, and quarrymen, provided most of the small number of tradesmen recorded later.[92] In the later 19th century Edwin Draper, who worked a smithy at Cockleford and kept the Green Dragon inn, appears to have been almost the only representative of trade in the parish.[93] In the 1880s there was a small brickworks by the Churn in the east corner of the parish.[94]

LOCAL GOVERNMENT. Frankpledge jurisdiction in Elkstone, which formed a single tithing with Syde for that purpose, was exercised by the Rapsgate hundred court.[95] Court rolls for the Elkstone manor court survive for the period 1571–1609[96] and for 1670.[97] It was presumably still being regularly held in 1735 when a lease of the manor farm reserved the use of the house for the court twice a year.[98]

Churchwardens' accounts from 1791 are the only records of parish government known to survive.[99] The appointment of churchwardens was one of several matters disputed between the rector William Prior and the parishioners. Another appears to have been the administration of poor-relief, for in 1699 Prior got an order from the magistrates that payments should be made monthly in church after Sunday service in the presence of the rector and leading parishioners.[1] In the early 19th century the cost of relief seems to have been about average for a parish of the size; c. 20 people were usually receiving permanent relief.[2] In 1836 Elkstone became part of the Cirencester poor-law union[3] and it passed into Cirencester rural district,[4] being absorbed by Cotswold district in 1974.

CHURCH. The church at Elkstone dates from the later 12th century. The living was a rectory in 1291[5] and has remained one. It was united with Syde in 1927,[6] and Winstone was added to the

[73] M.A.F. 68/26/19; M.A.F. 68/1609/1.
[74] M.A.F. 68/3295/5.
[75] M.A.F. 68/1609/1; M.A.F. 68/3295/5.
[76] Kelly's Dir. Glos. (1906), 156.
[77] Glos. Colln. J 10.63.
[78] Glos. R.O., D 184/T 36.
[79] Ibid. M 7; C 66/1069 mm. 25–6.
[80] Glos. R.O., D 184/M 24, p. 183.
[81] Deeds 1810, penes Mr. H. W. G. Elwes, of Colesbourne Pk.
[82] Cf. G.D.R., T 1/76.　　　　[83] Glos. R.O., D 184/M 7.
[84] Ibid. T 43; D 444/T 18.
[85] Ibid. D 184/P 1, f. 94.
[86] O.S. Map 6″, Glos. XLIII. NW. (1884 edn.); Glos. R.O., SL 414.
[87] Glos. R.O., D 184/T 48.
[88] Hockaday Abs. cxcii.
[89] Smith, Men and Armour, 255–6.

[90] Census, 1831.
[91] Glos. R.O., D 184/T 39.
[92] e.g. ibid. T 40, lease 1622; T 47; H.O. 107/1968.
[93] Kelly's Dir. Glos. (1856 and later edns.).
[94] O.S. Map 6″, Glos. XXXV. SW. (1883 edn.).
[95] Ciren. Cart. ii, p. 619.
[96] Glos. R.O., D 184/M 7.
[97] Ibid. M 8, which also has draft rolls and ct. papers for the early 17th cent.
[98] Ibid. D 181/III/T 40.
[99] B. & G. Par. Rec. 135.
[1] Glos. R.O., P 135/IN 1/2.
[2] Poor Law Abstract, 1804, 180–1; 1818, 154–5.
[3] Poor Law Com. 2nd Rep. p. 522.
[4] Census, 1911.
[5] Tax. Eccl. (Rec. Com.), 221.
[6] Lond. Gaz. 23 Dec. 1927, pp. 8224–5.

united benefice in 1949 but was replaced in it by Brimpsfield in 1972.[7] The advowson of Elkstone descended with the manor,[8] though in 1525 Thomas Poyntz exercised it for one turn,[9] in 1583 the Queen presented through lapse, and in 1625 trustees for the former lord, William Huntley, presented.[10]

The rector received all the tithes of the parish except for small portions that had been granted to religious houses. In 1291 Newent Priory was entitled to a portion worth 13s. 4d., Eynsham Abbey (Oxon.) to one of 6s. 8d., and Fontenay Abbey (Calvados) to one of 3s., though Fontenay's right was then being disputed by the rector.[11] In 1535, however, only a portion of 6s. 8d. owed to Fotheringhay College (Northants.), successor to Newent's endowments, was recorded.[12] By 1680 the owner of Combend had negotiated a composition with the rector for all the tithes of that estate. From the rest of the parish, however, tithes were still paid in kind, except those for young animals in cases where there were insufficient numbers to be tithed.[13] The tithes of the parish were commuted for a corn-rent-charge of £356 in 1841.[14] The rector's glebe in 1680 comprised 51 a. in closes and 52½ a. in the open fields with sheep- and beast-pastures.[15] After inclosure the total glebe amounted to 78 a.[16]

The rectory house standing north-east of the church was recorded from 1608.[17] It incorporates reset windows of the 14th and 17th centuries but otherwise appears to have been rebuilt in the early 18th century. The principal front, on the west, is of five bays and three storeys and has windows with semicircular heads and rusticated architraves.[18] The east front was partly of three and partly of two storeys over a basement until 1847 when that front was reconstructed to the designs of Francis Niblett;[19] it was raised to the same height as the main front, given projecting bays at each side, and refaced and refenestrated. At the same time the interior was remodelled and a new staircase put in. The house remained the residence of the incumbent of the united benefice until 1973.[20]

The rectory was valued at £10 in 1291[21] and at £12 9s. 2d. in 1535.[22] It was worth £80 in 1650,[23] c. £100 in 1727, c. £150 in 1797,[24] and £382 in 1856.[25]

In the post-medieval period the living was usually held by non-resident pluralists and served by stipendiary curates. James Huntley, who later succeeded to the manor, was rector from 1562 until 1570;[26] he was non-resident in 1563.[27] William Broad, rector 1583–1611, was also rector of Rendcomb, where he lived.[28] William Poole, who held the living from 1625 until his death in 1665, probably resided at Elkstone.[29] Poole was an unsuccessful claimant to North Cerney rectory and it was his rival there, Samuel Rich,[30] who succeeded him at Elkstone and held both livings until his death in 1683.[31] William Prior, rector 1683–1726,[32] lived at Elkstone where his relations with his parishioners were often troubled.[33] Humphrey Lloyd, 1727–79, was also portioner of Tredington (Worcs.), and his successor, Charles Bishop[34] (d. 1788), was also rector of Rudford but lived at Elmore Court where he kept a private school.[35] Fulwar Craven Fowle, rector 1788–1840, was later also vicar of Kintbury (Berks.). Thomas Hooper, who served Elkstone as curate from 1794[36] and later was also rector of Syde and curate of Winstone,[37] succeeded Fowle in the rectory and died in 1845.[38] In 1825 he was holding one Sunday service at Elkstone, alternating between mornings and evenings,[39] but in 1830 the bishop intervened to get full services at Elkstone and a rise in salary for Hooper.[40]

The church of *ST. JOHN THE EVANGELIST*, the dedication of which is recorded from 1506,[41] is built of rubble and ashlar and has a chancel, a nave with south porch, and a west tower. The chancel is in two vaulted compartments separated by a wide arch and it is suggested that in the later 12th century when the church was built the western compartment was the base of a central tower. Although small the church is notable for its sculptural decoration, including that of the corbel table and the south doorway, which has a carved tympanum depicting Christ in Majesty. The central tower was probably removed in the 13th century at the time when new windows were put into the south sides of both compartments of the chancel, and it was probably at the same remodelling that a chamber, later adapted as a columbarium, was formed over the eastern compartment. The nave was refenestrated in the 14th century and a new window put into the north wall of the

[7] *Glouc. Dioc. Yr. Bk.* (1971), 52; (1978), 38.
[8] C.P. 25(1)/75/39 no. 231; Worc. Episc. Reg., Reg. Brian, i, f. 32; Reg. Morgan, i, f. 11v.; Hockaday Abs. cxcii.
[9] Worc. Episc. Reg., Reg. Ghinucci, f. 18.
[10] Hockaday Abs. cxcii; cf. Glos. R.O., D 184/T 37, agreement 11 July 1623.
[11] *Tax. Eccl.* (Rec. Com.), 221.
[12] *Valor Eccl.* (Rec. Com.), ii. 496; cf. *V.C.H. Glos.* ii. 106.
[13] G.D.R., V 5/125T 1, 4.
[14] G.D.R., T 1/76.
[15] G.D.R., V 5/125T 1.
[16] G.D.R., T 1/76.
[17] Glos. R.O., D 184/T 41.
[18] See plate facing p. 125.
[19] G.D.R., F 4/1.
[20] *Glouc. Dioc. Yr. Bk.* (1973), 53, 76.
[21] *Tax. Eccl.* (Rec. Com.), 221.
[22] *Valor Eccl.* (Rec. Com.), ii. 496.
[23] *Trans. B.G.A.S.* lxxxiii. 93.

[24] Hockaday Abs. cxcii.
[25] G.D.R. vol. 384, f. 92.
[26] Hockaday Abs. cxcii.
[27] Bodl. MS. Rawl. C.790, f. 9v.
[28] Hockaday Abs. xlix, state of clergy 1584, f. 24; cxcii; cccxxii.
[29] Ibid. cxcii; Bigland, *Glos.* i. 559.
[30] C 107/112.
[31] Hockaday Abs. cxliii, cxcii.
[32] Hockaday Abs. cxcii.
[33] Glos. R.O., P 135/IN 1/2.
[34] Hockaday Abs. cxcii.
[35] *Glouc. Jnl.* 15 Dec. 1777; 31 Mar. 1788; G.D.R. vol. 319.
[36] Hockaday Abs. cxcii.
[37] Ibid. cccxxxviii, ccccix.
[38] Inscr. in ch.
[39] G.D.R. vol. 383, no. ccxxx.
[40] Hockaday Abs. cxcii.
[41] Ibid.

eastern part of the chancel. The tall west tower, which has a lofty, vaulted lower stage, was added in the 15th century.[42] The western chancel arch, which had become broken and misshapen as a result of the instability of its southern pier,[43] was carefully rebuilt in 1849.[44]

The church has an octagonal font of the 15th century.[45] The carved woodwork of the pulpit is of the early 17th century but rests on a medieval stone base, and the reading-desk, dated 1604, was apparently made from the sounding-board of the pulpit. A ring of four bells was cast by Edward Neale of Burford in 1657 and one bell recast by Abraham Rudhall in 1719;[46] a treble bell was added in 1927 when all were rehung.[47] The plate includes a paten-cover of 1576 and a chalice of 1634, the latter apparently acquired in 1720.[48] The churchyard monuments include two late-17th-century carved chest-tombs. The parish registers survive from 1592.[49]

NONCONFORMITY. Houses at Elkstone were registered for a group connected with Eastcombe Baptist chapel, in Bisley, in 1818 and 1822, and two other houses were registered by unidentified groups in 1829;[50] no later record of nonconformity in the parish has been found.

EDUCATION. By 1818 Elkstone had a Sunday school on the National plan in which 36 children were taught at the cost of one of the Milligan family of Cotswold House, North Cerney.[51] In 1833 a dame school, with 6 children attending, provided the only weekday education,[52] but by 1847 a church day-school, supported by subscriptions and pence, had been started and taught 26 children.[53] In 1867 the average attendance was 30–35 but varied considerably according to the weather and the state of the roads. An evening school for older boys was then held as well.[54] A new schoolroom was built in the north part of the village in 1871.[55] Average attendance was c. 30 in 1885[56] and rose to 42 by 1910 but fell back to c. 25 by the 1930s.[57] The school was closed in 1951 when the children, whose numbers had fallen to c. 12, were transferred to Cirencester schools.[58]

CHARITIES FOR THE POOR. Robert Rogers of Sandywell, Dowdeswell, by will proved 1628 gave £5 to the poor of Elkstone.[59] Before 1705 it was placed out at interest of 5s. a year[60] and the principal was later lost. A building given for an alms-house was mentioned in 1705 but appears to have been lost to the parish through the invalidity of the deed of gift.[61]

RENDCOMB

RENDCOMB, a small parish and estate village, lies in the valley of the river Churn 7.75 km. north of Cirencester. The parish is apparently named from the coomb south of the village, for the stream flowing through the coomb into the Churn was known as *hrindan broc* in 852.[62] Twenty acres transferred from North Cerney in 1935, when the boundary at the south was moved from the Churn to the Cheltenham–Cirencester road,[63] brought the area of Rendcomb parish up to 2,606 a. (1,055 ha.).[64]

The Churn valley is the central feature of the parish but on the east and west the boundaries take in the high wolds at 200–250 m. Smaller coombs lead into the Churn valley on either side and the deep Shawswell valley formed by the tributary stream of the Churn breaks into the high ground in the east. The high ground is on the Great Oolite while the underlying strata of the Upper Lias, the

Inferior Oolite, and fuller's earth, which forces out several springs, outcrop in the valleys.[65] The high ground was once cultivated as open fields while the Churn valley provided some rich meadow land. Most of the hillsides appear to have been wooded from ancient times. Cliffordine wood was granted c. 1180 to Bruern Abbey to form part of its Marsden estate[66] and Eycot wood was recorded in 1546.[67] In 1837 there was a total of 285 a. of woodland, all owned by the Rendcomb Park estate.[68] The landscaped park stretching along the east side of the Churn valley is a major feature of the landscape. The park existed by 1544[69] and in 1676 included 250 a.[70] The river Churn, which was incorporated as a feature of the park and formed into a lake at its northern end, has long provided trout-fishing for the owners of the manor; in 1477 100 trout were reported to have been poached from it.[71] Some of the high land of the parish near

[42] For a full description of the ch. with illustrations, see *Trans. B.G.A.S.* lii. 187–200; and see above, plate facing p. 140.
[43] Cf. S. Lysons, *Glos. Antiquities* (1803), plate IX.
[44] Glos. R.O., P 135/CW 2/1.
[45] *Trans. B.G.A.S.* xliv. 192.
[46] *Glos. Ch. Bells*, 46; cf. G.D.R., V 5/125T 2.
[47] Inscr. under tower. [48] *Glos. Ch. Plate*, 79.
[49] *B. & G. Par. Rec.* 135.
[50] Hockaday Abs. cxcii.
[51] *Educ. of Poor Digest*, 299.
[52] *Educ. Enquiry Abstract*, 314.
[53] *Church School Inquiry, 1846–7*, 8–9.
[54] *Rep. Com. Agric. Employment*, p. 99.
[55] Date on bldg.; cf. Ed. 7/34/133.
[56] *Kelly's Dir. Glos.* (1885), 452.
[57] *Bd. of Educ., List 21, 1911* (H.M.S.O.), 161; *1922*, 104; *1932*, 115; *1936*, 120.
[58] Glos. R.O., S 135. [59] Glos. R.O., D 444/T 19.
[60] G.D.R., V 5/125T 3–4. [61] Ibid. 4.
[62] *P.N. Glos.* (E.P.N.S.), i. 161; Grundy, *Saxon Charters*, 58. This account was written in 1978.
[63] *Census*, 1931 (pt. ii); cf. O.S. Map 6″, Glos. XLIII. NW. (1884 edn.).
[64] *Census*, 1951.
[65] Geol. Surv. Map 1″, drift, sheet 235 (1933 edn.).
[66] *Ancient Charters* (P.R.S. x), pp. 72–3.
[67] Glos. R.O., D 326/T 100.
[68] G.D.R., T 1/147.
[69] Leland, *Itin.* ed. Toulmin Smith, i. 130.
[70] Glos. R.O., D 2235/1.
[71] Staffs. R.O., D 641/1/4M/11.

Rendcomb Buildings together with adjoining land in North Cerney was used for an airfield by the Royal Flying Corps during the First World War.[72]

Before the building of the new Chelten-ham–Cirencester turnpike alongside the Churn in 1825[73] Rendcomb village in its wooded valley was in an isolated situation. The White way passing across the high ground to the east, presumably the ridgeway in Rendcomb south field mentioned in 1408,[74] was the only thoroughfare of any importance. The road on which the upper part of the village stands, continuing along the high ground at the top of the park and down to Marsden, perhaps provided access towards Cheltenham to the north, while Cirencester was presumably once reached by way of Woodmancote on the west side of the Churn valley or by a steep road which crossed the Shawswell valley to meet the White way near the south boundary of the parish.[75] About 1773, however, the owner of Rendcomb, Sir William Guise, improved access from the village to Cirencester by building a new road from the lower part of the village up through Conigree wood to meet the White way near its junction with the North Cerney–Calmsden road;[76] it was stopped up after the new Cheltenham–Cirencester road was built.[77]

The small village stands on the road up the hillside from a crossing of the Churn, where probably stood the Mill bridge mentioned in 1438,[78] and forms two separate groups of buildings, one of them, including the old mill, around the river crossing and the other higher up near the church. The Old School House in the lower group, named from a dame school that was once held in the small stone building in the garden,[79] is probably the oldest house in the village. Surviving 14th-century features—a stone doorway and a roof-truss, both *in situ*, and some reset window tracery—and a late-medieval fireplace in a first-floor room suggest that the north-east corner of the house formed the parlour end of a medieval house. To its west the hall range, which now has an upper-cruck roof of 3 bays, appears to have been reconstructed in the 16th or early 17th century, and to the south of the medieval block there is an extension of the 17th century. The other older houses of the village are small farm-houses and cottages of the 17th and 18th centuries and include in the upper part of the village the former farm-house of Rendcomb farm[80] (later used as the rectory), which is 17th-century in origin with later additions.

The character of the village is set, however, by the additions made by Sir Francis Goldsmid when he rebuilt the manor-house, Rendcomb Park, in the mid 1860s. They include the heavy ornamental bridge carrying the drive over the road, the imposing stable courtyard which dominates the upper part of the village, and the group of model cottages—six pairs and a trio—at the top of the village; all were designed by Philip Hardwick, the architect of the house.[81] Also in the upper part of the village are some houses and old people's bungalows built in the late 1960s and early 1970s.

The village, for so long dominated by the big house and estate of the Guise family and their successors, remained in the 20th century largely an adjunct of Rendcomb College, the school founded in the house in 1920 by F. N. H. Wills of Miserden. The pupils, whose numbers had risen to 60 by 1926, were at first all free scholars drawn from the elementary schools of the county and from preparatory schools but from 1923 fee-paying pupils were also taken. The school later bought the rectory house and adapted the stable courtyard, and a period of expansion in the 1960s, which brought the number of pupils up to 160, involved the addition of purpose-built buildings in the grounds of the house and in the village, including houses for the headmaster and other members of staff and in 1967 a new arts block.[82] A new boarding house was built on the north side of the house in the early 1970s and a new sports hall was under construction in the upper village in 1978. The school owned most of the village in 1978 and the houses were mainly occupied by its employees.[83]

In the Middle Ages the parish contained a small hamlet called Eycot, the centre of a separate manor which apparently comprised all the land lying west of the Churn. The hamlet had a chapel by the beginning of the 12th century[84] and 8 inhabitants were assessed for the subsidy in 1327[85] and c. 12 for the poll tax in 1381.[86] There were still a few tenants at Eycot in 1442[87] but no later record has been found of the hamlet, though the manor-house, which was absorbed with the rest of the manor into the Rendcomb estate, was recorded by the name Eycot Farm until 1732.[88] The name of the hamlet, derived from a cottage near an island or water-meadow,[89] suggests that the site of Eycot was down by the Churn and it seems likely that the manor-house survives as the oldest part of Lodge Farm (renamed Rendcomb Manor in the 20th century), which stands by a ford near the north end of Rendcomb park. If that is the case the final disappearance of the hamlet may possibly be associated with the creation of the park some time before 1544. In the late 18th century Lodge Farm, so called by 1777,[90] was the centre of farm which included Eycot field, evidently a former open field of the manor, and most of the other land on that

[72] Glos. R.O., D 2299/1585; Glos. Colln. JF 5.51.
[73] Cirencester Roads Act, 6 Geo. IV, c. 143.
[74] Staffs. R.O., D 641/1/4M/2.
[75] Cf. G.D.R., T 1/147.
[76] Glos. R.O., D 326/T 107; cf. Bryant, *Map of Glos.* (1824).
[77] Glos. R.O., Q/SRh 1828 B/2–3.
[78] Staffs. R.O., D 641/1/4M/5.
[79] Ex inf. the occupier, Mr. R. Kelsey.
[80] G.D.R., T 1/147.
[81] Verey, *Glos.* i. 378–80.

[82] C. H. C. Osborne, J. C. James, and K. L. James, *Hist. of Rendcomb Coll.* (Oxford, 1976), 23–4, 29, 121, 152–7.
[83] Ex inf. the headmaster, Mr. R. M. A. Medill.
[84] *Hist. & Cart. Mon. Glouc.* (Rolls Ser.), ii. 41.
[85] *Glos. Subsidy Roll, 1327,* 14.
[86] E 179/113/35A rot. 2A.
[87] Glos. R.O., D 678, ct. rolls 94.
[88] Ibid. D 326/T 10.
[89] *P.N. Glos.* i. 161.
[90] Taylor, *Map of Glos.* (1777).

side of the river.[91] The house dates partly from the 17th century but has an early-19th-century wing and some 20th-century additions in Cotswold style. The farm buildings at Eycot field were the only buildings on the high ground on that side of the river in 1837[92] but *c.* 1930 a large Cotswold-style residence, called Aycote House, designed by Norman Jewson, was built for the owner of a small estate established in that part of the parish after the break-up of the Rendcomb estate.[93]

Marsden, which takes its name from the coomb on the north boundary of the parish,[94] was the site of a manor belonging to Bruern Abbey in the Middle Ages. The manor was sometimes referred to as a grange[95] and probably never had a village or hamlet attached to it, though a house or houses recorded at Shawswell on the high ground to the east in 1676 were said to have once been part of the manor.[96] Shawswell Farm at the latter site, though remodelled in the 19th century, may incorporate a 17th-century house. On the other side of the Shawswell valley two farm-houses, Greenmeadow and Rendcomb Buildings, were established in the 19th century on former open-field land and a new house called Chittlegrove was built *c.* 1928 to the designs of V. A. Lawson.[97]

In 1086 a total of 39 inhabitants of Rendcomb and Eycot was recorded.[98] Nineteen people were assessed for the subsidy in 1327[99] and *c.* 36 for the poll tax in 1381.[1] There were said to be *c.* 61 communicants in the parish in 1551[2] and 12 households in 1563.[3] Later estimates of the population were 18 families in 1650,[4] about 120 inhabitants *c.* 1710,[5] and 139 inhabitants *c.* 1775.[6] In 1801 it stood at 147 and there was a slow rise to 264 by 1851. In the next 120 years the population fluctuated between 211 (reached in 1881) and 295 (reached in 1921), and in 1971, excluding the pupils of Rendcomb College, it stood at 218.[7]

There was an inn on the manor estate in 1732[8] but no later record of one at Rendcomb has been found. A reading-room, provided by the lord of the manor, existed in 1878[9] and there was a village hall in 1978.

Sir Thomas Roe (1581?–1644), ambassador and explorer,[10] was living at Rendcomb in 1608 when his mother Dame Eleanor Berkeley owned the manor.[11]

MANORS. In 1086 two estates at Rendcomb were held by Gilbert son of Turold; 5 hides had formerly belonged to Aluric and 3 hides were held from Gilbert by one Walter,[12] apparently his son-in-law.[13] Gilbert's estates had passed to the honor of Gloucester by the late 12th century[14] and it is possible that then and until the mid 13th century the manor which the de la Mare family held from the earls of Gloucester included all of the Rendcomb land.[15] In 1255, however, Earl Richard de Clare reserved to himself and his heirs 2 ploughlands[16] and that land, known as the manor of *RENDCOMB*, was retained by the earls together with lands in North Cerney and Woodmancote. After the death of Gilbert de Clare in 1314[17] his manor and the overlordship of the de la Mare's manor were assigned to his sister Margaret, wife of Hugh de Audley, earl of Gloucester (d. 1347). Hugh was succeeded by his daughter Margaret, wife of Ralph Stafford,[18] created earl of Stafford in 1351, and the manor and overlordship passed with the Stafford earldom, though Anne, widow of Thomas, the 3rd earl, and later wife of Edmund, the 5th earl, held them as dower[19] until her death in 1438.[20] Edward Stafford, duke of Buckingham and earl of Stafford, granted the Rendcomb land attached to the manor to Edmund Tame in 1508 but retained the manor-house, manorial rights,[21] and the North Cerney lands, which after his execution and attainder in 1521 were held for life by his widow Eleanor (d. 1531).[22] Later in 1531 the Crown leased the manor for 21 years to Sir William Kingston and Edmund Tame[23] and later the same year the reversion was granted for life to Anthony Kingston. In 1554 the reversion was granted to Henry Stafford, Lord Stafford, son of the duke, and his wife Ursula,[24] who evidently took possession on Anthony Kingston's death in 1556.[25] Henry died in 1563[26] and in 1566 Ursula and her son Edward, Lord Stafford, sold the estate, then called the manor or manors of Rendcomb, North Cerney, and Woodmancote, to Thomas Taylor, rector of North Cerney.[27]

Taylor sold the estate in 1576 to Richard Davies; Davies sold in 1585 to William Holliday; and Holliday sold in 1593 to Richard Poole, a Stroud mercer, who obtained a conveyance from Edward, Lord Stafford, in 1599. Poole's tenure of the estate was complicated by his many debts and at least two of his creditors appear to have gained temporary possession of the whole or part of the

[91] Glos. R.O., D 326/F 22.
[92] G.D.R., T 1/147.
[93] Verey, *Glos.* i. 380; *Kelly's Dir. Glos.* (1931), 60.
[94] *P.N. Glos.* i. 161.
[95] *L. & P. Hen. VIII*, xii (1), p. 513; Glos. R.O., D 326/T 10.
[96] Glos. R.O., D 2235/1.
[97] Verey, *Glos.* i. 380.
[98] *Dom. Bk.* (Rec. Com.), i. 164v., 168v.
[99] *Glos. Subsidy Roll, 1327*, 10, 14.
[1] E 179/113/35A rott. 2A, 14; E 179/113/31A rott. 2, 5.
[2] *E.H.R.* xix. 112.
[3] Bodl. MS. Rawl. C.790, f. 23v.
[4] *Trans. B.G.A.S.* lxxxiii. 93.
[5] Atkyns, *Glos.* 620.
[6] Rudder, *Glos.* 623.
[7] *Census*, 1801–1971.
[8] Glos. R.O., D 326/T 10.
[9] Ibid. D 1388/SL 6, no. 52.

[10] *D.N.B.*
[11] Wadham Coll., Oxford, Mun. 61/A 12.
[12] *Dom. Bk.* (Rec. Com.), i. 168v.
[13] *Trans. B.G.A.S.* iv. 160–1.
[14] *Ancient Charters* (P.R.S. x), pp. 72–3.
[15] That is implied by *Rot. Hund.* (Rec. Com.), i. 181.
[16] C.P. 25(1)/74/21 no. 453.
[17] *Cal. Inq. p.m.* v, p. 328.
[18] *Cal. Close*, 1313–18, 414–15; *Cal. Inq. p.m.* ix, p. 61.
[19] *Cal. Close*, 1392–6, 39, 47; 1402–5, 218.
[20] *Complete Peerage*, xii (1), 181.
[21] Glos. R.O., D 326/T 88.
[22] E 150/365 no. 4.
[23] *L. & P. Hen. VIII*, v, p. 129.
[24] *Cal. Pat.* 1553–4, 484.
[25] C 3/282/7; *V.C.H. Glos.* xi. 16.
[26] *Complete Peerage*, xii (1), 184.
[27] C 54/721 mm. 40–2.

estate. In 1610 Poole conveyed it to Henry Gastrell as a trustee for a sale but, according to Poole, Gastrell's sale of the estate to Sir Valentine Knightley in 1612 was made without his consent.[28] Sir Valentine later conveyed the estate to Richard Poole's brother William Poole of Long Newnton (Wilts. later Glos.) with reversion to Richard's son Abel Poole; William conveyed his interest to Abel in 1619.[29] It was later claimed that Abel made a conveyance in 1638 for the benefit of his creditors Richard Poole (apparently his cousin) and Thomas Freame, and that Richard Poole bought out Freame and was succeeded by his son Richard Poole of London. In 1683, however, the younger Richard was being challenged by Sir John Guise[30] whose claim derived from the Rich family. Thomas Rich of North Cerney (d. 1647) had acquired a long lease of the estate which he left to his wife Anne, and his grandson Thomas Rich,[31] who apparently claimed the freehold, sold the estate to Sir John before 1676.[32] In 1721 the Guises bought out a right claimed by Nathaniel Poole of Stonehouse, whose father Richard Poole of Painswick was devisee of Richard (fl. 1683), but in 1731 the Guises' claim to the estate, or at least to the Woodmancote manor that was attached to it, was once more being disputed, at that time by Jane Parry, apparently a great-niece of Richard (fl. 1683).[33] The Guises' right to the estate appears to have later remained unchallenged. The manor-house belonging to the estate, called the Earl's Court, still existed in 1566[34] but its site is not known.

The manor of RENDCOMB, held under the earls of Gloucester and their successors, was probably owned by Robert de la Mare, who was among the earl's knights in 1166.[35] William de la Mare held it c. 1180,[36] apparently in right of his wife: the gift of the manor and a manor in Hardwicke made by Robert son of Gregory to his sister Amfelice, wife ' of William de la Mare, was confirmed by John, as count of Mortain, c. 1190, the service due to the honor of Gloucester being that of 2 knights.[37] Thomas de la Mare was lord in the early 13th century when he made a grant of the service of the free tenants and other rights to his son William,[38] who held the manor in 1243.[39] In 1255 Richard de Clare confirmed the manor, with the reservation mentioned above, to one Simon and

Parnel his wife to hold with the Hardwicke manor for 9½ fees,[40] though later the two manors were usually assessed only at 2½ fees.[41] Parnel, then called Parnel de la Mare, died c. 1263 and was succeeded in the manor by her son William de la Mare[42] (d. by 1296).[43] John de la Mare held it in 1303[44] and in 1331 when he settled it on his son Thomas with contingent remainder to another son William,[45] presumably the William de la Mare who held it in 1347.[46] In 1387 Rendcomb and Hardwicke were held by Thomas and Robert de la Mare[47] and Thomas held Rendcomb in 1390 subject to dower rights of his mother.[48] Thomas died before 1414 leaving as his heir his son John who came of age in 1419.[49] John (d. by 1462) was succeeded by his son John[50] (fl. 1480).[51] By 1500 the second John had been succeeded by a kinsman John Westby who sold Rendcomb manor in 1503 to Edmund Tame of Fairford.[52]

Sir Edmund Tame, as he became, was succeeded at his death in 1534[53] by his son Sir Edmund (d. 1544),[54] whose widow Catherine held Rendcomb manor in 1547 when the reversion was assigned to the younger Edmund's sister Margaret, wife of Sir Humphrey Stafford.[55] Margaret's son Sir Humphrey Stafford[56] sold the manor in 1564 to Richard Berkeley (later knighted) of Stoke Gifford but that transaction may only have involved the reversionary right, for Roger Lygon, third husband of Catherine, granted a lease of the manor to Berkeley in 1566.[57] Sir Richard held the manor at his death in 1604 and his widow Eleanor[58] retained it until her death in 1629[59] when it passed to Sir Richard's grandson Richard Berkeley.[60] In 1635 Richard's son, Sir Maurice, sold his reversionary interest in the manor and in the family's other estates in the parish to Sir William Guise of Elmore,[61] whose grandson Sir Christopher Guise, Bt.,[62] took possession on Richard Berkeley's death in 1661.[63] From Sir Christopher (d. 1670) it descended in the Guise family from father to son, to Sir John (d. 1695), Sir John (d. 1732), Sir John (d. 1769), and Sir William (d. 1783). The estate, by then including the whole parish except for the rector's glebe,[64] was devised by Sir William to his sister Jane, wife of Shute Barrington, bishop of Salisbury, later bishop of Durham.[65] On Jane's death without issue in 1807 it passed to Sir

---

[28] C 107/112; C 3/260/29; Glos. R.O., D 293/4, transcr. of Chancery proceedings 1614.

[29] Glos. R.O., D 2525, N. Cerney man. 1611–20.

[30] Ibid. D 326/L 12.

[31] C 3/458/62; Visit. Glos. 1682–3, 142–4.

[32] Glos. R.O., D 2235/1.   [33] Ibid. D 326/L 12.

[34] C 54/721 m. 40.

[35] Red. Bk. Exch. (Rolls Ser.), i. 288.

[36] Ancient Charters (P.R.S. x), pp. 72–3.

[37] Earldom of Glouc. Charters, ed. R. B. Patterson (Oxford, 1973), p. 105.

[38] Glos. R.O., D 326/T 88.

[39] Bk. of Fees, ii. 819.

[40] C.P. 25(1)/74/21 no. 453.

[41] e.g. Cal. Inq. p.m. ix, p. 61; xvi, p. 166.

[42] Cal. Inq. p.m. i, p. 164; Feud. Aids, ii. 239.

[43] Cal. Inq. p.m. iii, p. 249.

[44] Feud. Aids, ii. 246.

[45] C.P. 25(1)/77/59 no. 76.

[46] Cal. Inq. p.m. ix, p. 61.

[47] Ibid. xvi, p. 166.

[48] Glos. R.O., D 326/T 88.

[49] Ibid.; Staffs. R.O., D 641/1/2/160.

[50] Glos. R.O., D 326/T 88.

[51] Staffs. R.O., D 641/1/4M/11.

[52] Glos. R.O., D 326/T 88.

[53] Hockaday Abs. cxciv, 1533; mon. in Fairford ch.

[54] C 142/71 no. 156.

[55] C.P. 40/1134 Carte rot. 2d.

[56] C.P. 25(2)/71/587 no. 39.

[57] Glos. R.O., D 326/T 96.   [58] C 142/285 no. 150.

[59] Bigland, Glos. iii, no. 214; Smith, Men and Armour, 253.

[60] Visit. Glos. 1623, 8–9, where Sir Ric. is called Sir Rob.

[61] Glos. R.O., D 326/T 96.

[62] For the Guise fam., see Trans. B.G.A.S. iii. 70–4.

[63] Rudder, Glos. 699. Richard's second wife Jane who would have had a life-interest in the man.-ho. and pk. had died in 1659: Glos. R.O., P 267/IN 1/1.

[64] Glos. R.O., D 326/E 15; G.D.R., T 1/147.

[65] Glos. R.O., D 326/F 22.

Berkeley William Guise,[66] son of Sir William's cousin and heir, and he was succeeded at his death in 1834 by his brother Sir John Wright Guise. Sir John sold the estate in 1864 to Sir Francis Goldsmid, Bt.,[67] M.P. for Reading and one of a family of successful Jewish financiers. Sir Francis (d. 1878) was succeeded by his nephew Sir Julian Goldsmid[68] who sold the estate, which with the North Cerney, Chedworth, and Colesbourne land attached to it comprised 4,775 a.,[69] in 1883 to James Taylor, a cotton-manufacturer of Bradford.[70] After Taylor's death in 1896 his widow Editha held the estate.[71] It later passed to James Herbert Taylor, who had a life-interest under Taylor's will, and in 1914 he and the trustees of the will sold the greater part of the Rendcomb land to William Mewburn.[72] It passed within a few years to a syndicate of owners which broke up the estate.[73]

The de la Mare family appears to have usually lived at Rendcomb[74] and later lords to use the manor-house there included the younger Sir Edmund Tame.[75] The Berkeleys, though usually described as of Stoke Gifford, also used the Rendcomb house on occasion,[76] and Sir Richard entertained Elizabeth I and her court there for two days in 1592.[77] In 1672 Sir John Guise was assessed for tax on 27 hearths in two houses,[78] the second perhaps being that of the estate formerly the Staffords'. About 1685 Sir John built a new house,[79] a substantial mansion of plain design,[80] which was used by the family as its chief residence during the 18th century.[81] It was demolished in the mid 1860s by Sir Francis Goldsmid who built a large Italianate mansion on the same site. The new house was designed by Philip Hardwick and built by the firm of Thomas Cubitt[82] and, though the workmanship and detail are of a high quality, the inappropriateness of such a building to its parkland setting in a narrow Cotswold valley has often been remarked on. Features contemporary with the house include the massive stable court with its tall tower, the ornamental bridges which carry the south drive over the village road and the river, and the south lodge, which apes the style of the house. A classical lodge of the late 18th or early 19th century survived at the north entrance to the park

until the mid 20th century.[83] In 1918 the house and village and the surrounding park-land were bought by F. N. H. Wills for the purpose of founding Rendcomb College.[84]

In 1086 the manor of EYCOT, extended at 1 hide, was held by Ordric from the bishop of Worcester as a member of the bishop's manor of Bibury.[85] An intermediate lordship between the bishop and the tenant-in-demesne was held by Gilbert de Mynors and Roger de Mynors at different times during the 12th century and a further lordship under Roger was held by Robert Mucegros.[86] In 1209 and later, however, the manor was said to be held directly from the bishop, being accounted as ⅓ knight's fee.[87] Early holders of the manor were Reynold and Richard of Beckford who made a grant of tithes in Eycot to Gloucester Abbey[88] before 1100.[89] At some time in the 12th century the manor was held by Robert Russel in right of his wife Basile, and his heir William[90] was perhaps the William Russel who held Eycot in 1209.[91] William was dead by 1232 when the right of his widow Alice to have the whole manor as dower was questioned by his heir John Russel on the grounds that it represented more than a third part of all William's possessions.[92] Robert Russel, to whom a small estate in Eycot was conveyed in 1241,[93] may have held the manor, and it later passed to John le Brun, apparently by his marriage to Margery, daughter of John Russel.[94] John le Brun, who in 1278 acquired from Walter Wyth ½ plough-land in Nether Rendcomb, Woodmancote, and North Cerney,[95] held Eycot in 1303[96] and in 1312 his widow Margery granted it to Thomas Neel of Purton. A contingent remainder in that grant was for the benefit of John of Burton and his heirs,[97] one of whom was presumably Thomas of Burton who held the manor in 1346.[98]

Thomas of Burton died in 1375 leaving as heir to Eycot his son Thomas, a minor,[99] and the manor was placed in the custody of William Archibald.[1] In 1385, however, Thomas, not yet of age, was impleaded by John Atwood who claimed Eycot under a grant made by a John Russel to his ancestors Robert and Margery Crook in Edward II's reign. John Atwood recovered seisin[2] and in

[66] Ibid. F 5.
[67] *Hist. Rendcomb Coll.* 15.
[68] *D.N.B.*
[69] Glos. R.O., D 1388/SL 6, no. 52.
[70] *Hist. Rendcomb Coll.* 16.
[71] Plaque in ch.; *Kelly's Dir. Glos.* (1897), 272.
[72] G.D.R., D 5/1/36.
[73] *Hist. Rendcomb Coll.* 16; cf. G.D.R., T 1/147, altered apportionment 1921.
[74] Glos. R.O., D 326/T 88; *Cat. Anct. D.* iv, A 9250, A 9378.
[75] Hockaday Abs. cccxxii, 1544.
[76] *Visit. Glos. 1623*, 8–9; Glos. R.O., D 326/T 96.
[77] *Glos. N. & Q.* ii. 380.
[78] E 179/247/13 rot. 29.
[79] Bodl. MS. Rawl. B.323, f. 58v.; cf. Atkyns, *Glos.* 619.
[80] Illustrated in Atkyns, *Glos.* plate at pp. 618–19; Rudder, *Glos.* plate at pp. 620–1; *Delineations of Glos.* plate facing p. 76.
[81] e.g. Glos. R.O., P 267/IN 1/2; D 326/F 15, T 10.
[82] Verey, *Glos.* i. 378–9; see above, plate facing p. 204.
[83] Min. of Housing and Loc. Govt., List of Bldgs. in Ciren. R.D. (1949); photog. in Glos. Colln. RV 248.1.

[84] *Hist. Rendcomb Coll.* 6, 23; see above.
[85] *Dom. Bk.* (Rec. Com.), i. 164v.
[86] *Red Bk. of Worc.* 414–15, 439.
[87] *Bk. of Fees*, i. 39; *Feud. Aids*, ii. 248; *Cal. Inq. p.m.* xiv, pp. 94–5.
[88] Glouc. Cath. Libr., Reg. Abb. Froucester B, pp. 83–4.
[89] *Hist. & Cart. Mon. Glouc.* (Rolls Ser.), ii. 41; cf. *Reg. Regum Anglo-Norm.* ii, no. 1041.
[90] Glouc. Cath. Libr., Reg. Abb. Froucester B, pp. 83–4; cf. *Red Bk. of Worc.* 439.
[91] *Bk. of Fees*, i. 39.
[92] *Cur. Reg. R.* xiv, p. 519.
[93] C.P. 25(1)/73/14 no. 262.
[94] Cf. *Year Bk. 1319* (Selden Soc. lxx), 131–2.
[95] C.P. 25(1)/75/31 no. 43; cf. *Reg. Mon. Winch.* ii, pp. 500–3.
[96] *Red Bk. of Worc.* 369; *Feud. Aids*, ii. 248.
[97] C.P. 25(1)/76/45 no. 86a.
[98] *Feud. Aids*, ii. 280.
[99] *Cal. Inq. p.m.* xiv, pp. 94–5.
[1] *Cal. Pat. 1374–7*, 100.
[2] *Reg. Mon. Winch.* ii, pp. 511–14.

1386 granted the manor to John Pouger[3] (d. 1405).[4] In 1410 John Pouger's son John made a settlement with John Warre, nephew and heir of the younger Thomas of Burton, under which he quitclaimed Eycot to Warre.[5] By 1421 the manor was in the possession of Winchcombe Abbey[6] but the abbey's title was not apparently secured until 1429 when it had quitclaims from feoffees acting for John Warre's sister Catherine and from Robert Andrew, another heir of the Burtons.[7] After the Dissolution the manor passed to Sir Edmund Tame, whose widow Catherine held it after his death, the reversion being assigned with Rendcomb to the Staffords.[8] It was perhaps included in the sale to Richard Berkeley in 1564 and it had certainly passed to the Berkeleys by 1605. The freehold then descended with Rendcomb manor[9] but Robert Berkeley, a younger son of the second Richard Berkeley, held the capital messuage and farm, which apparently then comprised the whole estate, under a long lease until his death in 1690.[10] As suggested above, the capital messuage may have been the house later called Lodge Farm.

Land in the north part of the parish was given to Bruern Abbey (Oxon.) by William de la Mare c. 1180 and by other members of his family at other times; it was added to adjoining land in Chedworth given to the abbey by Roger, earl of Warwick (d. 1153),[11] to form the manor of MARSDEN, based on a farmstead on the boundary between the two parishes. The abbey had a grant of free warren in the manor in 1366.[12] In 1537 the Crown granted Marsden, then held at farm by John Meysey,[13] to John Berkeley[14] (d. 1545) who settled it on his wife Isabel who survived him. She was succeeded by their son Richard, later Sir Richard,[15] who acquired Rendcomb manor. On Sir Richard's death in 1604 Marsden passed to his son Henry[16] (d. 1608) who was succeeded by his son Richard.[17] By the conveyance of 1635 it was to pass to the Guises on the deaths of Giles Hyett and his wife Edith, lessees under the Berkeleys.[18] It then descended as a farm on the Rendcomb estate[19] until the break-up of the estate when Marsden became a separate freehold, owned in 1927 by Mrs. M. M. Fitzgerald[20] and in 1978 by Mr. R. H. N. Worsley.

The manor-house at Marsden was recorded in the 1530s[21] and the house still contains two 16th-century roofs (though only one is in situ) as well as other features of the 16th and 17th centuries. It

was evidently much altered, however, in the 18th or early 19th century,[22] and before the extensive alterations and enlargements that were carried out in the early 1920s it apparently comprised two distinct structural blocks which abutted on one another but had no common axis. The remodelling of the 1920s was in 17th-century Cotswold style including careful reproductions in both stone and timber. At the same time a separate building was put up on the north side to house a library.[23]

The Knights Hospitallers had a claim to 40 a. of land in Rendcomb, which they had perhaps received with their Calmsden estate; in 1225 their right to the land was bought by Thomas de la Mare.[24]

ECONOMIC HISTORY. In 1086 1 team and 7 servi were recorded on the demesne of one of Gilbert son of Turold's estates while the other, held from him by Walter, had 2 teams and 6 servi.[25] In 1307 the part of Gilbert's former estates retained by the earls of Gloucester had in demesne 120 a. of arable and a small acreage of meadow and pasture.[26] At Eycot 2 teams and 2 servi were recorded on the demesne in 1086.[27] In 1375 the demesne arable on that manor covered 120 a. but half of it had by then gone out of cultivation and the other half was hilly and unprofitable land.[28] In the later Middle Ages the demesne land of the various manors, and presumably much of the tenant land too, was used extensively for sheep-raising; court records of the 15th century reflect continual pressure on the available sheep-pasture of the parish.[29] In the late 14th century the earl of Stafford's demesne was farmed by a shepherd,[30] and in 1402 a flock of 328 sheep was leased with it.[31] By 1413, however, the demesne flock of 211 animals was in hand, together with some meadow land to provide it with winter fodder. The flock suffered continual losses from murrain and was finally given up by the owners of the manor c. 1440.[32] John de la Mare retained part of his demesne land or pasture-rights for sheep-raising in 1435[33] and in 1443, when he was also lessee of the sheep-house belonging to the earl of Stafford's demesne.[34] Bruern Abbey had a sheep-house on its Marsden estate in the late 13th century[35] and its flock there numbered at least 500 in 1366.[36]

The tenants on one of Gilbert son of Turold's

[3] C.P. 25(1)/78/80 no. 61.
[4] C 137/55 no. 50.
[5] Cal. Close, 1409–13, 79–80, 82.
[6] Glos. R.O., D 678, ct. roll 61c.
[7] Reg. Mon. Winch. ii, pp. 505–11.
[8] C.P. 40/1134 Carte rot. 2d.
[9] Glos. R.O., D 326/T 96; D 2235/1.
[10] Visit. Glos. 1682–3, 15–16; Glos. R.O., D 326/T 101.
[11] Cal. Chart. R. 1341–1417, 221; Ancient Charters (P.R.S. x), pp. 72–3.
[12] Cal. Chart R. 1341–1417, 196.
[13] Glos. R.O., D 326/T 98.
[14] L. & P. Hen. VIII, xii (1), p. 513.
[15] C 142/73 no. 71; cf. Visit. Glos. 1623, 8.
[16] C 142/285 no. 150.
[17] C 142/304 no. 45.
[18] Glos. R.O., D 326/T 96.
[19] Ibid. T 10; G.D.R., T 1/147.
[20] Kelly's Dir. Glos. (1927), 303–4.

[21] Valor Eccl. (Rec. Com.), ii. 266.
[22] There are photogs. of the ho. in 1913 in Glos. Colln. RV 248.1.
[23] Ex inf. Mr. Worsley; the date 1924 appears on the ho. and the library.
[24] Cur. Reg. R. xii, p. 230.
[25] Dom. Bk. (Rec. Com.), i. 168v.
[26] Inq. p.m. Glos. 1301–58, 75.
[27] Dom. Bk. (Rec. Com.), i. 164v.
[28] Inq. p.m. Glos. 1359–1413, 88.
[29] Staffs. R.O., D 641/1/4M/2–11.
[30] Ibid. 2, cts. 14 Jan. 4 Hen. IV, 8 Nov. 10 Hen. IV; E 179/113/35A rot. 14.
[31] Staffs. R.O., D 641/1/2/156.
[32] Ibid. 160, 162–3, 169.
[33] Ibid. D 641/1/4M/4.
[34] Ibid. D 641/1/2/169.
[35] E 315/47 no. 216.
[36] Cal. Pat. 1364–7, 282.

estates in 1086 were 3 *villani* and 7 bordars, with 3 teams between them, and a Frenchman whose holding was equivalent to that of 2 *villani*. The other estate had 4 *villani* and 3 bordars with 2 teams.[37] The only tenants listed on the earl of Gloucester's estate in 1307 were 4 free tenants holding 2 yardlands,[38] but the survey apparently omitted the North Cerney and Woodmancote lands of the estate in which most of the customary holdings recorded in later centuries lay.[39] Details of the tenantry of the larger manor, held by the de la Mares, do not survive. On Eycot manor in 1086 there were 2 *villani* and 4 bordars with 2 teams.[40] In 1375 the lord of that manor received only 23s. 1d. rent from tenants-at-will,[41] a decline in the population having probably by then broken down the old system of tenures. There were still copyholds on the Rendcomb estate in the 1750s[42] but the larger farms were apparently already held on short leases before the main inclosures began at the end of that century.[43]

The north and south fields of Rendcomb, recorded from 1372,[44] occupied the high ground of the east part of the parish on either side of the Shawswell valley.[45] On the west side of the Churn valley the closes in the coomb below Eycot wood have names that suggest that they were inclosed at some date from an open field,[46] and further south Eycot field, an inclosed field covering 90 a. in 1795, probably represented other open-field land.[47] In Chittle grove on the east side of the parish some copyholders claimed customary rights of common in 1753 but Sir John Guise was able to establish that they held those rights under lease from him and not by right of their holdings;[48] the grove had in fact been an ancient manorial warren.[49] All the other woods of the estate were then held in severalty, though rights of common had been enjoyed in the Marsden woods until some time in the 13th century when Bruern Abbey secured their extinction.[50] The open fields, however, afforded customary rights of common for considerable flocks of sheep in the 18th century and the customs for the tithing of sheep recorded in 1705 suggest that some were regularly summered in the parish by non-parishioners.[51] The Churn valley provided the parish with a narrow but rich belt of meadow land and the practice of controlling the river to flood the meadows there is recorded from 1419.[52]

Plans to inclose the remaining open fields were made by Sir William Guise (d. 1783) but the main inclosure was apparently carried out under his successor Shute Barrington. The Rendcomb Park estate included the whole parish apart from the glebe, and c. 1785 almost all of the surviving open-field land was apparently comprised in the 843 a. belonging to the 1,030-acre Rendcomb farm; there were then three other farms—Shawswell with 485 a., Lodge farm with 387 a., Marsden with 82 a. in the parish but a much larger acreage in Chedworth—and some smaller holdings, all under 30 a.[53] In 1787 Barrington made exchanges with the rector under which all the glebe was inclosed[54] and by 1792 c. 100 a. had been taken from the open fields. Inclosure of the remainder was probably contemplated under the lease of Rendcomb farm granted in the latter year to Richard George.[55]

Rendcomb farm, which continued in the tenure of the George family, remained a farm of over 1,000 a. in the early 19th century.[56] By 1837, however, it had been divided, 490 a. remaining with the small farm-house in the upper part of the village and 472 a. attached to Greenmeadow in the east part of the parish. Shawswell farm then had 562 a. and Lodge farm 339 a.[57] There was some reorganization of the farms before 1878, involving the creation of a new one based on Rendcomb Buildings,[58] but by 1885 all the Rendcomb land of the estate had been taken in hand and was administered by a farm bailiff. That arrangement continued for some 20 years but by 1910 the land was once more leased, three large farms being based on Greenmeadow, Shawswell, and Rendcomb Buildings.[59] Later in the 20th century, after the break-up of the estate, there was a more varied pattern of individually owned farms. In 1976 10 farms, ranging in size from 10 to 300 ha., were returned, four of the smaller ones being worked on a part-time basis.[60]

Following the inclosures the land was cropped on one of the usual Cotswold rotations, under which roots or temporary grass leys were fed off by sheep whose manure provided fertility for corn-crops. The lease of Rendcomb farm in 1792 provided for two years of turnips, or alternatively turnips in the first year and clover and grass-seeds in the second, and two years of corn-crops,[61] and some such rotation evidently continued in the 19th century. In 1837 the parish contained 1,507 a. of arable and 708 a. of permanent grassland[62] and the division was much the same in 1866.[63] Later in the century the agricultural depression, presumably the main reason for the farms being taken in hand, resulted in a greater concentration on grassland

---

[37] *Dom. Bk.* (Rec. Com.), i. 168v.
[38] *Inq. p.m. Glos.* 1301–58, 75.
[39] Staffs. R.O., D 641/1/4M/2; C 54/721 m. 40.
[40] *Dom. Bk.* (Rec. Com.), i. 164v.
[41] *Inq. p.m. Glos.* 1359–1413, 88.
[42] Glos. R.O., D 326/L 18.
[43] Ibid. E 15.
[44] Ibid. T 92.
[45] G.D.R., V 5/248T 2.
[46] G.D.R., T 1/147.
[47] Ibid.; Glos. R.O., D 326/F 22.
[48] Glos. R.O., D 326/L 14, L 18.
[49] Ibid. F 22, marr. settlement 1732.
[50] *Cat. Anct. D.* ii, B 2481–3, B 2488–9, B 2503–4.

[51] G.D.R., V 5/248T 2.
[52] Staffs. R.O., D 641/1/2/160.
[53] Glos. R.O., D 326/E 15, where the val. dated 1778 must be for 1783×91, for Barrington, as bp. of Salisbury, is owner.
[54] G.D.R., V 5/248T 5.　　　[55] Glos. R.O., D 326/T 97.
[56] Ibid. E 64; D 182/III/156.
[57] G.D.R., T 1/147.
[58] Glos. R.O., D 1388/SL 6, no. 52.
[59] *Kelly's Dir. Glos.* (1879 and later edns.); Glos. Colln. RV 248.1.
[60] Agric. Returns 1976.
[61] Glos. R.O., D 326/T 97.
[62] G.D.R., T 1/147.
[63] M.A.F. 68/26/19.

farming. It was presumably for that purpose that James Taylor built a comprehensive system to supply water to the upland fields from a reservoir by the White way and rebuilt many of the farm buildings.[64] By 1896 the conversion of arable to permanent grass had produced a roughly equal acreage of each and the number of cattle returned was 263 compared with 131 in 1866. The flocks of sheep had also been much increased, 1,801 being returned compared with 847, and they were presumably then fed more on permanent grass, for the amount of turnips and pasture leys had suffered a considerable reduction in common with the wheat and barley crops; oats, however, had shown a marked increase.[65] The statistics for 1926 indicate a further contraction in the traditional pattern of agriculture, with only 258 a. returned for cereal and root crops and the number of sheep down again to 781. The effort to develop dairying and beef production as new sources of income had not apparently been pursued to any extent following the break-up of the estate.[66] In 1976, however, dairy and beef cattle were of considerable importance in the parish and there had been a revival in sheep-farming: of the 6 largest farms based there 3 specialized in cattle- and sheep-raising, 2 in cereal crops, and 1 in dairying. The total number of cattle returned was 768 and of sheep 2,660. The farms still gave employment to 33 people.[67]

In 1086 three mills were recorded in the parish, one on each of Gilbert's estates and one on Eycot manor[68] but only one site can be traced later, that on the Churn at the bottom of Rendcomb village. The village mill, probably the one recorded on the de la Mares' manor in the late Middle Ages[69] and on the Guises' estate in 1676,[70] continued to work until at least 1906.[71] That mill or another may have been a fulling-mill in the late 14th century, for William Walker, a tucker, was living at Rendcomb in 1381[72] and had responsibility for the upkeep of a watercourse in 1400.[73]

Rendcomb never had many tradesmen, probably only some four or five, including representatives of the usual village crafts and a shopkeeper or two, as was the case in the later 19th century;[74] the tallow-chandlers mentioned in 1779 and 1830[75] were the only tradesmen found recorded that are less usual for a small village. Only one tradesman, a smith, was listed in 1608[76] and only 5 families were supported by trade in 1831.[77]

LOCAL GOVERNMENT. View of frankpledge in Rendcomb and its members was exercised by the de la Mares in the early 13th century when Thomas de la Mare granted to his son the 'free hundred belonging to the manor of Rendcomb'.[78] In 1255, however, the overlord, Richard de Clare, earl of Gloucester, reserved the view of frankpledge to himself[79] and in 1287 his successor was holding a view at Rendcomb for a group of Cotswold estates of the honor of Gloucester.[80] The earl also laid claim in the late 13th century to return of writs and excluded the royal bailiffs from Rendcomb.[81] The tithings attending the Rendcomb view were Over and Nether Rendcomb, apparently the manors of the earl and the de la Mares respectively, Woodmancote and Calmsden in North Cerney, Aylworth and Harford in Naunton, and Coates and Trewsbury in Coates. Rolls of the court survive for about 30 years in the period 1387–1481 when it was held twice a year together with the court baron for the earl of Stafford's own manor.[82] The right to the view remained attached to that manor[83] and records survive of views held by the Guises in 1760 and 1819. At the latter date jurisdiction was claimed only over the Rendcomb and Cerney tithings and over Aylworth.[84]

The part of Bruern Abbey's Marsden estate that lay in Rendcomb had exemption from the earl's jurisdiction under a grant of 1246[85] but rights over Marsden were claimed by the hundred lord, Cirencester Abbey, whose bailiffs held a separate view at Marsden after the view at Rapsgate.[86] Eycot attended the view held at Bibury for the bishop of Worcester and his successors.[87] Manor court rolls for Eycot manor survive for 1421 and 1442.[88]

Churchwardens' accounts for Rendcomb survive from 1686 and there are a few late-18th-century overseers' records.[89] Land was leased for building a new poorhouse in 1832.[90] Poor-relief was probably never a very serious burden, for the inclusion of the parish in a single estate restricted any influx of poor families and the residence of the Guises at the manor-house, and the park and woodlands maintained around it, presumably provided useful supplementary sources of employment to farmwork for the small population. The cost of relief and the numbers receiving it on a regular basis, 23 in 1803 and 17 in 1813, were about average for a parish of that size in the early 19th century,[91] but at

[64] H. J. Elwes, *Memoirs of Travel, Sport, and Natural Hist.* (1930), 290; O.S. Map 6″, Glos. XLIII. NE. (1884 edn.); cf. Glos. Colln. RV 248.1.
[65] M.A.F. 68/25/16; M.A.F. 68/26/19; M.A.F. 68/1609/17.
[66] M.A.F. 68/3295/4.
[67] Agric. Returns 1976.
[68] *Dom. Bk.* (Rec. Com.), i. 164v., 168v.
[69] Staffs. R.O., D 641/1/4M/1–2, 11.
[70] Glos. R.O., D 2235/1.
[71] *Kelly's Dir. Glos.* (1906), 280.
[72] E 179/113/35A rot. 14.
[73] Staffs. R.O., D 641/1/4M/2.
[74] *Kelly's Dir. Glos.* (1856 and later edns.).
[75] Glos. R.O., D 326/T 105, T 109.
[76] Smith, *Men and Armour*, 253–4.
[77] *Census*, 1831.
[78] Glos. R.O., D 326/T 88; cf. *Rot. Hund.* (Rec. Com.), i,

181; *Lacock Abbey Charters*, ed. K. H. Rogers (Wilts. Rec. Soc. xxxiv), no. 376.
[79] C.P. 25(1)/74/21 no. 453.
[80] *Plac. de Quo Warr.* (Rec. Com.), ii. 253.
[81] *Rot. Hund.* (Rec. Com.), i. 181.
[82] Staffs. R.O., D 641/1/4M/1–11.
[83] Glos. R.O., D 293/4, transcr. of Chancery proceedings 1614; C 3/458/62.
[84] Glos. R.O., D 326/T 97, M 33.
[85] *Cal. Pat.* 1364–7, 344.
[86] *Ciren. Cart.* ii, p. 619.
[87] *Red Bk. of Worc.* 369, 376; Glos. R.O., D 678, Bibury ct. rolls.
[88] Glos. R.O., D 678, ct. rolls 61c, 94.
[89] *B. & G. Par. Rec.* 227.
[90] Glos. R.O., P 267/OV 9.
[91] *Poor Law Abstract, 1804*, 180–1; *1818*, 154–5.

a time of agricultural prosperity in the middle of the century there were not enough resident labourers to work the farms of the parish.[92] Rendcomb was included in the Cirencester union in 1836[93] and was later in Cirencester rural district[94] until the formation of Cotswold district in 1974.

CHURCH. The earliest record found of the church at Rendcomb was in 1255 when the earl of Gloucester reserved the advowson in his grant of the manor.[95] The living was a rectory in 1291[96] and remained one. From 1974, however, the living was served by a priest-in-charge, combining the role with that of chaplain to Rendcomb College, which supplied part of his income.[97]

The advowson descended with the earl of Gloucester's manor until the execution of the duke of Buckingham in 1521.[98] The Crown presented in 1535 and 1536[99] and again in 1576, though Ursula, Lady Stafford, claimed the advowson in 1563.[1] That claim was still made by the Staffords in 1625[2] but by 1603 the incumbent William Broad owned the advowson[3] and it evidently remained in his family until at least 1710[4] though exercised by various trustees or assignees.[5] In 1738 the incumbent George White conveyed the advowson to Charles Coxe[6] who presented in 1748. Thomas Jayne presented himself to the living in 1786. The advowson later belonged to the Pitt family: Joseph Pitt of Cirencester exercised it in 1798 and it passed to his son Cornelius, who held the living himself from 1831 until his death in 1840, and to Cornelius's son Joseph, who held the living from 1844[7] until 1887.[8] Sir Julian Goldsmid owned the advowson by 1879 and it passed with the manor.[9] F. N. H. Wills, the founder of Rendcomb College, bought it[10] before his death in 1927 and it passed to his widow Margery, later Mrs. H. M. Sinclair, who gave it c. 1970 to her son Mr. H. D. H. Wills.[11]

Half the demesne tithes of Eycot were granted by Reynold and Richard of Beckford to Gloucester Abbey before 1100 and were later commuted for a pension of 9s. The pension was to be paid to the abbey by the priest serving the chapel which existed at Eycot in the 12th and 13th centuries[12] and which may have been endowed with the rest of the tithes of the hamlet. The chapel had perhaps already gone out of use by 1291 when the rector of Rendcomb was held to be responsible for the pension and accused of detaining it.[13] It continued in dispute between him and the abbey until at least 1351.[14] In 1541 it was settled on the bishopric of Gloucester.[15]

The rector's tithes were commuted for a corn-rent of £440 in 1837.[16] In the 16th century his glebe comprised 1 yardland of arable, various small closes, and pasture for 60 sheep and 7 beasts.[17] In 1775 the rector exchanged his closes with Sir William Guise and in 1787 his open-field land, then comprising 35 a., was inclosed by agreement with Shute Barrington.[18] In 1837 the total acreage of glebe was 24 a.[19] The rectory house, east of the church, was rebuilt as a substantial residence by Cornelius Pitt in 1832–3.[20] In 1932 it was sold to Rendcomb College which used it as a headmaster's house and later as a junior house, adding a large new wing c. 1966.[21] The former farm-house of Rendcomb farm became the rectory.

In 1291 the rectory was valued at £8 6s. 8d.[22] and in 1535 it was let at farm to Sir Edmund Tame for £14 5s. 2d.[23] It was valued at £80 in 1650,[24] £120 c. 1710 and in 1743,[25] c. £130 in the 1770s,[26] and £381 in 1856.[27]

The medieval rectors of Rendcomb included William of Appleton who had licence for 7 years' study in 1305.[28] Humphrey Horton, rector from 1536,[29] was non-resident in 1551 when the curate serving the church was found unable to repeat the commandments.[30] Horton held two other benefices in 1576.[31] In that year he was succeeded by William Broad, the first of six members of that family to hold the living. William (d. 1611) was succeeded in the rectory in turn by his sons Samuel (d. 1612) and Thomas (d. 1635)[32] and Samuel's son Samuel was instituted in 1635 and ejected in 1649 because of his service with the royalist army.[33] Henry Prime, described as a preaching minister, held the living in 1650[34] and by 1653 it was held by William Warren[35] whose persecution at the hands

[92] Rep. Com. Agric. Employment, 101.
[93] Poor Law Com. 2nd Rep. p. 522.
[94] Census, 1911.
[95] C.P. 25(1)/74/21 no. 453.
[96] Tax. Eccl. (Rec. Com.), 222.
[97] Glouc. Dioc. Yr. Bk. (1975), 45; ex inf. Mr. Medill.
[98] e.g. Cal. Close, 1313–18, 137; 1392–6, 48; Worc. Episc. Reg., Reg. Carpenter, i. f. 54v.; C 142/80 no. 23.
[99] L. & P. Hen. VIII, ix, p. 309; xi, p. 566.
[1] Hockaday Abs. cccxxii.
[2] C 142/419 no. 72.
[3] Eccl. Misc. 95.
[4] C 142/326 no. 82; Atkyns, Glos. 620.
[5] Hockaday Abs. cccxxii.
[6] C.P. 25(2)/1128/12 Geo. II Mich. no. 28.
[7] Hockaday Abs. cccxxii; cf. Glos. R.O., D 1388, Pitt fam., deed of ho. in Dollar St., Ciren., 1858.
[8] Inscr. in ch.
[9] Kelly's Dir. Glos. (1879 and later edns.).
[10] Hist. Rendcomb Coll. 49.
[11] Burke, Peerage, (1975), 851; Glouc. Dioc. Yr. Bk. (1969), 50; (1970), 50.
[12] Glouc. Cath. Libr., Reg. Abb. Froucester B, pp. 83–4; Hist. & Cart. Mon. Glouc. (Rolls Ser.), ii. 41.

[13] Tax. Eccl. (Rec. Com.), 222.
[14] Glouc. Cath. Libr., Reg. Abb. Froucester B, pp. 16–18.
[15] Valor Eccl. (Rec. Com.), ii. 448; L. & P. Hen. VIII, xvi, p. 572.
[16] G.D.R., T 1/147.
[17] G.D.R., V 5/248T 1.
[18] Ibid. 5.
[19] G.D.R., T 1/147.
[20] Hockaday Abs. cccxxii.
[21] Hist. Rendcomb Coll. 29, 155–6.
[22] Tax. Eccl. (Rec. Com.), 222.
[23] Valor Eccl. (Rec. Com.), ii. 448.
[24] Trans. B.G.A.S. lxxxiii. 93.
[25] Atkyns, Glos. 620; G.D.R. vol. 397, f. 83.
[26] Rudder, Glos. 622.
[27] G.D.R. vol. 384, f. 164.
[28] Reg. Ginsborough, 115.
[29] L. & P. Hen. VIII, xi, p. 566.
[30] E.H.R. xix. 112.
[31] Hockaday Abs. xlvii, 1576 visit. f. 106.
[32] Ibid. cccxxii; cf. Prob. 11/118 (P.C.C. 98 Wood); Prob. 11/119 (P.C.C. 54 Fenner); Prob. 11/168 (P.C.C. 86 Sadler).
[33] C 107/112; Walker Revised, ed. Matthews, 172.
[34] Trans. B.G.A.S. lxxxiii. 93.
[35] Glos. R.O., P 267/IN 1/1.

of Samuel Broad and his supporters is said to have caused his death.[36] Broad, who perhaps lived at that time on the family estate at Woodmancote,[37] also organized opposition to the minister at Bagendon, ousting him from his pulpit in 1658.[38] He returned as rector of Rendcomb at the Restoration and at his death in 1679 was succeeded there by his son Samuel (d. 1710). The younger Samuel was also vicar of Down Hatherley, and the three succeeding rectors were also pluralists: Samuel Broad, 1710–12, was rector of Coln Rogers, George White, 1712–47, was rector of Colesbourne from 1729, and Thomas Shellard, 1748–85, was vicar of Tytherington.[39] From 1925 the parish church and its life were closely associated with Rendcomb College, which attended the services corporately and provided the choir, organist, and bellringers.[40]

The church of *ST. PETER*, which bore that dedication by 1508,[41] is built of coursed rubble and ashlar and has a chancel with south chapel and north vestry, a nave with south aisle and south porch, and a west tower. From the early church three piers of a 13th-century arcade, incorporated in the north wall, are all that survive. Otherwise the whole building is the product of a rebuilding carried out in the early 16th century, apparently by the elder Sir Edmund Tame,[42] whose initials appear in the glass of one of the nave windows. The new church is notable for the spacious arrangement of the interior which has a wide south aisle and chapel and no chancel arch. It retains the 16th-century wooden screens and nave roof but the chancel roof was renewed before 1887.[43] Restoration work was carried out under F. R. Kempson in 1895,[44] when the small vestry may have been added.

The Norman font, decorated with figures of the apostles,[45] came from the old chapel at Elmore Court and was used as a garden ornament at Rendcomb Park before being installed in the church in the mid 19th century.[46] It replaced a plainer tub-shaped font, also apparently Norman work.[47] Fragments of the early-16th-century stained glass survive.[48] In the south chapel are a

monument to Dame Eleanor Berkeley (d. 1629) and one to the Guise family in general, both of them rebuilt or remodelled in the 19th century; the monument to the Guises originally comprised a pyramid of marble and was completed in 1785 by John Bryan.[49] In the chancel is a baroque tablet to Jane (d. 1672), daughter of Robert Berkeley. There are three medieval bells and three that were recast by T. Mears in 1841 or 1842.[50] The plate includes a pair of Elizabethan flagons and some 17th-century pieces.[51] In the churchyard are the steps of a medieval cross, to which a new shaft and head were added in the mid 19th century.[52] The parish registers survive from 1566 with some gaps.[53]

NONCONFORMITY. None known.

EDUCATION. Sir Berkeley William Guise paid a woman to teach a charity school at Rendcomb from 1808,[54] and 16 children were being taught in 1818 when Sir Berkeley was also supporting a Sunday school.[55] Sixteen children were still being educated free at the day-school in 1833 and another 12 attended at their parents' expense.[56] A National school was built in the village in 1857 and in 1867 was supported mainly by Sir Francis Goldsmid and the rector Joseph Pitt, though pence were also charged. Average attendance was 25 at the latter date[57] but had fallen to 20 by 1885.[58] In the early 20th century average numbers in the school varied with the fluctuating population, reaching as high as 40 in 1922 but falling to c. 10 by 1930 when the school was closed.[59]

CHARITIES FOR THE POOR. Rendcomb shared in a Cirencester apprenticeship charity founded by Sir Thomas Roe in 1638; the parish was entitled to submit one child to the trustees every three years[60] but appears to have used the right only intermittently, if at all, before the early 19th century.[61]

SYDE

SYDE, one of the smallest rural parishes in Gloucestershire, covers 254 ha.[62] (629 a.) and lies on a high part of the Cotswolds 12 km. south of Cheltenham. The parish takes its name from the

hillside which it occupies,[63] extending from Ermin Street on the east down to the valley of the river Frome on the west.

The higher ground is formed by the Great Oolite

[36] *Walker Revised*, ed. Matthews, 172.
[37] C 60/525 mm. 29–31.
[38] *Cal. S.P. Dom.* 1658–9, 189.
[39] Hockaday Abs. cccxxii.
[40] *Hist. Rendcomb Coll.* 49.
[41] Glos. R.O., D 326/T 88.
[42] Bodl. MS. Rawl. B. 323, f. 58v. See above, plate facing p. 205.
[43] Inscr. in ch. to the Revd. Jos. Pitt.
[44] Verey, *Glos.* i. 377.
[45] *Trans. B.G.A.S.* xxxiii. 303.
[46] *Glos. N. & Q.* i. 108–9.
[47] S. Lysons, *Glos. Antiquities* (1803), plate LXII.
[48] *Trans. B.G.A.S.* xlvii. 330–1.
[49] Rudder, *Glos.* 623; *Glouc. Jnl.* 5 Sept. 1785.

[50] *Glos. Ch. Bells*, 60.
[51] *Glos. Ch. Plate*, 172–3.
[52] Inscr. in ch. to the Revd. Jos. Pitt.
[53] *B. & G. Par. Rec.* 227.
[54] Glos. R.O., D 326/F 5, F 8.
[55] *Educ. of Poor Digest*, 307.
[56] *Educ. Enquiry Abstract*, 325.
[57] Ed. 7/35/268; cf. *Rep. Com. Agric. Employment*, 101.
[58] *Kelly's Dir. Glos.* (1885), 554.
[59] Glos. R.O., S 267; *Bd. of Educ., List 21, 1922* (H.M.S.O.), 107; *1932*, 117.
[60] Glos. R.O., P 267/CH 1.
[61] *20th Rep. Com. Char.* 51–2.
[62] *Census*, 1971. This account was written in 1979.
[63] *P.N. Glos.* (E.P.N.S.), i. 162.

and the lower slopes by fuller's earth and the Inferior Oolite.[64] The main piece of woodland was Calley wood in the north-west corner, which may take its name from 13th-century owners of the manor; the lower slopes generally were fairly well wooded and along Ermin Street was a narrow belt of beech wood called Gloucester Beeches.[65] The woodland of the parish totalled 40 a. in 1838.[66] The east corner of the parish was crossed by an ancient salt-way, recorded as the Salt Street in 1301.[67] In 1678 it was called Tetbury way[68] and it apparently formed part of the Cheltenham–Tetbury turnpike between 1756 and 1774 when that route was moved further east to Beechpike.[69]

The parish contained only 17 houses c. 1710[70] and 11 in 1801.[71] The diminutive village stands above the Frome valley where a lane from Ermin Street to Caudle Green meets a bridle path from Brimpsfield. Apart from the substantial early manor-house the only dwelling of any size is Manor Farm, which was built in 1867 by the lord of the manor John Hall to provide a rectory house. His offer of the house to the church authorities was withdrawn, however, apparently when he was asked to establish his title to the building, and the house was occupied by the estate bailiff and later became the farm-house of Manor farm.[72] The only other dwellings in 1979 were five cottages, not all occupied, and a modern bungalow.

Haycroft, south of the village on the road to Caudle Green, was recorded from the early 15th century when Hawise atte Haycroft was mentioned as a former tenant in the parish.[73] Haycroft was described as a small hamlet c. 1710[74] and there were four cottages there in 1838.[75] Only one survived in 1979, a medieval building which is traditionally associated with the chantry founded at Syde in 1343[76] and may have been the chantry-priest's house. It comprises a small two-storeyed building of the 14th century with a large east doorway inserted in the early 16th; there were later alterations and additions. At Washbrook, below, named from a small tributary stream of the Frome,[77] there was a pair of cottages within Syde parish in the 18th century but in 1979 only a late-19th-century house. At Harcombe on the lane from Syde village to Ermin Street a farm-house was built near some earlier farm buildings in the mid 19th century,[78] and higher up the lane a new house was built in 1952.[79]

Eleven inhabitants of Syde were recorded in 1086[80] and 5 people were assessed for the subsidy in 1327.[81] There were said to be c. 35 communicants in the parish in 1551,[82] 6 households in 1563,[83] and 36 communicants in 1603.[84] Later estimates of the population were 28 families in 1650,[85] about 70 inhabitants c. 1710,[86] and 47 inhabitants c. 1775.[87] In 1801 the population stood at 41 and there were small fluctuations during the next 170 years, the highest number recorded being 55 in 1861 and 1871 and the lowest 29 in 1891. In 1971 the parish contained 40 people and, with Owlpen which had the same number, was the least populous in the county.[88]

MANOR AND OTHER ESTATES. The manor of *SYDE* was held by Lewin before the Conquest and in 1086 by Ansfrid de Cormeilles who had an under-tenant, Turstin.[89] The overlordship of the manor later passed with the honor of Cormeilles, descending after the early 13th century with Elkstone manor.[90]

In 1200 the manor of Syde was held by William Peto[91] who granted it in 1221 to Osbert Giffard, son of Ellis Giffard.[92] Osbert apparently granted the whole or part of the manor before 1228 to another Osbert Giffard, described as Osbert Giffard of Norfolk,[93] but in 1232 the manor was apparently divided between Maud Giffard, Adam of Kellaways (de Cayley) and Mabel his wife, Isabel de Frevill, and Llanthony Priory.[94] Adam of Kellaways held the whole or part of the manor in 1243[95] and in 1255 Mabel of Kellaways held ½ fee in Syde, over which Adam de Crumbe exercised an intermediate lordship between her and the overlord, John le Brun.[96] Simon of Kellaways held the manor under Simon de Crumbe in 1279 and 1285[97] and Robert of Kellaways held it in 1303.[98]

Before 1316[99] the manor was granted by Adam of Kellaways to John Giffard of Brimpsfield and his mother Margaret Giffard. After John Giffard's execution in 1322 it was granted to Hugh le Despenser, earl of Winchester, executed in 1326,

[64] Geol. Surv. Map 1″, drift, sheet 235 (1933 edn.).
[65] Bryant, *Map of Glos.* (1824); Glos. Colln. RX 271.1.
[66] G.D.R., T 1/176.
[67] *Cat. Anct. D.* iii, A 5920.
[68] G.D.R., V 5/298T 1.
[69] Tewkesbury and Cheltenham Roads Act, 29 Geo II, c.51; Cheltenham Roads Act, 14 Geo. III, c.111; notes on Glos. turnpikes by Mr. A. Cossons, *penes* the editor, V.C.H. Glos.
[70] Atkyns, *Glos.* 653.
[71] *Census,* 1801.
[72] W. C. Virgo, 'The Story of Syde' (TS. 1974, in Syde ch. chest), App. 8; Syde ch. chest, corres. about the new ho. 1866–9.
[73] *Ciren. Cart.* ii, p. 619.
[74] Atkyns, *Glos.* 653.
[75] G.D.R., T 1/176.
[76] Virgo, 'Syde', App. 3.
[77] Glos. R.O., D 1229, Syde deeds 1652–1713, deed 1694.
[78] Virgo, 'Syde', App. 8.
[79] Ibid. p. 55.

[80] *Dom. Bk.* (Rec. Com), i. 169v.
[81] *Glos. Subsidy Roll, 1327,* 10.
[82] *E.H.R.* xix. 115.
[83] Bodl. MS. Rawl. C.790, f. 9v.
[84] *Eccl. Misc.* 81.
[85] *Trans. B.G.A.S.* lxxxiii. 93.
[86] Atkyns, *Glos.* 653.   [87] Rudder, *Glos.* 663.
[88] *Census,* 1801–1971.
[89] *Dom. Bk.* (Rec. Com.), i. 169v.
[90] *Bk. of Fees,* i. 50; C.P. 25(1)/74/20 no. 420; *Feud. Aids,* ii. 240; *Cal. Inq. p.m.* vii, p. 43; see above.
[91] *Rot. Cur. Reg.* (Rec. Com.), ii. 214–15.
[92] *Eyre Rolls, 1221–2* (Selden Soc. lix), 127.
[93] *Cur. Reg. R.* xiii, p. 102.
[94] *Close R. 1231–4,* 142, 148.
[95] *Bk. of Fees,* ii. 819.
[96] C.P. 25(1)/74/20 no. 420.
[97] C.P. 25(1)/75/31 no. 37; *Feud. Aids,* ii. 240.
[98] *Feud. Aids,* ii. 247.
[99] Cf. Worc. Episc. Reg., Reg. Maidstone, f. 48v.

and in 1327 it was restored to Margaret Giffard.[1] In 1330 the reversion after Margaret's death was granted by John of Kellaways, heir to the Giffards, to John Mautravers,[2] whose lands were forfeited in 1331.[3] By the following year the reversion had been acquired by Thomas Berkeley, Lord Berkeley,[4] who gave the manor in 1349 to a younger son Thomas, on whose death the same year it reverted to his father.[5]

After the death of Thomas, Lord Berkeley, in 1361 his wife Catherine (d. 1385)[6] held Syde manor and was succeeded by her son John Berkeley. Before 1411 John granted the manor at farm for life to John Vey;[7] it had apparently reverted to John by 1419[8] and before his death in 1428 he made a grant for life to Robert Poyntz. It reverted to John's son Maurice Berkeley[9] of Beverstone (d. 1460). It descended to Maurice's son Maurice[10] (d. 1474), to the younger Maurice's son William[11] (d. 1485), and to William's uncle Edward Berkeley.[12] Edward's eldest son Thomas died in 1500 before his father and Syde eventually became divided among Thomas's daughters, Laura who married John Ashburnham, Anne who married John Brent, Elizabeth who married Sir George Herbert, and Alice who married George Whetenall.[13] In 1531 Sir George and Elizabeth granted their quarter share to Sir William Berkeley,[14] Elizabeth's uncle, who in the following year acquired another share from John Daniel and Laura his wife, presumably Thomas Berkeley's daughter and a second husband.[15] The Whetenalls conveyed their share in 1530 to Charles Bulkeley[16] but it and the Brents' share were presumably also acquired by Sir William, who at his death in 1551 was succeeded in the manor by his son John.[17]

John Berkeley sold the manor in 1560 to William Partridge[18] and it followed the descent of Wishanger in Miserden[19] until 1663 when Henry Partridge sold it to Nathaniel Ridler[20] of Edgeworth (d. 1707). Nathaniel Ridler left it to his son Walter[21] (d. 1749)[22] who left it for life to his brother Samuel, rector of Edgeworth.[23] It later passed to Nigel Kingscote of Kingscote (d. 1774), who was succeeded by his nephew Robert Kingscote.[24] Robert sold it before 1803 to Joseph Pitt[25] and the manor, which then comprised the whole parish except the glebe, descended with Brimps-

field manor[26] until 1870. Syde later passed to Thomas Ramsbottom of Bury (Lancs.), who died before 1879, and in 1893 Esther and Harriet Ramsbottom[27] sold it to Theodore Crewdson, a Manchester cotton-manufacturer. Crewdson (d. 1923) was succeeded by his son Joseph Dillworth Crewdson, after whose death in 1946 Syde passed through two firms which exploited the timber on the estate. In 1950 the estate was split up, most of it being bought by Mr. D. Whitaker, the tenant of Manor farm, who sold Manor farm to Mrs. G. Cox the same year but retained some land in the parish. Mrs. Cox sold the farm in 1961 to Maj. S. P. H. Simonds,[28] who owned it in 1979 when it covered 150 ha. (370 a.).

The manor-house, Syde Manor, a substantial gabled building of various dates, was the home of several of the lords, including John Partridge in the early 17th century[29] and Walter Ridler in the 18th.[30] For most of the 19th century it was used as the farm-house of the estate[31] but from the beginning of the 20th J. D. Crewdson made it his home.[32] In 1979 it belonged, without any land attached, to Mr. F. I. Fairlie. The oldest part of the house is at the north-west corner, and the short eastern wing, which has an upper cruck roof and 16th-century windows, appears to be an addition. With the possible exception of a buttress on the west front no medieval features survive. The main range appears to have been lengthened southwards in the 17th century, when it was also completely reroofed, and the west porch may have been added c. 1700. The south end may have been partly demolished in the later 18th century when a new south range was put on. The rooms in that range were refitted c. 1830 and minor additions were made in the late 19th century and early 20th. To the north of the house, adjoining the churchyard, a barn of five bays with a central transeptal entrance at the south may be of the 16th century, though its roof was renewed in the 20th. At its western end is a small late-medieval two-storeyed building, presumably originally a church house or priest's house, having diagonal buttresses and windows with ogee tracery. It was in use as stables in the early 20th century but was restored as a dwelling in the early 1950s.[33]

In 1201 William Peto granted 2 yardlands and

[1] Cal. Close, 1327–30, 122–3.
[2] Ibid. 1330–3, 140.
[3] Cal. Fine R. 1327–37, 258.
[4] C.P. 25(1)/77/62 no. 162.
[5] Berkeley MSS. i. 347–8; C.P. 25(1)/77/67 no. 295.
[6] Berkeley MSS. i. 346, 349–50.
[7] Worc. Episc. Reg., Reg. Whittlesey, f. 26; Reg. Peverell, f. 30v.
[8] Reg. Sede Vacante, 393.
[9] C 139/35 no. 50; for the Berkeleys of Beverstone, see Berkeley MSS. i. 349–55.
[10] C 139/179 no. 57.
[11] Worc. Episc. Reg., Reg. Alcock, f. 50.
[12] C.P. 25(1)/294/79 no. 14.   [13] C 1/526 no. 66.
[14] C.P. 25(2)/51/368 no. 2.
[15] C.P. 25(2)/51/369 no. 7.   [16] C.P. 25(2)/51/367 no. 25.
[17] C 142/95 no. 83.
[18] C.P. 25(2)/259/2 Eliz. East. no. 6.
[19] C 142/185 no. 85; C 142/268 no. 146; Inq. p.m. Glos. 1625–42, i. 9–11; V.C.H. Glos. xi. 51.

[20] C.P. 43/323 rot. 70.
[21] V.C.H. Glos. xi. 42; Glos. R.O., D 1801/26.
[22] Virgo, 'Syde', p. 12.
[23] Prob. 11/783 (P.C.C. 335 Greenly); V.C.H. Glos. xi. 46.
[24] Rudder, Glos. 512, 663; Hockaday Abs. cccxxxviii, 1772, 1796.
[25] Fosbrooke, Glos. ii. 529; Glos. R.O., Q/SO 12.
[26] Syde ch. chest, papers of Revd. Thos. Hooper 1813–46; Glos. R.O., D 1388/SL 3, no. 113A; cf. above.
[27] Kelly's Dir. Glos. (1870), 650; (1879), 759; Glos. Colln. RX 271.1. These sources conflict with details of the Ramsbottom fam. given in Virgo, 'Syde', pp. 48–9, and the statement there that they bought the man. from John Hall in 1867.
[28] Virgo, 'Syde', pp. 51–6.
[29] Glos. R.O., D 2525, N. Cerney man. 1552–1657, leases 1604, 1608.
[30] Prob. 11/783 (P.C.C. 335 Greenly).
[31] Glos. Colln. RV 56.1; G.D.R., T 1/176.
[32] Kelly's Dir. Glos. (1902 and later edns.).
[33] Virgo, 'Syde', p. 55.

pasture-rights at Syde to Llanthony Priory. In the late 13th and early 14th century the estate was held as a single villein tenement, owing services to the priory's manor of Colesbourne.[34] It was presumably retained by the priory until the Dissolution[35] but it has not been found recorded later.

ECONOMIC HISTORY. In 1086 there were 2 plough-teams and 6 *servi* on the demesne of Syde manor, and in 1327 the demesne comprised 200 a. of arable, 5 a. of meadow, and a pasture. The tenants in 1086 were a villein, a priest, and 3 bordars having a single team between them. In 1327 there were 4 free tenants, 5 customary half-yardlanders, and 3 other tenants, presumably cottagers.[36]

Later evidence about the pattern of landholding in Syde is almost entirely lacking until the early 19th century, by which time the parish formed a single manor farm. There were still at least six or seven small tenant or freehold farms in the late 17th century[37] and the declining population figures presumably reflect their disappearance during the 18th century, perhaps in connexion with the inclosure of the open fields; one small freehold at least remained independent of the manor in 1771.[38]

In the late 17th century the parish had two open fields, a north and south field, in the eastern half of the parish,[39] while the steeper slopes in the western half provided pasture closes and the Frome valley some meadow land. The fields had been inclosed by the early 19th century.[40]

By the 1820s all the farmland of the parish, including the glebe, formed a single tenant farm comprising 595 a.[41] The farm was taken in hand by the lord of the manor before 1863 and was usually managed by farm bailiffs[42] until 1920 when most of the estate was leased as two separate farms, Manor farm and Harcombe farm.[43] The parish remained divided between those two farms and one or two small holdings in the mid 20th century.[44]

The parish was mainly under the plough in the 18th century[45] and remained so in the mid 19th. There were 402 a. of arable to 167 a. of permanent meadow and pasture in 1838.[46] The usual rotation of the region, involving wheat, barley, oats, turnips, and leys of clover or grass, was followed on the manor farm and a considerable stock of beef cattle was kept, together with a flock of sheep; 80 cattle

and 422 sheep were returned in 1866.[47] The later 19th century saw the usual decline in barley and wheat production, the land being turned instead to permanent pasture or to growing more oats.[48] In the early 20th century more dairy and beef cattle were introduced by Theodore Crewdson who bred Aberdeen Angus cattle.[49] In the 1970s Manor farm was used for growing wheat and barley and raising sheep while Harcombe farm specialized in dairying.[50]

Syde had at least three tradesmen, a smith and two masons, in 1608.[51] In 1831 there were no tradesmen in the parish[52] and in 1851 a thatcher was the only tradesman enumerated with a shepherd and the farm labourers.[53]

LOCAL GOVERNMENT. No records of manorial government for Syde are known to survive. For view of frankpledge it was represented with Elkstone by a single tithingman at Cirencester Abbey's hundred court.[54]

The parish had two churchwardens in the 16th century[55] and apparently had its separate overseers of the poor in 1683.[56] In the early 19th century, however, the tenant of the manor farm, as the sole ratepayer, served the offices of churchwarden, overseer, and constable.[57] The annual cost of poor-relief rarely rose above £50 at that period, there being usually only one or two people on permanent relief.[58] In 1836 the parish became part of the Cirencester poor-law union[59] and was later in Cirencester rural district[60] until the formation of Cotswold district in 1974.

CHURCH. There was a priest at Syde and therefore presumably a church in 1086[61] and the surviving church dates from the early 12th century. The living was a rectory in 1319[62] and remained one. After being served for many years together with one or other of the neighbouring parishes it was united with Elkstone in 1927[63] and in 1979 formed a united benefice with that parish and Brimpsfield. The advowson descended with the manor,[64] though in 1592 it was exercised by Anthony Ockhold of Miserden, in 1644 by John Pleydell, and in 1714 by the queen because of a lapse.[65]

The rector owned all the tithes of the parish. In

[34] C 115/K 2/6683 ff. 263v.–5.
[35] It was perhaps included as one of the customary tenements at Colesbourne in *Valor Eccl.* (Rec. Com.), ii. 425 and S.C. 6/Hen. VIII/1224 m.15d.
[36] *Dom. Bk.* (Rec. Com.), i. 169v.; *Inq. p.m. Glos.* 1301–58, 209–10.
[37] G.D.R., V 5/298T 1.
[38] Glos. R.O., D 182/III/189.   [39] G.D.R., V 5/298T 1.
[40] Ibid. 5; Glos. Colln. RV 56.1.
[41] Glos. Colln. RV 56.1; Glos. R.O., D 1388/SL 3, no. 30.
[42] *Kelly's Dir. Glos.* (1863 and later edns.).
[43] Virgo, 'Syde', p. 53.
[44] M.A.F. 68/3295/5; Agric. Returns 1976.
[45] Atkyns, *Glos.* 653; Rudder, *Glos.* 662.
[46] G.D.R., T 1/176.
[47] M.A.F. 68/25/16; M.A.F. 68/26/19.
[48] M.A.F. 68/1609/18.
[49] M.A.F. 68/3295/5; Virgo, 'Syde', p. 51.

[50] Agric. Returns 1976; ex inf. Maj. S. P. H. Simonds, of Manor Fm.
[51] Smith, *Men and Armour*, 256.
[52] *Census*, 1831.
[53] H.O. 107/1968.   [54] *Ciren. Cart.* ii, p. 619.
[55] Hockaday Abs. xxviii, 1540 visit. f. 47; xlvii, 1576 visit. f. 97.
[56] G.D.R., V 5/298T 2.   [57] G.D.R. vol. 383, no. ccxlv.
[58] *Poor Law Abstract, 1804,* 180–1; *1818,* 154–5; *Poor Law Returns* (1830–1), p. 70; (1835), p. 69.
[59] *Poor Law Com. 2nd Rep.* p. 522.
[60] *Census,* 1911.
[61] *Dom. Bk.* (Rec. Com.), i. 169v.   [62] *Reg. Cobham,* 18.
[63] *Lond. Gaz.* 23 Dec. 1927, pp. 8224–5.
[64] e.g. Worc. Episc. Reg., Reg. Maidstone, f. 48v.; Reg. Brian, i, f. 33; Reg. Morgan, i, f. 19; Reg. Alcock, f. 50; Hockaday Abs. cccxxxviii.
[65] Hockaday Abs. cccxxxviii; G.D.R., D 7/1/19.

1706 they were paid in kind except for those of milk cows for which a modus had been established.[66] The glebe in the late 17th century comprised 30 a. of open-field land and a few acres in closes, together with sheep- and beast-pastures;[67] after inclosure it comprised 31 a.[68] By the early years of the 19th century it had become the practice for the rector to receive £50 a year from the tenant of the manor estate instead of the profits of the tithes and glebe. That payment had come to be regarded as a stipend and the rector Thomas Hooper appeared to be in danger of losing his rights to the rectorial assets before 1832 when he secured recognition of them from the lord of the manor William Lawrence. Lawrence then took a lease of the tithes and glebe from Hooper for a rent of £100.[69] The rector was awarded a corn-rent-charge of £100 for the tithes at commutation in 1838.[70] The living received an augmentation of £200 by lot from Queen Anne's Bounty in 1778[71] and the rector received £10 a year interest for this in the early 19th century.[72] The living was valued at 78s. 3d. in 1535,[73] £28 in 1650,[74] £20 c. 1710,[75] £40 in 1750,[76] and £106 in 1856.[77]

The parsonage house, recorded from 1678,[78] was described as a mere cottage with two rooms in 1817.[79] It appears to have been the small stone cottage beside which John Hall built the new house (later Manor Farm) that he intended for the rectory in 1867. Following the failure to establish the new house as the rectory only one rector apparently resided at Syde and his wife is said to have left him to live in London because of the inadequacy of the accommodation. In the 20th century the cottage was used as part of Manor Farm and was joined to it physically in 1951.[80]

The poverty of the living and the meagre accommodation for its incumbents meant that Syde was usually held by non-resident pluralists. It was probably one of the more neglected livings in the 16th century: the curate serving it in 1551 was unable to repeat the Commandments,[81] it lacked the book of homilies and a copy of the injunctions in 1563, and no quarter sermons were preached in 1572. Thomas Paine, who was rector from 1560 and held the living together with Cowley from 1582,[82] was one of the few rectors to reside in the parish.[83] The rector Thomas Knight, described as unlearned but honest in 1593,[84] retained the living until his death in 1644 when Thomas Goddard was

instituted.[85] Thomas Stephens held the living in 1650[86] and subscribed at the Restoration. John Laurence, rector 1714–30,[87] was also curate of St. Mary de Lode, Gloucester.[88] Thomas Davies, rector from 1731, later held the living with Duntisbourne Abbots rectory, as did Joseph Chapman who succeeded Davies in 1772.[89] In 1784 Chapman lived at Trinity College, Oxford, of which he was president as well as vice-chancellor of the university; Syde was served for him by another Joseph Chapman, apparently his father,[90] who had succeeded him at Duntisbourne.[91] Thomas Hooper, rector 1813–45, lived at Elkstone where he was curate and later rector.[92] In the early 20th century two successive rectors held Syde with Duntisbourne Abbots and another held it with Brimpsfield.[93] In the 18th century and the early 19th a single Sunday service was held at Syde, alternating between the morning and afternoon.[94]

A chantry was founded in Syde church by Thomas Berkeley in 1343, acting through his agent William of Syde. Dedicated to the Virgin, it was endowed with a house and 2 yardlands.[95] It appears to have lapsed before the dissolution of the chantries.

The church of *ST. MARY THE VIRGIN*, so called by 1343,[96] has a chancel with south vestry, nave with north porch, and west tower. The small nave is of the early 12th century and retains its original plain doorways, the northern one having a medieval door and the southern one being blocked. The chancel was probably rebuilt in the 13th century when the tower, which has a simple saddle-back roof, was added. In the 14th century an altar was set up on the north side of the chancel arch, evidently for the chantry of 1343, and a low window made in the north wall to light it. In the 15th century larger windows were put into both sides of the nave, that on the north retaining the rear arch of an original opening and that on the south only the reveals, and the nave was reroofed. About 1850 the chancel was rebuilt[97] and it was perhaps at the same restoration that the vestry and porch were added.

The church retains 18th-century box-pews and pulpit. The font is of the 15th century with an octagonal bowl and an unusual pentagonal base.[98] There are two medieval bells and one that was recast in 1771.[99] A new set of plate was provided in 1856.[1] The parish registers survive from 1686.[2]

[66] G.D.R., V 5/298T 4.
[67] Ibid. 1, 3.
[68] Ibid. 5.
[69] Syde ch. chest, papers of Revd. Thos. Hooper 1813–46.
[70] G.D.R., T 1/176.
[71] Hodgson, *Queen Anne's Bounty*, p. cclxxxvi.
[72] Syde ch. chest, papers of Revd. Thos. Hooper 1813–46.
[73] *Valor Eccl.* (Rec. Com.), ii. 497.
[74] *Trans. B.G.A.S.* lxxxiii. 93.
[75] Atkyns, *Glos.* 653.
[76] G.D.R. vol. 381A, f. 29.
[77] G.D.R. vol. 384, f. 177.
[78] G.D.R., V 5/298T 1.
[79] Hockaday Abs. cccxxxviii.
[80] Virgo, 'Syde', App. 4, 8.
[81] *E.H.R.* xix. 115.
[82] Hockaday Abs. clxxii, cccxxxviii.
[83] Ibid. xlix, state of clergy 1584, f. 29; Bodl. MS. Rawl. C.790, f. 9v.

[84] Hockaday Abs. lii, state of clergy 1593, f. 13.
[85] G.D.R., D 7/1/19.
[86] *Trans. B.G.A.S.* lxxxiii. 93.
[87] Hockaday Abs. cccxxxviii.
[88] Bigland, *Glos.* ii. 173.
[89] Hockaday Abs. clxxxiv, cccxxxviii.
[90] G.D.R. vol. 319; Foster, *Alum. Oxon.* 1715–1886, ii. 239.
[91] Hockaday Abs. clxxxiv.
[92] Ibid. cccxxxviii.
[93] *Kelly's Dir. Glos.* (1910–23 edns.).
[94] G.D.R. vol. 381A, f. 29; 383, no. ccxlv.
[95] *Reg. Bransford*, pp. xxxv, 110–11.
[96] Ibid. p. 110.
[97] *Kelly's Dir. Glos.* (1856), 367.
[98] *Trans. B.G.A.S.* xliv. 180, 199.
[99] *Glos. Ch. Bells*, 63; cf. Bodl. MS. Rawl. B.323, f. 210.
[1] *Glos. Ch. Plate*, 204.
[2] *B. & G. Par. Rec.* 266.

NONCONFORMITY. None known.

EDUCATION. The parish had no school of any kind in the first half of the 19th century.[3] By 1867 there was a dame school attended by 9 children, each paying 2*d.* a week and in that year the lord of the manor John Hall gave the use of a cottage for a parish school, to be maintained by the rector.[4] In the 1870s Esther and Harriet Ramsbottom ran a school for the younger children in part of the manor-house but it had apparently closed by 1885, and in 1889 the children of the parish attended Winstone school.[5]

CHARITIES FOR THE POOR. Syde was one of four parishes that shared in the charity of Thomas Muggleton (d. 1659), derived from land in Duntisbourne Abbots.[6] The poor of Syde were receiving 15*s.* from that source in 1683[7] and 20*s.* in 1807.[8] In 1979, when the income was derived from stock, Syde received *c.* £4 from the charity, which was left to accumulate against particular cases of need.[9]

[3] *Educ. of Poor Digest*, 311; *Educ. Enquiry Abstract*, 326; *Church School Inquiry, 1846–7*, 16–17.
[4] *Rep. Com. Agric. Employment*, p. 99.
[5] Virgo, 'Syde', p. 49; *Kelly's Dir. Glos.* (1879–89).

[6] *14th Rep. Com. Char.* H.C. 382, pp. 61–2 (1826), xii.
[7] G.D.R., V 5/298T 2.
[8] Ibid. 5.
[9] Ex inf. Maj. Simonds.

INDEX